World Literature

World Literature is an increasingly influential subject in literary studies, which has led to the reframing of contemporary ideas of "national literatures", language and translation.

World Literature: A Reader brings together thirty essential readings which display the theoretical foundations of the subject, as well as showing its conceptual development over a two-hundred-year period.

The book features:

- an illuminating introduction to the subject, with suggested reading paths to help readers navigate through the materials;
- texts exploring key themes such as globalization, cosmopolitanism, post/trans-nationalism, and translation and nationalism;
- writings by major figures including J. W. Goethe, Karl Marx, Friedrich Engels, Zhang Longxi, David Damrosch, Gayatri Chakravorty Spivak, Pascale Casanova and Milan Kundera.

The early explorations of the meaning of "Weltliteratur" are introduced, while twenty-first-century interpretations by leading scholars today show the latest critical developments in the field. The editors offer readers the ideal introduction to the theories and debates surrounding the impact of this crucial area on the modern literary landscape.

Theo D'haen is Professor of English and Comparative Literature at University of Leuven (KU Leuven), Belgium and has also worked in Holland, France and America. He is Editor-in-Chief of the *European Review*, and President of FILLM (Fédération Internationale des Langues et Littératures Modernes) 2008–12.

César Domínguez is Associate Professor of Comparative Literature at the University of Santiago de Compostela, Spain. He is a member of boards of the Spanish Comparative Literature Association and the European Network for Comparative Literary Studies, Chair of the ICLA (International Comparative Literature Association) Research Committee, and member of the ICLA Coordinating Committee and the Academia Europaea.

Mads Rosendahl Thomsen is Associate Professor in Comparative Literature at Aarhus University, Denmark. He is the author of *Mapping World Literature: International Canonization and Transnational Literatures*.

Routledge Literature Readers

Also available

Literature and Globalization

The History of Reading

For further information on this series visit: http://www.routledge.com/literature/series

World Literature

A Reader

Edited by

**Theo D'haen, César Domínguez and
Mads Rosendahl Thomsen**

Routledge
Taylor & Francis Group

LONDON AND NEW YORK

First published 2013
by Routledge
2 Park Square, Milton Park, Abingdon, Oxon OX14 4RN

Simultaneously published in the USA and Canada
by Routledge
711 Third Avenue, New York, NY 10017

Routledge is an imprint of the Taylor & Francis Group, an informa business

British Library Cataloguing in Publication Data
A catalogue record for this book is available from the British Library

Library of Congress Cataloging in Publication Data
World literature: a reader / edited by Theo D'Haen, César Domínguez, and Mads Rosendahl Thomsen.
    p. cm.
    Includes bibliographical references.
    1. Literature—History and criticism.—Theory, etc.   2. Comparative literature.
    3. Literature and globalization.   4. Literature and society.   I. Haen, Theo d'
    II. Domínguez, César.   III. Thomsen, Mads Rosendahl, 1972–
    PN441.W67 2012
    809—dc23
                                                                2011040937

ISBN: 978–0–415–60298–3 (hbk)
ISBN: 978–0–415–60299–0 (pbk)

Typeset in Perpetua and Bell Gothic
by RefineCatch Limited, Bungay, Suffolk

Printed and bound in Great Britain by the MPG Books Group

Contents

Acknowledgements

J. W. Goethe, "Comparative Literature: The Early Years" and Hugo Meltzl de Lomnitz "Comparative Literature: The Early Years", from *Comparative Literature: The Early Years* edited by Phillip H. Rhein and Hans Joachin Schultz. © 1973 University of North Carolina Press. Used by permission of the publisher. www.uncpress.unc.edu.

Werner P. Friederich, "The Teaching of World Literature: Proceedings of the Conference at the University of Wisconsin" from *The Teaching of World Literature* edited by Haskell M. Block. © 1960 University of North Carolina Press, renewed 1989 by Haskell M. Block. Used by permission of the publisher, www.uncpress.unc.edu.

René Étiemble, "Faut-il réviser la notion de *Weltliteratur?*" in *Essais de littérature (vraiment) générale*. © Editions Gallimard. Reprinted by permission of the publisher.

Irina Neupokoeva, "Dialectics Of Historical Development Of National And World Literature" used with kind permission from Springer Science + Business Media: Neohelicon, Dialectics of historical development of national and world literature, 1973, Volume 1, Issue 1–2, pp. 113–130, Irina Neupokoeva. © Springer Science + Business Media 1973.

"A Footnote to Weltliteratur" from *Le Mythe D'Étiemble* (1979) by George Steiner © Didier Erudition, Paris.

Excerpt from "The Universal in Literature" from *The Reemergence of World Literature* by A. Owen. Aldridge. University of Delaware Press (1986). Used by permission of Associated University Presses.

"Epilogue," in *The Tao and the Logos*, Longxi Zhang, pp. 189–199. © 1992 Duke University Press. All rights reserved. Reprinted by permission of the publisher.

"Weltliteratur," reprinted by permission of the publisher from *The Challenge of Comparative Literature* by Claudio Guillén, translated by Cola Franzen, pp. 37–45, Cambridge, Mass.: Harvard University Press. © 1993 President and Fellows of Harvard College.

Franco Moretti "Conjectures on World Literature" and "More Conjectures," from *New Left Review* 1, (January–February 2000, pp. 54–68) and *New Left Review* 20 (March–April 2003, pp. 73–81). Reproduced with permission of *New Left Review*.

"World Literature and Global Theory: Comparative Literature for the New Millennium" by Vilashini Cooppan, reproduced from *Symplokē* with permission from the University of Nebraska Press. © 2001.

Damrosch, David. *What is World Literature?* © 2003 Princeton University Press. Reprinted by Princeton University Press.

"Planetarity" from *Death of a Discipline* by Gayatri Chakravorty Spivak. © 2003 Columbia University Press. Reprinted with permission of the publisher.

Gerard Holden, "World Literature and World Politics: In Search of a Research Agenda" from *Global Society*, vol. 17, no. 3, 2003. Reprinted by permission of the publisher (Taylor & Francis Ltd, www.tandf.co.uk/journals).

"Anthologizing 'World Literature' " by Sarah Lawall, reprinted from *On Anthologies: Politics and Pedagogy*, edited by Jeffrey R. Di Leo, by permission of University of Nebraska Press. © 2004 University of Nebraska Press.

Shu–Mei Shih, "*Global Literature* and Technologies of Recognition." Reprinted by permission of the Modern Languages Association of America from *PMLA*, Volume 119, Number 1, January 2004, pp. 16–30. © 2004 Modern Languages Association of America.

Pascale Casanova, "Literature as a World" from New *Left Review* 31 (January–February 2005, pp. 71–90). Reproduced with permission of *New Left Review*.

"Die Weltliteratur" by Milan Kundera, originally published by *The New Yorker*. Reproduced with permission of the author.

Nirvana Tanoukhi, "The Scale of World Literature." *New Literary History* 39:3 (2008), 599–617. © 2009 *New Literary History*, University of Virginia. Reprinted with permission of The Johns Hopkins University Press.

"Canonization and World Literature: the Nobel Experience" by Horace Engdahl from *World Literature, World Culture: History, Theory, Analysis*, eds. Karen–Margrethe Simonsen and Jakob Stougaard–Nielsen (2008). Aarhus: Aarhus University Press. Reproduced with permission from the publisher and the author.

Mariano Siskind, "The Globalization of the Novel and the Novelization of the Global: A Critique of World Literature," in *Comparative Literature*, Volume 62, no. 4, pp. 336–360. © 2010 University of Oregon. All rights reserved. Reprinted by permission of the publisher, Duke University Press.

Introduction

THE CONCEPT OF WORLD LITERATURE has been around for well-nigh two centuries now, but for most of this time it has led a rather shadowy existence. Almost inevitably, this applies to its role in the national literary traditions and their reflection on their own place in the world. However, and rather surprisingly, it also holds true for its role in comparative literature's reflection on itself as an all-encompassing field of literary study. Still, in the late 1990s we saw a marked increase in interest in world literature from the part of comparative literature scholars. This has resulted in a series of attempts to redefine the concept and to develop new approaches to it. In this process, earlier ways of defining and making use of the concept remain valuable as a necessary foundation for considering new directions, aims and methods. The present *Reader* offers a series of seminal contributions to the field, from before Johann Wolfgang von Goethe, who has generally been credited with, if not, as we now know, actually coining the term then at least giving it its widest currency, to our present moment.

The reasons for the revival of the concept of world literature are multiple, but two important factors seem to hold a good deal of explanatory power. The first goes beyond the realm of literature and literary studies and is linked to the agenda of globalization and its effects on culture and on conceptions of identity. Seen in this light, the renewed interest in world literature is a response to a need for thinking of literature's role beyond the nation-state in a world where cultural exchanges are becoming increasingly more intense and far-reaching.

The other factor has to do with the internal organization of literary studies. Nominally, world literature for the longest time made its academic home in departments of comparative literature programs. However, for various reasons comparative literature in practice had difficulty living up to the ambition of being sufficiently inclusive to the literatures of the world. One reason certainly had to do with the enormity of the field. Another resided in a proven lack of interest in so-called "minor," and particularly non-Western literatures. Much of the world's literature was left to specialists in national or regional literatures to deal with, while comparative literature programs limited themselves to the larger Western literatures, even if many seminal works from all over the world became ever more widely available in translation.

A correction to this state of affairs set in with postcolonialism, addressing issues of a fixed and narrow canon as well as of methods commensurate to new orientations within studies of national identity, migrancy and cosmopolitanism. Yet for all its institutional success, in particular in English departments, postcolonial studies has to a large degree remained unsuccessful in integrating its canon and its approaches with those of comparative literature.

World literature can in this light be seen as a response to the shortcomings of both comparative literature and postcolonialism when it comes to the global study of literature. That is not to say that world literature has also solved those problems: new agendas also mean new challenges of definition and method.

Definitions and uses

Defining world literature has been and is likely to continue to be an open-ended discussion influenced by particular interests and by the uses made of the term in particular situations. Ideas of literary value, institutional constraints and the international reception of concrete works intersect in attempts to define what world literature is.

Historically, world literature has, often tacitly, been assumed to cover either one of two concepts that each in its own way makes sense, but at the same time seems limiting for the needs of a globalizing cultural situation. One definition holds world literature to refer to that part of the world's literature that is both "the best" of what literature has to offer and possesses universal appeal. This is a commonly held notion that implies a strict hierarchy in the organization and valuation of literature. The other definition is almost diametrically opposed to the first, and considers world literature to be all of the world's literature, without pronouncing on questions of quality and influence. While these definitions have the merit of being clear-cut, their extreme simplicity makes it impossible to address more intricate questions and avoid blind spots. It is for example obvious that much world literature according to the first definition in reality is Western literature, although claims of universalism are not retained for that reason. It is also unclear how there can be a dynamics between works of literature that have proven to be long-living international classics and works that may not have the same reputation. On the other hand, a complete openness to all of the world's literatures soon becomes uninteresting as questions of quality of writing and relevance of themes and historical description are bound to come up, as they should in any study of literature.

One crucial difference between the formerly dominant definitions of world literature and more recent attempts to redefine the concept could be summed up as a move from seeing world literature as an *object*, either as a small canon or a vast ocean of texts, to a *paradigm* for approaching texts from, or within, diverse contexts and making connections between them. The questions of canonization and all-inclusiveness enter into this paradigm, but they do so alongside a much wider array of problems. These range from questions of how literature travels across borders, how translations are used, how genres influence each other and how they move across literatures, whether there is a specific poetics of texts that gain global recognition, how highly canonized works can be read in conjunction with lesser known ones, what is the role of institutional factors such as changes in publishing and dissemination, reviewing, advertising, literary agents, teaching, anthologizing, etc.

Making use of this volume

The thirty texts in this anthology are ordered chronologically, and that order obviously tells one story of the development and uses of the idea of world literature. Among many other possible ways of making use of the material, we have suggested six reading paths or clusters of texts that more specifically address certain topics within the field. They are concerned with the debate revolving around Goethe's initial definition, basic theories of world literature, the relationship between comparative literature and world literature, the role of markets and literary systems, the pedagogical consequences of world literature, and of how expansion of the field takes place. The basic reading materials and the suggestions for further reading listed in the reading paths are detailed in the bibliography at the end of the volume.

Reading Paths

The Goethean debate

UNTIL RECENTLY IT HAS BEEN COMMONPLACE to credit the turn-of-the-nineteenth-century German writer Johann Wolfgang von Goethe (1749–1832) with having coined the term "*Weltliteratur*" in 1827. We now know that at least the historian August Ludwig von Schlözer and the writer Christoph Martin Wieland had used it earlier, but it does remain true that Goethe's use of it has had the greatest impact. Between 1827 and 1832, the year of his death, Goethe regularly used the term, as evidenced in altogether twenty-one brief passages from Goethe's own writings and his recorded conversation. These passages have served as the inevitable point of departure for all further discussions on the topic. Yet none of these passages provides a real definition of *Weltliteratur*. No wonder, then, that they have given rise to the kind of diametrically opposed interpretations briefly outlined in the preceding paragraphs. Scholars now generally agree, though, that Goethe himself meant neither of the two interpretations there given. At the time of Goethe's taking an interest in *Weltliteratur* Europe had only relatively recently emerged from a period of violent warfare occasioned by the French Revolution and the Napoleonic Wars. Goethe had himself been actively involved in some of these events. After the final defeat of Napoleon in 1815 Europe had entered upon a period of pacification and political restoration. Goethe noted that under these circumstances an increase in the production and circulation of periodicals facilitated the exchange of ideas across Europe, and though politically speaking Germany, divided as it still was in many smaller and larger entities, did not play a very important role in Europe, he saw possibilities for the German language and for German literature serving as mediators for the dissemination of work in foreign languages throughout Europe. Thus, a transnational literature would come into being that would serve the cause of understanding and toleration among nations and peoples.

Georg Brandes, at the end of the nineteenth century, concentrates on the uneven chances writers from different nations and writing in different languages have for making it into world literature. He concludes that it is only writers from some large nations, and writing in a (then) widely disseminated language such as French, English or German, and to a lesser extent Italian and Spanish, stand a fair chance, whether in the original or in translation. In fact, he claims, qualitatively lesser writers from great nations more easily become part of world literature than do outstanding writers from smaller nations. This does not really serve the cause of general understanding among people, or at best only promotes a one-way traffic of understanding.

Fritz Strich, writing in 1930, discusses the various concepts of world literature then existing, and concludes that what one means by the term depends on the use one wants to make of it. The most important question for him, though, is whether world literature is only something that can be ascertained and described as a historical reality, proof of the literary traffic among nations, or whether its coming into being is a necessary step on the road to achieving the highest goals of the human spirit. Strich does not hesitate to answer affirmatively, and does so by invoking Goethe.

René Étiemble, writing in the middle of the twentieth century, thinks that the exchange between literatures that Goethe talked about has in practice been too much restricted to European literatures, and worse, to only some of those. Therefore, he proposes to revise the concept of world literature to include the literatures of peoples beyond Europe, especially from the Islamic world, from China and Japan and India; only then will we be able to truly speak of "world literature."

George Steiner, at the end of the 1970s, explicitly situates Étiemble in the lineage of Goethe. Expressing his admiration for the sheer range of Goethe's interests, his grasp of so many languages and literatures, Steiner still feels that a true knowledge of world literature escaped even Goethe because of the sheer volume of materials to be read and studied, which made it impossible even in Goethe's time, and even for the greatest genius, to truly fathom it all. What remains valid in Goethe's concept of world literature, though, Steiner argues, is the idea of comparison, of gaining greater insight even into one's own language and literature by getting to know other languages and literatures, especially so through translation, an art Goethe practiced throughout his life.

David Damrosch, at the beginning of the twenty-first century, harks back to Goethe's world literature as the circulation of intellectual, and more precisely literary goods among nations. Damrosch starts from how Goethe's own pronouncements of world literature came to circulate among the writers and intellectuals of his own day, and subsequently traces different instances of circulation in the original or in translation, from the epic of Gilgamesh in ancient times to the autobiography of Rigoberta Menchú at the end of the twentieth century. Clearly, his intention, as was that of Goethe, Strich and Étiemble, is to further the cause of understanding among nations.

Basic readings: Goethe, Brandes, Strich, Étiemble, Steiner, Damrosch.

Further readings: Elster (1901), Meyer (1913), Beil (1915), Vossler (1928), Strich (1946), Hoflfeld (1953), Bender & Melzer (1958), Berczik (1967), Marino (1975), Prawer (1976), Aldridge (1983), Balakian (1983), Koppen (1984), Clüver (1986), Steinecke (1987), Weitz (1987), Boubia (1988), Steinmetz (1988), Dimić (1991), Gulya (1994), Birus (1999), Bollacher (2001), Gálik (2003), Hoesel-Uhlig (2004), Madsen (2004), Moretti (2006), Pizer (2006), Tihanov (2011), Wang (2011).

World literature theory

Theories of what world literature is and how it can and should be studied are unavoidable unless one settles for a definition of world literature as merely all the world's literature, a solution which does not provide any useful perspective from which to approach this enormous subject. Arguments for specific ways of differentiating the field of world literature from other approaches to literature have been put forth since scholars first became interested in the subject. Cultural activism and questions of method have been intertwined in these attempts to delimit the field. Goethe used national literatures as the primary opposition to world literature, which for him stood both as a description of the field as he saw it and a call for a radical change in the use and study of literature. At the beginning of the twentieth century, Richard Moulton's central methodological turn asserted the necessity of studying world literature as one indivisible entity, but from a local perspective. In the 1950s, Erich Auerbach suggested new approaches to close reading as a central component of his approach, which was designed to overcome the complexity of the vast subject of world literature. These scholars thus have very different perspectives on world literature corresponding with their different objectives and hopes for the future of the field. At the same time, they share an interest in sketching a meaningful context for world literature and proposing ways to study it.

For many years, contributions such as Auerbach's notwithstanding, there was little interest in developing theories of world literature, and the term was primarily used to designate either the best of the world's literature, largely meaning Western literature, or simply all foreign literature. Honouring the legacy of Goethe, critics such as Fritz Strich and George Steiner provided valuable reinterpretations, but in general the academic-institutional climate was not very conducive to further discussion of the subject.

Institutionally speaking, the discipline of comparative literature has been traditionally conceived as encompassing world literature. In reality, comparative literature programs tended to restrict themselves to Western literature, and they failed to develop concepts and strategies for including non-Western literature which can only be read in the original by specialists. Starting at the end of the 1970s, postcolonialism paved the way for the study of "new" literatures. Still, the latter's integration with the dominant Western canon remained problematic. Moreover, as postcolonial literatures in practice meant literatures written outside of Europe or the West but in European languages, large parts of the world's literature still were excluded from this development.

At the end of the twentieth century, after a decade of globalization discourse, world literature appeared on the agenda again. New theoretical contributions were made in the service of developing a cultural agenda as well as providing a methodological stance. The work of David Damrosch and Franco Moretti took the study of world literature in two opposing directions. While Moretti has focused on factors which have had a unifying effect on the literatures of the world primarily achieved through the spread of genres, Damrosch has explored how different literatures and works have been able to enter into dialogue. Damrosch's insistence on close reading and his focus on teaching world literature on the one hand, and, on the other hand, Moretti's provocative practice of "distant reading" and his focus on patterns of world literature, sum up the major tendencies of their theoretical contributions, although their work is more nuanced than our brief summary here suggests and displays a number of shared interests.

Criticism of both positions has been expressed by a number of scholars, either directly or indirectly. In this volume Gayatri Spivak's contribution employs the notion of "planetarity" to counter the concept of world, thereby urging us to rethink the relations between such concepts as nation, culture, area and world. Nirvana Tanoukhi questions the uses of geographical metaphors and the many scales and viewpoints from which world literature is approached, while Vilashini Cooppan, like many others, advocates that the strangeness of other literatures should not be erased by the will to see similarities everywhere.

Basic readings: Auerbach, Corstius, Guillén, Ďurišin, Moretti, Damrosch, Holden, Casanova, Tanoukhi.

Further readings: Ďurišin (1972), Neupokoyeva (1976), Balakian (1983), Ďurišin (1984), Vipper (1985), Steinmetz (1988), Ďurišin (1989), Miner (1990), Lambert (1991), Ďurišin (1992), Prendergast (2001), Gálik (2003), Prendergast (2004), Milner (2004),

Ruden (2004), Casas (2005), Garnier (2005), Pradeau (2005), Tlostanova (2005), Apter (2006), Cabo Aseguinolaza (2006), Damrosch (2006), Dong-il (2006), Moretti (2006), Pizer (2006), Saussy (2006), Arac (2007), Casanova (2007), Damrosch (2008), Pettersson (2008), Thomsen (2008), Bleiker (2009), Holden (2010), Puchner (2011), Tihanov (2011).

Comparative literature and world literature

The study and teaching of world literature have traditionally been seen as belonging to the province of the discipline of comparative literature. In fact, the actual teaching of something called "world literature" has been mainly confined to the United States, and we will return to it in a later reading path. As to the actual study of world literature, if in most writings on comparative literature there is the obligatory, but often also perfunctory, nod to the term, just as often the possibility of actually "doing" world literature has been dismissed out of hand. This is especially true of the so-called "French" school of comparative literature, which from the middle of the nineteenth to the middle of the twentieth century dominated the field, and which heavily insisted on the "comparative" element in the discipline's practice. In Europe or in the European tradition comparative literature, moreover, in practice was the domain of a cultured elite naturally schooled in a variety of languages, often because of the specific political or other conditions they found themselves in. It is certainly no coincidence that many of the nineteenth-century forerunners of comparative literature, and of its earlier practitioners in the twentieth century, were Swiss or worked in that country, or, like Meltzl, lived and worked in the often polyglot and multicultural-avant-la-lettre environment of Central and Eastern Europe. Moreover, the cultured elite in Europe during the nineteenth and early twentieth century as a matter of course understood, spoke and wrote French, and was educated with Latin and Greek as self-evident parts of the high school curriculum, with Latin often being a prerequisite for admission to university. Finally, scholars working in languages and literatures until World War II were almost invariably philologists, who already as a matter of course studied European rather than single national literatures. The ideal of a world literature studied by multilingual philologists clearly shines through in the writings of Strich and Auerbach, and even later in those of Friederich and Guillén, both comparatists trained in Europe but working in the United States.

In the United States circumstances were completely different, and when after World War II the lead in comparative literature passed from Europe to the US this also had immediate consequences for the study of world literature. Even before World War II American comparatists, even if they were Europeans such as Moulton and Guérard, but had made their academic home in the US from an early stage in their career, were much more open to studying numerous literatures in translation rather than a few literatures in the original. Hence, the scope of the literatures that could be studied broadened significantly, and concurrently no immediate filiation between various works studied need be demonstrated, and more general topics could be broached.

For various reasons, though, from the 1970s through the 1980s comparative literature, and world literature with it, in the United States was eclipsed by a rapid succession of theoretical movements that flourished in national literature, and particularly English departments, rather than comparative literature departments. The same thing, though perhaps to a somewhat lesser extent, was true of Europe, while in the rest of the world comparative literature only slowly succeeded in gaining ground next to the study of national literatures, and interest in world literature as a theoretical or practical issue was virtually nonexistent. This was a point noted, and discussed, by American comparatists venturing abroad, such as for instance Owen Aldridge. In Europe, Étiemble, as mentioned earlier, as of the 1960s had already been loudly pleading for casting the net of world literature, and of comparative literature, much wider. The recent renewal of interest in world literature, fueled by comparative literature departments, has returned the latter discipline to the center of American academe again. However, this is a much-changed comparative literature from what it was in earlier days, as can be seen from Cooppan's article here included.

Basic readings: Andrés, Meltzl, Moulton, Strich, Guérard, Auerbach, Friederich, Aldridge, Guillén, Cooppan.

Further readings: Neupokoyeva (1963), Jost (1972), Lange (1972), Rüdiger (1972), Träger (1974), Vajda (1974), Aldridge (1983), Clüver (1986), Lawall (1990), Spivak (2003), Madsen (2004), Spivak (2005), Tlostanova (2005), Apter (2006), Pizer (2006), Pizer (2007).

Market, systemic and materialist readings

In the 1780s Juan Andrés expressed surprise that during the previous few decades European scholars had known much more about Chinese and Indian literature than Chinese and Indian scholars did themselves. Still, he did not explore the bonds between this "new" knowledge and the European overseas colonies and trading posts. Some forty years later Johann Wolfgang von Goethe saw this connection straightaway and at least partially based his concept of *Weltliteratur* on it. According to the French journal *Le Globe*, as quoted by Goethe, even England, one of "the nations that devote themselves chiefly to trade and industry," looked forward to broadening her knowledge of foreign literatures (1973: 7). And it is this knowledge and the supporting communication network that would facilitate the emergence of world literature in Goethe's opinion: "a world literature, such as is inevitable with the ever-increasing facility of communication, is to be formed in the near future" (Goethe 1973: 10). Twenty years later, Karl Marx and Friedrich Engels supported Goethe's impressionistic description with a materialist theory of social change and economic expansion, for the formation of a world economy and a world literature went hand in hand. "The bourgeoisie has through its exploitation of the world-market given a cosmopolitan character to production and consumption in every country. [. . .] And as in material, so also in intellectual production. The intellectual creations of individual nations become common property [. . .] and from the numerous national and local literatures, there arises a world literature" (Marx & Engels 2009: 8 & 9).

Paradoxically, the market and material dimensions of world literature—as acknowledged by Goethe in relation to the role of translations, literary journals, travel and communications— did not form part of the main narrative about world literature until very recently. Mads Rosendahl Thomsen distinguishes the three most often cited recent approaches to world literature, by Franco Moretti, David Damrosch and Pascale Casanova, respectively, as follows: "Moretti is oriented toward research, whereas Damrosch is more focused on the teaching of world literature, while Casanova can be said to embrace a wider field of the sociology of criticism" (2008: 20). It has to be noted, though, that market issues are central to Moretti's research on "the evolution of genres and the ways in which local differences shape the techniques of certain genres" (Thomsen 2008: 20), and also, although in a different and perhaps more restricted way, to Casanova's research into the formulation of what she calls the "world republic of letters." Moreover, it is important not to overlook that other voices have been concerned precisely with material and market issues in relation to world literature.

In this respect it is interesting to note that the term "system" has played an important part in the renewed world literature studies (for an overview, see Apter 2009), and this in spite of the long-standing reluctance to systemic theories in US academe, in contrast to, for instance, their Canadian counterparts. Some recent proposals represent authentic tours de force when it comes to searching for new explanations of world literature. A case in point is the systemic typology proposed for the history of world literature by Alexander Beecroft (2008), which seriously challenges statements such as Moretti's that "the literature around us is *now* unmistakably a planetary system" (2000: 54; emphasis added). In other cases, "system" seems to be used as a shortcut to avoid the multifarious complexity of world literature. But what cannot be overlooked is that system, market and the material and institutional dimensions are interlaced aspects of an approach which, rooted in Russian formalism, tries to explain literature as a semiotic whole in constant communication with other social systems. Although one offshoot of Russian formalism, polysystem theory as formulated by Itamar Even-Zohar (1990), never aimed to explain world literature as such, it is obvious that its view of the literary institution, the role played by the market, and the distribution between canonized- and non-canonized strata may provide world literature studies with useful tools. This is even more true of other offshoots of Russian formalism such as Dionýz Ďurišin's theory of interliterary process, the ultimate goal of which is to provide an explanation of world literature as a changing system whose dynamics the restrictive disciplinary boundaries between national and comparative literary studies cannot address.

Recent debates in world literature studies about the role of anthologies, international literary prizes, government support of translations, simultaneous publication worldwide and other publishing house strategies, world fiction as commodity, hybridization of genres, transnational literary phenomena, book history, etc. are some examples of the relevance that the study of the material dimension of literature might have for understanding world literature from a systemic perspective.

Basic readings: Marx & Engels, Neupokoyeva, Ďurišin, Moretti, Casanova, Kundera, Engdahl.

Further readings: Guillén (1971), Lukács (1973), Prawer (1976), Neupokoyeva (1976), Ďurišin (1984), Vipper (1985), Jameson (1986), Ďurišin (1989), Lambert (1991), Bassel (1991), Azarov (1992), Wallerstein (1997), Braginsky (2001), Arac (2002), Kristal (2002), Milner (2004), Parla (2004), Casanova & Samoyault (2005), Epelboin (2005), Ruffel (2005), Moretti (2006), Julien (2006), Trumpener (2006), Casanova (2007), Apter (2008), Baggesgaard (2008), Beecroft (2008), Thomsen (2008), Apter (2009).

The pedagogical dimension

The idea of world literature as a holistic body whose meaning goes beyond the simple addition of the units—whichever they are—it embraces is the result of what Claudio Guillén has phrased as a "fruitful historical paradox," the one derived from a rising nationalism which laid "the foundation for a new internationalism" (1993: 27). Comparative literature is only possible as a discipline when the existence of a multiplicity of literatures is acknowledged. And one of the aims of the discipline is precisely the understanding of the unity within the diversity of literature, which cannot be the unity of an absolute (Eurocentric) poetics any longer.

Whereas the French foundations of comparative literature were linked to the study of "other" modern literatures qua *littératures étrangères* (foreign literatures; see Espagne

1993), the pre-disciplinary period (from the late eighteenth century to the 1820s) tried to provide a wide audience—from scholars to dilettantes gathered in public sessions of academies and arts associations—with a picture of the literatures of the world from ancient to modern times. This was a picture in constant change, for new information about both European and non-European literatures became more and more widely available. Whereas in the 1740s Francesco Saverio Quadrio considered that a knowledge of Greek, Latin and Italian literature was enough for the instruction of the average learned man, thirty years later Juan Andrés expanded the list to include Chinese, Indian, Persian, Phoenician, Chaldean, Hebrew, Greek, Latin, Arab, Spanish, Italian, Occitan, French, German, English, Polish, Russian, Swedish, Danish and Dutch literature, not to mention plans to gather information on sub-Saharan literatures. The old rhetorical rule that required the knowledge of the (Greek and Roman) *scriptores* for the formation of the individual as *cives* therefore came to cover as wide a field as stretched the admiration for the diversity of the literatures of the world. And both this new training and curiosity were satisfied, mainly with the aid of translations, within a pedagogical environment. Andrés's *Dell'origine, progressi e stato attuale d'ogni letteratura*, for instance, was used as a textbook to teach world literature in Madrid and Valencia in the early nineteenth century, whereas Friedrich Schlegel lectured on ancient and modern literatures in Vienna in the 1810s and Georg Weber, in accordance with his didactic eagerness as director of the Höhere Schule in Heidelberg, wrote for his students *Literaturhistorisches Lesebuch, enthaltend Proben aus den bedeutendsten Literaturwerken aller Völker und Zeiten* (1851–52; A Reader of Literary History, with the Most Important Works of all Nations and Times) and *Weltgeschichte in übersichtlicher Darstellung* (1866; World History in Overview).

A number of further examples might be cited, but those mentioned will suffice to qualify a recurrent statement of the US academia related to world literature and pedagogy. Sarah Lawall, for instance, has stated that, as an academic course, world literature is "a uniquely American institution" (1988: 53) and has "its own special horizons in American educational history" (1994: x). This seems to imply that current US theories on world literature deserve some kind of special recognition due to this pedagogical tradition, not to mention the fact that it also seems to justify that non-US theories may be overlooked. A more cautious approach might be to explore how different ideas about world literature emerge depending on specific pedagogical environments, be these either the history of education in nineteenth- and twentieth-century Western Europe, in the twentieth-century US (with the important contribution of World War II European exiles), or in former colonies, as illustrated by postcolonial studies, among many other possibilities. The importance of US contributions to the discussion about the pedagogy of world literature is, however, indisputable. A case in point is the 1959 conference on teaching world literature held at the University of Wisconsin (Block 1960), in which issues such as the problems of teaching literary texts in translation, the scope of introductory courses and the purposes of said courses within the humanities were discussed, not to mention the relevance of pooling actual experiences about teaching world literature. From 1959 to 2009, with the collective volume edited by David Damrosch, several important contributions to the pedagogical dimension of world literature have been made. For the period up to 2006, an extremely informative overview is presented by John Pizer (2006). These contributions may be singled out as a US-specific, pragmatic concern, namely, the relevance of a second-degree approach to world literature, the relevance of the reflection about how to teach world literature as opposed to the practice of teaching world literature without an explicit pedagogy. In contrast to the US, Europe has produced encyclopedic textbooks and histories of world literature without a preliminary reflection and questioning of the object (*littérature universelle*) they address, with the notable exceptions of German (Schmeling 1995) and Russian (Neupokoyeva 1976) contributions.

On a par with the far-reaching changes in US anthologies of world literature over the last fifty years or so (a case in point is the transition from the Norton anthology of world masterpieces to the Norton anthology of world literature), the array of pedagogical problems has broadened. Reading texts in the original languages and/or in translation, the ethical aims, the questioning of the idea of literature itself, the spatio-temporal expansion of the canon, the role attributed to "minor literatures," and how to handle the loss of cultural specificity because of distance in place and time, remain major concerns for the teaching of world literature.

Basic readings: Andrés, Moulton, Friederich, Aldridge, Damrosch, Lawall.

Further readings: Daghlian & Frenz (1950), Brown (1953), Alberson (1960), Block (1960), Laird (1961), Lawall (1990, 1993 & 1994), Ross (1993), Carroll (1996), Vinck (1996), Hassan (2000), McInturff (2003), Pizer (2006), Thomsen (2008), Damrosch (2008), McFarland (2008), Damrosch (2009a & 2009b).

Expanding world literature

It is obvious that there is too much literature in the world for an individual to read all of it. But the same point holds true for the literature of a single nation or in a single language, so selection is an inevitable part of our engagement with literature. Selection occurs in different settings, from the personal reading list to the curriculum of a course in world literature and the collective work of creating literary histories and anthologies. The idea of world literature also implies the need to expand national and comparative traditions and to take in more works, languages and literatures. However, the precondition for including more is to exclude others, as we are not able to add more hours to the day and more days to the year. The aspiration to expand the field of world literature thus revolves around redrawing canons to reflect greater diversity and inclusivity, inventing new uses for world literature, and describing how collective and individual work in the field might be carried out. It will hardly do to do what Goethe did: to call for an expansion of the literary outlook and then leave it up to future generations to figure out how to do so.

Writing in the late nineteenth century, Georg Brandes takes a realistic view of which authors actually leave their mark outside of their nation and which do not. Being part of the core canon of a large literature does not mean that one is part of the canon of world literature. At the same time, Brandes would like to see more authors from minor literatures get a chance to be evaluated in other cultures. Such hopes for an expansion of the canon are also at the heart of René Étiemble's concerns, whereas Claudio Guillén and Franco Moretti in different ways suggest that we focus on the systemic conditions for the circulation of world literature.

Another perspective on canons and world literature we find with David Damrosch, who proposes that we combine highly canonized works, that is world literature in the old sense of the world's best and most universal literature, with lesser known works which show a filiation with the established canon, an approach which he applies in *The Longman Anthology of World Literature*. This approach corresponds to one of his definitions of world literature as a mode of reading rather than as a fixed canon. This perspective on the pedagogical aspect of world literature is also central to Sarah Lawall's contribution.

Throughout the texts in this anthology, it is taken as a given that while canonization takes place and can reveal constellations in world literature, it should be challenged by the introduction of new authors and new constellations of work, not simply obeyed. For Horace Engdahl, this challenge to established canons is one of the values of the Nobel Prize in Literature, while Gayatri Spivak urges us not to let dominant narratives conceal the singular expressions that literature is capable of.

Basic readings: Andrés, Étiemble, Aldridge, Zhang, Holden, Spivak, Shih, Tanoukhi, Engdahl, Siskind.

Further readings: Alberson (1960), Marino (1975), Ivask (1977), Aldridge (1986), Spivak (1988), Miner (1990), Gnisci (1999), Spivak (1999), Damrosch (2000), Hillis Miller (2000), Appiah (2001), Asong (2002), Orsini (2002), Greene (2002), McInturff (2003), David (2005), Tlostanova (2005), Damrosch (2006), Dong-il (2006), Victor (2007), Walkowitz (2007), Larsen (2008), Pettersson (2008), Puchner (2011), Saussy (2011), Wang (2011).

Theo D'haen, César Domínguez and Mads Rosendahl Thomsen

Chapter 1

Juan Andrés

ON THE ORIGIN, PROGRESS AND PRESENT STATE OF ALL LITERATURE (EXCERPTS)

J UAN ANDRÉS was a Spanish Jesuit, *littérateur* and historian. When the Jesuits were expelled from Spain in 1767, Andrés moved to Corsica, where he spent a year, and then to Ferrara, where he lived until 1774 teaching philosophy at the Jesuit School. From 1774 to 1796 he stayed at Mantua working as private tutor of the marquis Bianchi's children. It is during this period, after collecting many materials while traveling across Italy, that he started writing a seven-volume world history of literature titled *Dell'origine, progressi e stato attuale d'ogni letteratura* (On the Origin, Progress and Present State of All Literature), which was published between 1782 and 1799. His brother, Carlos, translated it into Spanish, in a ten-volume version published between 1784 and 1806.

Whereas Goethe's reflection on world literature may be described as a future-oriented conceptual rumination without a practical application, Andrés's world history of literature may be described as a past-oriented practical application without a conceptual basis. In fact, Andrés never used in his world literary history concepts such as "universal literature" or "world literature." His closest phrases are *ogni letteratura* and *tutta la letteratura*, which may be translated as "all literature" or "the whole of literature." This notwithstanding, Andrés had a clear plan, namely "to provide a critical history of the work done by literature in all times and places [. . .] a philosophical account of its progress since its inception in every genre." Goethe several times used the concept of *Weltliteratur*, but never provided an exact and clear definition of it. Yet, contemporary discussion on world literature traces its genealogy back to Goethe, and not to Andrés or other literary historians who—like the Italian Francesco Saverio Quadrio in *Della storia e della ragione d'ogni poesia* (1734/1739–52)—aimed at providing a world literary overview. This opposition Goethe/Andrés represents in a nutshell another variety of the geopolitical division North/South of knowledge. Both Goethe and Herder, however, did know that in their respective travels to Italy they had to visit Andrés in Mantua, for he was one of the most famous scholars in Europe.

Mentioning here a geopolitical division of knowledge is not unwarranted inasmuch as Andrés's history is to a large extent a reply to both the North/South division—represented by the French attacks against Spain in general (the Black legend) and Spanish literature in particular (Masson de Morvilliers)—and a South/South division whereby the minor role of Italian literature within European literature was attributed to the negative influence of Spanish literature (Girolamo Tiraboschi, Saverio Bettinelli).

Andrés built his world literary history upon a critical, comparative approach and an epistemological and geographical universalism. His work deals with the origins of literature, including discussions of Chinese, Indian, Persian, Phoenician, Chaldean and Hebrew literature, the Greco-Roman foundations and a lengthy analysis of Arab literature and its key role for the development of European literature, which comprises Spanish, Italian, Occitan, French, German, English, Polish, Russian, Swedish, Danish and Dutch literatures up to the eighteenth century. As for African literature, Andrés suggests ``literary missions'' as a way to gather information about it. And regarding American literature, Andrés seems to envision a future geopolitical move to the Atlantic—even in literary terms (vol. 1, chap. 1)—as a result of the enlightened theories of universal *translatio*.

Andrés's world literary history was very successful during his lifetime and shortly after his death, as proven by the many editions and reprints of the Italian original from 1783 to 1838, its translation into Spanish (also with several editions and reprints) and into French (only the first volume). When the first chair of literary history was endowed in connection with the Real Colegio de San Isidro in Madrid in 1785, the librarians Francisco Meseguer y Arrufat and Miguel de Manuel asked permission of José Moñino y Redondo, count of Floridablanca and minister of Carlos III, to use the *Orígenes* as textbook, because all the other literary histories had a restricted national/regional scope. One hundred and fifty-four students attended this seminar on world literary history the first year. Some of the papers presented for the final exam were ``A Comparison of Ancient African and Asian Cultures'' (Baltasar Félix de Miñano y Las Casas), ``A Comparison of European Literary Cultures till Augustus (excluding Greece and Rome)'' (Alfonso de Manuel y Arriola) and ``On Hebrew Culture, Language and the Literary Value of the Old and New Testament'' (Juan José Heydek). The same permission was granted to the University of Valencia, with the result that these were the first European institutions where world literature was taught.

Passages reproduced from *Origen, progresos y estado actual de toda la literatura*, trans. Carlos Andrés, eds. Jesús García Gabaldón, Santiago Navarro Pastor and Carmen Valcárcel Rivera, vols. 1 & 2 (Madrid: Verbum, 1997) 1: 5–6, 8–14, 17–18, 381–82, 384 & 2: 20–23. Translated by César Domínguez.

Carlos Andrés. Preface by the translator (vol. 1)

Many scholars have stated that two people are necessary for writing a history of the whole literature, one for gathering materials and the other for organizing, classifying and assessing them, for such an enterprise would be too difficult for just a single person, even though the latter had made an extensive reading and enjoyed universal scholarship as well as a deep reflection and a remarkable critical capacity. And yet this hazardous enterprise has been undertaken by the author of the present work, *Del origen, progresos y estado actual de toda la literatura* (On the Origin, Progress and Present State of All Literature).[1] [. . .]

A reviewer from Modena, after having praised the first volume, has stated that it would have been better if the author had devoted less attention to Arabic literature and more to Greek and Roman literature. However, whoever takes into consideration the author's considerations will agree that his method was the best. Arabs have traditionally been considered a barbarian people who have destroyed literature. By assessing their literature extensively, the author has shown, on the one hand, how much modern culture is indebted to them and, on the other hand, their influence on the re-establishment of the belles lettres and, even more, of the sciences. This new opinion and the honorable role played by Spain for having stored Arabic literature and transmitted it to the other nations explain why the author has devoted so much attention to this issue. [. . .]

Juan Andrés. General preface by the author (vol. 1)

The aim of *On the Origin, Progress and Present State of All Literature* is fourfold. Firstly, it seeks to provide a critical history of the labors experienced by literature in all times and places. Secondly, it gives a philosophical account of its progress since its inception in every genre. Thirdly, it draws a picture of its present state. Fourthly, it argues what literature lacks, something which writers will enjoy even though my presentation is not the best one. My plan, which may be considered too impetuous and imprudent, is to provide a sketch of literature that cannot be found elsewhere. We have innumerable literary histories—some of nations, regions and cities, some of specific sciences and arts—which are extremely useful for the increase of knowledge. However, what we lack is a philosophical history which, by focusing on literature as a whole, critically describes its progress and present state and devises means of improving it.[2] The fact that the literary republic is in need of such a history has given me strength to undertake an ambitious enterprise like the present one. [. . .]

I shall give, therefore, exact information of the progress of both the whole literature and each of its genres. For doing so, it is necessary to say something about its origin, something we know very little of. That is why I have decided not to deal at length with such a complex matter. I will exclusively deal with the origin of each science in order to fix a starting point from which one can assess their progress. [. . .]

It is imperative to make distinctions between kinds of sciences [. . .]. The best classification is the one by Bacon, which has been adopted by contributors to the *Encyclopédie* and by Baron Bielfeld.[3] Bacon classifies human knowledge into three kinds in accordance with the three powers of our soul, that is, history, which belongs to memory, poetry, which belongs to the imagination, and philosophy, which belongs to the intellect. [. . .]

I will provide a general idea of the state of literature by dividing it into several ages since its origins to the present. The assessment of its state before the Greeks supplies abundant material for extensive research. However, after intense and endless speculation, one can only arrive at insubstantial and worthless conclusions. After much reading and thought, I have attempted to expound only what can be securely established.[4] Greek literature deserves more attention, as it can really be considered the origin of all literatures. I have tried to identify the origins of Greek literature, something which has not been done so far, and examine the causes of its progress. After describing Greek and Latin literatures separately, a comparison of both of them is most convenient. Some scholars may reject ecclesiastical literature as an independent category. But those who know how literature flourished after the Greek and Latin decadence will agree with me. The decay of literature may seem surprising, especially if one takes into consideration how kings and noblemen after Charlemagne promoted literature. I will try to identify the cause of such a disgraceful event.

Nobody has studied Arabic literature as it deserves. Pococke, Herbelot, Hottinger and some other scholars have provided much information about it, but we do not have a complete account.[5] The novelty of the matter has led me to extensive research. The catholic king Carlos III has given me as a present Casiri's *Bibliotheca Arabico-Hispana Escurialensis*.[6] My section on Arabic literature shows how much I am indebted to this work. As this catalogue is restricted to Arabic manuscripts held at the Biblioteca del Escorial, however, one cannot have all the required information in order to write a complete history of Arabic literature. Nonetheless, I have used all the sources at my disposal.

This research has shown me how much the re-establishment of European literature is indebted to Arabic literature. In order to support this argument, I had to deal with many complicated matters. To mention but a few, research into Spanish literature, which is as unknown as the Arabic; an analysis of ancient writers, who are now completely forgotten; a study of the origin and culture of modern languages and their poetry; a survey of ancient Spanish and Occitan poets.[7] These and other research fields have shed light on a particular thing which may seem a curious paradox to many people: Arabic literature is the mother of modern literature as far as the sciences and belles lettres are concerned. In order to show other aspects of the Arabic influence on Europe, I will talk about many inventions which some nations have wrongly claimed as their own, such as paper, numbers, gunpowder, and the compass, which have arrived to us thanks to the Arabs. Maybe the oscillatory clock and other brilliant inventions of modern times were first designed by them. Schools, observatories, academies and other literary institutions do not consider having their origins in the Arabic culture; most probably they will not feel very satisfied when I show them this ancient connection.

Once the bias against Arabic literature is corrected, it is also necessary to fight against a common opinion regarding Greek literature. It has been advocated that the re-establishment of literature in our area took place with the fall of Constantinople due to the cultural influence of the Greeks who fled to Italy during the 15th century, in the same way as they did in the past with their influence on the unpolished and wild Latium. I will advocate, on the contrary, that the fall of the Greek empire had few advantages for Latin literature, for Italy was more cultivated and had a better taste for the belles lettres than Greece. As for literature in later ages, I have experienced the same difficulty mentioned by Horace: "difficile est proprie communia dicere" (It is difficult to speak of what is common in a way of your own). This notwithstanding, what I will discuss about the literary worth of the 16th and 17th centuries and even more of the present time may seem new to many who do not look at the scholarship during this period in its several dimensions. The last thing that should be done regarding the present state of literature is to mention what aspects need to be improved. [. . .]

On the state of literature before the Greeks (vol. 1)

[. . .] It is not easy to conclude in which country or area literature was born. The regions which have fought for this honor are many. No wonder that, if many cities have fought for being recognized as the birth place of Homer, every scholar had fought for the glory of being the birth place of literature being attributed to their favorite nation. There are many divergent opinions between ancients and moderns. Some think that the cradle of the sciences is in Egypt, others in Assyria and others in India. Moderns [. . .] have learnt exotic languages and studied their main writings; many Europeans know more about Indian and Chinese literature than Indians and Chinese themselves. The *Sadder*, the *Zand-i-Avesta*, the *Shastah*, the *Vedas*, all have been translated to Europe with the Asian riches and have become fashionable among modern writers as drugs and fabrics have become fashionable among people of sophisticated taste.[8] [. . .]

It is necessary to reach the extreme parts of Asia to see China as the first nation that has cultivated the belles lettres. Who could have imagined that China, for so long unknown and foreign for Europe, would be so familiar and close that one may better know Chinese history than our own history? In our century we have more clear and specific information about the ancient times of the Chinese empire than we have of recent antiquities in European regions. [. . .] China provides us in its literature with a spectacle unseen elsewhere in the world. [. . .] I do not have arguments against either Mignot, who advocates the Indian origin of literature, or Guignes, Caylus and others, who advocate the Egyptian origin of literature.[9] But an indestructible wall kept apart China from Tartary and northern Asia, and an even stronger wall kept Chinese scholarship hidden from Egyptians and Europeans, blind at that time, as well as from Indians and Persians. Chinese literature has never gone beyond the limits of the empire. [. . .]

Juan Andrés. Origin, progress and present state of the belles lettres (vol. 2)

When one analyzes the history of literature as a whole, one realizes that the vicissitudes of the belles lettres are very different from those of the sciences. Sciences experience only two conditions, as they are either cultivated or in abandonment. Sciences had great splendor with the Greeks; they were abandoned during some time and, regaining splendor with the Arabs, they will reach perfection with the moderns. Belles lettres, however, change almost constantly, and show their diversity in every age and nation. The perfection in taste achieved in one century is destroyed by the efforts in other directions made in the next century. The path followed by a nation in the artistic course is left by another nation that wants to explore new frontiers. That is why the picture of vicissitudes experienced by belles lettres is more beautiful than that experienced by the sciences. [. . .]

The origin of literature (vol. 2)

Some scholars have tried to show how human beings have cultivated literature since the beginning of time. Madero [sic] has speculated about writings and libraries before the great flood.[10] Hilscher has compiled an Adamic book collection.[11] Reimann [sic] has written a pre-diluvian literary history.[12] Some other scholars have also devoted their free time to these learned hobbies. Heumann, however, has been more cautious by tracing the origin of literature to the times when Jacob's children lived in Egypt.[13] It is undeniable that, when Moses and his sister Mary sang a poem shortly after the Israelites abandoned Egypt, poetry had a previous history. The Book of Job has been dated to that time and is considered a proper poem with a literary style. After a short time, Moses wrote a long and important history in which gentiles themselves have found passages which are praiseworthy due to their sublime eloquence. Writing books on the most diverse matters was a practice so extended among Asian people and other neighboring communities—while the Greeks knew no writing at all— that Solomon regretted that there was such a huge amount of books. Josephus, in his first book of *Against Apion*, showed how whereas the Greeks did not know the art of writing, the Egyptians, Chaldeans, Tyrians, and Phoenicians had already written books on history, philosophy and politics. He also said that during his time the epistles between his king Hiram and the learned Solomon were conserved. One must therefore conclude that not only the sciences and arts, but also poetry, history and all the belles lettres were born in Asia and Egypt.

But, what about the style of those nations? The Greeks or, better said, the Romans have talked about the Asian style as pompous and hollow, redundant and vague, but they were only making reference to the Greeks who lived in Asia, and not to the Asians themselves. Cicero and Quintilian discussed the Asian taste of Caria, Mysia and other Greek colonies in contrast to the Athenian and the Rodian styles, but they said nothing about Indians, Israelites and other authentic Asian people, for their taste was not worth mentioning. We know almost nothing about Chinese literature. Some important Indian and Persian works, deemed to be very ancient, have recently been considered modern forgeries. We only have enough books by Israelites to grasp their style. However, as Chinese, Arabs and Persians have a style quite similar to the biblical, it is possible to conclude that all Asia shares a common style, which was not as pompous and redundant as the Romans believed.

Jean-Baptiste Du Halde, in his *Description de la Chine*, states that the Chinese style is mysterious, concise, allegorical, and obscure for those who are not competent enough in their language. Chinese say many things in few words, and their expressions are lively, vivacious, full of noble metaphors and audacious comparisons. And this very same statement may be applied to the taste of all Asia. [. . .] William Jones concludes in *On the Poetry of the Eastern Nations*, after dealing extensively with rhetorical figures, that allegories are the key difference between the Asian and the European styles. However, I think that this difference may be the result of the frequent use by Asians of paronomasia, word play and prosopopoeia not only for serious matters and deep affections—as used by the Greek and Romans—but also for love, games and everything.

It is possible for someone to attribute to Asians the Greek origin of belles lettres. In fact, as their first poets and historians were born in the Asian colonies and Homer has some passages very similar to the biblical books, as advocated by André Dacier and George Jubb, one may think that the Greeks received their first literary influences from the Asians.[14] Notwithstanding the oriental origin of Greek literature, the extraordinary literary progress should only be attributed to the Greeks, as both in prose and verse, in poetry, history and any kind of eloquence the Greeks showed their fertile imagination and balanced judgement. Their writings captivate readers with a natural and sweet charm. They do not achieve this with audacious figures, forged comparisons, and puns, but with proper and balanced figures, natural and noble expressions, sublime thoughts and authentic images. They do not only give delight to the ears with sweet sounds, but also give a great and warm feeling to the heart. [. . .]

Although the Greeks and Romans were very different as far as their character, genius and customs are concerned, both nations loved natural manners and nobility and with them the belles lettres were close to perfection.

Juan Andrés. Literary history (vol. 1)

We have now the *Histoire littéraire de la France*, although it has been abandoned by their authors, the erudite benedictine monks of St. Maur, Rivet and Clemencet. The Brothers Mohedano are publishing a *Historia literaria de España*, which is so vast that it seems not only difficult, but impossible that it could be concluded. We are enjoying the *Storia della letteratura italiana*, which has been recently finished by the erudite and sensible Tiraboschi. At this moment there is not a single nation, region or city which does not have a literary history of its own. This great national passion goes beyond any limit, and we even have histories of specific genres of every national literature. [. . .]

However, in order to better see all the history of literature's progress and vicissitudes, it is worth remembering here very briefly what I have proved in this volume. Literature was first cultivated in Asia and Egypt, but flourished in Greece, where it bore the most valuable and useful fruits in every branch of the sciences, belles lettres and liberal arts. Greek literature by spreading to Rome gave rise to Latin literature, which is completely Greek as far as its origins are concerned, both in its character and taste. But Latin literature, restricted to the belles lettres, did not spread as much as its mother did. After the decay of Greek and Latin literature, Christianity was the source of ecclesiastical literature, which declined very quickly. The light of scholarship faded in the western world until it shone again thanks to the eastern influence. The Arabs, with their translations and studies, partly increased Greek science and, via

Spain, introduced the natural sciences into Europe. They also, by cultivating all the branches of the belles lettres, gave rise to both a new kind of poetry in our regions and improved our culture and our vernacular languages. Literature was, therefore, reborn in Europe.

Notes

1   An important issue is how to translate into English the original Italian phrase "ogni letteratura" and its Spanish version "toda la literatura." Roberto Dainotto has chosen to render the original Italian title *Dell'origine, progressi e stato attuale d'ogni letteratura* as *Of the Origins, Progress, and Present State of All Literatures*; see Roberto M. Dainotto, *Europe (In Theory)* (Durham: Duke UP, 2007) 108. In my opinion, the plural use of "literature" is not the idea intended by Juan Andrés. Although Andrés makes many references to "universal histories," such as the *Discours sur l'histoire universelle* by Bossuet, he never uses such phrases as "universal literature" or "world literature". This notwithstanding, it seems clear that he thinks of *ogni letteratura* as "tutta la letteratura" / "toda la literatura," that is, as a single unity which spreads all over the world. For a phrase with this global sense, an example may be: "vediamo l'origine, i progressi, e lo stato attuale di tutta la bella letteratura," in Giovanni Andres, *Dell'origine, progressi e stato attuale d'ogni letteratura*, vol. 2 (Parma: Stamperia Reale, 1785) 19 (let us see the origin, progress and the present state of the whole beautiful literature). This global sense is also applied by Andrés to European literature: "la letteratura europea non può ricavare verun ajuto dal soccorso cinese," in Giovanni Andres, *Dell'origine, progressi e stato attuale d'ogni letteratura*, vol. 1 (Parma: Stamperia Reale, 1781) 9 (European literature could not get any help from Chinese literature). The French translation of the first volume, made by J. E. Ortolani in 1805, uses the phrase "histoire littéraire universelle." In accordance with such a global sense, I have decided to translate *ogni letteratura* as "all literature."

2   It is clear that Andrés uses the concept of "literature" in the sense of written culture, with two main branches, the sciences and belles lettres. However, many times "literature" is also used by Andrés with the modern sense of "imaginative literature." Belles lettres are divided into four broad categories, poetry (including epic and lyric poetry as well as narrative), eloquence, history, and grammar.

3   Andrés makes reference to the classification of the sciences included by Roger Bacon in *De dignitate et augmentis scientiarum* (1620). D'Alembert, in his famous *Discours préliminaire*, qualified Bacon's system of human knowledge. Baron Jakob Friedrich Bielfeld was a Prussian officer and a comparative Latinist; Andrés mentions here Bielfeld's work *Progrès des allemands dans les sciences, les belles lettres, et les arts* (1767).

4   Andrés is making reference here to the brothers Rafael and Pedro Rodríguez Mohedano's *Historia literaria de España* (1766–91), which, after ten volumes, only reached the 1st century with the "Hispano-Latin" poet Lucan notwithstanding their aim of writing "the literary history of Spain, the scientific progress of this nation and other fields of knowledge since its first inhabitants to *the present*", in F. Pedro Rodríguez Mohedano and Rafael Rodríguez Mohedano, *Historia literaria de España*, vol. 1 (Madrid: Antonio Pérez de Soto, 1766) i (emphasis added).

5   Richard Pococke (1704–65), an English prelate and anthropologist, published a *Description of the East* (1743–45), an account of his travels to Egypt, Jerusalem, Palestine, and Greece. He discussed the origins of the medieval Arabic document the *Achtiname* of Muhammad. Barthélemy d'Herbelot de Molainville (1625–95), a French orientalist, devoted his life to the *Bibliothèque orientale*, which consists of both an abridged translation of the *Kashf al-zunūn 'an asāmī al-kutub wa-al-funūn*, (The Removal of Doubt from the Names of Books and the Sciences), by the Ottoman Turk Kâtip Çelebi (1609–57), and other Arabic and Turkish manuscripts. Johann Heinrich Hottinger (1620–67) was a Swiss philologist and theologian who gained himself a reputation as an orientalist.

6   Miguel Casiri (1710–91) was a learned Maronite and orientalist who was employed in the Royal Library at Madrid. He was a member of the Royal Academy of History, an interpreter of oriental languages to the king, and a librarian at the Escorial. He published the two-volume *Bibliotheca Arabico-Hispana Escurialensis* (1760–70), a catalogue of more than 1,800 Arabic manuscripts at the Escorial which includes a number of quotations.

7   One needs to take into consideration that Andrés' *Origen* was written in the context of two controversies. On the one hand, the controversy caused by Masson de Morvillier's article on Spain for the *Encyclopédie*, wherein he wonders "[Q]ue doit on à l'Espagne? [. . .] qu'a-t-elle fait pour l'Europe?" and answers "nothing." The important influence of the Arabic culture on European literature and the sciences was a key argument for the defenders of Spanish culture, as it was argued that Arabic culture reached Europe precisely via Spain, not to mention the extensive number of

translations of Arabic and Hebrew works made in Spain. On the other hand, the controversy fueled by Italian scholars such as Ludovico Muratori, Saverio Bettinelli and Girolamo Tiraboschi, who attributed the decay of Italian literature to the Spanish influence.

8   The *Sadder* is a verse-history of the flight of the Parsis into India. The *Avesta* is a collection of sacred texts of Zoroastrianism composed over the course of several centuries. The *Zand-i-Avesta* is one manuscript form in which the *Avesta* has been transmitted, in this case including comments. The *Shastah* is Brahmins' first sacred law. The *Veda* are a large body of texts originating in India, which constitute the oldest layer of Sanskrit literature.

9   Abbé Étienne Mignot (1698–1771) advocated the Indian origins of Chinese literature in *Sur les anciens philosophes de l'Inde*. Joseph de Guignes (1721–1800) was a French orientalist and sinologist who maintained that the Chinese nation had originated in Egyptian colonization. Anne-Claude-Philippe de Tubières, count de Caylus (1692–1765), was a French archaeologist; his principal work is the seven-volume *Recueil d'antiquités égyptiennes, étrusques, grecques, romaines, et gauloises* (1752–67).

10 Joachim Johann Mader (1626–80) wrote *De bibliothecis atque archiuis virorum clarissimorum libelli et commentationes cum praefatione de scriptis et biblithecis antediluuianis* (1666), which is considered the first anthology on libraries and library science.

11 Paul Christian Hilscher (1666–1730) was a Lutheran theologian who wrote *De bibliotheca Adami* (1711).

12 Andrés makes reference here to the German theologian and bibliographer Jacob Friedrich Reimann (1668–1743); however, it is not clear which work/s he is mentioning. It may be either *Versuch einer Einleitung in die Historiam literariam* (1708–13) or the *Catalogus bibliothecae theologicae*, whose second volume is titled *Bibliotheca historiae literariae critica* (1731).

13 Andrés makes reference here to Kristophe August Heumann, founder of the *Acta Philosophorum*.

14 André Dacier (1651–1722) was a French classical scholar and George Jubb (1717–87) was a Professor of Hebrew.

Chapter 2

Johann Wolfgang (von) Goethe

ON WORLD LITERATURE (1827)

THE GERMAN WRITER JOHANN WOLFGANG (von) Goethe (1749–1832) did not coin the term "world literature" or, in Goethe's own language, *Weltliteratur*, though for the longest time he was thought to have done so. Undeniably, though, his use of it gained the term the wide currency it has ever since enjoyed.

Goethe had gained legendary fame with the publication of his *Sorrows of Young Werther* (*Die Leiden des jungen Werthers*, 1774). This epistolary novel became the rage all through Europe, and helped pave the way for Romanticism throughout the continent. First and foremost, though, it confirmed Goethe as one of the main exponents, next to Friedrich Schiller (1759–1805), of the short-lived "Storm and Stress" (*Sturm und Drang*) movement in Germany. This movement is usually considered a precursor of Romanticism proper. Preferring the emotions to reason, the Storm and Stress authors rebelled against the values usually associated with the Enlightenment. As the latter was seen as primarily the work of a number of French, and by the 1770s already rather aged, philosophers and writers, Storm and Stress saw itself as speaking up for both youth and Germany. In 1775 Goethe was called to the court of the Duke of Saxe-Weimar.

In Weimar, and following an extended trip to Italy from 1786 to 1788, Goethe reneged on his early Romanticism and became, again with Schiller, one of the leading lights of so-called Weimar Classicism. The adherents of this movement tried to reach a harmonious blend of classical, Enlightenment and Romantic elements in their search for a new humanism fit for the turn of the nineteenth century. During this period Goethe wrote his *Faust*, part I (1808, the complete play, including part II, was only published after Goethe's death) and *Wilhelm Meister's Apprenticeship* (*Wilhelm Meisters Wanderjahre*, 1795–96), a—some would say *the*—typical *Bildungsroman*.

In later life Goethe enjoyed the status of Europe's most famous man of letters, and his residence in Weimar became a place of literary pilgrimage. Goethe, however, was not only a writer of literature, but also a scientist with a lively interest in geology, botany and the study of nature in general. He wrote extensively on these subjects, and he himself considered his *Theory of Colours* (*Zur Farbenlehre*, 1810) his most important work.

Because of Goethe's fame his statements on *Weltliteratur* spread rapidly in European literary circles. In all, Goethe used the term *Weltliteratur* or world literature twenty-one times: in conversations with Johann Peter Eckermann, as recorded in the latter's *Conversations with Goethe* (*Gespräche mit Goethe*, 1836), his own diary, letters to various addressees, articles in his own journal *Art and Antiquity* (*Über Kunst und Ältertum*), an address to a Congress of Natural Scientists in Berlin, and drafts for, and the published version of, an introduction to the 1830 German translation of Thomas Carlyle's *Life of Schiller*. All passages date from between 1827 and 1831. All of them are brief to very brief, and nowhere does Goethe give a definition of what precisely he means with *Weltliteratur*. No wonder then that subsequent commentators have often strayed very widely in their interpretations of the term, as can be gauged from the further selections in the present volume. Goethe's pronouncements on world literature have formed the inevitable starting point for all subsequent reflections on the topic, though, and remain so to this day.

Broadly speaking, Goethe at various times during the years in which he used the term seems to have associated the following, sometimes contradictory, ideas with world literature. Most commonly Goethe is assumed to have seen world literature as the circulation of ideas, themes and forms between the literati of, in first instance, Europe, and possibly beyond. He saw this circulation as speeding up because of economic and technical developments, and particularly because of the rapid rise and spread of literary journals across Europe. This he saw as a positive development, knitting the peoples of Europe closer together, or at least promoting understanding and tolerance among them. These same developments, however, also held the danger of cheap commercialization. Goethe balked at this: he saw world literature as the province of the learned, not the rabble. His ideals of "understanding" and tolerance were intimately linked to his interest in humanism, both in its original Renaissance form and in the guise of the "new humanism" then spreading throughout German intellectual circles. He definitely did not perceive of world literature as a canon of world masterpieces, although this is the meaning that rapidly came to be associated with the term after Goethe's death with the rise of literary historiography as of the middle of the nineteenth century.

In what follows we publish Goethe's statements on world literature as they have been collected in the appendix to Fritz Strich's *Goethe and World Literature* (Transl. C.A. Sym, New York: Hafner Publishing Company, 1949, pp. 349–51, passages numbered 1, 3, 5, 6, 9, 10, 12, 13, 14, 16, 17, 21; English translation of *Goethe und die Weltliteratur*, Bern: Francke Verlag, 1945), and for some of the more important passages (2, 4, 7, 8, 11, 15, 18, 19) in the fuller version published in Hans-Joachim Schulz and Philip H. Rhein, eds., *Comparative Literature: The Early Years* (Chapel Hill: The University of North Carolina Press, 1973, pp. 5–11), in a translation (with some minor amendments by Schulz & Rhein) by Joel E. Spingarn, *Goethe's Literary Essays* (New York: Harcourt, Brace and Company, 1921).

    1. Diary, 15th January 1827: "Dictated to Schuchardt on the subject of French literature and world literature."

    2. *Über Kunst und Ältertum*, Vol. 6, part I, 1827 (Le Tasse, drame historique en cinq actes, par Monsieur Alexandre Duval): "I report about French journals not only to draw attention to myself and my work. I am aiming at something higher which, for the time being, I will indicate as follows:

Everywhere we hear and read of the progress of the human race, of the broader view of international and human relations. Since it is not my office here to define or qualify these broad generalities, I shall merely acquaint my friends with my conviction that there is being formed a universal world literature, in which an honorable role is reserved for us Germans. All the nations review our work; they praise, censure, accept, and reject, imitate and misrepresent us, open or close their hearts to us. All this we must accept with equanimity, since this attitude, taken as a whole, is of great value to us.

We experience the same thing from our own countrymen, and why should the nations agree among themselves if fellow citizens do not understand how to unite and cooperate with each other? In a literary sense we have a good start on the other nations; they will always be learning to prize us more, even if they only show it by borrowing from us without thanks, and making use of us without giving recognition of the fact.

As the military and physical strength of a nation develops from its internal unity and cohesion, so must its aesthetic and ethical strength grow gradually from a similar unanimity of feeling and ideas. This, however, can only be accomplished with time. I look back as a cooperator in this work over many years and reflect how a German literature has been brought together out of heterogeneous, if not conflicting, elements,—a literature which for that reason is only peculiarly one in the sense that it is composed in one language,—which, however, out of a variety of wholly different talents and abilities, minds and actions, criticisms and undertakings, gradually draws out to the light of day the true inner soul of a people."

3. Letter to Streckfuss, 27th January 1827: "I am convinced that a world literature is in process of formation, that the nations are in favour of it and for this reason make friendly overtures. The German can and should be most active in this respect; he has a fine part to play in this great mutual approach."

4. Conversation with Eckermann, 31st January 1827: "It is becoming more and more obvious to me that poetry is the common property of all mankind and that it is manifest everywhere and in all ages in hundreds and hundreds of people. The only difference is that some express themselves a little better and are on top a little longer. Herr von Matthison should not consider himself the poet, as I should not think that I am; everyone should be aware of the fact that the poetic talent is not very rare and should not pride himself on having composed a good poem. But of course, when we Germans do not look beyond the narrow confines of our immediate surroundings, we easily develop this pedantic pride. I therefore like to keep informed about foreign productions, and I advise everybody to do the same. National literature means little now, the age of Weltliteratur has begun; and everyone should further its course. But this esteem for foreign productions should not stop with specific characteristics and declare them models. We should not think that the truth is in Chinese or Serbian literature, in Calderón or the Nibelungen. In our pursuit of models, we ought always to return to the Greeks of antiquity in whose works beautiful man is represented. The rest we contemplate historically and assimilate from it the best as far as we can."

5. Conversation with Eckermann, 15th July 1827: "It really is a very good thing that with this close intercourse between Frenchmen, Englishmen and Germans we have a chance of correcting each other's errors. This is the great advantage that world literature affords, one which will in time become more and more obvious. Carlyle has written the life of Schiller and has estimated him throughout as it would have been difficult for a German to do. On the other hand we can judge Shakespeare and Byron, and know how to evaluate their merits perhaps better than the English themselves."

6. Letter to Boisserée, 12th October 1827: "In this connection it might be added that what I call world literature develops in the first place when the differences that prevail within one nation are resolved through the understanding and judgment of the rest."

7. Letter to Carlyle, 1st January 1828: "Now I should like to have your opinion on how far this *Tasso* can be considered *English*. You will greatly oblige me by informing me on this point; for it is just this connection between the original and the translation that expresses most clearly the relationship of nation to nation and that one must above all know if one wishes to encourage a common world literature transcending national limits."

8. *Über Kunst und Ältertum*, Vol. 6, part 2, 1828 (Relations to Other Countries):
"My sanguine suggestion that our present active epoch with its increasing communication between the nations might soon hope for a world literature has been taken up approvingly by our neighbors of the west, who indeed can accomplish great things in this same direction. They express themselves on the subject in the following manner:

> Le Globe, Tome V., No. 91.
>
> 'Every nation indeed, when its turn comes, feels that tension which, like the attractive power of physical bodies, draws one towards the other, and eventually will unite in one universal sympathy all the races of which humanity consists. The endeavor of scholars to understand one another and compare one another's work is by no means new; the Latin language in former times has provided an admirable vehicle for this purpose. But however they labored and strove, the barriers by which peoples were separated began to divide them also, and hurt their intellectual intercourse. The instrument of which they made use could only satisfy a certain range and course of ideas, so that they touched each other only through the intellect, instead of directly through the feelings and through poetry. Travel, the study of languages, periodical literature, have taken the place of that universal language, and establish many intimate and harmonious relations which it could never cultivate. Even the nations that devote themselves chiefly to trade and industry are most concerned with this exchange of ideas. England, whose home activity is so tremendous, whose life is so busy, that it seems as if it would be able to study nothing but itself, at the present time is showing a symptom of this need and desire to broaden its horizon. Its existing reviews are not enough for them; two new periodicals, devoted especially to foreign literature, and cooperating together towards that end, are to appear regularly.'

Of the first of these English journals, *The Foreign Quarterly Review*, there are already two volumes in our hands; the third we expect directly, and we shall in the course of these pages often refer to the views of important men who are giving proof, with so much insight and industry, of their interest in foreign literature.

But first of all we must confess that it made us smile to see, at the end of the old year, more than thirty literary almanacs (*Taschenbücher*), already noticed in an English journal—not indeed reviewed, but at least referred to with some characteristic comments. It is pleasant that our productions of this sort meet with approval and find a market over there, since we are also obliged to buy their similar works for good money. Little by little we shall discover, I suppose, whether the balance of this trade turns out to our advantage.

But these trivial considerations must give place to more serious ones. Left to itself every literature will exhaust its vitality, if it is not refreshed by the interest and contributions of a foreign one. What naturalist does not take pleasure in the wonderful things that he sees produced by reflection in a mirror? Now what a mirror in the field of ideas and morals means, everyone has experienced in himself, and once his attention is aroused, he will understand how much of his education he owes to it."

9. Letter to Zelter, 21st May 1828: "Please note that the world literature I have called for is deluging and threatening to drown me like the sorcerer's apprentice: Scotland and France pour forth almost daily, and in Milan they are publishing a most important daily paper called *l'Eco*."

10. Letter to the Editor of the journal *L'Eco*, 31st May 1828: "The first forty-seven numbers of the journal which you are launching in Milan have been a most pleasant surprise

to me; with their content, and the attractive form you have given them, they will make the most pleasing contribution to the universal world literature which is spreading with increasing energy, and I sincerely assure you of my interest."

11. *Über Kunst und Ältertum,* Vol. 6, part 2, 1828 *(Edinburgh Reviews)*: "The *Edinburgh Review*, as well as the current *Foreign* and *Foreign Quarterly Reviews*, we can only mention briefly here."

These journals, as they win an ever wider public, will contribute in the most effective way towards that universal world literature for which we are hoping. Only, we repeat, the idea is not that the nations shall think alike, but that they shall learn how to understand each other, and, if they do not care to love one another, at least that they will learn to tolerate one another. Several societies now exist for the purpose of making the British Isles acquainted with the continent, and are working effectively and with a practical unanimity of opinion. We continentals can learn from them the intellectual background of the time across the channel, what they are thinking and what their judgments about things are. On the whole, we acknowledge gladly that they go about the work with intense seriousness, with industry and tolerance and general goodwill. The result for us will be that we shall be compelled to think again of our own recent literature, which we have in some measure already put to one side, and to consider and examine it anew. Especially worthy of notice is their profitable method of starting with any considerable author, and going over the whole field in which he worked.

[. . .]

The methods and manners of these critics deserve our consideration in many ways. Although varying on many points, yet there is an agreement in criticism upon the main issues, which seems to indicate, if not a coterie, yet a number of contemporary critics who have come to a similar attitude and point of view. Worthy of our admiration are the honest and sincere application, the careful labors, which they devote to surveying our complex artistic and literary world, and to looking over it with a just and fair attitude and vision. We shall hope often to be able to return to them and their work.

12. The Congress of Natural Scientists in Berlin, 1828: "In venturing to announce a European, in fact a universal, world literature, we did not mean merely to say that the different nations should get to know each other and each other's productions; for in this sense it has long since been in existence, is propagating itself, and is constantly being added to. No, indeed! The matter is rather this—that the living, striving men of letters should learn to know each other, and through their own inclination and similarity of tastes, find the motive for corporate action."

13. From Makarie's *Archives* (probably 1829): "Now, in the first stages of world literature, if we look closely we can see that the German stands to lose most; he would do well to ponder this warning."

14. Letter to Zelter, 4th May 1829: "The exaggerations forced upon the theatres of Paris, that great wide-spread city, do harm to us who are still far from finding them necessary ourselves. Yet these are the consequences of advancing world literature, and we can find comfort only in the fact that though the common cause comes off badly yet individuals are helped and benefited; from time to time I receive very gratifying proofs of this."

15. Letter to C. F. v. Reinhard, 18th June 1829: "For some time now I have devoted myself almost exclusively to French books. To go through the eight volumes of the *Revue française*, which I have received only now, is no small endeavor, considering the variety and great significance of its articles. The authors use recent publications only as a pretext, so to speak, to air their well-founded opinions and honest attitudes. The acknowledgement of all merit suits the liberal well, particularly the kind of acknowledgement we find here. It offers us proofs of the sort of free and elevated point of view on diverse matters which, after all, alone characterizes objectivity.

It is truly amazing how far the French have advanced since they stopped being narrow and exclusive in outlook. How well they know their Germans, their Englishmen, better than those do themselves. How precisely they describe the egoistical man of the world in the former, the good-natured private citizen in the latter. The *Globe* too is dear to me, although its special political tendency makes me feel uneasy. But one does not have to be in complete agreement with excellent people to feel affection and admiration for them.

[. . .]

The mutual relationships between the elements of world literature are very forceful and strange; if I am not greatly mistaken, the French will profit most from them in terms of a higher perspective. They already have a certain self-confident feeling that their literature will again have the same influence upon Europe that it enjoyed in the first half of the eighteenth century—even in a more profound way than formerly."

16. Scheme for *Kunst und Ältertum*, Vol. 6, part 3, 1829: First Version: "World literature". Second Version: "European, in other words, World Literature".

17. Conversation with Willibald Alexis, 12th August 1829: "In this conversation also there appeared references to a common European or World literature, one of the favourite themes of the winter of his life which is still haunted by spirits of his imagination."

18. Introduction to Thomas Carlyle's *Life of Schiller,* 1830: "There has for some time been talk of a Universal World Literature, and indeed not without reason: for all the nations that had been flung together by frightful wars and had then settled down again became aware of having imbibed much that was foreign, and conscious of spiritual needs hitherto unknown. Hence arose a sense of their relationship as neighbours, and, instead of shutting themselves up as heretofore, the desire gradually awoke within them to become associated in a more or less free commerce." [Translation by C. E. Norton, *Correspondence between Goethe and Carlyle,* London, 1837.]

19. From the draft of the above Introduction (see 18) and, the passage beyond the second row of dots, from the published Introduction : "If a world literature, such as is inevitable with the ever-increasing facility of communication, is to be formed in the near future, we must expect from it nothing more and nothing different from what it can and does accomplish.

The wide world, extensive as it is, is only an expanded fatherland, and will, if looked at aright, be able to give us no more than what our home soil can endow us with also. What pleases the crowd spreads itself over a limitless field, and, as we already see, meets approval in all countries and regions. The serious and intellectual meets with less success, but those who are devoted to higher and more profitable things will learn to know each other more quickly and more intimately. For there are everywhere in the world such men, to whom the truth and the progress of humanity are of interest and concern. But the road which they pursue, the pace which they keep, is not to everybody's liking; the particularly aggressive wish to advance faster, and so turn aside, and prevent the furthering of that which in turn could further them. The serious-minded must therefore form a quiet, almost secret, company, since it would be futile to set themselves against the current of the day; rather must they manfully strive to maintain their position till the flood has passed.

Their principal consolation, and indeed encouragement, such men must find in the fact that truth is serviceable. If they can discover this relation, and exhibit its meaning and influence in a vital way, they will not fail to produce a powerful effect, indeed one that will extend over a range of years.

[. . .]

Not only what such men say about us should be of the greatest importance to us, but we should consider all their relations to other nations, the French and the Italians.

General world literature can only develop when nations get to know all the relations among all the nations. The inevitable result will be that they will find in each other something likeable and something repulsive, something to be imitated and something to be rejected.

This too will contribute to the expanding economic relations, for the recognition of common convictions will further a prompter and deeper confidence. On the other hand, when we are dealing with people who think very differently, we will be more cautious as well as more tolerant and forgiving.

[. . .]

There has been talk for some time of a general world literature, and indeed not without justice. For the nations, after they had been shaken into confusion and mutual conflict by the terrible wars, could not return to their settled and independent life again without noticing that they had learned many foreign ideas and ways, which they had unconsciously adopted, and had come to feel here and there previously unrecognized spiritual and intellectual needs. Out of this arose the feeling of neighborly relations, and, instead of shutting themselves up as before, they gradually came to desire to be part of some sort of more or less free spiritual intercourse.

This movement, it is true, has lasted only a short time, but still long enough to start considerable speculation, and to acquire from it, as one must always from any kind of foreign trade, both profit and enjoyment."

20. Draft of the above Introduction (see 18), 5th April 1830: "Not merely what such men write to us must be of first importance to us; we have also to consider their other relationships, how they stand with reference to the French and the Italians. For that after all is the only way towards a general world literature—for all nations to learn their relationships each to the other; and each is bound to find in the other something attractive and something repellent, something worthy of emulation and something to be avoided."

21. Letter to Boisserée, 24th April 1831: "In the case of the translation of my latest botanical studies I have had the same experience as you. Some passages of capital importance, which my friend Soret could not understand in my German, I translated into my kind of French; he rewrote them in his own, and I am quite convinced that in that language they will be more generally understood than perhaps in German. A certain French lady appears to have thought of using this system already; she has the German translated to her simply and literally, and then proceeds to endow it with a grace peculiar to her language and her sex. These are the immediate consequences of a general world literature; the nations will be quicker in benefiting by each other's advantages. I shall say no more on this subject, for it is one which calls for a good deal of elaboration."

Chapter 3

Karl Marx and Friedrich Engels

THE COMMUNIST MANIFESTO (1848)

KARL MARX (1818–83) AND FRIEDRICH Engels (1820–95) are well-known as social scientists, political theorists, philosophers, and fathers of Marxism, which is both an economic and socio-political worldview and a theory of the development, reproduction and transformation of capitalism. One of the main tenets of this theory is the distinction between the base—the forms of economic organization or modes of production (from cooperative tribalism and feudalism to capitalism and communism)—and the superstructure—ideology or forms of social consciousness, such as religion, law, politics and art. Although later interpretations of this distinction are rather restrictive and deterministic, Marx's definition and Engels's elaborations stressed that the superstructure is not a passive product of the base, for the former may work with a considerable degree of autonomy. This is of key importance when it comes to understanding the way both authors approached literature. Language in general and as the substance of literature in particular is another kind of social practice and, therefore, is rooted in the material conditions of the base. This notwithstanding, literature is relatively autonomous, for its relation with the base is not merely reflexive.

Statements on literature and the arts by both Marx and Engels are fragmentary and scattered throughout their huge mass of writing. In this sense, "Marxist" ideas on literature need to be treated with caution, for they are mostly the result of attempts by Marxist critics to comprehensively organize Marx and Engels's opinions, such as their predilection for literary realism, the issue of literary value and the relation between literature and politics. One example of such a fragmentary statement is that on world literature included in the *Manifest der Kommunistischen Partei* (1848; *Manifesto of the Communist Party*) (for a survey of Marx's arguments, see Prawer 1976). Whether the *Manifesto* was jointly authored by Marx and Engels is a matter of controversy. Engels is credited with having written two drafts, "Communist Credo" and "Principles of Communism," which undoubtedly influenced the final version attributed to Marx.[i] The reference to *Weltliteratur* (world

i   Hal Draper, *The Adventures of the Communist Manifesto* (Alameda, CA: Center for Socialist History, 2004) 11.

literature) is included in the first chapter ("Bourgeois and Proletarians"), wherein Marx and Engels examine the Marxist conception of society as a history of class struggles. In the modern era, industry has established a world market, to which the bourgeoisie has given a cosmopolitan character. Likewise, the intellectual creations of single nations, including literature, are not nation-specific any longer, but the common property of the world.

Interestingly, György Lukács traced the decadence of the novel to 1848, the year when the *Manifesto* was published and the European bourgeoisie abandoned its revolutionary role according to this leading Marxist critic. A suggestive triangulation of the issue of world literature between Goethe, Marx–Engels and Lukács may be explored if one takes into consideration Goethe's interest in technology as a driving force for international communication, the influence of *Faust* upon Marx and Engels's *Manifesto*, and Lukács's claims about Faust as the fulfillment of capitalist activity.[ii]

The passage we here reproduce is from page 16 of *The Communist Manifesto* available online at http://www.marxists.org/archive/marx/works/download/pdf/Manifesto.pdf, which is itself taken from Marx/Engels *Selected Works*, Vol. One, Progress Publishers, Moscow, 1969, pp. 98–137; as translated by Samuel Moore in cooperation with Frederick Engels in 1888.

The bourgeoisie cannot exist without constantly revolutionising the instruments of production, and thereby the relations of production, and with them the whole relations of society. Conservation of the old modes of production in unaltered form, was, on the contrary, the first condition of existence for all earlier industrial classes. Constant revolutionising of production, uninterrupted disturbance of all social conditions, everlasting uncertainty and agitation distinguish the bourgeois epoch from all earlier ones. All fixed, fast-frozen relations, with their train of ancient and venerable prejudices and opinions, are swept away, all new-formed ones become antiquated before they can ossify. All that is solid melts into air, all that is holy is profaned, and man is at last compelled to face with sober senses his real conditions of life, and his relations with his kind.

The need of a constantly expanding market for its products chases the bourgeoisie over the entire surface of the globe. It must nestle everywhere, settle everywhere, establish connexions everywhere.

The bourgeoisie has through its exploitation of the world market given a cosmopolitan character to production and consumption in every country. To the great chagrin of Reactionists, it has drawn from under the feet of industry the national ground on which it stood. All old-established national industries have been destroyed or are daily being destroyed. They are dislodged by new industries, whose introduction becomes a life and death question for all civilised nations, by industries that no longer work up indigenous raw material, but raw material drawn from the remotest zones; industries whose products are consumed, not only at home, but in every quarter of the globe. In place of the old wants, satisfied by the production of the country, we find new wants, requiring for their satisfaction the products of distant lands and climes. In place of the old local and national seclusion and self-sufficiency, we have intercourse in every direction, universal inter-dependence of nations. And as in material, so also in intellectual production. The intellectual creations of individual nations become common property. National one-sidedness and narrow-mindedness become more and more impossible, and from the numerous national and local literatures, there arises a world literature.

ii   Margaret M. Bullitt, "A Socialist Faust?," *Comparative Literature* 32.2 (1980): 184–95 (195).

Chapter 4

Hugo Meltzl

PRESENT TASKS OF COMPARATIVE LITERATURE (1877)

H UGO MELTZL (1846–1908; ALSO known as Hugo von Meltzl and Hugo Meltzl de Lomnitz) was a professor of German language and literature at the university of what is now Cluj (officially Cluj-Napoca) in Romania, but which at the time went by the names of Klausenburg in German and Kolozsvár in Hungarian, and which was the capital of the then province of Transylvania in the Austro-Hungarian Empire. Together with his older colleague Samuel Brassai (1800–97), Meltzl founded the first ever comparative literature journal in 1877. Originally appearing under a multilingual title, the journal as of 1879 was called *Acta Comparationis Litterarum Universarum*. Meltzl became the sole editor upon Brassai's retirement in 1883, and this continued until the journal's demise in 1888.

Meltzl actively promoted polyglottism as a standard for comparative literature. In a three-part programmatic article published in the first three issues of the journal, Meltzl outlined what he saw as the "Present Tasks of Comparative Literature." *Weltliteratur* he claimed to have been generally misunderstood in his day, with every nation clamoring for its own version. This, Meltzl argued, was the inevitable consequence of literary history, following the example of the German literary historian Gervinus, in the middle of the nineteenth century having been reduced to an "*ancilla nationis*" or handmaiden of the nation. True "world literature" for Meltzl could only remain "an unattainable ideal in the direction of which, nevertheless, all independent literatures, i.e. all nations, should strive." The means with which to pursue this ideal were translation and polyglottism. Eventually, Meltzl proposed ten working languages for the journal: German, English, French, Icelandic, Italian, Spanish, Portuguese, Swedish, Dutch and Hungarian, next to Latin. In practice, most articles were in German and Hungarian. In its later years the *Acta* increasingly concentrated on one of the aspects that Meltzl highlighted as the province of what he considered "world literature," that is to say the folkloric, offering examples from around the world in the original with adjacent translations. The *Acta*, notwithstanding its ambitions, and probably at least partially due to its relatively inauspicious site of publication, never had more than a few score subscribers and readers. By the end of the 1880s it had been overtaken, and in practice been replaced, by a German rival periodical edited by Max Koch (1855–1931).

Though Meltzl was never really forgotten, the relatively small dissemination his journal had enjoyed, and the fact that it was accessible at few libraries only, greatly limited his real impact. However, over the last decade or so the situation has changed dramatically, with especially a number of US comparative literature scholars such as David Damrosch and Haun Saussy reclaiming Meltzl as having shown the way towards a truly multilingual and globally oriented study of literature.

We here reprint "Present Tasks of Comparative Literature, Parts I and II" in the version also included in Hans-Joachim Schulz and Philip H. Rhein, *Comparative Literature: The Early Years* (Chapel Hill: The University of North Carolina Press, 1973, pp. 56–62) and as translated from *Acta Comparationis Litterarum Universarum* I (January 1877), 179–82 and II (October 1877), 307–15.

I

Since our polyglot journal has been mistaken for a philological one by some philologists, it may not be superfluous to discuss briefly once more the tasks of our journal which—being the very first such effort in this area—cannot rely on achievements of predecessors or other convenient advantages.

Comparative Literature—for which to our knowledge only the Germans, French and Italians already have an established designation—is nevertheless by no means a fully defined and established academic discipline. As a matter of fact, it is still far from that goal. The task, therefore, of an organ of this slowly emerging discipline of the future should not so much consist in definitely comparing the vast (though still insufficient) material at hand as in adding to it from all sides and in intensifying the effort, directly as well as indirectly. A journal like ours, then, must be devoted at the same time to the art of translation and to the Goethean *Weltliteratur* (a term which German literary historians, particularly Gervinus, have thoroughly misunderstood). Literature and language are closely related; the latter being substantially subservient to the former, without which the servant would have not only no autonomy but no existence at all. Therefore it should be understood that linguistic problems will also be touched upon now and then (though not methodically discussed), particularly with regard to exotic peoples. For similar reasons Comparative Literature touches upon the fields of philosophy, esthetics, even ethnology and anthropology. Without ethnological considerations, for instance, the literatures of remote regions could not be fully understood.

To these tasks we have to add the *reform of literary history,* a reform long awaited and long overdue which is possible only through an extensive application of the *comparative principle.* As every unbiased man of letters knows, modern literary history, as generally practiced today, is nothing but an *ancilla historiae politicae,* or even an *ancilla nationis,* at best an *ancilla philologiae* (in the modern sense of the latter term). Literary historians have gone so far as to base their divisions into literary epochs on political events, sometimes on the death-years of—kings! For these and similar reasons, even the best and best-known presentations of the literary history of all languages are thoroughly unacceptable to the mature taste and are quite unprofitable for serious literary (not political and philological) purposes. Only extensive work in the comparative fields, particularly translation, can eliminate gradually many preconceptions. Of those many preconceptions, we may mention one in the field of modern German literary history. In Koberstein's monumental work [*Grundriss der Geschichte der deutschen Nationalliteratur*], which is on the whole justly famous (5th ed., by the conscientious Bartsch, Leipzig, 1872, Vol. I, p. 218, footnote 7), there is a lengthy discussion of the question whether the "Tage- und Wächterlied" was invented by Wolfram von Eschenbach or by the Provençal poets. Finally the author agrees with the "thorough and cautious" Lachmann that Wolfram is the inventor of this genre. With all their thoroughness and caution they do not consider the fact that Lieder of this type were sung eighteen centuries ago in China (as those contained in the *I'Ching*) and are frequently found among the folksongs of modern peoples, for instance, the Hungarians.

There is no area of literary study today as overworked, unattractive and, in spite of this, frequented as that of literary history; and there is none that promises less. Lichtenberg already came to that conclusion before the writing of literary histories had properly begun. This is only confirmed by such rare exceptions as Scherr's and Minckwitz's historical works which—in spite of occasionally fitting literary phenomena into conventional schemes derived from certain preconceptions of liberalism—at least compensate for it by a fresh, intelligent and universal approach. There is no space here for an extensive discussion of these important questions. Let us conclude by repeating what has been said earlier in this journal: our journal intends to be a meeting place of authors, translators and philosophers of all nations. The established disciplines are excluded, particularly since they serve, openly or not, only practical purposes. Besides, these disciplines have their share of scholarly journals. Only one discipline does not have its journal yet, the one we intend to cultivate: the art of translation as it has been accepted in its full significance only since Goethe—whose consequence is nothing less than the emerging discipline of the future: Comparative Literature. The scruples that a discipline still in the process of consolidation should not have its own journal would raise violent objections if directed at our older sister, Comparative Philology, which is also still consolidating itself, although it is already well-structured in many of its vast areas. Besides, comparative literary history is already practiced directly, even in the classrooms of German universities (e.g., Carrière in Munich). Among its indirect representatives belongs the impressive group of German translators of literature (and I am not talking about the mass of second and third rate translators).

II

The principle of polyglottism

Our journal has changed its motto with the second volume. Instead of the beautiful one taken from Eötvös which is, after all, limited to the principle of true translation, we have found in Schiller's dictum a more precise and at the same time more universal expression of the tasks of this journal. This seemingly unimportant change of mottoes alone may justify our returning to, or rather, our continuing the above discussion. Besides, much that is important had to be left unsaid on the last occasion for lack of space. We hope that nobody misunderstands our beautiful motto from Schiller.

The art of translation is, and will remain, one of the most important and attractive tools for the realization of our high comparative aims. But the means should not be mistaken for the end. Goethe was still able to conceive of his "Weltliteratur" as basically, or even exclusively? (German) translation which for him was an end in itself. To us today it can only be the means to a higher end.

True comparison is possible only when we have before us the objects of our comparison in their original form. Although translations facilitate the international traffic or distribution of literary products immensely (particularly in the German language, which is poetically more adaptable than any other modern language), nobody will dispute Schopenhauer's opinion that even the best translation leaves something to be desired and can never replace the original. Therefore, the *principle of translation* has to be not replaced but accompanied by a considerably more important comparative tool, the *principle of polyglottism*. The limited space of our journal, of course, permits us only a limited realization of this principle. But this modern principle has to be realized above all if literary comparison is to do more than scratch the surface. (Incidentally, polyglottism is not something entirely modern since we are indebted to it for two quite modern disciplines which both deal with the antiquity of human culture: Egyptology and Assyriology. Without the polyglottism of the tablets of Rashid and Nineveh our knowledge would be considerably poorer.)

The principle of translation is confined to the *indirect* commerce of literature in contrast to the principle of polyglottism which is the *direct* commerce itself. This already indicates the great importance of polyglottism which can be applied in several ways. The most desirable and at the same time most practical way would be, for the time being, if the critical articles of a comparative journal would appear in that language with which they are principally concerned, so that, for instance, a Hungarian contribution to Camões scholarship would be written in Portuguese and a German contribution to Cervantes criticism would appear in Spanish. It should be obvious that in most cases this aim will remain an ideal and unattainable one for the time being. We on our part feel that we should strictly realize it at least with regard to Hungarian and German literature. (This is our reason for giving preference to German and Hungarian literature, which, besides, corresponds to our geographic and cultural situation; therefore the diglottism of the section *Revue*.)

Also, a proper use of the principle of polyglottism should not exclude polyglot original production entirely.

It should be obvious, however, that these polyglot efforts have nothing in common with any kind of universal fraternization or similar international *nephelozozzugia*. The ideals of Comparative Literature have nothing to do with foggy, "cosmopolitanizing" theories; the high aims (not to say tendencies) of a journal like ours would be gravely misunderstood or intentionally misrepresented if anybody expected us to infringe upon the national uniqueness of a people. To attempt that would be, for more than one reason, a ludicrous undertaking which even an association of internationally famous scholars would have to consider doomed from the start—supposing such an association would be foolish enough to get together for such a purpose. It can safely be assumed that the purposes of Comparative Literature are more solid than that. It is, on the contrary, the *purely national of all nations* that Comparative Literature means to cultivate lovingly—here within the narrow framework of a journal where every nation is made to institute healthy (or just attractive) comparisons, which would not result from other approaches. Our secret motto is: nationality as individuality of a people should be regarded as sacred and inviolable. Therefore, a people, be it ever so insignificant politically, is and will remain, from the standpoint of Comparative Literature, as important as the largest nation. The most unsophisticated language may offer us most precious and informative subjects for comparative philology. The same is true for the spiritual life of "literatureless peoples," as we might call them, whose ethnic individuality should not be impinged upon by the wrong kind of missionary zeal; rather, it is our duty to protect it honestly and preserve it, if possible, in its purity. (From this comparative-polyglot standpoint should be considered the *ukas* of the Censorship Office of the Russian Ministry of the Interior of May 16, 1876—mentioned already on page 30 [see original reading]—which prohibits the literary use of the Ukrainian language. It would appear as the greatest sin against the holy spirit even if it were directed only against the folksongs of an obscure horde of Kirghizes instead of a people of fifteen million.) To impede the folk literature of a people would mean to destroy arbitrarily an important expression of the human spirit. In a time when certain animal species such as the mountain goat and the European bison are protected against extinc-tion by elaborate and strict laws, the willful extinction of a human species (or its literature, which amounts to the same thing) should be impossible.

In this sense we want understood the term "world literature" which, along with the art of translation, we intend to cultivate, particularly since the latter has not yet had a journal to itself, while the former has been well represented for some time now by such good, fully recognized and elaborate journals as the *Magazin für die Litteratur des Auslands* and Herrig's *Archiv für das Studium der neueren Sprachen* in Berlin. In England and France, too, it has always been cultivated by all major journals with praiseworthy zeal and good success. However, it cannot be denied that the so-called "world literature" is generally misunderstood, as has been indicated above. For today every nation demands its own "world literature" without quite knowing what is meant by it. By now, every nation considers itself, for one good reason or another, superior to all other nations, and this hypothesis, worked out into a complete theory of *suffisance*, is even the basis of much of modern pedagogy which today practically every-where strives to be "national." This unhealthy "national principle" therefore constitutes the fundamental premise of the entire spiritual life of modern Europe—which may take such peculiar forms as the "national ethic" of a Viennese high school teacher who exhibits no little satisfaction with his achievement. In this way, all sound conceptions are undermined from the start, even with regard to the highest spiritual concerns which could otherwise have immeasurably rich consequences considering today's wonderfully intensified commerce of ideas in the world. Instead of giving free rein to polyglottism and reaping the fruits in the future (fruits that it would certainly bring), every nation today insists on the strictest monoglottism, by considering its own language superior or even destined to rule supreme. This is a childish race whose result will finally be that all of them remain—inferior. The bril-liant Dora d'Istria, in the foreword to her fine book *La Poesie des Ottomans* (the second edition appeared recently) confirms our opinion by exclaiming impatiently:

> Nous vivons en effet dans une époque fort peu littéraire, et l'Europe livrée aux haines des partis, aux luttes des races, aux querelles des sectes, aux rivalités des classes, n'attache qu'une médiocre importance aux questions qui semblaient, il y a quelques années, capables d'occuper tous les esprits cultivés. Trop de pays chrétiens ressemblent maintenant à la Turquie du XVIIIe siècle.

True "world literature," therefore, in our opinion, can only remain an unattainable ideal in the direction of which, nevertheless, all independent literatures, i.e., all nations, should strive. They should use, however, only those means which we have called the two most important comparative principles, translation and polyglottism, never acts of violence or barbaric hypotheses which will be profitable for nobody but which unfortunately appear occasionally even in the great European journals. It is therefore particularly satisfying to hear a voice from *Ultima Thule* which I may be permitted to quote here. Our collaborator in Iceland writes us in German (July 29):

> I have always considered it desirable that there would be a journal which would bring together the writers, or all thinkers, of various nations; or, better still, that they would form an international society against the barbaric powers of our time. An important step in this direction seems to be this journal, as a focal point for writers and thinkers, or, to put it humorously, an exhibition of the spirit.

This noble voice of the Icelandic translator of Shakespeare, Steingrimur Thorsteinsson, moves us to submit the following proposal to our collaborators: For a small journal like ours to bring together at least a small number of "writers and thinkers of various nations" effec-tively, we intend to begin, starting with our next number, a small polyglot parliament on various problems of Comparative Literature, including practical ones. After all, it is neces-sary to assemble stone by stone the edifice of the future which may be of profit only to future generations. . . .

Chapter 5

Georg Brandes

WORLD LITERATURE (1899)

G EORG BRANDES (1842–1927) was a Danish literary historian and critic. His *Main Currents in Nineteenth Century Literature* (1872), which traces the influence of migrant writers following the French Revolution, is considered a classic in comparative literature studies. He wrote extensively on Scandinavian and European writers alike, including book-length studies of Goethe and Shakespeare. Having lived in Berlin for several years, he continued to be involved with European authors after his return to Copenhagen in 1883, and his correspondence with and lectures on Friedrich Nietzsche are regarded as central elements in the revaluation of the philosopher's work.

In his 1899 article ''World Literature'', which was originally published both in German and Danish, Brandes reflects on the concept of world literature, taking as his starting point that he was living in much more nationalistic times than Goethe. The short text contains a number of observations on what constitutes great literature and what enables texts to make their mark outside of their original context, and Brandes's writings on the subject display elements of both idealism and realism. On the idealistic side, he emphasizes that literature must be read in its original language, and he laments how smaller literatures which might deserve more attention are disadvantaged in the circulation of literature across borders. Considering Danish literature, he argues that Søren Kierkegaard ought to be part of world literature, which he eventually did become.

But Brandes is a realist when describing the thresholds thrown up by the genres and dominant literatures that shape world literature and a pessimist about the prospects for change, which is a concern that also informs the work of the contemporary scholar Pascale Casanova. However, Brandes did not envision how the literary center of the world would gradually shift from Paris to the Anglophone capitals of culture, which has since made it more complicated to describe the world's literary circulation.

At the end of his text, Brandes formulates a very short poetics of world literature which states that a literary work without an affiliation to a local environment would not be able to succeed as world literature, and thus he formulates a basic paradox that internationally canonized literature appears to overcome: it can be rooted in local references without being so local that it does not make sense to others.

We here print a new English translation of the 1902 version of Brandes's text as published in the latter's *Samlede Skrifter*, vol. 12 (Copenhagen: Gyldendal, 1902), pp. 23–28; this version is slightly different, especially at the end, from the better-known 1899 version published as "Weltliteratur" in *Das literarische Echo* 2.1: 1–5. Translated by William Banks.

The term *world literature* comes from Goethe. He used it for the first time as a heading for the 1827 epigram *Wie David königlich zur Harfe sang*, to the effect that the poetry of all peoples amounts to a single, harmonious global song, and he concludes with a desire that all of the nations under the same sun must be at ease with and enjoy the same gifts. A year later in *Über Kunst und Altertum*, he employs the word a second time in the piece *Ferneres über Weltliteratur*. The French journal *Globe* had in an article at that time given a kind of answer to Goethe, confirming that it would now be possible to hope for a world literature, given the historical movements of the age and the greater communication between countries. The *Globe* article recalled that the Latin language had in a previous age provided such conditions, although with the limitation that in that language only the intellect of peoples, and not their hearts and poetry, could be exchanged. Now the effect of travel, language study, journals, and newspapers had brought about much more intimate communications between nations than there had been in previous times.

Goethe here made several different observations. He admitted that of those works which speak to the masses, only those which are not particularly serious or good will spread outward across borders. But he insists that in a world literature, "they who have given their lives to the highest and the best will get to know each other more quickly and more closely." He concludes by pointing out the benefit that not just newspapers, which in the past were so awful, but also critically engaged journals, had made to the intellectual communication between peoples.

When I now, without consideration to the great originator of these words, ask myself: What is world literature?—it occurs to me that we must in the first place think of the work of the scientific researchers and the explorers. That which Pasteur, Darwin, Bunsen and Helmholtz have written is unconditionally world literature, in that it addresses and enriches all of humanity. Certain travel writings such as Stanley's and Nansen's likewise doubtlessly belong to it.

The works of the historians, even the greatest, do not in the same way seem to me to belong to world literature, because according to their nature they are less definitive, and necessarily bear a quite personal mark and thereby rather address themselves to the countrymen of the author, who as a rule are closer to him as a personality. Such superb works as Carlyle's *Oliver Cromwell*, Michelet's *History of France* or Mommsen's *Roman History* are in spite of the learning and intellect of the authors not definitive as scientific works. Their status as world literature is indisputable only insofar as they are considered as works of art, which naturally does not exclude them from being known by the majority of Europe or America either in the original or in translation. When we really think of world literature, we think for the most part of *belles-lettres* in all its forms.

Over the books inherited from previous ages time has issued its judgments. Few writers of the many thousands, few works of the hundreds of thousands, belong to world literature. The names of such men and such works everyone has on his tongue. The *Divine Comedy* belongs not just to Italy, *Don Quixote* not just to Spain. Alongside the world-renowned works there further exist the innumerable books that are preserved, honored and from time to time read in the country in which they originated, without thereby becoming known outside of it. Shakespeare belongs to world literature, his great contemporary and forerunner Marlowe only that of the English. Likewise Klopstock is only German, Coleridge only English, Słowacki only Polish. For the world they do not exist.

In the meantime there is of course a great difference between our own time and earlier ages, in part because foreign languages are now learned better and more often, in part because the extraordinary upswing in the means of communication between peoples and the immense spread of the daily press have brought us much closer together, and finally because the enterprise of translation is much larger than ever before.

However many translations are taken up, it is nevertheless without a doubt that the writers of the various lands and languages differ widely with respect to the likelihood of acquiring world renown or just a certain measure of acknowledgement. Best of all is the position of the French, even though the French language is probably only fifth largest with regard to its use in the world. When an author is acknowledged in France, he is known across the entire earth. First in the second rank are the English and Germans, who nonetheless can however count on an immense reading public when they are successful. It is only the writers in these three lands who can hope of being read in the original by the most educated in all nations.

Italian and Spanish writers are much less advantageously positioned, but are nonetheless read by a certain public outside their homelands. Nearly the same is the situation among the French-language authors of Belgium and Switzerland, where only the exceptions (for example Cherbuliez, Rod and Maeterlinck) are fully adopted in France. The Russian writers are certainly not read in the original outside their country, but the Russian population in its millions is a remedy for that.

Those who write in Finnish, Hungarian, Swedish, Danish, Icelandic, Dutch, Greek, and so on are in the universal struggle for world renown clearly positioned most disadvantageously. In the contest for world renown these authors lack their weapon, their language, and for writers that about says it all.

It is impossible to write anything artistic in another language than one's own. On that we are all in agreement. But these translations! To these we all object. I confess to the heresy that I can only view them as a pitiful expedient. They eliminate the literary artistry precisely by which the author should validate himself, and the greater he is in his language, the more he loses.

The necessary imperfection of the translations has as a consequence the effect that an author of the sixth rank in a widespread language, a world language, can with ease become more known than an author of the second rank in a language spoken by only a few million. Anyone who knows the literature of the small and the large lands will readily grant this, but the large countries will as a rule not believe it.

We make a single concession: lyric poetry is translated with difficulty and in every case always loses much in so doing. Usually the effort to translate it to another language is not undertaken for the simple reason that nothing will be gained from such an effort. A German easily intuits that those who only know Goethe's poems from a prose translation or from a by necessity distant or forced rhymed rendering in another language cannot possibly enjoy or evaluate them. The Frenchman cannot even imagine the verse of Victor Hugo or Leconte de Lisle in a foreign tongue. But according to the received opinion, prose writing suffers no great loss in translation. But this is wrong. The loss remains immeasurable, albeit less striking than in poems. The selection and the sound of the words, the architecture of the sentences and the harmony, the peculiarity of literary expression; everything vanishes. Translations are not even replicas.

Even those who when considering artistically sensitive translations are inclined to hold the translator in high regard, will nevertheless not deny that the writers of the world's various lands are not equally apportioned with respect to world renown, even if we have seen that a poet like Ibsen, who writes in a small language, and even smaller minds than him, have been acknowledged everywhere.

But is this world renown among contemporaries, in the present, decisive? Does it mean that the master and the work really belong to world literature in a permanent sense? One must have an awfully sunny outlook on life to believe that. World renown seems to me a particularly poor measuring stick for the giving of due justice.

In the first place there are personalities who acquire world renown without lifting themselves discernibly above the level of the common. When the plane on which they stand accords with that of the average educated reader, and when they belong to a large land, it is therefore easy for them to be known everywhere. Georges Ohnet is read everywhere. And an author need not be literally insipid or unsophisticated to win over prevailing opinion; he can in an indirect way be shallow or trivial, as when in a vulgar, superficial manner and by virtue of a trivialized general culture he attacks the prevailing trivialized general culture; for example by declaiming the prejudices of monarchy, Church, aristocracy, the so-called conventional lies. We have also seen writers without any artistic cultivation and quite devoid of artistic sensibility become famous by tearing down the great artists, poets and thinkers of their age through coarse superciliousness and by patronizing them as weak-minded or demented. The great mob in most countries is impressed by this behavior, and careless scribblers count among world literature.

On the other hand it does not seem at all rare that by pure chance this or that author of the first rank dies unknown, and also after his death remains unknown; even in cases in which one can without difficulty see why an author of inferior rank has acquired world renown, the reason is by no means always commensurate with his talent.

Of all Danish authors and poets from the Middle Ages up to the present, only H.C. Andersen has won world renown. Holberg, our nation's great teacher, is hardly known by name outside of Scandinavia. Oehlenschläger is known only in Germany and is viewed poorly. Not a single person in Europe knows Christian Winther or Johan Ludvig Heiberg or Poul Møller or for that matter any of the many who in influence were the equals of Andersen and with respect to talent more than equal. Only Andersen, who cannot be considered our greatest, belongs by virtue of his fairytales to world literature.

Although Søren Kierkegaard is the most significant religious thinker in Nordic literature, he does not belong to world literature. One would assume that all of the advocates of Christianity in Europe would be occupied with him as they were a couple of hundred years ago with Pascal; but his language has locked him out.

No doubt, the best of the best eventually elbow their way through everywhere and in our time this process definitely takes considerably less time than in the past. But it must not be forgotten that everywhere also the great majority is lethargic, ignorant and of poor judgment. The best is inaccessible to the mob and the finest incomprehensible. The mob chases after the bellowing soap-boxers and the inscrutable crackpots, they follow fashion and worship success. That a writer at one point has pleased everybody is by no means enough that we may include him in world literature forever.

There does not at this moment seem to be any kind of flourishing period at hand in European literature. The best of the young writers are not replacing the greats of the recent past, not Kipling in England, not d'Annunzio in Italy. Yet they are by any standard more famous than any of their predecessors ever were in their lifetimes.

However, in our era a new phenomenon has appeared which earlier was unknown, when the idea of becoming universally recognized and read everywhere had not yet been envisioned by poets and writers. There are those who have begun to write for a general and unspecified public, and production has suffered thereby. Emile Zola provides an example. His great cycle of novels *Les Rougon-Macquart* he wrote for France, and it is therefore densely composed with great regard for the language. His trilogy *Lourdes-Rome-Paris* he wrote at the height of his fame for the entire world. It has accordingly become in certain sections more abstract than in the past, and as a whole also much less meticulous in its language. He has written as Sarah Bernhardt acts when she performs in Peru or Chicago. To make a powerful effect a writer must remain focused on his surroundings; he must work in the land in which he was born and write for his countrymen, whose paths of development he knows. In this way he will, if he has talent for greater things, step by step come to write for the world. That which from the first is intended for humanity as a whole loses in vigor that which it has gained in universal accessibility—it no longer carries the scent of the earth. He who would write immediately for Europe and America exposes himself to the danger of paying tribute to a foreign taste that is less cultivated than that of his own people. To look first for world renown and world literature carries a risk.

On the other hand it is apparent that one should not write for those who live on the same street or in the same town, which the polemical author always is tempted to do.

When Goethe coined the term *world literature*, humanism and the spirit of world citizenship were still ideas universally entertained. In the last decades of the 19th century, an ever stronger and more bellicose nationalism has pushed these ideas backward. The literatures of our day become ever more national. I by no means, however, mean to suggest that nationalism and world citizenship are mutually exclusive. The world literature of the future will become all the more captivating the more the mark of the national appears in it and the more heterogeneous it becomes, as long as it retains a universally human aspect as art and science. That which is written directly for the world will hardly do as a work of art.

Chapter 6

Richard Green Moulton

THE UNITY OF LANGUAGE AND THE CONCEPTION OF WORLD LITERATURE and WORLD LITERATURE THE AUTOBIOGRAPHY OF CIVILIZATION (1911)

RICHARD GREEN MOULTON (1849–1924) was a professor at the University of Chicago who wrote several works on the history of world literature and on literary theory. In his works he reacts against the departmental division of the academic study of literature and urges us to recognize the unity of literature: "Only world literature – literature studied apart from distinctions between particular languages – gives a body of literary material from which it is safe to make generalizations, only in world literature can the life history of literature be fully revealed" (Moulton 1915: 92). Moulton applies the distinction between universal and world literature to distinguish the totality of all literature and literature seen from a particular point of view. Moulton's claims are at once highly ambitious and modest; he both insists on the need to study all literature as being connected and he accepts the limits imposed by the history of cultures and individuals. His own work is thus anchored in British literary culture, and its rendering of a canon is simultaneously rather traditional and ambitious in scope.

In *World Literature and Its Place in General Culture*, Moulton makes the case for the use of translations, which he refuses to view as a loss. Instead, he focuses on what is gained by making works of literature available in other languages, and he seeks to describe how language and literature are, while of course intrinsically linked, not identical. The basic structure of this argument is repeated with reference to nations that have a great influence on literature, but which are countered by a general "Intrinsic Literary Interest" which crosses nations and opens up the possibility of pursuing connections over time and across borders. Many nuances are touched upon in his book that also concerns the development of civilizations and the practice of teaching literature across national boundaries.

We here reproduce Ch. 1, "The Unity of Literature and the Conception of World Literature" (pp. 1–9) and Ch. 10, "World Literature the Autobiography of Civilization" (pp. 429–437) from the 1921 (originally 1911) edition of Moulton's *World Literature and Its Place in General Culture*. New York: The Macmillan Company. See also his 1915 *The Modern Study of Literature: An Introduction to Literary Theory and Interpretation*. Chicago: University of Chicago Press.

The Unity of Literature and the Conception of World Literature

It has been among the signs of our times that popular inquiries have been started at intervals in reference to "The Best Books." Eminent individuals have been importuned to name the ten, the twenty-five, the hundred best books; or—since this is an age of democracy—the selection has been referred to newspaper voting. In all this there seems to be a certain simplicity mingled with a strain of deep wisdom. The simplicity is the naïve idea that every-thing knowable is of the nature of information, sure to be found in the right compendium; only, as universal wisdom has not yet been alphabetically indexed, it may be necessary to have recourse to an expert. The wisdom latent in such attempted selections is the suggestion that the popular mind, in however crude and shadowy a way, has grasped a principle ignored in more formal study—the essential unity of literature.

   This failure to recognize the unity of all literature accounts for the paradox that, while literary study is going on actively all around, yet the study of literature, in any adequate sense, has yet to begin. When we speak of the study of philosophy, what we have in mind is not the reading of Greek philosophic writers by persons interested in Greek studies, and the reading of German philosophers by persons interested in German studies, and the like: apart from all this we recognize that there is the thing philosophy, with an independent interest and history of its own, the whole being something quite different from the sum of the parts. In other words, we recognize the unity of philosophy. Similarly, we recognize the unity of history, the unity of art; even the separate languages of the world have coalesced into a unity in the study of philology. But when the question is of literature, it would seem as if the humanities side of the educational edifice has been built in water-tight compartments; what goes on in our schools and colleges is the study in one class room of English literature in connection with English history and language, in other class rooms Greek or Latin or French literature in connection with Greek or Latin or French history and language. We look in vain for an independent study of literature itself, and of literature as a whole.

   Perhaps it may be objected that such a thing is to be found under the name of Comparative Literature, or the Philosophy of Literature. Comparative Literature is an important advance towards recognizing unity for the whole literary field; but that it is only an advance the title infallibly marks. For who would speak of Comparative Philosophy, or Comparative Mathematics? Such names might indeed be used to denote specific pieces of work; they could never indicate a whole study. Similarly, the Philosophy of Literature can be nothing more than a single element in the whole study of literature. The most important part of any treat-ment of literature must be a detailed and loving acquaintance with a large number of actual literary works: in proportion as a reader possesses this will the philosophy of the subject be valuable. To offer it as equivalent to the study of literature would be as futile as to think that a course in economics would of itself make a good business man, or that text-books in psychology and ethics would give a knowledge of human nature.

   No doubt there are special difficulties in the way of our compassing the study of litera-ture as a whole. The first of these I should myself consider not so much a difficulty as a preju-dice. It is obvious that the study of literature as a whole is impossible without a free use of translations. Now, there is a widespread feeling that the reading of translated literature is a makeshift, and savors of second-hand scholarship. But this idea is itself a product of the

departmental study of literature which has prevailed hitherto, in which language and literature have been so inextricably intertwined that it has become difficult to think of the two
separately. The idea will not bear rational examination. If a man, instead of reading Homer
in Greek, reads him in English, he has unquestionably lost something. But the question arises,
Is what he has lost literature? Clearly, a great proportion of what goes to make literature has
not been lost; presentation of antique life, swing of epic narrative, conceptions of heroic
character and incident, skill of plot, poetical imagery—all these elements of Homeric literature are open to the reader of translations. But, it will be said, language itself is one of the
main factors in literature. This is true, but it must be remembered that the term "language"
covers two different things: a considerable proportion of linguistic phenomena is common to
related languages and will pass from one to the other, while other elements of language are
idiomatic and fixed. What the English reader of Homer has lost is not language, but Greek.
And he has not lost the whole of Greek; the skilled translator can convey something of the
ēthos of idiomatic Greek into his version, writing what may be correct English, but not such
English as an Englishman would write. When, however, all abatement has been made, the
reader of the translation has suffered a distinct loss; and the classical scholar knows how great
that loss is. But the point at issue is not the comparative value of literature and language, but
the possibility of realizing literature as a unity. One who accepts the use of translations where
necessary secures all factors of literature except language, and a considerable part even of
that. One who refuses translations by that fact cuts himself off from the major part of the
literary field; his literary scholarship, however polished and precise, can never rise above the
provincial.

To which it must be added that the prejudice against translations is of the nature
of a prophecy which can fulfil itself: where it has prevailed, the character of translations
has approximated to the schoolboy's "crib." On the other hand, it is noteworthy how
classical scholars of front rank have devoted themselves to translation as the best form of
commentary—Jowett, Munro, Conington, Jebb, Palmer, Gilbert Murray; how poets of
front rank have made themselves interpreters between one language and another—William
Morris, Edwin Arnold, Chapman, Dryden, Pope; when precise scholarship and poetic gifts
mingle in such men as Mr. Arthur S. Way and Mr. B. B. Rogers, it can be brought about that
Homer, Euripides, and Aristophanes shine equally as English and as Greek poetry. Again,
men of the highest literary refinement have made strong pronouncements on the side of
translated literature. "I do not hesitate," says Emerson in his Essay on Books, "to read all the
books I have named, and all good books, in translations. What is really best in any book is
translatable; any real insight or broad human sentiment. . . . I rarely read any Greek, Latin,
German, Italian—sometimes not a French book—in the original which I can procure in a
good version. I like to be beholden to the great metropolitan English speech, the sea which
receives tributaries from every region under heaven. I should as soon think of swimming
across Charles River when I wish to go to Boston, as of reading all my books in originals,
when I have them rendered for me in my mother tongue." Let an appeal, moreover, be made
to history. Luther's translation of the Bible, and the English Authorized Version, laid the
foundations of literary speech for two nations. Effects on some such wide scale may be looked
for when high linguistic scholarship from critical shall turn to creative, and apply itself to
naturalizing in each literature the best of all the rest.

Quite apart, however, from this question of translation there are real and formidable
difficulties that impede the study of literature as a whole. In such a subject as language the
unit is a word or a phrase: in literature the smallest unit is a whole poem. In philology, and
most other studies, we have to deal only with facts: with information, and that information
digested. But information on the subject of literature is of all things the most barren; what is
wanted in this study is imaginative knowledge, the reaction of the literary matter upon the

reader's taste, upon his artistic and spiritual susceptibility. How is it possible to compass the universal field, where the unit is so large, and the appreciation so deep seated?

With such a problem as this we are concerned in the present work only so far as it bears upon general culture. And that which seems to me the proper solution I am expressing by what is the title of this book—World Literature. It must be admitted that the term "world literature" may legitimately be used in more than one sense; I am throughout attaching to it a fixed and special significance. I take a distinction between Universal Literature and World Literature. Universal Literature can only mean the sum total of all literatures. World Literature, as I use the term, is this Universal Literature seen in perspective from a given point of view, presumably the national standpoint of the observer. The difference between the two may be illustrated by the different ways in which the science of Geography and the art of Landscape might deal with the same physical particulars. We have to do with a mountain ten thousand feet high, a tree-fringed pond not a quarter of an acre in extent, a sloping meadow rising perhaps to a hundred feet, a lake some four hundred miles in length. So far as Geography would take cognizance of these physical features, they must be taken all in their exact dimensions. But Landscape would begin by fixing a point of view: from that point the elements of the landscape would be seen to modify their relative proportions. The distant mountain would diminish to a point of snow; the pond would become the prominent centre, every tree distinct; the meadow would have some softening of remoteness; on the other side the huge lake would appear a silver streak upon the horizon. By a similar kind of perspective, World Literature will be a different thing to the Englishman and to the Japanese: the Shakespeare who bulks so large to the Englishman will be a small detail to the Japanese, while the Chinese literature which makes the foreground in the one literary landscape may be hardly discernible in the other. World Literature will be a different thing even to the Englishman and the Frenchman; only in this case the similar history of the two peoples will make the constituent elements of the two landscapes much the same, and the difference will be mainly in distribution of the parts. More than this, World Literature may be different for different individuals of the same nation: obviously, one man will have a wider outlook, taking in more of universal literature; or it may be that the individuality of the student, or of some teacher who has influenced him, has served as a lens focussing the multiplex particulars of the whole in its own individual arrangement. In each case the World Literature is a real unity; and it is a unity which is a reflection of the unity of all literature. That it is a reflection relative to the particular student or thinker is a thing inseparable from culture: is indeed what makes the difference between the purely scientific and the educational point of view.

The essential thing is that the observation of the whole field which gives us this World Literature should be correct; in other words, that there should be a sound philosophy at the basis of this perspective grouping. It is the absence of such underlying philosophy that takes the value out of mere lists of "best books" as representations of literature. And the theory on which a view of World Literature is to rest will resolve itself ultimately into two supplementary principles. One of these may be termed the National Literary Pedigree,—the train of historic considerations that connects the reader's nationality with its roots in the far past, and traces its relationship with other parts of the literary field. Here we are on the sure basis of history. But it will be history as seen from the standpoint of literature: literary pedigree may be very different from ethnological or linguistic descent. The other principle is Intrinsic Literary Interest. Quite apart from its association with history literature has an interest and values of its own. The individuality of an author (to take the most obvious cases) or the accidental flowering of some literary type may lift portions of a literature quite out of the position that would have been given them by their historic settings, just as in our landscape illustration the mountain was so distant as to have been invisible if it had not happened to be ten thousand feet in height. The individuality of a Dante or an Aristophanes has modified for all of us the general map of poetry. These two principles, then, of historic connection, and of intrinsic literary value, by their mutual interaction will elaborate a sound basis on which a conception of World Literature may rest.

Such World Literature, conceived from the English point of view, is the subject of the present work. And our first step is to trace the Literary Pedigree of the English-speaking peoples.

World Literature the Autobiography of Civilization

A national literature, it is generally recognized, is a reflection of the national history. Literature is much more than a product of the individual. A lunatic—to take the ad absurdum degree of individuality—may write a book, and, if he can command funds, may get his book printed and published: but it will take some degree of public acceptance, acceptance at the time or in the future, to convert that book into literature. Books as books reflect their authors; as literature, they reflect the public opinion which gives them endorsement. Thus a national literature as a whole is seen to reflect the successive stages, or accidental phases, through which the history of the nation has passed. And this principle will seem the truer in proportion as our conception of history is more adequate. At first, it might seem as if only certain kinds of literature would serve to reflect national history. Authors are free to take topics remote from their own day and generation; they may, and often do, create for them-selves purely ideal worlds. Swinburne, in the nineteenth century, produces dramas in Greek form which read as purely Greek in their matter and thought as if they were plays of Æschylus or Sophocles; Spenser's *Faerie Queene* depends for its main interest upon the degree in which its incidents are kept at a distance from real life: how, it might be objected, can the *Erechtheus* and the *Atalanta in Calydon* be said to reflect nineteenth-century England, or the *Faerie Queene* the age of Elizabeth? The answer depends upon the idea we hold as to the meaning of history. At a time when feudal conceptions were still strong, history meant dynastic history, and confined itself to the concerns of the reigning families and of those closely associated with them. Then history widened, and became the record of public events in general. It widened further, to take in the manners and customs of a country: instead of the history of England we had the history of the English people. Yet its scope is wider than this, and includes a nation's ideas and tastes. A man's character is not made by what he does only, but by what he loves and hates and wishes; the most important element in the character may be made by the man's unfulfilled aspirations. So it is an important item of English history that a nineteenth-century Englishman was profoundly interested, and could interest those about him, in the Greek point of view of two thousand years before; it is another item of English history that an Elizabethan reading public had strength of imagination to be enthusiastic over idealized shadows. The wider our sense of the historic, the more fully shall we see in a national litera-ture the reflection of the national history.

Now, the principle that is true for the smaller unit of the nation holds good equally for the larger unit of civilization.

The physical sciences have one advantage over the studies we group together under the name of the humanities: in the physical sciences it is so easy to realize the common ground between them. The geologist, the chemist, the physiologist, the psychologist, with all their differences of field and method, are perfectly aware that they are all studying the same one thing, which they call by some such name as nature. But what is the common ground between the humanity studies? We must not answer, Man: for that brings us into the sphere of sciences like anthropology or sociology. The question is difficult, but perhaps the best answer is that the common object of the humanity studies is Civilization. But if this is correct, then it must be admitted that our humanity studies are organized in a way to defeat their chief aim; they are found to concentrate attention on the surface variations of civilization, and to leave the thing itself almost untouched. Take four neighbor nations, English, French, German, Italian; bring representative men of these four nations together: it will immediately appear that the national distinctions separating the four are infinitesimally small in comparison with the common civilization that binds them together. If they have some means of getting over the practical difficulty of language, then they can converse together with easy community of feeling, to which their national peculiarities do no more than give a flavor of variety. Add to their company a Turk or a Malay: in contact with the strange civilization the first four feel themselves a unit. Yet it is the separate languages with their separate literatures and histories that make the humanity studies: the common civilization is almost entirely left out. The effect is as if, in studying grammar, we were painfully to memorize long lists of exceptions and forget to learn the rules; or as if, in medical art, we were to arrange elaborate systems of instruction separately for the training of expert oculists and expert aurists, while leaving the general physiology and pathology of the human body to be picked up by these oculists and aurists in chance readings of their leisure moments.

The Englishman naturally desires to understand English civilization and culture. But the knowledge of this will not be given him by the history of England. When the land of Britain was invaded by Julius Cæsar, and the English race was so immersed in the darkness of European antiquities that it is difficult to identify it—in other words, when the history of England was in its first faint beginnings—at that time the foundations of English civilization and culture had been laid long before, and the edifice was far advanced towards its completion. A foundation step had been taken centuries and centuries before, when, in the far-off region of Mesopotamia, Abraham had set out on his profoundly original journey of exploration, "to a country that God should give him": a migration to found a race that should be separated from other races, not by geography or ethnology, but by the cherishing of a spiritual instinct which should develop in the course of centuries into a force strong enough to determine the whole spiritual side of English and kindred civilizations. Again, for centuries and centuries before that opening of English history, another leading element of English civilization had been in progress, when, amid the ripening life of Greek races, competing rhapsodists, and later competing dramatists, filled with poetic enthusiasm, had been unconsciously framing the laws of rhythm and conceptions of what constitutes beauty, such as would eventually mould the taste and literary sense of English and European peoples. In the same remote period, though somewhat later, another stage in the creation of English civilization had been won when Greek sophists, searching into the mystery of the world around them no longer explained by religion, fell gradually into habits of thinking which were destined, eventually, to make for English culture its logical sense and impulse to scientific truth. Some three centuries before that beginning of English history the great crisis in the history of English and European civilization had been passed, when Macedonian conquerors, spreading on all sides Greek language and culture, unconsciously brought about the blending of Hellenic with Hebraic, which determined once for all the quality of human thought and character that should eventually dominate the western world. Before invasions like those of Hengist and Horsa had made a second beginning for the history of England, the structure of English civilization had attained its definite form in the Christianization of the Roman Empire, the interplay of State and Church, of imperial government and clerical culture, by which the modern world was to be slowly moulded. It is a worthy task of a history to trace the development of English nationality; but nationality is itself a late idea, belonging to the closing stages of mediævalism, and before this the real English culture is the culture of Europe. We hear of the introduction of Christianity into England in one century, of the Norman Conquest of England in another century: what these events mean is that solitary England is by revolution plunged into the life stream of European civilization. Later on, when it can be seen that the English people are strong in national individuality, it yet remains true that the main forces in the progress of their civilization are found outside—feudal courts and their circle of poetic aspirants; streams of traditional story from all quarters pouring in to a Europe that is a literary unity; Saracen civilization coming into rivalry and conflict with a Christian civilization thus led to feel still more strongly its own strength; clerical disputers uniting faith and philosophy in a new logic; clerical poets making an allegorical religion of love; Italian priestcraft playing against German zeal for reform, with renovated Greek learning as a third issue. When the whole area of the history of England has been traversed, nine-tenths of the history of English civilization and culture has been left outside.

Nor can the knowledge of our civilization and culture be attained by any process of simple addition. I suppose that the theory of the humanity studies—if there be a theory—is that we should master our English language and literature, and add to this French language and literature, to this German, Greek, Latin, and the rest. The programme seems a long one, enough to fill the whole length of an ordinary life. But when this programme has been carried to completion, we have still not really commenced our study of civilization: we have merely been getting our materials together. The civilization and culture in which we make a part can be studied only by a process similar in kind to that which in the present work has been applied to literature. We must take our stand at the point where we find ourselves, and, looking from that point in all directions, we must bring perspective into play: we must distinguish what from our viewpoint is great and what small, what is essential and what less essential, and with such perspective view ever maintained we must bring our constructive powers into action.

Of course, it is the function of history to do all this; history, besides dealing with individual nations or epochs, undertakes to trace for us the development of civilization. But just here the principle comes in which it is the purpose of this chapter to emphasize: namely, that as a national literature is the reflection of the national history, so in world literature is reflected the course of civilization. The literary unit we call the Holy Bible dramatizes for us, as we have seen, the evolution through the ages of those conceptions which are the foundation of our spiritual nature. Greek epics and dramas, not to mention other productions of the Greeks, not only gratify our poetic taste, but are the very instrument by which that taste has been created. Shakespeare appears before us, not simply as a representative of Elizabethan England—though of course that view of him is interesting—but as a force in civilization, by which the slow accumulations of romance were struck into new life by impact of a dramatizing power imported from the classical east. Mediæval culture, which is part of our culture, is highly complex, full of difficulties and unfamiliarities: in the *Divine Comedy* all that is most important in mediæval culture lights up for us with the illumination of supreme poetic genius. In the history of England, at the moment when the Restoration was a thing accomplished and the nation firmly determined to keep its monarchy, it became a matter of trifling importance whether the man Milton should be hanged as a warning to rebels, or as an extinct force be suffered to live on in obscurity. To civilization it was of prime import that he lived on, and his mind became a powerful reflector, which could catch rays coming from Puritan thought on the one side, and rays from classical form on the other side, and focus them into a clear image by which world literature gained what it could have gained from no other source. When the mediæval unity of Europe breaks up into modern nationalities the history of civilization becomes increasingly complex: we gain assistance from literature when we see some of these national differentiations—English Elizabethanism, Catholic Spain, German culture, nineteenth-century mysticism—obligingly cooperate in moulding the same Faust story to reflect for us their divergent points of view. In the study of world literature we get developed the comparative habit of mind, which acts as a lens to bring together resemblances and contrasts from all parts of the complex civilization. It is the function of history to lead us by philosophical analysis to the understanding of civilization and culture: world literature is civilization presented by itself.

Hence we may speak of World Literature as the Autobiography of Civilization. For what is autobiography? An individual, wise with advancing years, and at all events old enough to feel that his life is not an aggregation of accidents, but a unity with a significance, sets out to interpret his life to others. His interpretation may of course fall into error. But we feel that autobiography is never so soundly autobiographical as where the writer, instead of discussing his life, is presenting it: in his letters and correspondence, in his conversations and discourses, in his original compositions, whatever the special output of the life may be. The history of civilization corresponds to the formal discussion of the life. World Literature is autobiography in the sense that it is the presentation of civilization in its own best products, its most significant moments emphasized as they appear illuminated with the highest literary setting.

Chapter 7

Fritz Strich

WORLD LITERATURE AND COMPARATIVE LITERARY HISTORY (1930)

F RITZ STRICH (1883–1963) WAS a German scholar of literature. Strich was born in Königsberg, historically the capital of East Prussia, but since 1945 known as Kaliningrad in what today is the Russian enclave of the same name between Poland and Lithuania. Strich first taught at the University of Munich, and in 1929 became full professor at the University of Bern in Switzerland.

Strich has become particularly known for his *Goethe und die Weltliteratur*, published in Bern in 1946, and translated into English, as *Goethe and World Literature*, in 1949. Strich read Goethe as a spokesperson for a liberal humanism, and for freedom and understanding among nations. It was no coincidence that Strich published his book immediately after World War II, a period that had not been marked by any such understanding but rather by carnage on a scale unprecedented in European history. In fact, Strich's interest in Goethe dated back to immediately after World War I, when he had been invited to give a series of lectures on Goethe and world literature at London University. Strich drew clear parallels between the situation Goethe found himself, and Europe, at the end of the Napoleonic wars, and Europe after the two world wars that had devastated the old continent. For Strich, Goethe's interest in world literature had been spurred by what the latter saw as a unique opportunity for Europe to promote tolerance and understanding among its peoples, and perhaps at a later stage in the world at large, in an era marked by the aftermath of the downfall of a would-be European hegemon. In Goethe's time this hegemon had been France under Napoleon, in Strich's time it had been Germany, first under the Kaiser and the Prussian military, and later under Hitler.

Goethe had seen literature as the means by which to increase the circulation of ideas, and the mutual knowledge of one another's cultures, among Europe's writers and intellectuals. He had been able to do so before the age of nationalism had quelled the idea of a genuine world literature, free of national prejudices. Hitler and his Germany on the contrary were the evil end products of the worst kind of nationalist aberration. The defeat of Nazism created the opportunity to return to a more or less Goethean situation, and to shoe Europe on a new last, with world literature à la Goethe once again playing a mediating role. Strich in passing offered Switzerland, where he had been teaching all through the Nazi period and the war, as a working example of tolerance and understanding with its harmonious and peaceful co-existence of languages, cultures and peoples.

In the essay that here follows, and which dates from 1930, Strich frames a discussion of Goethe's ideas with a more general consideration of the relationship between world literature and comparative literature. Basically, he rejects the term "comparative literature" as being too narrow, and opts for "world literature" as the more encompassing term. After a wide-ranging discussion, informed by the ideas and using the terminology of the German philosopher Georg Wilhelm Friedrich Hegel—for whom history worked towards the realization of the fullest possible spirit of humanity, of what such world literature should and should not, can and cannot be, and which works unquestionably belong to it—he reaches his true goal: whether world literature, as a revised and updated form of comparative literature, is useful, and perhaps even necessary, in the world? Not surprisingly, he finds the answers to these questions with Goethe: a resounding "Yes!" Even though to our contemporary reader this may not be immediately obvious, and he or she might find the corresponding sentences even cryptic, in the final words of his essay Strich for his own contemporary reader clearly alludes to the evils threatening Europe once again in 1930. The coming to power of Hitler and the Nazis shortly thereafter would of course substantiate Strich's fears. It is precisely in order to counter such evils that world literature is absolutely necessary, is his conclusion. Strich's 1946 book on Goethe and world literature reiterates this remedy for yet another postwar world.

Fritz Strich, "Weltliteratur und Vergleichende Literaturgeschichte," in *Philosophie der Literaturwissenschaft*, Ed. Emil Ermatinger, Berlin: Junker & Dünnhaupt, 1930, pp. 422–41. Translated by Theo D'haen.

The name "comparative literary history," which in analogy to the natural sciences has been coined for the discipline that concerns itself with the international relations between the literatures of the various nations, and which is commonly used everywhere, in France, Germany, England, Italy, to me does not really seem very apt. After all, the method of comparison is not unique to this discipline. Every national literary history has to resort to comparison. One compares Goethe and Schiller, German classicism and German Romanticism, to establish the specificity of a writer's personality or a literary or cultural current, and to trace changes in the history of ideas. Comparison is also not so typical of the discipline that concerns itself with the international relations between literatures that it could meaningfully set apart this discipline from the other branches of literary scholarship. To this we have to add that the comparative method is also for this particular discipline not the only one with which it seeks to answer its questions. Comparison can only settle part of such questions, and not even the more important ones. Like every other literary discipline it also has to use other methods, philological and historical. When Wilhelm Wetz, one of the founding fathers of the discipline, in his *Shakespeare, vom Standpunkt der vergleichenden Literaturgeschichte* (Hamburg 1897) compares Shakespeare with Corneille and Racine and with the Spanish playwrights, in order to "penetrate by comparing analogous phenomena into the innermost being of each of these authors, and thus to discover the laws that have caused both the similarities and dissimilarities between them," we may correctly call this comparative literary history. Yet when the central organs of the discipline, such as Koch's *Zeitschrift für vergleichende Literaturgeschichte* and the *Revue de littérature comparée*, publish all kinds of articles on transformations of themes and forms, on the influence of one literature upon another, or upon the fate that the work of one poet meets with in the literature of another nation, this has no longer anything to do with comparative literary history. Therefore we would recommend another term which, even if not univocal, in any case does not lead to confusion, and the closest equivalent to this would then probably be "world literary history" or "world literature studies."

But also the concept of world literature is at the same time particularly glamorous and indefinite. The term is used differently in scholarship than in ordinary life. Yet neither in literature nor in ordinary life do two people ever use it with the same meaning. Everyone uses it one way at one moment, and in another way another moment, and there is no scholarly work from any one of these fields that does not suffer from any such confusion. This confusion makes understanding difficult and, worse, indicates in essence that the scholarship that concerns itself with world literature is not itself clear about what its subject is, and therefore also not about the questions that it should pose it. The concept is only used unequivocally in all those so-called "histories of world literature" which understand under this nothing but the written record of all times and all nations, those compilations of national literary histories of Germany, England, France, Italy, China, and India, and whose claim to comprehensiveness resides only in the fact that they are published by the same publisher and between the same cover. In other words clarity is here bought at the price of meaninglessness, and these world literary histories are not worth discussing.

There is not even a consensus as to what we should understand by "world" and "literature." If one talks about the world, one usually thinks primarily only of Europe, and world literature stands for European literature. Of course, in all scholarly endeavors it is indispensable and apt to limit oneself. Who can really completely and in detail master even one single literature. But Europe is not the world, and the question should precisely be asked whether world literature does not really begin where the borders of Europe are being transcended. After all, and regardless of the diversity of its peoples and literatures, Europe remains a self-enclosed and relatively homogeneous cultural community, and the international relations between its literatures only concern this particular community. One has to go beyond this Eurocentric perspective in order to gain the right to dare speak of world literature.

A literary work perhaps only then belongs to world literature when it does not belong to European literature only.

Now as to the concept of literature: do we here refer to creative literature only, or also to philosophy, history, rhetoric and criticism? Here too one should at least clarify what one wants to be understood by the concept used. Maybe it would be possible to agree on this: we reckon everything to literature that is cast in literary language and for which this language is an inner necessity. Tacitus, Montesquieu, Ranke and Mommsen would then belong to this concept as much as do Schopenhauer and Nietzsche, while Kant would not be considered part of world literature but rather of world philosophy.

It is clear, then, that there are many and very diverse possibilities to invest the concept of world literature with meaning, and to come up with concomitant sets of problems that are of interest to world literature scholarship. It is also clear however that not all such sets are equivalent when it comes to scope and importance, and that world literature studies is a layered construction.

Surveying all European national literatures, it is easy to see that regardless of their different national characteristics they still run a parallel course that transcends the purely national, and that they show a similar development. Romanesque and Gothic, Renaissance, Baroque, Classicism and Romanticism: none of these is restricted to only one literature. Moreover, they not only follow upon another in this way in only one literature. Rather, all European literatures, albeit with some temporal differences, show the same developments. A question that has hardly ever been raised is whether such parallel developments also pertain beyond Europe, and whether in the literatures of the Orient we find the same transformations of style and of ideas – and moreover at more or less the same moments as in European literature. Yet this is one of the most essential questions in the history of ideas. When we look at European literature in its totality it clearly shows a supranational course of development. Whether it is possible to also construct a world literature along these lines is a question that has not yet received a definitive answer. If however, for the sake of provisional limitation, one wants to understand world literature as European literature in the sense just mentioned, we can already draw up a first list of questions we want to pose to world literature studies. These questions have to do with how to ascertain this supranational and unitary development of these literatures and to establish the motives that have led to such a unity. Is such a construction raised on the common foundations of all European literatures, that is to say the Classics and Christianity, or is it the expression of a more general humanity, of unison which in essence is rooted in the human mind, or is it only because these peoples belong to the same moments in history, the same times, that they are destined to share the same ideas and styles? Is it the noble motif of competition that spurs people on to similar creations, or does it all rest on influence, imitation, and invention? Of course, there is also another side to this set of questions. It is not just a matter of examining the supranational unity of literature, but also the diverse national characteristics show up particularly tellingly against the background of such a supranational unity. This is where the method of comparison comes into play, and if one compares German and French Classicism or English and Italian Romanticism, one will recognize that within these common currents national differences perhaps even outweigh the shared traits. As is the case everywhere in life, here too unity manifests itself only in diversity and plenitude.

What is still missing from this concept of world literature, though, is the principle of selection. We have to admit that not everything belongs to world literature, not even when it fits this supranational development of literature. It is possible to define the concept of world literature more precisely: only pertains to world literature in this more restricted sense what really transcends the borders of the nation, what really has become known and appreciated by other nations by means of translation, and what has influenced other literatures; in other words, what participates in the exchange of ideas and in the world literary traffic between the nations. The fact that with concepts such as renown, appreciation, and influence we are dealing with very relative quantities, does not necessarily plead against such a vision of world literature. We will have to accept once and for all that concepts such as these, and with which the history of ideas concerns itself, always have only a relative value. It is impossible to ascertain in which, and in how many literatures, or to which degree or which depth, a literary work has to have penetrated and cast its influence, to be reckoned part of world literature. In any case, the task of world literature studies that follows from such a definition of world literature as we have been proffering here, exists in researching the real and active relations pertaining between literatures, in tracing how themes, motifs, forms, ideas and works move from one country to another, how they change according to the diversity of the soil on which they find themselves, how they have been received and elaborated, and how they play their rousing and fertilizing roles. When does a national literature gain entry to a world literature so conceived, and why does it do so at that particular moment? What did one nation give to the others, what did it receive from these others, and on which basis did this exchange happen?

These two last questions are certainly the most important ones from this set of questions.

As far as the first question is concerned, the historian will note that nations gain entry to world literature in sequence and that they take turns when it comes to creative leadership and dominance. After a people for hundreds of years has played only a receiving and assimilating part, it suddenly, when its hour has struck, comes to the fore with such individual and necessary human creations, that the world can no longer do without it, and this nation now itself becomes a leader and donor. This was the case of Italy during the Renaissance, France in the days of Classicism, and Germany in the era of *Werther*, *Faust*, and Romanticism. Throughout history, it is through this ever new infusion of national characteristics that all of humanity gradually develops itself to the fullest of its possibilities.

When, though, does the hour strike for a particular people?

In the course of history we can see how the spirit of humanity at all times advances such new and specific needs, on such a supranational level, that they are not limited to one single nation, but impose themselves everywhere, demanding to be satisfied everywhere. Such a movement, whether Renaissance, Gothic, or Baroque, assumes a European dimension. Yet we also see that every movement first originates with one specific nation, that there it is brought to completion, and that from there on it spreads amongst the nations. In one specific period movement only does a nation reveal its own innermost character and does it accomplish its mission in the world, while in other periods it can only play a receiving role. The historical hour of a nation therefore has arrived when the general needs of the historical moment coincide with the specific task and mission of this nation, when a nation by dint of its own most individual character and its own specific gifts succeeds in answering the demands the world historical moment imposes. That is the stellar moment of a nation, when it sets out upon its spiritual conquest of the world. Such a moment for instance came for the German spirit when towards the end of the eighteenth century French Classicism and the West-European Enlightenment, by which German intellectual and spiritual life had been dominated during that eighteenth century, grew tired, and when this culture had become so overripe that it had achieved its mission in the world, and the moment had arrived that a new spirit, that according to its own nature and mission would vanquish Classicism and was destined to usher in the period of Romanticism, had to take the lead. (See also my *Deutsche Klassik und Romantik*, 3rd edition, p. 386ff.)

With reference to the national character of a nation we can now also already answer this further question: what it is that a people has to give to world literature, and what it receives therefrom. There is something that is so rooted in a nation's own nature that it can only be achieved by this nation and no other, and what these other nations therefore can only receive, and must receive, from this particular nation when its time has come. And this nation receives what it cannot produce of its own accord but only with help from abroad. Whenever the time arrives for a classicist art, the German spirit has always had to draw upon the Classical and Romance cultures. But when the hour of freedom struck, of the breaking of bonds, of opening and loosening up, and when the spirit of humanity in Faustian flight swung upwards toward infinity, then it was the German flight that carried along the other nations. One of the most important tasks of world literature scholarship is to research how the specific nature of a nation determines its own creative mission in the world and also what it has to receive from other nations, and how thus the image of Man unfolds itself in history through a process of reciprocal addition and completion. Hence, world literature resembles a living organism for which the national literatures serve as members and in which each of these members has to fulfill its specific and necessary function.

A concept of world literature such as we are discussing here posits criteria of supranational appreciation and dissemination.

We should remark however that according to this concept Kotzebue is more of a world literary author than Goethe, Sudermann more than Hauptmann, Wallace with his detective stories more than Cervantes with his *Don Quixote*. In such a case it might offer a way out if one says: Kotzebue and Wallace do not belong to world literature because they do not belong to literature to begin with. But which works in fact do enjoy the greatest dissemination and easiest reception in the world? Obviously it is those which do not have an eternal but a topical relevance. The times, the identical moment, is obviously the supranational fate shared by all nations. These topical problems concern all nations because they all face them in the same way. Literary creations therefore that ask and answer questions related to their own times, that finger the wounds of the period and try to heal them, that is to say contemporary works, most easily conquer the world. That is also why the novel, which by its very nature tends towards a period picture, particularly easily achieves world literary status. But it is not just Goethe's *Werther*, Jacobsen's *Niels Lyhne* or Remarque's war novel that owe their acceptance into world literature to their topical subjects; the same goes for Ibsen's social dramas. When the problem has been solved and the illness cured they are forgotten, because they achieved their importance in the world only because of their topical interest. Homer's war poem is eternally valid. Whether this is also true for Remarque's war novel is very doubtful, to say the least. Goethe's *Wilhelm Meister* remains significant. The question is whether this will also be the case for Thomas Mann's *Magic Mountain*.

We should not try and play the prophet. Obviously, however, there is a yet deeper concept of world literature that comprises not just a spatial but also a temporal dimension. World literature is precisely that literature that has not been forgotten and that has not sunk below the horizon, even if once it may have enjoyed the widest dissemination and influence. Next to dissemination throughout the world this concept then also considers duration in the world, and next to supranational importance lasting validity. Certainly, the topical can coincide with the eternal in one and the same work, as we can see from Goethe's *Werther*. But *Werther* precisely belongs to world literature in this deeper sense because it does not only hold period interest but everlasting one, because it has not only for a certain period decisively influenced all literatures, but because it has continued to matter beyond its own time. It is quite possible that there are breaks in the total period of time that a work or an author enjoys world literary status. A work or a writer may become suppressed by a particular period movement, and temporarily forgotten. But when the work or the author really is of lasting value, it or he will always again, when its hour has struck, emerge from the river of forgetfulness, as happened with Shakespeare and Cervantes.

But we are not done yet with world dissemination and world duration. There is a certain popular taste that everywhere and at all times remains the same: the taste for Kotzebue. Notwithstanding his dissemination throughout the world and his lasting popularity, though, the eternal Kotzebue is still far from belonging to world literature. We also have to take into account the grounds for dissemination and duration.

But can we really say anything about the nature of a work of world literature? What is it that makes a work into world literature in this sense? Is there such a "nature," after all?

Maybe one will think that works with a cosmopolitan or, when one wants to limit oneself to European literature, with a European character, that because they do not have a distinctive national character address all Europeans, qualify in first instance.

There truly is a literature that owes its world literary importance to its spirit of world citizenship. That literature is French literature, whose central point of attention, and whose aims coincide with European civilization. It is with these ideas, and with its formal characteristics of clarity, order and unity that French literature gained entry into world literature. Montesquieu, Pascal, Larochefoucauld did not speak as individual personalities and also not as specific Frenchmen, but as representatives of the spirit of European civilization, as spokesmen for human reason, the bringing into being of which Europe saw as its task. We might recall here that law of French Classicism that the drama should respect the unities of place and time. The insistence on these unities in essence means that place and time do not have a truly distinctive function here. Such drama is without place and time. These formal requirements also function as simple, yet very representative symbols of the French spirit. These laws demand the rule of a reason transcending any place, any time.

But it is not mere wordplay when we say that this rational spirit of French literature is also a very national spirit, that is to say the spirit of France, whose national specificity rests precisely in this idea of a European mission. In general, a cosmopolitan mindset is not necessarily a part of world literature. On the contrary. If another work but a French one assumes such a character, this precisely makes it more difficult for it to find its way in the world. That Heinrich Mann for instance has not been able to secure himself a place in world literature, while his brother Thomas Mann did succeed in doing so, has nothing to do with a difference in literary value, but everything with the fact that Heinrich Mann's novels show the same cosmopolitan character as we find in French literature, and that therefore they have nothing to say to the world that it has not already heard from France. From Germany the world wants to hear something else and something specifically German. It is precisely works that show very distinctive national characteristics, then, that go to make up world literature. The position Goethe occupies in world literature rests in first instance on the most German of his works, *Faust*. After all, nations want to obtain from one another what they themselves do not have and what they cannot produce from their own inner selves. World literature is a harmony of voices of the most different sounds.

We should immediately add that this harmony only comes into being, and that a literary work can only then be understood and assimilated by the world, when the essence of the national character it gives voice to is also an essential trait of the figure of humanity, of the eternal image of Man, a necessary member of the overall human organism, that image of Man also that unfolds and realizes itself in the historical development of the spirit of humanity through the input of ever new nations. A work becomes world literature when it has to offer something to the world without which the overall spirit of humanity would not be complete, when its roots are firmly embedded in the soil of the nation, yet its crown reaches high into the space of eternal humanity, when it is fed by the blood of the nation, yet is infused with the spirit of general humanity. Shall we enumerate a few examples of works that in this way have succeeded in gaining entry into world literature? *The Odyssey*, the most Greek and the most human of poems, *Don Quixote*, the epitome of Spanish chivalry yet also of eternal human idealism. Dante's *Divine Comedy*, in which Italian Catholicism refined itself into the eternal human yearning for God. De Coster's *Uhlenspiegel*, in which rootedness in Flemish soil becomes a symbol of everyman's connection to the earth and to reality. *Hamlet*, whose very English skepticism deepens into Man's fundamental world-weariness. *Gulliver's Travels*, Byron's *Don Juan*, Rabelais' *Gargantua*, Tolstoy's *Resurrection*, Dostoyevsky's *Brothers Karamazov*, Flaubert's *Madame Bovary*. All have become myths, grown from their own particular landscape and begotten by the power of a nation, but all with their crowns reaching up into the eternal and common space of humanity, figures that represent their own nation in such a wonderful way, in whose veins runs unmistakably English, French, or Russian blood, but that at the same time are also so essentially human, that everyone, whether Englishman, Frenchman, Russian or German, as long as he or she is a human being, finds some of his own blood and his own spirit in them.

It is symbolical-mythical figures, then, that conquer the world, because in them a national spirit assumes the common shape of all humanity, as with Don Quixote, Gargantua, Till Uhlenspiegel, Faust, Don Juan, Ahasverus. In general, it is in popular works, in legends, myths and fairytales, in which the national character of a people dresses itself against the background of eternal humanity, which is also why all these kinds of works everywhere in the world show common traits.

It is also very instructive to find out with what ease or difficulty literatures gain their place in world literature. Because this does not at all depend on their value or lack of value, but from the nature and the characteristics that a specific literature can contribute to world literature on the basis of its own national inclination. Access to world literature was always most open to

French literature. Quite obviously, if faced least resistance, because from the very beginning, given its cosmopolitan character, it addressed general human reason and therefore was understood everywhere. German literature faced the most difficult road. Even the greatest of German poets, Hölderlin and Kleist, hitherto have not succeeded in carving out for themselves a position worthy of them in world literature. The difficulty lies in the nature of the contribution that German literature could make to the unfolding image of Man. It lies in the German idea of the value of the individual, and the German desire to express the free and creative power of the individual in literary works. When Mme de Staël, in her book on Germany, which prepared the way for German literature into the world, explained the distinction between German and French authors to reside in that the Germans have to lead their lives and write their works only for themselves, and that each of them has to start anew and fashion his own language, without the backing of a community, a national consensus, a tradition and a national set of customs, she not only pointed out a tragic fate, but also what lies at the heart of German literature and constitutes its specific value. But how could this concept of individual freedom, which in itself creates so little bonds, easily become a bond between nations. This concept made it difficult even for Goethe to gain entry into European literature, Goethe, whose individuality notwithstanding had refined itself into a general humanity such as no other German author ever before. Goethe's way of expressing his very personal experience in his writing and to use his works as both confession and as cure for himself was alien to other people and difficult to understand. In a French journal, the *Globe*, it was once said literally (in Goethe's own translation): "the slowness with which Goethe's reputation spreads with us is largely to be blamed on the most exemplary trait of his character, which is his originality. Everything that is original to the highest degree, that is to say heavily marked by the character of a special man or nation, will be difficult to the tastes of others, and originality is the outstanding quality of this poet. One could indeed maintain that, in his independence, he takes this quality, without which one cannot speak of genius, to excess. All other poets follow a uniform course, easy to recognize and follow; but he is so different from all others and from himself, it is often so difficult to guess where he is going, he confuses in such a way the ordinary expectations of criticism, even of those that admire him, that in order to truly enjoy him one should have just as few literary prejudices as he has himself, and maybe it would be just as difficult to find a reader that is completely free of them as it is to find a poet who, like him, has disregarded them all. Therefore it should not come as a surprise that he is not yet popular in France, where one eschews effort and study, and where everyone hastens to ridicule that which he does not understand, from fear that somebody else will do it first, with an audience that only admires when it is impossible to avoid doing so."

It is the German concept of individuality and originality then that formed an important part of the German contribution to the image of Man that put a first obstacle in the path of Germany's entry into the world. Closely linked to this concept is yet another one. German man, immersed in his own inner loneliness, only seldom, unwillingly and hesitatingly leaves this lonely interior to venture out into commonly shared space. It is only with difficulty and unwillingly that he gives his inner world an appearance, a form, gestures and a guise that can be grasped with the senses. He doesn't care to make himself commonly understood. He speaks in monologues, and strongly feels that no exterior form can adequately express the inner spirit. The concept is more important to him than the form, the truth of his feeling more than the word and the gestures, and sentiments more than a job well done. Precisely because of what is most precious to its nature, then, and because of its characteristic interiority, which at the same time make up his contribution to the image of Man, his literature lacks the bonding power and the general comprehensibility that only reside in a sensuous, graspable and measurable form.

Still, all these impediments vanish before what surely must be the most difficult and tragic of them all. The concept of world literature is inextricably bound up with the concept of civilization, the sharing, exchange and mutual tolerance among nations on the basis of a common set of morals, reason and contractual arrangements. Both these concepts originated and spread at the same time. But the German mission in the world, the most proper concept that the German spirit has to offer to the world, is inimical to civilization and seeks to save and to conserve precisely those values that threaten to be swallowed by civilization; to the ever growing mechanization it opposes the creative and organic life, to the hegemony of reason the irrational soul, to practical materialism the eternal ideal, to general leveling aristocratic values, to skepticism belief, to empiricism metaphysics. This is what we find with the most German of German poets: Hölderlin. Briefly put: it was Germany's fate that the German spirit would conquer the world at a time in which it had to try and halt that world's historically necessary progress, that it should become world literature with a contribution that threatened to explode the form of a world literature firmly founded on civilization.

All this it was then that, more so than anywhere else in the world, made it inevitable that in Germany there would first arise a genius hitherto unheard of, so that the German voice would be heard in the world and carry it along and master it. Such a genius only arrived with Goethe, and it was only he that succeeded in accomplishing this unspeakably difficult task.

We could also put it differently: that someone of his kind (not of his value) finds it easier than someone else to conquer the world after a period of classicism, because it is of the essence of the classical work that it transcends time and space, that it is typical and eternally human in its form, and that in its form it is measurable. This is much more difficult to do for a baroque or romantic literature.

In this respect the various literary genres are also very different. It is much more difficult for lyrical poetry to penetrate the world than it is for the novel and the reason for this is that a lyrical poem in its lyrical depth cannot be translated because it inevitably loses its highest beauty, its sound and its perfume in another language. The themes, the plot, and the forms of a novel on the contrary can be translated, and prose allows at least to a certain degree a translation that is fairly equivalent. There are no deeper layers here.

World literature in the sense we have just given to this ambiguous concept is then the literature that on the basis of its national and general human dimension achieves a validity transcending space and time.

Now one could perhaps object that it is not a matter of effective dissemination in space and duration in time, but of the eternal quality and value, the absolute validity, that can also adhere to a work that has not enjoyed duration or dissemination. Success cannot be the decisive factor.

Of course: success alone is not decisive, only success on the basis of absolute value. But also absolute value is not decisive in itself, but only that value that in the reality of history has been conserved through duration and dissemination. No science is able to hand us a criterion by which we might judge the absolute value of a work of art. Every judgment of this kind remains outside the scientific sphere because of its inevitable subjectivity. Of course, this does not deny us the right and the need to come up with a judgment on the absolute value of a work of art. Indeed, we can only welcome and rejoice that in a time in which everything is to be measured, counted and rationally proven we find in the realm of art a last refuge where man, without such sticks and crutches, can assume the personal responsibility for the truth of his judgment. But why does one always seek to identify world literature with literature in the absolute sense? The world is a reality and world literature is a reality, which by that very reason can serve as scientific object to the historian. World literature, as I have mentioned, is that literature which across space and over time has retained its validity, that has become realized itself in its reality. World history is world judgment, Schiller said, and he certainly did not revere success. With "over time," then, we mean what really lasts through the ages, with "across space" we mean what really transcends national borders.

As far as the history of world literature is concerned, that will look differently according to the various concepts of it we have given. Because according to what concept one follows it will be a different object with which the historian deals.

Often the question is asked: since when do we have a world literature? Is it a modern phenomenon, that started with Goethe, the creator of the term "Weltliteratur" (world literature)? Or is there already a world literature in the Middle Ages or even in the ancient world? Of course, the confusion when it comes to the answers to these questions is just as big as that with regard to the use of the term world literature. Did the classics have a world literature? If one understands by the term the period unity of all literatures it is well-nigh impossible to say anything about this as far as the ancient world is concerned. There still is a complete lack of research on whether the literatures known to us from these times have followed a supranational and uniform course of development. When we consider the international relations between literatures, we can already notice some early traces of this. Tacitus brings to the Romans news about Germany, Herodotus about Egypt to the Greeks. In the final periods of antiquity a vivid exchange of gods and cultures, and consequently of literary forms and figures took place between Asia, Greece and Rome. If by world literature we mean a repertoire of literary works shared by various peoples, then Roman literature enjoyed such dissemination and validity throughout the empire that we can truly say that this literature was the world literature of the classical world. But in the deepest sense of the word, that in which we do not talk of dissemination only but also of duration in the world, we can hardly speak of world literature in the antique world. A repertoire, in the traditional sense, of supranational and in time continuously present works did not exist. Still, Greek and Roman literature later on proved capable of becoming world literature to a greater degree than almost any other literature in the world. This literature became not only a part, but indeed the foundation of world literature, and this because of its foundational concept, without which no such world literature could have originated: the concept of "humanitas" and the ever self-realizing form of beauty which seems to coincide with the concept of a humanity transcending time and space.

Did the Middle Ages have a world literature? They certainly did in the sense that all European literatures shared a common development and a unitary character. The unified Christianity of the Middle Ages also produced a unified spiritual Europe. There was the common bond of one God, one religion, one church, and there also was one world language, Latin. There also already existed a lively international traffic between literatures, even between the literatures of Europe and Asia alongside that between the European literatures themselves. Themes, motifs, fables, legends, forms and figures moved from one country to another. Yet the Middle Ages also already knew a world literature in the final and deepest sense: the Bible and Roman literature, in as far as it then continued to be valid, specifically Virgil. But part of medieval literature itself was of such eternally human scope that it was capable of becoming world literature and thus part of the supranational repertoire of the mind of Man, as happened with Dante and with the figures of the Arthur-cycle, and who could even conceive of a world literature of which the Christian idea of the world would not be a part. The Middle Ages then put down the second foundation of world literature. To the classical idea of the beauty of Man was added the spirit of love, tolerance, brotherliness and humanity, and the awareness of a higher bond uniting all nations in God.

Did the Renaissance have a world literature? The unity of European literatures at the time is clear to us today. The Renaissance was a European movement. That there was a literary world traffic is undeniable. Italian literature became the common property of all nations. But the Renaissance also had a world literature in the sense of world dissemination and world duration: the Bible, Greek and Roman literature, and medieval literature in as far as it lasted beyond the Middle Ages. But Italian Renaissance literature, which at the time set the tone in the European world, proved itself capable of becoming part of world literature (Petrarca, Boccaccio, Ariosto and Tasso).

In this way one could trace the history of world literature according to the various meanings one attaches to the concept, and in particular it would be one of the most rewarding tasks of the history of ideas to comprehensively chart at which moments, in which ways, and for which reasons those literary works that transcend space and time conquered the world, when they disappeared and reappeared, what changes they wrought in the world and how throughout history, with the ever new input of nations and national creations, the common image of Man continues to unfold to its full capacities.

A last question remains: is world literature really only a historical given, whose existence and growth scholarship can chart, or is it something that the spirit of humanity demands and a supreme Good, the blessings of which can be critically proven? Should we demand, and further, all the efforts of all those go-betweens, journals and periodicals, and especially the translators, that strive to make the literatures of other people better known and more widely disseminated amongst their own people? This question too will receive a different answer according to the various ideas one has with regard to world literature. Here too the answer will never be unequivocal, and in each case one will have to weigh the pros and cons. In the first place one has to think of the problem of translation. World literature, in all senses of the word (except that which subsumes under this heading all the literature of the world existing at a particular moment in history), depends on translation, and each translation, even the best and most inspired one, always remains *Ersatz*, and hence of necessity a forgery. Every language labors under constraints of mind and sound that disqualify it from truly re-creating the spirit, sound and rhythm of a foreign literature. Every period is bounded by its own typical structures, language, and ideas that inevitably thwart the re-creation of literary works grounded in different phases of ideas and language. The difference between the personalities of the author and the translator is a further hindrance even in the case of the most gifted of interpreters. If one should propose though that a wider and deeper knowledge of foreign languages might make the use of translations superfluous, one would have to respond that even the most proficient speaker or reader of a foreign language is never able to experience a work in that language as he does in his own. Therefore we will have to accept that in world literature we will always have to make do with an insufficient second best.

A second reflection would have to be that the nature and the literature of a nation would lose some of their character and specificity if they let themselves be influenced too much by foreign minds. Undoubtedly, literary world traffic, the exchange of intellectual goods, demands sacrifices from all nations. The question then becomes whether the gain offsets the loss, and for Goethe, for whom world literature was not just a reality coming into being but truly a demand of the spirit of humanity, the answer was affirmative in any case.

For Goethe, who, as I already said before, coined the term world literature, and whose thoughts in the 1820s indefatigably circled around this idea, the term referred to the intellectual space in which the nations, through their literatures, no longer just addressed themselves but also one another. It was a space in which nations mutually heard and understood each other, where literary world traffic happened, of the exchange of intellectual goods, of a reciprocal giving and taking, a getting to know, to evaluate and to translate one another. But Goethe saw not only that this concept began to take shape with particular intensity in his own time. For him it was also an ideal that he propagated and that he tried to further with all his power. For him world literature had a task and a mission. World literature had as task for each nation to get to know itself after its own nature by holding up the mirror of other nations' literatures to itself, and to renew and bring to greater fruition each nation through foreign exposure and understanding. Because every literature — Goethe says — eventually reaches a dead end in itself when it is not renewed by contact with the foreign. Which nature researcher has not rejoiced in the wonders he recognizes through comparison? And what comparison, holding up the mirror to oneself, can do for a man's moral growth every man, even if unwittingly, has experienced for himself and will readily understand when he stops to think how much of his education he owes to it. Goethe also remarked how the distance of foreignness makes for a clearer and more rigorous approach to another literature. By his quiet, clear-sighted and intimate intervention in German literature, for instance, Carlyle was able to resolve in German literature the kind of conflict that inevitably rages within the literature of a nation. After all, to live and work also means taking sides and to attack. While such doings for many years may obscure the horizon of a nation's literature, the foreigner lets dust, fog and haze settle and disperse, and clear-sightedly looks upon these remote territories, with their sunny and shady sites, with the same ease of mind with which we are wont to look at the moon on a clear night.

This, then, is the advantage that world literature brings with it for national self-knowledge.

World literature's second aim, though, is that it lets nations become acquainted with one another, thus doing away with hate and chauvinism, and clearing the way for a general tolerance. It should bring this about by developing, and realizing to an ever higher degree the ideal of the eternally human. As a natural scientist Goethe had observed that one "Ur-phenomenon" was at the root of all of nature's metamorphoses, that in all variety there hid one basic form. In the same way all men are only metamorphoses of the one basic phenomenon "Man," and all nations only variations of basic "humanity." Goethe's idea of world literature ultimately springs from his belief in the idea of "Man," transcending all varieties of time and space. Clearly, he states somewhere, for quite some time now the efforts of the best authors and writers of all nations have aimed at what is common to humanity. In all that matters, and transcending nationality and personality, we will see this common humanity shine forth ever more clearly and radiantly. Whatever tends and works in this direction in the literatures of all nations is what all other nations should assume to themselves.

World literature, then, should strive to realize the figure of Man in a cleansing and purging way. In its development the coming into being of humanity acts itself out, and through it every nation should constitute itself as part of overall humanity in that it receives from the world what it does not yet possess itself.

World literature studies can also contribute to achieving these aims, and in this way it is itself a part of world literature. Indeed, it is not just that it is impossible to understand and describe a national literature without taking into account the relations it shows to other literatures. In that it compares literatures with each another, world literature also strives to further the knowledge of each nation's specific nature and its mission in the world. At the same time it aims to serve the causes of understanding, respect and tolerance between nations in that it demonstrates how nations are dependent upon one another in their intellectual life.

It is from motives such as these that world literature studies has sprung. The first reason for its emergence was national. When the idea of nation dawned in the Renaissance, several literatures tried, through comparison with others, to elevate themselves over these others, or to assert their own rights in the face of these others. This is what happened in the famous "Querelle des anciens et modernes" in France, where the issue was to prove the equality, even the pre-eminence of the more recent writers over the Greeks and Romans. For national reasons, too, Lessing compared the German drama with that of the French and English. Through comparison he wanted to wake the German spirit to its own nature and to its mission in the world.

With Herder it was as much his cosmopolitan as his national spirit that made of him one of the most important founding fathers of the world literature studies. It was his experience that the beauty of the spiritual world lies precisely in its plenty and variety. There is no such thing as a canon of art that would remain eternally valid, and that would be meaningful and right for all times and places. No aesthetics or poetics can proclaim universally binding laws or an absolute set of norms. Instead, there are endless possibilities and transformations. Homer, the Bible, Ossian, Dante, Shakespeare, Petrarca and Cervantes cannot be measured with the same rod. In many different tones the voices of the nations join in one symphony (anyway, this is something that even before Herder Voltaire had suggested in his "Essay sur les moeurs et l'esprit des nations" and "Essay sur la poésie épique"). Herder's cosmopolitanism, then, grew from an irrational world view: never ending, ever new, everywhere different life here confronted always and everywhere identical reason that thought it could impose general rules and laws.

But of course rationalism too might elevate world literature into a claim and an ideal. Only then we are not speaking of a harmony composed of the most variegated national voices, but of one and the same tone representing all humanity. Ever since in the eighteenth and nineteenth centuries it has come to be seen as the task of the European spirit to work towards the intellectualization, and hence also the equalization and standardization of life, literary scholarship has tried to prove the unity of all European literatures, or to advance it as a claim.

World literary studies, then, sprang from national and cosmopolitan motives, and we cannot ignore that in our day this discipline has gained greater urgency and importance than ever before. Because it is this discipline that is able to help us resolve the battle now raging between the idea of the nation and that of humanity.

Works cited

E. Beil, Zur Entwicklung des Begriffs der Weltliteratur, Leipzig 1915.

L. P. Betz, La Littérature comparée (Straßburg 1900).

F. Brunetière, La littérature européenne (Revue des deux mondes 1900, Bd. 161).

Georg Brandes, Hauptströmungen der Literatur des 19. Jahrhunderts. Endgültige Ausgabe. Berlin 1924.

B. Croce, La letteratura comparata (La critica I, 1903, S. 77, II, 1904, S. 483).

Derselbe, Weltliteratur (Literarisches Echo, Oktober 1899).

Ibid., Die Weltliteratur im 20. Jahrhundert vom deutschen Standpunkt aus betrachtet (Stuttgart und Berlin 1913). 2. Auflage. Fortgeführt von Paul Wiegler, Stuttgart und Berlin 1922.

Ibid., Weltliteratur, Goethe und R. M. Meyer (Beilage zur A. Z. 10. Nov. 1900).

Ibid., Literaturvergleichung (Literarisches Echo, Februar 1901).

E. Elster, Weltliteratur und Literaturvergleichung (A.f.d.St. d.n.Spr. Bd. 107).

M. Genast, Voltaire und die Entwicklung der Idee der Weltliteratur (Romanische *Forschungen* 1927).

Journal of Comparative Literature 1903.

M. Koch, Zeitschrift für vergleichende Literaturgeschichte, 1887 ff.

M. Koch, Studien zur vergleichenden Literaturgeschichte, 1901 ff.

E. Kühnemann, Zur Aufgabe der vergleichenden Literaturgeschichte (Zentralblatt für Bibliothekswesen 1901, Heft 1).

E. Martin, Goethe über Weltliteratur und Dialektpoesie (Straßburger Goethevorträge 1899).

R. M. Meyer, Die Weltliteratur und die Gegenwart (Deutsche Rundschau, August 1900).

Mazzini, Antologia 1829 (darin: d'una letteratura europea).

Posnett, Comparative litterature, 1886.

J. Petersen, Nationale oder vergleichende Literaturgeschichte (Deutsche Vierteljahrsschrift VI, Heft 1).

E. Quinet, De l'unité des littératures modernes (Revue des deux mondes 1838).

Revue de la littérature comparée, herausg. von Baldensperger und Hazard, 1921 ff.

G. Simmel, Logos III, S. 25.

F. Strich, Goethes Idee einer Weltliteratur (Dichtung und Zivilisation 1928, S. 58).

J. Texte, Rousseau et les origines du cosmopolitisme littéraire, Paris 1895.

K. Voßler, Nationalliteratur und Weltliteratur (Zeitwende, März 1928).

W. Wetz, Shakespeare vom Standpunkt der vergleichenden Literaturgeschichte, Hamburg 1897.

Chapter 8

Albert Guérard

WHAT IS WORLD LITERATURE?
and THE INDISPENSABLE
INSTRUMENT: TRANSLATION (1940)

ALBERT LÉON GUÉRARD (1880–1959) was a French scholar who, however, spent most of his adult life in the United States, primarily as Professor of Comparative Literature at Stanford University in California. Guérard was a staunch opponent of nationalism, and of the separation of the study of national literatures. Instead, in a Goethean spirit, he strove for bringing into being a world literature that would promote understanding among peoples of all nations and all cultures. In his writings of the 1930s, particularly after 1933 and up to 1940, when his *Preface to World Literature* appeared, Guérard blamed the German writer and philosopher Johann Gottfried Herder (1744–1803) for having laid the foundations of Romantic nationalism, the beginning of a development that Guérard saw leading straight to the excesses of National Socialism rampant in Germany at the time of his writing. Instead of to such starkly differentiated identities as posed by nationalism, Guérard adhered to the idea of universal humanity. In fact, for Guérard literature had always already been international, European-wide, and hence "world" literature, before the advent of Romanticism, which he blamed for the onset of nationalism and the study of national literatures as such. The Latin literature of the middle ages, the medieval fabliaux or romances, or the works of the Enlightenment philosophers, or in later ages children's classics such as *Pinocchio*, fairy tales, or even popular literature, in fact all works freely circulating either before or after the onset of Romanticism, transcended the boundaries of a nation or a language group, and was the common property of humanity, and hence properly "world literature." As he put it in *Preface to World Literature*: "The first, and lesser, benefit of World Literature is to reveal to us the picturesque, the delightful variety of mankind. The greater benefit is to make us conscious of its fundamental unity" (Guérard 1940: 24).

In readily accessible language Guérard touches upon many of the issues that would come to inform the discussion of world literature as it would flare up around the turn of the present century.

Albert Guérard. *Preface to World Literature*. New York: H. Holt, 1940. Excerpts from Chapter 1 "What is World Literature?" (pp. 3–16) and Chapter 2 "The Indispensable Instrument: Translation" (pp. 17–29).

What is World Literature?

The expression World Literature originated with Goethe. Our work could hardly be placed under a nobler or more fitting patronage. For Goethe is a perfect illustration of the conception that he named; to define his spirit is to define our subject. The supreme exponent of German culture, he was able to look beyond the political and linguistic boundaries of his tribe. Nothing human was alien to him. He considered the treasure house of mankind as his legitimate heritage; he enjoyed the masterpieces of ancient Greece and Rome, and those of modern France, Italy, Spain and England as well; he even sought to bridge the gulf between Oriental and Occidental cultures. Everywhere he assumed the freedom of a son of the house; he gave so convincing an interpretation of *Hamlet* that our critics accepted it for generations with scarcely a challenge. As he freely received, no less freely did he give. He had all Europe for his audience. Twice at least, in his early tale of frustration and despair, *The Sorrows of Young Werther,* and in the first part of his mighty philosophical drama, *Faust,* he reached, not scholarly and critical readers alone, but the multitude. For years before his death, his position as the head of European letters was unquestioned. Other prophets have arisen in his Germany, whose message can hardly be reconciled with Goethe's ideal; but the spirit that shone in Weimar shall outlive the fret and fury of our day.

There is some danger, however, in claiming Goethe as our master. It might foster the notion that World Literature is a formidable subject, fit only for such a titan of culture as he, or, at second-hand, for his learned disciples. We might as well imagine that religion is the exclusive privilege of St. Paul, St. Augustine, St. Thomas Aquinas, Martin Luther, with their following of professional theologians. We know that on the contrary, religion is a fact of common experience, not denied to the common man. So it is with World Literature. It is not reserved for a supercilious élite, doctors of philosophy or cosmopolitan sophisticates. We all read and enjoy World Literature in the same way as a character in Molière, Monsieur Jourdain, the *would-be gentleman,* had been talking prose all his life—without being aware of it. *World Literature begins, not in the graduate school, but in the nursery.* Our children are told immemorial tales, the fairy lore of all ages and climes. They do not object to the Grimm Brothers because they were Germans, to Charles Perrault because he was French, to Hans Christian Andersen because he was a Dane. The same blissful openness of heart and mind still prevails when they graduate from the nursery. *The Swiss Family Robinson, Heidi, Pinocchio,* are great favorites, although they were not born under the Stars and Stripes. Adolescent America finds delight in *The Three Musketeers* and *Monte Cristo,* by that lusty dusky giant among story-tellers, Alexandre Dumas; and youngsters still enjoy Jules Verne, even though many of his anticipations are now back numbers.

The common man retains this freedom from prejudice until he is taught better—I mean until he is taught worse. Adults are quite unconscious of national frontiers in the literary field. If there be but one book in the lone cabin, it will be the Book, the *Bible,* with its hoard of strange beauty as well as divine wisdom, a whole library of incomparable range within the covers of a single volume; and that book came to us down the ages, through men who spoke alien tongues and lived under alien skies. In the last century, the common man again was thrilled by the romances of Eugène Sue, *The Mysteries of Paris* or *The Wandering Jew;* he still enjoys, without the benefit of a university education, Victor Hugo's epic of redemption and social pity, *Les Misérables.* Among our best-sellers, read for sheer pleasure and not as class assignments, are many works of foreign origin: *Quo Vadis?* by Sienkiewicz, *The Four Horsemen of the Apocalypse* by Blasco Ibáñez, Ludwig's *Napoleon,* Remarque's *All Quiet on the Western Front,* Vicki Baum's *Grand Hotel,* Fallada's *Little Man, What Now?* World Literature, for the average reader, is not a theory, but a condition.

As our knowledge of literature expands, we realize more clearly that the best which has been thought and said in the world is not limited to our own bewildered generation, and to our terse and colorful American language. We become aware, not only of the best-sellers of today, but of those perennial good-sellers which are called the classics. Some day Homer swims into our ken; and Dante's *Divine Comedy,* and Goethe's *Faust,* and Tolstoy's *War and Peace*. Ignore these summits of human achievement, or grant them grudgingly a subordinate place, and you will stunt and warp the growth of your mind. This is not true only of the classics which rose to fame ages ago; anyone genuinely interested in contemporary literature has to get acquainted with Anatole France, Marcel Proust, Pirandello; with d'Annunzio, Gorky, Maeterlinck; with André Gide, Thomas Mann, Unamuno; with Jules Romains, Stefan Zweig, Ortega y Gasset.

From these plain facts, a plain conclusion must be drawn. *Literature should be taught as Literature in English, not as English Literature*. A selection there must be; but the basis of our selection should be excellence. It is far more important for us to know world masterpieces than to clutter up our minds with the names of local mediocrities. In the self-education which should continue throughout adult life, it would be wise to be guided by the same rule: let us read and enjoy the best, wherever the best may be found.

This simple suggestion may strike some readers as a willful paradox. We are used to a fairly rigid division into self-contained departments—English, Classical Languages, Modern Languages, History, Philosophy; and the disruption of these time-honored boundaries strikes us as a major heresy, like the confusion of the Three Powers in the Constitutional State. It would be well to remember that departments were made for man, and not man for departments. Above all, we should bear in mind that "time-honored" divisions are, in certain cases, surprisingly recent. In the long perspective of history, the study of literature from a strictly national point of view is a thing of yesterday. For centuries, the accepted approach was through the Humanities, that is to say through the Greek and Latin classics. When the present writer was a high-school boy in France, the same master taught French, Latin and Greek: the three formed a single whole. This long tradition is fading, but it has not completely disappeared. If Latin is still so extensively studied in America, it is not for utilitarian purposes, and not even for its very great intrinsic merits, but as the keystone of our culture. Latin may no longer be the indispensable bond among the nations; but few will deny that the disruption of Europe's spiritual unity involves a tragic loss.

The division of literature into separate language departments is defended on the plea that definite knowledge demands specialization. It is hard enough to know, accurately and intimately, a single literature, and that our own; it is out of the question even for a prodigy to take all literature as his domain. Such an attempt can lead only to shallowness, concealed at best under a pleasing film of generalities. As Professor C. H. C. Wright of Harvard put it with good-humored banter, the study of World Literature is apt to be "a breathless attempt to keep up with God and H. G. Wells."

This indicates a danger, not a radical impossibility. I agree with the professional scholars: the age of encyclopedic geniuses is past. But we must specialize far more than the departmental division would indicate. It is in fact impossible to know everything about a single literature. No man is expected to be a first-hand authority on *Beowulf* and James Joyce, extreme links in an enormous chain. In all cases, there must be selection, renunciation, and finally a confession of ignorance. We move in a little circle of trembling light; beyond that, a brief penumbra; and then, darkness absolute.

But, however limited our field may be, if we want to investigate it with any degree of thoroughness, we shall not be able to restrict it to national boundaries. Every great English writer had some foreign ancestor in the spirit, more important in shaping his art and thought than many of his English predecessors and contemporaries. No one could be a Chaucer scholar without some knowledge of Chaucer's French and Italian sources. A student of Milton will have to peer into Hebraic, Greek, Latin and Italian literatures. This is true even of our own darkly nationalistic age. We cannot fully understand Arnold Bennett without a knowledge of the influence of Maupassant, Edith Wharton without Paul Bourget, Katherine Mansfield without Chekhov, James Branch Cabell without Anatole France, George Bernard Shaw without Ibsen and Voltaire.

It may be contended, however, that foreign influences act only as modifiers of the national tradition, which remains the fundamental element. An Anglomaniac Frenchman like Voltaire remains a Frenchman all the same; a Gallophile and Gallicized Briton like Gibbon is none the less a thorough Briton. One man or one nation may borrow from another a set of terms, a doctrine, a technique, perhaps a new shade of thought or feeling; the underlying reality is unchanged. There are few things in literary history more dramatic than the success of Lord Byron on the Continent. Poets everywhere forsook their national masters to follow the lead of the prestigious English rebel. But Byron was so successful only because the Continent, through Rousseau, through Goethe and Schiller in their earliest works, through Chateaubriand, had independently reached the stage of Byronism.

Granted; but this only brings out the fact that all great literatures go through very much the same phases, almost at the same time. In other words, this emphasizes the unity of European culture. Within that unity, there are two sets of differences. The first are historical, and are manifested in the *periods;* the second are geographical, and separate the *nations*.

Between these two sets, nationality has the advantage of possessing a definite legal existence. Every man is registered as belonging to a nation, whereas the "spirit of the time" is but a shadowy sovereign. So we think more naturally of Edmund Spenser, for instance, as "an Englishman of the Renaissance" than as "a man of the Renaissance who happened to live in England." Yet, in the domain of culture, the period may actually be more real, more significant than the nation. There is greater resemblance among the European minds of a given age, such as the Enlightenment, than between a medieval Englishman and his distant mid-Victorian posterity. If you examine an old portrait, you will first of all be conscious of the period to which it belongs. It is only on closer scrutiny that you may be able to detect the nationality of the subject. There are fashions in clothes, but also fashions in expression and in modes of thought, which sweep the whole Western world. The proper unit for detailed study, then, would be a phase of civilization—the Romantic Revolt, for instance, or the Realistic Reaction—rather than any national group.

Nor should we fail to take into account, in pre-war Europe at any rate, the existence of class distinctions more rigid than national boundaries. For frontiers, now so sharply drawn, were long uncertain; what seems to us a vestige of feudal chaos survived into the Classical Age, and even after the French Revolution. Alsace, for instance, could at the same time be under the French crown and yet remain connected in many ways with the Holy Roman Empire. Less than a hundred years ago, Neuchâtel was still both a Prussian principality and a part of republican Switzerland. But, if a member of the nobility might hesitate about his national allegiance, he had no doubt whatever about his own rank, and the abyss that separated him from a commoner. Traces of such a state of mind can be found even in our own days. On the battlefield, all classes will fight with equal heroism for king and country. On the morrow, an aristocrat will give his daughter in marriage to a foreign aristocrat rather than to a plebeian of his own country.

This condition has a bearing upon literature. Members of the upper class, because they lived the same kind of life, inspired and enjoyed everywhere the same kind of art. Chrétien of Troyes, master of chivalric romance in the second half of the twelfth century, provided all Europe with patterns of refined love. Early in the sixteenth century, it was Baldassare Castiglione who, in his *Courtier,* defined the aristocratic ideal, for Englishmen and Frenchmen as well as for Italians. The spread of French literature under Louis XIV and Louis XV was due, not exclusively to its classic perfection, but in a large measure to the social prestige of Versailles and the Paris salons.

On the other hand, the common people also mingled with their kind across the uncertain border; they swapped stories, edifying or broadly satirical, on the market place and the fair ground, or along the pilgrimage routes. This prevented the formation of narrow regionalism, even in those days when communications were precarious and indeed perilous. It explains why the folk epic, *Reynard the Fox,* achieved such universal currency, and why the very same merry tales and farces, apparently home-grown and racy of the soil, are found in practically every land. There was a time when Christendom was a single pyramid, made up of the same social layers.

We must be cautious, however, not to over-emphasize the cleavage between these layers. There was, inevitably, a large amount of interpenetration. Lords, and even ladies, in all likelihood, enjoyed the rough-and-tumble humor of the populace. The "lower orders" have always craved for an insight into the magic existence of their "betters." There are, therefore, twilight zones between the cultures of the various classes, just as there are intermediate regions—Belgium, Switzerland—between the clashing worlds of Latin and Teuton. But the social class constitutes none the less a "climate" which influences literature more definitely than does the nation.

If the nation were but the political state, our demonstration would be fairly conclusive. But the idea of nation is complex. Ideally, the nation should be a territorial unit, under the same rule and *speaking the same language*. A genuine nation with a multiplicity of tongues, like Switzerland, is a miraculous exception.

Nowhere is this complete identity of linguistic and political boundaries fully attained. There are still many non-Germans within the Reich, and many Germans without. The English-speaking world is divided into two nations, and the Spanish world into twenty. France, so often supposed to be the model of a conscious nation, "one and indivisible," has to struggle even yet to impose linguistic unity within her European borders. It is perhaps because every nation is still in the making that national feeling is everywhere running so high.

From the point of view of culture, the *language group,* when it does not coincide with the political, is by far the more important factor. Indeed, in the study of what we call "national" literatures, the strictly political division is usually ignored. No one would think of eliminating Jean Jacques Rousseau from French literature because he was a citizen of Geneva. At the time when Germany was torn into hundreds of principalities, her literature was one—and great. In the nineteenth century, no *Anschluss* was required to bring the Austrian Grillparzer into the fold; and the Swiss Gottfried Keller is a German of the spirit. It would be an evil day for America if all the great British writers since the Revolution were voted *aliens*.

We may still maintain that a *language* is not the best natural unit for the study of literature; that the *period*, the *social class*, perhaps also the *theme* or the *kind*, would provide a better framework. But an artificial barrier, like a Maginot line of fortification, may be a formidable obstacle. World Literature is hampered by language differences far more than the other arts or than the sciences. Even mathematicians and chemists suffer through the lack of a common medium; but their basic symbols, at any rate, are universal, and the findings of Swedish or Italian research may be accurately checked in an American laboratory. The painting, the sculpture, and especially the music of foreign groups may at times demand special initiation; but their essential conventions, if not world-wide, are at any rate pan-European. Chinese music may be meaningless to us; but we can understand Debussy or Sibelius without the need of a translation. On the contrary, even for the most receptive and sensitive mind, the very best book in an unknown tongue is dead.

This difficulty can never be fully overcome. A universal language is a very remote possibility; and many lovers of literature doubt whether it would be clear gain.[1] We are

imprisoned within the confines of our own speech: a frontier harder to cross than the brist-
ling border between two hostile countries. *Yet World Literature does exist:* Germany knows
Shakespeare, and England knows Goethe. There is no more striking proof of Western unity
than this victory, however incomplete, over what might seem an impassable barrier.

At all times there were men, merchants and diplomats, whose business it was to cross
the frontier. Many of these were not wholly impervious to culture; yet their influence on
literary intercourse has not been very great. More important are those adventurous spirits for
whom a barrier is a challenge. They are not equally numerous in every age and nation, and
especially they are not evenly successful. In periods of serene self-satisfaction, conformity
and tradition prevail: Boileau knew something of Italian and Spanish writers, but only to
scorn them; the literatures of the North, for him, were lost in Cimmerian darkness; everything that was not bathed in clear, classical light vanished from his sight. But there are self-
critical moments when eternal conformity grows wearisome. These are not necessarily times
of decadence, self-depreciation and despair. They may be on the contrary periods of eagerness and hope, true *Renaissances,* with all the proud and joyous connotations of that word. It
is the most vigorous ages that dare to travel and to borrow. A culture afraid of the least wind
from across the border is confessing decrepitude.

There is therefore a fitful but unceasing process of interchange between national cultures.
The balance of spiritual trade may shift with brutal suddenness; then the infiltration of foreign
thoughts and phrases turns into an invasion; and the conservatives are appalled at what seems
to them a catastrophe. Thus, in France, the irruption of Italianism in the sixteenth century
was resented and denounced; so was the Romantic cult for English and German poets two
hundred years later; or, at the end of the nineteenth century, the craze for Russian novelists
and Scandinavian dramatists. Such a reaction is wholesome, when it seeks to check a mere
vogue, the passing favor attaching to forms, tricks or poses; no master is good simply because
he is foreign. But, on the other hand, no influence is bad simply because it is new and different.
It is foolish to reject a gift from abroad on the plea that it is "alien to our spirit"; if it were so
alien, our spirit would reject it automatically. The fact that Englishmen in the eighteenth
century appreciated French wit simply proves that French wit was not un-English. Anglo-
German romanticism would not have fructified so magnificently on French soil, if that soil
had not been ready for such a crop. A foreign influence simply liberates us from artificial
limitations, and reveals to us our own possibilities.

This process of international borrowing comprises several phases, which may or may not
be carried through by the same man. The first step is obviously the *actual learning of foreign
languages.* This is indispensable, but by no means sufficient. Many professional linguists,
traders, scholars, teachers, interpreters, do not help very directly in the diffusion of foreign
literatures. Two keys are needed, and if the first is, inevitably, knowledge, the second must
be *appreciation.*

Thus one pioneer forces the barrier, takes hold of foreign treasures. He must now bring
them back to his own people. This is done through *translation, propaganda,* and *conscious imitation:* three methods which do not invariably follow in the same order. To take a concrete
case, Voltaire knew English, appreciated Shakespeare, revealed the very existence of
Shakespeare to the general public in France, and showed, in his tragedies, faint but distinct
traces of Shakespearian influence. But it was reserved for an obscure hackwriter, Letourneur,
to give the first translation; for a forgotten dramatist, Ducis, to bring out the first stage
versions; while it was not until a whole generation later, about 1825, that the full impact of
Shakespeare's power was felt in France, with Vitet, Vigny, Dumas and Victor Hugo. The
process of assimilation, which in this case remains very incomplete, took nearly a hundred
years. Coleridge, to give another example, traveled in Germany, translated from the German
(in particular Schiller's *Wallenstein*), and showed in his philosophy and criticism the

unmistakable influence of German thought. In Carlyle, all the various stages of the process are found. He knew German, appreciated German, translated Goethe's *Wilhelm Meister,* imitated, in his *Sartor Resartus,* the style of the German romantic humorists, appointed himself the chief propaganda agent for German culture; in many of his pages, we do not know whether we are hearing Germany expressing herself with a Scotch burr, or Scotland with a German accent. It was William Archer who translated and staged Ibsen; but it was George Bernard Shaw who made himself, in his own irrepressible way, the apostle of Ibsenism. A crop of "would-be Ibsenians" was followed by a crop of "Ibsenians without knowing it": all that remained lacking was an English Ibsen. The very last stage, most important of all, and hardest to define, is that of *complete absorption. Madame Bovary* was the pattern that innumerable modern novels followed; but writers and public no longer realize their obligation to Gustave Flaubert.

This study of international influences is technically known as *Comparative Literature.* The term, thus restricted, is a misnomer. There is scarcely any valid kind of criticism that is not based upon comparison: comparison between authors in the same field, comparison with earlier work of the same author, comparison with "standards" which are themselves the result of comparison: Aristotle's *Poetics,* founded on the examination of all the Greek plays known to him, is a perfect example of the "comparative" method. To trace influences is "comparative," even when the writers concerned used the same language. What Keats consciously owed to Milton, for instance, is as well worth examining as what he borrowed from Boccaccio.

It is not invariably futile to fight against a misleading word; once the glorious period of St. Thomas Aquinas was known as "the Dark Ages"; now that expression is seldom used by reputable historians. So we register our protest against the term *Comparative Literature;* and we must confess in the same breath that we have no better one to suggest. Rightly or wrongly named, Comparative Literature is an extensive and fascinating subject. It tends to break down our inevitable tendency to parochialism. It places masterpieces in their proper line of descent, and among their peers. When we take it for granted that Milton is the product of European culture as a whole, and a factor in European culture, our understanding of Milton will be greatly deepened.

The weakness of Comparative Literature is that it emphasizes the accident of individual foreign influences, and minimizes the deeper reality of common elements. It does not much matter whether a thing was said first in English and then in French, and whether the Frenchman knew that the Englishman had said it before; what does matter is that both wanted and tried to say the same thing. The men who revealed England to eighteenth-century France, ahead of Voltaire and Montesquieu, were, as individuals, of secondary importance; they merely proved that the developments of England and France were then so synchronized that communications between the two could be established even through mediocrities. In other terms, *Comparative Literature* would be an extremely minor branch of study, if it did not lead to *General Literature;* and by that we mean the consideration of literary problems beyond the national field, such as period, theme, school, kind, spirit. This was the ambition of the Danish critic Georg Brandes in his *Main Currents in Nineteenth Century Literature.* It is interesting to note that the French masters who have created a very active school of Comparative Literature, Fernand Baldensperger, Paul Hazard, Paul Van Tieghem, are all advocates of the wider conception.

Certain authorities choose to establish a four-fold division: Universal Literature, World Literature, Comparative Literature, General Literature. *Universal Literature,* in this scheme, stands for the fullest possible expansion of our field: it embraces all literatures, of all ages, in all languages, without insisting on their unity or their relations. *World Literature* is limited to those works which are enjoyed in common, ideally by all mankind, practically by our own group of culture, the European or Western. In both these cases, the word *Literature* applies to a body of literary works, not to their critical study. *Comparative Literature* and *General Literature*, on the contrary, are methods of approach. The first is concerned with the mutual influences between various national literatures; the second with those problems which are present in the literature of every epoch and every country. We do not deny the validity and the convenience of these distinctions. But they should not be over-emphasized. They do not represent four separate branches of learning; they deal with the same material and use the same mental disciplines. They are four aspects of a single subject: *literature.*

Summary

Goethe was the godfather of World Literature. But this exalted patronage might give a wrong impression: World Literature begins in the nursery, not in the graduate school. The most modest readers have access to World Literature, in the form of the Bible, even when they have never heard of the term. World Literature is, "not a theory, but a condition." The division of literature into national compartments or departments, English, French, German, etc., is recent and not eternal. For centuries, the approach to the study of literature was through the ancient Classics, and the unity of Western Culture was fully recognized.

Within that unity, there are two sets of differences: in space and time, *nations* and *periods.* From the cultural point of view, the periods, although not so sharply defined, are actually more real than the nations, and form a better unit for study. Even the social classes are more influential in this respect than political geography. Repeatedly, the aristocracy of Europe enjoyed the same or similar books very much at the same time; and popular literature also had common themes and a common spirit throughout the Continent.

The unity of European literature is veiled, but not destroyed, by language differences. These create barriers worse even than military frontiers; yet there are explorers who venture beyond the border, and bring back the products of other groups. The study of these international influences is technically known as *Comparative Literature:* a misnomer, for most forms of criticism, in one way or another, make use of the comparative method.

For the sake of clearness, we shall then distinguish:

1. *Universal Literature:* the sum total of all writings in all languages at all times.
2. *World Literature:* the body of those works enjoyed in common, ideally by all mankind, practically by our own Western group of civilization.
3. *Comparative Literature:* the study of relations, in the literary field, between different national or linguistic groups.
4. *General Literature:* the study of problems common to all literatures; this study might also be called *Principles of Criticism;* it finds its best examples in the works which belong to World Literature.

Note

1   Prophecy and objection apply to a *universal* language, not to a neutral *auxiliary* language.

The indispensable instrument: translation

The first key to World Literature is the learning of foreign languages. But it is a key so unwieldy that most of us, it must be admitted, renounce every hope of possessing it.

Languages are actively studied in American high schools and colleges; but seldom are they thoroughly mastered. The pressure of technical and utilitarian subjects is too great; and even greater is the competition of sports and social pleasures. "We are so busy being human," said a youth in self-defense, "that we have no time for the humanities."

The situation could be remedied to some extent if the study of languages were frankly directed to the acquisition of a reading knowledge. To write and speak French or German with correctness, elegance and facility is indeed a heavy undertaking. It must remain a privilege and a luxury. The utilitarians, on their own chosen ground, are right: not one high school graduate in a thousand will have any practical need of writing and speaking any language but his own. On the contrary, a reading knowledge can be acquired with comparatively little effort, and the results it yields are immediate as well as abundant. There is no clerk in a country store whose life would not be enriched if he had direct access to the treasures of another literature. It would give him the exhilaration of release and of spiritual adventure, the welcome sense that the world is not a dismal interminable conglomeration of Gopher Prairies. It would enable him to look upon Gopher Prairie with critical eyes, and by critical, we mean understanding rather than depreciative: "What should they know of Gopher Prairie, who only Gopher Prairie know?"

For that deepening of experience, it is not necessary to be a Cardinal Mezzofanti, who spoke fifty or sixty languages with ease, and was acquainted with many others. The mastery of even a single foreign tongue is sufficient to break down the wall of provincialism. The reform we advocate, shifting the emphasis from the languages in themselves to the literatures they convey, has to face one great moral objection: it would make easy, and even pleasant, a branch of study at present proverbially hard. Our puritanical conscience balks at what might seem a capitulation to slackness. But the puritanical conscience is not always the best guide in matters of pedagogy; and a class in literature can be made as exacting, and if required, as forbidding, as a class in elementary grammar.

But even if the possession of several languages remained a necessary qualification for a scholar and a gentleman, it would not suffice. World masterpieces are found in more languages than even the professional philologist can be expected to master. Rare indeed are the men of culture who can read in the original, and with literary enjoyment, books in Chinese, Sanskrit, Arabic, Hebrew, and even Greek or Russian. It is an inexorable fact that our main line of approach must be through translation.

Nothing is so stubborn as a fact; but the refusal to face a fact may, for generations, be just as stubborn, and appear successful. To the present day, there are excellent scholars who decline to recognize the validity of any literature in translation. If we were to believe them, we should have no right to be moved by the beauty of the English Bible; it would have been better for Keats if he never had opened Chapman's Homer; it was a mistake for Chapman to translate Homer at all; and we should deny ourselves the illicit pleasure of reading Tolstoy or Dostoevsky in any language but the original Russian. I am hardly exaggerating: I have a letter from a great American critic, who happens to know Russian, but not German. He has stoically deprived himself of the great experience of reading *Buddenbrooks* and *The Magic Mountain,* although the perspicuous beauty of Thomas Mann's style survives particularly well the ordeal of translation.

However, it would not be safe to dismiss as absurd the opinion of men whose achievements and judgment we are bound to respect. Their reluctance to accept translation as genuine literature, although excessive, is not difficult to understand. The literary experience, whether in creation or appreciation, requires the intimate fusion of matter and form. The true poetical note is absolutely unique; the same feeling, expressed in different words, no longer is quite the same feeling. It is the exquisitely personal accent that creates *style;* and honest writing, without style, is business or science, but not literature.

There is profound truth in this contention. But it should not be turned into a rigid dogma; for in literature, truth, no less than beauty, depends on delicate and elusive shades rather than upon hard and fast distinctions. There are cases in which translation stands condemned; there are others in which, however inadequate, it will serve; there are others still in which the gain is immeasurably greater than the loss.

It is on the lowest level that the impossibility of translation is most apparent: hardly any pun can be rendered into another language. In French, *Pierre* means both Peter and a rock; in English, the identity disappears. Rostand's *Cyrano de Bergerac* is a crackling machine-gun fire of puns, including the aggravated kind known as *à peu près*, or near-pun. The play was none the less a brilliant success in many languages. Rough equivalents did the trick. What signified was not the actual pun, a poor thing at best, but the punning spirit, an evidence of insolent gaiety and bravado, as prominent a feature in Cyrano's picturesque figure as his waving plume or his enormous nose.

Almost as untranslatable as the pun is the melody of words. If a poem is sheer music in the material sense, if sound is emphasized at the expense of thought or feeling, then the magic disappears when the medium of expression is changed. Swinburne's alliterations, excessive even in English, would become nonsensical in French. Edgar Poe's *The Bells* would turn into a jarring jingle. The opulent rhymes and sprightly rhythms of Théodore de Banville, which, in French, have a lovely, lightsome, fantastic effect, would, in any other language, seem mere verbal acrobatics. There again, the loss is small: no poem is supreme by virtue of music alone. If literal translation is an impossibility, imitation remains open, provided it be deemed worth while.

There is, however, a subtler, less obtrusive kind of music which is the very essence of poetry, and which evaporates in transposition. The lines

> Break, break, break,
> On thy cold gray stones, o sea!

have in their absolute simplicity the true Tennysonian ring, which is not to be despised. George du Maurier, in his delightful *Vers Nonsensiques à l'Usage des Familles Anglaises,* offered this rendering:

> Cassez vous, cassez vous, cassez vous,
> O mer, sur vos froids gris cailloux!

which is literally perfect, and perfectly ludicrous. This is willful parody; but it clearly indicates a line which translation can hardly attempt to cross without self-destruction. The difficulty is not the same in every language and with every poet; and there may be translators whose miraculous gifts push back the limits of possibility; but, if the danger line is flexible, it is none the less inexorable.

It would be idle to deny that certain authors can never be fully known in translation. Byron's obvious attitude made him a European figure; Shelley's unearthly music is appreciated abroad only by a handful of thorough scholars. All that most Americans understand of Victor Hugo's verse is the resounding rhetoric. The marvelous orchestration, the poignant delicacy which constantly accompanies the enormous blare and is not drowned by it, the underlying sense of tragic mystery and awe, all this is lost on the foreign reader; so that Victor Hugo in World Literature remains the very great popular romancer of *Les Misérables,* rather than the supreme lyric and epic poet of *Contemplations* and *The Legend of the Centuries.*

However, Mark Van Doren's daring and very successful *Anthology of World Poetry* has proved that there was at least a craving for the enlargement of our lyrical experience beyond the confines of our native speech. Granted that the best of these efforts are adaptations rather than literal renderings; in the case of the *Rubáiyát* of Omar Khayyám *and* Fitzgerald, a hybrid, the fruit of remote collaboration, rather than even an adaptation; still we are the richer by this straining toward the unattainable. Goethe's *Wanderer's Nightsongs,* done into English by Longfellow, are not quite Goethe's, but they are better than anything else in Longfellow.

Poetry, or that poetical element which is the essence of all style worthy of the name, is music as well as sense. But the music does not necessarily reside in the words. The overtones which make expression truly great are in the soul, not in the voice. This may sound like idealistic nonsense: let us take a concrete illustration. There is magic in the distant sound of bugle or hunting horn in the woods at eve. On this obvious theme, Tennyson wrote *"The splendour falls . . ."* in *The Princess;* Alfred de Vigny, *The Horn.* Tennyson's lyric is a masterly technical achievement. He is coolly aware of the opportunities offered by the theme, and coolly determined to display the resources of his art. With the unerring selection of glamorous echoing words, with inner rhymes, alliterations, repetitions, he transcribes the effect of music with a skill we frankly—and coolly—admire. Tennyson is untranslatable: a transcription of this marvelous transcription would fall flat. It would be another *Cassez vous, cassez vous, cassez vous.* Vigny is not a virtuoso, but a stoic. We hear no audible music: we feel by inner response the deep vibrations of music in a grave and tender soul. The words are not indifferent; they are perfect in French, in their quiet restraint. But equally perfect words in English could restore exactly the innermost song that is in Vigny. This, of course, could be achieved only by a great poet, with the dramatist's gift of sympathetic insight; but it is not inconceivable. Vigny's poem is at least a candidate for World Literature; Tennyson's cannot leave its native soil.

The truth in this matter was expressed by the Greek critic Longinus many centuries ago: there is a sublimity which is inherent in the thought, and which therefore is universal. Longinus gave as an example: "Let there be light"—perhaps the first time the Bible was appreciated purely as literature. The stark majesty of these words stands unaltered in Hebrew, in Greek, in English; and it would lose nothing in Tagalog or in Esperanto.

In every great writer, there are verbal felicities, which must remain within the circle of the original language, and deeper notes, capable of appealing to all mankind. If the quips and pranks and spirited conceits cannot be translated, they may, in many cases, be imitated very much in the same vein; the call of the soul to the soul is direct, profound and universal. The Elizabethan clevernesses of Shakespeare are delightful because of their English accent. There are moments when Shakespeare is not "Elizabethan," not "English" and not "clever": he is Shakespeare. "To be or not to be," "The rest is silence," belong to the world.

So there is a *World Literature* even in the realm of poetry, which seems hopelessly divided by language barriers. The greatest French poet of our age, Paul Claudel, learned his art from the Bible, Walt Whitman, and perhaps even Nietzsche, not from Boileau, Lamartine, or Verlaine. American lovers of poetry are more deeply influenced by Villon, Baudelaire, Mallarmé, and, in a limited field, Heredia, than by certain American classics that every child knows by heart.

In the case of prose, the objection is slightly different. The harmonics and overtones which, it is alleged, belong to the language and cannot be translated, are not strictly musical, but cultural. Two words like *king* and *roi,* like *boy* and *garçon,* may be given as equivalent in the dictionary, but their connotations are different. He who was not brought up in the American scene, whose ears were not attuned to American speech, whose palate does not respond to American savors, will never fully understand American letters. Whatever lexicographers may say, no *flan au potiron* can ever hope to be *pumpkin pie.* Conversely, it is argued that no American can ever read a foreign book without inflicting upon it some distortion, at times frankly ludicrous.

That translation is impossible is one of those impressive assertions in which profundity is artfully blended with mystification. Every book is "translated" by every reader into terms of his own experience. When he comes across the word *hills,* his imagination, if it be vivid at all, will evoke the hills which are familiar to his eyes. The experiences of all Americans do not by any means coincide; much of the "American Scene" remains, geographically or socially, foreign to most of us. *Death Comes for the Archbishop,* by Willa Cather, is an American master-piece, written by an American and for Americans; the scene is laid in America; the subject is an authentic part of American history. But, among the thousands who have read this great book with delight, many have never been within hundreds of miles of Santa Fe; there is nothing in their memory that corresponds with the austere and yet friendly majesty of its landscape; nothing that will give them a clue to Indian or Mexican mentality; nothing that will enable them to fathom the soul of a priest.

If we could appreciate only the things of our own daily life, we never could enjoy any book with a setting remote in space or time. All exotic, all historical, as well as all foreign, literature, would be sealed against us. Even the masterpieces of England, and Shakespeare's first of all, would be meaningless. Fortunately, this is not the case. For the plain man as well as for the man of culture, literature is no mere reproduction of experience, but an extension and a deepening.

The desire for extension is obvious. We all crave to travel, in the spirit, beyond the circle of our petty cares; to reach strange lands of thought, and plow unknown seas; to asso-ciate with great kings, great lovers and great criminals. Adolescent romanticism if you like; but phonographic realism and sociological reports will never quite supplant it. The deep-ening of experience does not require that we should start from the humble details of our daily existence. On the contrary, it may be clear gain to brush them aside. It is good that our spirit should escape from its immediate environment, so that we may better realize what is profoundly and eternally human in ourselves. The first, and lesser, benefit of World Literature is to reveal to us the picturesque, the delightful variety of mankind. The greater benefit is to make us conscious of its fundamental unity.

When Jack Smith of Middletown translates Henry James into terms of Jack Smith's experience, there is an obvious wastage; still Jack Smith will be the richer even for his faulty reading. When Charles Grandgent or Melville Best Anderson, great Dante scholars, pondered over the *Divine Comedy,* there was, even for them, a loss. They could never know all that Dante knew, they could never see all that he had seen. To such a loss they were resigned; they thought only of the immeasurable gain. I may not catch in *Buddenbrooks* the fine details and the subtle shades which are obvious to a Lübeck burgher. But I see far more in *Buddenbrooks* than in many novels about my own California. It is not inconceivable that you will enjoy Victor Hugo's *Notre Dame* better than Sinclair Lewis's *Work of Art,* that matchless handbook for hotel managers. If such be the case, let no abstract dogma stand in the way of your legitimate enjoyment.

It must be confessed that many translations are bad; and so are not a few original works. Translation is a thankless task: difficult, ill-rewarded, despised. For that reason, it is too often abandoned to hackwriters of doubtful competence. Because we have such a poor opinion of translations and translators, we are contemptuously tolerant of inferior work. *Traduttore, traditore:* translator, betrayer, is an ancient, but not ill-humored jibe; the poor devil is doing his best. And when Woodrow Wilson said: "To hear one's words translated is to witness the compound fracture of an idea," he did so with a smile. If we realized the essential part that translation must play in world culture, we should grow less scornful and more exacting.

No art is to be despised as parasitic because it depends upon some other art. All performers—conductors, instrumentalists, vocalists, actors—are only interpreters; the composer, the dramatist, alone can claim full originality. Yet a performer is an artist in his own right, and may be a great artist. He does not mechanically transmit a work of art: he interprets and re-creates it. Paradoxically, a singer may be greater than his song, an actor than the text he is using as his medium. Sarah Bernhardt gave some semblance of poetical life to the gaudy melodramas of Victorien Sardou, and Sir Henry Irving to even cheaper plays, like *The Bells*.

But if the common run of translations is poor, it should not be forgotten that the art has been practiced by the very greatest, Goethe and Schiller translated both masterpieces and trifles. In England, Chaucer, Milton, Dryden, Pope, Fielding, Coleridge, Carlyle, George Eliot, did not spurn the lowly craft. Nor is the tradition in abeyance; for among translators in the twentieth century could be mentioned the leaders in French literature, Maurice Maeterlinck, Paul Claudel, André Gide, Marcel Proust, Jules Romains;[1] in America, George Santayana, Ludwig Lewisohn, Van Wyck Brooks, Edna St. Vincent Millay. . . . The contributors of translations to Mark Van Doren's *Anthology of World Poetry* constitute a very creditable roll of fame.

That great writers should consent to act as translators need not surprise us. In one respect, the translator's attitude is one of humility; he abdicates initiative; he is willing to serve, not to command. In another respect, translation means proud collaboration. What exultation if Goethe, at the height of his fame, had consented to accept our aid! Now that he can no longer help himself, we are free to impose our partnership upon him. But that partnership possesses to a high degree the same merits as co-operation with the living man. It compels us to attune ourselves to his thoughts, to his moods, to his familiar and unconscious tricks. We must create in ourselves a self after Goethe's image, before we can translate Goethe at all. Every word not of the obvious kind is a challenge. We have to surmise the exact shade that Goethe had in mind, even—sacrilegious thought!—when Goethe's mind had remained in a convenient haze. So every translation worthy of the name becomes an interpretation, a commentary, a criticism. Nothing should be more ennobling than this wrestling with a great spirit. Like Jacob with the angel, we can compel a blessing.

This great dignity of translation should be more fully recognized in our universities. We need advanced courses—and very arduous courses they would be—in thorough translation. A version of some foreign classic, combining scholarly care with literary merit, might very well be accepted in lieu of a Master's thesis. And, in self-defense against botchers, conscientious translators should band themselves into an effective guild. They should insist that the work even of their qualified members be submitted to a competent board of revision; the editors of the very best firms are notoriously slack in this respect. Authors, publishers, public, need to be protected against unscrupulous middlemen.

There is one advantage that a translation possesses over an original work: it can be amended, and if need be discarded and superseded. We may feel that Proust's last volumes were left in a very imperfect condition; but we have no right to correct or complete his manuscript. And, when a masterpiece grows archaic, like Chaucer's *Canterbury Tales,* we greatly hesitate (far more than our ancestors did) before attempting to modernize it. Classic rank imposes upon a text a frozen dignity perilously akin to death. With a translation, our freedom is restored. Professor Zeitlin, for instance, in his very fine edition of Montaigne's *Essays,* did not feel compelled to reprint Cotton's version *verbatim*. The French are still trying to translate Shakespeare: it is to be hoped that each new version is both more Shakespearian and more French than the last. It is meet that every century, nay every generation, should have its own Homer and its own Dante. T. E. Lawrence's *Odyssey* and W. H. D. Rouse's *Story of Odysseus,* in a most welcome fashion, have renewed the freshness of that great tale of adventure.

Our conception of World Literature, to sum up this long discussion, is but the negation of a negation. It is the refusal to accept as final, in matters of the spirit, the limitations of political allegiance or local dialect. Our field is *living literature*. Whatever quickens in us the sense of life is part of *our* literature, even though it was first said in Hebrew or in Greek. Conversely, a writer may still be active, and he may use the purest "American": if he means nothing to us, he is dead.

In thus defining the domain of literature without reference to the map, we are not preaching internationalism: we are only noting elementary and uncontroverted facts. It is those who would introduce the question of nationality into the esthetic field who are guilty of injecting a political element where it does not belong. This is as futile as to inject it into religion or science. In culture, internationalism is the basic fact. Isolation, *autarky,* is delusion or self-mutilation.

But this brand of internationalism is perfectly compatible with the highest patriotism. If we love our own community, we shall be all the more eager to enrich it with the best which has been thought and said in the world; and, reciprocally, we shall desire to contribute our best to the common hoard of mankind. There is no place in all this for an inferiority complex. English Literature, of which the American branch is no less vigorous and no less legitimate than the British, is, by universal consent, second to none. We give, and we are more than willing to give, fully as much as we receive. Let us have the freest trade in spiritual goods: we need not be afraid of an adverse balance.

Summary

For World Literature to come into existence, the language barrier must be overcome. This cannot be done except through the acquisition of foreign languages—a formidable task, if by acquisition we mean thorough mastery. But a mere reading knowledge is far more accessible, and would bring abundant reward to every high school student.

However, not even professional scholars can know even all the major culture languages, and the indispensable instrument of World Literature is translation. But translation is still distrusted, and even despised. It is claimed that in art intention and form are inseparable, and that every translation is bound to destroy this vital unity.

Obviously no translation can render literally that which depends altogether upon the sounds of a particular language: puns or verbal music. Only equivalents can be offered. Lyric poetry is far more difficult to render into a foreign tongue than narrative or drama. Plain sense, on the other hand, can easily be translated; and, beyond plain sense, there is a poetry which lies in the ideas or feelings themselves and their association. This deeper poetry also can be translated: the supreme passages in the Bible and Shakespeare are universal in their appeal.

Every book, even in our own language and dealing with our own country, requires a *translation* from the terms of the writer's experience to those of the reader's. Fortunately, man is able to make such an adjustment, and to feel the human element under the infinite variety of forms. Without such a capacity, there could be no communication between man and man. It is the extension of this capacity that makes communication possible between age and age, nation and nation, language and language, and accounts for the undeniable existence of World Literature.

In spite of grievous handicaps, translation has been practiced by great writers in the past, and the tradition is not lost. It is an exacting but ennobling task to co-operate with a foreign genius, to attune yourself to his thought, and to make his words your words.

Translation offers one advantage over original work: it can more readily be corrected, perfected, brought up to date, by successive generations. Every age has, and should have, its new translation of Homer or Dante.

The essential thought of these two introductory chapters is that World Literature is the negation of a negation. It is the refusal to accept as final, in matters of the spirit, the limitations of political allegiance or local dialect. Our field is not this or that national literature, but *Living Literature*. Whatever quickens in us the sense of life is part of *our* literature, even if it was first said in Hebrew, Greek or German.

This is an internationalism of the spirit which is not merely compatible with the highest patriotism, but identical with it. We want to enrich our community with the best which has been thought and said in the world.

Note

1   A striking example of *World Literature* was offered by the success, in Paris, of Ben Jonson's *Volpone*, adapted by Jules Romains and Stefan Zweig.

Chapter 9

Erich Auerbach

PHILOLOGY AND *WELTLITERATUR* (1952)

E RICH AUERBACH (1892–1957) WAS a German literary scholar who after the Second World War came to the United States, where he began teaching at Yale University in 1950. He wrote major works on Dante and public life in the Middle Ages, yet the work that defines him most clearly in comparative literature is the book he wrote in Istanbul during the war: *Mimesis. Dargestellte Wirklichkeit in der abendländischen Literatur* (*Mimesis: The Representation of Reality in Western Literature*). This work spans the long history of the representation of reality, starting with Homer and the Bible and ending with contemporary (which for Auerbach was modernist) literature. Each chapter begins with an excerpt from a literary work, and the elegant combination of attention to the details of the text with a grand narrative of how reality has been approached in canonical literature has been much lauded despite its relative lack of philological detail. While *Mimesis* does not address the issue of world literature, it exemplifies a methodological approach that Auerbach described in his 1952 essay "Philologie der Weltliteratur" (translated by Edward W. Said as "Philology and *Weltliteratur*").

In this essay, Auerbach strikes a pessimistic chord as he regrets the loss of linguistic capabilities among scholars as well as of the humanist spirit of Goethe's age. He also draws attention to the possibility that English might become the dominant world language, which would paradoxically both destroy and fulfill the dream of a world literature, while acknowledging the vastness of world literatures and the impossibility of their being mastered by an individual. His suggested approach, which must be seen as an extension of the strategy taken in *Mimesis*, resembles Clifford Geertz's later use of "thick description." Auerbach's technique later inspired New Historicism to focus on extracting all of the discourses found in particular examples in order to avoid syntheses that are not in touch with the texts themselves.

This is a daring approach which raises a number of methodological problems. At the same time, the New Historicist approach never presents itself as being in a closed circuit, but remains in a continued dialogue with other exemplary investigations. The juxtaposition of dissimilar works suggested by David Damrosch and the idea of literary history as a series of related experiments suggested by Franco Moretti can both be connected to ideas running through Auerbach's work although in contrast to Auerbach, both later scholars strongly suggest that collective work is necessary in the study of world literature.

The essay reprinted here originally appeared in *Weltliteratur: Festgabe für Fritz Strich,* eds. Walter Muschg and Emil Staiger in 1952, and was translated as "Philology and *Weltliteratur"* by Maire Said and Edward W. Said for the *Centennial Review* 13:1 (1969), 1–17.

Nonnulla pars inventionis est nosse quid quaeras. [Not a small part of discovery consists in knowing what you are looking for.]

Augustine, Quest. in Hept., Prooem.

I

It is time to ask what meaning the word *Weltliteratur* can still have if we relate it, as Goethe did, both to the past and to the future. Our earth, the domain of *Weltliteratur,* is growing smaller and losing its diversity. Yet *Weltliteratur* does not merely refer to what is generically common and human; rather it considers humanity to be the product of fruitful intercourse between its members. The presupposition of *Weltliteratur* is a *felix culpa:* mankind's division into many cultures. Today, however, human life is becoming standardized. The process of imposed uniformity, which originally derived from Europe, continues its work, and hence serves to undermine all individual traditions. To be sure, national wills are stronger and louder than ever, yet in every case they promote the same standards and forms for modern life; and it is clear to the impartial observer that the inner bases of national existence are decaying. The European cultures, which have long enjoyed their fruitful interrelation, and which have always been supported by the consciousness of their worth, these cultures still retain their individualities. Nevertheless, even among them the process of levelling proceeds with a greater rapidity than ever before. Standardization, in short, dominates everywhere. All human activity is being concentrated either into European-American or into Russian-Bolshevist patterns; no matter how great they seem to us, the differences between the two patterns are comparatively minimal when they are both contrasted with the basic patterns underlying the Islamic, Indian or Chinese traditions. Should mankind succeed in withstanding the shock of so mighty and rapid a process of concentration—for which the spiritual preparation has been poor—then man will have to accustom himself to existence in a standardized world, to a single literary culture, only a few literary languages, and perhaps even a single literary language. And herewith the notion of *Weltliteratur* would be at once realized and destroyed.

If I assess it correctly, in its compulsion and in its dependence on mass movements, this contemporary situation is not what Goethe had in mind. For he gladly avoided thoughts about what later history has made inevitable. He occasionally acknowledged the depressing tendencies of our world, yet no one could then suspect how radically, how unexpectedly, an unpleasant potential could be realized. His epoch was brief indeed; and yet those of us who are members of an older generation actually experienced its passing away. It is approximately five hundred years since the national European literatures won their self-consciousness from and their superiority over Latin civilization; scarcely two hundred years have passed since the awakening of our sense of historicism, a sense that permitted the formation of the concept of *Weltliteratur.* By the example and the stimulation of his work Goethe himself, who died one hundred and twenty years ago, contributed decisively to the development of historicism and to the philological research that was generated out of it. And already in our own time a world is emerging for which this sense no longer has much practical significance.

Although the period of Goethean humanism was brief indeed, it not only had important contemporary effects but it also initiated a great deal that continues, and is ramifying today.

The world literatures that were available to Goethe at the end of his life were more numerous than those which were known at the time of his birth; compared to what is available to us today, however, the number was small. Our knowledge of world literatures is indebted to the impulse given that epoch by historicist humanism; the concern of that humanism was not only the overt discovery of materials and the development of methods of research, but beyond that their penetration and evaluation so that an inner history of mankind—which thereby created a conception of man unified in his multiplicity—could be written. Ever since Vico and Herder this humanism has been the true purpose of philology: because of this purpose philology became the dominant branch of the humanities. It drew the history of the other arts, the history of religion, law, and politics after itself, and wove itself variously with them into certain fixed aims and commonly achieved concepts of order. What was thereby gained, in terms of scholarship and synthesis, need not be recalled for the present reader.

Can such an activity be continued with meaning in wholly changed circumstances and prospects? The simple fact that it is continued, that it continues to be widespread, should not be overstressed. What has once become a habit or an institution continues for a long time, especially if those who are aware of a radical change in the circumstances of life are often neither ready nor able to make their awareness practically operative. There is hope to be gained from the passionate commitment to philological and historicist activity of a small number of young people who are distinguished for their talent and originality. It is encouraging to hope that their instinct for this work of theirs does not betray them, and that this activity still has relevance for the present and the future.

A scientifically ordered and conducted research of reality fills and rules our life; it is, if one wishes to name one, our Myth: we do not possess another that has such general validity. History is the science of reality that affects us most immediately, stirs us most deeply and compels us most forcibly to a consciousness of ourselves. It is the only science in which human beings step before us in their totality. Under the rubric of history one is to understand not only the past, but the progression of events in general; history therefore includes the present. The inner history of the last thousand years is the history of mankind achieving self-expression: this is what philology, a historicist discipline, treats. This history contains the records of man's mighty, adventurous advance to a consciousness of his human condition and to the realization of his given potential; and this advance, whose final goal (even in its wholly fragmentary present form) was barely imaginable for a long time, still seems to have proceeded as if according to a plan, in spite of its twisted course. All the rich tensions of which our being is capable are contained within this course. An inner dream unfolds whose scope and depth entirely animate the spectator, enabling him at the same time to find peace in his given potential by the enrichment he gains from having witnessed the drama. The loss of such a spectacle—whose appearance is thoroughly dependent on presentation and inter-pretation—would be an impoverishment for which there can be no possible compensation. To be sure, only those who have not totally sustained this loss would be aware of privation. Even so, we must do everything within our power to prevent so grievous a loss. If my reflec-tions on the future, with which I began this essay, have any validity, then the duty of collecting material and forming it into a whole that will continue to have effect is an urgent one. For we are still basically capable of fulfilling this duty, not only because we have a great deal of mate-rial at our disposal, but above all because we also have inherited the sense of historic perspec-tivism which is so necessary for the job. The reason we still possess this sense is that we live the experience of historical multiplicity, and without this experience, I fear, the sense would quickly lose its living concreteness. It also appears to me that we live at a time *(Kairos)* when the fullest potential of reflective historiography is capable of being realized; whether many succeeding generations will still be part of such a time is questionable. We are already threat-ened with the impoverishment that results from an ahistorical system of education; not only does that threat exist but it also lays claim to dominating us. Whatever we are, we became in history, and only in history can we remain the way we are and develop therefrom: it is the task of philologists, whose province is the world of human history, to demonstrate this so that it penetrates our lives unforgettably. At the end of the chapter called "The Approach" in Adalbert Stifter's *Nachsommer* one of the characters says: "The highest of wishes is to imagine that after human life had concluded its period on earth, a spirit might survey and summarize all of the human arts from their inception to their disappearance." Stifter, however, only refers to the fine arts. Moreover, I do not believe it possible now to speak of the conclusion of human life. But it is correct to speak of our time as a period of conclusive change in which a hitherto unique survey appears to have become possible.

This conception of *Weltliteratur* and its philology seems less active, less practical and less political than its predecessor. There is no more talk now—as there had been—of a spiritual exchange between peoples, of the refinement of customs and of a reconciliation of races. In part these goals have failed of attainment, in part they have been superseded by historical developments. Certain distinguished individuals, small groups of highly cultivated men always have enjoyed, under the auspices of these goals, an organized cultural exchange: they will continue to do so. Yet this sort of activity has little effect on culture or on the reconciliation of peoples: it cannot withstand the storm of opposed vested interests—from which an intensified propaganda emerges—and so its results are immediately dissipated. An exchange that is effective is the kind that takes place between partners already brought together into a rapport based on political developments: such a cultural dialogue has an internally cohesive effect, hastens mutual understanding and serves a common purpose. But for those cultures not bound together thus there has been a disturbing (to a humanist with Goethean ideals) general rapport in which the antitheses that persist nonetheless [as those, for example, between differing national identities] are not being resolved except, paradoxically, through ordeals of sheer strength. The conception of *Weltliteratur* advocated in this essay—a conception of the diverse background of a common fate—does not seek to affect or alter that which has already begun to occur, albeit contrary to expectation; the present conception accepts as an inevitable fact that world-culture is being standardized. Yet this conception wishes to render precisely and, so that it may be retained, consciously to articulate the fateful coalescence of cultures for those people who are in the midst of the terminal phase of fruitful multiplicity: thus this coalescence, so rendered and articulated, will become their myth. In this manner, the full range of the spiritual movements of the last thousand years will not atrophy within them. One cannot speculate with much result about the future effects of such an effort. It is our task to create the possibility for such an effect; and only this much *can* be said, that for an age of transition such as ours the effect *could* be very significant. It may well be that this effect might also help to make us accept our fate with more equanimity so that we will not hate whoever opposes us—even when we are forced into a posture of antagonism. By token of this, our conception of *Weltliteratur* is no less human, no less humanistic, than its antecedent; the implicit comprehension of history—which underlies this conception of *Weltliteratur*—is not the same as the former one, yet it is a development of it and unthinkable without it.

II

It was noted above that we are fundamentally capable of performing the task of a philology of *Weltliteratur* because we command unlimited, steadily growing material, and because of our historic perspectivist sense, which is our heritage from the historicism of Goethe's time. Yet no matter how hopeful the outlook seems for such a task, the practical difficulties are truly great. In order for someone to penetrate and then construct an adequate presentation of the material of *Weltliteratur* he must command that material—or at least a major part of it—himself. Because, however, of the superabundance of materials, of methods and of points of view, a mastery of that sort has become virtually impossible. We possess literatures ranging over six thousand years, from all parts of the world, in perhaps fifty literary languages. Many cultures known to us today were unknown a hundred years ago; many of the ones already known to us in the past were known only partially. As for those cultural epochs most familiar to scholars for hundreds of years, so much that is new has been found out about them that our conception of these epochs has been radically altered—and entirely new problems have arisen. In addition to all of these difficulties, there is the consideration that one cannot concern himself solely with the literature of a given period; one must study the conditions under which this literature developed; one must take into account religion, philosophy, politics, economics, fine arts and music; in every one of these disciplines there must be sustained, active and individual research. Hence more and more exact specialization follows; special methods evolve, so that in each of the individual fields—even within each special point of view on a given field—a kind of esoteric language is generated. This is not all. Foreign, nonphilological or scientific methods and concepts begin to be felt in philology: sociology, psychology, certain kinds of philosophy, and contemporary literary criticism figure prominently among these influences from the outside. Thus all these elements must be assimilated and ordered even if only to be able to demonstrate, in good conscience, the uselessness of one of them for philology. The scholar who does not consistently limit himself to a narrow field of specialization and to a world of concepts held in common with a small circle of like-minded colleagues, lives in the midst of a tumult of impressions and claims on him: for the scholar to do justice to these is almost impossible. Still, it is becoming increasingly unsatisfactory to limit oneself to only one field of specialization. To be a Provençal specialist in our day and age, for example, and to command only the immediately relevant linguistic, paleological and historical facts, is hardly enough to be a good specialist. On the other hand, there are fields of specialization that have become so widely various that their mastery has become the task of a lifetime. Such fields are, for instance, the study of Dante (who can scarcely be called a "field of specialization" since doing him justice takes one practically everywhere), or the courtly romance, with its three related (and problematic) subtopics, courtly love, Celtic matter and Grail literature. How many scholars have really made one of these fields entirely their own? How can anyone go on to speak of a scholarly and synthesizing philology of *Weltliteratur?*

A few individuals today do have a commanding overview of the European material; so far as I know, however, they all belong to the generation that matured before the two World Wars. These scholars cannot be replaced very easily, for since their generation the academic study of Greek, Latin and the Bible—which was a mainstay of the late period of bourgeois humanistic culture—has collapsed nearly everywhere. If I may draw conclusions from my own experiences in Turkey, then it is easy to note corresponding changes in non-European, but equally ancient, cultures. Formerly, what could be taken for granted in the university (and, in the English-speaking countries, at the post-graduate level) must now be acquired there; most often such acquirements are either made too late or they are inadequate. Moreover, the intellectual center of gravity within the university or graduate school has shifted; there is a greater emphasis on the most modern literature and criticism, and, when earlier periods are favored with scholarly attention, they are usually periods like the baroque, which have been recently rediscovered, perhaps because they lie within the scope of modern literary prejudices and catchalls. It is obviously from within the situation and mentality of our own time that the whole of history has to be comprehended if it is to have significance for us. But a talented student possesses and is possessed by the spirit of his own time anyway: it seems to me that he should not need academic instruction in order to appropriate the work of Rilke or Gide or Yeats. He does need instruction, however, to understand the verbal conventions and the forms of life of the ancient world, the Middle Ages, the Renaissance, and also to learn to know the methods and means for exploring earlier periods. The problematics and the ordering categories of contemporary literary criticism are always significant, not only because they often are ingenious and illuminating in themselves, but also because they express the inner will of their period. Nevertheless only a few of them have an immediate use in historicist philology or as substitutes for genuinely transmitted concepts. Most of them are too abstract and ambiguous, and frequently they have too private a slant. They confirm a temptation to which neophytes (and acolytes) are frequently inclined to submit: the desire to master a great mass of material through the introduction of hypostatized, abstract concepts of order; this leads to the effacement of what is being studied, to the discussion of illusory problems and finally to a bare nothing.

Though they appear to be disturbing, such scholarly tendencies do not strike me as being truly dangerous, at least not for the sincere and gifted student of literature. Furthermore, there are talented people who manage to acquire for themselves whatever is indispensable for historical and philological study, and who also manage to adopt the proper attitudes of open-mindedness and independence toward modish intellectual currents. In many respects these young people have a distinct advantage over their predecessors. During the past forty years events have enlarged our intellectual perspectives, new outlooks on history and on reality have been revealed, and the view of the structure of inter-human processes has been enriched and renewed. We have participated—indeed, we are still participating—in a practical seminar on world history; accordingly, our insight and our conceptual powers with regard to historical matters have developed considerably. Thus even many extraordinary works, which had previously seemed to us to be outstanding philological achievements of late bourgeois humanism now appear unrealistic and restricted in their positing of the problems they set themselves. Today we have it somewhat easier than forty years ago.

But how is the problem of synthesis to be solved? A single lifetime seems too short to create even the preliminaries. The organized work of a group is no answer, even if a group has high uses otherwise. The historical synthesis of which I am speaking, although it has significance only when it is based on a scholarly penetration of the material, is a product of personal intuition and hence can only be expected from an individual. Should it succeed perfectly we would be given a scholarly achievement and a work of art at the same time. Even the discovery of a point of departure [*Ansatzpunkt*]—of which I shall speak later—is a matter of intuition: the performance of the synthesis is a form which must be unified and suggestive if it is to fulfill its potential. Surely the really noteworthy achievement of such a work is due to a coadunatory intuition; in order to achieve its effect historical synthesis must in addition appear to be a work of art. The traditional protestation, that literary art must possess the freedom to be itself—which means that it must not be bound to scientific truth—can scarcely be voiced: for as they present themselves today historical subjects offer the imagination quite enough freedom in the questions of choice, of the problems they seem to generate, of their combination with each other, and of their formulation. One can say in fact that scientific truth is a good restriction on the philologist; scientific truth preserves and guarantees the probable in the "real," so that the great temptation to withdraw from reality (be it by trivial glossing or by shadowy distortion) is thereby foiled, for reality is the criterion of the probable. Besides, we are concerned with the need for a synthetic history-from-within, with history, that is, as the *genos* of the European tradition of literary art: the historiography of classical antiquity was a literary *genos*, for example, and similarly the philosophic and historicist criticism created by German Classicism and Romanticism strove for its own form of literary art and expression.

III

Thus we return to the individual. How is he to achieve synthesis? It seems to me that he certainly cannot do it by encyclopedic collecting. A wider perspective than mere fact gathering is an imperative condition, but it should be gained very early in the process, unintentionally, and with an instinctive personal interest for its only guidepost. Yet the experience of recent decades has shown us that the accumulation of material in one field, an accumulation that strives for the exhaustiveness of the great handbooks that treat a national literature, a great epoch or a literary *genos,* can hardly lead to synthesis and formulation. The difficulty lies not only in the copiousness of the material that is scarcely within the grasp of a single individual (so much so that a group project seems to be required), but also in the structure of the material itself. The traditional divisions of the material, chronological, geographical or typological, are no longer suitable and cannot guarantee any sort of energetic, unified advance. The fields covered by such divisions do not coincide with the problematic areas with which the synthesis is coping. It has even become a matter of some doubt to me whether monographs—and there are many excellent ones—on single, significant authors are suited to be points of departure for the kind of synthesis that I have been speaking about. Certainly a single author embodies as complete and concrete a unity of life as any, and this is always better than an invented unity; but at the same time such a unity is finally ungraspable because it has passed into the ahistorical inviolability into which individuality always flows.

The most impressive recent book in which a synthesizing historical view is accomplished is Ernst Robert Curtius's book on European literature and the Latin Middle Ages. It seems to me that this book owes its success to the fact that despite its comprehensive, general title, it proceeds from a clearly prescribed, almost narrow, single phenomenon: the survival of the scholastic rhetorical tradition. Despite the monstrosity of the materials it mobilizes, in its best parts this book is not a mere agglomeration of many items, but a radiation outwards from a few items. Its general subject is the survival of the ancient world in the Latin Middle Ages, and the effect on the new European literature of the medieval forms taken by classical culture. When one has so general and comprehensive an intention one can at first do nothing. The author, who in the earliest stages of his project intends only the presentation of so broadly stated a theme, stands before an unsurveyable mass of various material that defies order. If it were to be collected mechanistically—for example, according to the survival of a set of individual writers, or according to the survival of the whole ancient world in the succession of one medieval century after another—the mere outlines of such a bulk would make a formulated intention towards this material impossible. Only by the discovery of a phenomenon at once firmly circumscribed, comprehensible and central enough to be a point of departure (in this case, the rhetorical tradition, and especially the *topoi*) was the execution of Curtius's plan made possible. Whether Curtius's choice for a point of departure was satisfactory, or whether it was the best of all possible choices for his intention, is not being debated; precisely because one might contend that Curtius's point of departure was inadequate one ought to admire the resulting achievement all the more. For Curtius's achievement is obligated to the following methodological principle: in order to accomplish a major work of synthesis it is imperative to locate a point of departure [*Ansatzpunkt*], a handle, as it were, by which the subject can be seized. The point of departure must be the election of a firmly circumscribed, easily comprehensible set of phenomena whose interpretation is a radiation out from them and which orders and interprets a greater region than they themselves occupy.

This method has been known to scholars for a long time. The discipline of stylistics, for example, has long availed itself of the method in order to describe a style's individuality in terms of a few fixed characteristics. Yet it seems to me to be necessary to emphasize the method's general significance, which is that it is the only method that makes it possible for us now to write a history-from-within against a broader background, to write synthetically and suggestively. The method also makes it possible for a younger scholar, even a beginner, to accomplish that end; a comparatively modest general knowledge buttressed by advice can suffice once intuition has found an auspicious point of departure. In the elaboration of this point of departure, the intellectual perspective enlarges itself both sufficiently and naturally, since the choice of material to be drawn is determined by the point of departure. Elaboration therefore is so concrete, its component parts hang together with such necessity, that what is thereby gained cannot easily be lost: the result, in its ordered exposition, possesses unity and universality.

Of course in practice the general intention does not always precede the concrete point of departure. Sometimes one discovers a single point of departure [*Ansatzphänomen*] that releases the recognition and formulation of the general problem. Naturally, this can only occur when a predisposition for the problem already exists. It is essential to remark that a general, synthetic intention or problem does not suffice in and of itself. Rather, what needs to be found is a partially apprehendable phenomenon that is as circumscribed and concrete as possible, and therefore describable in technical, philological terms. Problems will therefore roll forth from it, so that a formulation of one's intention can become feasible. At other times, a single point of departure will not be sufficient—several will be necessary; if the first one is present, however, others are more easily available, particularly as they must be of the kind that not only links itself to others, but also converges on a central intention. It is therefore a question of specialization—not a specializing of the traditional modes of classifying material—but of the subject at hand, which needs constant rediscovery.

Points of departure can be very various; to enumerate all the possibilities here is quite impracticable. The characteristic of a good point of departure is its concreteness and its precision on the one hand, and on the other, its potential for centrifugal radiation. A semantic interpretation, a rhetorical trope, a syntactic sequence, the interpretation of one sentence, or a set of remarks made at a given time and in a given place—any of these can be a point of departure, but once chosen it must have radiating power, so that with it we can deal with world history [*Weltgeschichte*]. If one were to investigate the position of the writer in the nineteenth century—in either one country or in the whole of Europe—the investigation would produce a useful reference book (if it contained all the necessary material for such a study) for which we would be very grateful. Such a book has its uses, but the synthesis of which we have been speaking would more likely be achieved if one were to proceed from a few remarks made by writers about the public. Similarly, such subjects as the enduring reputation (*la fortuna*) of various poets can only be studied if a concrete point of departure is found to coerce the general theme. Existing works on Dante's reputation in various countries are certainly indispensable: a still more interesting work would emerge (and I am indebted to Erwin Panofsky for this suggestion) were one to trace the interpretation of individual portions of the *Commedia* from its earliest commentators to the sixteenth century, and then again since Romanticism. *That* would be an accurate type of spiritual history [*Geistesgeschichte*].

A good point of departure must be exact and objective; abstract categories of one sort or another will not serve. Thus concepts like "the Baroque" or "the Romantic," "the dramatic" or "the idea of fate," "intensity" or "myth," or "the concept of time" and "perspectivism" are dangerous. They can be used when their meaning is made clear in a specific context, but they are too ambiguous and inexact to be points of departure. For a point of departure should not be a generality imposed on a theme from the outside, but ought rather to be an organic inner part of the theme itself. What is being studied should speak for itself, but that can never happen if the point of departure is neither concrete nor clearly defined. In any event, a great deal of skill is necessary—even if one has the best point of departure possible—in order to keep oneself focused on the object of study. Ready-made, though rarely suitable, concepts whose appeal is deceptive because it is based on their attractive sound and their modishness, lie in wait, ready to spring in on the work of a scholar who has lost contact with the energy of the object of study. Thus the writer of a scholarly work is often tricked into accepting the substitution of a cliché for the true object; surely a great many readers can also be deceived. Since readers are all too prone to this sort of substitution, it is the scholar's job to make such evasions impossible. The phenomena treated by the philologist whose intention is synthesis contain their own objectivity, and this objectivity must not disappear in the synthesis: it is most difficult to achieve this aim. Certainly one ought not to aim at a complacent exultation in the particular, but rather at being moved and stirred by the movement of a whole. Yet the movement can be discovered in its purity only when all the particulars that make it up are grasped as essences.

So far as I know we possess no attempts at a philological synthesis of *Weltliteratur;* only a few preliminary efforts in this direction are to be found within western culture. But the more our earth grows closer together, the more must historicist synthesis balance the contraction by expanding its activity. To make men conscious of themselves in their own history is a great task, yet the task is small—more like a renunciation—when one considers that man not only lives on earth, but that he is in the world and in the universe. But what earlier epochs dared to do—to designate man's place in the universe—now appears to be a very far-off objective.

In any event, our philological home is the earth: it can no longer be the nation. The most priceless and indispensable part of a philologist's heritage is still his own nation's culture and language. Only when he is first separated from this heritage, however, and then transcends it does it become truly effective. We must return, in admittedly altered circumstances, to the knowledge that prenational medieval culture already possessed: the knowledge that the spirit [*Geist*] is not national. *Paupertas* and *terra aliena*: this or something to this effect, can be read in Bernard of Chartres, John of Salisbury, Jean de Meun and many others.* *Magnum virtutis principium est,* Hugo of St. Victor writes (Didascalicon III, 20), *ut discat paulatim exercitatus animus visibilia haec et transitoria primum commutare, ut postmodum possit etiam derelinquere. Delicatus ille est adhuc cui patria dulcis est, fortis autem cui omne solum patria est, perfectus vero cui mundus totus exilium est. . . .†* Hugo intended these lines for one whose aim is to free himself from a love of the world. But it is a good way also for one who wishes to earn a proper love for the world.

---

* *paupertas*: poverty; *terra aliena*: foreign ground
† Translation: It is, therefore, a source of great virtue for the wise man to learn, bit by bit, first to detach himself from visible and transitory things, so that later he may be able to relinquish them altogether. He to whom his homeland is sweet is still a tender beginner, strong already is to whom every soil is as his native land, but truly perfect is he to whom the entire world is a place of exile.

Chapter 10

Werner P. Friederich

ON THE INTEGRITY OF OUR PLANNING
(1960)

A NATIVE OF SWITZERLAND, WERNER P. FRIEDERICH (1905–93) was educated at the University of Bern, the Sorbonne and Harvard University, where he received his PhD in comparative literature in 1932. Friederich joined the faculty of the University of North Carolina in 1935 and in 1956 was appointed chairman of comparative literature. He founded and served as an early president for both the American and the International Comparative Literature Association. He also started the Comparative Literature Section of the Modern Language Association of America, co-founded the journal *Comparative Literature*, and founded and edited the *Yearbook of Comparative and General Literature*. Friederich conceived of this latter journal as a "bridge between Comparative Literature and World Literature." In March 1945, Friederich was hired by the Office of War Information as a translator for the American Army in Germany and soon fired due to the protests by Chapel Hill people, who unjustly claimed Friederich's Nazi sympathies to be shown in his 1938 pamphlet, "Political Problems in Present-Day Europe."[i] In 1972 Friederich established the Marcel Bataillon Professorship in Comparative Literature at UNC in honor of his French friend.

Author of key research tools for comparative literature, such as the *Bibliography of Comparative Literature* (1950; in collaboration with Fernand Baldensperger) and the *Outline of Comparative Literature from Dante Alighieri to Eugene O'Neill* (1954; co-authored with David Malone), Friederich mainly understood comparative literature as comparative literary history, as in *Dante's Fame Abroad, 1350–1850* (1950) and *Australia in Western Imaginative Prose Writings, 1600–1960* (1967). He also wrote histories of German literature (*An Outline-History of German Literature*, 1948; *History of German Literature*, 1958). The former studies are extremely ambitious works which only a scholar with the knowledge of languages and literatures Friederich had could successfully undertake. "There is much joy and satisfaction in this kind of labor," Friederich states, "although it may not display original research on every page."[ii] His

---

i   Laurence G. Avery, ed., *A Southern Life. Letters of Paul Green, 1916–1991* ([Chapel Hill]: The U of North Carolina P, 1994) 410n1.

ii Werner P. Friederich, *Dante's Fame Abroad, 1350–1850* (Roma: Edizioni di Storia e Letteratura, 1950) 7.

disciples remember him for bringing "intertextuality to life [. . .] by first showing his students how interlaced and interdependent all the literatures of Europe were and then requiring us to track down every last allusion and influence we could find."[iii].

The importance Friederich allotted to pedagogy is evident from his 1959 lecture at the University of Wisconsin, "On the Integrity of our Planning." Friederich addresses the problem of teaching world literature in translation (into English), whose legitimacy is denied by "traditional" comparatists. Ironically, his main argument is based on rejecting world literature (and anthologies of world literature), "a presumptuous and arrogant term" which most frequently stands for "NATO literatures."

Werner P. Friederich, "On the Integrity of Our Planning," *The Teaching of World Literature: Proceedings of the Conference at the University of Wisconsin*, Ed. Haskell M. Block, Chapel Hill: U of North Carolina, 1960, pp. 9–22.

I am sure that all of you, present here, will join me in extending our sincere gratitude to the University of Wisconsin for having made possible our getting together and discussing the very challenging problem of teaching so-called World Literature courses in English translation.

For that task, that goal of teaching the great masters of World Literature, is by no means easy to achieve. Your group is constantly being doubted and heckled on two fronts: on the left by nationalists and isolationists who garb their own intellectual inability of ever being able to look beyond the frontiers of their own chosen literature, in the mantle of patriotic ardor— for, far worse than the relatively tolerant Thoreau, "they travel much—in Concord" and therefore see no reason why they should bother with the literature of the world at large. And on the other hand, there are the most high-minded comparatists among us who attack your group because they insist that World Literature in English translation is *not* Comparative Literature and that it must always be restricted to undergraduate instruction (and I agree with these two assertions)—and therefore they look down upon World Literature courses and perhaps deny their legitimacy (and with this attitude I do *not* agree.) At this meeting, I am sure, we all will quite lustily attack the nationalists in the Humanities, for to be narrow-minded is the very negation of the concept of Humanism, and so they deserve to be over-whelmed with criticism from all sides. But, after this attack on the left flank, there should be an opening towards the right, a never-tiring attempt to establish a *modus vivendi*, a constructive and profitable relationship between World Literature courses and Comparative Literature.

In fact, I should like to emphasize right here that I tried to build a bridge between Comparative Literature and World Literature some eight years ago when I founded the *Yearbook of Comparative and General Literature* which began to appear in Chapel Hill in 1952. That *Yearbook* was born out of a certain sense of disappointment, because the journal, *Comparative Literature,* in Oregon, which Chandler Beall and I had founded in 1949 decided to remain true-blue comparative. I was voted down, 6 to 1, when I suggested to its Editorial Board that we should attempt an opening to the left and collaborate with certain colleagues who, to be sure, might not be "comparatists" in the strictest sense of that word, but who shared with us an enthusiastically cosmopolitan approach to literature. When this suggestion was turned down, I got in touch with my friend Horst Frenz from Indiana and other internationalists in the National Council of Teachers of English—and the *Yearbook* was started simply because it seemed imperative that you and we should learn to understand each other and to work together. To be sure, the *Yearbook* costs me about $1400 of my own money per

iii Patricia Galloway, *Practicing Ethnohistory. Mining Archives, Hearing Testimony, Constructing Narrative* (Lincoln: U of Nebraska P, 2006) 6.

year—but then we happily usually sell about $1500 worth of it *per annum,* so that I have never yet lost money on it. Horst Frenz, the loyal Associate Editor, suggested that it should be called *Yearbook of Comparative and World Literature*—but since, as you will soon notice, I do not particularly like the term World Literature and since, at any rate, it would not have been judicious to wave, shall we say, a red flag in front of those very men whom I hoped to lead to the altar with you, we finally settled on the term *Yearbook of Comparative and General Literature*. The trouble only is that I do not quite know what General Literature is, and for years I have been trying to find a learned article by some learned man who would unscramble the various definitions by Van Tieghem, Wellek, Guérard and others of what General Literature really encompasses, so that, *post facto,* we will at last know what exactly our *Yearbook* is supposed to do. In the meantime, in spite of the absence of a proper definition, we publish in Part I of every *Yearbook* articles on the scope and the methodology either of Comparative Literature or of World Literature courses; in Part II we honor great representatives of the two groups—for instance, in your case, men like Philo Buck or Arthur Christy; in Part III we give descriptions of departmental set-ups and "états présents des travaux" both of Comparative and of World Literature curricula in at least 20 American universities; in Part IV, exclusively for your group, we provide useful reviews and evaluations of the most recent English translations of World's classics; while Part V, mostly for the comparatists, contains an annual supplement to the basic Baldensperger-Friederich *Bibliography of Comparative Literature* of 1950.

But to return to our topic: the enemies on your left and on your right. Let us not, upon second thought, attack the enemies on your left, for they are discredited enough: the Anglicists whose world stops at the cliffs of Dover, the Hispanists or Italianists who would never look beyond the Pyrenées and the Alps, respectively; the Germanists and the "Françisants" for whom the Rhine used to be—please note the past tense, *used* to be—a ditch deeper than the Grand Canyon. They and their American counterparts definitely are on the way out—in New England and even in the Old South perhaps more so than in the Middle West. Let us, instead, dwell on the two groups closest to our hearts: the Comparative and the World Literature people, and let us, at this very meeting, attempt again to get them more closely together. Which, in the last analysis, perhaps means, to put it bluntly, that *my* friends should surrender some of their pride and begin to practice the Christian virtues of understanding and cooperation—while ever so many among *your* friends should acquire greater respectability and integrity in their academic endeavors. For surely, that which unites us, our faith is a common great cultural heritage of mankind, which we should gratefully acknowledge and share with our peers in distant lands, and our utter abhorrence of what Professor Guérard has so aptly called literary McCarthyism, is far stronger than what separates us. In fact, if we reduce our problems to the simplest formula, there should be absolutely nothing to separate us from the moment on that we recognize clearly that World Literature courses in English translation in 99% of all cases are meant to be undergraduate courses, and that out of this preparatory labor there then may—but not necessarily will—grow distinctly comparative courses for our graduate students. From the moment on that we recognize this, all our arguments should be over—for surely people of our kind, with the same cosmopolitan and tolerant attitude towards the cultures and the viewpoints of the world at large, should not, in the back-alleys of our own American institutions of higher learning, indulge in petty fights about irrelevant qualitative distinctions between ourselves. A few years ago, I preached a little sermon on that in an article entitled "Our Common Purpose" contained in the 1955 *Yearbook*—and I do not need to repeat myself.

With the bond of friendship and mutual respect thus firmly established between our two groups, I hope that it will not be amiss to discuss what I should call sound and useful courses in English translation. For we are faced with such an abundance of possibilities here in

America, that we may well envy the Europeans where—apart from far greater linguistic abilities—mere geographical facts may induce the Swiss to be concerned with such neighbors as Germany, France, and Italy, but not with Spanish literature, because there is no common border between the two—while the Spaniards in turn may disregard such geographically or ideologically distant lands and literatures as those of Russia or Poland. We, in America, on the contrary, are facing Europe as a whole, as the cradle of our civilization, as the former homeland of all our people—and thus Sweden and Portugal, Yugoslavia and Holland are no less important to many among us than the Big Two or Three of that continent. And so, what should be chosen?

The foremost consideration surely is to choose the classical Greek and Latin literatures in English translation. It is bad enough that Greek and Latin keep on fighting a losing battle for decent survival; let us not add to this tragedy by disregarding the rich heritage of classical Antiquity that is available even in English translation. We, whether teachers of World Literature or of Comparative Literature, are and must remain the most loyal, the most respectful friends of our Classics Departments, giving them a never-tiring moral support against all those perversions of academic values that may emanate from our Education or Commerce departments. That, then, seems an absolute must; if nothing else, our curricula must offer the great Greeks and Romans in translation.

Little need be said about the customary great literatures of Europe which, in one form or another, should be offered in translation to all those non-language majors who have a love of literature and are entitled to know about it, even if they cannot read their texts in the original. Perhaps I might remark that only French literature is of a constantly sufficiently high quality to deserve a complete survey course from beginning to end—while with the other literatures we might go into depth rather than width. Germany, for instance, in spite of the Golden Age of Barbarossa and the deep significance of the Reformation, would offer the richest harvest in the 200 years from Lessing to the Weimar Republic. Even narrower, and therefore deeper, could be the basis for Italy, Spain, or Russia—let us say merely the *trecento* and the *cinquecento* for Italy, the *Siglo de Oro* for Spain, from Charles V to Philip IV—for surely if, instead of piling up endless lists of meaningless names, the student knows the Renaissance of the former and the Counter-Reformation of the latter, he has begun to grasp the very soul, the very quintessence of Italy and Spain. That is after all what he wants—for, remember, if he wants to know more than that and become a little specialist, he has no business being in a translation course. As to the soul of Russia, we find it best in the novel of the nineteenth century—and that should be enough. Indeed, quite often the contribution of an entire nation might be built around the life and works of one single man—and thereby constitute yet another variety in depth rather than width of those courses: for Scandinavia, for instance, I am thinking of a very detailed study of Ibsen—which, in a way, would become an analysis not only of Norway, but of the whole technique of the modern drama in general.

Things are getting far more difficult when we come to Asian literatures—for how many among us are linguistically qualified to teach such courses? In spite of our desperate need to know far more about Asia than we actually do, we are in a particularly deplorable predicament right now—for the old sons of Christian missionaries in China or India who grew up bilingual, are slowly dying out, while the bright young men trained by our State Department, for obvious reasons, have not yet begun to forsake their political assignments and to turn to the teaching of Asian cultures and literatures instead. Nevertheless, if our universities are so bold or so farsighted as to want you to venture into the field of Asian literatures in translation, I would point to four distinct centers of which each one, separately, deserves at least one full semester course to begin with: the Mahometan World, especially the Arabs, though one might extend this to Iran and perhaps even farther east; India, China, and Japan. To devote less than one semester to each one of these four centers would be unworthy of our academic integrity.

From these remarks about great literatures in English translation, from Greece to France to Russia to India, I should like to derive various observations and discuss them in some detail: about the absurdity of the term World Literature and the inadvisability of using anthologies; about my preference for nationally restricted courses on that undergraduate level—and, if one wishes to reject such national restrictions, about the need of substituting so-called Great Books courses for sweeping international survey courses.

First of all: World Literature. It is not only a challenging, but also a presumptuous and arrogant term—and we should refrain from using it. Asia and Europe and, for good measure, Emerson and Whitman comprise, at best, 2½ continents—and the other 2½ continents of our world are left out, without even a word of apology. World literature would mean also the *Kalevala* from Finland, Camoens from Portugal, Mickiewicz from Poland, Petöfi from Hungary; it would mean the Armenian theatre, the lyrical poetry from Vietnam; the works produced in Egypt or Abyssinia, or the French novels of Algiers, or the British or Dutch works of South Africa; it would mean Sarmiento and Rubén Darío among many others in Latin America; it would mean at least ten or twelve Australian novels that I happen to have read. Yet of all these, in our critical age of national sensitivity, we do not deign to speak; the World means *our* World plus, perhaps at best, the *Sakuntala* and the *Arabian Nights*. Apart from the fact that such a presumptuous term makes for shallowness and partisanship which should not be tolerated in a good university, it is simply bad public relations to use this term and to offend more than half of humanity that has been left out. It is bad enough, for instance, that the term "Americans" is nowadays applied to the citizens of the United States, as though Canadians, Brazilians or Chileans had no right to it; let us not compound this psychological *faux pas* by stating that World Literature in reality is centered somewhere between the Ebro, the Arno, and the Rhine—and that the rest does not really count. Just because our own intelligence is limited, we feel justified in making such atrociously arbitrary decisions—just as our limited religious tolerance insists on calling a truly virtuous man a fine "Christian" because somehow it seems inconceivable to us that this exalted adjective might be applicable to Mahometans or Buddhists. We all share, collectively, in our frequent failure to acquire the good will of other nations and continents—and for that reason, too, the term World Literature, for what we are trying to do with our undergraduate students, simply should be abolished for academic, political as well as psychological reasons. Sometimes, in flippant moments, I think we should call our programs NATO Literatures—yet even that would be extravagant, for we do not usually deal with more than one fourth of the 15 NATO-Nations.

As to the inadmissibility of translation courses for undergraduates along anything but severely restricted national lines: I believe in that simply because I am bitterly opposed to such sweeping survey courses as The Novel in World Literature, 3 hours per week, in one semester—or The Drama from Aeschylus to Tennessee Williams, also in 3 hours per week, in one semester. It is because of courses like these that the bricks have kept on flying from the left and from the right, from the solid language departments snorting that this is the flimsiest kind of sheer amateurism, and from the solid comparatists complaining that it is because of such courses that Comparative Literature, ever since the 1920s, has gotten a black eye and an ill-repute from which it has not yet completely recovered, in spite of our intensified efforts during the past 15 years. It is here that the concept of integrity must be applied most strictly in our planning and—if an all-too-enthusiastic World Literature teacher is not capable of such self-discipline and renunciation—that the course committee on his own campus must restrain him most emphatically and insist on the inviolability of fairly stiff academic standards. Translation courses concerned with one entire nation (France), or with one or two centuries of a nation (Germany from 1750 to 1950), or with a genre in a limited time (The Russian novel of the nineteenth century), or with just one author (Cervantes), or even only with just one work of an author (*La Divina Commedia*) are more than legitimate; but any weaving across ten nations and twenty centuries must be rejected categorically. A comparatist, later, may discuss a handful of nations during a given period, for instance in the Baroque or in the Age of Enlightenment, and he will show the interrelationships of literary trends; but he, after all, will deal with mature graduate students, with Ph.D. candidates able to read at least three literatures in the original—while our surveys here are meant for sophomores and juniors who have not yet learned the ABC of literatures and languages and whom we simply must not throw on all this thin ice. At North Carolina, we have about 8 or 10 translation courses: the Greek Drama, French Classicism, Goethe—but we do not have a single Survey of World Literature; our people would not stand for it.

And while we are on this rather painful subject: there should be no anthologies of world literature either. Except for lyrical poetry, where entire poems can be given and where they are fully justified, anthologies with piddling little excerpts from dramas and novels simply should have no place in our way of thinking. Some people may argue that it is better to know a little bit of something about and by an author instead of nothing at all—for instance, the Francesca da Rimini episode from the *Inferno,* Faust's famous monologue, a chapter from *War and Peace* and the third act from *Doll's House.* I do not think so; instead, I fear, that such excerpts, scores of them, only add to the confusion of our bewildered sophomores. Neither for its contents, nor for its poetic beauty will such an excerpt make a lasting impression upon our young students—and that means that we miss the whole purpose of a course. To be sure, he would acquire a flimsy knowledge—less than a nodding acquaintance—with maybe 30 or 60 of the world's great authors—but that, sometimes, can be worse than nothing. All the more so since our students probably likewise know next to nothing about the great political, national, or historical background of these authors and the 25 centuries covered—and thus our work is quite as bad as though it were written on sand or water.

Instead, in our age of cheap paper-back classics, it stands to reason, if such big transnational surveys of literature are really ordered by the Humanities Division and the Dean's Office, that we should substitute Great Books courses instead. Let us give up the idea of total coverage and strict historical coherence; let us, instead, after a lot of soul-searching, devise a program of, say, 12 great masterpieces for an entire academic year, and let us give at least 8 to 10 hours to each of them. The fine choice of these masterpieces which, after further mature consideration, may be changed in different years, should perhaps emphasize, first, the genre and explain, by means of completely read paper-backs, the quintessence of epic, of tragedy, of comedy, of novel—or, perhaps, in the only anthology to be tolerated in that course, of lyrical poetry. Next, by its very selection, the course might turn to explaining the distinctly unique contributions of individual nations—the Greek tragedy, the Roman epic, the Spanish picaresque novel, the Italian comedy. Likewise, a discussion of these maximum 12 authors during an entire year would also permit one to say something about the greatness of true giants in literature—Aeschylus, Virgil, perhaps Petrarch, Molière, Schiller, Dostoevski. Finally there might be time to illustrate, again by means of these same 12 authors, the basic meaning of Antiquity, Middle Ages, Renaissance, Classicism, Romanticism, Realism, Naturalism. In such a way, a survey course could really serve a multitude of purposes; the student would learn to read entire masterpieces under guidance, he would learn to know about genres, literary movements, would be initiated into the rudimentary beginnings of literary criticism—and he would surely be more intelligent instead of more bewildered when his initiation into literature is over. After that, if he is a non-language major, he could take a course or two of just one or two national literatures or figures in English translation—and, if he should be a language major, he would, of course, turn to his languages and to his literatures in the original. Either way, his Great Books course would have helped him enormously.

One more worried remark before we turn to far more pleasant and optimistic matters. Till now I have expressed my concern only with regard to courses, programs, and students—what we must do and must not do in order to preserve our professional integrity and the standards of our colleges and universities which should be getting harder as we face the rising influx of candidates, instead of constantly getting easier and cheaper. But now we should also have a look at the men who will teach these courses. I am not fearful about the national literature courses in translation—those about French literature or the Russian Novel in the Nineteenth Century, or Homer in English, for I presume that these are always given by men from these departments and that all is well with these specialists. But what about The Great Books courses, or worse, the Surveys of World Literature from A to Z? Who is the A. W. Schlegel or the Fernand Baldensperger among us to teach these? And worse: since these big survey courses are mostly on the sophomore level, with hundreds of students split up into scores of sections: who on earth are the graduate assistants and the youngish Ph.D.s and quickly drafted assistant professors who can talk intelligently about the *Gilgamesh* epic in September, St. Augustine's *City of God* in November, Machiavelli's *Prince* in January, Voltaire in March, and Kafka in May? I do not even dare to answer this question—but I feel I must raise it, for we must ever be mindful of the enemies to the left and the enemies to the right who will snort whenever they can, and gleefully seize upon any weakness in your armor. And I submit, for your prayerful consideration, the greatest danger to our personal and academic integrity—if we are really resolved to introduce these sweeping World Literature courses and to have them taught by one man alone instead of a committee of at least ten specialists—lies not only in actually forcing such courses into our curricula, but in not being able to staff them decently. Here again I beg you, if such courses must be, at least not to make them Surveys of World Literature, but more humbly and correctly to call them Great Books courses—for a young instructor, after a few years, might actually learn to master 12 or 15 milestones in World Literature well enough to speak enthusiastically and inspiringly about them and their beauties.

These, then, in brief, are some of the viewpoints worth considering: That Foreign Literature in English Translation is a much needed field for undergraduate instruction, while Comparative Literature should be distinctly for graduate students only. Indeed, at North Carolina, we increasingly encourage comparatism for graduates only who already have a certain minimum knowledge of foreign languages and literatures, though we still do have a small number of undergraduates majoring in our field, too. Foreign Literature in English Translation might start with a Great Books course on the sophomore level which would initiate the student into a few great figures, genres and national contributions; afterwards, as upper classman, he should delve into narrower, yet deeper courses on the Orient or Greece, on the Spanish Golden Century or on Goethe. Whatever his later career will be, whether he will become a business man, a physician, or a professor of English—this will give him a truly liberal education. It will be a program of which we can all be proud.

In conclusion, lumping together our two groups, the comparatists and the Foreign Literature in English Translation people, I should like to speak rather glowingly of the great future that lies ahead of us. Two years ago I dwelled on that promising future in an address which I made at the University of Zürich and which, last year, was published in Tübingen—when I thought I should explain why America had more than caught up with the leadership of France in the field of Comparative Literature, and why the United States, by its very nature and geographical location, was destined to be an even finer intermediary between nations and continents than such ideal intermediaries of the past, Switzerland and Holland, had been.

For with our millions of non-Anglo-Saxon immigrants, we have a vested and loving interest in all the literatures of the Old World. Our leading American comparatists very often are foreign born: the Orsinis and Poggiolis from Italy, the Hatzfelds and Frenz from Germany, the Welleks from Czechoslovakia, the Guérards, Chinards and Peyres from

France—or then they are typical Americans in the sense that three of their four grandmothers are non-English: Dutch, Irish, Swedish, Jewish. With such a background, we are apt to be far juster in our evaluation of foreign literatures than ever so many so-called comparatists from Europe who in the past often prostituted the high calling and the lofty political challenge of Comparative Literature by making use of it only in order to prove the glory of their own national literature and the insignificance of the literatures of their neighbors. Such things, thank God, are not apt to happen here in America—not only because 3000 miles of distance have given us the necessary objectivity, but also because our racial make-up in the United States does not favor such pettiness as it existed in Western Europe prior to 1945. This great psychological advantage—plus the fact that, generally speaking, we have better financial resources and finer libraries than the war-ravaged Europeans—more than makes up for the disadvantage that because of our geographical distances from Rome, Paris, or Vienna, our students from the viewpoint of linguistic proficiency, are discouragingly handicapped if compared with Belgian, Swiss, or Polish students.

And it is not only this happy and unprejudiced racial mixture—it is even more our important geographical location which fills me with hope about the great, not only political, but also cultural and intermediary role we will be able to play in the future. We need not dwell on European-American relations; they always have been and always will be the subject of particularly intensive investigations—as evidenced, most strikingly, with regard to German-American literary relations, by the fine book of Professor Pochmann here at Wisconsin—a book that will remain a classic for many decades to come. Let us look, instead, at our role with regard to Latin America. Here we not only exert our own literary influence—for instance, the impact of Longfellow, Whitman, or Hemingway upon Latin America; we increasingly become an intermediary too, the clearing-house between Europe and Latin America. Formerly, the impact came directly from Europe—such as the influence of Chateaubriand or Lamartine upon Brazilian Romanticism, or the intimate connections between France and Cuba in the days of José María de Heredia. Now, much of that European influence first filters through the United States, where it may receive a twist of its own before being passed on to Buenos Aires or to Santiago de Chile. Men like Rubén Darío were apt to stop over in New York before or after going to Europe—and the strained relations between Franco's Spain and certain American states—think of Mexico and all its Spanish refugees—have, in turn, enhanced the importance of the United States as a fountainhead and a symbol of the world abroad.

Or let us look at Asia, where the aftermath of the last War created not only a multitude of political entanglements like SEATO, but also a wealth of new and promising cultural connections. We have never been as close to Japan since the days of Lafcadio Hearn, or to Korea, the Philippines, Pakistan and even India as we are right now—and whatever Western influences these nations receive, for better or worse, are apt to come by way of New York or San Francisco, rather than directly from Rome, Paris, or even London. With one villain blocking off the Suez Canal and another villain pushing down from the North as far as Baghdad, it may well be that soon all political, commercial, and cultural connections with Asia will have to be re-routed through the land of the middle, the United States—and that the traveller from London to Singapore will have to go west instead of east. There again, in spite of all calamity, is a new and great chance for the United States, of which we must prove ourselves worthy by cultivating among our academic youth a deep and abiding knowledge of, and interest in, the old literatures of the East and those of the West, between which we now find ourselves placed as the sole solid link between these two cradles of civilization. My hope that we should begin with at least four national survey courses, the friendly cultures of Japan and India, the at present aloof culture of Mahometanism, and the at present hostile culture of China, before establishing thorough graduate centers for Asian Studies over and above what the State Department is trying to do, is therefore no mere daydream; it is based upon the hard geopolitical and geocultural realities of our days.

And then, of course, there are Australia and New Zealand—the latter still so very English, the former already half American in its outlook and re-adjustment—they, too, aware that, with the Suez blocked, the influence, the cultural resources and, if it should come to the worst, the military help of the West is apt to come by way of America rather than through an uncertain Suez. Cautiously enough, I am not giving an evaluation whether from the viewpoint of Canberra or Christchurch it is a desirable thing that New York and Washington should have replaced London and Paris as the centers of Western strength; I am merely stating a fact and, I repeat it, an enormous, a wonderful challenge to all of us to be worthy of the task thrust upon us.

And finally, there is Africa—an Africa that is no longer European and that is in dire need of a friend. We can qualify for that role because we have the immense advantage that the voice of Africa was heard for the first time not on the Congo, but on the Mississippi. I am referring, of course, not to the literature of the white man in Africa—the Foreign Legion of *Beau Geste* by Christopher Wren, *La peste* by Camus, *Les Nourritures terrestres* by Gide, *Volk ohne Raum* by Grimm, *Cry, the Beloved Country* by Alan Paton, but to the soul of the Black Man, the former slave in America, to the fear, the despair, the deep religion, the hope and defiance as it burst forth, not so much in the days of Booker T. Washington, but in the novels and especially the poems of Richard Wright, Langston Hughes, James Weldon Johnson, Claude McKay. Here, in spite of the heartbreaks of the past, there are the rich promises of the future—promises painfully slow in materializing, yet even so, so infinitely better than the coming doom of *apartheid* in Cape Town—and here again ours is a chance which we must not forfeit.

And so, with Indians and Negroes in our midst, with our population made up of Anglo-Saxons, Celts, Latins, Teutons, Slavs, and Semites, with our cultural and political bonds with Western Europe stronger than ever before, and with a thousand threads extending from us to Latin America, Asia, the Commonwealth Down Under and, indeed, perhaps to Africa thanks to an ancient curse that may turn into a blessing: we just can't miss, we can't close our eyes, we can't turn the clock back: we are—not only the leader of the free world, politically and, I hope, slowly also culturally—but we are also the Land of the Middle. And we, assembled here in this center of learning of the American Midwest, have a very very important task assigned to us indeed: That of making American youth become aware of this throbbing and fascinating interplay with the rest of the world, and of making our students approach the best in the literary culture of our friends with respect and with gratitude.

Chapter 11

Jan C. Brandt Corstius

WRITING HISTORIES OF
WORLD LITERATURE (1963)

J AN C. (JOHANNES CHRISTIAAN) BRANDT CORSTIUS (1908–85) was a
Dutch literary scholar who taught at the Utrecht Gymnasium until 1959 and from
1960 to 1975 was Professor of Comparative Literature at the University of Utrecht,
where he also directed the Institute of Comparative Literature. His 1934 doctoral
dissertation dealt with the work of the Dutch poet Herman Gorter. Some of his most
important publications on Dutch literature are *De literatuur van de Nederlanden in de
moderne tijd* (1959; Literature of the Netherlands in Modern Times) and *Geschiedenis
van de Nederlandse literatuur* (1959; History of Dutch Literature). His approach,
however, was always comparative, as in, for instance, *De Muze in het morgenlicht.
Inleiding tot de geschiedenis van de eenheid der westerse literatuur* (1957; The Muses at
Dawn: Introduction to the History of the Unity of Western Literature). The textbook
Introduction to the Comparative Study of Literature (1968) was his major contribution
to the discipline. Influenced by the formalism of the New Criticism (Northrop Frye) and
Leo Spitzer, Corstius advocated a comparative close analysis of texts with the aim of
"showing what is original in a poet" through the comparatist's wider knowledge of the
international context (1968: 133). Another key feature of this textbook is Corstius's
emphasis on the role played by the socio-historical context to comparatively understand a
literary work. By recovering the historical background of the textual construction, and
most specially of the frequently used terms in a work, writer or period, they "reveal something of their nature" (1968: 172).

Distrustful about the study of "literature *qua* literature," his 1963 article "Writing
Histories of World Literature" surveys key examples of such histories from 1899 to 1955
by stressing the influence of the audience they address. For Corstius, all these histories
were based on outdated concepts and organized around two principles, overviews by
periods and juxtaposition of "national histories." The article concludes with some brief
but interesting remarks about the aim such a history should pursue.

Jan C. Brandt Corstius, "Writing Histories of World Literature," *Yearbook of Comparative and
General Literature* 12 (1963): 5–14.

An article on the writing of histories of world literature would seem to be out of place in a scholarly publication, since there are good reasons for denying that such histories meet the requirements of true literary historiography. Often such surveys are mere compilations which could easily be undertaken by clerks. They are aimed at a public believing in a shallow *Allgemeinbildung* [general knowledge] and wanting to inform itself about literature without reading the works themselves. For the student seriously concerned with literature, on the other hand, such manuals are of little use, of considerably less value, at any rate, than are histories of specific literatures or of literatures organically related to each other. Histories of world literature, to be sure, may be used as reference works, but in this respect they are generally inferior to dictionaries.

Traditionally, general histories of literature tend to be histories of civilization or of the evolution of the human mind. In them, literature proper is often subordinated to this broader purpose. If this is the announced intent, however, the underlying concept is incompatible with the aims of literary study embraced in our time. Modern scholars, on the whole, are disinclined toward viewing literature largely as a historical document or as a vehicle of ideas. They want to study literature *qua* literature, that is, primarily as an esthetic phenomenon. And literary history respects this view when it defines the place which a given work occupies in the history of literature in order to demonstrate the uniqueness of that work as well as its relation to other works. This is clearly the function of a history of national literature as well as of a history of literatures organically related to each other. It remains to be seen whether, seen in this manner, literary historiography on a universal scale makes sense. But as long as such histories are written for reasons extrinsic to literature itself, this question must be answered in the negative.

Yet there remains the fact that a number of well-known literary historians have engaged in the task of writing histories of world literature. Here we do not deal with industrious compilations but with serious attempts to make such surveys useful for the student. The authors of such histories can be counted on to have carefully worked out a plan and to have devised a method of presenting their material conscientiously and with the utmost possible objectivity. It is obvious, however, that these scholars, too, will often be forced to repeat what other scholars have said before them, since no one individual can be expected to know all the works that must be screened in the course of such an undertaking.

It depends, therefore, largely on the taste, erudition, and intelligence of the author whether or not his product is one of those "traurig stimmenden Versuche, in denen ein einziger Autor die Weltliteratur in einem einzigen Bande abhandelt" [sorry attempts, in which one single author deals with world literature in a single volume].[1] Maturity of outlook will be demonstrated in a number of ways: by the freshness and appropriateness of the critical views, by the degree of attention paid to the problem of how the author's own literature should be treated in relation to those that are closely related to or remote from it, by the aptness of the notion of what constitutes world literature, and by the discretion used in the selection of authors and works to be included in the survey. Often the scholarly author of a history of world literature will harbor doubts as to the feasibility of his undertaking. Nevertheless, he will seek to overcome the difficulties in his way. We shall examine the fruits of some of these endeavors to see whether enterprises of this kind are feasible.

Taken as a whole, histories of world literature are addressed to and consulted by the public of the country in which they are written. Exceptions to this rule are made in the case of certain histories written by Western authors and translated into Oriental languages as well as in that of foreign readers conversant with the language in which the survey is composed. But these exceptions only tend to confirm the rule; for authors and publishers hold that the above-mentioned circumstance calls for a special treatment, within the framework of the universal survey, of the literature of the country in which it is published. This special treatment often implies a more detailed description of and a more extended reference to minor authors as well as to minor works composed in the author's mother tongue. This procedure inevitably causes the overall balance to be destroyed and the value of the enterprise to be substantially lessened. In the past, authors occasionally shirked the problem by omitting the history of their national literature. The German literary historian Otto von Leixner, for example, wrote a *Geschichte der fremden Literaturen* (1899, 2nd ed.) and his compatriot Paul Wiegler a *Geschichte der fremdsprachigen Weltliteratur* (1913). Yet von Leixner implicitly speaks about German literature only when paying special attention to those foreign works which exerted an influence upon it.

To leave out one literature in the act of presenting an international literary panorama wherein that literature has its place would seem to be an illegitimate means to a national end. Such an omission can be more or less accepted only when the survey is presented in the form of a collection of histories of national literatures. But what about a true history of world literature? We shall reach some conclusions regarding this matter after having completed our examination of some recent works of this nature. Already we can take it for granted, however, that the writing of such histories in itself seems, in many respects, so willful an undertaking—since they are bound to remain incomplete—that to omit one single literature can hardly be regarded as a major crime.

Not all modern histories of world literature have solved this problem satisfactorily. The *Historia de la literatura universal* (1957–59), of Martín de Riquer and José María Valverde follows a traditional pattern. Considerably more space is allotted to Spanish literature than its contribution to European letters would seem to justify; for example, 80 pages out of a total of 244 dealing with twentieth-century literature. In the same chapter—the last of volume III—only 40 pages are assigned to contemporary French literature and 32 to English. Obviously, the work seems to combine two incompatible aims: that of presenting a history of world literature and that of stressing the Spanish contribution to it.[2]

The *Histoire des littératures*, edited by Raymond Queneau in the Bibliothéque de la Pléiade, fails in another respect with regard to the same problem.[3] The work was designed on the principle of allotting an equal number of pages to the history of every important Western literature. But this policy could not be enforced in the case of French letters. No French literary historian willing to perform a task gladly shouldered by his foreign colleagues could be found. Thus, in the end, one entire volume was reserved for the literature of the country in which the project originated. It would seem, then, as if this practice harks back to a situation of the past; for histories of world literature as written by von Leixner and Paul Wiegler presupposed the existence of a separate history of German literature, such as the one actually written by the former. But the case of the *Histoire des littératures* is not quite so simple; for here the history of French literature is covered in Volume III. This inconsistency is all the more striking since the work pays otherwise close attention to the interrelationship of the various national literatures forming among themselves an organic whole.

The Italian literary historian Giacomo Prampolini did not succumb to the same error when he wrote his *Storia universale della letteratura*, although he, too, could have been assured that his compatriots would have liked to see Italy's contribution more heavily emphasized. In Prampolini's work, Italian literature is given the scope due to it in its European context.[4]

But in the writing of histories of world literature still another problem of balance has to be solved by authors of Western origin; for the question arises as to how much space should be devoted to Western literature relative to its Eastern equivalent. In his inaugural address at the University of Lyon in 1901, Fernand Baldensperger, in dealing with the notion of European literature, exclaimed: "La littérature européenne!—ou encore, suivant la désignation plus ambitieuse qu'emploient nos voisins, la littérature mondiale, ou universelle" [European literature, or even, resorting to the more ambitious label used by our neighbors, world or universal literature.] In this way the French scholar pointed to a trend in literary historiography which to us moderns must seem erroneous. In writing about world literature, we have no excuse for paying more attention to the West than to the East. But for several reasons Western literature is usually favored.

Most histories of world literature, for one, are produced by Western authors, few of whose Eastern colleagues enter into competition. The chapters in them which deal with non-Western literature are mostly compilations of secondary sources; and there exists a traditional prejudice in the choice of Oriental literatures to be covered. This prejudice is an outgrowth of the type of study of non-Western literatures made by Western philologists and historians in the nineteenth century, when emphasis was placed on the earliest phases of these literatures, as in the case of Hebrew, Egyptian, Indian and Arabic letters. The effect of this was and still is noticeable in many histories. Usually such histories start with a survey of these initial phases. Next come Greek and Latin literatures, followed by the modern history of Western literature, whereas the modern history of Oriental literature is often slighted.

Prior to 1900, Leixner's book was one of the few exceptions to this rule, and the same applies to Fr. Loliée's *Histoire des littératures comparées* (1903).[5] This latter book, to be sure, reveals the author's enthusiasm for a future universal literature rather than his knowledge of literary history. But this enthusiasm is at least directed at both Western and non-Western letters. This may account for the fact that the book was subsequently translated into Chinese. For the most part, however, the histories of Chinese and Japanese literature were dealt with in a handful of pages at the conclusion of the survey (as in Paul Wiegler's *Geschichte der fremdsprachigen Weltliteratur*).

This fault has not been amended in all recent histories. In his *Panorama de las literaturas* (Buenos Aires, 1946) Ezequiel Martínez Estrada places his chapter on the history of Chinese and Japanese literatures (embracing three pages and brought up to date) between a chapter on medieval mystics and one on medieval heroic epic. The *Historia de la literatura universal* pays little attention to China and Japan, a practice defended by the editors with a view toward the circumstance that the literature of these countries exerted less influence on European letters than did other non-Western literatures. In the same survey, the history of Indian literature is not carried forward to the present (only Tagore is mentioned in the small section "other writers of the Commonwealth," Vol. III, p. 544), while at least some information about modern Hebrew and Arabic literature is provided.

The Dutch literary historian F. W. van Heerikhuizen (*Gestalten der Tyden*, Leiden, I, 1951, II, 1956) proceeds much in the same manner with Oriental literature. And so does the Swiss writer Eduard von Tunk in his *Illustrierte Weltliteraturgeschichte* (Zürich, I–II, 1954–55). In volume II of this survey the histories of Indian, Japanese, and Chinese literature, along with those of the Slavic, Hungarian, and Rumanian literatures, are brought up to date in approximately 90 pages. Von Tunk's compatriot Lavalette (*Literaturgeschichte der Welt* in one volume, Zürich, 1948, 1954), after dealing with the ancient histories of Indian, Egyptian, Assyrian, Babylonian, and Aryan literature, passes on to Greek and Roman literature and, from then on, exclusively concentrates on the literature of the West.

It is obvious that Western literary historians concerned with surveying world literature do not like to go outside the domain traditionally theirs, modern Western literature. This means, however, that the writing of universal literary history is not really their business. Their catholic aims inevitably clash with their limited experience and their methods, consequently, are often objectionable. Some of these writers, such as Martín de Riquer and José María Valverde, frankly admit that they write from the Western point of view and that non-Western literature figures only to the extent in which it impinges upon that of the West. The same authors also state their intention to treat works that constitute the universal patrimony of the literature of the civilized nations.

This general trend is formulated very well by Erwin Laaths, when he informs the readers of the author's concept of *Geschichte der Weltliteratur* (*Knaurs Geschichte der Weltliteratur.* München, 1953), using the term *Weltliteratur* in the sense of the Great Books. "Berücksichtigt er den deutschen Anteil auch ein wenig grosszügiger, so bildet doch die abendländische Weltliteratur vor den anderen Weltliteraturen—etwa der indischen oder ostasiatischen—das eigentliche Thema. Es wird hier versucht, abendländische Weltliteratur als einen grossen, sich entwickelnden oder entfaltenden Organismus zu schildern. Die anderen Weltliteraturen finden in diesem lebendigen Gefüge jedoch insofern einen Platz, als deren wichtigste Erscheinungen nach dem Mass einer abendländischen Anknüpfung einbezogen werden." [Even if he is a little bit more generous when it comes to German literature, his real topic is European world literature rather than other world literatures such as for instance Indian or East Asian literature. The aim is to present European world literature as one comprehensive organic whole that grows and unfolds itself. Still, other world literatures do find a place in this living organism in so far as their most important manifestations are included when they have some relation to European literature.]

On this point two other above-mentioned histories of world literature published at approximately the same time, namely Prampolini's *Storia universale della letteratura* and the Pléiade *Histoire des littératures,* go their own different ways, because they endeavor to cover the history of as many literatures as possible, i.e., the literatures of large as well as small nations, which not everybody takes to belong to the "civilized countries." Nor are these two works composed in such a way as to favor the Western literatures unduly.

Prampolini's *Storia universale della letteratura* is a work that commands respect. In its original form it dates from the years immediately preceding World War II and should therefore be excluded from this survey of histories of world literature written in the last fifteen or twenty years. But having lost all his materials during the bombardment of Torino in 1943, Prampolini started all over again and considerably expanded his work. The seven volumes of this second version appeared between 1948 and 1953. Their publication marks the greatest and most important single-handed effort of its kind. Prampolini's phenomenal command of languages enabled him to obtain first-hand knowledge of numerous literatures. Less than anybody else he was forced to rely on work done by his fellow-scholars. It is this circumstance which lends his vast panorama its remarkable unity and consistency.

As histories of literature go, however, it is quite conventional insofar as the brief introductions to the individual sections and the descriptions of literary texts and historical developments closely ally it with social and political historiography. Prampolini not only pays sufficient attention to the smaller literatures but, on the whole, manages to do them justice. He respects the historical landmarks of a national literature, which are not always those of literature in general. In each volume he maintains an exact balance between major and minor writers and works. And due to its vast scope his work can be effectively used as a dictionary, its index listing more than 20,000 references.

Yet in spite of this, Prampolini's *Storia universale della letteratura* is of little use to the serious student of literature. It remains a work mainly aimed at the general reader eager to gain an overall impression. The critical views it offers too closely resemble the conventional, stereotyped ones of sweeping surveys. The fact that Prampolini's knowledge is so vast cannot be used as an argument favoring the view that, in our time, a history of world literature can be written by one scholar, no matter how cosmopolitan his mind, how complete his mastery of languages, and how exceptional his erudition. Parts of Prampolini's work remain unsatisfactory because of the author's lack of intimacy with his subject. This is especially true of twentieth-century developments in non-Western countries (such as Indonesia). But histories of world literature written by teams of experts are by no means free of such defects. These seemingly inevitable shortcomings simply point to the enormous difficulties involved in writing a history of world literature in the mid-twentieth century.

In order to perform the task single-handedly attempted by Prampolini, the editor of the *Histoire des littératures,* Raymond Queneau, assembled a team of collaborators. This history, too, deserves the credit of having presented a sweeping panorama of world literature. Both it and Prampolini's work confirm our present view that, in spite of their differences and mutual controversies, the continents form one single world marked by an endless variety of forms and ideas that are increasingly international in scope. The *Histoire des littératures* impresses this state of affairs even more strongly on our minds than does Prampolini's survey. The difference in degree stems from some of the principles which underlie the plan of the latter publication.

I do not mean to imply, however, that the *Histoire des littératures* gives a satisfying account of the history of each literature dealt with. Sometimes, the outlines are sketchier than seems justified by the scope of the undertaking. As a source of reference, too, the work is sometimes disappointing. The index has no system in the presentation of the titles. Willfully they are given either in their original forms or in their French translations, sometimes in both. Thus: *Dame ne veut pas brûler (La); Death of a Salesman; Importance d'être constant (L'); Mourning Becomes Electra.* When only the French translation is given, difficulties may arise if no international terms, such as ballad or ode, are part of the title; for example: *Ascension de Hannelé (L');* *Eventail de Lady Windermere (L'); Par-delà le Bien et le Mal; Un gars du Shropshire.*

The literature of our own time, on the other hand, is treated so well that it supplies a wealth of interesting material for the study of the international aspect of modern literary history, especially with regard to the interchange of forms and ideas, the extent of which is truly unprecedented. A vivid impression of the steadily growing cosmopolitanism is conveyed, and that in spite of the fact that the national histories are treated independently. The order in which the literatures are dealt with is based on their geographical grouping. This method so convincingly projects the literary map of the modern world that a strong impression of the omnipresence of literature is conveyed.

Histories of world literature cannot be written without a firm basis in literary criticism. All too often, the range of such undertakings compels their authors to summarize traditional views concerning the works, authors, and movements they are concerned with. This explains why histories of world literature are sometimes insipid.

An exception is made by de Riquer and Valverde, who have successfully ventured to write a critical history. Their activity is directed toward an evaluation of individual works, since they aim at creating a "panorama crítico" designed to underline the specifically literary values of the works. Their evaluations are actually based on critical readings of those works in the original, at least in the case of books written in Greek, Latin, the Romance languages, German, and English. For the rest they used translations into one of these tongues. Although de Riquer and Valverde do not claim to offer highly personal criticisms and although they desire to express a general opinion, they boldly declare that the opinions given in their work are essentially theirs: We communicate to the reader our own experiences, instead of restricting ourselves to furnishing extracts from historical manuals.

In doing so, they present a history of world literature that is both remarkable and attractive, especially since they want it understood that their work is a polemical reaction against the excesses of the "culturalism" of our age. Their criticism is chiefly concerned with some of the classic works of the important literatures, for the information given about the classic books of other literatures does not convey the impression that the authors of the *Historia de la literatura universal* have read these books. Especially the third volume (19th and 20th centuries), written by Valverde, offers specimens of fine literary criticism. To both authors the history of the human mind is important only in view of its literary outgrowths; and they are less interested in literary generations than in the personalities of the writers as revealed through their works. However, they are concerned with the various literary periods, which they treat concisely and excellently. They evaluate without indulging in the use of technical terms and by no means overlook the results of historical studies that have led to factual discoveries.

It is an old complaint that the histories of the literature of great civilizations—especially of the Western world—as well as universal literary histories, however limited in scope, employ the method of stringing up national literary histories arranged, or not arranged, according to periods. Historiography of this kind is open to objection as soon as the notions of general and comparative literature develop.

For von Leixner the only way of writing the history of world literature lay in dealing successively with the national literary histories. However, he already thought of connecting the various literatures within the traditional periods. Yet in doing so, he felt, it would be necessary to deal with works partly or entirely derived from others, and thereby circumscribing the nature of the *Zeitgeist*. Methodologically, however, this program could not be carried out since, according to von Leixner, many works of small literary value and works of great value to one literature but insignificant for the others, would have to be taken into consideration.

As far as the comparative approach was concerned, von Leixner felt that it was still too early to make use of it: "Die vergleichende Literaturwissenschaft ist eine sehr junge Wissenschaft. Ihre Ergebnisse sind weder so gesichtet noch so feststehend, dass sie heute schon durch ein volkstümlich geschriebenes Werk der Allgemeinheit vermittelt werden könnten." [Comparative literature is a very young discipline. Its results are neither so spectacular nor secure that they might already be popularized.] Moreover, the method of dealing separately with the histories of the various national literatures was supported by the view, held by many literary historians, that literary historiography was a means of familiarizing the reader with the spirit of a nation.

One of the results of the historical approach to literatures in the nineteenth and twentieth centuries was a deeper understanding of the international character of such literary phenomena as themes, genres, motives, fashions, all of which taken together form the pattern of the literature of a truly international culture. Literary histories exceeding national boundaries could thus convey an idea of this universal character.

Around 1920, Paul Van Tieghem asked for *littérature générale,* i.e., for the history of the main literary traits of a given civilization and common to several nations.[6] I shall not discuss to what extent the literary historian of our day regards the notion of *littérature générale* as being identical with that of comparative literature. Van Tieghem, at any rate, clearly distinguished between the two, since comparative literature, in his view, was the study of the literary relations between two or more nations. More than once he objected to histories of European and world literature, while, at the same time, asserting the rights of a synthetic international literary history. Having undertaken various preparatory studies, he himself wrote such a history of Western literature, the *Histoire littéraire de l'Europe et de l'Amérique de la Renaissance à nos jours* (Paris, 1945).

In the meantime, the study of literary phenomena and their international history has advanced, especially with regard to Western literature. It now increasingly concentrates on structural elements, traditions, the international context of works of literature, and the basic presuppositions concerning literature and literary activity. Such studies, both analytic and historical in nature, tend to sharpen our awareness of Western literature as a whole. "Was wir gewonnen haben, ist eine neue Anschauung vom innern Zusammenhang der europäischen Literatur" [What we have gained is a new view of the inner coherence of European literature], says Curtius.

This view of the inner coherence of Western literature is demonstrated, among other works, by the studies of Curtius and Lausberg on the European tradition of ancient rhetoric, by Highet's *The Classical Tradition,* Weinberg's book on the poetics of the Italian Renaissance, Wellek's history of criticism, Lovejoy's studies in the history of ideas, Van Tieghem's investigation of *préromantisme* and M. H. Abrams' study of romantic criticism. All these works provide a basis for the writing of the history of Western literature in its entirety. The attempts made by Van Tieghem, Cohen, and Friederich/Malone will be followed by other histories availing themselves of the cumulative results of such studies in order to outline Western literature with a view toward its inner coherence.

But can what applies to the writing of Western literary history in our day also apply to the writing of its global equivalent? The Swiss literary historian Robert Lavalette, in his *Literaturgeschichte der Welt,* rejects the serialization of national histories of literature.[7] He also refrains from introducing the traditional periods (antiquity, the Middle Ages, the Renaissance, etc.). This practice does not reflect his conviction of the existence of one universal pattern of literature but characterizes his intention, "die tieferen geistigen Beweggründe des weltliterarischen Geschehens aufzudekken" [to discover the deeper motives of world literary events].

Lavalette writes a history of world literature in order to come to grips with the spiritual problems of our time. This purpose governs the organization of his book. The literatures of Babylonia, Assyria, Egypt, and ancient Israel are grouped together under the heading "Götter, Könige und Propheten" [Gods, Kings and Prophets], whereas the history of Greek literature is dealt with under the title "Schicksal und Menschlichkeit" [Fate and Humanity]. The chapter on Roman literary history is entitled "Die Ratio" [Reason] and the one concerned with the medieval literature of Europe "Diesseits und Jenseits" [Here and Beyond]. The basic principle of organization seems to be the idea underlying the spirit of each epoch. World literature as written by Lavalette is a survey of the spiritual life of mankind (mainly of its European branch) that makes use of literary works.

The vast panorama of literatures offered by the Pléiade *Histoire des littératures* is headed by two essays, the first one dealing with Oriental literature and the second with its European counterpart. By dint of their mutual differences, both essays greatly enhance the value of this history of world literature.

The second of these essays describes the traits characteristic of each period in the history of European literature. It views its subject under the heading of unity in variety. Specialists in the literature of each period—R. R. Bezzola for medieval literature, V. L. Saulnier for the Renaissance, Jean Rousset for the Baroque, Henri Peyre for Classicism, and Gaëtan Picon for the modern age—collaborate in a manner sanctioned by the tradition of literary historiography. Thus Volume I offers the reader a synthetic historical survey of European literature before embarking on a long series of national literary histories, and the idea of European literature prevails.

The peculiar nature of this literature is plainly shown by a comparison with Oriental literature as treated by Raymond Schwab in his essay entitled "Domaine orientale." In the preface to Volume I, Raymond Queneau, the editor, calls Schwab's contribution to the *Histoire des littératures* "sans doute la première vue synthétique, en langue française, de l'ensemble des littératures asiatiques" [without doubt the first survey in French of all Asian literatures]. And it is, without question, the most interesting part of the volume.

The author reduces the complexity of his subject, which is caused by the multiplicity and the extreme old age of Oriental literatures, to a number of aspects which serve both to accentuate and to conquer it. Schwab proceeds by abandoning the idea of historical development and evolution. He does not divide into periods, movements, or literary currents but replaces these concepts by pairs of antithetic notions, such as stability and motion, time and duration, quantity and quality, continuity and discontinuity. He also points to the interrelation between words, rhythm, and melody as well as to that between literature and knowledge, religion and the cosmos.

There is little use asking at this point whether the history of Western literature might not be viewed in the same manner, i.e., by means of basic antitheses, such as classic-romantic, idealistic-realistic, dream-reality, individualism-collectivism, and through its relations to mysticism, nothingness, the chaos. The tradition of the Western historiography of literature simply is not based on the aspects just mentioned. Its basic principles are chronology and the division into periods. That it is a Western scholar who projects a synthetic version of Asiatic literature does not matter. Naturally, Schwab's handling of Oriental literary history has a personal touch; but his contribution to the *Histoire des littératures* does not seem to differ significantly from surveys of Eastern literature written by other Western or Oriental scholars. What is important is the fact that Schwab has the basic differences between East and West constantly in mind.

One may think of Western and Oriental literature as sharing in equal parts in the Indo-European heritage; but "lorsque la moitié gréco-latine . . . se trouve en face de la moitié asiatique, elle n'a pas du tout l'impression qu'elle va se recoller" (I, 103; when the Greco-Latin half meets the Asian half, [this heritage] does not at all give the impression that it is going to mend itself). Still it is one heritage, so that "a moins de faire cause commune avec les génies non européens, nous n'aurons jamais qu'une idée boiteuse de ce que nous-mêmes appelons la littérature" (I, 104; unless we join with the non-European writers we will never have but a foreshortened idea of what we ourselves call literature).

Quite rightly Schwab sympathizes neither with "synthèses anticipées" (a priori syntheses) nor with "panoramas où l'ampleur [est] peu conciliable avec la précision" (I, 105; panoramas whose scope is hardly compatible with precision). On this point he is in accord with Raymond Queneau, who in his preface to the first volume of the *Histoire des littératures* remarks as follows about general analogies between East and West: "Je n'ignore pas du tout ce que ce genre de coincidences a de superficiel et de simplement anecdotique. A défaut de méthode scientifique encore inexistante, de tels rapprochements aident à une compréhension de l'unité de la littérature universelle de l'existence de laquelle on peut avoir, je l'avoue, de multiples raisons de douter" (I, xix; I am aware of how superficial and incidental these analogies may be. As long as we do not have at our disposal a scientific method, such analogies may help us to understand the unity of that universal literature of which, I admit, there are many reasons to doubt whether it actually exists).

Schwab speaks of Oriental literature as being of "cette pensée jumelle et antagoniste de la nôtre" (I, 105; this thought that is both twin and antagonistic to ours). Thus "le corpus strictement européen des littératures qu'on enseigne dans nos écoles a l'air d'un estropié congénital ou d'un mutilé volontaire" (I, 106; the strictly European literary corpus that is taught in our schools looks like a congenital cripple or a voluntary disabled person). And he concludes his introductory chapter with the words: "Je puis prédire à coup sûr qu'avant la fin de ce siècle on ne pourra plus analyser des grands processus historiques, en littérature grecque, française, ou américaine, sans puiser des éléments de comparaison dans les séries orientales" (1,108; I can predict for certain that before the end of this century it will be impossible to analyze major historical processes related to Greek, French or American literature without comparing them with Oriental literatures).

Schwab points out that it is impossible to think and speak properly of literature and literary history as long as Oriental literature is ignored. His opinion is shared by others (such as René Étiemble) who are conscious of the fact that in this regard the first move has still to be made in the fields of literary theory, stylistics, and comparative literature. For in these areas knowledge is still almost exclusively based on Western literature. We only know that the writing of literature is quite another thing in the West from what it is in the East. There are scarcely any corresponding esthetic categories. And the question, still unsatisfactorily answered, can be put if there are in East and West similar literary conditions, traditions and aims.

After what has been said it seems obvious that the aims for writing a history of world literature in the synthetic manner has not yet arrived. There is some difficulty in using the term world literature in connection with literary historiography. This term surely cannot be understood in the Goethean sense of the conditions favorable to cosmopolitanism in literature. For the history of world literature is neither a history of the preliminaries of a cosmopolitan literature nor the history of that literature itself. It cannot be taken in the canonic sense of the Great Books; the history of world literature cannot use this concept as an organizing principle, because we do not possess the knowledge demanded by such a task. It would perhaps be better simply to speak of the history of literature.

But this shift of terms will not be helpful if there is no corresponding shift in meaning, that is, if the term history of literature continues to apply to the compilation of histories of individual literatures instead of denoting the history of the international conditions of literature, the international views concerning the function of literature, the primeval forms, the similarities between various formal developments originating in these forms, and the world-wide diffusion of literary phenomena in modern times. The writing of histories of world literature today is usually still based on the outdated concepts; and the tradition of gathering histories of national literatures into volumes entitled histories of world literature, universal histories of literature, or histories of universal literature, respectively, is carried on, often with great skill, admirable erudition, and sound critical opinions. But as far as the study of literature is concerned, this tradition is definitely superannuated.

Notes

1   Horst Rüdiger, "Nationalliteraturen und europäische Literatur: Methoden und Ziele der vergleichenden Literaturwissenschaft," *Schweizer Monatshefte* 42 (1962): 195–211 (200).

2   [Editors' note: Martín de Riquer and José María Valverde, *Historia de la literatura universal*, 3 vols. (Barcelona: Noguer, 1958–68).]

3   [Editors' note: Raymond Queneau, ed., *Histoire des littératures*, 3 vols. (Paris: Gallimard, 1955–58).]

4   [Editors' note: Giacomo Prampolini, *Storia universal della letteratura*, 3rd ed., 7 vols. (Torino: Utet, 1959–61).]

5   [Editors' note: Frédéric Loliée, *Histoire des littératures comparées des origines au XXe siècle* (Paris, C. Delagrave, 1903).]

6   [Editors' note: Corstius makes reference here to Paul Van Tieghem, "La Synthèse en histoire littéraire: Littérature comparée et Littérature générale," *Revue de Synthèse historique* 31 (1921): 1–27.]

7   [Editors' note: Robert Lavalette, *Literaturgeschichte der Welt* (Zürich: Füssli, 1948).]

Chapter 12

René Étiemble

DO WE HAVE TO REVISE THE NOTION OF WORLD LITERATURE? (1964)

RENÉ ÉTIEMBLE (1909–2002) WAS the enfant terrible of French comparatism. He first gained notoriety also beyond France with the publication, in 1963, of *Comparaison n'est pas raison: la crise de la littérature comparée,* a pamphlet meant as rejoinder to René Wellek's famous 1958 address on "The Crisis in Comparative Literature," given to the Third World Congress of the International Comparative Literature Associaton. Étiemble was a polyglot, with an intimate knowledge of especially Arab and Chinese culture. He published widely on the concomitant literatures, and on their relation to European literature, as for example his two-volume *L'Europe chinoise* (1988–89). At the Fourth World Congress of the ICLA, held in Fribourg, Switzerland, in 1964, Étiemble held an impassioned plea for extending world literature to really include all of the world's literatures, and not just a few major European literatures. His provocative speech, entitled "Faut-il réviser la notion de *Weltliteratur*?" was published in 1966 in the proceedings of the 1964 Conference edited by François Jost. In the preface to his *Essais de littérature (vraiment) générale* (1975; *Essays in [Truly] General Literature*), in which his 1964 ICLA speech was included, Étiemble gave an example of how Japanese literature rendered void all theories of literature based on European examples, and he concluded that "any literary theory built only on European phenomena will not fare any better from now on" (*toute théorie littéraire qui s'élabore a partir des seuls phénoménes européens ne vaudra pas mieux désormais*). Albert Guérard, though in a much less provocative way, had already in his 1940 *Preface to World Literature* lamented that in what commonly passed as the canon of world litera-ture (his concrete example and point of departure had been a list drawn up by Sir John Lubbock in 1885 but he maintained that things had not really altered much for the better since then) "the East is woefully under-represented." Étiemble enlarged Guérard's argu-ment to encompass the entire world, and he abundantly referred to authors from the most diverse, yet always non-European, origin. We here offer the (to our knowledge) first English translation of Étiemble's text.

René Étiemble, "Faut-il réviser la notion de *Weltliteratur?*" *Proceedings of the IVth Congress of the International Comparative Literature Association / Actes du IVe Congrès de l'Association Internationale de Littérature Comparée (Fribourg, 1964)*, The Hague: Mouton, 1966, pp. 5–16. Version used taken from *Essais de littérature (vraiment) générale*, Paris: Gallimard, 1975, pp. 15–36. Translated by Theo D'haen.

How can we avoid being struck by the criticisms formulated these days against the concept of world literature [*Weltliteratur*]? Mr. Árpád Berczik compares it to a *Monstre-Konzert* and suspects that it is only an intellectual form of internationalism, guilty after all of serving an eternal idea of the beautiful.[1] The reservations of this Hungarian are echoed by a Czech, Mr. Jan Mukařovský, who relates world literature [*Weltliteratur*] to the rise of the bourgeoisie, and therefore sees it as something that needs to be overcome, because "for the first time in the history of human culture, we now witness the birth of a truly universal literature," born from the October Revolution, a literature that finally condemns "the subordination of the overwhelming majority of national literatures to that of some (so-called) *great literatures*, the privileged source of all creative initiative."[2]

It is not because these arguments have been put forward by academics from the socialist world that we should spurn them.

In fact, when I reread the two passages from [Eckermann's] *Conversations* [with Goethe] where there is talk of world literature [*Weltliteratur*], I can approve of the passage in which Goethe rejoices that world literature offers us the opportunity to mutually correct ourselves: "so that we can correct one another" [*In den Fall kommen uns einander zu korrigieren*], and in which he praises Carlyle to have judged Schiller so aptly as would not have been possible for a German. But I am astonished that his idea of world literature [*Weltliteratur*] came to him on the basis of some superficial judgments on a few mediocre Chinese novels and on a couple of songs of Béranger: the Chinese novels being so utterly moralistic [*so sittlich*] and the works of the French poet being so little moralistic [*so unsittlich*]. With Mr. Árpád Berczik, I would also object to an altogether too naïve interpretation of poetry on the part of Goethe that it is the common good of mankind: "I see ever clearer that poetry is the common property of all men" [*Ich sehe immer mehr dass die Poesie ein Gemeingut der Menschheit ist*]. Of course, I am happy that Goethe composed his *Diwan*; but in order for poetry to be common to all humanity it suffices to consider that the poetic sensibility is in fact equitably distributed throughout the human species. The poem, on the other hand, only belongs to those that know and that are able to savor perfectly the language in which it was written. The most universal linguistic art is the least poetic prose.[3]

All this does not prevent me from supporting Goethe when he is looking for the invariable features of all literary beauty in world literature [*Weltliteratur*].

Still, how could I forget that this world literature [*Weltliteratur*] that may well have been the product of a bourgeois conscience during the period of free-trade liberalism has illiberally participated in the denigration or even the systematic destruction of the African, Indian, Amerindian, Madagascan, Indonesian, Vietnamese and other literatures. Like free-trade liberalism, colonialist imperialism constitutes one moment of bourgeois consciousness. The European priests, soldiers, and merchants have in effect replaced Goethe's generous conception with one in which literature is divided between that of the masters and that of the slaves. In this sense our socialist colleagues are right. But if their conception of world literature [*littérature universelle*] may seem to be more open, I still have to conclude that not one word of Goethe on world literature [*Weltliteratur*] allows us to see in him a conscious or unconscious agent of imperialism. On the contrary, his elevated idea of world literature implicitly condemns German nationalism and along with it all nationalism. Let us therefore simply admit that Goethe is not any more guilty of the destruction of the Amerindian literatures than is the Jew Karl Marx, the theoretician of socialism, of the anti-Semitic and anti-Yiddish excesses of Stalin.

Renouncing, then, all political perspective, because too exclusionary, let us return to language, as our disagreements are always in the first place linguistic. Because the concept of world literature [*Weltliteratur*] was coined in German (and by what a German!) it has always retained, at least for certain people, the taint of a germanocentrism. Some have proposed alternative terms such as universal literature [*littérature universelle*], or general literature [*littérature générale*], or *World literature*, or мировая ялитература. There is even at least one Spaniard, Guillermo de Torre, who conflates world literature [*Weltliteratur*] and comparative literature when he wonders "whether the only field close to that envisaged by *Weltliteratur* is not comparative literature." For M. Hankiss, on the contrary, comparative literature does not deal with overall literary production, but restricts itself to "research involving more than one national literature."[4] As if things were not complicated enough yet, Mrs. Nieoupokoyeva, of the Academy of Sciences of the Soviet Union, conflates general literature and мировая ялитература, something that more than one proponent of general literature would contest.

Rather than trip over the adjectives clinging to the notion of literature and so in the last analysis turn out just as ridiculous as the various supporters of "proximate power" [*pouvoir prochain*] in the first [of Blaise Pascal's] *Provincial Letters*, let us candidly admit that the totality of all national literatures simply makes up *literature*, without adjective? In so far as I have understood the program and the projects of the Gorky Institute for world literature as they have been explained to me by our colleague Anissimov, who at the time was the director of that Institute, the literature in question, мировая ялитература, to me seems closer to universal literature [*littérature universelle*], or world literature, than to *littérature générale* or general literature. Let me add that in order to study this literature without adjective we have at our disposal – independent of works of literary history, sociology or criticism on separate literatures – the comparatist method, which can be subdivided into several sub-disciplines: comparative literary history, comparative sociology of literatures, genre theory, general aesthetics, and general literature [by which Étiemble means something that in our day we would probably call "theory of literature"]. If comparative literature, then, can be considered in relation to world literature [*Weltliteratur*], this is not because it is identical with the latter, but only in so far as it allows us to gain access to it.

If we agree on this we could also now serenely move on to more serious things and ask ourselves if in the twentieth century we should not revise that notion of world literature [*Weltliteratur*] that we have inherited from our predecessors.

The Soviet Orientalist N. I. Conrad thinks that indeed we should enlarge the historical and geographical scope of comparative literature, that is to say of the method that opens up world literature [*Weltliteratur*] for us, and the Harvard sinologist James Hightower concurs. Fine! I think to have found out that to understand the genesis of *The Chanson de Roland*, and to properly evaluate the *Légendes épiques* of Bédier, it is at least very useful to have some knowledge of the works of Jirmounsky on the epic in Central Asia, of Rolf A. Stein on the Tibetan *Gesar de Ling*, the ballads of the Oranian bard Mest'fa ben Brahim, even if the latter lived in the nineteenth century, the Armenian epic *David de Sassoun*, and, why not, half a dozen African epics?[5]

We no longer live in a time such as that of the Hungarian scholar Hugo von Meltzl, a follower of Goethe and a supporter of world literature [*Weltliteratur*], who could still preach a *Dekaglottismus* of civilized languages: German, English, Spanish, Dutch, Icelandic, Italian, Portuguese, Swedish and French – to which he added Latin. Literatures in all other languages for him amounted to no more than *Volkslied-literaturen* or, if they were *Kunstliteraturen,* they were of too recent origin. For anyone with any idea of the wealth, the age, and the quality of the Sanskrit, Chinese, Tamil, Japanese, Bengali, Iranian, Arab or Marathi literatures, all, or at least some, of which had already produced their master works at a time when the majority of the *Dekaglottismus* literatures did not yet exist, or were still in their infancy, this stingy idea of world literature [*Weltliteratur*] definitely seems to have had its day. Observe, moreover, that even Greek literature plays no part in this concert, to say nothing about Pharaonic literature (still little known in the time of Metzl, but without which it would now be impossible to understand anything at all about the history of the theater or of the novella in the Mediterranean world!)

Following Conrad, the Soviet scholar, and Hightower, the American scholar, let us proclaim that literature from now on can only mean the totality of all literatures, whether alive or dead, of which there remain written, or even only oral, traces, without further discrimination as to language, politics or religion.

Thus replacing the world literature [*Weltliteratur*] of *Dekaglottismus* with literature *tout court* I am immediately seized by a kind of panic terror, which reminds me of the proverb "grasp all, lose all." What would such theoretical openness of spirit to all literatures, whether present or past, bring us given that any human mind, however capacious we may imagine it, is limited by the average length of our lives? Fortunately, another German, Hermann Hesse, has already come up with the basic reply to this question in his *Eine Bibliothek der Weltliteratur*:[6] on the one hand nobody can effectively get to know even the totality of one literature, let alone that of all literatures; on the other hand each of us, in order to become a fully rounded human being, can and hence must construct his own personal library of world literature [*Weltliteratur*]. In short, that for us and even more so for those that we educate, one route only lies open to world literature [*Weltliteratur*], that of our affinities, of love: "He [the reader] must travel the road of love, not that of duty" [*Er [der Leser] muss den Weg der Liebe gehen, nicht den der Pflicht*].[7]

I see more proof that we have arrived at a point in history where what occupies us is a question that faces every thinking man in the inquiry that Raymond Queneau conducted on the *Bibliothèque idéale* or ideal library. He asked several dozen writers to pick from a list of approximately 3500 works their ideal library of one hundred titles. Some authors refused to reply and motivated their decision. Yvon Belaval, for instance, replies in the spirit of Hermann Hesse: "the ideal library for me is that which I am reading at the moment."[8] Gaston Bachelard replied: "my ideal library remains essentially open."[9] We do not even mention those that, like Hervé Bazin, reject the very idea: "there is no such thing as an ideal library. The times, nationality, taste, temperament, the specialization that culture imposes make impossible any common denominator."[10]

After having sorted through the 61 replies he received, Queneau drew up a table of one hundred titles. At the top of the list figured Shakespeare and the Bible, in this order, followed by Marcel Proust. What worries me from the beginning is that there are 60 French titles and 39 foreign titles. And what worries me even more is that of these 39 foreign titles 9 are of English or American authors, 8 belong to Greek literature, 6 to German literature, 6 are Russian, 4 are Latin authors, 3 Spanish; while Arab, Danish, Hebrew and Italian literature all can boast one title. You can easily guess that 58 of the 61 writers that replied were French: Henry Miller, Marion Moore and Frederick Prokosch represent foreign opinion.

As Apollinaire's *Alcools* is inadvertently cited twice, as numbers 25 and 85 respectively, I take the liberty to suggest that instead of one of these two *Alcools* we should insert the [Japanese] *Genji monogatari* [*Tale of Genji*], the [Chinese] *Hong leou mong* [*The Dream of the Red Chamber*, also called *The Story of the Stone*], the [Sanskrit] *Pançatantra* [*Five Principles*], the [Sanskrit] *Jataka*, the [Japanese] *Tzurezuregusa* [*Essays in Idleness*, also called *The Harvest of Leisure*], the *Zhuangzi*, Wang Chong, the *Prolegomenon* [*Muqaddimah*] of Ibn Khaldoun, or one or other of the thousands of titles that are worth more or at least as much as *Alcools*? The great merit of this inquiry surely is to demonstrate how far removed French writers are from acceding to the wish of Goethe, or to answering the hopes of Karl Marx.[11] Werner Kraus would undoubtedly be more indulgent than I am for the French men of letters, as he is of the opinion that until the 19th century French literature was in fact the model for all other literatures: "serving as example to all other literatures" [*Für alle andern Literaturen beispielgebend gewesen*]. To which I would respond, with the frankness of friendship, admiration even, that another literature has enjoyed, and continues to enjoy, and this since millennia, a situation that is as privileged as ours has been for eight centuries: the Chinese, which is not represented, not even with one title, in the *Bibliothèque idéale*.

Maybe one will object that one hundred titles, one hundred names, imposes impossible restrictions? Give us one thousand titles, ten thousand titles, and you will see something else. Well then, let's see! Let us first have a look at Adolf Spermann's *Vergleichende Zeittafel der Weltliteratur, von Mittelalter bis zur Neuzeit 1150–1939*, published in 1951, after the defeat of Nazism. Let us leave aside that, given this work's chronological limitations, three quarters at least of all literature is excluded, and let us probe the little we are presented with. We do not find Lu Hsun, Kouo Mojo, Hou Zhe, Premchand, Taha Hussein, Tawfiq al-Hakim, Jorge Luis Borges, Octavio Paz, Haldor Laxness, Rafael Alberti, Federico García Lorca, Miguel Hernández. Eugène Brieux, on the contrary, is included. No mention of Henry Miller or Arthur Miller, but a listing for the eighteenth-century Johann Miller [Johannes von Müller?]. As if aware of all that is missing, the author confesses that the war prevented him from seriously occupying himself with the literatures of Asia. This really is a pitiful excuse, because Murasaki Shikibu, Sei Shonagon, Kenkô, Zeami, Saikaku and Jippensha Ikku, to name only six of the masters of Japanese prose accessible in translation, were not unknown before 1939: in Europe, I mean. Or let us suppose that, putting together a world literature [*Weltliteratur*] following his own judgment, a Japanese scholar would overlook Goethe, Schiller, Nietzsche, Jean-Paul, Hölderlin and Thomas Mann, how would this go over this side of Eurasia? If on a list of eleven thousand titles one assigns twenty to Mr Joséphin Péladan but one ignores, or neglects, the [Japanese Jippensha Ikku's] *Hizakurige* [*Shank's Mare*], the [Vietnamese Du Nguyên's] *Kim-Vân-Kiêu*, the [Japanese Ueda Akinari's] *Ugetsu Monogatari* [*Tales of Moonlight and Rain*] and the oeuvre of [the British-Indian-Pakistani] Muhammad Iqbal, is one qualified – I allow myself to ask – to compose the list of honor of world literature [*Weltliteratur*]? Finally, if French writers give to France two thirds of world literature [*Weltliteratur*], Mr. Spemann gives to German literature of the twentieth century exactly the same role that some of us claim (who at least have the excuse of being writers only, and not scholars). Should we be more content with the three fat volumes of *Die Weltliteratur* published in Austria in the same year 1951 by a group of specialists, serious ones this time? Some ten thousand names here too. Doumic, Estaunié, Péladan are there in honor of France, but I look in vain for Cavafy, Rastko Petrovich, Mao Dun, Jean Paulhan, Dai Wangshu (one of the three or four Chinese poets of the twentieth century), Mulk Raj Anand, whose Indian novels have more strength and beauty than those of our Octave Feuillet, who is included. Again, there is a scandalous disproportion between Europe's part, from which the worst are highlighted, and that of Asia, where even the best are excluded from the paradise of world literature [*Weltliteratur*]; that is to say from a biased [*orientée*] world literature: see what part Islam, Buddhism, and atheism play in this world literature, and you will see that it is very small, justifying the criticisms of our colleagues from the socialist world. Presented thus, world literature [*Weltliteratur*] is nothing but a celebration of bourgeois and Christian values.[12]

I have much the same to say with regard to the work of a French scholar who is the zealous, and more unfortunate even than zealous, author of a universal literature with a comprehensive list from the Middle Ages until the present: Alice Berthet.[13] On her list we find the inevitable Brieux, we also encounter Blasco Ibáñez and Victor Cherbuliez, and three hundred more such individuals of this kind, all of them coming from our part of the world:

Western Europe. As far as the romantic lyric in Russia is concerned you are entitled to just the following three words: "Pushkin, lyrical poet." Asia is represented by Tagore, along with Okakura Kakuzo "who studied – as did Tagore – in England."[14] The reader might conclude that an Asian writer is only acceptable when he has studied at a British public school. If this is not a case of a colonialist spirit I really do not know what these words might mean.

Let us finally take a look at *Les Écrivains célèbres*, a volume edited by Raymond Queneau and Pierre Josserand. About ten thousand names. A pleasant surprise: here we find Mao Dun and Kouo Mojo, Cao Yu and Lao Tse, Ai Qing and Lu Hsun, Hou Zhe and Liu E for China past and present, which is a good thing, a very good thing even; for Greece we see Cavafy, Sikelianos, Kazantzakis, Seferis and even Engonopoulos, which is not bad either. For Japan, next to Tanizaki, I notice Shiga Naoya, Mori Ogai, Natsume Soseki, Ueda Bin, which always gives pleasure; for Iran, Sadegh Hedayat, with his admirable *Blind Owl*, is not overlooked. With just a little bit of competence and courage it is thus possible from now on to draw up a fair list of [world] literature, and even of the literature of the first 30 or 40 years of the twentieth century, and this, let us reassure ourselves, without sacrificing Estaunié or Brieux, who continue to figure on our list, or anything else.[15]

That it is possible to present a more or less correct idea of world literature [*Weltliteratur*] in the form of a manual is proved abundantly (literally so) by the *Histoire universelle synchronoptique* of Arno Peters, especially so in the French edition here mentioned as revised and enlarged under the editorship of M. Minder.

I fear, however, that we will have to wait yet a long time before the spirit of the *Écrivains célèbres*, which overall is also that of this synchronoptic history, triumphs over the idols of the different tribes. Our side of the world an insidious Eurocentrism continues to throw a false light on everything, while on the other side of the world for a while yet one will continue to celebrate well-meaning mediocrities for the sole reason that they celebrate the revolution, or atheism. Let us for instance have a look at the recent and, I agree on this, very useful work of Elizabeth Frenzel: *Stoffe der Weltliteratur*.[16] Three examples will do. In the article on *Cäsar* (pp. 94–98) I looked in vain for any reference to the Tibetan *Gesar*, an epic on which a lot of work had been done even before Stein's dissertation on it. And yet this is an exciting theme: a Roman Emperor that dominates the great epic of Tibet! The article on *Buddha* refers me to *Balaam and Josaphat*. Nothing more. Now as far as I know Buddha has not been less of an inspiration for world literature [*Weltliteratur*], that is to say for literature *tout court*, than has Jesus. He has even inspired many a literary craftsman in Western Europe. Final example: *Ann Boleyn* and even *Die Schöne Iren* receive the accolade of being considered "themes," but I look in vain for Yang Kwei-fei, who certainly can hold the candle to them in this respect, and who has found literary echoes in Europe, and even in the United States, up to our days.[17]

What other way is there to improve future repertories of names, those bio-bibliographies to which unfortunately until now most works on world literature [*Weltliteratur*] limit themselves, than to confide them to a truly international association of comparative literature in which all adherents to our discipline, whether they work in the socialist or in the capitalist world, can collaborate without too much difficulty when it comes to ascertaining facts. In this way, for instance, I have during my first stay in Japan discovered a list of one hundred titles, selected by qualified Japanese – namely the Rector of the University of Tokyo, Mr. Watanabe Kazuo, and Mr. Nakano, Professor of English Literature and a well-known Marxist sympathizer, a counterpart to Raymond Queneau's ideal library. Mr. Araki Toru has been so good as to translate this document, which is published as an appendix to all volumes in the collection Iwanami, the best world literature [*Weltliteratur*] or *literature* collection one can find in Tokyo, recommended to all students from fifteen to twenty-five years of age. This is an encouraging list in the sense that, notwithstanding the riches and variety of Japanese literature itself, two thirds of the one hundred titles are taken from foreign literatures: China, Germany,

England, France, Russia, Denmark, Norway, and the United States. That is to say that in spite of their Chikamatsu and Zeami, the Japanese also know about Shakespeare, Corneille, Molière, *Faust*, *The Cherry Orchard*, and *A Doll's House*, while with us Shakespeare or Molière keep us away from Chikamatsu, *Cyrano* from the nô [theatre], and the *Hamburgische Dramaturgie* from the *Treatises* of Zeami.[18] Still, two lacunae come as a surprise, and suggest that the Japanese themselves, as cosmopolitan as they may be in the best sense of this word, yet have some way to go in this respect: India is absent from the list, and so is the Arab world. *The Arabian Nights* apparently do not merit mention, while *Tonio Kröger* and *Quo Vadis?* do. It is evident that it would profit the Japanese to acquire a better knowledge of these two literary worlds. I've also asked Mr. Attia Naboul Naga to forward me the program of a forthcoming Egyptian collection called *Deux mille chefs-d'oeuvre, patrimoine de l'humanité*, or Two Thousand Masterpieces, The Heritage of Mankind. That the *Odyssey* does not figure in this repertory does not worry me too much, because even if it is also absent from Queneau's ideal library (where it is replaced by its modern subversion, James Joyce's *Ulysses*), it does figure among the one hundred Japanese titles. Moreover, one cannot judge an undertaking of this kind by one isolated title. Let us rather rejoice that next to Ibn Rouchid [Averroes], Ibn Sinna [Avicenna], Ben Arabi, Ibn Hazm, Al Farabi, Al Ghazali and the Brethern of Purity, the list also contains the names of Aristotle, Hegel, Heidegger, Hume, Husserl, Kant, Leibniz, Nietzsche, Plato, Plotinus, Schopenhauer and – as the only French philosopher – Sartre, with *Being and Nothingness*. Let us not be surprised if, with names to choose from such as the *Mu'allaqat*, Abul 'Ala al Ma'arri, El Moutannabi, Abou Nuwas for literature in Arabic, and the *Shahnameh*, *the Rubaiyat*, Hafiz and Saadi for the Persian, the Egyptians retain only a few poems by Blake, Burns, Byron, Shelley, Lamartine and Musset. If poets, as I believe at variance with what Goethe says, belong only to those knowing their language, this choice seems judicious. Let us rather express our appreciation that while among the two thousand masterpieces figure the *Seances* of Hariri, the novels of Tara Hussein, Tawfiq al-Hakim and Mahmoud Taymour, all of which I looked for in vain in most of our works on *Weltliteratur*, *Gil Blas*, *Zadig*, *Werther*, and twenty other European novels are not forgotten. Still, how could we not notice some omissions here too? Latin literature, the literatures of India, China and Japan have no place among these two thousand masterpieces. Another case of faulty procedures, you say? Not even. Simply that, victims of their own particularisms, of the idols of their tribe, we still have a long way to go before we are ready to shoulder the task that Goethe assigned to us a century and a half ago: to hasten the dawn of world literature [*Weltliteratur*].

Of course it makes sense that a German should know his own literature much better than that of the Persians or Japanese, and vice versa; but could we not agree that henceforth nobody has the right to meddle with world literature [*Weltliteratur*], or better with *literature*, if he or she has not done his or her best to escape the determinism of his or her birth. One day at the Sorbonne I overheard a number of sociologists discuss which authors should be part of a program on the origins of their discipline. None of them mentioned Ibn Khaldoun. Having admired, in French translation, the *Prolegomenon* and the *History of the Berbers*, and having read, amongst other things, the thesis of Taha Hussein on *La Pensée sociale d'Ibn Khaldoun*, I, layman here, allowed myself to suggest that the founding father of sociology, and this several centuries before Montesquieu, was the Arab-speaking Berber from Tunisia. They pitilessly told me that I spoke of what I did not know, that my intervention was only pose, or even imposture; and they refused to take it into consideration. Well then, I maintain that it is inadmissible to talk of sociology without knowing the *Prolegomenon*, and I think that from now on nobody will be able to talk seriously about the theater if he has not read the *Treatises* of Zeami, or if he has not taken cognizance of the nô, or of the Peking opera.

In one sense, this amounts to saying that the world literature [*Weltliteratur*] of the future, that is to say *literature*, will merit, even more than does the *Weltliteratur* of which Goethe dreamed, Mr. Árpád Berczik's reproach that it largely depends upon translations.[19] In fact, the good use to which each of us will put literature will depend on the progress made in an art usually looked down upon. This also means that whoever wants to really educate himself in literature will have to read Saikaku in translation rather than Péladan in the original, Ilango Idagal in translation rather than Françoise Sagan in the original, Hallaj in translation rather than Géraldy in the original, Kabir in translation rather than Anna de Noailles in the original. Indeed, do the sum yourself: give yourself fifty years of life without one day of illness or rest, or altogether 18,262 days. Rigorously taking into account periods of sleep, meals, the obligations and the pleasures of life, and of your profession, estimate the time left to you for reading masterpieces with the sole purpose of finding out what precisely is literature. As I'm extremely generous, I will grant you the privilege of reading every day – good ones as well as bad ones – one very beautiful book of all those that are accessible to you in your own language and in the foreign languages you have mastered, in the original, or in translation. You know that it will take you more than one day to read *The Magic Mountain* or the *Arabian nights*; but I also take into account that with a little bit of luck and zeal you might read in one day the *Hojoki*, the *Romancero gitano*, the *Menexenos* and *The Spirit of Conquest* of Benjamin Constant. This will give you the couple of days extra that you will need to read *And Quiet Flows the Don,* which for the longest time was thought to have been written by Sholokhov, but which is not any less good for actually being mostly the work of Krioukov. In any case better than *Cleared Land* by the same Sholokhov. Now, when measured against the total number of very beautiful books that exist in the world, what are 18,262 titles? Sheer misery.

And yet one will not be able to get it out of my head that, if there is a future for man, it is that in which our students will know how to read, and will want to read, Jippensha Ikku and Rabelais, Wang Chong and Hobbes, the *Risalat ul ghufran* and the *Li Sao*, the *Vita* of Cellini and the *Confessions* of St. Augustine and that, the world of men being what it is, it is to this ideal that we have to dedicate what in a previous century was world literature [*Weltliteratur*]. This means that instead of wasting one's time with reading a thousand bad books of which the whole world talks, one will be able to choose from the tens of thousands of great works that are only awaiting our goodwill. Maybe this also means that, while we may continue to educate specialists in the Romance languages, the Germanic languages, or the Slav languages, or Dravidian, or Sino-Tibetan, or Turkish-Mongolian, or Finno-Ugrian, or Semitic, and many Africanists, we will also educate another type of scholar: people that will know well a Semitic language, a Dravidian language, a Sino-Tibetan language, and a Malay language. These are the people that would be particularly apt to enrich and define more precisely the notion of literature. And let no-one object that I am dreaming, that I am wallowing in utopia. In Paris I know a few very gifted students that are beginning to acquire this kind of education. It is they that one day might write this history of literature, and of literatures, that we unfortunately still lack. They are the ones that one day might elaborate a history and theory of literary genres. Our traditional teachings should therefore be complemented with those offered by institutes of literature conceived in such a spirit. They are the people that, building on the work done by scholars of Slavic, Germanic, Chinese, Romance, and Semitic literatures, might try to put together those syntheses of literary history, criticism and aesthetics that still continue to elude us because, owing to a lack of means, but also to a lack of foresight and imagination, we continue in our usual groove.

But I sense that I risk falling foul of the complaint that a famous comparatist, Arturo Farinelli, formulated in a review of a book by Richard M. Meyer, *Die Weltliteratur der Gegenwart von Deutschland aus überblickt*. "Let us not be envious of the luster of faraway meteors and let us not yearn to roam the tempting meadows of the loud world, looking for bliss, and forgetting our own quiet and green home" [*Beneiden wir den Glanz der Fernleuchtenden Meteore nicht und trachten wir nicht danach, wonnesuchend, der stillen grünen Heimat vergessend, die lockenden*

Fluren der lärmenden Welt su durchschweifen].[20] After which, and by way of conclusion, he cites a few lines of verse by Theodor Fontane, among which the following two lines:

> *Das Haus, die Heimat, die Beschränkung,*
> *Die sind das Glück und sind die Welt.*
> [House, home, limitation,
> In these lie happiness and the world.]

One word above all strikes me, and worries me while it yet also reassures me: limitation [*Beschränkung*], because it reminds me that it is precisely the champion of world literature [*Weltliteratur*] who is responsible for putting into my head the following precept which I find at the same time so judicious and so difficult to respect:

> *In der Beschränkung zeigt sich erst der Meister.*
> [The true master knows what to limit himself to.]

Goethe himself, then, at one and the same time calls upon us to contribute with all our might to the dawn of world literature [*Weltliteratur*] and to know how to limit ourselves or otherwise never to excel at anything. This is where I see eye to eye with Hermann Hesse who refuses to back any preconceived program of world literature [*Weltliteratur*]; and yet I propose to organize our studies via a truly international association of comparatists that might even serve to distribute the great tasks that face us.

 Do I contradict myself? Am I caught in full aporia? Not at all, it seems to me. On the one hand I think that it is to be wished, that it is necessary even, that from now on an educated person should be able to take whatever suits him or her from anywhere: even though neither of them knows Chinese, Cyril Connolly in England and Jean Grenier in France have understood and assimilated part of Taoism. Of course, we have to be wary of the traps of exoticism. The present fashion for a *Zen* little understood ill serves the cause of world literature [*Weltliteratur*]. World literature should not be allowed to become mere pap. But if I'm allowed to draw on my own experience, I owe as much to Confucius and Zhuangzi as to Montaigne, almost as much to Sun Tzu as to Kant, and much more to Wang Chong than to Hegel. Without this detour by way of China I would probably never have encountered my own truth, my own moral universe and my happiness. [Mansur al-]Hallaj, the crucified, the Indian mystics Toukaram and Kabir, have helped me to better appreciate St. John of the Cross and Teresa of Avila. One can put literature to humanist purposes, then: as amateur (in the favorable sense of *he who loves*, like Hermann Hesse). In this case, following the precept of Goethe, everyone limits his choice according to his own appetite, his preferences, his moral or intellectual stature. But let us not confound this *usage*, this *enjoyment*, this *assimilation* of world literature [*Weltliteratur*] with the *knowledge* it behooves us to compile about it in the form of repertories, treatises, histories, dictionaries. In that case our only limits should be comprehensiveness and truth. A true history of literature and of literatures will have to be as truthful as possible, acceptable for all peoples involved. If it does not satisfy these criteria, it is worth nothing. In order to bring such an enterprise to a fruitful end, there will be need of teams of men that have an extraordinary capacity, indefatigable scholars, men of a totally different affective and intellectual caliber than Jean Grenier or Cyril Connolly. Perhaps we will be able to reconcile these two requirements. Because after all, as since 1929 I have never ceased to work on Rimbaud and his myth, from Mexico to Russia, from Turkey to China, and I've only succeeded in coming to understand what maybe there is to be understood in [Rimbaud's sonnet] "*Voyelles*," I know that the pleasure that the [Malagasy] *Hain-tenys* or the *Tzurezuregusa* give me can never be more than that of an amateur;[21] but why should I deprive myself of that? This is one of the contradictions of the world in which we live, in which our students will live: we are at one and the same time filled with information and overwhelmed by its excess. To the point even that at precisely the moment at which world literature [*Weltliteratur*] finally becomes possible it becomes at the same time almost impossible. Of course, I hope that everyone of us feels under obligation to the impossible.

Notes

1   "Goethe's concept of world literature can be compared to a 'Monstre-Konzert,' in which singular phrases sound the voices of the various nations and the whole yet fuses into one superb symphony. All this is to say that the Goethean world literature idea constituted an internationalism of the mind. As such it does not absorb into itself the separate literatures, as these become participants in world literature precisely because of their specific national characteristics, and the separate nations make what is really of value in their literatures into the common property of mankind through well-crafted translations and adaptations." "A Hungarian Conception of Wold Literature," in *Comparative Literature in Eastern Europe*, Budapest Conference, 26–29 October 1962, edited by I. Söter, of the Hungarian Academy of Sciences and K. Bor, T. Klaniczay Gy. M. Vajda (Budapest, Akadémiai Kiadó, 1963), p. 289.

2   "With the emergence of the bourgeoisie, the relations between the national literatures have even intensified, and become more varied, with literary contacts being facilitated by improved means of transport and becoming at the same time profitable from the point of view of economic exchanges too, etc. One even arrives at positing the idea of a set of literary values common to all humanity – the world literature of Goethe. But what is coming into being before our very eyes is deeply and fundamentally different from anything that ever went before. For the first time in the history of human culture we witness, etc." "What literary scholarship owes to contemporary world literature," ibid, p. 184.

3   Johann Peter Eckermann, *Gespräche mit Goethe* . . . ., [*Conversations with Goethe* . . . .], herausgegeben von Prof. Dr. H.H. Hausman (Wiesbaden, F. Brockhaus, 1959). See entries for 31 January 1827, pp. 172–174 and 15 July 1827, p. 199.

4   Jean Hankiss, "Littérature universelle?," *Helicon* (Debreczen, 1938), nos 1–2, p. 159.

5   *Mest'fa Ben Brahim et Turoldus, Gesar et Roland*, Paper given at the Congress of the French Comparative Literature Association in Rennes, 1963, and "Une épopée tibétaine," *Nouvelle Revue Française*, Septembre 1963.

6   Zürich, Werner Classen Verlag, 1946.

7   "Nobody could even then completely study the entire literature of even one single cultured nation, and get to know it, let alone that of all of humanity," p. 12, the quotation from the text is on p. 15. See also p. 17: "Education without heart is one of the worst sins against the spirit," in which we recognize the German equivalent ["Bildung ohne Herz ist eine der schlimmsten Sünden gegen den Geist"] to our French *science without conscience only leads to the ruin of the soul* [*science sans conscience n'est que ruine de l'âme*].

8   *Pour une bibliothèque idéale, enquête présentée par* [*For an ideal library, inquiry presented by*] Raymond Queneau, de l'académie Goncourt (Paris, Gallimard, 1946), p. 40.

9   *Ibid*, p. 28.

10   *Ibid*, p. 38.

11   "The age of Weltliteratur has begun; and everyone should further its course," Goethe, *loc. cit.*, p. 174. [See the Goethe selections in this volume.]

12   See *Vergleichende Zeittafel* . . . . (Stuttgart, Engelman Verlag Adolf Spemann, 1951), *passim*. In 1906, over against 34 German and 6 Austrian titles, Spemann mentions 8 English titles, 8 American, 1 Irish, 10 French, 1 Flemish, 1 Dutch, 3 Danish, 2 Norwegian, 2 Swedish, 1 Belgian, 1 Italian, 3 Spanish, 1 Hungarian, 1 Polish, 1 Japanese, 1 Russian. In 1915, while I find 31 German and 7 Austrian titles, I find 1 Swiss, 2 Danish, 1 Icelandic, 2 Norwegian, 1 Swedish, 14 English, 1 Irish, 7 American, 3 Australian, 4 French, 1 Italian, 1 Romanian, 1 Guatemalan, 1 Hungarian, 1 Polish, 2 Russian, 1 Japanese, 2 Indian. For 1939, the Germans are entitled to 70 titles, Austria to 11, and German Switzerland to 8; Flemish counts for 1, like Dutch, Danish, Swedish, Scottish, Irish, Finnish, English gets 10, American 11, French 15. And so on for each year. – In *Die Weltliteratur*, herausgegeben von E. Frauwallner, H. Giebisch, E. Heinzel (Wien [Vienne], Verlag Brüder Hollinek, 1951), three fat volumes (2118 pages with double columns), one does not have the excuse that there is not enough space.

13 *Tout ce qu'il faut savoir de la littérature universelle*, [Everything one has to know about world literature], par Alice Berthet (Paris, édition du Fauconnier, s.d.).

14 *Loc. cit.*, p. 67.

15 *Les écrivains célèbres*, [*The Famous Authors*], in three volumes, appeared with the publisher Lucien Mazenod, 1951–1952. Occasionally one here confuses, in Japanese, name and first name, because our first name in Japanese becomes an *after name*.

16 Elizabeth Frenzel, *Stoffe der Weltliteratur, Ein Lexikon dichtunggeschichtlicher Längsschnitte* [*Themes of World Literature, A Literary-Historical Lexicon*], (Stuttgart, Alfred Kröner Verlag, 1962), XV + 670 very dense pages. In her preface the author clarifies what method she used: "The various articles in my lexicon base themselves in the numerous researches into literary themes (dt. Stoff), that in the course of the last one hundred years have been published in the form of books, articles, and above all dissertations, and that already feature in bibliographies, the German by K. Bauerhorst (1932) and its continuation by F.A. Schmitt (1959) as well as the international one by F. Baldensperger/W.P Friederich (1950) and the 'Yearbook of Comparative and General Literature' meant as the latter's continuation." This implicitly also indicates the limitations of Frenzel's sources.

17 I have briefly dealt with this theme in my article "Yang Kwei-fei" in the encyclopedia *Les Femmes célèbres* [*Famous Women*], in two volumes, published with Lucien Mazenod, 1960–1961.

18 One should do a study on the affinities between *Cyrano de Bergerac* and the Japanese *kabuki* theatre. I outline such a study in "Shirano Benjuro et le nô," *Nouvelle Revue Française*, July and October 1964.

19 "Is primarily fed by translations, indeed, it is almost identical with translation." *loc. cit.*, p. 288.

20 "Let us not be envious of the luster of faraway meteors and let us not yearn to roam the tempting meadows of the loud world, looking for bliss, and forgetting our own quiet and green home" "Contemporary World Literature seen from Germany," in *Aufsätze, Reden und Charakteristiken zur Weltliteratur* [*Essays, Speeches and Definitions on World Literature*] (Bonn and Leipzig, Kurt Schroeder Verlag, 1925), p. 421. – The author of the book that serves as pretext for this review: Richard M. Meyer, to whom we owe *Die Weltliteratur im zwanzigsten Jahrhundert. Vom deutschen Standpunkt aus betrachtet* [*World Literature in the Twentieth Century: Seen from a German Perspective*] (Stuttgart and Berlin, Deutsche Verlagsanstalt, 1913), in the very terms he uses goes against the idea that Goethe had formed himself about this discipline, and abuses the term *Weltliteratur*. *Weltliteratur* is pressed into the service of Prussian imperialism: "there is being formed a universal world literature, in which an honorable role is reserved for us Germans [. . .]", French literature, on the contrary, is "the most unmodern," and this in 1913. As Farinelli says, we stand "before the tribunal of a Berlin judge", a judge that deplores that "contemporary world literature is still less imbued with German spirit than it is with the French one", which is just a pitiful argument if one compares it to the requirements of *Weltliteratur* according to Goethe: "correcting each other's errors".

By giving over one volume to *German Literature*, and another to *World Literature*, the Dalp collection (Bern, A. Francke A.G. Verlag, 1946) commits the reverse error of that of the *History of Literatures* of [the French series] the Pléiade: one volume for literatures in French, and two volumes for all other literatures. If I do not refer to the great work of Fritz Strich, *Goethe and World Literature* (Bern, A. Francke A.G. Verlag, 1946) it is because I intend to deal with the following question: "*Should we revise the notion of world literature?*", Not *Goethe and World Literature*.

21 Kenkô's work, *Les Heures oisives* [*Essays in Idleness*], is now available in French, in *Connaissance de l'Orient* [*Knowledge of the Orient*], Unesco collection of representative works, no. 27, Gallimard, 1968, together with the *Hôjô-ki, Notes de ma cabane de moine* [*Hôjô-ki, Notes from my monk's cabin*], by Kamo no Chômei.

Chapter 13

Irina Grigorevna Neupokoyeva

DIALECTICS OF HISTORICAL DEVELOPMENT OF NATIONAL AND WORLD LITERATURE (1973)

I RINA GRIGOREVNA NEUPOKOYEVA (1917–77) WAS a Russian scholar who mainly worked on Romantic literature. In her dissertation she dealt with the "principles" of Romanticism through an analysis of the work of the English poet Percy Bysshe Shelley. The choice of this poet within the context of Soviet literary scholarship was not unexpected, for Shelley—as opposed to Byron according to Marx and Engels—was a rebel "enshrined for homage in the political culture of Stalinism."[i] One of the main studies on Shelley by Neupokoyeva was, therefore, aptly entitled *P. B. Shelli: k voprosu ob estet-icheskikh printsipakh revolyutsionnogo romantizma* (1956; P. B. Shelley: On the Aesthetic Principles of Revolutionary Romanticism). The fact that Neupokoeyeva's research was carried out during the late Stalin period should not be overlooked, for it explains her disagreements with both Western scholars (or scholars working in the Western academia) and comparative literature, a discipline which at that moment was considered a dangerous pursuit as a result of its so-called aesthetic- and bourgeois-oriented values (for her critique of Western comparative literature, see Neupokoyeva 1963). In *Comparative Literature Today*, René Wellek recalled how papers by Russian scholars—including Neupokoyeva's—were "wholesale condemnations of all that we were doing" (1965: 331), whereas Harry Levin, in his presidential address at the ACLA meeting at Indiana University, described Neupokoyeva as a "polemical lady" who had not given up her "commitment to nationalism or, at any rate, to Pan-Slavism, anti-Westernism, and propaganda."[ii]

Neupokoyeva became a member of the Communist Party in 1957. At the Gorki Institute of World Literature, her initial research on English Romanticism progressively expanded to European Romanticism by focusing on the problems of literary interactions and relationships.[iii] Her interest in methodological issues as derived from the empirical

---

i   Rachel Polonsky, "Revolutionary Etudes: The Reception of Shelley in Russia," *The Reception of P. B. Shelley*, eds. Susanne Schmid & Michael Rosington (London: Continuum, 2008) 229–46 (239).

ii Harry Levin, "Comparing the Literature," *Yearbook of Comparative and General Literature* 17 (1968): 5–16 (14).

iii See István Sötér and I. G. Neupokoyeva, eds., *European Romanticism* (Budapest: Akadémiai Kiadó, 1977).

research on Romanticism simultaneously led to one of the most ambitious projects at the Gorki Institute, namely, the multi-volume *Istorii vsemirnoj literatury* (1983–89; History of World Literature). Neupokoyeva's contribution materialized in a series of preliminary publications on the problems posed by a history of world literature, a genre which she considered biased due to its *zapadnoevropocentrizm* (Western-Eurocentrism). A comprehensive synthesis of her main arguments on world literature may be found in her 1976 book, *Istorija vsemirnoj literatury. Problemy sistemnogo i sravnitel'nogo analiza* (History of World Literature: Problems of Systemic and Comparative Analysis), whereas in her 1969 article "The Comparative Aspects in the 'History of World Literature',") she discussed the methodological principles of the Gorki Institute's *Istorii*.

The interest of her 1973 article "Dialectics of Historical Development of National and World Literature" lies not only in the fact of providing a brief and seminal summary of her theory on world literature. What is more important is the fact that this paper was presented at the Colloque Méthodologique de Littérature Comparée held in Budapest in 1971, in which the leading comparatists of the moment participated (see the special issue of *Neohelicon* 1–2 (1973)). For Neupokoyeva, a theory of world literature had not addressed as yet a key issue, namely, the problem of regional literary development as an intermediate stage between national and world literature. The specific participation of a single national literature within world literature cannot be understood if its links with other national literatures as a result of a zonal development are neglected. This is tantamount to overlooking that any single literature includes both national and international elements. As these links are multifarious, world literature needs to be conceived as a "moving map." In the discussion following Neupokoyeva's presentation, except for A. O. Aldridge, all the other scholars—Claudio Guillén, Eva Kushner, Werner Bahner, Alexandre Dima, Jacques Voisine, Paul Cornea, Milan V. Dimić, Aleksandar Flaker, and Jean Weisgerber—acknowledged the importance of her contribution on the concept of "literary zone" and qualified it in important directions. This is relevant insofar as in this Colloque the manuscript for the first volume of the ICLA series "Comparative History of Literatures in European Languages" was presented. And literary zones were to play an increasingly important key role within this project.

Irina Grigorevna Neupokoyeva, "Dialectics of Historical Development of National and World Literature," *Neohelicon* 1–2 (1973): 115–30.

It is probably correct to say that in recent times world philology, besides showing an interest in various quantitative methods of research, has been increasingly attracted by broad philosophical-historical examination of the major processes in literature. Evidence of this is found in the appearance of several types of research:

—   comparative research into various national literatures within the chronological limits of the major literary periods (e.g., works differing in their subject material but similar by the very idea of synthesis in the field of Slav literature in ancient times[1] and in the nineteenth century;[2] study of the emergence and development of socialist artistic culture;[3] research into the history of the multinational Soviet literature;[4])

—   researches on a broad regional plane (e.g., general characteristics of the Latin-American[5] or Indian literatures[6]);

—   the appearance of histories of world literature in different countries;

—   *theoretical* interest in the problems of historical and literary synthesis and attention to the role the comparative-typological approach should play in it.

In recent years Soviet scholars have had serious discussions on problems of the Renaissance and the Enlightenment in world literature, on whether these concepts, elaborated mainly on the basis of European material, are applicable to the history of world literature and if so, to what extent. Problems of historical and literary synthesis are increasingly attracting the attention of different international forums.

In all this one cannot fail to see a serious positive basis, namely the concern of contemporary science for humanitarian problems. There can hardly be any justification for the occasional assertion that in researches of such a broad plane and freely touching on history, sociology, the history of social thought, the history of literature loses sight of its specific object. On the contrary, this may be seen as evidence that literary science is coming closer to its object, which has many forms of connection with the various spheres of social and spiritual life.

Historical and literary synthesis may have various orientations: "horizontal" (characterizing some particular zone in the development of literature or one of its major regional units); "vertical" (characterizing a definite period and based on comparative material from the literatures of a given zone or region); "global" (generalizing the laws of the world literary process). Each of these orientations has its particular tasks and difficulties, but there are also substantial common problems which inevitably face any work of literary criticism of the synthesizing type and can be solved only in works of this type, since the sphere of action of a single national literature is too narrow for them. It is understandable that these problems attract the greatest interest—it is precisely here that the search for optimum solutions of synthesis is concentrated. At the same time, precisely these problems become the object of the sharpest methodological discussions.

One such problem is that of national literature in the system of world literature. Without exaggeration it can be called the key problem—as regards both the methodology of synthesizing works and their very structure (insofar as in such works the type of their structure is itself a solution on the methodological plane).

The object of the present paper is not to polemize against any particular conceptions of the history of world literature or against any practical solutions in the field of its synthetic study.[7] We shall concentrate attention on one question of historical and literary synthesis which, in our view, has not yet been sufficiently elucidated—that of the dialectics of national and regional literary development.

1. First of all, it is necessary to note the gap existing in contemporary science between the practical research into regional cultures (including literature) which has recently been carried out on a broad scale, and the obvious backwardness in elaborating a *theory* of regional literary development in its relationship to national and world development. Such a theory has not yet been produced, and the practical study of the literatures of separate regions may apparently be considered as one of the necessary ways of approaching it.

A fair amount of work has already been done in this practical sphere, i.e., in the various *historical and literary* characterizations of separate aspects of the regional literary process (e.g., the closeness or community of the literary language of one region or another; the community of cultural and properly artistic traditions; the system of development of the genres specific to a given region, and so on). A certain amount of experience has also been accumulated in regional literary characterization, including both positive experience and experience of failure or incomplete success (which may also be of substantial significance in the history of science). All this seems to indicate that we may already pass on to some general theoretical problems of regional development in its relationship to the history of the national literatures, on the one hand and to the world literary process, on the other. One can already speak of the specific features, of regional literary development as one of the substantial factors and at the same time as one of the laws in the history of world literature.

An objective historical and philosophical premise of the possibility of producing a theory of regional literary development is the materialist teaching on the unity of the world historical process and on the general laws governing the development of artistic culture; as well as on the infinite variety of the forms and paths of this development. Regional literary development, as also its profound internal differentiation (zonal, national, and, within the national literature, the differentiation of the various ideological and aesthetic trends) is *one* of the manifestations of this variety.

2. One of the most important problems in the relationship of regional literary development to national and international development is the historical *dynamics* of this relationship. The history of world literature can be imagined as a *moving* map on which profound, many-sided changes are taking place all the time under the influence of both historical causes and processes belonging to the properly literary order.

The very composition of the literatures operating in a given period within a given region is historically fluid.[8] The balance of forces changes within a given region—some literatures have already attained a high level of development, while others are still in the process of formation. There appear symptoms of a kind of literary symbiosis. (For instance the emergence in the Middle Ages of the most interesting phenomenon of Arab-Spanish literature which, accordingly, must be considered as belonging to the region of Arab artistic culture, as well as to the European region. In the most recent period, this literary phenomenon, after substantially influencing the literature of both regions, ceases to exist as an independent whole.)

At definite stages there is *differentiation* of the literatures within the major regional communities. (For instance, Old Slav literature and the subsequent development of the national Slav literatures out of its historically formed system of ideas and art; the Iranian literature of the Middle Ages and the subsequent development of the Persian and Tajik literatures on its basis. It is in this order that we can consider the appearance of new national literatures—Swiss, Belgian, and Austrian on the map of the already highly developed literatures of the European region. These new literatures took shape inside larger literary cultures or at the juncture between them. While naturally retaining firm links with literatures akin to them by language and traditions, these European literatures are already independent national formations.)

With the development of universal links between nations (a process, noted in the *Manifesto of the Communist Party*) there arises in the world literary process *historically new communities of literatures*. In such cases regional links continue to function but now as a factor concomitant to the main trends of development of the new community. On the other hand, these new communities of literatures absorb also literatures which had formerly been developing in a system of different historical and artistic traditions. The formation of that significant phenomenon of socialist artistic culture—the multinational unity of Soviet literature—was one such process. Such were also the historical bases for the emergence, after the formation of the world socialist system, of a new historical community of literatures—the literatures of the socialist world—and also for the development of socialist realism as a phenomenon in international artistic culture.

No regional community of literature remains equal to itself at various stages. It is a community developing in its geographical contours, its composition, its cultural and its historical content.

The historically moving map of world literature registers the changes in the processes within the regions and also the changes in the relationship of a given region to world literature. It shows the changes in the historical function of the literatures of a given region (or of any of the national literatures which that region comprises) in the world literary process (e.g., the role of ancient literature at the various stages in the history of culture; the role of French or Russian literature in the modern European or world history of culture).

The problem of the regional development of literature is thus an historical problem. The concept of an historical and cultural region is not static. In its concrete content, as applied to a given stage in the development of society and its culture, it is inseparable from the concept of the historical and literary period.

3. There is a need also to stress another aspect of regional literary development, namely its *relative historical stability*. In the history of world literature processes of considerable historical duration are linked with this concept. It involves the spiritual activity of the peoples at still relatively early phases of their development, before they have taken shape as nations, when the national literature has not yet branched out as an independent unit in the world literary process with its own national language, when the written literature in the language in question is still in the process of formation. At the same time, regional literary community includes also most important features of similarity in the development of many mature national literatures in modern times. A great tradition in art dating back to centuries is preserved within the limits of the region and the significance of this tradition in the development of the national cultures is enormous.[9] Within the bounds of the regions there is the possibility for fruitful study of the most important artistic trends and currents (which can be studied both in their variety and in their resemblance within the world literary process only by the comparative method).

Among the "distinctive marks" of regional development which demand comparative study, we may mention the breadth and stability of links within the region. They operate along the main lines on the development of the literatures in a given region, enrich the literatures of that region, and, at the same time, promote the creation and strengthening of the region's own type of artistic culture. (Among European conditions such links may be illustrated by their significance in romantic literature and by the development of the realistic novel.)

Thus, a characteristic of the regional literary process is the dialectics of stability, tradition, of a definite *type* of literary development and the uninterrupted *development* of that type.

4. How, then, does an historically fluid system function, in which the main elements are—national, regional, and world literature (*main* elements, since the regional literary whole has its internal differentiations)? What links exist between these elements?

A national literature does not enter into the general movement of world literature "on its own". Its place on the map of world literature is side by side with other literatures close to it by their history and artistic traditions and to which it is linked by many "valencies"—ethical, geographical, linguistic, community of folklore heritage or the heritage of the classical period of written literature, the historical community of the peoples. These historically more closely linked groups of literatures, as it were, form within the bounds of a large historical and cultural region zones of literary development within the region. (For instance, in the European region we clearly distinguish the zonal features of the West European, Slav, Central and South European, and Scandinavian literatures.)

There are various and multiform factors determining the zonal closeness of literatures (e.g. West European and Slav), and, as a rule, they operate in every case in their aggregate, one of them, however, being basic in a given historical situation, the others, as it were, concomitant. Thus, at the early stage the predominance went to factors of ethnic, geographic and linguistic closeness, whereas at later stages closeness of the peoples' social and political development played an increasing role. (This same law was observed also in regional development.) The degree of internal closeness of literatures within a given zone also varied with the different periods.

It should also be noted that zonal literary development is not seclusive, the literature of the different zones are linked with each other by highly diverse threads. In the process of historical development these links grow increasingly wider and more intensive.

Attention to this zonal specific really existing in regional literary development is extremely important in a comparative study which aims not at collating separate facts isolated from their general historical context, but at studying the *processes* of world literature. The comparative study of the literatures within a given zone (taking into account the historical fluidity of zonal community itself and of links of the literatures in a given zone with other literatures outside it), as well as subsequent comparison of the literary process in various zones of a given region allow us to establish certain common tendencies characteristic of that zone, and also some equally characteristic exclusions.

Within the literary zones we observe with especial clearness such phenomena in the dialectics of the national and the more general as the following:

The presence in a large, complex regional whole of various *artistic systems* (or types of literary development) taking shape in a given zonal group of literatures. For example, a special type of development of romanticism in the literatures of Central and Southeast Europe and the Balkans, which, by virtue of a specific historical development, constitutes, as it were, a symbiosis of elements of Enlightenment and romanticism. At the same time, here too, as a result of the general tendencies in the regional literary process and of the non-seclusiveness of zonal development, there appear such manifestations of a general regional type of romanticism as Petar II Petrovih Negosh's *Lucha mikro-kozma* (The Ray of the Microcosm) or Petőfi's *Az apostol* (The Apostle).

We observe that the role of literature in social development varies from zone to zone, always in connection with the varying historical conditions.

Within zonal development especially close links between separate literatures are observable—links of synchronically developing literary processes and also use of common cultural sources. At the same time we must take into account the sometimes firm links which each of the literatures has outside the given zone (e.g., the links between the Russian and the French; the Hungarian and Italian literatures). The role of such binary links both in the national literatures themselves, and in regional and world literature is also quite significant.

When speaking of the zonal differentiation of the process within a large region, we must not overlook the fact that in certain historic periods, some literatures, which formerly developed within the bounds of a definite zone, "fall out," as it were, of that type of development as a result of a change in the historical situation. For instance, Italian literature, which developed in the epoch of the Renaissance as a classical West European type of literature, in the nineteenth century drew closer in many ways to the literatures of Central and Southeast Europe, as regards the very type of its development. There has been little research into the development of Spanish literature (in the general European context) in the nineteenth century.

There can be no doubt about the substantial successes scored in the past two decades by the historical and literary study of zonal specifics.[10] Nevertheless, on the theoretical plane there has been insufficient elaboration of questions concerning zonal development and its relationship both to the national and, on the other hand, to the zonal and the world literary process. In the approach to this problem it is important to stress that it is a question not of establishing *separate* features of resemblance between literatures, but of discovering, as has already been said, the *artistic system* which is characteristic of the given group of literatures and which has taken shape as one of the variants of regional literary development (which, in similar historical conditions, can have typological parallels in other regions). It is a question of determining that system's links with the historical and cultural traditions of the given group of literatures and broader traditions; as well as of elucidating how that system is connected with the contemporary tasks in the spiritual life of the peoples.

The study of the big regional literary processes (European, Latin American, Far Eastern, Near Eastern) leads to the conviction that there are *objective grounds* for grouping the European literatures (in a work such as the *History of World Literature*) according to the historical zones of their development, or—to speak a language closer to the very nature of art—according to the historically determined similarity of their artistic system, in order to provide more historic grounds for comparative analysis.

Elucidation of the specifics of zonal development (just as, on another "level" of comparative analysis,[11] elucidation of the national specifics) provides the researcher with historically more reliable aesthetic criteria for comparison, with the main object of understanding the correlation between the general and the particular in a given literary process. It helps free the comparative aspect of the study of world literature from contra-indicated appraisement (for example, whether the estimation of the whole depends on the greater or lesser degree of development of some artistic element in the literature of one zone or another—e.g., of the folklore element in the Slav, Central and South European literatures in modern times as compared with the West European literatures).

5. What specific possibilities, then, does the regional (and within it the zonal) aspect offer for understanding both national and world literary processes?

First of all, we are provided with a broad field for the comparative study of synchronic (within a definite period) literary processes. This allows us to discover both historically similar and nationally different variants of literary trends, tendencies and genres. (For example: types of the development of romanticism and realism in the European literary process of the nineteenth century or the development in its separate zones; the development in the European literatures of the novel genre in all the varieties of its historical and national types and genre forms; the emergence and development of the literature of socialist realism in all the wealth of national originality of this phenomenon in the artistic culture of the world.)

The data received from such a comparative analysis (on a regional scale) are of considerable importance, both for research into a national literature and for understanding the more general processes.

On the one hand, we can elucidate what in a given *national* "variant" of this phenomenon (trend, current, genre) is specific from the viewpoint of its real content and artistic form. Without comparison the specific cannot be revealed: attempts to reveal it within the bounds of a seclusive national study end either in positivistic descriptiveness or in predominance of statement over analysis. As for the regional (or narrower-zonal) context, it creates that feeling of historical space and perspective that is indispensable for understanding a given phenomenon in its multiformity.

On the other hand, the data received by a regional comparative analysis are necessary to understand the *general* laws governing the emergence and development of one aesthetic phenomenon or another in order to understand its *deep-down* aesthetic essence (and consequently the historical necessity of precisely that aesthetic solution). General regional characteristics are necessary as a basis for studying such cardinal problems in the history of world literature as the progressing development of human artistic awareness; the historical continuity of this development; its dialectics of tradition and innovation; the socio-ideological and aesthetic differentiation of literature on national and also broader scales.

6. The regional aspect allows a more accurate definition of the initial and final boundaries of main literary trends. This allows us to see at what stage of their development this or that literature joins them. The problems of periodization of national literatures thus fuses with the problems of periodization of zonal (where it is historically justified), regional and world literature. In tracing the historical sequence in which the literatures of a given region join a new aesthetic "system," we often enough reveal far greater significance in the literary process of the so-called "small" literatures than was assumed, owing to their having been insufficiently studied. On the other hand, there is a widening of our idea of the general chronological and geographical bounds of a given trend (which formerly seemed limited to the chronology and "geography" of separate literatures which had been the object of greater

study)—and this is of substantial importance for elucidating general processes in the development of world literature.

In the subsequent comparative study of interregional literary processes[12] we are enabled to see both the unequal ways of the artistic development of the world and also its increasing synchronization in modern conditions.

The regional approach opens up many possibilities also for understanding the social bases of the dynamics of literary development. In analysing on the comparative plane, the links of aesthetic phenomena with the social and historical processes, we see that what could often enough appear, in the narrow limits of one literature or the creative destiny of one writer, to be peculiar to one national or individual path, widens out into a general law of artistic development, inherent in the given stage in history (this is precisely what the well-known nineteenth century Finnish man of letters Snellman had in mind when he said that the Chartist literature was a phenomenon on the international type). Quite characteristic material in this respect is offered by a broad comparative examination (in the world, regional and zonal aspects) of the main streams of the modern literary processes.[13]

*

It is necessary to dwell on one of the serious difficulties attendant upon research into regional (and to a far greater degree zonal) processes. In conditions of constant contacts between literatures (not only in modern times, when the breadth and significance of these contacts become one of the obvious and most important factors of international literary development, but even in far more remote periods),[14] situations of a "purely" typological order not complicated by multiform possible influences, although frequently encountered in the real literary process, must be verified with special care. Otherwise, what in reality is a case of purely typological similarity, may, given a certain concurrence of facts, appear as the result of direct or mediated contacts. And conversely, the enormous role played by international cultural links in the process of the spiritual, including the artistic, development of humanity, may be diminished without any justification if the typological aspect hides from the researcher the picture of a real, highly complicated literary process and leads to the construction—artificial as regards the history of culture—of "parallel orders."

But precisely what is a serious difficulty in the study of a regional (or zonal) literary process gives us the most fruitful results. Precisely because within these cultural and historical bounds the intertwining of typological and contact links is so close, a given (regional or zonal) field of research presents one of the best natural laboratories for studying the live literary process in the real dialectics of its *general* laws (expressed in typologically similar processes) and the unique specific of a national literature's development (revealed to the world through the mediacy of contacts between artistic cultures of different nations).

Nevertheless, still one circumstance must be mentioned which is of fundamental significance both for methodology and for the method of comparative study of wide multinational literary processes. The path from regional characterizations to synthesis on the scale of world literature cannot be that of simply multiplying the results obtained. It is the path of a new stage in comparative analysis, the path of its new "level," this time *interregional*. Precisely on this level it is possible to elaborate and define more precisely the conceptual and terminological universals which are so important for philology.

Naturally, there are various possible alternatives in solving these or those problems in literary synthesis, whether on the scale of zonal, regional, or world development. But at the same time there are definite "conditions" imposed by the very object of research, without the fulfilment of which there can hardly be any objective scientific synthesis. One of them is to take into account the *dialectics* of national and international factors in literary development.

The general processes and problems cannot be fruitfully studied without taking into account their real national expression, since artistic culture does not exist outside its national embodiment. This specific of the object of research must necessarily be taken into account also in the higher, synthesizing stage of its study. On the other hand, and this is no less important, national processes cannot be understood if they are studied in seclusion.

It is important that in any case the choice of the work's structure, the selection of the material, the determination of its proportions and other correlations should be carried out proceeding from the premise that in historical and literary synthesis the conception of the national specific must not disappear, be dissolved in bigger zonal, regional, or world formations. Unacceptable to the Marxist student of literature is the idea of "supernational" literature. Just as the national is not exclusive, but is only part of the general history of humanity, so also the world literary process is not "supernational," but is manifested in the development of the national literatures, in their mutual links and interaction.

It is precisely by means of comparative analysis on various levels that history and theory of literature are able to approach the study of the complex, historically developing system of links between national literature and the world's literary process.

Notes

[Editors' note: Texts in Cyrillic in the original have been transliterated.]

1   D.S. Lihachev, "Drevneslavjanskie literatury kak sistema" [Old Slavic Literature as a System], *Slavjanskie literatury VI. Meždunar. s'ezd slavistov* (Moscow: Nauka 1968) 5–48; A.H. Robinson, "Literatura Kievskoj Rusi sredi evropejskih srednevekovyh literatur (tipologija, original'nost', metod)" [Kievan-Russian Literature among European Medieval Literatures (Typology, Originality and Technique)], *Slavjanskie literatury VI. Meždunar. s'ezd slavistov* (Moscow: Nauka, 1968) 49–116.

2   S.V. Nikol'skij, A.N. and B.F. Staheev, *O romantizme v slavjanskih literaturah* [Romanticism in Slavic Literatures] (Moscow: Izdatel'stvo AN SSSR, 1958); E.I. Georgiev, *Obshho i sravnitelno slavjansko literaturozvanie* [General and Comparative Slavonic Literary Theory] (Sofia: Nauka and izkustvo, 1965).

3   D.F. Markov, *Genezis socialisticheskogo realizma. Iz opyta juzhnoslavjanskih i zapadnoslavjanskih literatur* [Genesis of Socialist Realism from the Experience of South and West Slavic Literatures] (Moscow: Nauka, 1970).

4   G.I. Lomidze, *Istorija sovetskoj mnogonacional'noj literatury* [History of the Soviet Multinational Literature], vols. 1–2 (Moscow: Nauka, 1970–71); and *Internacional'nyj pafos sovetskoj literatury* [The International Pathos of Soviet Literature] (Moscow: Sovetskij pisatel', 1970.)

5   P. Henríquez Ureña, *Las corrientes literarias en la América hispana* (México: Fondo de Cultura Económica, 1954); W. Crawford, *A Century of Latin-American Thought* (Cambridge; MA: Harvard University Press, 1961); L. Harss, *Into the Main Stream* (London: Harper & Row, 1967); J. Franco, *The Modern Culture of Latin America: Society and the Artist* (New York: Frederick A. Praeger, 1967); Institut mirovoj literatury imeni A.M. Gor'kogo, *Formirovanie nacional'nyh literatur Latinskoj Ameriki* [The Formation of National Literatures of Latin America] (Moscow: Nauka, 1970).

6   D. Nagendra, ed., *Indian Literature* (Agra: Lakshmi Narain Agarwal, 1959); Prabhakar Mathve, *Bharat aur Ashia ka sahitya* (Aimar: Times Printing Press, 1967).

7   Here we do not touch on the differences between the methodological approaches to historical and literary synthesis which are especially apparent in works on the history of world literature. On this subject see I.I. Anisimov, I.G. Neupokoyeva and I.A. Terterian, *Sovremennye burzhuaznye koncepcii istorii vsemirnoj literatury* [Modern Bourgeois Conceptions of the History of World Literature] (Moscow: Nauka, 1967). On the methodological principles for the structure of a History of World Literature, on which Soviet scholars are working now, see I.G. Neupokoyeva, "Metodologicheskie voprosy postroenija 'Istorii vsemirnoj literatury'" [Methodological Issues for the Elaboration of a "History of World Literature"] *Vestnik Akademii nauk SSSR* 7 (1965); I.G. Neupokoyeva, "The Comparative Aspects in the 'History of World Literature'," *Proceedings of the Fifth Congress of International Comparative Literature Association*, ed. Nikola Banaševic (Amsterdam: Swets and Zeitlinger, 1969) 37–43.

8   N.I. Konrad, *West-East. The Inseparable Twins* (Moscow: Nauka, 1967).

9   One such tradition common to the European literatures is traced by E.R. Curtius in *European Literature and the Latin Middle Ages*, trans. W.R. Trask (Princeton: Princeton University Press, 1953).

10   Abundant material on this subject is provided by the International Slavistic Congresses. See also the documents of the Budapest Conference of scientists of the socialist countries on the comparative study of literature in the special issue of the *Acta Litteraria Academiae Scientiarum Hungaricae* 5 (1962).

11   A most fruitful setting of the problem of the various tasks and, accordingly, methods of comparative study is given by M.B. Hrapchenko. There are various "levels", as it is agreed to call them today, of typological study. Besides the typology of literary trends, the typology of genres is also of great significance. For a long time, especially in art criticism, there has been intense development of the typology of style. Of extreme interest and great importance is the typology of historical literary development—the elucidation of species, types, in the literary process of the different historical periods among the peoples of different countries. For example, the typology of literary trends naturally touches upon questions concerning not only their species, how they appeared in the history of world literature, but also the types, say, of romanticism or realism, including the national types of these literary trends. See M.B. Hrapchenko, *Tvorcheskaja individual'nost' pisatelja i razvitie literatury* [The Creative Personality of the Writer and the Development of Literature] (Moscow: Sovetskij pisatel', 1970) 257. See also M.B. Hrapchenko, "Typologische Literaturforschung und ihre Prinzipien," *Aktuelle Probleme der vergleichenden Literaturforschung*, eds. G. Ziegengeist and L. Richter (Berlin: Akademie, 1968) 7–25.

12   A considerable contribution to this field of comparative research has been made by the well-known Soviet scholars N.I. Konrad and V.M. Zhirmunsky.

13   B. Suchkov, *Istoricheskie sud'by realizma* [The Historical Fate of Realism] (Moscow: Sovetskij pisatel', 1970); French translation: *Les destinées historiques du réalisme* (Moscow: Edition du Progrès, 1971).

14   See, for example, P.A. Grinker, *Tipologija i vzaimosvjazi literatur drevnego mira* [Typology and Interliterary Relationships in the Ancient World] (Moscow: Nauka, 1971).

Chapter 14

George Steiner

A FOOTNOTE TO *WELTLITERATUR* (1979)

G EORGE STEINER (B. 1929) IS A French-born scholar and translator of Jewish-Austrian decent, and naturalized American citizen, who has held positions at the universities of Geneva, Cambridge and Oxford and at Harvard University. His publications cover an extraordinarily wide range of topics and authorships from classical to modern literature. Problems of metaphysics, translation and the aftermath of the Holocaust are among the central issues of his work. A pessimist about changes in culture and the loss of literacy in its widest sense, Steiner has repeatedly made the case for the expressions and experiences which only art and literature can bring about.

His most extensive work on translation, *After Babel*, considerably broadens the definition of translation and argues that translation is a fundamental process of communication that also applies to reading texts from one's first language. Even if Steiner's thesis is controversial, it has at least partially been responsible for the increased attention drawn to translation in world literature studies by such scholars as Susan Bassnett and Emily Apter.

In "A Footnote to *Weltliteratur*," Steiner demonstrates how important translation was to Goethe throughout his life and reveals the sophistication of Goethe's theory of translation, which balances between a number of influences, from the original's demand to be authentically represented and the limits set by the literary culture on the other. Even more importantly, Steiner interprets Goethe's use of the term *Weltliteratur* to designate the interrelation of all of the world's literature, which is more than just the sum total of diverse literatures. He notes that these interrelations are not given, but need to be nurtured.

Steiner also focuses attention on Goethe's cultural situation and describes the paradoxical time at which he introduced the term *Weltliteratur*. On the one hand, there was a rise in the scholarly understanding of particularly Middle and Far Eastern languages and culture; on the other hand, nationalism was beginning to dominate the cultural organization of Europe. If a parallel to our time can be drawn, a ground for optimism might be the contemporary prevalence of Goethe's cosmopolitan stance, which has had a much more enduring influence than that of any inward-looking author or intellectual.

George Steiner, "A Footnote to Weltliteratur," *Le Mythe d'Étiemble*, Paris: Didier, 1979, pp. 261–69.

The facts are known, but worth recalling. Goethe translates from eighteen languages: French, Italian, German, Serbo-Croatian (which he calls *das Morlakische*), an Indian language from Brasil (for which he finds a source in Montaigne), Greek, Latin, Finnish, Sicilian, Old Irish, Old Czech *(Altbömisch)*, modern Greek (which he designates as *Neugriechisch-epirotisch*), classical Arabic, Dutch, Gaelic, classical Chinese, Hebrew, Persian. In a number of cases, to be sure, his translations are made at second hand: when translating a Finnish text, Goethe uses the French version of a Swedish 'original'; the source of his Old Irish is a dubious imitation in Caroline Lamb's novel *Glenarvon* (1817); Goethe's Arabic derives from a Spanish version of 1822 and a preceding 'translation' made by Herder in 1779; his Dutch and Gaelic texts are taken from English adaptations; Goethe's resplendent version of the Song of Songs, composed in 1775, is based on the Vulgate and on Luther; the *Divan*, of course, draws extensively on Josef Hammer's adaptations from the Persian published seven years before, in 1812. Nevertheless, the range of linguistic-literary awareness and active involvement is formidable.

So, also, is the relevant time-span. Goethe starts translating in 1757—a fragment from Lipsius. He is still translating in 1830 when scrutinizing the pages on himself in Carlyle's short biography of Schiller. In other words, his activity as a translator covers seventy-three years. The range and diversity of material are vast. Roughly one third comprises verse, two-thirds prose. The young universalist and self-educator begins by translating Latin texts in January 1757; one year later, he is translating from Greek; in the period from 1765 to 1767, he is writing more or less fluent letters in French and English and making efforts to write passably in Italian. He sets himself frequent exercises in multi-lingual translation from a political journal published in Latin in Leipzig until 1786. But it is around the turn of the century that Goethe's performance as a translator is most intense. He works on his version of Cellini's autobiography from 1796 to 1803. The famous translation of Diderot's *Le Neveu de Rameau* occupies Goethe from December 1804 to January 1805 (it will itself be re-translated into French in 1821). Voltaire's *Mahomet* and *Tancrède* are translated for the Weimar stage in 1799 and 1800. To this should be added the translation of significant fragments from Corneille's *Le Menteur* and Racine's *Athalie*. But there is scarcely a year in Goethe's active life without some translation (note the turn towards Czech in the Marienbad summer of 1822).

"He who is ignorant of foreign languages", says Goethe—and observe the plural— "knows nothing of his own". He will reiterate this axiom and the assertion that French is to him a second native tongue *(eine zweite Muttersprache)* at numerous points in his writings: notably in *Dichtung und Wahrheit*, in the lines *Zum Brüderlichen Andenken Wielands*, in the notes to the *West-Östlicher Divan*, and in various contributions to *Kunst und Ältertum*. It is there that he publishes a statement at once central to his work and exemplified throughout it:

> Wer die deutsche Sprache versteht und studiert, befindet sich auf dem Markte, wo alle Nationen ihre Waren anbieten; er spielt den Dolmetscher, indem er sich selbst bereichert. Und so ist jeder Uebersetzer anzusehen, dass er sich als Vermittler dieses allgemein-geistigen Handels bemüht und den Wechseltausch zu befördern sich zum Geschäft macht. Denn was man auch von der Unzulänglichkeit des Uebersetzens sagen mag, so ist und bleibt es doch eines der wichtigsten und würdigsten Geschäfte in dem allgemeinen Weltverkehr.

> [Whoever understands and studies the German language finds himself on the market on which all nations peddle their wares; he plays the role of interpreter while at the same time enriching himself. And so it is obvious that every translator acts as go-between in this general trade of culture and makes it his business to promote this general exchange. Because whatever one may say about the insufficiency of translation, it is and remains one of the most important and honorable activities in the world's traffic.]

The idiom is unmistakable: *Markte, Waren anbieten, bereichert, Handels, Wechseltausch* and *Geschäft* belong to the world of free mercantile exchange (as does *Dolmetscher*, which here signifies a commercial interpreter, a *truchement*, rather than a literary translator). By virtue of this utilitarian, positivist vocabulary, Goethe is specifically countering the monoglot mystique of the German-language cult as it arises from Hamann and Herder and assumes chauvinist virulence after 1813.

The excursus on translation in the ancillary material to the *Divan* is couched in an altogether different style. Though the secondary literature devoted to Goethe's translations and involvement with foreign writers is substantial, this text of 1819 seems to me to remain highly problematical[1].

It follows the tripartite organisation which almost all theoretical discourse on translation has exhibited since Cicero and Quintilian. But whereas virtually all discussions of the various principal modes of translation are synchronic—they discriminate between three different levels or ideals of the craft—Goethe adopts a chronological, almost Hegelian scheme. He postulates that all mature cultures will witness three successive stages of translation (perhaps one ought, instead of 'cultures', to use the term 'literate communities', for this, plainly, is Goethe's underlying concept).

The initial stage is one of didactic appropriation. Using a *schlicht-prosaisch* idiom, the translator 'surprises us' by introducing into our 'national domesticity' *(in unsere nationale Häuslichkeit)* that which is of particular distinction or virtue from abroad *(des fremden Vortrefflichen)*. This importation into our native 'homeliness' has a direct impact on sensibility. It elevates our mood, it literally 'edifies' us *(und erbaut uns indem sie uns eine höhere Stimmung verleiht)*. This description is odd enough; it implies, logically, that literate communities evolve at different speeds, that there are always somewhere sources of foreign excellence more advanced than is our home ground. But it is made even odder by the example which Goethe adduces: Luther's translations from scripture. Now there can be no doubt as to the profoundly educative and edifying function of these translations in the development of German speech and sentiment. But one cannot argue that Luther's Bible is representative of some rudimentary form of translation or that its style is *schlicht-prosaisch*. Like the Authorized Version of the Bible in English, Luther's work represents a highly intricate amalgam of personal idiosyncracy, of radical invention, and of baroque emphasis. Goethe knew this, of course; hence the opaqueness of his reference.

The second phase is one in which "man sich in die Zustände des Auslandes zwar zu versetzen, aber eigentlich nur fremden Sinn sich anzueignen und mit eigenem Sinn wieder darzustellen bemüht ist." Again, the formulation is cryptic. Some kind of primal but unelucidated dichotomy between 'form' and 'sense' is operative. The translator seeks to situate himself amid the ambience of the foreign culture. Yet he achieves this transference solely in order to appropriate to himself the 'alien sense' *(fremden Sinn)*. He will then represent this sense in native guise. The distinction in regard to the first phase seems to be this: the initial mode of translation is one of direct import, with a view to enriching and edifying the native stock. There is 'surprise' and self-educative acceptance. In the second phase there is metamorphosis or creative echo (of the kind Dryden understands by *paraphrase*). The aim would be that already enunciated by Quintilian and St. Jerome: the translation represents an operative fiction whereby the original author has been induced to, has been conceived to be, writing in our own tongue.

Usually such re-creative parallelism is regarded as an exacting ideal and benefit. But Goethe's gloss on this second phase is markedly ambivalent. The appropriation and transformative re-production of sense of which he speaks is a business at which the French excel *(ein Geschäft zu dem Franzosen besonders berufen sind)*. There is no mistaking the pejorative inflection of the comment. This inflection is given stress by the example which Goethe cites: that of the copious translations of l'abbé Delille. Now as we know, Goethe was familiar with Delille's translations, notably his Virgil, but did not admire them. Goethe elucidates further: once the alien sense has been apprehended and brought home, a process of substitution must come about. For each foreign fruit, a surrogate is called for *(wirt ein Surrogate gefordert)* "das auf seinem eignen Grund und Boden gewachsen ist" (which is grown from its own soil and land). The notion of 'surrogate' carries a taint of artifice, of not altogether legitimate *Ersatz*. Goethe seems to underline this connotation when he says that the type of 'surrogate' he has in mind was achieved most particularly by Wieland. The latter found "seine Konvenienz" in classical and in foreign literatures. The phrase is scarcely translatable—'took his ease', 'found his advantage', 'took what was convenient for him'?—but its irony, its negativity are indubitable. The expression is the more puzzling when we recall how often and how warmly Goethe had praised Wieland's translations of Horace, of Cicero, of Cervantes, of Shakespeare and of Richardson, and how crucial he deemed these translations to have been to the enlightenment of German consciousness (a sentiment eloquently voiced in the *In memoriam* to Wieland). Why this thinly-veiled critique, why this identification of the major period in German literary translation with a suspect French precedent and the notion of impure substitution?

The third stage is both summit and finality *(welche der höchste und letzte zu nennen ist)*. In it, the translation is to be made identical with the original: "so dass eins nicht anstatt des andern, sondern an der Stelle des andern gelten soll." Just what does Goethe intend by this gnomic contrast? The crux is *anstatt;* and it is precisely this riddling use which Grimm cites in the *Wörterbuch* in order to instance an eccentric contrastive locution (Goethe's usage, he observes, is not *Sprachüblich*). In earlier German, moreover, *anstatt* frequently carries an adversative value. If we relate Goethe's sentence to the second rubric in his threefold historicist model, we get something like this: 'in the highest, final stage of translation, the translator creates a work which is both identical with the original yet also autonomous; this paradox of integral homology means that we do not, in our own native literature, have a surrogate for the foreign source, but a perfectly equivalent construct.' Such a phenomenology of 'independent identity' is difficult enough to grasp; but Goethe complicates matters further. In this third 'epoch', the translator renounces the 'originality' of his own nation: "Der Uebersetzer gibt mehr oder weniger die Originalität seiner Nation auf." The product of this renunciation is a *tertium datur* ("es ensteht eine dritte Art") towards which public taste will have to be gradually oriented and elevated. (In this complex of suggestions would seem to lodge one of the sources for Walter Benjamin's reflections on the occult 'third term' latent in all linguistic transfer from one language to another. It is the hermetic in Goethe which so often draws Benjamin.) In this highest moment, continues Goethe, Ariosto, Tasso, Shakespeare and Calderon become 'germanized aliens', *eingedeutschte Fremde*. (We are only a short step from Rudolf Borchardt's *Dante deutsch*.) The one concrete example Goethe offers of this climactic naturalization is "the never to be sufficiently esteemed" Voss.

Goethe's scheme is Delphic in its concision and elusiveness. One is confident neither of following its general argument nor of interpreting rightly the very private tactics which seem to generate Goethe's use of examples. Does he really mean to say that Wieland's Shakespeare is a case of exploitative or self-serving substitution? Would he really have us believe that Voss's Homer, inspired as it doubtless is, can be put 'in the place of' the original? There is no straightforward answer to these questions, and Goethe's own view of the role of 'translation' in the *West-Ostlicher Divan* obviously shaped and complicated his argument on translation as a whole. But there may be a way in which we can come nearer to grasping what he meant by the third and highest ideal of autonomous equivalence, of re-created identity. (Ought we to look to his crystalographic writings for an example of a perfectly translucent yet also integral, organic structure?) Though he cites only Voss, it is almost certain that he has his own practices and aims in mind, particularly when he adds that such practices and aims are not readily accessible to the *Geschmack der Menge* (taste of the masses). If there is a text which concretely exemplifies the ideal paradox of a translation which stands "nicht anstatt . . . sondern an der Stelle" of a great original, it is Goethe's *Nachdichtung* (literally *re-composition*) of Manzoni's *Il Cinque Maggio*.

Manzoni wrote his sovereign ode shortly after Napoleon's death, in July 1821; Goethe translated it in January 1822 and published it the following year in the fourth issue of *Über Kunst und Ältertum*. Any close study of the relationship between the Italian original and the German version lies entirely outside the scope of this note[2]. But a few obvious points can be made in reference to Goethe's enigmatic model of independent identity.

Goethe does not attempt a counterpart to Manzoni's rhymes. But wherever possible, he seeks equivalence in line-units, number of syllables and phrasing. The whole opening stanza, and its closing verse in particular, illustrates the fidelity of Goethe's rendition:

> Ei fu. Siecome immobile,
> dato il mortal sospiro,
> stette la spoglia immemore
> orba di tanto spiro,
> cosi percossa, attonita
> la terra al nunzio sta,
>
> Er war—und, wie, bewegungslos
> Nach letztem Hauche-Seufzer,
> Die Hülle lag, uneingedenk,
> Verwaist von solchem Geiste;
> So tief gretroffen, starr erstaunt
> Die Erde steht der Botschaft.

If Goethe alters the *enjambement* which leads, dynamically, to the second stanza, it is probably because the lapidariness and 'strangeness' of the German phrase demanded finality. Often, Goethe is able to preserve Manzoni's word-order:

> oh! quante volte, al tacito
> morir d'un giorno inerte,
> chinati i rai fulminei,
> le braccia al sen conserte,
> stette, e dei dì che furono
> l'assalse il sovvenir!

The reading of *rai fulminei* is masterful: Goethe conveys in *blitzenden Augenstrahl* both pertinent inferences: the Emperor's lightning-glance and the imperial sun. And if he misses the concrete Napoleonic gesture in *al sen*, Goethe's *bestürmt* is inspired in that it exactly mirrors the military implications of *l'assalse*:

> O! wie so oft beym schweigsamen
> Sterben des Tags, des leeren,
> Gesenkt den blitzenden Augenstrahl,
> Die Arme übergefaltet,
> Stand er, von Tagen vergangenen
> Bestürmt ihn die Erinn'rung.

Here, truly, is enacted that resolve to make "die Uebersetzung dem Original identisch" (the translation identical to the original). But this translation also instances most graphically the translator's necessary abandonment of the proper or natural spirit of his native tongue:

> e l'avviò, pei floridi
> sentier della speranza,
> ai campi eterni, al premio
> che i desideri avanza,
> dov'è silenzio e tenebre
> la gloria che passò.

> Und leitet ihn auf blühende
> Fusspfade die hoffnungsreichen,
> Zu ewigen Feldern, zum höchsten Lohn
> Der alle Begierden beschämet;
> Er sieht, wie auf Schweigen und Finsterniss.
> Auf den Ruhm den er durchdrungen.

Even if we take into account the wish to reproduce the echo of Dante in *che i desideri avanza*, and the metrical grounds for the elision of the article before *ewigen Feldern*, the sense of a drastic and willed strangeness remains. It is heightened, moreover, by the decision to put *die hoffnungsreichen* in apposition, though there is no warrant for this construction in the banal genitive of the original. The effect comes close to that of the parataxic translations made by Hölderlin (and, at the time, so brusquely denied by Goethe himself). In *Der fünfte May*, "ensteht eine dritte Art", a metamorphic, intermediary form of idiom. It may make of Manzoni an "eingedeuchtscher Fremde", but it also makes of Goethe's German an alien energy, an experiment conducted against the native grain. But because it emerges as a major poem, Goethe's ode seems indeed to accomplish the paradox of being a counter-presence and not a surrogate.

It is from his life-long activity as a translator and from his vision of the German language and of German literature as a mediator between and especial host to foreign genius, that Goethe's coinage of *Weltliteratur* derives its significance. The term occurs twenty-one times in Goethe's writings and recorded conversations. We find it for the first time in a diary entry for January 15th 1827. It is used almost immediately thereafter in the sixth instalment of *Über Kunst und Ältertum*. It is used in a well-known passage from the 1830 preface to Carlyle's *Leben Schillers*. The last occasion on which we come across it is in a letter from Goethe to Boisserée dated 24th April 1831 (a letter of considerable importance to our entire theme as in it Goethe discusses his intention to translate something of his own work into French as a pattern for future translators).

Weltliteratur is, therefore, a turn of phrase which is to be found only in the very last phase of Goethe's thought and activities. It is not to be confused with earlier uses of *Weltpoesie*, a characteristically romantic expression—we find close analogues to it in both Herder and Humboldt—signifying the universal human faculty for verbal invention, the ubiquity of *poiesis* in man. *Weltliteratur* does not carry psychological, organicist overtones. It designates a programmatic view of all literatures as relevant to man's understanding of his history and civil condition, and of all literatures as potentially interrelated (most notably via reciprocal study and translation). It is a concept embryonic in Montesquieu's and Leibniz's sense of the likely importance of 'exotic' civilizations and their written documents, and fully implicit in the taxonomic universalism of the *encyclopédistes* of the Enlightenment. If it carries a particular intensity in Goethe's usage, that intensity is moral-political. By the late 1820s, the ageing and partially isolated Olympian had a vivid apprehension of the new forces of nationalism, of militant chauvinism which were gathering in Europe and notably in Germany. He knew and feared the pan-Teutonic verbiage and symbolism which he observed in the German youth movements and in the archaicizing fervour of the new German philology and historiography. (To a degree which has not yet been assessed with adequate precision, it is such semi-conscious intimations which may have been involved in Goethe's repudiations of Kleist and even of Hölderlin.) Thus, while being a new term, and one which Goethe only launches at the close of his career, *Weltliteratur*, in fact, embodies ideals and categories of sensibility which belong to the universalist civilities, to the 'trans-national' freemasonry of enlightened spirits characteristic of high culture in the eighteenth century. The paradox is worth under-lining: technically, Goethe's programme for the awareness of *Weltliteratur* hinges on those philological and ethnographic advances, particularly in regard to Sanskrit, to Chinese, to Arabic, which mark the beginnings of modern scholarship in the early nineteenth century. But the politics, the moral tone implicit in *Weltliteratur* are decisively 'reactionary', in that they seek to counter the new nationalism by appealing to an eighteenth-century mundanity (the root of the word is, of course, that of the interplay between 'world' and 'worldliness').

But although the actual term *Weltliteratur* comes very late in Goethe's vocabulary, the practices which it entails had marked his whole performance. Even an incomplete listing of Goethe's writings on foreign literature and on the interactions between literatures amounts to a unique achievement in what the later nineteenth century was to call *littérature générale* and which we now know as 'comparative literature'[3]. As early as February 1776, Goethe composed a *Diesseitige Antwort auf Bürgers Anfrage Wegen Uebersetzung des Homers im 'Teutschen Merkur'*. Such inquiries into translation and understanding (witness the pioneering *Versuch, eine Homerische Dunkle Stelle zu Erklären* of June 1787) were to accompany Goethe's produc-tion to the very last.

The range is awesome. The investigation of classical authors in the light of modern schol-arly and critical practices leads Goethe to comment on Plato, to discuss translations of Lucretius, to write on Euripides, on Aristotle's *Poetics*, on Benjamin Constant's views on Homer, on Roman poetry (whose domestic and satiric modes so deeply influenced his own). Goethe studies St. Augustine—a master predecessor in the arts of self-revelation. He writes about Saxo-Grammaticus' Amlet and his possible relations to the Shakespearean figure. Shakespeare is a constant concern, a pervasiveness embodied in the title of the 1815 paper on *Shakespeare und kein Ende*. Goethe turns to Dante, to Manzoni, to Spanish drama and romances in order to elucidate the meaning of 'romantic', in order to trace the underlying fibres of continuity between the 'romanic' and 'the romantic'. These considerations, in turn, lead him to the attempt to define the 'Nordic', the anti-Mediterranean elements in the spurious prim-itivism of Ossian and in the authentic particularities of Byron and Sir Walter Scott (two titular presences in his sense of his own stature and location in modern letters). Hence also Goethe's study of and commentary on Campbell's *Lectures on Poetry* of 1821.

In the years from 1817 to 1828, Goethe directed much of his attention to Indian, Chinese, Arabic and Persian verse and prose. He toyed with various projects intended to increase the acquaintance of the European literate community with these great extraterrito-rial literatures. But he also looked nearer home: to Néroulos's *Cours de littérature grecque moderne*, to Old Lithuanian and its folk-songs, to Serbo-Croatian ballads, to popular poetry in *niederösterreichischer Mundart* (Goethe had an amateur interest in dialect-literature), to Laurence Sterne whose wayward genius fascinated him. He kept a magisterial eye on foreign versions of his writings (as in his considerations on Stapfer's French translation of *Faust* with illustrations by Delacroix). To which one must add a highly original and prophetic concern with the growing problem of the understanding and translation of scientific publications in different languages. Thus an almost unrivalled plenitude of personal knowledge and contri-bution lies behind the proud statement which Goethe made in Weimar in March 1830: "Die weite Welt, so ausgedehnt sie auch sei, ist immer nur ein erweitertes Vaterland" (The whole wide world, as wide as it may be, is always only a wider fatherland).

As we know, Prussian expansion was to give to this sentiment an altogether different and ultimately catastrophic direction. Even as Goethe spoke, populist-nationalist instincts were to blaze into antagonistic life throughout Europe. Towards the close of his career, Goethe, like Nietzsche, like Rilke after him, was a German whose vision of German identity and of the German language lay outside of, was tangential to the actual centres of German energy. His *erweitertes Vaterland* is the spiritualized, Enlightenment alternative to the new nation state.

But Goethe's concept of *Weltliteratur* was not only untimely in the political sense. It already exceeded the capacities of any individual, however catholic of spirit, however tireless. Too often, Goethe's inquiries into and judgements on texts with which he is not immediately at home, are derivative and amateurish. Even with reference to Greek and to Latin authors, Goethe's findings, though animate with the presence of his own 'neoclassicism', lay behind those of contemporary scholars. He could not cover the world (even in the rather diagrammatic sense in which Leibniz had still endeavoured to do so).

But the comparative approach, as Goethe exemplifies it, the insistence on the interrelations between literatures, the conviction that no man knows his own language thoroughly if he knows it alone—these stand. They are at the living root of our hopes (however Utopian), of our practices (however fragmentary) as comparatists. It is, in consequence, no accident, but essential historical justice and logic, that twentieth-century academic comparative literature may be said to have begun with Baldensperger's monograph on *Goethe en France* of 1904 or that Fritz Strich's *Goethe und die Weltliteratur*, which appeared in the tragic year 1945, should embody and articulate the ideals of the universalist and comparative method.

To an extent one might have thought impossible in our era of rancorous specialization, it is precisely these ideals which the teaching, the writings and the person of René Étiemble, master across frontiers, have sustained and adorned. Goethe would have acknowledged a kindred temper.

Notes

1   Goethe's translations are assembled in vol. XIV of the Cotta'sche *Neue Gesamtausgabe*, edited by Karl Maurer; and in vol. XV of the Artemis edition, with a *Nachwort* by Fritz Ernst. Both collections are informative but we do not have, until now, any single authoritative study of Goethe's activities and methods as a translator.

2   Cf. Horst Rüdiger's essay on this translation, as a "Versuch im Dienste der Weltliteratur-Idee" in *Studi in onore di Lorenzo Bianchi* (Bologna, 1960).

3   Siegfried Siedel has collected almost all the relevant texts *as Aufsätze zur Weltliteratur* in vol. XVIII of the Aufbau-Verlag edition of Goethe's works. But dicta on foreign writers and writings are scattered throughout the entirety of Goethe's works and conversations.

A. Owen Aldridge

THE UNIVERSAL IN LITERATURE
(1986)

A. OWEN ALDRIDGE (1915–2005) WAS EDUCATED at Indiana University, the University of Georgia and Duke University, where he received his PhD in English in 1942. In 1952–53, he started the Fulbright Program in France and earned a second PhD in comparative literature at the Université de Paris in 1955. He taught in the Department of English at the University of Maryland and in 1967 became professor of French and Comparative Literature at the University of Illinois. His first field of expertise was the spread of Enlightenment ideology, particularly Deism (*Shaftesbury and the Deist Manifesto*, 1951), and cosmopolitan figures with transatlantic careers, such as Thomas Paine (*Man of Reason: The Life of Thomas Paine*, 1960), Benjamin Franklin (*Benjamin Franklin, Philosopher and Man*, 1965), and Voltaire (*Voltaire and the Century of Light*, 1975). Another field to which he made important contributions was colonial American Literature (*Early American Literature: A Comparatist Approach*, 1982). It has been argued that his approach in this field anticipated the current hemispheric turn. Later on he became interested in a third field, East–West Studies. In 1963, together with Melvin J. Friedman, A. Owen Aldridge founded *Comparative Literature Studies*. This journal every two years devotes one of its regular issues to East–West literary relations. Aldridge has been honored with a separate Festschrift for each of these three fields.[i]

Fluent in several modern languages, Aldridge mastered Japanese in his sixties. In 1963 he used the parallels of a poem by Victor Hugo with a Chinese poem to illustrate René Étiemble's technique of comparison. His more intense involvement with Asian literatures, however, began some years later, when he was invited to attend the first international conference on comparative literature held in Taiwan in 1971, where he presented a paper on the influence of China on Voltaire. From then on he became fascinated with Asian literatures. His most important contributions to East–West Studies are *Fiction in*

---

[i] See Joseph A. Leo Lemay, ed., *Deism, Masonry, and the Enlightenment: Essays Honoring Alfred Owen Aldridge* (Newark: U of Delaware P, 1987); François Jost, *Aesthetics and the Literature of Ideas: Essays in Honor of A. Owen Aldridge* (Cranbury, NJ: Associated University Presses, 1990); and Mayasuki Akiyama and Yiu-nam Leung, eds., *Crosscurrents in the Literatures of Asia and the West* (Cranbury, NJ: Associated University Presses, 1997).

Japan and the West (1985), *The Reemergence of World Literature: A Study of Asia and the West* (1986), and *The Dragon and the Eagle: The Presence of China in the American Enlightenment* (1993). "While most scholars increasingly narrow their optics as they grow older," as Friedman put it, "Aldridge has vastly enlarged his."[ii]

"The Universal in Literature" is the second chapter of *The Reemergence of World Literature*. Aldridge's main argument takes as its point of departure the acknowledgement that a "revived awareness of world literature" needs to recognize "Africa and Asia as equal partners" (1986: 9). After surveying the history of comparative literature in West and East and illustrating the key concept of East–West Studies, namely, typological affinities, Aldridge advocates an understanding of world literature in accordance with his assertion that the "most important of all literary relationships is that between literature and life" (Introduction to the first issue of *CLS* at Illinois).

A. Owen Aldridge, *The Reemergence of World Literature*, Newark: University of Delaware Press, 1986. Excerpts from Chapter 2, "The Universal in Literature" (pp. 49–56).

In the year 1863, according to western chronology, a Chinese observer made the following statement: "For twenty years we have maintained relations with the foreigners. Some of them know our language and are able to write it and also read our classics. Among our mandarins and literate people, however, nobody knows the foreign culture" (Jost 1974: 272). Essentially the same opinion was expressed in the West a century earlier by Voltaire, who despite his belief in the essential unity of mankind, was aware of various physical and cultural differences. "The fact is," he wrote, "nature has from the very beginning placed west of us and east of us multitudes of beings of our species whom we became acquainted with only yesterday. We are on this globe like insects in a garden: those who live on an oak rarely encounter those who pass their short life on an elm" (1836: 29). In contrast to this state of affairs, many Chinese and Japanese at the present time, prominent among them being students of comparative literature, possess a sound knowledge of many aspects of English and American writing; whereas very few Americans or English, including even professors of comparative literature, have anything more than a superficial acquaintance with the literature of the East, even in translation.

The argument has been advanced that every Sinologist is in a sense a comparatist since he has absorbed the culture of his own country in the course of his daily life and his profession consists in studying the culture of China. The same logic has been applied to Chinese and Japanese professors of English. Much as mutual acquaintance and cultural understanding are to be desired and highly prized, however, familiarity with a national culture other than one's own is not what constitutes the academic discipline known as comparative literature. Even eastern professors of English and American professors of Chinese or Japanese are not comparatists merely because they are experts in an exotic literature. They become comparatists only when they bring their own and a second national literature into contact—when they place examples from each of two literatures side by side in such a manner as to furnish mutual illumination or to make possible an interpretation of a phenomenon in one literature which would not be apparent without reference to the other. It is certainly true that the Sinologist knows the cultures of both East and West, but his professional duties require him to explore that of China alone, not to bring the two cultures together for joint study. A Sinologist,

ii   Melvin J. Friedman, "Alfred Owen Aldridge: A Profile," *Aesthetics and the Literature of Ideas: Essays in Honor of A. Owen Aldridge*, ed. François Jost (Cranbury, NJ: Associated University Presses, 1990) 9–12 (9).

moreover, may live out a distinguished career without referring to a single literary work from a western country, or indeed without even treating literature at all.

As far as translations are concerned, a scholar in the East who knows thoroughly the history of Chinese drama and who has also studied all of the works of Shakespeare in a Chinese version is better equipped to handle East–West relations than the Sinologist, whether resident in the East or the West, who concerns himself exclusively with Chinese letters. To be sure, the eastern scholar who knows Shakespeare only through translation is not qualified to teach Shakespeare or English drama but he is in a better position to make comparisons than a colleague who has read nothing but Chinese drama. This may seem equivalent to stating that a person who reads Shakespeare in translation is not a qualified teacher of Shakespeare, but a person who makes comparisons between Chinese works in their original and Shakespeare in translation is indeed a capable Shakespearean. This is not the meaning at all. What is suggested is that the Chinese scholar who has read Shakespeare merely in translation is better equipped to teach Chinese drama than he would be if he knew only Chinese drama and no dramatist from any other culture. If he makes comparisons between Chinese and western works, however, these comparisons should throw some new light on one of the works compared. Otherwise there is no point whatsoever in demonstrating resemblances or differences.

Before proceeding to discussion of specific techniques and methods of comparative literature, it is appropriate to provide a definition of literature itself. In answer to the frequently-asked question "What is literature?" I would reply that literature consists of communication by means of written words or symbols when the purpose of communication involves some degree of emotional or esthetic response as well as mere transference of information (Aldridge 1977: 6: 2648). Here we are approaching one of the meanings of universal literature, which I shall discuss later. The definition of literature in the most comprehensive sense embraces not only the broad conventional genres such as poetry, fiction and drama, but also ideological prose such as most works of history and philosophy together with some textbooks and even some advertising. It may also include nonsense verse. Obviously this definition excludes utilitarian compilations such as telephone directories as well as classified advertising, most textbooks and dictionaries. It excludes, moreover, two very closely related artistic genres on the grounds that they do not represent the written word; these are motion pictures, and songs and epics in oral form. Once the latter have been recorded, however, they become literature.

To go from literature as such to comparative literature is a progress from unity to plurality. It is obvious that comparison requires two or more elements to be analyzed jointly. At the same time it is a reductive process, going from literature in the mass to constituent elements of two separate national literatures. Even if we consider the concept of literature in the broadest sense as comprising all works of verbal expression in existence, this mass of materials must be broken down into parts or units in order for comparisons to take place. Paradoxically in this process of considering units or individual works rather than entire literatures, the comparatist tends to reveal the totality or universality of literature. To adapt an English esthetic maxim from the eighteenth century, the comparatist does not seek to demonstrate variety . . . in the midst of uniformity, but instead the reverse, to demonstrate uniformity or esthetic unity in the midst of variety.

In ordinary usage, the term comparative literature refers to relations between two or more national literatures, but it may also be used to indicate the relations between literature and other humanistic areas of study such as art, music, cinema, the social structure or science. "Briefly defined, comparative literature can be considered the study of any literary phenomenon from the perspective of more than one national literature or in conjunction with another intellectual discipline or even several" (Aldridge 1969: 1).

In a rigorous sense, the term has historically been confined to studies involving at least two different languages as well as separate cultures. The application of western critical methods to eastern literatures represents a special problem; in one sense the process seems to represent the interaction of two literatures, but in another it seems to be merely an exercise involving a single literature. The treatment of relations between English and American works or between Spanish and Argentinian ones has not in the past been classified under comparative literature on the grounds that only a single language is involved. By the same token, the perception of relations between works in British literature and those in Indian or other Commonwealth literatures in English has been regarded as comparative culture, but not strictly comparative literature. If the use of translations in studying East–West relations is to be accepted as comparative literature, however, it would seem to be illogical not to accept as well the study of literary relations between two separate cultures which happen to use the same language. Recently an attempt has been made to classify literatures in English other than those of the United States and Great Britain under the rubric of Literature in English or Anglophone literatures. The situation has been succinctly stated by a contemporary Australian poet, A. D. Hope (1980: 165).

> What we are faced with today and from now on, when English is a first or second language in more than forty countries, each with its own social back-ground and its own cultural tradition, is actually the end of what used to be called English Literature and its replacement by something which we should call Literature in English. Just as in the British Isles themselves, the main writers over the last two hundred years have belonged to the region as a whole and form part of one literature even if their source and character is English, Scottish, Irish, or Welsh, while in England, Scotland, Wales and Ireland there is a regional literature specific to that background—so now this pattern is being reproduced on a world scale. Gone is the concept of a tree with minor branches in which the English of England has dominance and priority, except perhaps as an historical image. Each region is independent of the others, free to develop its form of English and its national character as literature yet bound together by a commu-nity of language. The major writers in English in Australia, Pakistan, The United States, India, Singapore, Malaysia, Oceania, New Zealand, the West Indies, Canada, South Africa and so on will belong to the whole, will be read all over and exert a literary and cultural influence in all the regions concerned. Within each one, however, there will be a regional or national literature with its roots in native soil and more or less confined to its own borders.
> [. . .]

The term *comparative literature* was first used in 1816 in the title of a book in the French language *Cours de littérature comparée* by Jean-François Michel Noël, but its first appearance in anything like the modern sense took place in 1886 when a British professor Hutcheson Macaulay Posnett published a book with the simple title *Comparative Literature*, which estab-lished the term throughout the English-speaking world and had repercussions from Japan to the United States. Four years later Professor Tsubouchi Shoyo introduced the book to his students at Waseda University in Japan (Aldridge 1972: 149), and in 1911 an American professor Alastair S. Mackenzie published a book heavily indebted to Posnett, *The Evolution of Literature*. Posnett believed that the critical method he set forth was already being widely practised in England, for he rapturously described it as "the peculiar glory of our nineteenth century," much as French philosophers a century earlier had hailed Diderot's *Encyclopédie* as the glory of the Enlightenment. As a matter of fact, prominent aspects of Posnett's system may be traced back to eighteenth-century theories of Hugh Blair in Scotland and Herder in Germany. In essence, Posnett believed that literature was an echo of sociological change, a means of measuring the upward evolutionary process of social organization. Unlike structuralists and formalists of today, who are largely concerned with description of literary artifacts and are indifferent to their origins, Posnett's main concern was to discover the manner in which great works came to be written. Rejecting equally "the theory that literature is the detached lifework of individuals who are to be worshipped like images fallen down from heaven" and the kindred one "that imagination transcends the associations of space and time," Posnett believed that a scientific explanation of literature may be found by studying the orderly changes in history in the relationship between the individual and the group. He traced, therefore, the reflection in literature of "the gradual expansion of social life, from clan to city, from city to nation, (and) from both of these to cosmopolitan humanity."

In keeping with much of the thought of the late nineteenth century and of that of some critics of the twentieth, Posnett believed that the study of literature could be considered a science, and his book was published in an international scientific series immediately following the titles *Anthropoid Apes* and *The Mammalia in their Relation to Primeval Times*. Apart from his fascination with sociological concepts, now considered old fashioned, Posnett espoused some belletristic ones which are today considered quite modern, for example, that the function of the literary critic is to examine not only the works themselves, but also the cause of the esthetic pleasure which they arouse in human emotions and intellect. But what is most important in Posnett's book is the cosmopolitan range of his interests and illustrations, covering the literatures of Asia as well as the West. Today few comparatists discuss more than one western and one eastern literature, but Posnett treats extensively the Japanese, Indian and Chinese along with the major ones of Europe. His century-old treatise makes a significant contribution to the study of East–West relations, even by today's standards.

Posnett's theories despite their international success seem to have had negligible influence upon British education, perhaps because he published his system while employed as a professor in New Zealand. He called in vain for the establishment of chairs of comparative literature in British universities; indeed at the present time—almost a century after the publication of his book—only three departments of comparative literature exist in the British Isles.

Posnett clearly reflected the sociological theories of a famous French critic Hippolyte Taine, who looked at works of artistic creation as reflections of race, environment and the historical moment. For Taine, as René Wellek has pointed out, literary criticism is "analogous to botany, which studies the orange, the laurel, the pine, and the birch with equal interest," except that literary criticism seeks to reveal how the individual work reflects humanity in general, a particular nation, and a historical age (1973: I, 600).

The scientific or positivistic orientation of Posnett and Taine strongly conditioned the next important stage in the development of comparative literature—that of the first half of the twentieth century—which was dominated by French thought and French scholarship. The University of Paris established an Institute of Comparative Literature early in the century, and the *Revue de littérature comparée* began publishing in 1921. One must observe, however, that this was by no means the first journal devoted entirely to comparative literature or with the term "comparative" in its title. This distinction belongs to the *Acta Comparationis Litterarum Universarum*, published first under a Hungarian title between 1877–88 in Transylvania, the time segment during which Bram Stoker was writing his famous novel *Dracula* concerning this fascinating part of the world. The professors of the Sorbonne during the period between the two world wars specialized in the tracing of literary influences from one nation to another. Unlike Posnett, who had treated the relations between the individual and society in his own culture, the Paris professors concerned themselves with the relations between different cultures. They treated particularly the fortunes of single authors; the impressions which one country made upon the writers of another, or the literary "mirage" as it is called; and the impact of narratives of travel and discovery. Although some critics with strong formalistic proclivities have sought to disparage studies of this kind, their usefulness has recently been reaffirmed by an official publication of the Australian Comparative Literature Association (Veit 1972).

In the East, the study of comparative literature developed directly under the influence of western trends. The pioneer Japanese association of comparatists, the Comparative Literature Society of Japan, which was founded in 1948 originally turned to the principles and methods of the Sorbonne for guidance. According to Professor Saburo Ota, one of the early members of the Society,

> the positive method of France presented difficulties. First there were relatively few cases in which such a method was applicable. There were many areas of investigation that could not be treated. Second, our study had to be limited chiefly to the Meiji Era, that is, 1869–1912, when the introduction of certain foreign authors or books could be traced fairly minutely, because the readers of foreign literature were pretty much limited to a narrow literary circle. But we see a far wider introduction and influence of foreign literatures in the present day. Thus we began to form two groups: one which closely adhered to the French school, and another which was trying to find a new method applicable to present day conditions and which was unwilling to follow blindly the pattern of the Sorbonne. The result was that the spring meeting of the society for 1954 was devoted to the discussion of the character and methodology of Comparative Literature. . . . Five persons expressed their opinion, of whom one followed the French school, keeping to strict positivism. Others insisted that we should devise a number of methods, which could be applied to the literature of different ages.

At about this time, the center of comparatist activity shifted from France to the United States. The Second Congress of the International Comparative Literature Association, which met in Chapel Hill, North Carolina in 1958, was organized to feature the topics and themes traditionally favored by the University of Paris, but René Wellek in a paper on the crisis in the discipline announced that this emphasis was all wrong and that attention should be shifted from extrinsic to intrinsic matters. The congress occurred at a time when most English departments in American universities were dominated by the so-called "new criticism," which was in fact an elaboration of a European movement begun a century before in Italy. For the next dozen or so years, therefore, most American comparatists decried influence studies, inveighed against positivistic aims and methods, and concentrated on the literary work itself. Since it is impossible to be comparative while examining merely a single artifact, the method of confrontation or "rapprochement" was developed.

During this period, the method of comparative literature continued to expand in the East, where emphasis was naturally placed upon East–West relations. In the western world, however, comparatist study and critical theory still concentrated for the most part upon European literatures until the 1970s, when a demand began to be expressed for a truly universal perspective. Sections devoted to East–West relations started to appear in meetings of the American and the International Comparative Literature Associations, in a trend led by scholars such as Étiemble in Europe, and Horst Frenz and Earl Miner in the United States.

[. . .]

The vast majority of studies in comparative literature at the present time in all parts of the world are devoted to an exploration and presentation of resemblances in particular works of two or more national literatures. Resemblance studies are completely different from studies of reception. They may include influence, but the majority concern works by authors who have had no direct contact with each other and who may not even have been aware of each other's existence. Parenthetically, influence may be studied under the rubrics of both reception and resemblance. The method of studying resemblance is variously described in western countries, most commonly as "rapprochement." The process consists in pointing out analogies, similarities and differences, or common elements of any kind in two or more literary works selected because in some way or other they are artistically akin. . .

Regardless of the value of reception studies among European literatures, there is no question that they have only a limited application to the relations between East and West. To concentrate briefly upon Japan, there were no significant literary relations of any kind with the West during the first period of contact from the middle of the sixteenth century until the middle of the nineteenth. Even in the subsequent period ending with the Second World War, very few direct exchanges took place. Western writers most affected by Japanese models were Claudel, Lafcadio Hearn, Louis Viaud (Pierre Loti), Ezra Pound, and William Butler Yeats (Miner 1958: 66–76). Perhaps the greatest contribution in the West during this period to the study of resemblances was the translation in the 1920s of the *Tale of Genji* by Arthur Waley, which made the great Japanese classic available throughout all western countries. Waley's edition illustrates the service which translations may perform in the transmission of literature between the two hemispheres. A contemporary German critic, Max Kommerell, perhaps the most eminent of the century from his country, has written a sensitive characterization of the *Tale of Genji*, using the English translation (Wellek 1975: 487). This is a remarkable example of literary criticism based upon the use of a translated text, perhaps all the more remarkable because it has been highly praised by René Wellek, who is otherwise ranked among the staunch opponents of translations in comparatist study.

Resemblances in literary works may conveniently be divided into three major groups: those of form, those of idea, and those of human relationships.

Form represents the major kinds or types of literature, such as poetry, drama and fiction. These categories may be broken down into an almost endless variety of sub-genres. In poetry, the Japanese form which has had greatest impact upon the West is that of the haiku, practised in Europe and America so extensively during the last three-quarters of a century that a bibliography of the genre in western languages has recently been published in the United States (Brower 1972) to which the eminent French comparatist Étiemble in a superb review has added many missing items (1974 (ii):1–19). At a recent international meeting, Professor Yuzo Saito of Nihon University compared the poetic sensibility of the Japanese poet Basho to that of the English poet John Keats (1966: 1399–1403). The epic is usually considered in the West to be the highest of poetic forms, and modern critical opinion accepts the Japanese *Heike monogatari* as appropriate to be compared to the Greek *Iliad* or the French *Chanson de Roland* (Étiemble 1974 (i):168). In the realm of drama, moreover, some direct contact may be demonstrated. The Japanese *nō* play has inspired several of the dramas of the Irish playwright William Butler Yeats. There is good reason, moreover, for comparatists to look for resemblances in earlier western dramatists even though no possibility of direct influence exists (Miner 1958: 251–64). Some of the major western types of prose fiction which undoubtedly have their counterparts in the East are the Bildungsroman or apprenticeship novel, the picaresque, the science-fiction tale, the mystery story, the epistolary novel and the historical novel.

Resemblances in ideas are to be found in all literary genres, but most extensively in philosophical and religious treatises, miscellaneous essays, histories, books of travel and political propaganda. An early American comparatist, Irving Babbitt, for example, has compared the primitivistic notions of the French Enlightenment philosopher, Jean-Jacques Rousseau, with those of Taoist philosophy, and a Japanese scholar has compared these same notions with those of a contemporary Japanese thinker, Andô Shoeki (Komiya 1974: 3). Few complete books, however, have been devoted to the subject of intellectual communications between East and West with the exception of those in the area of comparative religion. A good example of work in the latter discipline is a doctoral dissertation by a Japanese Christian, Jacob Yuroh Teshima, submitted to the Jewish Theological Seminary of America on "Zen Buddhism and Hasidism, a Comparative Study" (*New York Times*, 31 May 1977).

The richest field for comparative investigation is that of human relationships as they are portrayed in all genres, but primarily in narrative poetry, drama and fiction. The complexities of human behavior are depicted, of course, by means of plot, characterization and theme, the latter of which ordinarily depends upon the first two. In the Japanese novel, *The Setting Sun*, by Osamu Dazai, for example, the plot concerns the love of a daughter toward her mother, her ambivalent love-animosity toward her brother, her proposing herself in writing as a mistress to an elderly novelist whom she has not seen for six years, and her eventually becoming pregnant through him. Characterization in this novel reveals the development of bitterness and frustration in her personality as the result of a series of tragic incidents, including divorce from a none-too-happy marriage, the condition of childlessness, the horror of war, and the loss of her family's fortune and status in society. The theme of the novel as symbolized by the title, on one hand, is the decline of the institution of aristocracy and imperial Japan, and, on the other, the disintegration of the maladjusted personality of the protagonist. The comparatist could illustrate the universal application of these elements by presenting parallels in western literature. Although very few readers in the modern world may have actually experienced the precise trials and conditions of the protagonist of *The Setting Sun*, nearly all will have been witness to situations closely approaching them. There is one aspect perhaps about which the comparatist could do nothing toward revealing or clarifying the artistry of the author and that is the area of poetic expression, symbol, sound and metaphor. Drawing upon related considerations, however, the comparatist could explain the relevance of the author's frequent reference to such western esthetic materials as the painters Renoir and Monet.

Professor Robert Clements of New York University has isolated three major segments of comparative literature as it is presently practiced in the United States. "The narrowest dimension is the Western Heritage and its traditional minimal components French–English, German–French, Latin–English, etc. This narrowest dimension, when restricted to only two authors or literatures within the Western Heritage, is to be discouraged at the level of academic discipline. The second dimension is East–West, an area in which some exploration has been undertaken. The third dimension is World Literature, a much abused term in America" (1978: 7). Clements adds that these dimensions "are not static terms, not passively conjoined, but they must as fiefs of comparative literature, follow the methodology of Western Heritage comparative literature," which embodies essentially five approaches: "the study of (1) themes/myths, (2) genres/forms, (3) movements/eras, (4) interrelations of literature with other arts and disciplines, and (5) the involvement of literature as illustrative of evolving literary theory and criticism."

John J. Deeney of the Chinese University of Hong Kong has objected to Clements' placing of the East–West dimension among the "fiefs of comparative literature," considering this classification as a condescending and patronizing attitude, smacking of western chauvinism or colonialism. I do not believe for a moment, however, that Clements intended to suggest that the study of East–West relations is in any way inferior or subordinate to the study of the Western Heritage. He undoubtedly meant merely that East–West studies should be classified in the academic system among the properties or "fiefs" of comparative literature programs. In this sense, I fully agree with him. I part company, however, in regard to the use of the term "World Literature" to describe his third and broadest dimension. I would use instead "Universal Literature," as the most comprehensive term, and instead of treating world literature as a dimension of comparative literature, would consider the latter as a part of universal literature. As generally understood, World Literature possesses two almost contrary meanings: (1) the masterpieces of the major literatures of the world, and (2) all of the literatures of the world themselves. Since the term is imprecise (Clements indicates that it is much abused), a distinction must be made between world literature and universal literature, confining the former to masterpieces but according to the latter the fullest and broadest signification. I also believe that it is more fruitful in the East–West context to emphasize form, idea, and human relationships rather than the five approaches enumerated by Clements to illuminate the Western Heritage.

The concept of world literature was originally introduced by Goethe, who proclaimed in 1827, "National literature has little meaning today; the time has come for the epoch of world literature to begin, and everyone must now do his share to hasten its realization" (Jost 1974: 16). Goethe was so advanced beyond his times, moreover, that he included Chinese works among those to be studied. No one will quarrel with Goethe's view that people should not limit their reading to works of their own countrymen or to those in their own language, but considerable opposition has been raised to the corollary of this opinion that an attempt should be made to select as a nucleus of attention the most valuable works or the world's masterpieces. Recent objections to this theory have come from socialist countries in eastern Europe, who argue that the concept is elitist, linked to bourgeois culture, and a type of intellectual internationalism based on the theory of an absolute idea of the beautiful. The French critic Étiemble agrees with these strictures and observes in addition that the concept has been used by western critics to overvalue the works of the major European nations and to minimize those of smaller European nations and the nations of the East. The concept, moreover, works against the aspirations of the emerging literatures of our times (1974 (i): 13–35). Despite these objections to the cultural elitism implicit in attempts to rank the hundred best books of all mankind or to select a list of books for an ideal library, most critics are willing to accept the view that some works which have stood the test of time are worthy to rank as "classics" in their respective literatures and to be treated with appropriate respect. One must still make an effort, as Étiemble warns, to escape the determinism of one's birth. As we are all blessed or afflicted with the language and religion of our parents, we also acquire associated literary prejudices. Only those fortunate enough to possess leisure, industry, economic freedom and a large degree of intellectual independence are able to transcend these limitations and prejudices.

Among those so emancipated, the term "universal literature" is gradually acquiring popularity, but critics are still arguing about what it signifies. In the broadest sense, it represents the definition of literature in general which we gave earlier in this paper, the sum total of all texts and works throughout the world, or the combination of all national literatures. As the concept universal represents a broader perspective than world in the cosmic sense, so universal covers a greater area in the literary one. "Universal" also suggests that the study of comparative literature rests upon the assumption of the fundamental unity of all mankind. As Voltaire observed in the eighteenth century, "men are born everywhere more or less the same; . . . it is government which changes manners, which elevates or debases nations" (Voltaire 1953: 8133). Taoist philosophy also supports the view that "men under all skies regardless of the structure of their language are able to develop the same thoughts, the same philosophical systems" (Étiemble 1980: lxxix). Even allowing for political and cultural differences, the basic human relationships described in all literatures, ancient and modern, are fundamentally identical.

In recent years, however, the concept of universality has encountered opposition or competition from various sources, particularly from ethnic, nationalistic and special interest groups. Feminists, homosexuals, Freudians, for example, subject literary works to interpretive schemes reflecting their particular ideology, while others insist on isolating literatures written by and about blacks, Chicanos, Puerto Ricans or Cajuns. On the surface this literary splintering seems to suggest that the notion of universality is an illusion or an impractical ideal.

The claims of various national literatures for preferential treatment, moreover, are just as confusing, and they have been in existence for a much longer period of time. Some critics in the eighteenth century, for example, maintained that French letters were of such paramount importance that they should serve as the model for the rest of the world. Naturally these critics belonged to the French nation. One of them, a professor at the Parisian school which Voltaire attended, proposed as a subject for public discussion, "whether the French could properly claim the glory of outweighing the other nations of Europe in that which concerns literary works" (Riesz 1975: 227). This is an extreme example of the kind of nationalistic pride which still finds expression in the opinion that European literatures are supreme above all others. The French claims of superiority in the eighteenth century were hotly disputed by critics of the other European nations, and eventually all were admitted on a more or less equal basis. European literature came to mean universal literature. Various nations occasionally attempted to place themselves in the dominating position, but by the end of the nineteenth century general opinion had conceded that no single European literature was superior to the others.

A contemporary Rumanian critic, Adrian Marino, has formulated a conception of universal literature according to which it represents "the *sum* or *totality* of the literatures of the world without any discrimination" (Marino 1975: 79). According to this conception, individual works are not considered to be of a privileged caste merely because they belong to a national literature which has glorious historical antecedents. Competition exists among individual writers of all cultures, but they are judged entirely on the merits of their own productions, not on the basis of the national literature to which they belong. The concept of universal literature does not represent a homogenizing process in which all forms of literary expression, any more than all peoples, gradually adopt a greater uniformity than they have had in the past. Nor does it represent the use of modern technology, including mass-media, to produce a supranational literature comparable to supranational industrial conglomerates (Marino 1975: 70, 74). Rather, it is an outgrowth of the cosmopolitanism concept of the eighteenth century, of an indivisible "republic of letters," the recognition of common elements in the human race to which all literatures conform. In this perspective, historical chronology is considered irrelevant and all works are regarded as contemporary in the sense of existing today and being judged by the needs of modern society. The Irish playwright William Butler Yeats, for example, affirmed that the men who devised the Japanese *nō* drama had more in common with modern Europeans and Americans than with the ancient Greeks or Shakespeare and Corneille (Miner 1958: 268). One of the most eminent contemporary novelists of Africa, the Guinean Camara Laye, unlike many supranationalists of that continent, strongly expresses in his work the themes of cultural syncretism and ethnic reciprocity. In an interview, he described "the cultures of the world as all participating in one dance, each with its own special movement, contributing something significant to the total world rhythm. Any attempt to suppress one of them takes away an essential unit or beat from the cohesion of the whole" (Larson 1980: 3, 18). This does not imply, however, that a single system of music or rhythm exists for all peoples. The "high-floating" sound of Bach, Brahms and Mozart may be suitable for the verse of Yeats, Pound and Williams, but may have nothing in common with poetry in other parts of the world (Narasimhaiah 1976: 8).

The concept of the universal in literature corresponds to that of universality in the plastic arts which was expressed early in the twentieth century by Ernest F. Fenollosa, the art critic who in large measure introduced Ezra Pound to the culture of the East. According to Fenollosa, "we are approaching the time when the art work of all the world of man may be looked upon as one, as infinite variations in a single kind of mental and social effort. . . .

Oriental Art has been excluded from most serious art history because of the supposition that its law and form were incommensurate with established European classes. But if we come to see that classification is only a convenience . . . and that the real variations are as infinite as the human spirit, though educed by social and spiritual changes, we come to grasp the real and larger unity of effort that underlies the vast number of technical varieties. A universal scheme or logic of art unfolds, which as easily subsumes all forms of Asiatic and of savage art and the efforts of children as it does accepted European schools" (Fenollosa 1913: xxiv).

The conception of the universality of literature may seem to be based primarily on a quantitative perspective but universality may also be viewed in a qualitative sense. Even before Goethe propounded his notion of world literature his countryman Friedrich Schlegel pointed toward an "*Universalpoesie*," by which he meant a synthesis of both prose and poetry, artistic and popular, comprising essentially everything which exists from the largest to the smallest literary system or artistic manifestation (Aldridge 1969: 2). The subject matter of literature must be comprehensive, embracing every possible facet of human experience. After Schlegel, the term *universal* in a qualitative sense has acquired still further meanings. From the perspective of content, *universal literature* may refer to any work which reflects attitudes, situations or experiences which are felt or understood by human beings in all cultures, for example, respect for parents or revolt from them, success or failure in a career. From the perspective of the reader's response, universal literature refers to any work which contains elements broad enough to appeal to the average person in any literary culture. Response to these elements is highly subjective, and it is, of course, frequently impossible to state objectively exactly which characteristics of an artistic work are responsible for its broad appeal. Here reader response is far more important than subject matter although subject matter is much easier for the critic to analyze.

In recent years considerable attention has been devoted to the concept of reader response on both the individual and the group level. Various theories concerning psychological reactions have been proposed under the heading of reception esthetics, and sociologists have studied and quantified the reading habits of various classes in society. The latter studies have provided a basis for the principle that the test of a great book consists in its being widely read with approval by a public different from that for which it was originally intended. Obviously popularity, not intrinsic value, is being measured here, but no valid criteria for the latter have ever been devised. It seems reasonable, therefore, to accept this sociological-esthetic principle as an important contribution to the concept of universal literature, particularly for the appraisal of writings in the East–West context.

At first glance it would seem that the reader would ordinarily identify himself with the protagonist of a literary text and that he would respond most readily to the works which portray situations and feelings which he has encountered himself. Brief reflection will indicate that this is not at all true. To cite one of the most popular works of western literature, *Hamlet*, almost none of its readers is likely to be a young prince required by circumstances to avenge his father's death at the hands of an uncle living in incestuous relations with his mother. Nor are many of the admirers of the Japanese novel *The Temple of the Golden Pavilion* young priests whose psychological quirks lead them to burn down the temple in which they worship. It is not that readers see themselves in these works, but that they find something in the plot or presentation which gives them esthetic pleasure. In this sense, therefore, universal literature is the concrete manifestation of "the universality of taste," a concept which the Japanese critic Soseki, among others, has proclaimed (Tsukamoto 1969: xiv). The literary critic may affirm with slight risk of contradiction that such works as *Hamlet* and *The Temple of the Golden Pavilion* belong to universal literature, but the student of comparative literature must do more than make declarations. He must reveal parallels or relationships with similar works in other literatures.

The method of comparative literature, moreover, resolves a giant paradox existing in the concept of universal literature, no matter in which of the several senses it is understood. The paradox consists in the fact that universal is an international concept growing in importance at a time when nationalism is becoming increasingly more vociferous, illustrated, for example, by the demands for attention by "emerging" literatures, including some in the Far East. The techniques of comparative literature succeed in relaxing the tension between nationalism and internationalism by recognizing cultural differences as a basic premise, but at the same time calling attention to similarities which reflect the universality of psychological and esthetic reactions. The problem for Japanese writers, according to Armando Martins Janeira, "is to become universal without dissolving into a vacuous cosmopolitanism." Janeira cites André Gide as the final authority on the question: "It is by becoming national that a literature takes its place in humanity. . . . Is there anything more Spanish than Cervantes, more French than Voltaire, than Descartes, or Pascal, more Russian than Dostoevski; and more universally human than each one of them?" (142) The comparatist is always aware of the national or ethnic character of the literary works he treats while perceiving them from the universal perspective...

References

Aldridge, A. Owen, *Comparative Literature: Matter and Method* (Urbana: University of Illinois Press, 1969).

Aldridge, A. Owen and Shunsuke, Kamei, "Problems and Vistas of Comparative Literature in Japan and the United States: a Dialogue", *Mosaic*, 5 (1972), 149–63.

Aldridge, A. Owen, "Literature (Field of Study)", *International Encyclopedia of Higher Education* (San Francisco: Jossey-Bass Publishers, 1977), 6, 2648–52.

Brower, G. L. and W. Foster, *Haiku in Western Languages; An Annotated Bibliography* (Metuchen, New Jersey: Scarecrow Press, 1972).

Clements, Robert, *Comparative Literature as Academic Discipline* (New York: Modern Language Association of America, 1978).

Deeney, John J. "Comparative Literature for Scholars and Administrators", *Tamkang Review*, 11 (1980), 79–106.

Étiemble, René, *Essais de littérature (vraiment) générale* (Paris: Gallimard, 1974).

Étiemble, René, Review of Brower and Foster, *Haiku in Western Languages. Comparative Literature Studies*, 11 (1974), 1–19.

Étiemble, René ed., *Philosophes taoïstes.* (Paris: Gallimard, 1980).

Hope, A. D., "Teaching Australian Literature", *The Literary Criterion*, 15 (1980), 157–65.

Janeira, Armando Martins, *Japanese and Western Literature. A Comparative Study* (Rutland, Vermont: Charles E. Tuttle Co., 1970).

Jost, François, *Introduction to Comparative Literature* (Indianapolis: Bobbs-Merrill Company, 1974).

Komiya, Akira, "Andô Shôeki et Jean-Jacques Rousseau", *Hikaku Bungaku Kenkyu. Etudes de Littératures Comparées*. No. 26 (1974), 3 [abstract].

Larson, Charles R., "Master of the Word", *New York Times Book Review*, 16 March, (1980), 3, 18.

Marino, Adrian, "Où situer la 'littérature universelle'?" *Cahiers roumains d'études littéraires 3/1975*, 64–81.

Miner, Earl, *The Japanese Tradition in British and American Literature* (Princeton: Princeton University Press, 1958).

Narasimhaiah, C. D. *Commonwealth Literature. A Handbook of Select Reading Lists* (Delhi: Oxford University Press, 1976).

Posnett, Hutcheson Macaulay, *Comparative Literature* (New York: D. Appleton Company, 1886).

Riesz, János, "Einer Metzer Edition . . . von Beat Ludwig von Muralt", B. Alleman and E. Koppen eds, *Teilnahme und Spiegelung* (Berlin: Walter D. Gruyter, 1975).

Saito, Yuzo, "The Sensibility of Basho and Keats", François Jost ed., *Proceedings of the IVth Congress of the International Comparative Literature Association* (The Hague: Mouton, 1966), II, 1399–1403.

Tsukamoto, Toshiaki, "Problems of Sōseki's Bungaku-Hyôron", *Hikaku Bungaku. Journal of Comparative Literature*, 12 (1969), xiv [abstract].

Veit, Walter ed., *Captain James Cook; Image and Impact* (Melbourne: The Hawthorne Press, 1972).

Voltaire, "Fragments sur l'histoire", *Œuvres complètes* (Paris: Furne, Librairie-Editeur) 5 (1836), 225–84.

Voltaire, *Correspondance*. Theodore Besterman ed. (Geneva: Musée Voltaire, 1953–65), Letters are identified by number, not volume and page.

Wellek, René, "Literary Criticism", Philip P. Wiener, ed., *Dictionary of the History of Ideas* (New York: Charles Scribner's Sons. 1 (1973), 596–607).

Wellek, René, "Max Kommerell as Critic of Literature", B. Alleman and E. Koppen eds., *Teilnahme und Spiegelung* (Berlin: Walter D. Gruyter, 1975).

Chapter 16

Zhang Longxi

TOWARD INTERPRETIVE PLURALISM (1992)

Z HANG LONGXI (B. 1947) IS A professor at the City University of Hong Kong. Educated at Peking University and Harvard University, and a former professor at the University of California Riverside, he has worked extensively on the exchanges in culture and literature between Asia and the West, most notably in *Mighty Opposites: From Dichotomies to Differences in the Comparative Study of China* (Stanford: Stanford University Press, 1998).

Asia is home to a number of extensive literatures which are far older than Western literatures. The exchange between East and West, however, is for many reasons relatively limited, not just by obstacles of language but also by cultural barriers of understanding and lack of knowledge about other genres. This is particularly so when it comes to the influence of the East on the West, whereas the Western influence on modern Asian litera- ture has been more significant.

Zhang is not overly optimistic about the possibility of a truly global literary history which might overcome all such obstacles, and his ambition is more modest; his work attempts to make the difference between East and West productive in relation to the understanding of literature.[i] He most particularly does so in *The Tao and the Logos: Literary Hermeneutics, East and West*, in which he crafts an elaborate dialogue between literatures and interpretative traditions from both the East and the West. Rather than focusing on canonical works which could be called world literature, Zhang compares discourses on literature and its uses with reference to literary examples, an approach which again facilitates a deeper understanding of the plurality of world literatures, and helps to inspire new approaches to one's own inherited traditions.

"Toward Interpretive Pluralism" is the epilogue of *The Tao and the Logos: Literary Hermeneutics, East and West*, Durham: Duke University Press, 1992, pp. 191–98.

---

i   Zhang Longxi, 2006. "Two Questions for Global Literary History." In *Studying Transcultural Literary History*. Gunilla Lindberg-Wada, ed., Berlin and New York: Walter de Gruyter, 52–59.

Literature is valuable for its richness and variety. Why should all comments and appreciations be unified as if coming out of one mouth?
—Ge Hong, *Baopuzi*

The person who understands must not reject the possibility of changing or even abandoning his already prepared viewpoints and positions. In the act of understanding a struggle occurs which results in mutual change and enrichment.
—Mikhail Bakhtin, "Notes (1970–71)"

This book has argued for the recognition of the shared, the common, and the same in the literary and critical traditions of the East and the West beyond their cultural and historical differences, and yet what is recognized as the same is the presence of difference in all understanding and interpretation, the hermeneutic difference in aesthetic experience and literary criticism. The realization that meaning is always changing, that it is not determined once and for all by the author who permanently inscribes it in the text but is contingent upon the reader in a personal confrontation with the literary work, inevitably leads to the acknowledgment of the plurality of meaning and interpretation and to an appreciation of the principles of interpretive pluralism. In other words, the search for the same in this intercultural study has arrived at the sameness by way of difference, for it has come to emphasize the presence of hermeneutic difference and the necessity of opening up one's mind to different views and different positions. In contemporary Western literary theory, difference is certainly very much emphasized, but this very emphasis on difference, as Steven Connor argues, often ironically turns Western postmodernist theory into a totalizing discourse of consensus, a discourse that "closes off the very world of cultural difference and plurality which it allegedly brings to visibility," because this emphasis on difference tends to preclude the possibility of the same and thus results in a total "consensus in postmodernist discourse that there is no longer any possibility of consensus, the authoritative announcements of the disappearance of final authority and the promotion and recirculation of a total and comprehensive narrative of a cultural condition in which totality is no longer thinkable."[1] In contemporary literary theory, this totalizing tendency often manifests itself as attachment to one particular concept, term, or critical method as the exclusively valid or correct one; and it manifests itself first and foremost in the claim that the recognition of difference is of the highest value in criticism. Each of the various "schools" of critical theory obstinately insists on the value of one view, one opinion, one approach, or one way—its own way—of reading the literary text. For Wimsatt and Beardsley, the text is the only thing that matters; considerations of the author and the reader are all irrelevant fallacies. For E. D. Hirsch, every interpretation must conform to the authorial intention as the only objective criterion for its validity. For Stanley Fish, the reader or the interpretive community is the sole arbitrator of meaning, while "the objectivity of the text is an illusion."[2] In recognizing the indeterminacy of meaning and the importance of cultural, ethnic, gender, or other differences, modern critics are often rather determinate about their own interpretation. But why do we have to choose just one of the many different factors and approaches that contribute to the production of meaning and the understanding of a literary work? Why must the birth of the reader be at the cost of the death of the author? Why is the value of literary criticism said to lie in promoting a single view or method at the cost of a more balanced and sensible view of the hermeneutic process? Of course, we do not have to make such a limiting choice. We do not have to eliminate the text and its formal features to recognize the role of the reader, nor do we have to conceive of the reader as locked up in a prison of communal, collective thinking. Indeed, nothing needs to be excluded from contributing to the understanding of literature: the author, the text, and the reader all have their claims and specific ways of affecting the formation of meaning, and a deeper understanding of literature results from the synthesis of all these claims, a tentative agreement or balance of such competing forces, a moment of learning and cultivation in the fusion of horizons.

Contrary to the totalizing discourse in much of contemporary theory and criticism, literary hermeneutics as we have understood it has as its inevitable consequence the advocacy of interpretive pluralism, the emphasis on the importance of an open-ended and truly reciprocal dialogue as the paradigm of communication. Of course, there are different kinds of pluralism; the very form or formulation of pluralism is in itself pluralistic. An essay by Richard McKeon articulates one view of interpretive or critical pluralism. Taking his example from the different readings of Aristotle in the history of the interpretation of Aristotle's works, McKeon acknowledges that some interpretations are sound and suggestive whereas others are less sound and less suggestive but that the important task is not so much to identify the true interpretation as to be open to the plurality of interpretations, "to read interpretations of Aristotle which depart from one's own in the expectation that they may bring to attention insights into neglected facts, or thoughts that might be borrowed, or that they might suggest methods and principles that go beyond either interpretation or either critical method. Critical pluralism opens the way to a continuing history of interpretation which will enrich our understanding of works which have undetermined and indefinite potentialities of meanings and values in successive readings."[3] In pursuit of fruitful and suggestive interpretations, critical pluralism thus requires the willingness to engage other views and interpretations and to let one's own prepared viewpoints be challenged, tested, and modified by the Other. Interpretive pluralism thus formulated is surely not without its discontents, and one complaint against it is the skeptic's view that pluralism is too naively idealistic, that in reality "we are all dogmatists in one way or another," and that, worse still, pluralism may serve as "a strategy of 'repressive toleration.'"[4] Pluralism can be insincere, says another critic; it may claim "to encourage multiplicity while in fact championing the opposite."[5] Still another complains from an antipluralist point of view that pluralism is "a polemic for inclusion coupled with a programmatic commitment to exclusions," and specifically the exclusion of Marxism.[6]

The doubt of the practicality or sincerity of critical pluralism, however, does not in itself discredit its principle, nor does it invalidate the open orientation of literary hermeneutics. As for the charge of exclusion, one may answer that exclusion is not inherently an attribute of interpretive pluralism; rather, interpretation becomes pluralistic at the very moment when it engages opposing views and positions. Gadamer speaks of "a potentiality for being other [Andersseins]" in the experience of a true dialogue, the necessity "to expose oneself and to risk oneself."[7] Dialogue or conversation characterizes the hermeneutic process of coming to an understanding, and it involves the willingness to accept the challenges of the Other: "Thus it belongs to every true conversation that each person opens himself to the other, truly accepts his point of view as valid and transposes himself into the other to such an extent that he understands not the particular individual but what he says."[8] In reading a literary work, therefore, it is important to be aware of interpretations or critical views that are different from one's own. This means that one does not commit oneself to a particular interpretation or a particular approach to the work of literature but critically examines the very interpretation and approach that seem to make sense in one's reading. We can begin by examining the critical views that are generally accepted or predominant in contemporary literary theory and criticism.

The reader, for example, gets much attention and emphasis that he richly deserves in contemporary critical theory, but there is a related tendency to see the text as of less and less importance. In this connection, it is helpful to remember that the text as the object of aesthetic experience and interpretation offers the space for the fusion of horizons. It has its own voice and claim that must enter into the hermeneutic process and become the ground on which the reader builds up his or her individual concretization. "Literary art can be understood," as Gadamer argues, "only from the ontology of the work of art, and not from the aesthetic experiences that occur in the course of the reading." This is, however, not simply going back to the ontological text as advocated in New Criticism, for Gadamer goes on to say: "But this has a further consequence. The concept of literature is not unrelated to the reader. Literature does not exist as the dead remnant of an alienated being, left over for a later time as simultaneous with its experiential reality. Literature is a function of being intellectually preserved and handed down, and therefore brings its hidden history into every age."[9] In reading Gadamer's work, one often feels that a tension seems to exist between his emphasis on the interpreter's historicity and his effort to ground interpretation in the ontology of the work of art. Gadamer has most eloquently argued for the excess of meaning, the "inexhaustibility" of interpretation, and the positive value of "prejudice," understood as each individual's fore-structure of understanding, but at the same time he firmly rejects what he calls "an untenable hermeneutic nihilism"—namely, the view that there is no criterion of an appropriate reaction, that one understanding is just as legitimate as any other.[10] Such a tension, however, is not so much a critical self-contradiction in theory as a sign of a healthy fluidity of thinking, determined by the essential open-ended orientation of the hermeneutic process itself. In literary hermeneutics, therefore, the plurality of meaning and interpretation are well balanced by the ontology of the work of art, its specific mode of existence; and the emphasis of one element does not exclude the contribution of the other or others.

The author of a literary work, though largely neglected in contemporary theory, remains an important factor in understanding and interpretation. Annabel Patterson shows convincingly how the discredit of the authorial intention in New Criticism comes as a result of "an emergent new discipline, the academic and professionalized study of English Literature," in which the evaluative function and the interpretive authority are transferred from the author to the critic.[11] The authorial intention then falls further into "a new and potent form of disesteem, as a result of the convergence of a number of disparate attacks on the related ideas of human subjectivity, of selfhood, of the individual as a locus of subjectivity or an (even partially) free agent capable of having intentions, and hence on the very idea of authorship."[12] The disintegration of the self into different psychic functions in Freudian psychoanalysis, the critique of the individual as a product of bourgeois false consciousness in classical and especially structuralist Marxism, and finally the promotion of an impersonal and anonymous discourse in Foucault and Derrida, Patterson argues, have all contributed not so much to the solution of the problem of intention as to the denial or elimination of this problem. However, the problem of intention keeps coming back to haunt even the most anti-intentionalist and antihermeneutic readings of literature. For example, says Patterson, "by deconstructing Proust's text de Man was only, by his own admission, 'trying to come closer to being as rigorous a reader as the author had to be in order to write the sentence in the first place.'"[13] To put the disesteem of the authorial intention in historical perspective is then to understand the complexity of the problem and to avoid a simplistic elimination of intention. "It is undeniable," as Patterson remarks, "that literary critics and theorists do not publish their essays anonymously, and that their own intentions are part of the complex structure of professional practice that contributes to the meaning of the positions they take."[14] It certainly takes an author to make the authoritative announcement of the death of the author, and in thinking critically about literature and literary theory, we must bear in mind not just the problematic nature of the author's intention but the critic's or the theorist's intention as well. From the perspective of interpretive pluralism, then, the author and his intention need not be ignored in order to arrive at an appropriately creative understanding. Understanding is always a teleological process toward the resolution of textual difficulties and inconsistencies, the falling in place of the disparate textual elements that otherwise seem to cancel one another out and block the formation of meaning. The resolution of such hermeneutic problems, however, is never final and fixed, but only temporarily allows us to construct a coherent frame of reference within which the meaning of the work emerges. The validity in interpretation is therefore not absolute but temporary and contingent, and the best interpretation is the one that accounts for the most elements in the process of reading, offers the most coherent explanation of the text, and simply makes the best sense of the literary work as a whole.

In the Chinese tradition, differing means of understanding and interpretation appear to have been more readily acknowledged than in the West and accepted with greater tolerance; relativism does not seem to be the bugbear that every critic holds in absolute abhorrence. Despite their moralistic tendency and intentionalist hermeneutics, even the Confucian scholars recognize the arbitrary nature of language and readily acknowledge the basic plurality of meaning. Their very effort to "rectify names [zhengming]" that is, to fix the correspondence between the sign and the object it signifies, already testifies to their awareness of the radical dissonance of verbal expression. They also advocate a suggestive style and economy of expression. As Mencius puts it: "Words that speak of things near at hand but with far-reaching import are good words."[15] The Book of Changes, which the Confucians adopted as one of the canonical classics, is praised for its conciseness, as it "names the small but implies the great; its import is far-reaching, its style is elegant, and its words are indirect but right to the point."[16] If the nature of language is recognized as inherently metaphorical, its way of expression indirect and symbolic, and its meaning always exceeding the boundaries of the text, it is then only logical to infer that interpretation must be varied and flexible. Dong Zhongshu (176–104 B.C.), who was instrumental in establishing Confucianism as the predominant orthodoxy in early imperial China, declared that "[The Book of] Poetry has no direct interpretation."[17] He made that claim at a time when Confucian scholars were trying hard to reinterpret ancient writings to achieve a synthesis of ancient thoughts in the framework of Confucianism, which in itself constitutes a fascinating episode in the history of Chinese hermeneutic thinking. What Dong Zhongshu meant by that phrase was no more than a denial of the more straightforward, literal interpretation of The Book of Poetry, and he thereby justifies and sets up the ground for allegorical interpretation of ancient verse in terms of Confucian ethical and political philosophy.

Nevertheless, once it is admitted that poetic language is not to be taken literally, a door is opened to various divergent interpretations. The famous pronouncement in The Book of Changes that the benevolent and the wise will have different visions of the tao already serves to legitimize hermeneutic differences, and critics always refer to it as authorization of their different interpretations. By the same token, Dong Zhongshu's phrase can also be used to justify an interpretive plurality in reading poetry, though originally Dong was speaking of a specific work, The Book of Poetry. This is apparently how Shen Deqian (1673–1769) understands Dong's phrase when he argues that readers of poetry should just immerse themselves in reading and not seek "a forced uniformity" in understanding and making an aesthetic judgment. Moreover, he goes on to say, "the words of the ancients contain an infinitude of meaning, which is then experienced by posterity in various ways as according to their different dispositions, shallow or deep, high or low. . . . This is what Master Dong meant when he said that poetry has no direct interpretation."[18] The infinite possibility of meaning is finitely and temporarily realized by each reader in his or her own way; thus the reading of poetry may yield many interpretations that cannot be leveled into one by imposing a forced uniformity. In the works of Wang Fuzhi (1619–92), the role of the reader and the plurality of interpretation are even more clearly acknowledged. By citing different readings of some ancient verses as interpretive models, he virtually argues for the legitimacy of hermeneutic difference and emphasizes the importance of emotion and aesthetic pleasure. "Readers find in the author's one single intent whatever is in keeping with their own dispositions," says Wang. "There is no limit to the possible permutations of human emotion, but each reader can find in poetry what suits his own emotion; and that is precisely why poetry is so valuable."[19] The idea underlying all such critical opinions in the Chinese tradition is an open-minded accept-ance of different readings so long as they come from real enjoyment, as a result of the pleasure of the text. Speaking of reading and understanding in a tone reminiscent of Tao Qian's Mr. Five Willows, the critic Xie Zhen (1495–1575) declares boldly: "Of poems some can be understood, some cannot, and some need not be. They are like the moon in water or flowers in a mirror; so don't trace every line too doggedly."[20] This statement does not of course mean to abandon critical discrimination or responsibility, but it does express the spirit of tolerance and enjoyment, the spirit of interpretive pluralism, which accepts and even celebrates the divergence of meaning as a matter of course. What is implied in this statement is not only the realization that nothing should be excluded from understanding and interpretation, that the reader should be free to choose whatever is available to him or her, but more radically that the reader should also be free *not* to choose but to declare his enjoyment without thorough understanding.

In agreement with this pluralistic spirit of the pleasure of reading, it should be noted that the emphasis on silence and the blank as the source of textuality, which forms the centerpiece of the argument in this book, should also be taken as one approach among many to the study of hermeneutic problems in the reading of literature, and that the kinds of texts discussed in this book are by no means the only kinds that merit extensive critical inquiry. If the herme-neutic phenomenon is an ontological given rather than a purely theoretical issue, then herme-neutics, which promises to bring what is experienced to the level of conscious understanding and thereby enlarge and enrich the potential of aesthetic experience, ultimately teaches nothing that is not already experienced in life; and all that is discussed here, following the advice of Mauthner and Wittgenstein, can be discarded like the ladder after its proper use. Gadamer's notorious suspicion of any systematic approach or method can also be understood in this connection. The point is that we should not feel constrained by any theoretical concept or approach but should take all relevant factors into consideration in the reading and enjoy-ment of literature. Both the reading of literature for enjoyment and the scholarship of literary studies are essentially personal pursuits, which should not be constrained to one fixed perspective or one methodology. Perhaps this may sound incredibly syncretic or represent a typically Chinese eclectic attitude, but by virtue of its very open-mindedness and common sense, and in the context of many debated issues about author, text, and reader in contem-porary Western literary theory, this eclecticism may open a new vista on the critical scene and promise some new insights into the nature of literary hermeneutics.

Notes

1   Connor, *Postmodernist Culture*, pp. 9–10.
2   Fish, "Literature in the Reader: Affective Stylistics," in *Is There a Text?* p. 43.
3   Richard McKeon, "Pluralism of Interpretations and Pluralism of Objects, Actions, and Statements Interpreted," *Critical Inquiry* 12, a special issue on "Pluralism and Its Discontents" (Spring 1986): 596.
4   W. J. T. Mitchell, "Pluralism as Dogmatism," *Critical Inquiry* 12 (Spring 1986): 497, 499.
5   Bruce Erlich, "Amphibolies: On the Critical Self-Contradictions of 'Pluralism,'" *Critical Inquiry* 12 (Spring 1986): 523.
6   Ellen Rooney, "Who's Left Out? A Rose by Any Other Name Is Still Red; Or, The Politics of Pluralism," *Critical Inquiry* 12 (Spring 1986): 561.
7   Gadamer, "Text and Interpretation," in *Dialogue and Deconstruction*, ed, Michelfelder and Palmer, p. 110
8   Gadamer, *Truth and Method*, p. 385.

9   Ibid., p. 161.
10   Ibid., p. 95.
11   Annabel Patterson, "Intention," in *Critical Terms for Literary Study*, ed. Lentricchia and McLaughlin, p. 141.
12   Ibid., p. 143.
13   Ibid., p. 145.
14   Ibid., p. 144.
15   Mencius, *Mengzi zhengyi* [The Works of Mencius], 7b, p. 594.
16   *Zhouyi zhengyi* [The Book of Changes], in *Shisan jing zhushu* [Thirteen Classics], ed. Ruan Yuan, 77b, 1:89.
17   Dong Zhongshu, *Chunqiu fanlu* [The Luxuriant Gems of Spring and Autumn] (Shanghai: Shangwu, 1926), p. 6b.
18   Shen Deqian, *Tang shi biecai* [A Selection of Tang Poetry], 4 vols. (Beijing: Zhonghua shuju, 1964), 1:1.
19   Wang Fuzhi, *Jiangzhai shihua jianzhu* [Annotated Jiangzhai's Remarks on Poetry], ed. Dai Hongsen (Beijing: Renmin wenxue, 1981), pp. 4, 5.
20   Xie Zhen, *Siming shihua* [Siming's Remarks on Poetry], in *Lidai shihua xubian* [A Sequel to Remarks on Poetry from Various Dynasties], 3 vols., ed. Ding Fubao (Beijing: Zhonghua shuju, 1983), p. 1137.

Works cited

Connor, Steven. *Postmodernist Culture: An Introduction to Theories of the Contemporary*. Oxford: Basil Blackwell, 1989.

Dong Zhongshu (179?–93 B.C.). *Chunqiu fanlu* [The Luxuriant Gems of Spring and Autumn]. Shanghai: Shangwu, 1926.

Erlich, Bruce. "Amphibolies: On the Critical Self-Contradictions of 'Pluralism.'" *Critical Inquiry* 12 (Spring 1986): 521–49.

Fish, Stanley. *Is There a Text in This Class? The Authority of Interpretive Communities*. Cambridge; Mass.: Harvard University Press, 1980.

Gadamer, Hans-Georg. *Dialogue and Deconstruction: The Gadamer–Derrida Encounter*. Albany: State University of New York Press, 1989.

—. *Truth and Method*, 2d rev. ed. English translation revised by Joel Weinsheimer and Donald G. Marshall. New York: Crossroad, 1991.

McKeon, Richard. "Pluralism of Interpretations and Pluralism of Objects, Actions, and Statements Interpreted." *Critical Inquiry 12* (Spring 1986): 577–96.

Mencius (371?–289 B.C.). *Mengzi zhengyi* [The Works of Mencius with Exegesis]. Ed. Jiao Xun (1763–1820). In vol 1 of *Zhuzi jicheng*. (See *Mencius*, trans. D. C. Lau, Harmondsworth: Penguin, 1970.)

Mitchell, W. J. T. "Pluralism as Dogmatism." *Critical Inquiry* 12 (Spring 1986): 494–502.

Patterson, Annabel. "Intention," in *Critical Terms for Literary Study*, ed. Lentricchia and McLaughlin. Baltimore: Johns Hopkins UP: 1990.

Rooney, Ellen. "Who's Left Out? A Rose by Any Other Name Is Still Red; Or, The Politics of Pluralism." *Critical Inquiry* 12 (Spring 1986): 550–63.

Shen Deqian (1673–1769), ed. *Tang shi biecai* [A Selection of Tang Poetry]. 4 vols. Beijing: Zhonghua shuju, 1964.

Wang Fuzhi (1619–92). *Jiangzhai shihua jianzhu* [Annotated Jiangzhai's Remarks on Poetry]. Ed. Dai Hongsen. Beijing: Renmin wenxue, 1981.

Chapter 17

Claudio Guillén

WELTLITERATUR (1993)

BORN IN PARIS AND BROUGHT up partly in that city in a bilingual environment (to Spanish and French he soon added English and German), Claudio Guillén (1924–2007) was the most important Spanish comparatist of the twentieth century (Villanueva 1999). At the outbreak of the Spanish Civil War in 1936, he was sent to live with his grandmother in Paris, where he was joined by his mother (Germaine Cahen) in 1937. His cosmopolitan education was punctuated by his father's (the famous Generation of 1927 poet Jorge Guillén) positions at the universities of Murcia, Seville and Oxford. In 1938 Jorge Guillén left Spain to live in exile in the US. The family joined him in 1939, shortly before the poet began lecturing at Wellesley College. Claudio Guillén obtained a baccalaureate in 1940. He joined Charles de Gaulle's Free Forces and fought in northern Africa between 1943 and 1946 and on the French eastern front. After graduating from Williams College, in 1953 Guillén received his PhD in comparative literature at Harvard University, where his mentors were Harry Levin and Renato Poggioli. The topic of his dissertation was a comparative study of the origins of picaresque literature, a substantial part of which was written in Cologne, where he had obtained a teaching position. He taught comparative literature at Princeton University, the University of California at San Diego and Harvard University, where in 1983 he became the first Harry Levin Professor of Literature. During the 1980s, Guillén took leaves from Harvard and started teaching in Spain, first as extraordinary chair of comparative literature at the Universitat Autònoma de Barcelona and later as Emeritus at the Universitat Pompeu Fabra.

In 1957 Guillén published an article entitled "Literatura como sistema. Sobre fuentes, influencias y valores literarios" (Literature as System. On Literary Sources, Influences and Values), which led to one of his seminal books, *Literature as System*, 1971. His main thesis is that in literature there is a "will to order" which the comparatist has to address by taking into consideration a spatio-temporal dialectics, namely, the tension between evolution and continuity, between locality and world. It is here where the heuristic concept of "system" plays a key role, for (world) literature is "the larger configuration embracing one set after another in historical time".[i] Although neither *Weltliteratur*

---

i   Claudio Guillén, *Literature as System: Essays toward the Theory of Literary History* (Princeton: Princeton University Press, 1971), 376.

nor world literature are discussed as such concepts in *Literature as System*, it is clear that Guillén's systemic approach is a way to understand literature as a totality without over-looking both the intra-historicity and inter-historicity of its structures. It is in his 1985 textbook *Entre lo uno y lo diverso. Introducción a la literatura comparada*, translated into English as *The Challenge of Comparative Literature*, that Guillén discusses the concept of *Weltliteratur* (Chapter 6), which should be translated in his opinion as "litera-ture of the world" (1993: 39).

One may think that Guillén only addresses the issue of world literature as a stage in the disciplinary history of comparative literature. In fact, Chapter 6 of *The Challenge* is located between the sections devoted to positivism and the French school. It should be noted, however, that after dealing with Goethe's phrase and Marx and Engels's arguments about literary and economic relations, Guillén links the issue of the "litera-ture of the world" to his distinction between the international and the supranational, which is of key importance for he defines comparative literature precisely as the disci-pline which studies the latter dimension. Whereas the international stresses national literatures as the point of departure, supranationality makes reference to genres, forms and themes which have shaped the history of literature qua literature. Guillén distin-guishes three degrees of supranationality, of which the third one — typological affinities — represents what he considers to be not uprooted worldliness, but coherence and unity.

Claudio Guillén, *The Challenge of Comparative Literature*, Trans. Cola Franzen, Cambridge: Harvard UP, 1993, pp. 37–45 ("Weltliteratur"). Originally published in Spanish, 1985.

It is well known that Goethe coined the term [*Weltliteratur*] in his old age, in the year 1827, when a French adaptation of his *Torquato Tasso* appeared: "a general *Weltliteratur* is in the making in which an honorable role is reserved for us Germans."[1] Equally certain are the eighteenth-century origins of such an idea: Voltaire, J. G. Hamann, Herder. It was common-place to use the term "the Republic of Letters," whose aim, according to the Abbé Prévost, would be "to bring together into one confederation all the individual republics into which the Republic of Letters can be divided up to the present time."[2] Note that the existence of indi-vidual republics is pointed out in passing. Indeed, in order for the concept of a world litera-ture to develop it was necessary to describe first the diverse character of literature, that is, the insufficiently representative character of any one of its components alone, the limited nature of the contributions of any one nation or era to the culture in question. Something similar had happened in connection with the possibility of a universal history. Jacques Bénigne Bossuet in his *Discours sur l'histoire universelle* (1681) considered only those who in his judg-ment had raised their voices in song as part of God's design—the Hebrews, Greeks, Romans, and French. Not so Voltaire, who treated the Christian faith in a relativistic fashion in his *Essai sur les moeurs* (1753–58), thus opening the door of the world community to China, India, and the Arab countries.[3]

The term *Weltliteratur* is extremely vague—or should we say in a more positive way, it is too suggestive, and is therefore open to many misunderstandings. Let us look at three accepted meanings. In German, the juxtapositions of two nouns can lend an adjectival func-tion to the first noun. In such a case the range of meaning of the synthetic adjective can go so far as to imply that literature *itself* is worldwide, or that all literature is, or that only literature that is totally worldwide can be considered to be literature. What can one make of such an idea? The sum total of all national literatures? A wild idea, unattainable in practice, worthy not of an actual reader but of a deluded keeper of archives who is also a multimillionaire. The most harebrained editor has never aspired to such a thing.

As for the second meaning, one might think of a compendium of masterworks or of universal authors, if such words were understood to apply to those works that have been read and appreciated beyond the frontiers of their countries of origin: in sum, those authors hallowed either by a few respected critics, or by multitudes of readers. Quite a few historians have held this opinion, for example, Ferdinand Brunetière. Here is his definition of *littérature européenne*: "The works of a great literature belong to us only insofar as they have come in contact with other literatures, and to the extent that the contacts or encounters have had visible results."[4] At bottom he is speaking of European literature, and let us not call it world literature, a concept that, according to Luigi Foscolo Benedetto, came to be accepted in France. A disagreeable idea, in my opinion, and snobbish too, that recognizes success, and success only, together with its political, ephemeral, or contingent causes. It would be foolish of us to tell the history of our past in that manner, emphasizing its worst side: Vicente Blasco Ibáñez, Emil Ludwig and Erich Maria Remarque, Vicki Baum and Hans Fallada, Eugène Sue and Paul de Kock, Margaret Mitchell and Harold Robbins, Lajos Zilahy and Emilio Salgari and Corín Tellado. As far as our present-day evaluations of literature in Spain are concerned, it is more important that Juan Goytisolo admire and comment on the *Lozana andaluza* of Francisco Delicado, ignored in his own time, or on *Estebanillo González*, or the letters of Blanco White. Otherwise we find ourselves faced with the sad recapitulation of one trivial status quo after another, each one based on the influences and the influential writers of the past, and, of those, only those most visible and most widely known. That is what Guillermo de Torre, in an essay in *Las metamorfosis de Proteo* (1956), called "cosmopolitan literature," a literature that in many cases can hardly be considered even literary.[5] Unfortunately this conception is still bothersome as relic and bad habit of the old attachment of comparatists to the study of influences.

But there is more. There is a third accepted meaning of *Weltliteratur* that cuts across the second one, limiting it to the works of writers of the first or very highest rank. With more reason, the proposal is made to select great universal classics, as Martín de Riquer and José María Valverde write in the prologue to their *Historia de la literatura universal* (1957–74): "understanding as universal every literary creation capable of being of interest to everyone."[6] The universities (in the United States, the Great Books program of Chicago or of St. John's College, the courses of general education) and certain publishers put this attitude into practice. I am not questioning their pedagogical virtues. The Cyclopean task of writing a universal history of literature has produced some valuable results, such as the *Historia* of Riquer and Valverde, livelier and closer to the original texts than others, although it does not include Oriental literatures; and then there are Giacomo Prampolini's overwhelming fat tomes stuffed with knowledge.[7] But one should reread or take note of Étiemble, for whom the adjective "world" or "universal" turns out to be hyperbolical most of the time.[8] Can one call the collection of "La Pléiade" classics universal? It is no less Gallic-centered than the inquiry carried out some years ago by Raymond Queneau, who asked sixty-one writers what their "ideal library" would be. Since fifty-eight of those asked were French, the results surprised nobody.[9] And looking back, the historical perspectives—that is, looking at the past from the past—on the whole have been narrow and restrictive. The works of neither Dante nor Shakespeare nor Cervantes were considered classics by many European readers until well after the beginning of the nineteenth century. Vittorio Alfieri was of the opinion that in his day it would have been difficult to find more than thirty Italians who had read the *Divina commedia*. The chapter "Curriculum Authors" in Curtius's great book, translated as *European Literature and the Latin Middle Ages* (1973), brings out unexpected facts. As an example of historiographic method, there are more commendable ways to examine the past. And we would not think of implying that our own era is exemplary. However difficult it may be to learn Hungarian, isn't the quality of the poetry of Endre Ady (1877–1919) amazing even in translation? Without going farther afield, why don't we read *Max Havelaar* (1860), the charming and powerful novel by Multatuli of the Netherlands?

The attitudes that we have been discussing have little or nothing to do with Goethe, who had in mind the peculiarities of his own time and above all was looking toward the future. To come closer to his meaning, perhaps we should translate *Weltliteratur* as "literature of the world." And we should remember that Goethe started from the existence of some national literatures—thus making possible a dialogue between the local and the universal, between the one and the many, a dialogue that from that day to this has continued to breathe life into the best comparative studies. We are confronted then by three other groups of meanings. First: the presence of some poets and some poetries that can be "of the world" and for all the world, for everybody. Not limited to watertight national compartments, literatures can be accessible to future readers of a growing number of countries. The universality of the literary phenomenon is increasing. Second: works that in their real itinerary, their acceptance or rejection by different readers, critics, or translators, have circulated throughout the world. These necessarily include translations, transits, studies of reception aesthetics, close to what the first French comparative studies would become, a theme intertwined with the second accepted meaning of my previous paragraph but without normative, valorative, or anthological intentions—without bells and whistles. Bridges are built from country to country. János Hankiss once asked himself whether a universal literature could exist in the organic sense, in the truly unified sense of the term.[10] There is no such evidence for the idea which we are discussing, whose foundation is pluralistic.

And the third meaning: poems that reflect the world, that speak perhaps for all men and all women of the deepest, most common, or most lasting human experiences: the romantic exaltation of the poet, his symbolizing imagination, which may, as Coleridge wrote, "make the changeful God be felt in the river, the lion and the flame," the dream of historians such as Arturo Farinelli.[11] Thus we have three accepted meanings of "literature of the world," in brief outline, two of an international nature, and the third and last one better characterized as supranational.

In his conversation with J. P. Eckermann on January 31st, 1827, Goethe sees "more and more" that poetry is the universal possession, or common patrimony *(Gemeingut)*, of humanity, and that poetry reveals itself everywhere and in all eras, in hundreds and hundreds of men. (Herder had already emphasized this fact: the romances, folk songs, and other forms conserved by the common people show very clearly the widespread nature of this "poetry of the world," *Weltpoesie*.[12] That was the lesson of eastern Europe, from Latvia to Serbia. Vuk Karadžić, established in Vienna since 1813, had begun to publish his collections of popular Serbian poems with extraordinary success.) Translations and the study of foreign languages make it possible for the writings of great poets to enrapture vast and diverse audiences. In this manner—says Goethe—anyone can come out of his corner and breathe foreign airs: "National literature is now rather an unmeaning term; the epoch of world literature is at hand." A progressive expansion can be seen. The ancient Greeks did indeed fulfill an exemplary function. But it would be futile today to select a single nation or literature and try to convert it into a perfect "example"—whether it is "the Chinese, or the Serbian, or Calderón, or the *Nibelungen*," Goethe goes on to say. The earliest perfection remains in the past, the glory that was Greece. The future will be different. "All the rest we must look at only historically, appropriating to ourselves what is good, as far as it goes."[13] That is, the future will depend on a plurality of nations and their capacity for mutual understanding.

The starting point, Goethe explains elsewhere, consists of a national literature, but not of nationalism. "There is no patriotic art and no patriotic science." National literature is a beginning that will soon reveal its inadequacies. The reader, the critic, the curious man, the friend of peace and understanding between peoples are nourished more and more each day by works produced in myriad countries. So what the aged Goethe discovers and finds congenial is the growth of international exchanges. Note that Goethe emphasized what we call today the *reception* of literary works, a reception that becomes more and more international. He makes clear that increasing ease of communication is characteristic of modern times.[14] And he is interested in a class of phenomena that would later become a specialty of some comparatists: voyages and voyagers, magazines, reviews, and especially translations, such as those of Schiller into English, of Carlyle into German, or the French versions of *Faust*. There is the beginning of what Guillermo de Torre in *Las metamorfosis de Proteo* calls a "dialogue of literatures." There remains Goethe's hint of the connection between this dialogue of literatures and world trade, between the growth of economic relations and the expansion of cultural relations. Gerhard Kaiser emphasizes this connection with good reason: "The history of the concept of a literature of the world in the nineteenth century . . . can be understood only as a result of the change to which national as well as international thought was subjected in connection with the assumption of power by the bourgeoisie, a power that was, if not political, at least economic and social in nature."[15] But the increase of commercial interchanges and the growing power of the bourgeoisie are not considered here as threatening events. According to Goethe, they all contribute to peace and understanding—to the realization of the eighteenth-century ideal of a human community that was better informed, more tolerant, its components less isolated from one another. After the Napoleonic wars, achieving such a goal seemed more urgent than ever. The cannons of Waterloo still resounded in memory. The idea of *Weltliteratur* (like comparativism later) came out of a postwar atmosphere.

Such an idea would naturally become linked with similar, more innovative conceptions in the areas of politics and culture: with the Europeanism of Giuseppe Mazzini and with the new socialist internationalism.[16] As for Goethe's comments on the connection between literary and economic relations, *mutatis mutandis* Marx and Engels pick up the project of a *Weltliteratur* in the *Communist Manifesto* of 1848. The old economic self-sufficiency—they write—is giving way to international commerce. The same process is happening in intellectual as in material production. The spiritual products of individual nations are now "common property" *(Gemeingut)*; and a world literature will be formed from the local literatures: "In place of the old local and national seclusion and self-sufficiency, we have intercourse in every direction, universal interdependence of nations. And so in material, so also in intellectual production. The intellectual creations of individual nations become common property. National one-sidedness and narrow-mindedness become more and more impossible, and from the numerous national and local literatures, there arises a world literature."[17]

Today the concept of *Weltliteratur* raises certain difficulties, as we have already seen. Perhaps the most interesting and suggestive one is the distinction between the international and the supranational. These two dimensions implicate each other and should not suppress but rather foster the encounter between localization and meaning, an encounter that gives rise to a certain literary impulse, as we pointed out earlier. The greatest distances, those that most impede communication and understanding, are perhaps not international but intertemporal. And yet, are there not metaphors, similes, forms that persist and, after thousands of years, still reach us and speak to us? We are still moved—thanks perhaps to a simile, a metaphor, a dynamic form in crescendo—by the expression of jealousy in a famous poem by Sappho, who was born in Lesbos around 612 B.C.:

He seems as fortunate as the gods to me, the man who sits opposite you and listens nearby to your sweet voice and lovely laughter. Truly that sets my heart trembling in my breast. For when I look at you for a moment, then it is no longer possible for me to speak; my tongue has snapped, at once a subtle fire has stolen beneath my flesh, I see nothing with my eyes, my ears hum, sweat pours from me, a trembling seizes me all over, I am greener than grass, and it seems to me that I am little short of dying.[18]

This color green, between living and dying, cannot be simplified. The splendid verses of the Renaissance poet Garcilaso de la Vega come to mind, taken from his third Eclogue. The cadaver of a nymph lies beside the Tajo River:

> Cerca del agua, en un lugar florido,
> estaba entre las hierbas degollada
> cual queda el blanco cisne cuando pierde
> la dulce vida entre la hierba verde.

> Near the water, in a flowery spot, she lay among the
> grass with severed throat as the white swan lies when
> he loses his sweet life among the green grasses.[19]

Going much further back in time, I will cite a passage from an Egyptian poem of the XIIth dynasty (1900 B.C.) with its symmetries and comparisons (the final rain, so ambiguous), the poem called by Adolf Erman "Gespräch eines Lebensmüden mit seiner Seele" (Dialogue of One Tired of Life with His Soul). The poet, eager for suicide, has a conversation with himself:

> Today I have Death before me,
> like the aroma of myrrh,
> like someone resting beneath the sail on a windy day.

> Today I have Death before me,
> like the aroma of the lotus flower,
> like someone feeling on the verge of drunkenness.

> Today I have Death before me,
> like a rain moving away
> like someone returning to his house after a battle.[20]

It is well known that countless readers, not only westerners but Orientals also—for example, the Japanese—have read the works of Dostoevsky with passion. André Gide, who knew Dostoevsky's works well and admired them, declared that the most national writer is also the most universal. In our century, according to Harry Levin, no one fits that description as well as James Joyce:

> If Joyce departs from nationalism to arrive at internationalism, he follows a path different from Dante's: if Dante particularizes the universals, Joyce universalizes the particulars. Dante had fulfilled the conditions for beauty, as they had been laid down by Saint Thomas Aquinas: *integritas, consonantia, claritas*. The problem, as it was presented to Joyce, was more complicated: starting from fragments to create a whole; from discords, consonance; and from obscurities, clarity.[21]

Although a fragment does not necessarily express the whole or a unified entity, let us agree that since we are speaking of literature, the fragment is at least no longer merely local or particular. In the context of literature, internationalism does not mean a triumphant hetero-geneity. When fragment A and fragment B belonging to different localities come into contact, deeper and wider strata of sense are revealed, strata no longer confined to narrow spaces and moments, to a time *a* and a place *b*. Just as we leave the national sphere and approach a different one, we encounter not only the possibility of differences but also a confirmation of common values and questions. That is to say, matters of supranationality. Matters of transit and process that Goethe himself lived. Read again, for example, his 1828 review of Carlyle's *German Romance*, in which Goethe already supports the idea that it is the unique quality of the poet and of his nation that allows his literary work to illuminate *das allgemein Menschliche*, "the human quality in general":

> Evidently for a considerable time already the efforts of the best poets and best artistic writers of all nations have been directed toward the human quality in a general sense. In every particular aspect, whether historical, mythological, fabu-lous, or more or less arbitrarily invented, one will see that general dimension illuminating and shining through nationality and personality.[22]

The concurrence of these critical attitudes with the practices of Goethe the poet is evident—the poet who was interested in the rebirth of modern Greek literature, who translated one of the heroic Serbian cantos, "Lament for the Noblewomen of Asan Aga," who studied Czech during his summer vacations in Bohemia, and who—reader of Arabic, Persian, and Chinese poetry—wrote the *West-Östlicher Divan* (1819) and the "Chinesisch-Deutsche Jahres und Tageszeiten" (1830). As we will see later, the distinctions sketched by Goethe are funda-mental to the theory of literary genres.

There is no doubt that most of his contemporaries held a narrower conception of cosmo-politanism or "universality" than he did. Quite frequently some of them adopted pan-Euro-pean attitudes (Mazzini, Brunetière, Texte) or pan-Occidental stances. Or they perpetuated the hegemony of a half-dozen western European literatures. In the twentieth century the situation has changed appreciably; today writers confront literary groupings that include works and authors, procedures and styles originating in the most widely varying latitudes. As the Rumanian comparatist Adrian Marino explained so aptly, a unitary system of communica-tion is functioning nowadays with ever-increasing force, a world colloquy quite similar to the one glimpsed by Goethe:

> Time as well as space tends to expand more and more, to become superimposed, transformed into a unified cultural consciousness of the world, permanent and simultaneous. Thanks to the universal system of communication that is litera-ture, all literatures are on the way to becoming "contemporary" . . . Thus "universal literature" becomes the community of all literatures, past and present, no matter what their traditions, their languages, their historical dimensions and their geographical locations may be . . . The literary dialogue assumes a perma-nent and international character. Literary communication and community tend to merge.[23]

Notes

1   J.E. Spingarn, ed., *Goethe's Literary Essays* (New York: Harcourt, Brace and Company, 1921), 89.

2   Quoted in A. Marino, "Où situer la literature universelle," *Cahiers Roumains d'Études Littéraires* 3 (1975): 64–81 (71).

3   See E. Merian-Genast, "Voltaire und die Entwicklung der Idee der Weltliteratur," *Romanische Forschungen* 40 (1927): 1–226; and H. Bender and U. Melzer, "Zur Geschichte des Begriffes 'Weltliteratur'," *Saeculum* 9 (1958): 113–23.

4   F. Brunetière, *Variétés littéraires* (Paris: Calmann-Lévy, 1900), 23.

5   [Editors' note: G. de Torre, "Goethe y la 'literatura universal'," *Las metamorfosis de Proteo* (Buenos Aires: Losada, 1956), 278–89.]

6   [Editors' note: Martín de Riquer and José María Valverde, *Historia de la literatura universal*, 3 vols. (Barcelona: Noguer, 1958-68), 1:i.]

7   G. Prampolini, *Storia universale cedella letteratura*, 3rd ed., 7 vols. (Torino: Utet, 1959–61). On universal histories of literature, see J.C. Brandt Corstius, "Writing Histories of World Literature," *Yearbook of Comparative and General Literature* 12 (1963): 5–14 [Reproduced in this volume]. The Dutch comparatist makes a distinction between the historical surveys arranged by eras (like that of Riquer and Valverde, 1957–74) and the juxtapositions of national literatures (such as the three volumes edited by Queneau, 1955–58). Brandt Corstius was not able to read the meritorious (and aptly named) eight-volume *História da Literatura Ocidental* of O.M. Carpeaux (Rio de Janeiro: Cruzeiro, 1959–66). E. Martínez Estrada's *Panorama de las literaturas* (Buenos Aires: Claridad, 1946) is a lively personal essay.

8   For example, R. Étiemble, "Faut-il réviser la notion de Weltliteratur," *Proceedings of the IVth Congress of the International Comparative Literature Association/Actes du IVᵉ Congrès de l'Association Internationale de Littérature Comparée (Fribourg, 1964)*, ed. François Jost, 2 vols. (The Hague: Mouton, 1966) 1: 5–16. [Reproduced in this volume.]

9   See *Pour une bibliothèque idéale. Enquête présentée par Raymond Queneau* (Paris: Gallimard, 1956). Obviously these conceptions of universal literature leave aside or are unaware of the literatures of nations less studied or translated. See the commentaries of D. Ďurišin, *Vergleichende Literaturforschung* (Berlin: Akademie, 1972), 39–43.

10 J. Hankiss, "Littérature Universelle?," *Helicon* 1 (1938): 156–71.

11 A. Farinelli, *Petrarca, Manzoni, Leopardi. Il sogno di una letteratura "mondiale"* (Torino: Fratelli Bocca, 1925).

12 See Fr. Strich, *Goethe und die Weltliteratur* (Bern: Francke, 1946), 25. On *Weltliteratur*, see K. Vossler, "Nationalliteratur und Weltliteratur," *Zeitwende* 4.1 (1928): 193–204; E.R. Curtius, "Goethe als Kritiker," *Kritische Essays zur europäischen Literatur* (Bern: Francke, 1950), 25–58; E. Auerbach, "Philologie der Weltliteratur," *Weltliteratur: Festgabe für Fritz Strich zum 70. Geburtstag* (Bern: Francke, 1952): 39–50 [English translation reproduced in this volume]; H.J. Schrimpf, *Goethes Begriff der Weltliteratur* (Stuttgart: Metzler, 1968); Fr. Jost, *Introduction to Comparative Literature* (Indianapolis: Bobs Merrill, 1974), chap. 2; and G.R. Kaiser, *Einführung in die vergleichende Literaturwissenschaft* (Darmstadt: Wissenschaftliche Buchgesellschaft, 1980), chap. 2.

13 J.P. Eckermann, *Conversations with Goethe* (Oxford: Da Capo, 1998): 165–66.

14 [Editors' note: J.W. von Goethe, *Maxims and Reflections*, ed. P. Hutchinson, trans. E. Stopp (London: Penguin, 1999).]

15 Kaiser, 19. See the summary of G.M. Vajda, "Goethes Anregung zur vergleichenden Literaturbetrachtung," *Acta Litteraria Academiae Scientiarum Hungaricae* 10.3–4 (1968): 211–38.

16 R.V. Foa, *L'arte e la vita in Giuseppe Mazzini* (Genova: Associazione Mazziniana Italiana, 1956); and L.F. Benedetto, "La letteratura mondiale," *Uomini e tempi* (Milano: Ricciardi, 1953): 3–20.

17 See G.M. Vajda, "Essai d'une histoire de la literature compare en Hongrie," *Littérature hongroise, Littérature européenne*, eds. I. Söter and O. Süpek (Budapest: Akadémiai Kiadó, 1964): 525–88. [Editors' note: as for the excerpts from the *Manifesto of the Communist Party*, see the reproduction in this volume.]

18 D.A. Campbell, trans., *Sappho and Alcaeus* (Cambridge, Mass.: Harvard University Press, 1982) 79–81.

19 E.L. Rivers, *Renaissance and Baroque Poetry of Spain* (Prospect Heights, IL: Waveland Press, 1988): 76.

20 A. Erman, "Gespräch eines Lebensmüden mit seiner Seele," *Abhandlungen der Königl. Akademie der Wissenschaften zu Berlin* 2 (1896): 67–68; and S. Donadoni, *Storia della letteratura egiziana antica* (Milano: Accademia 1957): 81.

21 H. Levin, *Contexts of Criticism* (Cambridge, Mass.: Harvard University Press, 1958): 284. See also H. Levin, "Towards World Literature," *Tamkang Review* 6–7 (1975–76): 21–30.

22 Wolfgang Franzen's translation from the German: *Goethes Werke* (Weimar, 1903) 41.2: 305.

23 Marino, 68.

Chapter 18

Dionýz Ďurišin

WORLD LITERATURE AS A TARGET LITERARY-HISTORICAL CATEGORY (1993)

Dionýz Ďurišin (1929–97), PhD Comenius University (1952), was a leading Slovak comparatist who worked and researched in Bratislava throughout his life. He taught at the Teachers' College (1952–59), worked for the Commission on Agriculture (1959–60), as a researcher at the Czechoslovak–Soviet Institute of the Slovak Academy of Sciences (1960–64), and from 1964 onwards at the Institute of World Literature of the same Academy. Ďurišin's first monograph (1966), which was devoted to the analysis of the influence of Gogol on the realistic Slovak short story, led him to immediately reformulate theories of influence and reception and, therefore, the whole basis of comparative literature. This reformulation was presented in his 1967 *Problémy literárnej komparatistiky* (Problems of Literary Comparatism). Contrary to the rationale of key concepts of the French School of comparative literature ("source" and "influence"), which advocated the authority of the source-literature and the passive role of reception, Ďurišin argued that the act of reception is as creative and original as the act of literary creation proper, for it is the receiver who selects materials in accordance with, on the one hand, the needs of the literary system wherein these new materials are to be integrated and, on the other, the position of this system within a network of literary relations. Consequently, for Ďurišin the distinction between national and international influences was artificial and misleading, an argument which recalls René Wellek's discussion on the impossibility of distinguishing between national and international comparisons.

For Ďurišin, who drew on a synthesis of Alexander N. Veselovsky's historical poetics, Russian formalism, Jan Mukařovský's aesthetics, Felix Vodička's and Mikuláš Bakoš's functional structuralism, and Frank Wollman's comparatism, to which he applied a phenomenological approach, both national and comparative literary studies should be replaced by a single discipline, which he called the theory of interliterary process. The aim of this theory is to explain "the relationships arising from interliterary contactual co-existence and the adequacy of development of the literary processes" (Ďurišin 1984: 100). Theoretically, one has to differentiate between literary dis/similarities which are the result of either "genetical contacts," that is, the incorporation of materials from a precedent work through a specific kind of exposure, or "typological affinities," that is, affinities which cannot be explained by contact, as analyzed by, for instance, East–West

Studies. In practice, many causes make such a distinction impossible, for both kinds of dis/similarities are mutually conditioned. Ďurišin offered a comprehensive picture of these dis/similarities and their problems in *Theory of Literary Comparatistics* (1984), for they represent the network of literary relations, which, from single unities (national literatures) proceeds through intermediate stages (groups of national literatures called "interliterary communities") to the final stage, namely, world literature.

In 1992 Ďurišin published *Čo je svetová literatúra?* (What Is World Literature?), which he considered "the first [study] of its kind, even on a global scale" and "a synthesis of my own literary research" (196). *Čo je svetová literatúra?* is indeed the first book-length systemic study of world literature. It is also the most concise and detailed summary of Ďurišin's work on world literature since his 1967 textbook on comparative literature. Furthermore, *Čo je svetová literatúra?* laid out the rationale for two collective projects devoted to categories that lie between national and world literature. The first project on specific interliterary communities offered an alternative to the comparative histories sponsored by the Gorki Institute in Moscow and the ICLA Coordinating Committee. The second project dealt with literary areas which connected several communities, such as, for example, the Mediterranean. Ďurišin defined world literature as the structured system of literary phenomena that are either genetically or typologically related (1992: 200). In "World Literature as a Target Literary-Historical Category," Ďurišin surveys the traditional meanings attributed to world literature by comparative scholarship (compendium of literatures of the world, selection of masterpieces), and advocates an understanding of world literature as the result of the interliterary process.

Dionýz Ďurišin, From: "World Literature as a Target Literary-Historical Category," *Slovak Review* 2.1 (1993): 7–15.

I understand "world literature" to be the ultimate target category for literary scholarship, in a broad sense of the term. From experience we know that the designation "world literature," which is so frequently employed, is not without ambiguities, nor is it quite clear. This is true not only of the current literary designation, but also with regard to a basic category of literary scholarship. To my mind, this term deserves serious attention.

Despite its wide use in culture, and even in relation to literature nowadays, "world literature" is not an incidental concept. It does not merely express a global characteristic of the literary movement—in reflections on literature it is far more than an auxiliary factor. However, from a simplistic standpoint, "world literature" may in fact mean everything, and simultaneously almost nothing. The term is so comprehensive and all-encompassing that we cannot express it empirically, abstractly or theoretically. In this sense, world literature is being understood as something boundless and undefinable, something with only a general meaning and therefore of little instructive value to thinking.

This simplistic definition is flawed, not solely from the aspect of theory and literary history, but also from that of literary criticism, which evaluates literature in the strictest sense of the term. This has practical consequences in literary criticism, when a literary phenomenon is assessed against practical criteria of the literary movement. There is even greater significance for literary history, which requires a precise assignment of a work or an author to the developmental process, and a definite notion about the literary process. In this case, evaluation without the use of criteria deriving from the highest literary-historical unit—that is, from world literature—is just unthinkable.

It is thus evident that a definite, clear-cut comprehension of world literature was, is and will continue to be an important part of literary scholarship. Hence, the question "What is world literature?" is quite justified.

A direct question deserves a direct answer: world literature is a compendium of literary works of the whole world. However, we know that this answer fails to satisfy us, not only because it is a perfunctory statement, but especially because it fails to express the essence of the developmental movement. The answer begs further questions—what is a "compendium of literary works of the whole world"? How is it prepared and where is it evident? Can such a complex and living organism of human activity be described by the term "compendium" or even "sum"?

We see that such an answer fails to elucidate even general questions relating to world literature and its history. It does not answer some fundamental questions—what concepts of world literature existed in the past and what concepts exist at the present time? Since when has this designation been employed in thinking about literature? What is the relationship between national and world literature? In order to answer these questions, we must first define our own concept of world literature.

A perception of world literature can be gained through an understanding of literary-historical units such as national literatures and other analogous historical entities that existed and still exist today. This allows us to see world literature in action, to define its beginning and its final anchorage.

This perception also determines, both historically and in current explorations, such complex and differentiated literary-historical units as interliterary associations and groupings of literatures that came, or are coming into being, as the field continues to develop. Such examples are associations of Slavonic, Romance, Germanic, Central-European and other literatures, such as Swiss, Anglo-American and Baltic literatures. An investigation of these literary associations enables us to formulate the laws of interliterary development and thereby to define the corresponding basic conceptual apparatus in our discipline.

With this aim in mind, an investigation of world literature proceeds towards an under-standing of literary-historical concepts and categories such as literary tradition, convention, style, genre, genre form, artistic translation, periodization of literature and so on. It is becoming apparent that the concept of world literature need not be abstract, but can be quite concrete, compelling us to formulate new literary-historical, but mainly theoretical catego-ries. Thus far, many of them have only been dealt with empirically. One reason for this is the fact that world literature was understood as a fictive and inaccessible category, yet we know that it is both a basic and a main target literary concept. Literature, literary events and the literary process cannot be fully understood without the criteria which are implied within them. Hence, "world literature" is an indispensable gauge to a reader, helping him to find his bearings in national and foreign literary trends. Consequently, the term has formative significance.

From this function, it follows that world literature is not a rigid category, but a very flexible, vivid and fundamental element of literature and literary life. It is a historical and therefore mutable entity: it changes, as do epochs, literatures and readers' habits. Historicism of world literature applies to its categories, which permits us to write a history of literature; that is, to apply historical principles to the literary output of practically the whole world. A history of literature without generalization of the interliterary process is only a partial history. Work on the history of world literature thereby necessitates a restructuring of the traditional procedures and practices in literary history.

As a result of historicism and transformations in the literary movement, we meet with various concepts of world literature in the history of thought on literature. Prevailing views fluctuate between two extreme positions: on the one hand, world literature as a sum of national literatures, or analogous historical units, and, on the other hand, an inaccessible fiction diffused into literary infinity. These extreme positions reveal that the question of world literature is not dealt with scientifically, but empirically. Between the two poles, which lead to a literary-historical agnosticism, we find various notions regarding world literature, deriving from a conviction that this extensive material can be investigated, generalized and arranged into a hierarchical system. Past attempts at formulating a concept of world literature show that practically every literary historian and theoretician has in some way come into contact with this topical issue relating to the existence of world literature. A case in point is the Hungarian comparatist János Hankiss who, awed by the magnitude and diversity of this problem, recommends the use of the term "European" or "general" literature, since the concept "world literature" can uniquely be grasped through manifold relations and connections among the literatures of the world.[1] The German literary scholar Erwin Laaths divides world literatures regionally: Western European, Indian, East Asian and so on; and considers Western European literature to be at the centre of the world's literary development.[2] This is the standpoint of so-called Western European centrism. The Swiss literary historian Eduard von Tunk, without attempting a methodically-founded exposition of world literature, likewise proclaims the priority of European world literature.[3] A similar view is held by his countryman Robert Lavalette, who also includes the results of Eastern European literatures in his concept, but solely in terms of the extent to which these have been incorporated into Western European literatures.[4] We should also mention the French comparatist Albert Guérard, who includes all the works in world literature that have gained universal recognition.[5] He makes use here of the term "universal literature," comprising all significant works, regardless of the place and time of their origin.

Many such concepts of world literature exist today. One may consider a French edition of the *History of Literatures* (1958), then *Literatures of the World in an Oral and Written Form* (Zürich, 1964); and the work by the Austrian Slavist J. Matla, *Europe and the Slavs* (1964).[6] This methodological orientation also includes earlier German authors—O. Leixner (1898), O. Hauser (1910), K. Busse (1910), A. Bertels (1911), E.M. Mayer (1913), as well as works by numerous English, French and other authors.

As in Western European scholarship, considerable pressure was felt in Eastern European countries for a solution to the question of world literature. A certain unification of these two streams of literary-historic initiative took place in Belgrade in 1967, at the Fifth Congress of the International Association of Comparative Literature, where efforts were made to introduce a common methodology for the History of European Literature or History of Literatures of European Languages.[7]

An effort to understand the history of world literature on the basis of a conceptual synthesis of the interliterary process is also evident in the attempt by a team of Russian literary scholars at the Institute of World Literature in Moscow to edit a ten-volume *History of World Literature*.[8] The publication of such a comprehensive history of world literature marks a certain dividing line, if not a breakthrough, on a worldwide scale. The methodological preparation of this wide-ranging work is the start of historiographic studies which signal the necessity of a systematic approach to the literary process and bring in numerous methodological stimuli.

It should be observed here that new syntheses of world literature have lately appeared in other countries, including compendia of world literature in Poland, Hungary, Yugoslavia (eight volumes), the Czech Republic and Slovakia. Two volumes of a Slovak edition of the *Dejiny svetovej literatúry* (History of World Literature), published by Obzor in 1963, meant a certain breakthrough in the historiography of Slovak literature. Their publication raised the question of how to incorporate the development of Slovak literature into the context of a higher literary-historical entity. Towards the end of the 1980s a new, analogous *History of World Literature* was prepared, but the communist system was incapable of publishing it, although it was editorially ready for print.

*

What is of interest now is an answer to the question "What in fact is world literature?" Our theory and practice so far have brought three principles into the foreground, which in my opinion may be considered to be three steps towards formulating the concept of "world literature." I hasten to add that there is an inherent question regarding principles whose measure of conceptualization differs on particular points. Thus, dissimilarity, but also conditionality of these principles comes to the forefront, as they acquire the character of relatively valid, or even occasionally, dominant concepts.

The first principle involves a concept traditionally formulated as a set of national literatures or analogous literary-historical units, placed side by side more or less mechanically.

The second principle represents a selection of the best authors, works, processes and so on, decided according to the transitory value of a concrete literary situation.

Lastly, the third principle is bound to literary phenomena, comprising the same relations and affinities, which are therefore mutually genetically and typologically conditioned. I consider these principles—which represent my notion of world literature in its complex understanding—to be relatively interdependent. They may not be separated from one another, but have to be understood as having a certain mutual influence and connection. Furthermore, their adequate explication (and also the methodological instructiveness of such clarification), resides precisely in their close connection. Taking this as a starting point, I shall try to analyze these concepts, endeavoring to point out their mutual influence and contradictions, and in particular their role in a constantly evolving notion of world literature and its history—a notion that is living, topical, historically indispensable, but changeable. Therein resides the essence of the issue at stake.

World literature as a complex or a compendium of literatures of the world

This is essentially an elemental concept, since it more or less straightforwardly places national and other literatures next to each other. Historically it is the earliest and evidently the simplest concept. We have termed it "additive" or "parallel." It is traditionally said to be defined by a mechanical principle of structure, devoid of a unifying system; one that does not create the history of world literature as a unified whole. It thereby prevents us from uncovering the inner relationship between the specificity of national literatures, or analogous literary-historical units, and the universal literary process. Although the additive concept fails systematically to reveal the laws of the interliterary process, it nevertheless does point to their existence and thereby evokes the necessity of their investigation, thereby stimulating research along this line.

As becomes clear from the argument above, negative features predominate in this definition of the concept. As a matter of fact, the definition is given *per negationem* and is accompanied by numerous reservations. There are even voices demanding that it should not be considered at all as a concept, since its "mechanical essence" does not comprise any activity which would express the presence of a concept; any inherent creative principle is an organic outcome of a certain generalization of phenomena and processes.

However, we cannot fail to notice that this concept of world literature, although it has been criticized and refuted, is the most frequently implemented in literary-historical practice. Examples of this are the Slovak compilations of a *History of World Literature*: I have in mind the work of 1963, and partly also that completed in 1990.[9] Both of these syntheses were of an additive character, essentially adjunctive or parallel. Both provide a history by application of the mechanical organizing principle.

A dominant position is ascribed to literatures which enjoy a considerable temporal advance in comparison with European literatures; that is, those of the Far, Near and Middle East; with a geographic principle of construction as the starting point. This history also partially respects the genetic principle which, in this case, is of a functional character, pointing to the developmental progression in world literature. I am aware that the geographic principle of construction and periodization has an auxiliary classificatory function, although historically it has often acted as an inner amalgamator—as in the case of central European, Nordic, Mediterranean literatures and so on. In the Slovak *History of World Literature*, the geographic principle fulfilled the role of an auxiliary periodizing criterion. The aim of that edition was to set up a complex of informative data on a synchronous platform.

The eight-volume *Povijest svjetskej književnosti* (History of World Literature) is also essentially additive but, like the Slovak publication, tried to go beyond this limited goal.[10] This ambitious project was not only permitted to encompass the extensive historic material, but also to select exacting methodological principles and procedures. In some measure, the various volumes together provide rounded periodizing wholes—I say in some measure, because the Croatian *History of World Literature* is wholly of the additive type. This additive nature, however, is overcome through efforts at characterizing certain literary entities—attempts to capture their functionality, and, in places, also through the authors' ambition to preserve integrity and unity.

Even a cursory observation of the additive concept of world literature reveals that this simplest of approaches best corresponds to the needs of the reader community, for which it provides a factographic base and enables it to form an idea of literary events on a worldwide scale. This approach derives from the principle of a summation of concepts, and less from their classification and evaluation. Although it has until now been the most frequently applied principle, it is not satisfactory from a gnoseological aspect, for it ultimately leads to a certain disinformation.

The literary-historical view takes this fact into account and therefore, alongside the summation concept, it creates a more exacting model of world literature from the literary and conceptual point of view.

A selective concept of world literature

This concept of world literature overcomes the principle of summation; it is guided by principles deriving from systemic selectivity. Selection is based on an application of literary-historical criteria within an evaluation of literary facts. It prefers the peak phenomena of the literary evolution: leading personalities, works, trends and processes. It is devoid of empirical relativity and is determined by specific principles of classification.

The selective concept is also termed a "reader concept." It is real and has practical justification. We are governed by it, for example, in teaching literature, and in the publishing, editing and marketing industries. The literary-historical, evaluative concept of world literature enjoys considerable popularity among readers and is also accepted by literary scholars, due to its operative, dynamic and productive nature. Occasionally it is referred to as a concept of world classicism, which shows that it is oriented toward a strict selectiveness. Numerous one-sided views have been expressed regarding this point, and were especially evident when the value or selective concept of world literature was discussed from centralist literary-historical aspects. It then became an instrument of abstract value criteria, *a priori* defined with the aid of territorial determinants.

Leaving aside these extremes and adhering to objective measures of artistic value, we may overlook the fact that however significant these values are, they are not the only indicators of classification. The rating of authors or works is often subject to changes brought about by the various bonds affecting such a rating. This may be, for instance, a socially determined factor behind the rating, the cultural type or the social function—agents that may be subsumed under the term "socio-literary convention" in its widest sense.

Often they are agents which are subject to the prevailing taste. Such was, for example, the wave of interest in K. May's works, or the popularity once enjoyed by Dumas's writings. Nonetheless, the value concept of world literature remains considerably attractive. As a matter of fact, literary development does not solely comprise clear values representing literary progress, but also includes a decline of aesthetic values as a result of the literary production of second- and even third-rate authors, which is often turned to good profit by the editing and publishing industries.

Were we to compare these two concepts of world literature from the aspect of the relationship between the national and world processes, we would note that the former derives from a certain predominance of national literary historiography and the latter is the result of so-called supranational notions about literary development. While the former process reinforces the aspect of individuality at the expense of universality, the latter favors the universal without taking into account the appropriate connections with the individual.

A description of the value concept should also point out certain problems that are often overlooked. The point is that this concept of world classics cannot be left to stagnate in isolationist positions on the basis of a narrowly and formally understood immanence. I have in mind its creative relationship to the triumvirate which forms the starting point of world literature, namely, the additive, the selective and the relational principles. The concept of world literature cannot be the sum of an unequivocal, isolated selection of the best authors, works, processes and outputs of world literature without consideration of the milieu which had molded them, either directly or indirectly.

From this it follows that not even a selective concept of world literature can comprehensively deal with the issue of value. It must also take into account the results of literary-historical research and abide by them, because value—as a constituent element of the literary-critical approach to phenomena—is ultimately rooted in the results of literary-historical knowledge. For example, Shakespeare, Molière, Balzac, Dostoyevsky, or Gorky may not be assigned *ad hoc* in the history of world literature, but only on the basis of a consistent study and evaluation of their historico-genetic, developmental and actual significance. Knowledge of the fates of literary classics in the interliterary process constitutes a precondition of selectivity. We see that these three concepts of world literature—namely additive, selective and literary-historical—mutually condition and internally complete one another.

The value-selective concept of the history of world literature is represented by numerous syntheses in European and other literatures. This is a concept which, by its nature, suits practice and also authors' pragmatic aspirations. A case in point is *A világirodalom története* (History of World Literature) by the Hungarian literary historian Antal Szerb.[11] This work is a typical compendium of the old type, as evidenced by the evaluative criteria and the method of explanation. It is marked by a subjective treatment of history as a process and also as a value, with its inevitable mutability which accepts the developmental mode of Hungarian literary consciousness.

A value-selective history of world literature also comprises compendia destined for teaching practice, such as the *History of World Literature* of the Philosophical Faculty, Charles University in Prague (under Prof. Ján O. Fischer), or a work by the Philosophical Faculty, Palacký University at Olomouc (Z. Brančíková).[12] Both these works are of a selective character from the aspect of their function, although they simultaneously follow the process of literary development.

Developmental concept of world literature

The concepts of world literature dealt with here—namely, the additive and value concepts—are the result of certain stages of literary thinking and therefore, at a specific developmental phase in thinking, were well-grounded and justified. However, they are now regarded as outdated, having been replaced by a new system in literary history which, instead of separating one layer from another, investigates their reciprocal synthesis and wholeness. Although I have expressed certain reservations about the preceding concepts, it does not mean that I refute them. Each of them has positive attributes. A literary-historical concept absorbs the two preceding concepts and creatively completes them. It integrates and synthesizes some of their attributes, especially those expressing objective reality. Such an approach to the concept of world literature reflects the dialectics of the cognitive process, which is neither rectilinear nor mechanical. The literary-historical concept of world literature is more complex, more comprehensive and has a greater measure of objectivity.

An integration of the various concepts does not proceed mechanically and in linear fashion. Therefore, certain problems are likely to arise in an explication of the literary-historical material. The first such problem is embodied in the question: which literary facts form part of world literature?

The answer is: those facts that are the bearers of mutual relationships and affinities, those that are genetically and typologically mutually conditioned and systematized. The measure of their influence in the literary-historical system is the measure of their share in the progressively developmental trends of the interliterary process. Developmental progressiveness is not an *a priori* evaluative phenomenon; it embodies the criteria of developmental dynamism, which are also realized during periods of stagnation and decline. The moment and the measure of progressiveness are factors determining the structures of world literature as a system. They tend toward a transformation of the hierarchy of the components of world literature.

Therein lies the guarantee of development in the "interliterary association" of this system, which is realized on the synchronous, as well as the diachronous plane. It is a living, flexible, developmentally stimulating formation. Thus understood, the concept of world literature might be said to be more complex and thereby also theoretically ineffective. This would indeed be true if we failed to take into account the fact that the concept of world literature is a reflection of the objective reality of a certain historical sector in our awareness. This reflection, however, is not identical to reality.

The concept and the content of world literature depend upon the extent of our knowledge of the literary process. This knowledge corresponds to the development of literary thinking in a given period. Our explanation of world literature should have the characteristic of a system to which would respond both literary scholarship and a notion of world literature, subjectively transposed into human consciousness at a given degree of development. In relation to the natural, material system, existing independently of our consciousness and embodying all existing phenomena, the system of world literature is distinguished by a certain measure of completeness and exactness. The relationship between world literature as a factual system and concepts of world literature as ideational systems is necessarily variable and expresses the dialectical tension of the cognitive effort of taking objective reality under control, or getting as close to it as possible.

Therefore, the concept of world literature is not an immutable phenomenon. On the contrary, it is subject to constant modification—an inner restructuring as the consequence of: (a) changes in the level of lower systematic planes; hence, it depends on the developmental paths of artistic literature, and (b) sign-projection of these literary facts, realized within the system of literary scholarship, involving a compact stream of notions yielded by the research of interliterary relationships and affinities; and of the interliterary process as such.

This justifies retrospective attempts at formulating the concept of world literature, as with those undertaken by traditional comparative studies and literary history. An exhaustive and final, or absolute, definition of world literature is, in fact, impossible. A historically living and dynamic concept reaches out to meet the needs of the theory of literature in that it fulfills the function of a basic methodological instruction. Herein lies the source of numerous discussions and polemics relating to the concept of world literature which create prospects of future research.

Our notion of world literature as a target, or final literary-historical category—of the interliterary community—can also be graphically outlined (see scheme below). We see that the structure of world literature consists of several gnoseological-ontological strata: genetic-contact relationships, structural-typological affinities, interliterary communities and centrisms. This complex is the object of the interliterary process in its "supranational" inter-literary projection, which proceeds towards world literature. This explains why I consider it to be a final interliterary association.

*

The functionality of and justifications for an attempt to formulate a concept of world literature have been documented by the fact that the Slovak literary scholarship has, within a relatively short time, presented two projects on the *History of World Literature*. As mentioned above, the first of these was published in 1963 and the second was prepared for print in 1990. The latter of the two projects of literary synthesis is an expression of dissatisfaction with the interpretation of interliterariness as understood by contemporary European and international literary scholarship.

A formulation of the concept of world literature has also been elicited by the fact that, as yet, this concept has no theoretically elaborated category of literature and poetry that would tend from the national literary-historical unit towards the final historical unit which is world literature.

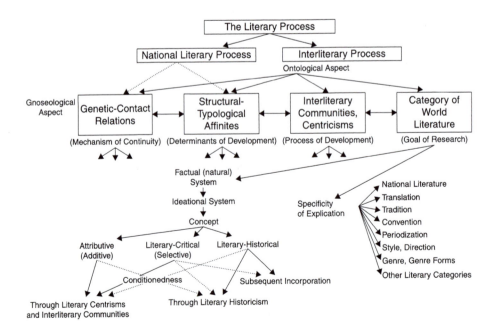

A qualitatively new explication of the concepts and categories of the traditional theory of literature may be heard from podia of interliterary associations and communities. In studies by interliterary communities, basic functions—particularly the integrating, differentiating and especially the complementary functions—tend to acquire new content. In this manner, a whole series of concepts come to be modified, such as dioecism and polyoecism, biliterariness and polyliterariness, polyfunctionality, syncretism of literary traditions, stimulative-fictive analogy, and so on. A new interpretation is beginning to be applied to artistic translation, tradition and convention, and a whole series of further theoretical categories are being innovated in a similar manner. That, however, is a further aspect of the inner structure of the theory of interliterariness and world literature, and is dealt with in another section of our study.

Notes

[Editors' note: This article by Ďurišin was translated from an unpublished Slovak original into English by an unknown translator and published in 1993. Due to the great number of grammatical errors, the text presented here has been corrected and substantially modified.]

1   [Editors' note: János Hankiss, "Littérature universelle?" *Helicon* 1 (1938): 156–71.]
2   [Editors' note: Erwin Laaths, *Geschichte der Weltliteratur* (München: Droemersche, 1953).]
3   [Editors' note: Eduard von Tunk, *Illustrierte Weltliteraturgeschichte*, 3 vols. (Zürich: Stauffacher, 1954–55).]
4   [Editors' note: Robert Lavalette, *Literaturgeschichte der Welt* (Zürich: Füssli, 1948).]
5   [Editors' note: see Guérard's text included in this volume.]
6   [Editors' note: as for a "French edition," Ďurišin is most probably making reference here to Raymond Queneau, ed., *Histoire des littératures*, 3 vols. (Paris: Gallimard, 1955–58); W. von Einsiedel, ed. *Die Literaturen der Welt in ihrer mündlichen und schriftlichen Überlieferung* (Zürich: Kindler, 1964).]
7   [Editors' note: Ďurišin makes reference here to the comparative literary histories sponsored by the ICLA's Coordinating Committee for a Comparative History of Literatures in European Languages.]
8   [Editors' note: J.S. Braginsky, ed., *Istorija vsemirnoj literatury*, 6 vols. (Moscow: Nauka, 1983–89).]
9   [Editors' note: Ďurišin is most probably making reference here to Jaroslava Pašiaková, *Dejiny svetovej literatúry* (Bratislava: Univerzita Komenského 1990).]
10   [Editors' note: Dušan Karpatský and Aleksandar Flaker, *Povijest svjetske književnosti* (Zagreb: Mladost, 1975).]
11   [Editors' note: Antal Szerb, *A világirodalom története* (Budapest: Magvetökönyvkiadó, 1962).]
12   [Editors' note: Ďurišin makes reference here to the series coordinated by Ján O. Fischer, "Dejiny svetových literatur." Zdenka Brančíková, *Kapitoly ze světové literatury* [Chapters of World Literature] (Olomouc: Rektorát Univerzity Palackého, 1977).]

Chapter 19

Franco Moretti

CONJECTURES ON WORLD LITERATURE and MORE CONJECTURES (2000/2003)

F RANCO MORETTI (B. 1950) HAS BEEN a professor of English and comparative literature at Stanford University since 2000. He previously held positions at Columbia University and at Italian universities. His main area of study is the novel and the way this genre has evolved and spread around the world. Moretti is an unconventional literary scholar who seeks to explain the uses of certain genres in society by means of both statistical methods and a well-developed analytical grip on the literary texts themselves. This approach is also a key element of his major edited work, *The Novel*.

Moretti has written a few short but highly influential articles on the subject of world literature which are often contrasted with the contributions of David Damrosch and Pascale Casanova in the context of the renewed interest in world literature which emerged around 2000. Moretti's earlier work foreshadowed that interest in different ways. *Modern Epic* (1996) investigated foundational classics in world literature with an emphasis on their ability to present a large vision of the world, while *Atlas of the European Novel 1800–1900* (1998) attempted to quantify streams of exchange between nations and the directions in which influence flowed.

In the seminal theoretical article "Conjectures on World Literature" Moretti weighs the pros and cons of expanding the scope of a traditional comparative approach which investigates three or four literatures to the enormous task of dealing with world literature. The concept of "distant reading" is introduced as shorthand for focusing second-hand, so to speak, on literary phenomena such as a particular narrative device across a number of literatures. Since no one is capable of mastering the enormous corpus of languages and literatures of the world such research of necessity has to rely on the previous work of other scholars that have done the hands-on primary research in one, or at best a few, literatures in the original.

Instead of doing close readings of all texts in the corpus, distant reading allows us to trace the dissemination of the novel around the world and to research how similarities and differences are created when a new literature adopts, and adapts, the form of the novel. Moretti uses the metaphors of waves and trees to describe two ways of looking at literatures. The wave approach is interested in the spread of influences in the form of genres and their features, while the tree focuses on what makes a national or local literature specific and separate from others. While both approaches can be valuable, Moretti clearly prefers the former.

In "More Conjectures", written in response to criticism of his initial article on world literature, Moretti stresses that the novel is not the only genre which has had a wavelike influence, and he downplays the role of language differences and points to cultural understandings as elements which are often much more complicated to export. It is in this respect that genres facilitate the comprehension of unfamiliar contents: by means of a similarity in genre.

Franco Moretti, "Conjectures on World Literature," *New Left Review* 1 (2000): 54–68 and "More Conjectures," *New Left Review* 20 (2003): 73–81.

CONJECTURES ON WORLD LITERATURE (2000)

My mission: to say it more simply than I understand it.

Schönberg, *Moses and Aaron*

'Nowadays, national literature doesn't mean much: the age of world literature is beginning, and everybody should contribute to hasten its advent.' This was Goethe, of course, talking to Eckermann in 1827; and these are Marx and Engels, twenty years later, in 1848: 'National one-sidedness and narrow-mindedness become more and more impossible, and from the many national and local literatures, a world literature arises.' *Weltliteratur*: this is what Goethe and Marx have in mind. Not 'comparative', but world literature: the Chinese novel that Goethe was reading at the time of that exchange, or the bourgeoisie of the *Manifesto*, which has 'given a cosmopolitan character to production and consumption in every country'. Well, let me put it very simply: comparative literature has not lived up to these beginnings. It's been a much more modest intellectual enterprise, fundamentally limited to Western Europe, and mostly revolving around the river Rhine (German philologists working on French literature). Not much more.

This is my own intellectual formation, and scientific work always has limits. But limits change, and I think it's time we returned to that old ambition of *Weltliteratur*: after all, the literature around us is now unmistakably a planetary system. The question is not really *what* we should do—the question is *how*. What does it mean, studying world literature? How do we do it? I work on West European narrative between 1790 and 1930, and already feel like a charlatan outside of Britain or France. World literature?

Many people have read more and better than I have, of course, but still, we are talking of hundreds of languages and literatures here. Reading 'more' seems hardly to be the solution. Especially because we've just started rediscovering what Margaret Cohen calls the 'great unread'. 'I work on West European narrative, etc. . . . .' Not really, I work on its canonical fraction, which is not even one per cent of published literature. And again, some people have read more, but the point is that there are thirty thousand nineteenth-century British novels out there, forty, fifty, sixty thousand—no one really knows, no one has read them, no one ever will. And then there are French novels, Chinese, Argentinian, American. . . . Reading 'more' is always a good thing, but not the solution.[1]

Perhaps it's too much, tackling the world and the unread at the same time. But I actually think that it's our greatest chance, because the sheer enormity of the task makes it clear that world literature cannot be literature, bigger; what we are already doing, just more of it. It has to be different. The *categories* have to be different. 'It is not the "actual" interconnection of "things"', Max Weber wrote, 'but the *conceptual* interconnection of *problems* which define the scope of the various sciences. A new "science" emerges where a new problem is pursued by a new method.'[2] That's the point: world literature is not an object, it's a *problem*, and a problem that asks for a new critical method: and no one has ever found a method by just reading more texts. That's not how theories come into being; they need a leap, a wager—a hypothesis, to get started.

World literature: one and unequal

I will borrow this initial hypothesis from the world-system school of economic history, for which international capitalism is a system that is simultaneously *one*, and *unequal*: with a core, and a periphery (and a semiperiphery) that are bound together in a relationship of growing inequality. One, and unequal: *one* literature (*Weltliteratur*, singular, as in Goethe and Marx), or perhaps, better, one world literary system (of inter-related literatures); but a system which is different from what Goethe and Marx had hoped for, because it's profoundly unequal. 'Foreign debt is as inevitable in Brazilian letters as in any other field', writes Roberto Schwarz in a splendid essay on 'The Importing of the Novel to Brazil': 'it's not simply an easily dispensable part of the work in which it appears, but a complex feature of it';[3] and Itamar Even-Zohar, reflecting on Hebrew literature: 'Interference [is] a relationship between literatures, whereby a . . . source literature may become a source of direct or indirect loans [*Importing* of the novel, direct and indirect loans, foreign debt: see how economic metaphors have been subterraneously at work in literary history]—a source of loans for . . . a target literature . . . *There is no symmetry in literary interference. A target literature is, more often than not, interfered with by a source literature which completely ignores it.*'[4]

This is what one and unequal means: the destiny of a culture (usually a culture of the periphery, as Montserrat Iglesias Santos has specified)[5] is intersected and altered by another culture (from the core) that 'completely ignores it'. A familiar scenario, this asymmetry in international power—and later I will say more about Schwarz's 'foreign debt' as a complex literary feature. Right now, let me spell out the consequences of taking an explanatory matrix from social history and applying it to literary history.

Distant reading

Writing about comparative social history, Marc Bloch once coined a lovely 'slogan', as he himself called it: 'years of analysis for a day of synthesis';[6] and if you read Braudel or Wallerstein you immediately see what Bloch had in mind. The text which is strictly Wallerstein's, his 'day of synthesis', occupies one third of a page, one fourth, maybe half; the rest are quotations (fourteen hundred, in the first volume of *The Modern World-System*). Years of analysis; other people's analysis, which Wallerstein's page synthesizes into a system.

Now, if we take this model seriously, the study of world literature will somehow have to reproduce this 'page'—which is to say: this relationship between analysis and synthesis—for the literary field. But in that case, literary history will quickly become very different from what it is now: it will become 'second hand': a patchwork of other people's research, *without a single direct textual reading*. Still ambitious, and actually even more so than before (world literature!); but the ambition is now directly proportional *to the distance from the text*: the more ambitious the project, the greater must the distance be.

The United States is the country of close reading, so I don't expect this idea to be particularly popular. But the trouble with close reading (in all of its incarnations, from the new criticism to deconstruction) is that it necessarily depends on an extremely small canon. This may have become an unconscious and invisible premiss by now, but it is an iron one nonetheless: you invest so much in individual texts *only* if you think that very few of them really matter. Otherwise, it doesn't make sense. And if you want to look beyond the canon (and of course, world literature will do so: it would be absurd if it didn't!) close reading will not do it. It's not designed to do it, it's designed to do the opposite. At bottom, it's a theological exercise—very solemn treatment of very few texts taken very seriously—whereas what we really need is a little pact with the devil: we know how to read texts, now let's learn how *not* to read them. Distant reading: where distance, let me repeat it, *is a condition of knowledge*: it allows you to focus on units that are much smaller or much larger than the text: devices, themes, tropes—or genres and systems. And if, between the very small and the very large, the text itself disappears, well, it is one of those cases when one can justifiably say, Less is more. If we want to understand the system in its entirety, we must accept losing something. We always pay a price for theoretical knowledge: reality is infinitely rich; concepts are abstract, are poor. But it's precisely this 'poverty' that makes it possible to handle them, and therefore to know. This is why less is actually more.[7]

The Western European novel: rule or exception?

Let me give you an example of the conjunction of distant reading and world literature. An example, not a model; and of course my example, based on the field I know (elsewhere, things may be very different). A few years ago, introducing Kojin Karatani's *Origins of Modern Japanese Literature*, Fredric Jameson noticed that in the take-off of the modern Japanese novel, 'the raw material of Japanese social experience and the abstract formal patterns of Western novel construction cannot always be welded together seamlessly'; and he referred in this respect to Masao Miyoshi's *Accomplices of Silence*, and Meenakshi Mukherjee's *Realism and Reality* (a study of the early Indian novel).[8] And it's true, these books return quite often to the complicated 'problems' (Mukherjee's term) arising from the encounter of western form and Japanese or Indian reality.

Now, that the same configuration should occur in such different cultures as India and Japan—this was curious; and it became even more curious when I realized that Roberto Schwarz had independently discovered very much the same pattern in Brazil. So, eventually, I started using these pieces of evidence to reflect on the relationship between markets and forms; and then, without really knowing what I was doing, began to treat Jameson's insight as if it were—one should always be cautious with these claims, but there is really no other way to say it—as if it were a *law of literary evolution*: in cultures that belong to the periphery of the literary system (which means: almost all cultures, inside and outside Europe), the modern novel first arises not as an autonomous development but as a compromise between a western formal influence (usually French or English) and local materials.

This first idea expanded into a little cluster of laws,[9] and it was all very interesting, but . . . it was still just an idea; a conjecture that had to be tested, possibly on a large scale, and so I decided to follow the wave of diffusion of the modern novel (roughly: from 1750 to 1950) in the pages of literary history. Gasperetti and Goscilo on late eighteenth-century Eastern Europe;[10] Toschi and Martí-López on early nineteenth-century Southern Europe;[11] Franco and Sommer on mid-century Latin America;[12] Frieden on the Yiddish novels of the 1860s;[13] Moosa, Said and Allen on the Arabic novels of the 1870s;[14] Evin and Parla on the Turkish novels of the same years;[15] Anderson on the Filipino *Noli Me Tangere*, of 1887; Zhao and Wang on turn-of-the-century Qing fiction;[16] Obiechina, Irele and Quayson on West African novels between the 1920s and the 1950s[17] (plus of course Karatani, Miyoshi, Mukherjee, Even-Zohar and Schwarz). Four continents, two hundred years, over twenty independent critical studies, and they all agreed: when a culture starts moving towards the modern novel, it's *always* as a compromise between foreign form and local materials.

Jameson's 'law' had passed the test—the first test, anyway.[18, 19] And actually more than that: it had completely reversed the received historical explanation of these matters: because if the compromise between the foreign and the local is so ubiquitous, then those independent paths that are usually taken to be the rule of the rise of the novel (the Spanish, the French, and especially the British case)—*well, they're not the rule at all, they're the exception*. They come first, yes, but they're not at all typical. The 'typical' rise of the novel is Krasicki, Kemal, Rizal, Maran—not Defoe.

Experiments with history

See the beauty of distant reading plus world literature: they go against the grain of national historiography. And they do so in the form of *an experiment*. You define a unit of analysis (like here, the formal compromise),[20] and then follow its metamorphoses in a variety of environments[21]—until, ideally, *all* of literary history becomes a long chain of related experiments: a 'dialogue between fact and fancy', as Peter Medawar calls it: 'between what could be true, and what is in fact the case'.[22] Apt words for this research, in the course of which, as I was reading my fellow historians, it became clear that the encounter of western forms and local reality did indeed produce everywhere a structural compromise—as the law predicted—but also, that the compromise itself was taking rather different forms. At times, especially in the second half of the nineteenth century and in Asia, it tended to be very unstable:[23] an 'impossible programme', as Miyoshi says of Japan.[24] At other times it was not so: at the beginning and at the end of the wave, for instance (Poland, Italy and Spain at one extreme; and West Africa on the other), historians describe novels that had, certainly, their own problems—but not problems arising from the clash of irreconcilable elements.[25]

I hadn't expected such a spectrum of outcomes, so at first I was taken aback, and only later realized that this was probably the most valuable finding of them all, because it showed that world literature was indeed a system—but a system *of variations*. The system was one, not uniform. The pressure from the Anglo-French core *tried* to make it uniform, but it could never fully erase the reality of difference. (See here, by the way, how the study of world literature is—inevitably—a study of the struggle for symbolic hegemony across the world.) The system was one, not uniform. And, retrospectively, of course it had to be like this: if after 1750 the novel arises just about everywhere as a compromise between West European patterns and local reality—well, local reality was different in the various places, just as western influence was also very uneven: much stronger in Southern Europe around 1800, to return to my example, than in West Africa around 1940. The forces in play kept changing, and so did the compromise that resulted from their interaction. And this, incidentally, opens a fantastic field of inquiry for comparative morphology (the systematic study of how forms vary in space and time, which is also the only reason to keep the adjective 'comparative' in comparative literature): but comparative morphology is a complex issue, that deserves its own paper.

Forms as abstracts of social relationships

Let me now add a few words on that term 'compromise'—by which I mean something a little different from what Jameson had in mind in his introduction to Karatani. For him, the relationship is fundamentally a binary one: 'the abstract formal patterns of Western novel construction' and 'the raw material of Japanese social experience': form and content, basically.[26] For me, it's more of a triangle: foreign form, local material—*and local form*. Simplifying somewhat: foreign *plot*; local *characters*; and then, local *narrative voice*: and it's precisely in this third dimension that these novels seem to be most unstable—most uneasy, as Zhao says of the late Qing narrator. Which makes sense: the narrator is the pole of comment, of explanation, of evaluation, and when foreign 'formal patterns' (or actual foreign presence, for that matter) make characters behave in strange ways (like Bunzo, or Ibarra, or Bràs Cubas), then of course comment becomes uneasy—garrulous, erratic, rudderless.

'Interferences', Even-Zohar calls them: powerful literatures making life hard for the others—making *structure* hard. And Schwarz: 'a part of the original historical conditions re-appears as a sociological form . . . In this sense, forms are the abstract of specific social rela-tionships.'[27] Yes, and in our case the historical conditions reappear as a sort of 'crack' in the form; as a faultline running between story and discourse, world and worldview: the world goes in the strange direction dictated by an outside power; the worldview tries to make sense of it, and is thrown off balance all the time. Like Rizal's voice (oscillating between Catholic melodrama and Enlightenment sarcasm),[28] or Futabatei's (caught between Bunzo's 'Russian' behaviour, and the Japanese audience inscribed in the text), or Zhao's hypertrophic narrator, who has completely lost control of the plot, but still tries to dominate it at all costs. This is what Schwarz meant with that 'foreign debt' that becomes a 'complex feature' of the text: the foreign presence 'interferes' with the very *utterance* of the novel.[29] The one-and-unequal literary system is not just an external network here, it doesn't remain *outside* the text: it's embedded well into its form.

Trees, waves and cultural history

Forms are the abstract of social relationships: so, formal analysis is in its own modest way an analysis of power. (That's why comparative morphology is such a fascinating field: studying how forms vary, you discover how symbolic *power* varies from place to place.) And indeed, sociological formalism has always been my interpretive method, and I think that it's particu-larly appropriate for world literature . . . But, unfortunately, at this point I must stop, because my competence stops. Once it became clear that the key variable of the experiment was the narrator's voice, well, a genuine formal analysis was off limits for me, because it required a linguistic competence that I couldn't even dream of (French, English, Spanish, Russian, Japanese, Chinese and Portuguese, just for the core of the argument). And prob-ably, no matter what the object of analysis is, there will always be a point where the study of world literature must yield to the specialist of the national literature, in a sort of cosmic and inevitable division of labour. Inevitable not just for practical reasons, but for theoretical ones. This is a large issue, but let me at least sketch its outline.

When historians have analysed culture on a world scale (or on a large scale anyway), they have tended to use two basic cognitive metaphors: the tree and the wave. The tree, the phylogenetic tree derived from Darwin, was the tool of comparative philology: language families branching off from each other—Slavo-Germanic from Aryan-Greco-Italo-Celtic, then Balto-Slavic from Germanic, then Lithuanian from Slavic. And this kind of tree allowed comparative philology to solve that great puzzle which was also perhaps the first world system of culture: Indo-European: a family of languages spreading from India to Ireland (and perhaps not just languages, a common cultural repertoire, too: but here the evidence is notoriously shakier). The other metaphor, the wave, was also used in historical linguistics (as in Schmidt's 'wave hypothesis', that explained certain overlaps among languages), but it played a role in many other fields as well: the study of technological diffusion, for instance, or the fantastic interdisciplinary theory of the 'wave of advance' by Cavalli-Sforza and Ammerman (a genet-icist and an archaeologist), which explains how agriculture spread from the fertile crescent in the Middle East towards the North-West and then throughout Europe.

Now, trees and waves are both metaphors—but except for this, they have absolutely nothing in common. The tree describes the passage from unity to diversity: one tree, with many branches: from Indo-European, to dozens of different languages. The wave is the opposite: it observes uniformity engulfing an initial diversity: Hollywood films conquering one market after another (or English swallowing language after language). Trees need geographical *discontinuity* (in order to branch off from each other, languages must first be separated in space, just like animal species); waves dislike barriers, and thrive on geographical *continuity* (from the viewpoint of a wave, the ideal world is a pond). Trees and branches are what nation-states cling to; waves are what markets do. And so on. Nothing in common, between the two metaphors. But—*they both work*. Cultural history is made of trees *and* waves—the wave of agricultural advance supporting the tree of Indo-European languages, which is then swept by new waves of linguistic and cultural contact . . . And as world culture oscillates between the two mechanisms, its products are inevitably composite ones. Compromises, as in Jameson's law. That's why the law works: because it intuitively captures the intersection of the two mechanisms. Think of the modern novel: certainly a wave (and I've actually called it a wave a few times)—but a wave that runs into the branches of local traditions,[30] and is always significantly transformed by them.

This, then, is the basis for the division of labour between national and world literature: national literature, for people who see trees; world literature, for people who see waves. Division of labour . . . and challenge; because both metaphors work, yes, but that doesn't mean that they work equally well. The products of cultural history are always composite ones: but which is the dominant mechanism in their composition? The internal, or the external one? The nation or the world? The tree or the wave? There is no way to settle this controversy once and for all—fortunately: because comparatists need controversy. They have always been too shy in the presence of national literatures, too diplomatic: as if one had English, American, German literature—and then, next door, a sort of little parallel universe where comparatists studied a second set of literatures, trying not to disturb the first set. No; the universe is the same, the literatures are the same, we just look at them from a different viewpoint; and you become a comparatist for a very simple reason: *because you are convinced that that viewpoint is better*. It has greater explanatory power; it's conceptually more elegant; it avoids that ugly 'one-sidedness and narrow-mindedness'; whatever. The point is that there is no other justification for the study of world literature (and for the existence of departments of comparative literature) but this: to be a thorn in the side, a permanent intellectual challenge to national literatures—especially the local literature. If comparative literature is not this, it's nothing. Nothing. 'Don't delude yourself', writes Stendhal of his favourite character: 'for you, there is no middle road.' The same is true for us.

Notes

1   I address the problem of the great unread in a companion piece to this article, 'The Slaughterhouse of Literature', forthcoming in a special issue of *Modern Language Quarterly* on 'Formalism and Literary History', spring 2000.

2   Max Weber, 'Objectivity in Social Science and Social Policy' [1904], in *The Methodology of the Social Sciences*, New York 1949, p. 68.

3   Roberto Schwarz, 'The Importing of the Novel to Brazil and Its Contradictions in the Work of Roberto Alencar' [1977], in *Misplaced Ideas*, London 1992, p. 50.

4   Itamar Even-Zohar, 'Laws of Literary Interference', in *Poetics Today*, 1990, pp. 54, 62.

5   Montserrat Iglesias Santos, 'El sistema literario: teoría empírica y teoría de los polisistemas', in Darío Villanueva (ed.), *Avances en teoría de la literatura*, Santiago de Compostela 1994, p. 339: 'It is important to emphasize that interferences occur most often at the periphery of the system.'

6   Marc Bloch, 'Pour une histoire comparée des sociétés européennes', *Revue de synthèse historique*, 1928.

7   Or to quote Weber again: 'concepts are primarily analytical instruments for the intellectual mastery of empirical data'. ('Objectivity in Social Science and Social Policy', p. 106.) Inevitably, the larger the field one wants to study, the greater the need for abstract 'instruments' capable of mastering empirical reality.

8   Fredric Jameson, 'In the Mirror of Alternate Modernities', in Karatani Kojin, *Origins of Modern Japanese Literature*, Durham–London 1993, p. xiii.

9   I have begun to sketch them out in the last chapter of the *Atlas of the European Novel 1800–1900* (Verso: London 1998), and this is more or less how they sound: second, the formal compromise is usually prepared by a massive wave of West European translations; third, the compromise itself is generally unstable (Miyoshi has a great image for this: the 'impossible programme' of Japanese novels); but fourth, in those rare instances when the impossible programme succeeds, we have genuine formal revolutions.

10   'Given the history of its formative stage, it is no surprise that the early Russian novel contains a host of conventions popularized in French and British literature', writes David Gasperetti in *The Rise of the Russian Novel* (De Kalb 1998, p. 5). And Helena Goscilo, in her 'Introduction' to Krasicki's *Adventures of Mr. Nicholas Wisdom*: '*The Adventures* is read most fruitfully in the context of the West European literature on which it drew heavily for inspiration.' (Ignacy Krasicki, *The Adventures of Mr. Nicholas Wisdom*, Evanston 1992, p. xv.)

11   'There was a demand for foreign products, and production had to comply', explains Luca Toschi speaking of the Italian narrative market around 1800 ('Alle origini della narrativa di romanzo in Italia', in Massimo Saltafuso (ed.), *Il viaggio del narrare*, Florence 1989, p. 19). A generation later, in Spain, 'readers are not interested in the originality of the Spanish novel; their only desire is that it would adhere to those foreign models with which they have become familiar': and so, concludes Elisa Martí-López, one may well say that between 1800 and 1850 'the Spanish novel is being written in France' (Elisa Martí-López, 'La orfandad de la novela española: política editorial y creación literaria a mediados del siglo XIX', *Bulletin Hispanique*, 1997).

12   'Obviously, lofty ambitions were not enough. All too often the nineteenth century Spanish-American novel is clumsy and inept, with a plot derived at second hand from the contemporary European Romantic novel.' (Jean Franco, *Spanish-American Literature*, Cambridge 1969, p. 56.) 'If heroes and heroines in mid-nineteenth century Latin American novels were passionately desiring one another across traditional lines . . . those passions might not have prospered a generation earlier. In fact, modernizing lovers were learning how to dream their erotic fantasies by reading the European romances they hoped to realize.' (Doris Sommer, *Foundational Fictions: The National Romances of Latin America*, Berkeley–Los Angeles 1991, pp. 31–32.)

13   'Yiddish writers parodied—appropriated, incorporated, and modified—diverse elements from European novels and stories.' (Ken Frieden, *Classic Yiddish Fiction*, Albany 1995, p. x.)

14   Matti Moosa quotes the novelist Yahya Haqqi: 'there is no harm in admitting that the modern story came to us from the West. Those who laid down its foundations were persons influenced by European literature, particularly French literature. Although masterpieces of English literature were translated into Arabic, French literature was the fountain of our story.' (Matti Moosa, *The Origins of Modern Arabic Fiction* [1970], 2nd ed. 1997, p. 93.) For Edward Said, 'at some point writers in Arabic became aware of European novels and began to write works like them' (Edward Said, *Beginnings* [1975], New York 1985, p. 81). And Roger Allen: 'In more literary terms, increasing contacts with Western literatures led to translations of works of European fiction into Arabic, followed by their adaptation and imitation, and culminating in the appearance of an indigenous tradition of modern fiction in Arabic.' (Roger Allen, *The Arabic Novel*, Syracuse 1995, p. 12.)

15   'The first novels in Turkey were written by members of the new intelligentsia, trained in government service and well-exposed to French literature', writes Ahmet O. Evin (*Origins and Development of the Turkish Novel*, Minneapolis 1983, p. 10); and Jale Parla: 'the early Turkish novelists combined the traditional narrative forms with the examples of the western novel' ('Desiring Tellers, Fugitive Tales: Don Quixote Rides Again, This Time in Istanbul', forthcoming).

16   'The narrative dislocation of the sequential order of events is perhaps the most outstanding impression late Qing writers received when they read or translated Western fiction. At first, they tried to tidy up the sequence of the events back into their pre-narrated order. When such tidying was not feasible during translation, an apologetic note would be inserted . . . Paradoxically, when he alters rather than follows the original, the translator does not feel it necessary to add an apologetic note.' (Henry Y. H. Zhao, *The Uneasy Narrator: Chinese Fiction from the Traditional to the Modern*, Oxford 1995, p. 150.) 'Late Qing writers enthusiastically renewed their heritage with the help of foreign models', writes David Der-wei Wang: 'I see the late Qing as the beginning of the Chinese literary "modern" because writers' pursuit of novelty was no longer contained within indigenously defined

barriers but was inextricably defined by the multilingual, crosscultural trafficking of ideas, technologies, and powers in the wake of nineteenth-century Western expansionism.' (*Fin-de-siècle Splendor: Repressed Modernities of Late Qing Fiction*, 1849–1911, Stanford 1997, pp. 5, 19.)

17   'One essential factor shaping West African novels by indigenous writers was the fact that they appeared after the novels on Africa written by non-Africans . . . the foreign novels embody elements which indigenous writers had to react against when they set out to write.' (Emmanuel Obiechina, *Culture, Tradition and Society in the West African Novel*, Cambridge 1975, p. 17.) 'The first Dahomean novel, *Doguicimi* . . . is interesting as an experiment in recasting the oral literature of Africa within the form of a French novel.' (Abiola Irele, *The African Experience in Literature and Ideology*, Bloomington 1990, p. 147.) 'It was the rationality of realism that seemed adequate to the task of forging a national identity at the conjuncture of global realities . . . the rationalism of realism dispersed in texts as varied as newspapers, Onitsha market literature, and in the earliest titles of the African Writers Series that dominated the discourses of the period.' (Ato Quayson, *Strategic Transformations in Nigerian Writing*, Bloomington 1997, p. 162.)

18   In the seminar where I first presented this 'second-hand' criticism, Sarah Golstein asked a very good, Candide-like question: You decide to rely on another critic. Fine. But what if he's wrong? My reply: If he's wrong, you are wrong too, and you soon know, because you don't find any corroboration— you don't find Goscilo, Martí-López, Sommer, Evin, Zhao, Irele . . . And it's not just that you don't find positive corroboration; sooner or later you find all sorts of facts you cannot explain, and your hypothesis is falsified, in Popper's famous formulation, and you must throw it away. Fortunately, this hasn't been the case so far, and Jameson's insight still stands.

19   OK, I confess, in order to test the conjecture I actually did read some of these 'first novels' in the end (Krasicki's *Adventures of Mr. Nicholas Wisdom*, Abramowitsch's *Little Man*, Rizal's *Noli Me Tangere*, Futabatei's *Ukigumo*, René Maran's *Batouala*, Paul Hazoumé's *Doguicimi*). This kind of 'reading', however, no longer produces interpretations but merely *tests* them: it's not the beginning of the critical enterprise, but its appendix. And then, here you don't really read the *text* anymore, but rather through the text, looking for your unit of analysis. The task is constrained from the start; it's a reading without freedom.

20   For practical purposes, the larger the geographical space one wants to study, the smaller should the unit of analysis be: a concept (in our case), a device, a trope, a limited narrative unit—something like this. In a follow-up paper, I hope to sketch out the diffusion of stylistic 'seriousness' (Auerbach's keyword in *Mimesis*) in nineteenth- and twentieth-century novels.

21   How to set up a reliable sample—that is to say, what series of national literatures and individual novels provide a satisfactory test of a theory's predictions—is of course quite a complex issue. In this preliminary sketch, my sample (and its justification) leave much to be desired.

22   Scientific research 'begins as a story about a Possible World', Medawar goes on, 'and ends by being, as nearly as we can make it, a story about real life.' His words are quoted by James Bird in *The Changing World of Geography*, Oxford 1993, p. 5. Bird himself offers a very elegant version of the experimental model.

23   Aside from Miyoshi and Karatani (for Japan), Mukherjee (for India), and Schwarz (for Brazil), the compositional paradoxes and the instability of the formal compromise are often mentioned in the literature on the Turkish, Chinese and Arabic novel. Discussing Namik Kemal's *Intibah*, Ahmet Evin points out how 'the merger of the two themes, one based on the traditional family life and the other on the yearnings of a prostitute, constitute the first attempt in Turkish fiction to achieve a type of psychological dimension observed in European novels within a thematic framework based on Turkish life. *However, due both to the incompatibility of the themes and to the difference in the degree of emphasis placed on each, the unity of the novel is blemished. The structural defects of* Intibah *are symptomatic of the differences between the methodology and concerns of the Turkish literary tradition on the one hand and those of the European novel on the other.*' (Ahmet O. Evin, *Origins and Development of the Turkish Novel*, p. 68; emphasis mine.) Jale Parla's evaluation of the Tanzimat period sounds a similar note: 'behind the inclination towards renovation stood a dominant and dominating Ottoman ideology that recast the new ideas into a mould fit for the Ottoman society. The mould, however, was supposed to hold two different epistemologies that rested on irreconcilable axioms. *It was inevitable that this mould would crack and literature, in one way or another, reflects the cracks.*' ('Desiring Tellers, Fugitive Tales: Don Quixote Rides Again, This Time in Istanbul', emphasis mine.) In his discussion of the 1913 novel *Zaynab*, by Husayn Haykal, Roger Allen echoes Schwarz and Mukherjee ('*it is all too easy to point to the problems of psychological fallacy here*, as Hamid, the student in Cairo acquainted with Western works on liberty and justice such as those of John Stuart Mill and Herbert Spencer, proceeds to discuss the question of marriage in Egyptian society on such a lofty plane with his parents, who have always lived deep in the Egyptian countryside': *The Arabic Novel*, p. 34; emphasis mine). Henry Zhao emphasizes from his very

title—*The Uneasy Narrator*: and see the splendid discussion of uneasiness that opens the book—the complications generated by the encounter of western plots and Chinese narrative: 'A salient feature of late Qing fiction', he writes, 'is the greater frequency of narrative intrusions than in any previous period of Chinese vernacular fiction . . . The huge amount of directions trying to explain the newly adopted techniques betrays the narrator's uneasiness about the instability of his status . . . the narrator feels the threat of interpretive diversification . . . moral commentaries become more tendentious to make the judgments unequivocal', and at times the drift towards narratorial overkill is so overpowering that a writer may sacrifice narrative suspense 'to show that he is morally impeccable' (*The Uneasy Narrator*, pp. 69–71).

24 In some cases, even *translations* of European novels went through all sorts of incredible somersaults. In Japan, in 1880, Tsubouchi's translation of *The Bride of Lammermoor* appeared under the title *Shumpu jowa* [*Spring breeze love story*], and Tsubouchi himself 'was not beyond excising the original text when the material proved inappropriate for his audience, or converting Scott's imagery into expressions corresponding more closely to the language of traditional Japanese literature' (Marleigh Grayer Ryan, 'Commentary' to Futabatei Shimei's *Ukigumo*, New York 1967, pp. 41–42). In the Arabic world, writes Matti Moosa, 'in many instances the translators of Western fiction took extensive and sometimes unwarranted liberties with the original text of a work. Yaqub Sarruf not only changed the title of Scott's *Talisman* to *Qalb al-Asad wa Salah al-Din* (*The Lion Heart and Saladin*), but also admitted that he had taken the liberty of omitting, adding, and changing parts of this romance to suit what he believed to be his audience's taste . . . Other translators changed the titles and the names of the characters and the contents, in order, they claimed, to make the translated work more acceptable to their readers and more consistent with the native literary tradition.' (*The Origins of Modern Arabic Fiction*, p. 106.) The same general pattern holds for late Qing literature, where 'translations were almost without exception tampered with . . . the most serious way of tampering was to paraphrase the whole novel to make it a story with Chinese characters and Chinese background . . . Almost all of these translations suffered from abridgement . . . Western novels became sketchy and speedy, and looked more like Chinese traditional fiction.' (Henry Zhao, *The Uneasy Narrator*, p. 229.)

25 Why this difference? Probably, because in Southern Europe the wave of French translations encountered a local reality (and local narrative traditions) that weren't that different after all, and as a consequence, the composition of foreign form and local material proved easy. In West Africa, the opposite situation: although the novelists themselves had been influenced by Western literature, the wave of translations had been much weaker than elsewhere, and local narrative conventions were for their part extremely different from European ones (just think of orality); as the desire for the 'foreign technology' was relatively bland—and further discouraged, of course, by the anti-colonial politics of the 1950s—local conventions could play their role relatively undisturbed. Obiechina and Quayson emphasize the polemical relationship of early West African novels vis-à-vis European narrative: 'The most noticeable difference between novels by native West Africans and those by non-natives using the West African setting, is the important position which the representation of oral tradition is given by the first, and its almost total absence in the second.' (Emmanuel Obiechina, *Culture, Tradition and Society in the West African Novel*, p. 25.) 'Continuity in the literary strategic formation we have identified is best defined in terms of the continuing affirmation of mythopeia rather than of realism for the definition of identity . . . That this derives from a conceptual opposition to what is perceived as a Western form of realism is difficult to doubt. It is even pertinent to note in this regard that in the work of major African writers such as Achebe, Armah, and Ngugi, the movement of their work has been from protocols of realist representation to those of mythopeic experimentation.' (Ato Quayson, *Strategic Transformations in Nigerian Writing*, p. 164.)

26 The same point is made in a great article by António Cándido: 'We [Latin American literatures] never create original expressive forms or basic expressive techniques, in the sense that we mean by romanticism, on the level of literary movements; the psychological novel, on the level of genres; free indirect style, on that of writing . . . the various nativisms never rejected the use of the imported literary *forms* . . . what was demanded was the choice of new *themes*, of different *sentiments*. ('Literature and Underdevelopment', in César Fernández Moreno, Julio Ortega, Ivan A. Shulman (eds), *Latin America in Its Literature*, New York 1980, pp. 272–73.)

27 'The Importing of the Novel to Brazil', p. 53.

28 Rizal's solution, or lack thereof, is probably also related to his extraordinarily wide social spectrum (*Noli Me Tangere*, among other things, is the text that inspired Benedict Anderson to link the novel and the nation-state): in a nation with no independence, an ill-defined ruling class, no common language and hundreds of disparate characters, it's hard to speak 'for the whole', and the narrator's voice cracks under the effort.

29   In a few lucky cases, the structural weakness may turn into a strength, as in Schwarz's interpretation of Machado, where the 'volatility' of the narrator becomes 'the stylization of the behaviour of the Brazilian ruling class': not a flaw any longer, but the very point of the novel: 'Everything in Machado de Assis's novels is coloured by the *volatility*—used and abused in different degrees—of their narrators. The critics usually look at it from the point of view of literary technique or of the author's humour. There are great advantages in seeing it as the stylization of the behaviour of the Brazilian ruling class. Instead of seeking disinterestedness, and the confidence provided by impartiality, Machado's narrator shows off his impudence, in a gamut which runs from cheap gibes, to literary exhibitionism, and even to critical acts.' (Roberto Schwarz, 'The Poor Old Woman and Her Portraitist' [1983], in *Misplaced Ideas*, p. 94.)

30   '*Grafting* processes', Miyoshi calls them; Schwarz speaks of 'the *implantation* of the novel, and of its realist *strand* in particular', and Wang of '*transplanting* Western narrative typologies'. And indeed, Belinsky had already described Russian literature as 'a *transplanted* rather than indigenous growth' in 1843.

MORE CONJECTURES (2003)

In the past year or so, several articles have addressed the issues raised in 'Conjectures on World Literature': Christopher Prendergast, Francesca Orsini, Efraín Kristal and Jonathan Arac in *New Left Review*, Emily Apter and Jale Parla elsewhere.[1] My thanks to all of them; and as I obviously cannot respond to every point in detail, I will focus here on the three main areas of disagreement among us: the (questionable) paradigmatic status of the novel; the relationship between core and periphery, and its consequences for literary form; and the nature of comparative analysis.

I

One must begin somewhere, and 'Conjectures' tried to sketch how the literary world-system works by focusing on the rise of the modern novel: a phenomenon which is easy to isolate, has been studied all the world over, and thus lends itself well to comparative work. I also added that the novel was 'an example, not a model; and of course my example, based on the field I know (elsewhere, things may be very different)'. Elsewhere things are different indeed: 'If the novel can be seen as heavily freighted with the political, this is not patently the case for other literary genres. Drama seems to travel less anxiously . . . How might the . . . construct work with lyric poetry?', asks Prendergast; and Kristal: 'Why doesn't poetry follow the laws of the novel?'.[2]

It doesn't? I wonder. What about Petrarchism? Propelled by its formalized lyrical conventions, Petrarchism spread to (at least) Spain, Portugal, France, England, Wales, the Low Countries, the German territories, Poland, Scandinavia, Dalmatia (and, according to Roland Greene, the New World). As for its depth and duration, I am sceptical about the old Italian claim that by the end of the sixteenth century over two hundred *thousand* sonnets had been written in Europe in imitation of Petrarch; still, the main disagreement seems to be, not on the enormity of the facts, but on the enormity of their enormity—ranging from a century (Navarrete, Fucilla), to two (Manero Sorolla, Kennedy), three (Hoffmeister, Kristal himself), or five (Greene). Compared to the wavelike diffusion of this '*lingua franca* for love poets', as Hoffmeister calls it, western novelistic 'realism' looks like a rather ephemeral vogue.[3]

Other things being equal, anyway, I would imagine literary movements to depend on three broad variables—a genre's potential market, its overall formalization and its use of language—and to range from the rapid wave-like diffusion of forms with a large market, rigid formulas and simplified style (say, adventure novels), to the relative stasis of those characterized by a small market, deliberate singularity and linguistic density (say, experimental poetry). Within this matrix, novels would be representative, not of the *entire* system, but of its most mobile strata, and by concentrating only on them we would probably overstate the mobility of world literature. If 'Conjectures' erred in that direction it was a mistake, easily corrected as we learn more about the international diffusion of drama, poetry and so on (here, Donald Sassoon's current work on cultural markets will be invaluable).[4] Truth be told, I would be very disappointed if all of literature turned out to 'follow the laws of the novel': that a single explanation may work *everywhere* is both very implausible and extraordinarily boring. But before indulging in speculations at a more abstract level, we must learn to share the significant facts of literary history across our specialized niches. Without collective work, world literature will always remain a mirage.

II

Is world-system theory, with its strong emphasis on a rigid international division of labour, a good model for the study of world literature? On this, the strongest objection comes from Kristal: 'I am arguing, however, in favour of a view of world literature', he writes, 'in which the West does not have a monopoly over the creation of forms that count; in which themes and forms can move in several directions—from the centre to the periphery, from the periphery to the centre, from one periphery to another, while some original forms of consequence may not move much at all'.[5]

Yes, forms *can* move in several directions. But *do* they? This is the point, and a theory of literary history should reflect on the constraints on their movements, and the reasons behind them. What I know about European novels, for instance, suggests that hardly any forms 'of consequence' don't move at all; that movement from one periphery to another (without passing through the centre) is almost unheard of;[6] that movement from the periphery to the centre is less rare, but still quite unusual, while that from the centre to the periphery is by far the most frequent.[7] Do these facts imply that the West has 'a monopoly over the creation of the forms that count'? Of course not.[8] Cultures from the centre have more resources to pour into innovation (literary and otherwise), and are thus more likely to produce it: but a monopoly over creation is a theological attribute, not an historical judgment.[9] The model proposed in 'Conjectures' does not reserve invention to a few cultures and deny it to the others: it specifies *the conditions under which it is more likely to occur*, and the forms it may take. Theories will never abolish inequality: they can only hope to explain it.

III

Kristal also objects to what he calls the 'postulate of a general homology between the inequalities of the world economic and literary systems': in other words, 'the assumption that literary and economic relationships run parallel may work in some cases, but not in others'.[10] Even-Zohar's argument is a partial response to the objection; but there is another sense in which Kristal is right, and the simplifying euphoria of an article originally conceived as a 30-minute talk is seriously misleading. By reducing the literary world-system to core and periphery, I erased from the picture the transitional area (the semi-periphery) where cultures move in and out of the core; as a consequence, I also understated the fact that in many (and perhaps most) instances, material and intellectual hegemony are indeed very close, but not quite identical.

Let me give some examples. In the 18th and 19th centuries, the long struggle for hegemony between Britain and France ended with Britain's victory on all fronts—except one: in the world of narrative, the verdict was reversed, and French novels were both more successful and formally more significant than British ones. Elsewhere I have tried to explain the reasons for the morphological supremacy of German tragedy from the mid-eighteenth century on; or the key role of semi-peripheral realities in the production of modern epic forms. Petrarchism, which reached its international zenith when its wealthy area of origin had already cata-strophically declined (like those stars which are still shining long after their death), is a particularly spooky instance of this state of affairs.

All these examples (and more) have two features in common. First, they arise from cultures which are close to, or inside the core of the system—but are not hegemonic in the economic sphere. France may be the paradigm here, as if being an eternal second in the political and economic arena encouraged investment in culture (as in its feverish post-Napoleonic creativity, compared to the postprandial somnolence of the victorious Victorians). A—limited—discrepancy between material and literary hegemony does therefore exist: wider in the case of innovation *per se* (which does not require a powerful apparatus of production and distribution), and narrower, or absent, in the case of diffusion (which does).[11] Yet, and this is the second feature in common, all these examples *confirm the inequality of the world literary system:* an inequality which does not coincide with economic inequality, true, and allows some mobility—but a mobility *internal* to the unequal system, not alternative to it. At times, even the dialectic between semi-periphery and core may actually widen the overall gap (as in the instances mentioned in footnote 11, or when Hollywood quickly 'remakes' successful foreign films, effectively strengthening its own position). At any rate, this is clearly another field where progress will only be possible through the good coordination of specific local knowledge.

IV

The central morphological point of 'Conjectures' was the contrast between the rise of the novel in the core as an 'autonomous development', and the rise in the periphery as a 'compromise' between a Western influence and local materials. As Parla and Arac point out, however, early English novels were written, in Fielding's words, 'after the manner of Cervantes' (or of someone else), thus making clear that a compromise between local and foreign forms occurred there as well.[12] And if this was the case, then there was no 'autonomous development' in western Europe, and the idea that forms have, so to speak, *a different history* at the core and at the periphery crumbles. The world-system model may be useful at other levels, but has no explanatory power at the level of form.

Here things are easy: Parla and Arac are right—and I should have known better. After all, the thesis that literary form is *always* a compromise between opposite forces has been a Leitmotiv of my intellectual formation, from Francesco Orlando's Freudian aesthetics to Gould's 'Panda principle', or Lukács' conception of realism. How on earth could I 'forget' all this? In all likelihood, because the core/periphery opposition made me look (or wish . . .) for a parallel morphological pattern, which I then couched in the wrong conceptual terms.[13]

So let me try again. 'Probably all systems known to us have emerged and developed with interference playing a prominent role', writes Even-Zohar: 'there is not one single literature which did not emerge through interference with a more established literature: and no literature could manage without interference at one time or another during its history'.[14] No literature without interference . . . hence, also, no literature without compromises between the local and the foreign. But does this mean that all types of interference and compromise *are the same?* Of course not: the picaresque, captivity narratives, even the *Bildungsroman* could not exert the same pressure over French or British novelists that the historical novel or the *mystéres* exerted over European and Latin American writers: and we should find a way to express this difference. To recognize when a compromise occurs as it were *under duress*, and is thus likely to produce more unstable and dissonant results—what Zhao calls the 'uneasiness' of the late Qing narrator.

The key point, here, is this: if there is a strong, systematic constraint exerted by some literatures over the others (and we all seem to agree that there is),[15] then we should be able to recognize its effects *within literary form itself*: because forms are indeed, in Schwarz's words, 'the abstract of specific social relationships'. In 'Conjectures', the diagram of forces was embodied in the sharp qualitative opposition of 'autonomous developments' and 'compromises'; but as that solution has been falsified, we must try something else. And, yes, 'measuring' the extent of foreign pressure on a text, or its structural instability, or a narrator's uneasiness, will be complicated, at times even unfeasible. But a diagram of symbolic power is an ambitious goal, and it makes sense that it would be hard to achieve.

V

Two areas for future discussion emerge from all this. The first concerns the type of knowledge literary history should pursue. 'No science, no laws' is Arac's crisp description of Auerbach's project; and there are similar hints in other articles too. This is of course the old question of whether the proper object of historical disciplines are individual cases or abstract models; and as I will argue at extravagant length for the latter in a series of forthcoming articles, here I will simply say that we have a lot to learn from the methods of the social and of the natural sciences. Will we then find ourselves, in Apter's words, 'in a city of bits, where micro and macro literary units are awash in a global system with no obvious sorting device'? I hope so . . . it would be a very interesting universe.

So, let's start looking for good sorting devices. 'Formalism without close reading', Arac calls the project of 'Conjectures', and I can't think of a better definition. Hopefully, it will also be a formalism where the 'details' so dear to him and to Prendergast will be highlighted, not erased by models and 'schemas'.[16]

Finally, politics. Several articles mention the political pressure behind Auerbach's *Mimesis*, or Casanova's *République mondiale des lettres*. To them I would add Lukács's two versions of comparative literature: the one which crystallized around World War I, when *The Theory of the Novel*, and its (never completed) companion study on Dostoevsky mused on whether a world beyond capitalism could even still be imagined; and the one which took shape in the Thirties, as a long meditation on the opposite political significance of German and French literature (with Russia again in the background). Lukács' spatio-temporal horizon was narrow (the nineteenth century, and three European literatures, plus Cervantes in *The Theory of the Novel* and Scott in *The Historical Novel*); his answers were often opaque, scholastic, philistine—or worse. But his lesson lies in how the articulation of his comparative scenario (western Europe or Russia; Germany or France) is simultaneously an attempt to understand the great political dilemmas of his day. Or in other words: *the way we imagine comparative literature is a mirror of how we see the world*. 'Conjectures' tried to do so against the background of the unprecedented possibility that the entire world may be subject to a single centre of power—and a centre which has long exerted an equally unprecedented symbolic hegemony. In charting an aspect of the pre-history of our present, and sketching some possible outcomes, the article may well have overstated its case, or taken some wrong turns altogether. But the relationship between project and background stands, and I believe it will give significance and seriousness to our work in the future. Early March 2003, when these pages are being written, is in this respect a wonderfully paradoxical moment, when, after twenty years of unchallenched American hegemony, millions of people everywhere in the world have expressed their enormous distance from American politics. As human beings, this is cause to rejoice. As cultural historians, it is cause to reflect.

Notes

1 'Conjectures on World Literature', NLR I; Christopher Prendergast, 'Negotiating World Literature', NLR 8; Francesca Orsini, 'Maps of Indian Writing', NLR 13; Efraín Kristal, ' "Considering Coldly . . .": A Response to Franco Moretti', NLR 15; Jonathan Arac, 'Anglo-Globalism?' NLR 16; Emily Apter, 'Global *Translatio:* The "Invention" of Comparative Literature, Istanbul, 1933', *Critical Inquiry,* 29, 2003; Jale Parla's essay ('The object of comparison') will be published in a special issue of *Comparative Literature Studies* edited by Djelal Kadir in January 2004.

2 'Conjectures', p. 58; 'Negotiating World Literature', pp. 120–21; ' "Considering Coldly . . ." ', p. 62. Orsini makes a similar point for Indian literature: 'Moretti's novel-based theses would seem to have little application to the Subcontinent, where the major nineteenth and twentieth-century forms have been poetry, drama and the short story, whose evolution may show quite different patterns of change': 'Maps', p. 79.

3 See Antero Meozzi, *Il petrarchismo europeo (secolo xvi),* Pisa 1934; Leonard Forster, *The Icy Fire: Five studies in European Petrarchism,* Cambridge 1969; Joseph Fucilla, *Estudios sobre el petrarquismo en España,* Madrid 1960; Ignacio Navarrete, *Orphans of Petrarch,* California 1994; William Kennedy, *Authorizing Petrarch,* Ithaca 1994; Maria Pilar Manero Sorolla, *Introducción al estudio del petrarquismo en España,* Barcelona 1987; Gerhart Hoffmeister, *Petrarkistische Lyrik,* Stuttgart 1973; Roland Greene, *Post-Petrarchism: Origins and Innovations of the Western Lyric Sequence,* Princeton 1991. Kristal's implicit acknowledgement of the hegemony of Petrarchism over European and Latin American poetry comes where he writes that 'the lyrical conventions of modern Spanish poetry were developed in the 16th century by Boscán and Garcilaso de la Vega . . . The first signs of a reaction against the strictest conventions of Spanish prosody did not take place in Spain but in Spanish America in the 1830s': ' "Considering Coldly . . ." ', p. 64.

4 See, for a preliminary account, 'On Cultural Markets', NLR 17.

5 ' "Considering Coldly . . ." ', pp. 73–74.

6 I mean here the movement between peripheral cultures which do not belong to the same 'region': from, say, Norway to Portugal (or vice versa), not from Norway to Iceland or Sweden, or from Colombia to Guatemala and Peru. Sub-systems made relatively homogeneous by language, religion or politics—of which Latin America is the most interesting and powerful instance—are a great field for comparative study, and may add interesting complications to the larger picture (like Darío's modernism, evoked by Kristal).

7 The reason why literary products flow from the centre to the periphery is spelt out by Even-Zohar in his work on polysystems, extensively quoted at the beginning of 'Conjectures': peripheral (or, as he calls them, 'weak') literatures 'often do not develop the same full range of literary activities . . . observable in adjacent larger literatures (which in consequence may create a feeling that they are indispensable)'; 'a weak . . . system is unable to function by confining itself to its home repertoire only', and the ensuing lack 'may be filled, wholly or partly, by translated literature'. Literary weakness, Even-Zohar goes on, 'does not necessarily result from political or economic weakness, although rather often it seems to be correlated with material conditions'; as a consequence, 'since peripheral literatures in the Western hemisphere tend more often than not to be identical with literatures of smaller nations, as unpalatable as this idea may seem to us, we have no choice but to admit that within a group of relatable national literatures, such as the literatures of Europe, hierarchical relations have been established since the very beginnings of these literatures. Within this (macro-)polysystem some literatures have taken peripheral positions, which is only to say that they were often modelled to a large extent upon an exterior literature.' Itamar Even-Zohar, 'Polysystem Studies', in *Poetics Today,* spring 1990, pp. 47, 81, 80, 48.

8 Nor does it have a monopoly over criticism that counts. Of the twenty critics on whose work the argument of 'Conjectures' rests, writes Arac, 'one is quoted in Spanish, one in Italian, and eighteen in English'; so, 'the impressive diversity of surveying some twenty national literatures diminishes into little more than one single means by which they may be known. English in culture, like the dollar in economics, serves as the medium through which knowledge may be translated from the local to the global': 'Anglo-Globalism?', p. 40. True, eighteen critics are quoted in English. But as far as I know only four or five are from the country of the dollar, while the others belong to a dozen different

cultures. Is this less significant than the language they use? I doubt it. Sure, global English may end up impoverishing our thinking, as American films do. But for now, the rapid wide public exchanges it makes possible far exceed its potential dangers. Parla puts it well: 'To unmask the hegemony [of imperialism] is an intellectual task. It does not harm to know English as one sets out for the task.'

9   After all, my last two books end on the formal revolutions of Russian and Latin American narrative—a point also made (not 'conceded', as Kristal puts it, suggesting reluctance on my part) in an article on European literature ('an importer of those formal novelties that it is no longer capable of producing'), another one on Hollywood exports ('a counter-force at work within the world literary system') and in 'Conjectures' itself. See 'Modern European Literature: A Geographical Sketch', NLR I/206, July-August 1994, p. 109; 'Planet Hollywood', NLR 9, May-June 2001, p. 101.

     'Conjectures' pointed out that 'in those rare instances when the impossible programme succeeds, we have genuine formal revolutions' (p. 59, footnote 9), and that 'in a few lucky cases, the structural weakness may turn into a strength, as in Schwarz's interpretation of Machado' (p. 66, footnote 29).

10   'Considering Coldly . . .', pp. 69, 73.

11   The fact that innovations may arise in the semi-periphery, but then be captured and diffused by the core of the core, emerges from several studies on the early history of the novel (by Armstrong, Resina, Trumpener and others: all written in total independence from world-system theory), which have pointed out how often the culture industry of London and Paris discovers a foreign form, introduces a few improvements, and then retails it as its own throughout Europe (ending in the masterstroke of the 'English' novelist Walter Scott). As the picaresque declines in its native country, Gil Blas and Moll Flanders and Marianne and Tom Jones spread it all over Europe; epistolary novels, first written in Spain and Italy, become a continental craze thanks to Montesquieu and Richardson (and then Goethe); American 'captivity narratives' acquire international currency through Clarissa and the Gothic; the Italian 'melodramatic imagination' conquers the world through Parisian feuilletons; the German Bildungsroman is intercepted by Stendhal, Balzac, Dickens, Bronte, Flaubert, Eliot . . . This is of course not the only path of literary innovation, perhaps not even the main one; but the mechanism is certainly there—half swindle, half international division of labour—and has an interesting similarity to larger economic constraints.

12   'Anglo-Globalism?', p. 38.

13   This seems a good illustration of the 'Kuhnian' point that theoretical expectations will shape facts according to your wishes—and an even better illustration of the 'Popperian' point that facts (usually gathered by those who disagree with you) will be finally stronger.

14   'Polysystem Studies', p. 59. A page later, in a footnote, Even-Zohar adds: 'This is true of almost all literatures of the Western hemisphere. As for the Eastern hemisphere, admittedly, Chinese is still a riddle as regards its emergence and early development.'

15   Except Orsini: 'Implicit in [Casanova's] view—explicit in Moretti's—is the traditional assumption of a "source" language, or culture—invariably carrying an aura of authenticity—and a "target" one, seen as in some way imitative. In place of this, Lydia Liu much more usefully proposed the concept of "guest" and "host" languages, to focus attention on the translingual practice through which the hosts may appropriate concepts and forms . . . Cultural influence becomes a study of appropriation, rather than of centres and peripheries': 'Maps', pp. 81–82. The culture industry as a 'guest' invited by a 'host' who 'appropriates' its forms . . . Are these concepts—or daydreams?

16   'Anglo-Globalism?', pp. 41, 38; 'Global translatio', p. 255.

Chapter 20

Vilashini Cooppan

WORLD LITERATURE AND GLOBAL THEORY: COMPARATIVE LITERATURE FOR THE NEW MILLENNIUM (2001)

VILASHINI COOPPAN (B. 1967) IN THE 1990s taught Comparative Literature at Yale University, and now teaches at the University of California at Santa Cruz, where she does research in, and teaches, postcolonial studies, comparative and world literature, literatures of slavery and diaspora, globalization studies, and cultural theory of race and ethnicity. She has published *Worlds Within: National Narratives and Global Connections in Postcolonial Writing* (Stanford University Press, 2009), as well as essays in *symplokē, Comparative Literature Studies, Gramma, Concentric,* and a number of collective volumes.

In the article by Cooppan we here republish she discusses the position of "world literature" within the discipline of comparative literature. Although throughout the twentieth century the study of world literature was recognized as part of that discipline, it was most often also condemned to playing a minor role. Particularly, the teaching of world literature, which of necessity had to be done in translation, was routinely looked down upon and relegated to other departments, particularly the English department. Cooppan at the end of the 1990s was part of a group of scholars at Yale reintroducing the teaching of world literature into the comparative literature curriculum. Specifically, Cooppan argues that comparative literature in the US might rejuvenate itself by translating the challenge of globalization into an opportunity for devising radically different "world literatures" courses. In order to do so, she argues, it is not necessary to engage in the wholesale overhaul of existing canons. Rather, she advocates what she calls "globalized reading" in which works from different traditions, different regions, different times are read concurrently, thus revealing unexpected, but not necessarily unrelated, lineages, parallels, contrasts. Importantly, such globalized reading does not presuppose the hegemony of any kind of center, geographically, culturally, historically, but rather starts from the equality of all texts read. With this article Cooppan showed herself particularly attuned to then developing trends in especially American comparative literary scholarship.

Vilashini Cooppan, "World Literature and Global Theory: Comparative Literature for the New Millennium," in *symplokē* 9 (2001) 1–2: 15–43.

It has become a sign of living in the present to note the increasing globalization of the world – the transnationalism of the currents along which capital, goods, labor, persons, and information flow; the interconnectedness of diverse cultures; the networks and internets that, despite their inequitable distribution, have nonetheless become the icons of rapidly changing, intricately interlinked societies. Global consciousness, speaking everywhere with the inexorable voice of the new, also appears to tow traditional academic bodies of knowledge within its orbit: "adapt," it seems to say, "or die." This Darwinian choice between adaptation and death has of course already been made, its iteration in the present tense serving to obscure the creeping changes long wrought on our disciplinary institutions, critical theories, and pedagogical practices by an ever more heterogeneous global sensibility. Globalization, understood as a process of cross-cultural interaction, exchange, and transformation, is certainly as old as any currently recognized academic field and in most cases far older, whether we take as its starting point the postmodern, post-colonial acceleration of spatio-temporal connection, the nineteenth-century capitalist expansion of imperial nations, the fifteenth-century formation of a world system dominated by mercantilist states and divided into core and peripheral zones, or even the trade routes of the ancient and medieval world.[1] But contemporary globalization is of course far more than the mirror image of its various historical antecedents, bearing at its disposal unprecedented economic and cultural forces of connection (if one is utopian) or homogenization (if one is dystopian).[2]

Fredric Jameson suggests that the distinction may depend on whether one focuses on the cultural or economic axes of globalization. As cultural process, globalization names the explosion of a plurality of mutually intersecting, individually syncretic, local differences; the emergence of new, hitherto suppressed identities; and the expansion of a world-wide media and technology culture with the promise of popular democratization. As economic process, globalization works on the principle not of ever increasing difference but forced identity: the assimilation or integration of markets, of labor, of nations. Jameson goes on to note that we are of course free to switch things around, and to lament globalization's standardization of culture (McDonald's in Beijing) while celebrating the productive diversities and differences of the new global free market (Jameson 1998, 56–58). Globalization, by no means reducible to the universal reign of commodification, is for many of its scholars an inherently mixed phenomenon, a process encompassing both sameness and difference, compression and expansion, convergence and divergence, nationalism and internationalism, universalism and particularism (Robertson; Lowe 1997). Consistently contradictory, deeply double, the "global" has less to do with the concept of a hegemonic, homogeneous universal than with what Stuart Hall terms the practice of relational thinking. Attune to the various ways in which "the global/local reciprocally re-organise and re-shape one another," relational thinking proceeds under the sign of difference and plurality and through the method of articulation (Hall 1996, 247; 1991a, b).

Although globalization theorists differ in the critical discourses they bring to their topic, the historical periodization they assign to it, and the political and cultural effects they diagnose from it, they nonetheless share, in Anthony D. King's words,

> at least two perspectives: the rejection of the nationally-constituted society as the appropriate object of discourse, or unit of social and cultural analysis, and to varying degrees, a commitment to conceptualising "the world as a whole."
>
> (ix)

If globalization demands the perpetual realization that the national is not the only paradigm, what does it then mean to conceive of globalized models for literary study, globalized futures for literary disciplines? Beyond the simple acquisition of the globe by certain well-established and often nationalized disciplinary methods (a process resembling critical McDonaldization), we must instead envision the making of new method, the learning and teaching of a different, double, dialectical way of thinking for which globalization's own dualities provide the model.[3]

No contemporary institution, academic or otherwise, can choose to ignore globalization. Fareed Zakaria intuits the problem and identifies a form suitable to its expression: "If I had to write a bumper sticker to describe the climate of today's world, it would read: 'Globalization – Love It or Leave It' " (Zakaria 16). The punch of the postmodern, atomized form of the homily that is the bumper sticker relies on the presentation of a largely false choice. The Hotel California of capitalist systems, globalization is that which you cannot leave and cannot love. One solution to this impasse may lie in Giles Gunn's recent call, in a special issue of PMLA devoted to the globalization of literary studies, for "the critical engagement of globalization."

> [M]ore than an acknowledgment that many of the materials we study, not to mention the methods by which we study them, are produced or at least influenced by globalizing trends . . . to engage globalization critically will also necessitate a much more careful analysis of just how many of the materials in which we profess an interest, whether from the remote past or the emergent present, have themselves subjected aspects of globalization to careful scrutiny and to serious critique and revaluation.
>
> (Gunn 21)

What is required, Gunn seems to suggest, is a critical method that recognizes itself a part of globalization yet also seeks to stand in some degree apart, both subject to globalization's privileged narratives and capable of discerning alternative ones. This essay focuses on a particular kind of disciplinary "material," namely the undergraduate world literature course. Global thinking in curricular form, the world literature course critically engages globalization not only in its presentation of literary texts as the products of local moments and global movements, but also insofar as that very presentation can be seen to derive from, participate in, and occasionally intervene into, broader academic debate on globalization. How does global theory or the theory of globalism look when seen from the vantage point of globalized pedagogy? And how do such basic categories of the contemporary critical discussion of globalization as homogeneity and heterogeneity, moment and movement, local and global, operate when translated into the project of curricular design? Finally, how does the undergraduate world literature course provide a window onto the disciplinary formation of comparative literature, from its cosmopolitan origins to its global future?

World literature: the history of an idea

Comparative literature has always questioned and often transgressed boundaries; boundaries of national literatures and national histories, of literary periods and literary genres, of disciplinary practices and critical theories. While the rise of comparative literature as an academic discipline clearly coincided with the flowering of European nationalism, the field has also reached out, from its very beginning, to grasp some vision of globalism. Certainly comparative literature finds an inaugural moment in Madame de Staël's resolutely nationalizing *De la Littérature* (1800), with its differentiation of the literatures and characters of the dour, philosophical Germans, the joking English, the passionate Italians, and the French, blessed with "more charm, taste, and levity" than any other European nation (Staël-Holstein 1: 45). But comparative literature equally looks back to Johann von Goethe's roughly contemporaneous elaboration of the expansive, supranational concept of *Weltliteratur* [world literature].

Weltliteratur was Goethe's term for a specific class of texts that even as they represented particular national spirits, also managed to traverse, even to transcend, their national, linguistic, and temporal origins. More a prophecy than a program, *Weltliteratur* was not a list of the great masterworks of prior traditions so much as the conjuring forth of a particular literary and political order, indeed, the envisioning of the one in the other. In one of the twenty or so allusions in personal journals, public lectures, letters, and reported conversations from which scholars have pieced together the idea of *Weltliteratur*, Goethe identified its goal: "not that the nations shall think alike, but that they shall learn how to understand each other, and, if they do not care to love one another, at least that they will learn to tolerate one another" (Goethe 8).

Goethe, notes Fritz Strich in his extensive examination of *Weltliteratur*, regularly employed the rhetoric of trade to describe a new order that would see, in Strich's words, "a traffic in ideas between peoples, a literary market to which the nations bring their intellectual treasures for exchange" (Strich 13). The use of economic terminology for cultural phenomena, while it suggests an analogy between Goethe's vision of *Weltliteratur* and the contemporary discourse of globalization, by no means constitutes the sole evidence for such a claim. As a dream of works yet to be written in which Goethe foresaw an important place for German authors and the eventual revitalization of German and other national literatures through foreign contact, *Weltliteratur* reflected early nineteenth-century tenets of nationalist thinking, particularly the Herderian concept of national soul embedded in spirit and language. At the same time, in its aspirations for the literary text as cultural ambassador, *Weltliteratur* constituted an internationalist reaction against the rising tide of ever more virulent nationalisms in post-Napoleonic Europe.[4] That the rise of nationalism as a principle of differentiation coincided with a culture of cosmopolitanism argues for a long historical interpenetration of nation and globe, that very interpenetration which contemporary theorists have also found constitutive of globalization in its various historical eras.[5] The history of comparative literature, then, is also to some degree the history of globalization.

Well recognized as a shaping paradigm in standard histories of the development of comparative literature, *Weltliteratur* now finds itself reanimated as a "concept [that] anticipates current cultural trans-nationalism" (Pizer 216).[6] Both the older and newer discussions of *Weltliteratur* look to it as an alternative to the narrowness of national thinking and the tragedies of nationalist sentiment. While most critics privilege *Weltliteratur*'s vision of exchange across the boundaries of nation, culture, and language, they have had collectively little to say about the term's pedagogical implications. With the notable exception of Sarah Lawall's 1987 *Reading World Literature*, the contemporary expression of *Weltliteratur* that is the undergraduate world literature course has gone largely unexamined.[7] To read the undergraduate world literature course as an expression of the border-crossing that defines comparative literature, to take the project of world literature as in some sense the philosophical heart of the discipline, is little short of heretical. For comparative literature has long positioned the world literature course outside its own characteristic concerns with original language scholarship and continental theory, consciously ceded the teaching of that course to other, less translation-wary departments in the university, and blatantly derided it as both "needlessly grandiose," in the words of René Wellek and Austin Warren, and hopelessly limited.

"Existing courses in world literature," write Wellek and Warren in their 1942 *Theory of Literature*, "like the textbooks and handbooks written for them, often supply us with snippets from famous authors and great books ranging from the *Rig-Veda* to Oscar Wilde and encourage an indiscriminate smattering, a vague, sentimental cosmopolitanism" (Wellek 1949, 41). In a 1959 address to a University of Wisconsin conference on the teaching of world literature, Werner Friederich similarly warns against the dangers of unrestricted literary sampling. Goethe's "unfortunate term of 'Weltliteratur'," he writes, "is not for us," limited as we are by our abilities to perceive "only a few facets, and never the whole totality of God's creation" (Friederich 1959, 30–31).[8] The 1965 Levin Report to the American Comparative Literature

Association, like the subsequent 1975 Greene Report, sharply distinguishes between world literature on the undergraduate level and comparative literature as a graduate discipline open to a select, polyglot few.[9]

Repudiations of world literature notwithstanding, recent years have witnessed an intensified call to integrate new parts of the world, new texts, and new methods into comparative literature's predominately European tradition of knowledge. The emergence over the past three decades of new disciplinary sites such as ethnic studies, cultural studies, and post-colonial studies has reoriented the academic map around the global phenomena of exile, diaspora, forced migrancy, and immigration. In these phenomena scholars have come to see not only the new identities of the present, but also the unacknowledged historical undersides of some of our most privileged cultural narratives – the very narratives that have often passed as "World History" or "World Culture." The history of modern European capitalism we now know to be unthinkable without the tri-continental history of the slave trade and the various histories of colonial and imperial penetration of three-quarters of the globe. European Enlightenment rationalism, as Paul Gilroy has so powerfully demonstrated, defines itself in part through and against the institutions and rhetorics of racialized slavery. Finally, the categorization of what we label European culture takes us to historical moments and places deeply marked by cultural contact – an ancient Greece shaped by Canaanite and Phoenician cultures, a Golden Age Spain filigreed with Islamic influences, an eighteenth-century England finding its national sensibility through imperial adventures.

If the contemporary call to do world literature emanates from broader intellectual trends outside comparative literature, it also represents a very particular engagement on the part of that field with aspects of its history and senses of its selfhood. The 1995 volume of essays *Comparative Literature in the Age of Multiculturalism*, sparked by the much-debated 1993 Bernheimer Report to the ACLA, reveals the various passions that disciplinary self-interrogation stands to unleash. Some contributors to the volume staunchly defend comparative literature as a kind of last bastion against the gradual infiltration of literary studies by a host of upstart disciplines and methods. Others, speaking as practitioners both of comparative literature and of gender and ethnic studies, cultural studies, and post-colonial studies, praise the possibilities of what Mary Louise Pratt figures as "unforeseen matings and crossbreedings" (Pratt 58).[10]

One scholar's disciplinary hybridization is of course another's withering on the vine. In a masterful 1994 overview of the history, practice, and future of comparative literature George Steiner describes the etiolation of the field:

> In too many universities and colleges, comparative literature today is conducted, if at all, nearly entirely via translation. The amalgamation with threatened departments of modern languages, with "core courses" on Western civilization and with the new demands for pan-ethnicity, for "global" studies, lies readily to hand. In more and more curricula, "comparative literature" has come to signify "a reading of great books which one ought to have read anyway in, preferably paperback and in the Anglo-American tongue." Or a resolve, assuredly arguable, to set classics too long prepotent, too long dusty beside, often in the boisterous shadow of, the Afro-American, the Chicano, the Amazonian traditions. . . .
>
> (Steiner 8)

Steiner speaks as if the recent critical turn toward questions of the globe and globality sounds comparative literature's death knell. In fact, it might well be the occasion for the field's revitalization and reinvention. From Steiner's "boisterous shadow" sounds a global clamor – the very opposite of white noise – that, far from receding into the background, instead presses new voices into literary studies' foreground. There is no great surprise in this observation, which has become commonplace on both sides of the canon wars. More unusual, and more evocative of comparative literature's unique position on that contested terrain, is Steiner's further claim that "comparative literature listens and reads after Babel" and that it has done so from its inception, ever dedicated to the "commerce between tongues, between texts of different historical periods or literary forms, [and to] the complex interactions between a new translation and those that have gone before . . ." (9, 11). To read the history of comparative literature in terms of a polyphonous, chaotically global present suddenly encroaching upon a hitherto intact disciplinary past is thus in no small sense to misread comparative literature's own history, in which the global has long been an operative category.

Comparative literature's global vision was enlarged in the middle of the twentieth century by an expanding frame around what constituted the world, from Ernst Robert Curtius's Latinate Europe to Leo Spitzer's Roman and Christian empires to the broadly Western tradition of Auerbach's *Mimesis*, whose inspired plotting of the representation of reality from Homer to Woolf was famously imagined not in the libraries of Europe but in Istanbul, where Auerbach waited out World War II. As the site of what Steiner calls an "inward diaspora" (7), Auerbach's Turkish exile limns a zone in which both texts and textual theorists may be seen to migrate. It is in this zone of displacement and reconnection, of transmission across time and scattering across space, that comparative literature paradoxically finds its disciplinary home. This home has sometimes been as small as the little world of England, France, and Germany (long the obligatory national literatures for comparative literature students), sometimes as large as the globe itself.[11]

In 1952 Auerbach published an essay entitled "Philologie der *Weltliteratur*," a manifesto and methodology for a global comparative literature. Auerbach wrote at a moment when he perceived, on the one hand, the decay of "the inner bases of national existence," the concentration of human activity into Euro-American or Soviet patterns, and the general standardization of world culture; and, on the other hand, the sheer "superabundance" of literary material beyond the grasp of any single individual and the incursion of new methods and concepts into philological research (Auerbach 1969, 2). In this state of affairs, whose simultaneous homogenization and heterogenization surely earns for it the descriptor "globalized," Auerbach notes the waning of *Weltliteratur* as practical ideal. The traditions of cultural exchange between "small groups of highly cultivated men" cannot triumph over a dichotomized, propagandizing world and must necessarily fail to bring about that "spiritual exchange between peoples" and "reconciliation of races" towards which Goethe yearned. Auerbach goes on to imagine a new *Weltliteratur*, one animated by a different understanding of history and historical method and therefore able to "articulate the fateful coalescence of cultures for those people who are in the midst of the terminal phase of fruitful multiplicity" (6–7). "[T]he more our earth grows closer together, the more must historicist synthesis balance the contraction by expanding its activity," writes Auerbach in a statement of globalizing aspiration that stands as the methodological corollary to the article of cosmopolitan faith with which the essay concludes: ". . . our philological home is the earth: it can no longer be the nation" (17).[12]

Auerbach's idiom of philological citizenship found distinctly more nationalist expression in a 1964 address by his fellow emigré Werner Friederich, founder of the program in comparative literature at the University of North Carolina. Speaking to the Australasian Language and Literature Congress from the adopted position of a United States "in the very hub of developments," Friederich analogized programs of comparative literature to the departments of Foreign Affairs that "every well-run government" maintains for the "constant scrutiny of its political and cultural relationships with the nations around it" (Friederich 1964, 47, 36). For Friederich, this espionage-like vision of comparatism was both "a political creed" and a utopian alternative to what he perceived as "the narrowness of ever so much in merely nationally conceived literary scholarship" (48). To the emigré critic René Wellek, the espousal of comparatism as politics by other means portended the unhappy bureaucratization of literary study, the specter of "cultural expansionism," and the impoverishment of literature itself. Departing from those who endowed literary works with the capacities of nationalist representation in an internationalizing world, Wellek urged that literature be considered "not as an argument in the warfare of cultural *prestige*, or as a commodity of foreign trade, or even as an indicator of national psychology" but rather as an aesthetic imperium, a "new world of the imagination [in which] national vanities will disappear" (Wellek 1959, 285 & 295).

As this abbreviated disciplinary history suggests, comparative literature has always been concerned to imagine and articulate some notion of the global, often alongside some vision, however beleaguered or disavowed, of the national. And comparative literature has always been deeply tied to the political and economic structures of its day, from the burgeoning European nationalism that informs Madame de Staël and is in part transformed by Goethe into the possibility of a supranational cosmopolitanism, to Auerbach's, Friederich's, and Wellek's very different responses to cold war ideology, to current efforts to think through what globalization and transnationalism might mean for disciplinary practice. Certainly the global confronts comparative literature and other disciplines now in a different way than it has in the past, as a distinct kind of epistemological object, with an altered form of address to those of us located within the metropolitan academy. To suggest otherwise would be to close the gap between the world in *Weltliteratur* and the globe in globalization, to obscure the very real difference between the relative coherence that marks the rise of European nationalism, with which comparative literature's beginning coincided, and the unmistakable shattering of the national paradigm that is one of the hallmarks of our own moment.[13]

Goethe's nineteenth-century vision of a conversation conducted between nations through their most representative and greatest works of literature, a vision that at once over-flows national boundaries and reconfirms them, cannot be rendered simply prefigurative of the more atomizing and anonymous, displaced and displacing, flows associated with the twenty-first-century transnational. But however new the contemporary addresses of the transnational is, however yoked to the latest advances in communication technology and the material conditions of what Stuart Hall calls "the global post-modern," as cultural discourse it represents something more than the wholly autonomous sign of the present (Hall 1991a, 33). The transnational, like that larger global whose contours it sketches, can equally be understood as the uncanny return in ever more powerful and penetrating forms of certain long-standing aspirations, once familiar but since forgotten, towards cross-cultural exchange.

In the particular species of forgetting practiced by disciplinary history, the global vistas of Goethe's *Weltliteratur* and Auerbach's philological citizenship of the earth have loomed larger for the ideal of unbound lettered privilege they envisioned than for the various constraints under which they labored – the predominantly European compass of their worlds, the rising nationalisms that their cosmopolitanism sought to escape, and the exile and dispos-session that marked Auerbach and his entire generation of emigré intellectuals. In recent years a handful of critics have taken this invisible material as the starting point for a differently globalized version of disciplinary history. This comparative literature, richly textured by the experiences of exile and diaspora, signally uneasy about the work of cultural hegemony, and constantly negotiating the poles of global aspiration and nationalist interpellation, offers the tantalizing prospect of a disciplinary past that coincides with the guiding preoccupations of the present.[14] But if the project of disciplinary redefinition and renewal is not to take on the aspect of a journey back to the future in which we look behind for the already written script of what lies ahead – reanimating the Goethes and Auerbachs as globalization theorists before their time – attention must be paid to the distinction between history, which binds disciplinary futures to their pasts, and historical method, which tells a different story (or ought to) of changing practices, emergent paradigms, new methodologies.[15] Our task then is to learn to read the past for its differences from, as well as its similarities to, the present; to locate our ghostly forefathers within their own historical and ideological moment, and to discern in them the skeleton of a method that might visit us again.

World literature in the classroom: making of a method

Although comparative literature has long been global in its ambitions, it has not been altogether global in its approaches. Friederich's analogy of departments of comparative literature to government "departments of Foreign Affairs" recalls the existence, long dominant, of what Paul Jay calls "a curricular world organized along the lines of a political map, the borders of which have neatly duplicated those between modern nation-states" (Jay 32). In this particular curricular world national thinking prevails. It underwrites the powerful critical narrative of homogeneous, continuous traditions within individual literatures, as well as the very institutional logic that subdivides universities into distinct departments of national literatures and a comparative literature that has historically confined its work to a selective exchange among like, predominantly European, traditions. At the center of this paradigm lies the notion of a mimetic compact between nations and narratives, as present in Madame de Staël's outmoded romantic sketches of national characters and national literatures as in Benedict Anderson's influential thesis that the novel and the newspaper provided "the technical means for 're-presenting' the *kind* of imagined community that is the nation" (Anderson 25). The cultural fact of transnational traffic and exchange disrupts this mimetic compact in our present moment, as well as in the late nineteenth-century cases Anderson focuses on, and the early nineteenth-century context of Staël.

In an age of globalization – and that age can be, if we wish, very broadly defined – national perspectives do not wither, any more than nation-states themselves do. However, national perspectives do require to be thought of somewhat differently. Globalization, taken as in part a reading strategy, might challenge us to look anew at literary texts, seeking not the mimetic compact between nation and narrative but rather the presence of certain intranational and extra-national forces of affiliation and disaffiliation. The globalization of literary studies does not involve simply leaving the nation for that other social, political, and imaginative space, shaped by the dual forces of human migration and electronic media communication, which Arjun Appadurai evocatively dubs the "transnation" (Appadurai 172–77). Rather, the globalization of literary studies entails the learning (and teaching) of a kind of relational thinking in which we see the nation through the local yet as part of the global.

The globalizing effort to expand what is studied and taught can go in two directions. We can produce updated versions of Jay's curricular map that include new and different texts but continue to read them representatively, in the spirit of that famous map of Africa whose indexes of colonial character Conrad's Marlow ponders in the waiting room of the Brussels trading company. "There was," Marlow recalls with undisguised praise for British efficiency,

> a vast amount of red – good to see at any time because one knows that some real
> work is done in there – a deuce of lot of blue, a little green, smears of orange,
> and, on the East Coast, a purple patch, to show where the jolly pioneers of
> progress drink the jolly lager-beer.

> (Conrad 13)

A representative reading of the terrain of world literature would introduce particular works as embodiments of national sensibility, examples to be assimilated into the compass of worldly knowledge. Alternatively, we can conceive of the curricular map less in the mode of territorial specification and acquisition than in that of defamiliarization and displacement. Any map presents the global as a local utterance, for any attempt to represent "the world" inevitably bespeaks the mapmaker's own placement. To change a map, then, is to change not only what we look at, but also the very place and premises from which we look. It is to encounter not just the strangeness of the world, but our own selves made strange. It is to inhabit, most productively, what the late Charles Bernheimer called "the anxieties of comparison."

These anxieties are not those conjured by Harold Bloom in his characterization of canons as "achieved anxieties"; indeed, they represent a quite different engagement with the idea and ideology of the canon (Bloom 38). For Bloom, the distinguishing mark of the canonical is "strangeness, a mode of originality that either cannot be assimilated, or that so assimilates us that we cease to see it as strange" (3). Dante offers the prime example of the first, Shakespeare of the second. Whereas for Bloom the canonical work of art effects the experience of strangeness, in the alternative mapping I have sketched it is the readerly act that produces the shock of alienation and subsequent realization of difference. What the cartographers of the new curriculum confront is the possibility that literatures may not follow what have become the naturalized lines of territorial maps. The path of literary movement in fact suggests a far more porous and shifting structure to the borders of nation and region, language and culture, a structure that admits, even encourages, contact and change.

I focus for the remainder of this essay on a single undertaking of readerly reorientation: the 1999–2000 introduction by Yale's Comparative Literature department of a new undergraduate course in "World Literatures." The debut of this course coincided with a significant restructuring of the undergraduate Literature major in order to accommodate a new track devoted to interdisciplinary literary studies, for which "World Literatures" and another new course on "World Cinema" serve as prerequisites. It is too soon to advance predictions on the final shape this course may take, and too hubristic to present the course and the larger changes of which it is a part as a definitive model for a new comparative literature. But as academic institutions continue to ponder how to globalize existing disciplines and programs, it may perhaps be useful to provide an account of how Yale's literature faculty conceptualized this demand and the structures we invented to answer it.

Over the course of two years, faculty in Comparative Literature and representatives from nearly every other university department of language and literature met regularly to discuss and design what eventually became a team-taught, two semester undergraduate lecture course with a weekly discussion section. During the planning period I also incorporated discussion of the course into my own undergraduate teaching. Students in an introductory comparative literature seminar read excerpts from Bloom's *The Western Canon* and the *Norton Anthology of World Masterpieces* and then designed their own world literature courses. One student's reading list began with the following questions:

What is the point of a World Lit class? Is it to expose students to as many narratives as possible? Is it to show that different persons/nations/minorities/publics produce the same type of literature? Is it to isolate great themes? Is it about similarities? Differences?

Like the French literary critic Ferdinand Brunetière, who in 1900 lamented the "few points of contrast" and "few possibilities of comparison" between certain "faraway and mysterious civilizations" and the little world of Europe, this student quickly isolated comparison as the central dilemma of a world literature course (Brunetière 157–58). It is relatively easy to expand the range of what is read, less clear how one might create and transmit a coherent principle for making sense of that range as some kind of whole.[16]

Like the larger process of globalization, which both homogenizes and heterogenizes the world, at once integrating distinct entities and causing differences to proliferate, our effort to globalize literary studies inhabited distinctly contradictory terrain. The challenge was to find a pedagogical form that would allow our students to register a plurality of particularities while seeking those aspects of similarity and connection without which a world literature course quickly dissolves into precisely that "vague, sentimental cosmopolitanism" scorned by an earlier generation of comparative literature scholars, mere coverage for coverage's sake (Wellek 1949, 41). For Brunetière, an ardent believer in the possibility of applying evolutionary theory to literary history, the law of progressive development presented itself as the paramount principle of connection. Just as "*Astrée* begot *Polexandre* and *Endymion*, which begot *Artamène* and *Clélie*, which begot the *Princess de Clèves* and *Zayde*" [he cites a series of seventeenth- and eighteenth-century French romances and novels], so too does genre for Brunetière evolve from the lyrical to the elegiacal, from drama to epic to narrative (Brunetière 177, 167). Our course, while it retained the organizational rubric of a particular sequence of genres (sacred and wisdom literatures, lyric poetry, and drama in the fall semester, epic and novel in the spring), [it] nonetheless eschewed the teleological plot of generic evolution in favor of more lateral networks of influence and adaptation.

To study genre is to study change. Genres are systems in constant transformation, always inverting, displacing, or combining earlier genres and, equally, ever in the process of being themselves remade (Todorov 15, 18). As the sites where poetics and history, form and ideology meet, genres afford a vantage point from which to learn something about the individual societies that codify and popularize certain genres as the formal mirrors of conceptual belief. The study of the changing history of literary genres further stands to teach us something about a larger cultural story of cross-societal contact, transmission, and hybridization.[17]

Globalization's pedagogical injunction is to think both locally and globally, both nationally and transnationally, both through the particular and towards the universal in its reconceptualized form as network, intersection, routes. We can find one model for how to think world literature in an age of globalization in Auerbach's essay on *Weltliteratur*, focused as it is on the redemptive project of a historical synthesis that is as much a spatial location as an intellectual vocation. Citing Curtius's *European Literature and the Latin Middle Ages* as an emblematic instance of that ever expanding historical synthesis to which *Weltliteratur* must aspire in an globalizing age of increasing contraction, Auerbach observes Curtius's debt to the following "methodological principle":

> [I]n order to accomplish a major work of synthesis it is imperative to locate a point of departure [*Ansantzpunkt*], a handle, as it were, by which the subject can be seized. The point of departure must be the election of a firmly circumscribed, easily comprehensible set of phenomena whose interpretation is a radiation out from them and which orders and interprets a greater region than they themselves occupy.
>
> (Auerbach 1969, 13–14)

Although points of departure may be several and of various kinds ("a semantic interpretation, a rhetorical trope, a syntactic sequence, the interpretation of one sentence, or a set of remarks made at a given time and in a given place"), they are inevitably characterized by both their solid grounding or "concreteness," and their centrifugal movement (15). Of the many possible points of departure conceivable for a world literature course, we singled out two, both marked by the *ansatzpunkt*'s doubling of location and diffusion: the practice of reading and the structure of genre.

One reads, of course, from some place. *Mimesis*, for all the vastness of its historical range (historical relativism to its harsher critics) and for all the loving audacity of its attempt to provide what Hayden White calls "the diachronic 'plot' of the history of western literature," was still, in Auerbach's words, "quite consciously a book written by a particular person in a particular place during the early 1940's."[18] But reading is also that which defies the grounding of place, a handle that rather than presenting itself for seizure seems endlessly to slip from our grasp, transform in our hands, never stay the same. To conceive a world literature course from the *ansatzpunkt* of reading is to give up on the illusion that one could, from some central location, cover everything, contain all the texts, represent the globe, hold firm in the face of dizzying difference. Such an illusion produces as its most powerful fantasy the list, from the ancient classical syllabus of writers deemed worthy of grammatical and rhetorical imitation, to the early Church fathers' canon of orthodox, as opposed to heretical, writers, to such recruits in our contemporary cultural wars as E.D. Hirsch's *Cultural Literacy: What Every American Needs to Know*, with an appendix, *What Literate Americans Know* (1987); Harold Bloom's *The Western Canon* (1994) with its "survivor's list" of 26 canonical writers and accompanying appendix of some several hundred masterworks of world literature; and, at the other end of the ideological spectrum, the dauntingly comprehensive *Norton Anthology of World Masterpieces* (1995). To take as the *ansatzpunkt* of a world literature course not the making of the list but rather the question of how to read the items on the list is to seek a more pointilist vision of knowledge, a vision of world literature not as something we get or give, inherit or overthrow, but rather a way we learn to think.

The alternative to the list is the system, by which I understand those larger networks of textual influence and broader structures of historical and social inscription which surround individual texts. Read systemically, world literature is not so much an ontology, a catalogue of what is, as a particular epistemological mode. As a way of knowing, world literature does not attempt to place its students in a single tradition or cultural lineage, as the "Great Books" courses instituted in American universities and colleges in the period of World War I aspired to do.[19] Instead, world literature displaces its students, obliging them to shuttle and shift like literary texts themselves across the borders of geography and time, language and culture. Against the "Great Books" or "Western Civilization" models which underwrote the twentieth-century convergence between the idea of world literature and a particular canon, comparative literature's version of the world literature course logically enough seeks its own methodological imprimatur, a literal disciplining of the classroom in which the act of comparison prevails over the codification of the canonical.

Such a reconceptualization of the project of world literature may well be the pedagogical corollary to Wai Chee Dimock's recent theorization of "the centrifugal force of literature." For Dimock the singular elasticity of the spatio-temporal "fabric" of literature "mess[es] up territorial sovereignty and numerical chronology," and causes contractions of the sort that bring two authors as geographically, linguistically, and historically distinct as Dante and his ardent student, the twentieth-century Russian poet Osip Mandelstam, into an Einsteinian "relativity of simultaneity" in which non-synchronous entities collide (Dimock 2001, 178). Such contractions coexist with an ever expanding movement of words in "dimensions of space and time so far-flung and so deeply recessional that they can never be made to coincide with the synchronic plane of the geopolitical map." We are obliged instead to imagine an endlessly warped "continuum" of linguistic contacts and an "evolving radius of literary action." Reading is not the single central point of this radius but rather a multiplying and dispersing process of "extension, elaboration, and randomization," the constantly deterritorializing work of a "global readership" that is anything but unified (174–75).

Translating the concentric patterns of literary history into an undergraduate survey course, Yale's faculty sought, rather than the syllabus's customary regime of chronological progression and territorial coverage, a series of polychronic encounters between texts. Although we began with the Bible, our juxtaposition of the story of Job and Proverbs with significantly earlier Near Eastern "Just Sufferer" compositions and proverb collections from the Akkadian, Egyptian, and Sumerian traditions (11th c., 12th c., and 18th c. BCE respectively) enabled students to conceive of the Bible as something other than a beginning. The foundational text of the Judeo-Christian tradition indeed emerged as a latecomer, an inheritor of ancient stories and long-existing expressive forms. This initial questioning of the very concept of origin and originality in literary history, accompanied by a constantly shifting cartography of literary migration, provided the guiding themes of the course.

Even in a two-semester survey, time is short and so our methodological aspirations regularly exceeded our grasp. For example, we read only one of the vast number of texts radiating outward from the *Paen in a t*, an ancient Sanskrit collection of animal tales which gave rise to some 200 translations and retellings, including individual tales in Chaucer's *Canterbury Tales*, the *Thousand and One Nights*, Boccaccio's *Decameron*, the fables of Aesop, Marie de France, and La Fontaine, and the fairy tales of the brothers Grimm. Though we read only one of these many retellings, the pairing of *Pathe fable* with Marie de France's medieval *Fables*, like the pairing of the Bible and its various Near Eastern antecedents, or the pairing of Homer's *Odyssey* with such twentieth-century echoes as Ralph Ellison's *Invisible Man*, Derek Walcott's *Omeros*, and David Dabydeen's poem "Coolie Odyssey," laid out the grounds of a method. I will call this method globalized reading.

Globalized reading does not attempt to create an alternative canon so much as to change the prevalent positioning of the canonical and the non-canonical as one another's opposites, with the election of the one appearing to dictate the disappearance of the other. Taking a text considered world-making and placing it alongside one from another tradition and time, globalized reading changes the way we see. It displaces the hegemonic sense of "world" as fictive universality in favor of a vision of many worlds, individually distinct and variously connected. In this model, if Caribbean and African American retellings of the *Odyssey* confirm a powerful critical narrative that holds Homer's poem great precisely because it has been so often imitated, the retellings equally invite construction of a different narrative, one that reads in the migratory movements of literary texts a far less unidirectional plot than the simple creeping expansion of a particular Western tradition. In its various New World adaptations and reinventions, refracted through the experiences of forced migration, slavery, and colonization, the *Odyssey* tells a different story. The heroes of these later *Odysseys* cannot, like Odysseus, return home but they nonetheless make of their dispossession a particular kind of voice and a unique form of literary possession. For Franco Moretti it is such echoes of a dominant literary original from the peripheral or semi-peripheral zones of the globe that most properly deserve the title of "*world*" texts." World texts are distinguished by a "geographical frame of reference [that] is no longer the nation-state, but a broader entity – a continent, or the world-system as a whole" (Moretti 1996, 50).[20]

In the new pedagogy I am sketching it is not just a question of recognizing the modern emergence of a transnational, transregional global literature. We must also learn to read older works and older categories of belonging (culture, language, region, nation) in global ways. The "terrains of world literature" are indeed, as Homi K. Bhabha writes, now less those of national traditions than of the colonized, the migrants, the refugees – human products of the changing world-system (Bhabha 12). These border identities, while constitutive of the particular swath of modernity encompassed by post-colonial studies, also extend backwards in time to earlier eras. Given the past-heavy nature of the introductory survey course, we could not simply rush students towards a set of properly "world" or global texts whose emergence signals the demise of national thinking. Nor would such an approach go very far towards defining what globalization might mean as a pedagogical project with the potential to reconfigure how we locate, approach, and teach our oldest, most canonical works. By contrast, Yale's "World Literatures" course sought to re-present texts spanning nearly four millennia in a globalized way: locally inflected and translocally mobile, open for reading not only in themselves or for some abstract notion of canonical value, but furthermore (and differently) through the modes of resonance, contrapuntality, textual interconnection, and systemic inscription.[21] Globalized reading discerns two dimensions in literary texts; location in history and dispersal across time and space. Even more importantly, globalized reading actively articulates location to dispersal, in the spirit of those Auerbachian *ansatzpunkte* "whose interpretation is a radiation out from them and which orders and interprets a greater region than they themselves occupy" (Auerbach 1969, 13–14).

Moretti offers one visualization of such a reading method. He proposes that we think of literature as a series of branches and of literary history itself as a tree (Moretti 2000). Individual branches represent certain formal choices that shape the larger, changing history of literary genres. Read through the figure of the tree, genres reveal themselves as "wide field[s] of diverging moves," most of which dead end into the vast unread (217). Against the close analysis that underpins the notion of canonical greatness, Moretti calls instead for a "maximum of methodological boldness" which would bring the statistics, charts, graphs, and maps of sociological analysis to literary studies thereby allowing for the retrieval of the unread and the identification of patterns as broad and diverse as "the uncharted expanse of literature" itself (227). Sadly, perhaps inevitably, the course we designed had little place for what Moretti identifies as the 99.5% of non-canonical literature. We included the Zulu *izibongo* [oral praise poem] here, a little-read example of the early Soviet social realist novel there, but we largely concentrated on a selection of major works from both Western and non-Western traditions. Where Moretti's "methodological boldness" did impact the design of the course was in the style of reading we sought to transmit. This globalized style, if it did not approach Moretti's controversial call for the wholesale abandonment of close reading (surely unwise in an introductory course), nonetheless attempted to pair the work of formal analysis with the larger history of form itself. Through a method that looked both closely and distantly or, to use another lexicon, both textually and systemically, we sought to trace similarities in the intratextual functional unit Moretti names "device" in order to map changes and transformations in the supratextual unit he names "genre."

The team-taught format of the course enabled the careful documentation of such aspects of device as language, style, and figure (all too often lost in courses taught in translation), as well as the brief presentation of necessary historical and cultural context for each text. For nearly every class, we brought in a specialist from the relevant department and prefaced his or her lecture with a short introduction that related the day's text to earlier readings, drew connections, and named patterns.[22] If the specialists' deeply detailed lectures embedded each text in a highly particular culture, our generalist's introductions attested to a changing critical paradigm of literature as a global system of expansion, transmission, and exchange. The academy has long been intellectually wedded and institutionally bound to the notion that a single instructor should be agent of both the aerial and the ground view thanks to his or her specialization in a nationally or linguistically delimited realm. That model, however, profoundly constricts the possible range of what can be taught.

However clumsy our course's particular division of labor was and however prone to the difficulties of inevitably different lecturers, our collaborative, interdepartmental structure nonetheless provided a means for students to perceive a specificity within the texts they read and a continuity across them. They came to know something, I hope, about the differing forms the didactic impulse of wisdom literature takes, from the proverbs, prayers, and instructions of the ancient Near East, to the *Pae texts t*'s and Marie de France's treatises on wise governance, to the *Analects* of Confucius (5th – 4th c. BCE), the Koranic suras (7th c.), and Minamoto no Tamenori's Japanese Buddist tale *Sanboe* (10th c.). With regard to the lyric, students considered the structures of memorialization through which a poem seeks to arrest time and reverse loss. Their reading led them through Sappho's odes (Greek, 7th c. BCE), the *Nine Songs* (Chinese, 4th c. BCE), the *Man'yoshu* of Kakinomoto no Hitomaro (Japanese, 8th c.) the erotic ghazals of Umar ibn Abi-Rabi'a and Waddah al-Yaman (Arabic, 8th c.), the troubador lyrics of Arnaut Daniel and Bernart de Ventadorn (Provençal, 12th c.), Petrarch's *canzoniere* (Italian, 15th c.), Ronsard's sonnets (French, 16th c.), Keats's "Ode on a Grecian Urn" (English, 19th c.), Goethe's Teutonization of the Arabic ghazal in his *West-öestlicher Divan* (German, 19th c.), and Pushkin's "Exegi Monumentum" (Russian, 19th c.).

In contrast to poetry's freezing of time, drama unfolds action over time. Although we introduced students to this and other aspects of Aristotle's theory of drama, this particular unit began not with the freshman survey's customary Greek tragedy but rather with *sakuntala*. Written in the 4th c. by Kalidasa, the preeminent classical poet of the Sanskrit tradition, *sakuntala* became a frequently translated, repeatedly staged staple of the nineteenth-century European Orientalist tradition. With its mixture of verse and prose and the happy ending characteristic of Sanskrit dramatic plays, *sakuntala* is hardly legible through Aristotelian terms such as the triad of epic, lyric, and dramatic poetry or the essential division between tragedy and comedy. To read the play requires some understanding of the mixed prose-verse *campu* form, of the distinction between *drsya* and *sravya* (dramatic and non-dramatic works), and of the elaborate theory of the *rasas*, the nine emotional moods produced in listeners by works of art. To be sure, our students probably did not retain a complete grasp of these aspects of Sanskrit literary aesthetics. But our Sanskritist colleague's presentation of them in his reading of *sakuntala* opened the students' eyes to the cultural specificity of literary categories and the illogic of any theory of genre that would simply transplant literary form across the globe.

The drama unit subsequently paired Shakespeare's *Macbeth* with Akira Kurosawa's Japanese film version, *Throne of Blood*, and a fifteenth-century Japanese Nø drama with Bertolt Brecht's twentieth-century German plays *The Measures Taken* and *He Who Says Yes; He Who Says No*. These selections restaged the question of cultural difference even while attesting to the translatability of certain narratives and narrative forms. The method of globalized reading did not always turn on the explicit juxtaposition of textual "model" to textual "echo." The final selection of *Evam Indrajit*, a twentieth-century Bengali play, in fact obliged the lecturer to read backwards, introducing Pirandello's *Six Characters in Search of an Author* and Brecht's *Caucasian Chalk Circle* (neither of which the students had time to read) as the sources of certain absurdist aspects of the Indian play.

Our tracing of individual textual themes and devices, coupled with a pedagogical narrative about the migratory patterns of literary form, produced at least a partial sense that our heterogeneous material might also coalesce at various moments and in various places into something approaching a new literary history of genre. We told this story differently in the second semester, when our treatment of lengthier epics and novels allowed for fewer lecturers and more consistent development of particular connective threads. Genres, despite their emergence from a particular history of Western literary criticism, are dynamic and changing forms. Subject to a variety of historical conditions, they take particular inflections in different cultures and often trace out distinctly cross-cultural, cross-linguistic patterns of transmission and circulation. While genres cannot be simply transported from culture to culture, as an *ansatzpunkt* they can be understood to radiate out from a specific point of origin, becoming ever more multiplicious.

Readers of Bakhtin will recognize the previous description as the exclusive provenance of the novel, whose heteroglossia, polychronism, and "decentralizing, centrifugal forces" contrast with the monologic, centralizing, characterologically flat, temporally immediate nature of epic (Bakhtin 273). For Moretti, on the other hand, this model of centripetal epic and centrifugal novel is persuasive only up until the end of the eighteenth century. Then, in a curious instance of literary devolution, the epic emerges as the properly "polyphonic form of the modern West" – global in its aspirations, as heterogeneous in its forms as the space of the world-system itself (Moretti 1996, 56–57). For the purposes of our "World Literatures" course the point was not to endorse one or the other claim for generic ascendancy. We sought instead to apply the centrifugal method implicit in both accounts to epic and novel equally, thereby recasting their relationship less as a Bakhtinian break than as a discernible continuity.

To read in this manner we had to accord epic, against the claims of Bakhtin or Lukacs or Auerbach, a certain interiority and interpretability. We had furthermore to place epic within that very trajectory of outward movement and adaptive dissemination which we have come to think of as predominantly novelistic.[23] In "World Literatures" the *Odyssey*, read nearly in its entirety, was prefaced by the Akkadian *Epic of Gilgamesh*, which predates Homer by some eight centuries, and immediately followed by a series of twentieth-century Caribbean reappropriations. We then proceeded to selections from the *Ramayana* (Sanskrit, 6th c. BCE), the *Song of Roland* (Old French, 12th c.), and selected books of Camoes's *Lusiads* (Portuguese, 15th c.). We read portions of the *Aeneid* as precursor to Camoes's chronicle of African discovery, the fifteenth-century Malian *Epic of Sundiata* as contemporary and counter-point, and "Rounding the Cape" by the twentieth-century South African poet and critic Roy Campbell as long historical resonance, in which the figure of Adamastor rises as the voice of indigenous Africa. From the epic we moved into the novel, beginning with the sixteenth-century Spanish picaresque of *Lazarillo de Tormes* and Aphra Behn's seventeenth-century *Oroonoko*. *Oroonoko* is notable (like Defoe's *Robinson Crusoe*, with which it vies for title of the first English novel) for its mixing of narrative forms and its foregrounding of the slave trade and mercantile capitalism. Having established through their reading of *Oroonoko* an intimate bond between the consolidation of the modern world-system and the rise of the novel, students were prepared for later considerations of the the novelistic impact of capitalism (Balzac's *Père Goriot*); socialism (Nikolai Ostrovsky's *How the Steel was Tempered*); colonialism (Ralph Ellison's *Invisible Man* and Ngugi wa Thiong'o's *Devil on the Cross*); and underdevelopment (*The Harp and the Shadow* by Alejo Carpentier and *Crossing the Mangrove* by Maryse Condé).

Changing degrees of realism – atmospheric, socialist, mythical, magical – provided one recognizably Auerbachian account of the sequential development of the novel, the increasing polyphony of narration another. The growing incursion of vernacular and oral speech in Ellison, Ngugi, and Condé, for example, tells a now familiar story about the novel as the formal result of ever more daring negotiations between a dominant foreign form and the indigenous materials of local culture. Curiously, however, *Oroonoko*'s jarring combination of confession, romance, tragedy, and travelogue is as preoccupied by the magic and wonder of the New World, as mixed in its registers, and as heteroglossic in its narration as *The Harp and the Shadow*. The latter's retelling of Columbus's discovery of the New World incorporates his own invented confession, actual fragments of his diaries, historical chronicle, popular legend, and a vast intertextual web of allusion to such epic forebears as the *Odyssey*, the *Song of Roland*, and the *Divine Comedy*. Strangely secret sharers at opposite ends of three hundred years of novelistic history, *Oroonoko* and *The Harp and the Shadow* dispense with the model of a pure generic origin increasingly contaminated or irradiated by the process of dissemination. Against a purely teleological reading of literary movement (from singular origin to plural copies), they propose very different mappings of literary time and space, recalling Moretti's tree and Dimock's radii, which encourage us to see every text in multiple dimensions.

The inclusion of *The Tale of Genji* by the Japanese woman of letters Murasaki Shikibu offers a case in point. The text might be seen to invite various readings: a contrapuntal counterpart to Aphra Behn, another female chronicler of court life; a prefigurative version of that interiorization of character and intricacy of plot which we consider properly novelistic; and finally, the altogether distinct status of a mixed prose-verse work [*monogatari*] from a tenth-century culture whose novels would only be written many centuries later and in direct dialogue with Western forms. *The Tale of Genji* is much more than the prehistory of the novel, just as Latin American, Caribbean, African, and Indian magical realism are much more than its post-colonial present. The key was to get students to see an equally powerful, less teleological, critical narrative in the shape of the syllabus itself – chronological certainly but also centrifugal, plotted along the familiar lines and lineages of literary history but also taking each point on that line as the origin of a widening circle of influence and imitation.

Conclusion: globalized reading and global form

In a recent article Ian Baucom defines global form as a "strictly regulated flow dynamics that balances the relentless centrifugal distributions of capital with their inevitable centripetal return to a seat of high finance." He suggests we view global form through three laws: "expansion contracts, contraction enriches, and enrichment haunts" (Baucom 160). This haunting effect is as visible for Baucom in globalization – whose flows find their "dematerializing, dedifferentiating logic of exchange" troubled by the return of cultural, spatial, and temporal difference – as in genre. Genre, Baucom writes in a gloss on Jameson, is

> a cognitive space of flow – an epistemological structure that, as it achieves a (generally metropolitan) hegemony, is capable of expanding its range of address and subordinating virtually every corner of the globe to its designs but that, when it does so, and so helps to define the specifically historical ideology of its age, finds its articulations haunted by a ghost language that subordinates its ideology of the present age to the ideology "of all the dead generations."
>
> (162–63)

The internal haunting of one genre by another illustrates a crucial aspect of the law of global form. In this "finance capital moment of literary study" genres and schools of genre criticism first expand, then contract, leaving in circulation the ghostly imprint of their externalized others and their anteriorized models. This elegant reading of the flows of literary-critical history relies on an implicit connection between the structure of globalization and the structure of genre quite similar to that which I have argued for here (although I would insist more on their dual tendencies to heterogenize as they expand). It is no doubt true, as Baucom cautions, that global literary study holds out the distinctly unsavory possibility of "making the literary market a corporate partner *of*, as well as an analogue *for*, global capital." But the "challenge of the global" remains, in Baucom's words, "rethinking the form of the globe" (169–70). This form, I have tried to suggest, exists on both theoretical and pedagogical planes and in fact demands that we imagine their coincidence.

For the American political subject globalization too often conjures a sense of standing at the center of an ever expanding radius where we contemplate the increasing symmetry between ourselves and the world (McDonald's in Beijing, literary criticism in the mode of finance capital). But globalization is equally the shock of confronting the plurality and prevalence of difference, the largeness of a world that surpasses our narratives and our categories. This is to say nothing of the extent to which the triumphal story of world-wide Americanization itself depends on the simultaneous denial and exploitation of the racial, ethnic, and class differentiations that structure United States society internally and the division of labor globally. If we want to globalize comparative literature and literary studies more broadly we must seek the sheer inassimilable strangeness of difference, not erase it out of the pedagogical moment.

For those of us who introduced "World Literatures" into Yale's Department of Comparative Literature, globalization meant reimagining a course historically despised by our discipline, reconceiving the shape of our teaching and our students' learning, and inventing a means by which we could all of us begin to read globally. Globalized reading meant giving up on the certitudes of the center in favor of the difficulties of dissemination; striving to grasp both the larger systems or networks of influence into which individual literary texts fit and their individual historical and formal particularities; not so much placing ourselves in a linear national or linguistic tradition as persistently displacing ourselves through a sequence of shifting, migrating, radiating materials. A two-semester course cannot deliver the world, but that is no reason to shrink from the task of globalizing disciplines and programs. Auerbach's prediction that "the more our earth grows closer together, the more must historicist synthesis balance the contraction by expanding its activity" serves us well as motto and method for the expansion and diversification, centrifugalization and heterogenization not only of "world literature" but of literature itself. We should, Auerbach tells us, be big in the face of a shrinking world, creating through new frameworks of comparison and connection a theoretical and pedagogical practice that claims neither to be the globe nor to represent it, but simply to learn to think in a global fashion.

Notes

1   References refer respectively to Harvey (1990), Appadurai (1996), Giddens (1990), Wallerstein (1974), and Hodgson (1993).
2   On global culture's homogenizing aspects and global capital's standardizing effects, see Smith (1990) and Miyoshi (1996). Beneath globalization's specter of homogenization of course lies the fact of growing social differentiation. See, for example, Zygmunt Bauman's argument that the spatial mobility created by globalization constitutes a new and potent factor of social stratification dividing learned cosmopolitan elites from the common population (1998, 18). On cosmopolitanism's emblematic figuration of an increasingly diverse and complexly connected global sensibility, see Hannerz (1990 & 1996); Robbins (1998 & 1992); and, for a more critical viewpoint, see Friedman (1997).
3   According to Jameson, dialectical thinking "no longer attempts to resolve the dilemma head on, according to its own terms, but rather com[es] to understand the dilemma itself as the mark of the profound contradictions latent in the very mode of posing the problem" (Jameson 1974, 343). A dialectical thinking of globalization would thus take as its most urgent work the elaboration of an intellectual method that reflects rather than resolves the tension, observed by so many of globalization's critics, between the homogeneous and the heterogeneous, the national and the transnational, the universal and the particular.
4   On the simultaneously nationalist and internationalist aspects of *Weltliteratur*, see Steiner (1995, 6); Pizer (2000, 216–18); and Lawall (1994, 13–20).
5   See especially Robertson's claim that "the *idea* of nationalism (or particularism) develops *only* in tandem with internationalism" (Robertson 103).
6   Pizer, in addition to himself offering an example of current theorizing about the connections between *Weltliteratur* and globalization, also provides a succinct survey of several standard studies of comparative literature that place *Weltliteratur* at the conceptual center of the discipline. He cites Ulrich Weisstein's *Comparative Literature and Literary Theory* (1973), François Jost's *Introduction to Comparative Literature* (1974), and Claudio Guillén's *The Challenge of Comparative Literature* (1993).
7   Lawall's volume of essays should be read in conjunction with *The Norton Anthology of World Masterpieces*, of which she is an editor. Also see Ross (1993) and Lindenberger (1989) for useful histories of world literature or world civilization initiatives at the University of California at Santa Cruz and Stanford University. For a model of theoretical speculation on pedagogical practice, see Brooks's description of Yale's "Literature X" undergraduate course and the broader Literature Major, dedicated to

"literature in transcendence of national and linguistic boundaries," "fictions beyond the specific institution of literature," and "a wider context for the study of literature" (Brooks 1973, 179).

8   Deriding "that awfully facile and arrogant concept of World Literature courses" which promises totality only to deliver woefully incomplete "snippets" of "NATO-literature . . . from ancient Greece through the Mediterranean and German literatures to the modern Anglo-Americans," Friederich proposes an alternative Great Books model. He envisions an academic year devoted to twelve masterpieces that together present the essence of epic, tragedy, comedy, novel, and lyric poetry, and the distinctive achievements of individual nations and literary movements. Sustained encounters with the literatures of Europe, Asia, Africa, and the Americas should, Friederich suggests, be reserved for upperclass seminars, while comparative literature should be restricted to graduate students alone.

9   Levin (1996), Greene (1996). For a similar statement of division, see Guérard (1940).

10 Pratt's essay, joined by those by Michael Riffaterre, Emily Apter, Rey Chow, Françoise Lionnet, and David Damrosch articulates a vision of a new, multidisciplinary and multicultural comparative literature in contrast to the more traditional disciplinary vision advocated by other contributors.

11 On exile as a crucial problematic both in the careers of modern comparative literature's founding fathers, many of whom found their way to American universities after the war, and in the discipline itself, see Apter (1996).

12 On the possibilities that Auerbach's essay affords to literary criticism and intellectual culture, see Said (1975, esp. 68–69, 72–73, 76, 324); and Bové (1986, 131–208).

13 For critiques of national thinking see Gilroy (1993), Chow (1993), Appadurai (1996), and Lowe (1996).

14 Several of these critics cite Auerbach's production of the seminal text of comparative literature from Turkish exile as a defining aspect of the discipline. See Said (1983, esp. 5–9), Apter (1996), Holquist (1993), and Mufti (1998). Also useful are the extended models for a transnational, transcultural comparative literature offered in Said (1993) and Apter (1999).

15 I am thinking of the differences between Pizer's suggestion that "Goethe's musings on world literature also anticipate, and could thereby help to define, 'transnational literary studies' in the present, just as they helped to define 'comparative literature' in the past" (214), and Fredric Jameson's call, in his much-maligned "Third World Literature in the Era of Multinational Capitalism" for the "reinvention, in a new situation, of what Goethe long ago theorized as 'world literature'" (Jameson 1986, 68).

16 The student-designed syllabi offered valuable indexes to those questions of methodological coherence which students correctly assumed would trouble the course, as well as to students' own investments in such a course. One would expect the repeated inclusion of the *Odyssey* and the *Iliad*, the Bible and the Koran, Dante, Shakespeare, Cervantes, and Joyce; more unusual was the repetition in about a fifth of the syllabi of Confucius, the *Tales of a Thousand and One Nights*, *Faust*, and *Eugene Onegin*. With twentieth-century materials the syllabi emerged at their most idiosyncratic, incorporating texts as varied as Lu Xun's *Diary of a Madman*, Sigmund Freud's *Dora*, Virginia Woolf's *To the Lighthouse*, Vladimir Nabokov's *Lolita*, Jorge Luis Borges's *Ficciones*, Naguib Mahfouz's *Arabian Days and Nights*, Audre Lorde's *Zami*, and William Gibson's *Neuromancer*.

17 On genre as the meeting point of form and ideology see Jameson (1981), especially Chapter 2.

18 White (1996, 129); Auerbach (1953, 18) as quoted in Lindenberger (1996, 199, fn. 17). On the "dangerous relativism" of *Mimesis*, see Wellek (1954).

19 On this history see Lawall (1994, 20–34). On the broader issue of the canon and its history, see Guillory (1993 & 1995).

20 Moretti's periphery is by no means exclusively non-Western. He includes Goethe's divided Germany, Melville's emergent America, and Joyce's colonized Ireland alongside García Márquez's underdeveloped Colombia, all distinct from the "highly homogeneous national cultures of France and England, at the core of the world-system." What most distinguishes periphery from core in this "possible geography of literary forms" is the dominance of the epic with its "global ambition" and non-homogeneous nature in the periphery, and the reign of the more controlling and controlled, rigorously nationalized, novel in the core.

21 See Dimock (1997), Said (1993), and Moretti (1996 & 2000).

22 Faculty lecturers were drawn from the departments of Comparative Literature, Asian Languages and Literatures, Classics, English, French, German, Slavic, Spanish and Portuguese, and Near Eastern Studies. The introductions to the lectures were given alternately by myself and Michael Holquist, co-instructors of the course.

23 See Lukacs (1971) and Auerbach (1953a).

References

Anderson, Benedict. *Imagined Communities: Reflections on the Origin and Spread of Nationalism*. New York: Verso, 1983, rev. ed. 1991.

Appadurai, Arjun. *Modernity at Large: Cultural Dimensions of Globalization*. Minneapolis: U of Minnesota P, 1996.

Apter, Emily. "Comparative Exile: Competing Margins in the History of Comparative Literature." *Comparative Literature in the Age of Multiculturalism*. Ed. Charles Bernheimer. Baltimore: Johns Hopkins UP, 1996: 86–96.

—. *Continental Drift: From National Characters to Virtual Subjects*. Chicago and London: U of Chicago P, 1999.

Auerbach, Erich. "Philology and *Weltliteratur*." Trans. Edward Said and Marie Said. *The Centennial Review* 13 (1969): 1–17.

—. *Mimesis: The Representation of Reality in Western Literature*. Princeton: Princeton UP, 1953a.

—. "Epilegomena zu *Mimesis*." *Romanische Forschungen* 65 (1953b): 1–18.

—. "Philologie der Weltliteratur." *Weltliteratur: Festgabe für Fritz Strich zum 70. Geburtstag*. Bern: Francke, 1952.

Bakhtin, Mikhail. *The Dialogic Imagination*. Trans. Michael J. Holquist and Caryl Emerson. Austin: U of Texas P, 1981.

Baucom, Ian. "Globalit, Inc.; or, The Cultural Logic of Global Literary Studies." *PMLA* 116.1 (January 2001): 158–72.

Bauman, Zygmunt. *Globalization: The Human Consequences*. New York: Columbia UP, 1998.

Bernheimer, Charles. "Introduction: The Anxieties of Comparison." *Comparative Literature in the Age of Multiculturalism*. Ed. Bernheimer. Baltimore: Johns Hopkins UP, 1996: 1–17.

Bhabha, Homi K. "Introduction." *The Location of Culture*. London and New York: Routledge, 1994: 1–18.

Bloom, Harold. *The Western Canon: The Books and Schools of the Ages*. New York: Harcourt Brace and Company, 1994.

Bové, Paul. *Intellectuals in Power: A Genealogy of Critical Humanism*. New York: Columbia UP, 1986.

Brooks, Peter. "Man and His Fictions: One Approach to the Teaching of Literature." *College English* (October 1973): 40–49.

Brunetière, Ferdinand. "European Literature," *Revue des Deux Mondes* (1900). Rpt. in *Comparative Literature: The Early Years*. Eds. Hans-Joachim Schulz and Philip Rhein. Chapel Hill: U of North Carolina P, 1973. 155–82.

Chow, Rey. *Writing Diaspora: Tactics of Intervention in Contemporary Cultural Studies*. Bloomington and Indianapolis: Indiana UP, 1993.

Conrad, Joseph. *Heart of Darkness*. Ed. Robert Kimbrough. 3rd edition. New York: W.W. Norton, 1988.

Curtius, Ernst Robert. *European Literature and the Latin Middle Ages*. New York: Pantheon, 1953.

Dimock, Wai Chee. "Literature for the Planet." *PMLA* 116.1 (January 2001): 173–88.

—. "A Theory of Resonance." *PMLA* 112.5 (October 1997): 1060–71.

Friederich, Werner. "The Challenge of Comparative Literature" (1964). *The Challenge of Comparative Literature and Other Addresses*. Ed. William J. DeSua. Chapel Hill, NC: U of North Carolina P, 1970. 36–50.

—. "Great Books versus 'World Literature'" (1959). *The Challenge of Comparative Literature and Other Addresses*. Ed. William J. DeSua. Chapel Hill, NC: U of North Carolina P, 1970: 25–35.

Friedman, Jonathan. "Global Crises, The Struggle for Cultural Identity and Intellectual Porkbarrelling: Cosmopolitans versus Locals, Ethnics and Nationals in an Era of

De-hegemonisation." *Debating Cultural Hybridity*. Eds. Pnina Werbner and Tariq Modood. London: Zed Books, 1997: 70–89.

Giddens, Anthony. *The Consequences of Modernity*. London: Polity, 1990.

Gilroy, Paul. *The Black Atlantic: Modernity and Double Consciousness*. Cambridge, MA: Harvard UP, 1993.

Goethe, Johann W. von. "Some Passages Pertaining to the Concept of World Literature." *Comparative Literature: The Early Years*. Eds. Hans-Joachim Schulz and Philip Rhein. Chapel Hill, NC: U of North Carolina P, 1973. 3–11.

Greene, Thomas M. *et al*. "The Greene Report." *Comparative Literature in the Age of Multiculturalism*. Ed. Charles Berhheimer. Baltimore: Johns Hopkins UP, 1996: 28–38.

Guérard, Albert. *Preface to World Literature*. New York: Henry Holt, 1940.

Guillory, John. "Canon." *Critical Terms for Literary Study*. Eds. Frank Lentricchia and Thomas McLaughlin. 2nd ed. Chicago: U of Chicago P, 1995. 233–49.

—. *Cultural Capital: The Problem of Literary Canon Formation*. Chicago: U of Chicago P, 1993.

Gunn, Giles. "Introduction: Globalizing Literary Studies." *PMLA* 116.1 (January 2001): 16–31.

Hall, Stuart. "When Was 'the Post-Colonial'? Thinking at the Limit." *The Post-Colonial Question: Common Skies, Divided Horizons*. Eds. Iain Chambers and Lidia Curti. New York: Routledge, 1996: 242–60.

—. "The Local and the Global: Globalization and Ethnicity." *Culture, Globalization, and the World-System*. Ed. Anthony D. King. Binghamton, NY: Department of Art and Art History, State U of New York at Binghamton P, 1991a. 19–39.

—. "Old and New Identities, Old and New Ethnicities." *Culture, Globalization, and the World-System*. Ed. Anthony D. King. Binghamton, NY: Department of Art and Art History, State U of New York at Binghamton P, 1991b. 41–68.

Hannerz, Ulf. *Transnational Connections: Culture, People, Places*. New York: Routledge, 1996.

—. "Cosmopolitans and Locals in World Culture." *Theory, Culture & Society* 7.2–3 (1990): 237–52.

Harvey, David. *The Condition of Postmodernity: An Enquiry into the Origins of Cultural Change*. New York: Blackwell, 1990.

Hirsch, E. D., Joseph F. Kett, and James Trefil. *Cultural Literacy: What Every American Needs to Know*. Boston: Houghton Mifflin, 1987.

Hodgson, Marshall. *Rethinking World History: Essays in Europe, Islam, and World History*. Cambridge: Cambridge UP, 1993.

Holquist, Michael. "The Last European: Erich Auerbach as Precursor in the History of Cultural Criticism." *Modern Language Quarterly* 54.3 (September 1993): 371–91.

Jameson, Fredric. "Notes on Globalization as a Philosophical Issue." *The Cultures of Globalization*. Eds. Fredric Jameson and Masao Miyoshi. Durham: Duke UP, 1998: 54–77.

—. "Third World Literature in the Era of Multinational Capitalism." *Social Text* 14/15 (1986): 65–88.

—. *The Political Unconscious: Narrative as a Socially Symbolic Act*. Ithaca: Cornell UP, 1981.

—. *Marxism and Form*. 2nd ed. Princeton, N.J.: Princeton UP, 1971, 1974.

Jay, Paul. "Beyond Discipline? Globalization and the Future of English." *PMLA*. 116.1 (January 2001): 32–47.

King, Anthony D., ed. *Culture, Globalization, and the World-System*. Binghamton, N.Y.: Department of Art and Art History, State U of New York at Binghamton P, 1991.

Lawall, Sarah. "Introduction: Reading World Literature." *Reading World Literature: Theory, History, Practice*. Ed. Sarah Lawall. Austin: U of Texas P, 1994: 1–64.

Levin, Harry, *et al*. "The Levin Report." *Comparative Literature in the Age of Multiculturalism*. Ed. Charles Bernheimer. Baltimore: Johns Hopkins UP, 1996. 21–27.

Lindenberger, Herbert. "On the Reception of *Mimesis*." *Literary History and the Challenge of Philology: The Legacy of Erich Auerbach*. Ed. Seth Lerer. Stanford: Stanford UP, 1996. 195–213.

—. "The Western Culture Debate at Stanford University." *Comparative Criticism* 11 (1989): 225–34.

Lowe, Lisa. *Immigrant Acts: On Asian American Cultural Politics*. Durham: Duke UP, 1996.

Lowe, Lisa and David Lloyd, eds. *The Politics of Culture in the Shadow of Capital*. Durham: Duke UP, 1997.

Lukacs, Georg. *The Theory of the Novel: A Historico-Philosophical Essay on the Epic Forms of Great Literature*. Trans. Anna Bostock. Cambridge: MIT Press, 1971.

Mack, Maynard, ed. *The Norton Anthology of World Masterpieces*. Expanded Edition in 2 vols. New York: W. W. Norton, 1995.

Miyoshi, Masao. "A Borderless World? From Colonialism to Trans-nationalism and the Decline of the Nation-State." *Global/Local: Cultural Production and the Transnational Imaginary*. Eds. Rob Wilson and Wimal Dissanayake. Durham: Duke UP, 1996. 78–106.

Moretti, Franco. "The Slaughterhouse of Literature." *Modern Language Quarterly* (March 2000): 207–27.

—. *Modern Epic: The World-System from Goethe to García Márquez*. Trans. Quintin Hoare. New York: Verso, 1996.

Mufti, Aamir. "Auerbach in Istanbul: Edward Said, Secular Criticism, and the Question of Minority Culture." *Critical Inquiry* 25.1 (Autumn 1998): 95–125.

Pizer, John. "Goethe's 'World Literature' Paradigm and Contemporary Cultural Globalization." *Comparative Literature* 52.3 (Summer 2000): 213–27.

Pratt, Mary Louise. "Comparative Literature and Global Citizenship." *Comparative Literature in the Age of Multiculturalism*. Ed. Charles Bernheimer. Baltimore: Johns Hopkins UP, 1995. 58–65.

Robbins, Bruce, and Pheng Cheah, eds. *Cosmopolitics: Thinking and Feeling Beyond the Nation*. Minneapolis: U of Minnesota P, 1998.

—. "Comparative Cosmopolitanism." *Social Text* 31/32 (1992): 169–86.

Robertson, Roland. *Globalization: Social Theory and Global Culture*. London: Sage, 1992.

Ross, Kristin. "The World Literature and Cultural Studies Program." *Critical Inquiry* 19.4 (Summer 1993): 666–76.

Said, Edward W. *The World, the Text, and the Critic*. Cambridge, MA: Harvard UP, 1983.

—. *Culture and Imperialism*. New York: Alfred A. Knopf, 1993.

—. *Beginnings: Intention and Method*. New York: Basic Books, 1975.

Smith, Anthony D. "Towards a Global Culture?" *Theory, Culture & Society* 7.2–3 (1990): 171–93.

Spitzer, Leo. *Classical and Christian Ideas of World Harmony*. Baltimore: Johns Hopkins UP, 1963.

Staël-Holstein, Anne Louise Germaine. *De la Littérature Considérée dans ses Rapports avec les Institutions Sociales*. 2 vols. Paris and London: Colburn, 1812.

Steiner, George. "What is Comparative Literature?" An Inaugural Lecture delivered before the University of Oxford on 11 October 1994. Oxford: Clarendon Press, 1995. 1–19.

Strich, Fritz. *Goethe and World Literature*. London: Routledge & Kegan Paul, 1949.

Todorov, Tzvetan. *The Poetics of Prose*. Trans. Richard Howard. Ithaca: Cornell UP, 1977.

Wallerstein, Immanuel. *The Modern World System*. New York: Academic, 1974.

Wellek, René. "The Crisis of Comparative Literature" (1959). *Concepts of Criticism*. Ed. Stephen G. Nichols, Jr. New Haven, CT: Yale UP, 1963. 282–95.

—. "Auerbach's Special Realism." *Kenyon Review* 16 (Winter 1954): 299–307.

Wellek, René and Austin Warren. *Theory of Literature*. New York: Harcourt, Brace and Company, 1949, 3rd ed. 1962.

White, Hayden. "Auerbach's Literary History: Figural Causation and Modernist Historicism." *Literary History and the Challenge of Philology: The Legacy of Erich Auerbach.* Ed. Seth Lerer. Stanford: Stanford UP, 1996. 124–39.

Zakaria, Fareed. "Passing the Bucks." Review of John Gray's *False Dawn: The Delusions of Global Capitalism* (1999). *The New York Times Book Review* (April 25, 1999): 16–18.

Chapter 21

David Damrosch

WHAT IS WORLD LITERATURE? (2003)

D AVID DAMROSCH (B. 1953) SINCE 2009 holds the Chair of Comparative Literature at Harvard University, where he is also Ernest Birnbaum Professor of Literature. Before, he taught for many years at Columbia University as a colleague of Edward Said and Gayatri Spivak. He obtained his PhD in Comparative Literature from Yale, where he pursued interests in a wide range of ancient and modern languages and literatures. A prolific author of both scholarly and more popular material (he has written very entertainingly on *The Buried Book: The Loss and Recovery of the Great Epic of Gilgamesh*, 2006), his work has been translated into a variety of languages, including Chinese, Estonian, Hungarian, Turkish and Vietnamese. Although he had already started writing on world literature in the 1990s, Damrosch in 2003 established himself as the leading expert in the field with *What is World Literature?* Damrosch also served as editor-in-chief of the multi-volume *Longman Anthology of World Literature*; which as of its appearance in the early years of the twenty-first century quickly established itself as the most widely used anthology in the field.

We here reproduce a generous selection from *What is World Literature?*, with passages detailing Damrosch's oft-cited definition of world literature as all literature that circulates, either in translation or in the original, beyond its own national or linguistic-cultural borders, of his "ellipse" metaphor approach to world literature, and his views on translation. Many of these points had been made before, by Moulton, Strich, Guérard, Étiemble and others, but Damrosch succeeded in brilliantly distilling them all into one briskly and entertainingly written book, which goes at least some way towards explaining its instant success.

David Damrosch, *What is World Literature?* Princeton: Princeton UP, 2003.

Introduction: Goethe coins a phrase

[. . .]

For Marx and Engels, as for Goethe, world literature is the quintessential literature of modern times.

The dramatic acceleration of globalization since their era, however, has greatly complicated the idea of a world literature. Most immediately, the sheer scope of the term today can breed a kind of scholarly panic. "What can one make of such an idea?" Claudio Guillén has asked. "The sum total of all national literatures? A wild idea, unattainable in practice, worthy not of an actual reader but of a deluded keeper of archives who is also a multimillionaire. The most harebrained editor has never aspired to such a thing" (*The Challenge of Comparative Literature*, 38).[1] Though it has a certain surface plausibility, Guillén's objection is hardly decisive; after all, no one denies that the term "insect" is viable, even though there are so many billions of insects in the world that no one person can ever be bitten by each of them. Still, the sum total of the world's literatures can be sufficiently expressed by the blanket term "literature." The idea of world literature can usefully continue to mean a subset of the plenum of literature. I take world literature to encompass all literary works that circulate beyond their culture of origin, either in translation or in their original language (Virgil was long read in Latin in Europe). In its most expansive sense, world literature could include any work that has ever reached beyond its home base, but Guillén's cautionary focus on actual readers makes good sense: a work only has an *effective* life as world literature whenever, and wherever, it is actively present within a literary system beyond that of its original culture.

A viable concept when delimited in this way, world literature still consists of a huge corpus of works. These works, moreover, stem from widely disparate societies, with very different histories, frames of cultural reference, and poetics. A specialist in classical Chinese poetry can gradually, over years of labor, develop a close familiarity with the vast substratum beneath each brief T'ang Dynasty poem, but most of this context is lost to foreign readers when the poem travels abroad. Lacking specialized knowledge, the foreign reader is likely to impose domestic literary values on the foreign work, and even careful scholarly attempts to read a foreign work in light of a Western critical theory are deeply problematic. As A. Owen Aldridge has said, "it is difficult to point to remarkably successful examples of the pragmatic application of critical systems in a comparative context. The various theories cancel each other out" (*The Reemergence of World Literature*, 33).[2] Or as the Indian scholar D. Prempati has pointedly remarked, "I do not know whether the innumerable Western critical models which, like multinationals, have taken over the Indian critical scene would meaningfully serve any critical purpose at this juncture." ("Why Comparative Literature in India?", 63).[3]

Some scholars have argued that literary works across cultures do exhibit what Northrop Frye thought of as archetypes or what more recently the French comparatist Étiemble has called "invariants." In his lively polemic *Ouverture(s) sur un comparatisme planétaire*, Étiemble argued that common literary patterns must provide the necessary basis for any truly global understanding of literature. Yet such universals quickly shade into vague generalities that hold less and less appeal today, at a time when ideals of melting-pot harmony have faded in favor. Scholars of world literature risk becoming little more than the literary ecotourists described by Susan Lanser, people "who dwell mentally in one or two (usually Western) countries, summer metaphorically in a third, and visit other places for brief interludes" ("Compared to What?" 281).[4]

A central argument of this book will be that, properly understood, world literature is not at all fated to disintegrate into the conflicting multiplicity of separate national traditions; nor, on the other hand, need it be swallowed up in the white noise that Janet Abu-Lughod has called "global babble." My claim is that world literature is not an infinite, ungraspable canon of works but rather a mode of circulation and of reading, a mode that is as applicable to individual works as to bodies of material, available for reading established classics and new discoveries alike. This book is intended to explore this mode of circulation and to clarify the ways in which works of world literature can best be read. It is important from the outset to realize that just as there never has been a single set canon of world literature, so too no single way of reading can be appropriate to all texts, or even to any one text at all times. The variability of a work of world literature is one of its constitutive features—one of its greatest strengths when the work is well presented and read well, and its greatest vulnerability when it is mishandled or misappropriated by its newfound foreign friends.

A work enters into world literature by a double process: first, by being read *as* literature; second, by circulating out into a broader world beyond its linguistic and cultural point of origin. A given work can enter into world literature and then fall out of it again if it shifts beyond a threshold point along either axis, the literary or the worldly. Over the centuries, an unusually shifty work can come in and out of the sphere of world literature several different times; and at any given point, a work may function as world literature for some readers but not others, and for some kinds of reading but not others. The shifts a work may undergo, moreover, do not reflect the unfolding of some internal logic of the work in itself but come about through often complex dynamics of cultural change and contestation. Very few works secure a quick and permanent place in the limited company of perennial World Masterpieces; most works shift around over time, even moving into and out of the category of "the masterpiece," [. . .]

As it moves into the sphere of world literature, far from inevitably suffering a loss of authenticity or essence, a work can gain in many ways. To follow this process, it is necessary to look closely at the transformations a work undergoes in particular circumstances, which is why this book highlights the issues of circulation and translation and focuses on detailed case studies throughout. To understand the workings of world literature, we need more a phenomenology than an ontology of the work of art: a literary work *manifests* differently abroad than it does at home.

[. . .]

But how to mediate between broad, but often reductive, overviews and intensive, but often atomistic, close readings?

One solution is to recognize that we don't face an either/or choice between global systematicity and infinite textual multiplicity, for world literature itself is constituted very differently in different cultures. Much can be learned from a close attention to the workings of a given cultural system, at a scale of analysis that also allows for extended discussion of specific works. A culture's norms and needs profoundly shape the selection of works that enter into it as world literature, influencing the ways they are translated, marketed, and read.

[. . .]

For any given observer, even a genuinely global perspective remains a perspective *from somewhere*, and global patterns of the circulation of world literature take shape in their local manifestations.

[. . .]

Conclusion: world enough and time

And so, what *is* world literature? I have conceived this book as a demonstration as much as an essay in definition, seeking to show the kinds of work now in our view and some of the ways they can be approached. I have dwelt on some of the texts that have obsessed me over the years and that seemed particularly suggestive on issues of circulation, translation, and production. In the process, much as Eckermann gives us *his* Goethe, I have given you my world literature, or at least a representative cross-section of it, while recognizing that the world now presents us with material so varied as to call into question any logic of representation, any single framework that everyone should adopt and in which these particular works would all have a central role. A leading characteristic of world literature today is its variability: different readers will be obsessed by very different constellations of texts. While figures like Dante and Kafka retain a powerful canonical status, these authors function today less as a common patrimony than as rich nodes of overlap among many different and highly individual groupings.

Amid all this variety, family resemblances can be found among the different forms of world literature circulating today, emergent patterns that lead me to propose a threefold definition focused on the world, the text, and the reader:

1.   *World literature is an elliptical refraction of national literatures.*
2.   *World literature is writing that gains in translation.*
3.   *World literature is not a set canon of texts but a mode of reading: a form of detached engagement with worlds beyond our own place and time.*

Each of these points merits discussion.

Elliptical refraction of national literatures. For the past half-century, world literature in its North American guises has usually been opposed to national literature. A genial disregard, if not outright hostility, often obtained between the devotees of the two. With most literature faculty based in departments organized along national lines, in many schools "world literature" was treated as an introductory course, suitable for beginning students but fundamentally vague in conception and unrigorous in application, a preliminary stage prior to serious work in a literature major based on close study of a culture and its language.

[. . .]

Comparatists in the postwar era often returned the specialists' disregard, holding out messianic hopes for world literature as the cure for the ills of nationalistic separatism, jingoism, and internecine violence—and, by implication, advancing the comparatist as the transcendent heir to the narrowness of monolingual specialization. Comparative literature was to be the grand corrective for "the nationalistic heresy," as Albert Guérard put it in a lead article in the *Yearbook of Comparative and General Literature* in 1958.

[. . .]

Understanding the term "national" broadly, we can say that works continue to bear the marks of their national origin even after they circulate into world literature, and yet these traces are increasingly diffused and become ever more sharply refracted as a work travels farther from home.

This refraction, moreover, is double in nature: works become world literature by being received *into* the space of a foreign culture, a space defined in many ways by the host culture's national tradition and the present needs of its own writers. Even a single work of world literature is the locus of a negotiation between two different cultures. The receiving culture can use the foreign material in all sorts of ways: as a positive model for the future development of its own tradition; as a negative case of a primitive, or decadent, strand that must be avoided or rooted out at home; or, more neutrally, as an image of radical otherness against which the home tradition can more clearly be defined. World literature is thus always as much about the host culture's values and needs as it is about a work's source culture; hence it is a double refraction, one that can be described through the figure of the ellipse, with the source and host cultures providing the two foci that generate the elliptical space within which a work lives as world literature, connected to both cultures, circumscribed by neither alone.

[. . .]

Whether it is pursued individually or collaboratively work on world literature should be acknowledged as *different in kind* from work within a national tradition, just as the works themselves manifest differently abroad than at home. This does not mean that we should simply ignore the local knowledge that specialists possess, as literary theorists of the past generation often did when developing their comprehensive theories. [. . .] A student of world literature has much to gain from an active engagement with specialized knowledge.

At the same time, though, this knowledge is best deployed selectively, with a kind of scholarly tact. When our purpose is not to delve into a culture in detail, the reader and even the work itself may benefit by being spared the full force of our local knowledge.

[. . .]

Intimately aware of a work's life at home, the specialist is not always in the best position to assess the dramatically different terms on which it may engage with a distant culture. Looking at such new contexts, the generalist will find that much of the specialist's information about the work's origins is no longer relevant and not only can but should be set aside. At the same time, any work that has not been wholly assimilated to its new context will still carry with it many elements that can best be understood by exploring why they came to be there in the first place. The specialist's knowledge is the major safeguard against the generalist's own will to power over texts that otherwise all too easily become grist for the mill of a preformed historical argument or theoretical system.

When I distinguish "specialists" from "generalists," I mean to characterize approaches as much as individuals. Just as a work can function either at home or abroad, so too any given person can be both a specialist in some areas and a generalist in others. When we are employing a generalist approach, we should not simply cast off our specialist selves—or our specialist colleagues. Generalists have much to learn from specialists, and should always try to build honestly, though selectively, on the specialists' understandings, ideally even inspiring the specialists to revise their understandings in turn. Too often, a generalist who alludes dismissively to the narrow-minded concerns of specialists merely ends up retailing a warmed-over version of what specialists had been saying a generation earlier. Instead, the generalist should feel the same ethical responsibility toward specialized scholarship that a translator has toward a text's original language: to understand the work effectively in its new cultural or theoretical context while at the same time *getting it right* in a fundamental way with reference to the source culture.

This brings us to my second point: *World literature is writing that gains in translation.* There is a significant difference between literary language and the various forms of ordinary, denotative language, whose meaning we take to be largely expressed as information. A text is read as literature if we dwell on the beauties of its language, its form, and its themes, and don't take it as primarily factual in intent; but the same text can cease to work as literature if a reader turns to it primarily to extract information from it, as when George Smith read *The Epic of Gilgamesh* to confirm the biblical history of the Flood, regretting that the account had been "disfigured by poetical adornments." Informational texts neither gain nor lose in a good translation: their meaning is simply carried over with little or no effective change. Treaties and contracts can be complex documents, but if well drafted and well translated, they are understandable to all parties concerned. They may be breached from the pressure of changing circumstances or through misinterpretations that apply to all the document's versions, but treaties rarely fail because of problems arising from translation per se.

At the other extreme, some works are so inextricably connected to their original language and moment that they really cannot be effectively translated at all. Purist views of literary language often take all poetry as "what is lost in translation," in Robert Frost's famous phrase, since whatever meaning a new language can convey is irretrievably sundered from the verbal music of the original. "A poem should not mean/But be," as Archibald Macleish wrote in 1926 in his "Ars Poetica," in lines that convey their own declarative meaning with surprising success. Much poetry, including Frost's and Macleish's, has been translated with great effect into many languages. It is more accurate to say that *some* works are not translatable without substantial loss, and so they remain largely within their local or national context, never achieving an effective life as world literature.

It is important to recognize that the question of translatability is distinct from questions of value. A work can hold a prominent place within its own culture but read poorly elsewhere, either because its language doesn't translate well or because its cultural assumptions don't travel. Snorri Sturluson's dynastic saga *Heimskringla* is a major document in medieval Nordic culture, but it only makes compelling reading if you are fairly knowledgeable about the political history of Norway and Iceland, and it remains unknown abroad outside specialist circles. By contrast, Norse mythological texts like the Elder Edda and Snorri's own *Prose Edda* have been widely translated and much appreciated. They are actually harder to understand than the *Heimskringla*, but they treat themes of broad interest in striking, if often mysterious, language. Equally, a work's viability as world literature has little to do with its author's perspective on the world. There can be no more global work, conceptually speaking, than *Finnegans Wake*, yet its prose is so intricate and irreproducible that it becomes a sort of curiosity in translation. *Dubliners*, a far more localized work, has been much more widely translated and has had a far greater impact in other languages.

Literary language is thus language that either gains *or* loses in translation, in contrast to nonliterary language, which typically does neither. The balance of credit and loss remains a distinguishing mark of national versus world literature: literature stays within its national or regional tradition when it usually loses in translation, whereas works become world literature when they gain on balance in translation, stylistic losses offset by an expansion in depth as they increase their range, as is the case with such widely disparate works as *The Epic of Gilgamesh* and *Dictionary of the Khazars*. It follows from this that the study of world literature should embrace translation far more actively than it has usually done to date.

[. . .]

It is often said that quite apart from individual innovation, literary language is particularly hard to translate since so much of the meaning depends on culture-specific patterns of connotation and nuance. Yet one could equally make a very different argument: after all, literature is often distinguished from film and television by the fact that the reader is *required* to fill in the scene, which is not given outright as it is on the screen. As Wolfgang Iser argued in *The Act of Reading*, literary narratives work less by communicating fixed information than by creating suggestive gaps that the reader must fill in. Iser further emphasized (against Roman Ingarden) that different readers will necessarily, and productively, fill in these gaps in different ways.

What is true of any literary work is doubly true of world literature. A book read in one language and within one cultural context presents a situation in which, as Iser says, readers will differ but "the text itself cannot change" and exerts a powerful limiting force on the variability of readerly response (167).[5] Traveling abroad, though, a text does indeed change, both in its frame of reference and usually in language as well. In an excellent translation, the result is not the loss of an unmediated original vision but instead a *heightening* of the naturally creative interaction of reader and text. In this respect a poem or novel can be seen to achieve its lasting effect precisely by virtue of its adaptability to our private experience.

[. . .]

Of course, some elements of a literary work are more freely variable than others, and a large part of a translator's interpretive responsibility lies in determining which particular patterns of sound, imagery, or implication are important to carry over as directly as possible. Yet even elements that cannot be directly reproduced in the new language can often be conveyed at a different level of the text. Some of Kafka's self-deconstructing sentences really can't be rendered in English without a substantial loss of ironic play, and yet the irony we label "Kafkaesque" is fully conveyed at the levels of the paragraph and of the scene, even if not always at the level of the individual sentence.

[. . .]

To use translations means to accept the reality that texts come to us mediated by existing frameworks of reception and interpretation. We necessarily work in collaboration with others who have shaped what we read and how we read it. Indeed, any works written in an earlier period in our own country reach us in much the same way that Walter Benjamin describes translation itself: "a translation issues from the original—not so much from its life as from its afterlife. For a translation comes later than the original, and since the important works of world literature never find their chosen translators at the time of their origin, their translation marks their stage of continued life" ("The Task of the Translator," 71).[6] A specialist equipped with ample research materials can do much to approximate a return to the world in which an old or foreign poem was composed. The generalist, concerned with the poem's worldly afterlife, doesn't have that luxury, or even that necessity.

Its relative freedom from context does not require the work of world literature to be subjected to anything like an absolute disconnect from its culture of origin. Anyone involved in translating or teaching works from other cultures must always weigh how much cultural information is needed and how it should be presented. One healthy consequence of the increasing acknowledgment that a translation *is* a translation has been a greater openness in providing contextual information. Often in the past, translators gave no such information at all, or folded it silently into the translation itself so as to preserve the seeming purity of the text—though in reality they had to distort the text in order to avoid disrupting a supposedly direct encounter of reader and work. Especially when the text in question was both old and foreign, translations were forced either to become very loose paraphrases (Burton's *Arabian Nights*) or to assimilate closely to host-country norms (Edward Fitzgerald's *Rubáiyat of Omar Kháyyâm*). Scholarly readers, by contrast, would be given heavily annotated bilingual editions, full of cultural information but with the translation often only marginally readable.

[. . .]

Whereas the specialist attempts to enter as fully as possible into the source culture, the student of world literature stands outside, very much as Benjamin describes translation itself standing outside a work's original language, facing a wooded ridge that each of us will forest with our own favorite trees: "Unlike a work of literature, translation does not find itself in the center of the language forest but on the outside facing the wooded ridge; it calls into it without entering, aiming at that single spot where the echo is able to give, in its own language, the reverberation of the work in the alien one" (76).

And so to the final part of my definition of world literature: *not a set canon of texts but a mode of reading, a detached engagement with a world beyond our own*. At any given time, a fluctuating number of foreign works will circulate actively within a culture, and a subset of these will be widely shared and enjoy a canonical status, but different groups within a society, and different individuals within any group, will create distinctive congeries of works, blending canonical and noncanonical works into effective microcanons.

[. . .]

The texts themselves exist both together and alone: when we read Dante, we are aware that we are encountering a major work of world literature, one that draws on a wealth of previous writing and that casts its shadow ahead onto much that will follow it. Yet even as we register such connections, we are also immersed within Dante's singular world, an imagined universe very unlike any envisioned by Virgil or by Saint Paul, and one that Milton, Gogol, and Walcott will radically revise in turn for very different purposes of their own.

[. . .]

The great conversation of world literature takes place on two very different levels: among authors who know and react to one another's work, and in the mind of the reader, where works meet and interact in ways that may have little to do with cultural and historical proximity. Someone who reads *Swann's Way* and *The Tale of Genji* together is likely to find them resonating in multiple and profound ways, engaging one another at least as closely as a reader who is attentive to national traditions will find Proust engaging with Balzac, or the *Genji* with *The Tale of the Heike*. World literature is fully in play once several foreign works begin to resonate together in our mind. This provides a further solution to the comparatist's lurking panic: world literature is not an immense body of material that must somehow, impossibly, be mastered; it is a mode of reading that can be experienced *intensively* with a few works just as effectively as it can be explored *extensively* with a large number.

[. . .]

Immersion in a single culture represents a mode of relatively direct engagement with it, aptly symbolized by efforts to acquire "near-native fluency" in the culture's language. Reading and studying world literature, by contrast, is inherently a more detached mode of engagement; it enters into a different kind of dialogue with the work, not one involving identification or mastery but the discipline of distance and of difference. We encounter the work not at the heart of its source culture but in the field of force generated among works that may come from very different cultures and eras.

This elliptical relation already characterizes our experience of a foreign national tradition, but there is likely to be a significant difference of degree, both because the ellipses multiply and because the angle of refraction increases. Works of world literature interact in a charged field defined by a fluid and multiple set of possibilities of juxtaposition and combination: "intercourse in every direction," in Marx and Engels's apt phrase. As we triangulate between our own present situation and the enormous variety of other cultures around and before us, we won't see works of world literature so fully enshrined within their cultural context as we do when reading those works within their own traditions, but a degree of distance from the home tradition can help us to appreciate the ways in which a literary work reaches out and away from its point of origin. If we then observe ourselves seeing the work's abstraction from its origins, we gain a new vantage point on our own moment. The result may be almost the opposite of the "fusion of horizons" that Friedrich Schleiermacher envisioned when we encounter a distant text; we may actually experience our customary horizon being set askew, under the influence of works whose foreignness remains fully in view.

Notes

1   See the Guillén selection in this volume.
2   See the Owen selection in this volume.
3   Prempati, D. "Why Comparative Literature in India?" In R.K. Dhawan, *Comparative Literature*, New Delhi: Bahri, 1987, pp. 53–65.

4   Lanser, Susan Sniader. "Compared to What? Global Feminism, Comparatism, and the Master's Tools." In Margaret Higonnet, ed., *Borderwork: Feminine Engagements with Comparative Literature*, Ithaca: Cornell University Press, 1994, pp. 280–300.

5   Iser, Wolfgang. *The Act of Reading: A Theory of Aesthetic Response*. Tr. David Henry Wilson. Baltimore: Johns Hopkins University Press, 1978.

6   Benjamin, Walter. "The Task of the Translator." In *Illuminations*, ed. Hannah Arendt, tr. Harry Zohn, 69–82. New York: Schocken Books.

Chapter 22

Gayatri Chakravorty Spivak

PLANETARITY (2003)

G AYATRI CHAKRAVORTY SPIVAK (B. 1942) is an Indian-American university professor at Columbia University. She was educated in India and the US and taught at different American universities prior to her appointment at Columbia in 1991. A prolific figure in postcolonial studies, she has been influential in a number of central debates in the literary theory of recent decades, ranging from deconstruction, feminism and Marxism to the future of literary studies. Having addressed issues of translation frequently, she has herself translated Jacques Derrida's *Of Grammatology* and works of Indian literature.

In *Death of a Discipline* she uses the concept of "planetarity" to move beyond the dominant idea of globalization and to critique the disciplinary organization of the study of literature. Spivak evaluates postcolonialism, comparative literature and area studies for their different perspectives, and she examines the often unfortunate consequences of the power exercised by their way of looking at the world. Like Wlad Godzich in *The Culture of Literacy* (Godzich 1994: 26), Spivak wants to maintain a place for the unique voice and the singular literary experience which are not appropriated by a foregone conclusion: "so must the new Comparative Literature persistently and repeatedly undermine and undo the definitive tendency of the dominant to appropriate the emergent." However, as her constant involvement with different modes of reading and different cultural codifications suggests, the planetary position cannot stand alone; rather, it serves as a reminder of the openness towards the world which appears to be a constant value of literature regardless of culture.

The passages here reprinted are from "Planetarity," the final chapter of Gayatri Ch. Spivak, *Death of a Discipline*, New York: Columbia University Press, 2003, pp. 84–102.

All my examples so far have been postcolonial, tied to New Immigrant groups in the United States: Maryse Condé, J. M. Coetzee, Tayeb Salih, Mahasweta Devi; with Conrad as control. Cultural Studies is heavily invested in new immigrant groups. It seems to me that a planetary Comparative Literature must attempt to move away from this base. What I write in closing will give some indication of the way out, as far as a nonexpert can imagine it. These words are no more than scattered speculations, to mark the limits of my rather conventional U.S. Comparative Literature training: English, French, German, poetry and literary theory, romantic and modernist.

As I hope above, the new Comparative Literature will touch the older minorities: African, Asian, Hispanic. It will take in its sweep the new postcoloniality of the post-Soviet sector and the special place of Islam in today's breaking world. Not everything for everyone, all at once. But a Comparative Literature format—historical and linguistic—possible for any slice chosen from any of these places, the background filled in by new reference tools on Franco Moretti's model.

I am writing these words in Hong Kong. I come here as often as I can, and go on to other Chinas, to get a sense of the immensely changeful and vast scenario of the evolving Asia–Pacific. The three papers I heard from Wu Hung this time would be a way into the Comparative Literature of the future, if seen through the eyes of a critic for whom gender is not just for special cases.[1] This is no more than an example, of course, and it touches only the People's Republic of China. The Asia–Pacific spans Southeast Asia, Micronesia, Polynesia, New Zealand, perhaps Australia, Hawai'i, California—each with different histories of the movements of power. It is with this ensemble that the divided and diversified story of Asian America, old and new immigrants, must be imaginatively cobbled to make for a robust Comparative Literature. The time for producing historically thin "theory" describing the feeling of migrants in pseudopsychoanalytic vocabulary is over. It was exhausted in the first phase of the Comparative Literature dispute reflected in the Bernheimer collection.[1a]

The old postcolonial model—very much "India" plus the Sartrian "Fanon"—will not serve now as the master model for transnational to global cultural studies on the way to planetarity. We are dealing with heterogeneity on a different scale and related to imperialisms on another model:

> Over the time that the world has known substantial states . . . empires have been the dominant and largest state form. . . . Only now . . . do we seem to be leaving the age of massive Eurasian empires that began in earnest across a band from the Mediterranean to East Asia almost four thousand years ago. To the extent that we regard such international compacts as the European Union, GATT, and NAFTA as embodying imperial designs, furthermore, even today's requiem may prove premature.[2]

To this compact we must add the financialization of the globe.

Globalization plays with all the constituencies I have announced in this chapter, but in a different way with the postcoloniality announced by the breakup of the old Russian imperial formation, competing with the Habsburgs and the Ottomans, that managed to appropriate the dream of international socialism and was propelled by the historical moment into new imperial competitions. In this sector of Comparative Literature, my example for the moment is Mark von Hagen's "From Russia to Soviet Union to Eurasia: A View from New York Ten Years After the End of the Soviet Union," a piece rich in suggestions for new work.[3]

The study of this new postcoloniality will not necessarily find the best directions from the proliferating collections of post-Soviet feminist anthologies in translation—first because, like much earlier postcolonial studies, they still follow the lines of empire, and therefore Central Asia is liable to find a less than interesting place, with little careful historical textualizing or tracing. And second, it is well known that the Soviets made women the vehicle of modernization in the area.[4] Thus here too the division among women on either side of the tradition-modernity line is one agenda for the new Comparative Literature as it weighs in with metropolitan Ethnic Studies. That particular division is quite often marked by access to Russian. The in-depth study of language is crucial here.

As Hamid Dabashi writes: "from the scattered memories of a sacred imagination that once congealed in the Arabia of the sixth (Christian) century, competing 'Islams' were invented by contending political forces dominant from Transoxiana to Spain."[5] The tribalities of Central Asia had paradoxically written a "freer," more eclectic Islam than the more publicized conflicts in the residue of medieval Islamic cosmopolitanism or the recent puritanism and orthodoxy of the Wahabis, and, in a different formation, the Taliban. Close as I am to Bangladesh, I am very aware of the paradoxical freedoms within peripheral Islams. In Central Asia we can tap the consequences of an earlier modernization of women and a current tradi-tionalization of Islam. I have discussed the tracks of planetarity in this formation elsewhere.[6]

The range and diversity of the Islamic diaspora is immense. It is altogether appropriate that Comparative Literature should undo the politically monolithized view of Islam that rules the globe today, without compromising the strong unifying ideology potentially alive in that particular cultural formation.

Comparative Literature can also find its own unacknowledged prehistory in this sector, and thus do a long-range historical revision of the record of its apparently European prov-enance. Muslim Europe and Arabic–Persian cosmopolitanism have both been abundantly studied in Middle Eastern studies and comparative history.[7] Because of the special nature of Comparative Literature, we, on the other hand, have spent considerable energy on Leo Spitzer and Erich Auerbach in Turkey, as if they were explorers for the cause of literary criticism.[8]

To a certain extent, Islamic feminism has also been relegated to its own ghetto. The introduction to Deniz Kandiyoti's "Contemporary Feminist Scholarship and Middle East Studies" summarizes a great deal of information about this phenomenon.[9] I have attempted to work against such ghettoization in my work on Assia Djebar.[10]

Can the foothold for planetarity be located in the texts of these spread-out sectors of the world's literatures and cultures? Perhaps. The new comparativist is not obliged to look for them, of course. One cannot adjudicate the task of an entire discipline, in spite of the efforts of the world literaturists, the Encyclopedists. I think this drastic epistemic change must be imagined by Comparative Literature. But I cannot will everyone to think so.

I would like to close this section of the chapter with no more than a gesture toward the two older minorities, the African American and the Hispanic. I am very far indeed from expertise in these areas. I have no doubt that intimations of planetarity in my sense have been documented in the vast critical literature in these areas. I give witness by quoting two passages from my own work, one on a passage from Toni Morrison, another on a passage from Diamela Eltit.[11] No plot summaries. As in the case of those teasers of the next mystery included at the end of thrillers, I hope the reader will move to the text if the bits tantalize. *Beloved* is a much-read text in the U.S. mainstream, Eltit not so.

First, then, a moment in *Beloved*:

> The lesson of the impossibility of translation in the general sense, as Toni Morrison shows it, readily points at absolute contingency. Not the sequentiality of time, not even the cycle of seasons, but only weather, as in these words, summing up the conclusion of the terrible story of maternal sacrifice, an opening into a specifically African-American history. If Mahasweta undoes the division between Aboriginal and Indo-European India by the experience of an impossible planetarity; Morrison undoes the difference between Africa and African-America by the experience of a planetarity equally inaccessible to human time:

"By and by, all traces gone. And what is forgotten is not only the footprints but the water and what it is down there. The rest is weather. Not the breath of the disremembered and unaccounted-for; but wind in the eaves, or spring ice thawing too quickly. Just weather" (B275).

That too is time. Geological time, however slow, is also time. One must not *make* history in a deliberate way. One must respect the earth's tone. One might be obliged to claim history from the violent perpetrator of it, in order to turn violation into the enablement of the individual, but that is another story. After the effacement of the trace, no project for restoring the origin. That is "just weather," here today as yesterday.

With this invocation of contingency, where nature may be the great body without organs of woman, we can begin to see that the project of translating culture within the politics of identity is not a quick fix.

And now "I give you the briefest glimpse of Diamela Eltit's *The Fourth World*, written during the so-called economic miracle following General Pinochet's repressive regime in Chile."[12]

Eltit achieves a sustained superrealism that signals another lexicon—an allegory to be explored—by its very seamlessness. The language mimes the tone of the child-analyst who knows that metaphor and reality—inner and outer—have not separated themselves in the child's consciousness. "Whole persons" have not congealed here. We are in a world of negotiable sexual identities, twin brother vanishing into twin sister. I repeat, nothing, except an uneasy sense of everything, tells us that there is an entire body of political meaning here—in order to discover which we must move into the social text. Far from being self-referential, the text signals beyond itself. Yet there will be no referential connection, I can promise. As soon as you decide this is a veiled description of a devastated country, you will be obliged to remind yourself what Melanie Klein teaches us: that this is the normal landscape of the infantile psyche that enters "social normality" precariously, in depression and mourning, which may or may not be informed with postcolonial content. Eltit does not permit negotiation between autobiography and the political: two discontinuous structures of violence.

The narrative, such as it is, begins with the primal scene of violence: "On that April 7, enshrouded in my mother's fever, I not only was conceived, but also must have shared her dream because I suffered the horrible feminine attack of dread" (FW3). After one hundred and eleven pages of violent shuttling and reality testing inching towards some unnameable conclusion, the last page asks for a reading in Kleinian language, as the birth of a political super-ego. When the beginning of the final section says "Outside . . .," we are convinced that it is a description of a city on a certain map. There can be little doubt that "[t]he money from the sky return [ing] to the sky . . . hungry for urban emptiness but also sowing emptiness upon the fields . . . [upon which] contempt for the sudaca race [the immiserated female race, especially from the South—*sud*] is clearly printed" (FW 112–13) speaks of the empty promise of "economic growth" as the immiseration not only of some place like Chile but of the entire South, of "Development"-as-exploitation. This is not post-colonial*ism* as some latter-day psychomachia of territorial imperialism. It is the recognition of a globality that cannot be captured by our computers. Autobiography is easy here—the collectors of testimonies are waiting with their tape recorders—but irrelevant. "Far away," the book concludes, "in a house abandoned to brotherhood, between

April 7 and 8, diamela eltit, assisted by her twin brother, gives birth to a baby girl. The sudaca baby will go up for sale"—code name "democratization."

Today I would suggest that, by attempting to write the self at its othermost and blurring the outlines between that graphic and globalization, Eltit's text stages the lineaments of the planetary.

[In response to objections from my first best reader, I had jettisoned what I include in this extended parenthesis. Perhaps it would have been wiser to excise. Let me at least give my reasons for pasting the cut text back in.

All you're saying is that these two pluralize, my friend had said. I cannot see how that can be read as planetarity.

What I am attempting is to force a reading. I would like to see if the text could possibly sustain the turning of identitarian monuments into documents for reconstellation. Twenty-five years ago I attempted such a forced reading of *To the Lighthouse*, timidly attesting that it might not be "correct."[13] I still recall a mainstream feminist critic mockingly commenting that it was certainly an incorrect reading. I realize now that I have not lost my obstinacy. I read in Miller's *Others:* "This other calling on us to respond, this future that comes into being by way of the response, can only get here, arrive on this shore, speaking in tongues, in a multitude of overlapping and contradictory voices."[14] In Mark von Hagen's groundbreaking "From Russia to Soviet Union to Eurasia," I read that a "consequence of this feature [the retelling of the history of the Russian empire and Soviet Union from multiple vantage points] of pluralization has been a decentering of Russian history"; that in the fourth issue of *Kritika*, a journal associated with this new pluralization, "the editors defend their tolerance of cultural studies approaches to 'representations of alterity.'" I keep feeling that there are connections to be made that I cannot make, that pluralization may allow the imagining of a necessary yet impossible planetarity in ways that neither my reader nor I know yet. In this last chapter of scattered speculations, I include this imperfect parenthesis in the hope that the connection will be made by a future reader. As follows:

Identity politics is neither smart nor good. Comparative Literature laced with Area Studies goes rather toward the other. With this confidence, I approach two widely known, heroic figures from the older minorities, writers of a previous dispensation: José Martí (1853–95) and W. E. B. Du Bois (1868–1963). The task is to find moments in these earlier texts that can be reinscribed for what I am calling planetarity.

José Martí, the Cuban activist intellectual who lived in New York from 1881 to 1895 and died in action in the Cuban revolution against Spanish colonialism, could still seem to generalize a binary opposition: "Spanish America, *his* America . . . [as] 'Our America' and . . . Anglo-Saxon America, 'the Other America.'"[15] If we look more closely at his writings, however, we see this fervent nationalist going beyond mere nationalism to a more general and heterogeneous version of "Latin America," a phrase coming into circulation even as he was writing.[16] I believe it is possible to read the concept-metaphors of Martí's ruralist left-humanism for undoing named binaries, nationalism giving way not only to a heterogeneous continentalism but also to an internationalism that can, today, shelter planetarity. I will read only one passage here, but examples can be multiplied. To read one passage is not to under-demonstrate the argument.

Forcing Martí onto the tracks of planetarity is particularly fraught with the temptation to "ruralism." I have written about the spectralization of the rural (altogether distinct from ruralism)—conversion of "the rural" into a database for pharmaceutical dumping, chemical fertilizers, patenting of indigenous knowledge, big dam building and the like—as the forgotten front of globalization for which the urban is an instrument.[17] In my open-plan fieldwork, I consider the Indian rural poor as the largest sector of the electorate. The urban subproletariat should certainly not be ignored. In order, however, to access cultural systems—long dysfunctional because of delegitimation—for the source of an ethical instruction that may supplement socialism, the isolation of the rural may be helpful. To romanticize this group as the primitive will defeat the purpose and annul effort. And indeed, I always insist that we should make a further effort, at the same time, to insert them into the social productivity of capital through education, a risky undertaking. But otherwise, the current material wretchedness of their normality is not perceived as due to the remote depradations of capitalist exploitation without capital's social productivity.[18]

It is from this position, far from a primitivist romanticization of the rural, that I ask, Is it possible to make Martí's ruralism into a *mochlos* for planetarity?[19] Since the Earth is a bigger concept-metaphor than bounded nations, located cities, can we read it against Martí's grain and turn the text around for planetarity? Perhaps not. As I have already indicated, I write for a future reader. In the meantime, let me not be taken to be a ruralist, quite in the grain of Martí's text.

My plane is flying now over the land between Baghdad, Beirut, Haifa, and Tripoli, into Turkey and Romania. I am making a clandestine entry into "Europe." Yet the land looks the same—hilly sand. I know the cartographic markers because of the TV in the arm of my seat. Planetarity cannot deny globalization. But in search of a springboard for planetarity, I am looking not at Martí's invocation of the rural but at the figure of land that seems to undergird it. The view of the Earth from the window brings this home to me.

It is of course an established, even banal connection that exists between the rural and the Earth, Nature capital N. But even at its most banal it provides a countertext to the idea of city/nation. This is particularly noticeable when Martí speaks of education. Martí is no primitivist. His civic planning, however untested, inspired Fidel Castro as well as the Florida Cubans. His ideas of the education of the rural population are closer to Booker T. Washington than to Du Bois and more like the Chautauqua in form. But the logic of the metaphors rather than, necessarily, the substantive argument allows a way out of nationalism, and not in the direction of the North American diaspora. Nowhere is this clearer than in his account of the memorial service on the death of Karl Marx, where the idea of a labor international is embellished in the following way: "By operating the forces of Nature, they become as beautiful as Nature" (MR 43; translation modified).

It is when he is writing of the education of the peasant that the metaphor of nature releases its potential for displacement. In this account as well, he speaks of education. However bourgeois, sometimes even feudal, Martí's language might be, he intuits the same problem that Perry Anderson describes a hundred years later: the tension between structure and subject in Marx's thought. "Being in a hurry, and somewhat away from real life, he did not see that children who have not had a natural and laborious gestation are not born viable, whether in the womb of the people, in history, or from the womb of woman in the home" (MR 44; translation modified).[20] Again, the link is banal: nature, woman, and history by way of fertility. But the logic of the metaphor connects internationalism and nature, by placing history itself in the forces of nature and thus away from the specificity of nations. The common Spanish word for "people"—*el pueblo*—one of whose strong current meanings is "village," as one among a range of possible groupings of people, from a small local group to a tribe to a nation—manages the contrast between city/nation and nature.

Parallel structural contrasts—between nature and trade, universality and the nation—are present and managed in Martí's best-known piece on education, "Wandering Teachers" (MR 46–50). Here is the passage I will read: "The farmer's children cannot leave the paternal farm and day after day, go mile after mile, to learn Latin declensions and short division. And yet"—there is the contrast—

The farmers comprise the best, most healthful, and succulent national mass, because they receive from up close and in full measure the emanations and the loving contact of the earth from whose loving give-and-take they live. Cities are the minds of nations; but their hearts, where the blood rushes back and from where it is redistributed, are in the countryside. Men are still eating machines. We must make every man a torch.

(MR 48; translation modified)

The country here is not simply the prenational as opposed to the national. It is also the *hylè* or mass of the national, to which the blood rushes first and that becomes continuous with the exchange with the Earth. The Earth is a paranational image that can substitute for international and can perhaps provide, today, a displaced site for the imagination of planetarity. The choice of the blood rushing *back* as the first move, the description of the rural as a specifically *national* mass, and the inclusion of the trade-related word "redistribution" (*se repartir*) in its activity seeks to undo the contradiction between the national and the rural.[21] If you read these essays in the context of Martí's own development, the vision of the countryside as the place of national production and redistribution rather than consumption—leading to exchange—is clear. Martí's was a necessarily proleptic choice for a specifically *postcolonial* internationality. We will see this to be true of Du Bois's choice as well. In our conjuncture, I am asking if there is anything in these stirrings of a postcolonialism before the letter that can displace itself into planetarity. Can the figure of the rural in Martí gives us leverage for such a reading?

Martí was acutely aware of the internal line of *cultural* difference within "the same culture." He was against the establishment of a Creole oligarchy in postcolonial Cuba. This combines with left-ruralism in his work to reverse and displace the direction of progressive change, however imperfectly. This tendency can be developed to make his work consonant with the planetary imagination of the new Comparative Literature. We are outlining a politics of reading. Marx's preference for the city over the country could not think the spectralization of the rural yet.[22]

The question of the possible displacement into planetarity may be a necessary supplement to the reconfiguration of "Our America" for cultural studies, which suggests that "Martí's U.S. writing belongs to that tradition of exilic representation which counterpoises the lived experience of being 'left alone' in the Anglo United States with the reconstructed collective memories of homelands which lie elsewhere."[23] Martí is not quite so distant from Cuba when he writes from New York; he is constantly planning for his country's future. "Reconstructed collective memories" gives a sense of nostalgia that, for me, is absent from Martí's feisty text, except for some stylized poetry where the genre asks for that sentiment.[24] I think part of this sentimentalization is precisely because the text is being reconfigured for the "twentieth-century migration [that] has seen the reassertion of Our America's *cultural* claims to" the Other America. The essays in the collection from which I quote, especially those by Rosaura Sánchez and Donald Pease, redress the balance, pointing at the historical difference rather than effacing it by appropriation. I seek not only to correct but also to displace.

José Martí was killed fighting the Spanish at the age of forty-two. Du Bois was ninety-five when he died. We can see the possibility of being pulled into the track of planetarity more clearly in the latter. W. E. B. Du Bois undid African American continent-think, reversing and displacing the violence and violation of slavery and imperialism. In our historical moment, we must try persistently to reverse and displace globalization into planetarity—an impossible figure and therefore calling on *teleopoiesis* rather than *istoria*.

The Souls of Black Folk is the prototype of the best (nationalist) vision of metropolitan Cultural Studies.[25] Du Bois acknowledges the responsibility of the African *American* because "the shadow," as yet unpluralized, "of a mighty Negro past"—this metaphor of the shadow is important for him—must be claimed as part of an American past as well. The price is high. We can read a reversal of Aristotle's definition of friendship—one soul in two bodies—as we can read an echo of Faust's lament in Du Bois's description of the African American at the end of the last century as "two souls . . . in one dark body, whose dogged strength alone keeps it from being torn asunder" (SB 52).[26] Writing from the Indian subcontinent, Ashis Nandy had spoken of Britain as the intimate enemy.[27] For the African American, the intimate enemy resides inside. This difference animates what I discuss next, a prescient essay called "The Negro Mind Reaches Out," written twenty-five years later, where Du Bois gives us the first taste of colonial discourse studies and even a preview of what was to follow from it—postcolonial criticism. Du Bois the pan-Africanist knew the continent of Africa to be heterogeneous.

Du Bois's movement from exceptionalism to egalitarianism—pushing for "the talented tenth" in the early phase to communism in the later—is well known. If, however, we look at the two texts without explicit reference to his intellectual life, what seems most striking is that, writing as a member of the metropolitan minority, Du Bois is exceptionalist and individualist; whereas, writing as a member of a global colonial world looking forward to postcoloniality, Du Bois is altogether aware that the production of the exceptionalist and individualist colonial subject creates a class division among the colonized, and that the colonizer often and paradoxically preferred the "primitive" rather than the "mimic man" he himself produced. Du Bois was writing on the internal class line of which I spoke above. Today, when these class divisions have altered the demographics of the former colonies and their diasporas, the metropolitan comparativist must imagine planetarity, displace the "primitivism" of the colonizer into the subaltern of the postcolonial, existing now in a cultural formation historically compromised by centuries of delegitimization; through the transforming work of imagining the impossible other as that figured other imagines us.

In ripe colonialism, Du Bois writes of

> the new democratic problems of colonization . . . fostered by a certain type of white colonial official who was interested in the black man and wanted him to develop. But this official was interested in the primitive black and not in the educated black. He feared and despised the educated West African and did not believe him capable of leading his primitive brother. He sowed seeds of dissension between these two.
>
> (NM 399)

*Post*colonially, the relationship between "the educated West African"—the Black European—and the "primitive" has continued in a class apartheid. The call for planetarity in the reading subject may be a training for at least recognizing that scandal in the history of the present.

Du Bois is aware of the results, first, of the difference among the imperial policies of the various European powers; and, second, of the difference in the imperial policy of the same power toward its various constituencies. Thus for Du Bois the production of the colonial subject is diversified, yet another lesson that some postcolonial work forgets explicitly, though its mark is historically evident upon its body, as academic interest broadens out into Development and human rights.

Let us consider these two points separately. As we do so, we must of course note that Du Bois presupposes the difference in the production of the New World African—historically a double ancestry claimed by struggle, and, in 1924, the date of "The Negro Mind Reaches Out," an economic and educational status more rooted, by that fact, as "American" than the Black European gentleman of whom he speaks.

Observing the difference in policy among the various European powers, or, as he puts it more picturesquely, the "shadows" of Portugal, Belgium, France, and England, Du Bois notices that "for nearly two centuries France has known educated and well-bred persons of Negro descent. . . . It was not that the French loved or hated Negroes as such; they simply grew to regard them as men with the possibilities and shortcomings of men, added to an unusual natural personal appearance" (NM 392). Alas, the situation is sadly changed today. And indeed, Du Bois did not see the shadow of France as an unquestioned good. Only in Boineuf of Martinique does he discover an exception: "One black deputy alone, Boineuf of Martinique, has the vision. His voice rings in Parliament. He made the American soldiers keep their hands off the Senegalese. He made the governor of Congo apologize and explain; he made Poincaré issue that extraordinary warning against American prejudice. Is Boineuf an exception or a prophecy?" (NM 397). Frantz Fanon is born in Martinique the next year.

We cannot know if Du Bois was aware that anticolonialism would not lead to productive continentalism. If so, he never put it down in published writing. We can turn to Wole Soyinka, "Arms and the Arts," to find a clue, English to English, class-fixed.[28] The project for the new Comparative Literature would have been to make it possible to trace this multiform trajectory (or its restricted permeability) in the African languages, thickening each nation-state invoked by Soyinka through persistently depoliticized Area Studies resources. Insofar as such pluralization decenters the idea of "Africa," it is possible to think our way into considerations of subalternity, eminently present in African studies from Amadiume to Mudimbe (I am no expert), and perhaps take a step, learning to learn from below, toward imagining planetarity.[29]]

Just as socialism at its best would persistently and repeatedly wrench capital away from capitalism, so must the new Comparative Literature persistently and repeatedly undermine and undo the definitive tendency of the dominant to appropriate the emergent. It must not let itself be constituted by the demands of liberal multiculturalism alone. Training in such persistent and repetitive gestures comes, necessarily, in the classroom. Insofar as the tertiary student is in the service of the dominant (although often unwilling or unable to acknowledge it), such training might seem to undermine their self-assurance. This is not an easy "positional skepticism of postmodernist literary and cultural studies," but something to be worked through in the interest of yoking the humanities, however distantly, with however few guarantees, to a just world.[30] I appreciate gestures to shore up the humanities institutionally. I can, however, concur less with John Guillory's recent suggestion that "the appropriate alternative to this strategy is to define and develop a knowledge of culture fully integrated into the spectrum of human sciences" than I can with Moretti's scopic generic morphology (see chapter 2, note 1 [see original reading]), which promises excellent reference tools, at least. Legitimating the humanities by making them scientific was already tried by the extremes of symbolic logic and structuralism, which were and are, in their own sphere, useful developments. Our own North American player Northrop Frye put in a strong bid for literary studies on the model of the "natural sciences," although he did grant that "the presence of incommunicable experience in the center of criticism will always keep criticism an art." This incommunicable experience had nothing to do with Frye's remarkably impersonal view of the ethical, as witness his "Second Essay: Ethical Criticism."[31] To confuse the ethical as the experience of the impossible with positional skepticism and prescribe scientific procedure, as does Guillory, speaks perhaps to the occupational hazard of wanting a science of criticism. If we want to compete with the hard "science"(s) and the social sciences at their hardest as "human science," we have already lost, as one loses institutional competition. In the arena of the humanities as the uncoercive rearrangement of desire, he who wins loses. If this sounds vague, what we learn (to imagine what we know) rather than know in the humanities remains vague, unverifiable, iterable. You don't put it aside in order to be literary critical.

The planetarity of which I have been speaking in these pages is perhaps best imagined from the precapitalist cultures of the planet. In this era of global capital triumphant, to keep responsibility alive in the reading and teaching of the textual is at first sight impractical. It is, however, the right of the textual to be so responsible, responsive, answerable. The "planet" is, here, as perhaps always, a catachresis for inscribing collective responsibility as right. Its alterity, determining experience, is mysterious and discontinuous—an experience of the impossible. It is such collectivities that must be opened up with the question "How many are we?" when cultural origin is detranscendentalized into fiction—the toughest task in the diaspora.

Notes

1   Wu Hung, "Public Time, Public Portrait, and the Renewal of Urban Monumentality," "Photography and the Birth of a Modern Visual Culture of Fragments," and "Reinventing Exhibition Spaces in Post-Cul tural Revolution China," conference on "Public Criticism and Visual Culture," Hong Kong University, June 6–10, 2002. Leo Ou-fan Lee and Liuo Ping-hueh presented brilliant discussions of spectacular nineteenth- and early twentieth-century verbal and visual texts focused toward correcting views expressed in Benedict Anderson's latest book, *The Spectre of Comparisons: Nationalism, South East Asia, and the World* (New York: Verso, 1998). The new Comparative Literature would find comparable efforts in other colonized countries, in India (there are parallels), and in North and sub-Saharan Africa, and make visible patterns in colonial production by the colonized middle class that would, incidentally, correct Anderson.

1a   [Editors' note: Bernheimer, Charles, ed., 1996. *Comparative Literature in the Age of Multiculturalism.* Baltimore: Johns Hopkins University Press.]

2   Charles Tilly, "How Empires End," in Karen Barkey and Mark von Hagen, eds., *After Empire: Multiethnic Societies and Nation-Building; The Soviet Union and the Russian, Ottoman, and Habsburg Empires* (New York: Westview, 1997), 2.

3   Paper presented at conference on "Ten Years of Post-Soviet Historiography," Ost und Sudosteuropa-Institut, University of Vienna, September 2001, and under consideration at *American History Review.*

4   Gregory Massell, *The Surrogate Proletariat: Moslem Women and Revolutionary Strategies in Soviet Central Asia, 1919–1929* (Princeton: Princeton University Press, 1974).

5   Hamid Dabashi, *Truth and Narrative: The Untimely Thoughts of 'Ayn Al-Qudat Al-Hamadhani* (Richmond, Surrey: Curzon Press, 1999), 109.

6   With the opening of the Oil Road, we will see a quick restructuring of Central Asian economies to accommodate aggressive financialization. Women's microcredit initiatives without infrastructural involvement become a part of this. For my discussion of planetarity in tribal Islam, see *Imperatives to Re-Imagine the Planets*/Imperative zur Neuerfindung des Planeten, ed. Willi Goetschel (Vienna: Passagen, 1999).

7   For Muslim Europe, Reinhart Dozy, *Spanish Islam*, tr. Francis Griffin Stokes (London: Chatto and Windus, 1913); H. A. R. Gibb, *The Influence of Islamic Culture on Medieval Europe* (Manchester: John Rylands Library, 1955); and Jean Lacam, *Les Sarrazins dans le haut moyen-age français* (Paris: Maisonneuve, 1965) represent the tip of the iceberg, indicating the monumental, the secondary, and the orientalist tendencies. For Islamic cosmopolitanism, see George Makdisi, *The Rise of Colleges: Institutions of Learning in Islam and the West* (Edinburgh: Edinburgh University Press, 1981), and *The Rise of Humanism in Classical Islam and the Christian West with Special Reference to Scholasticism* (Edinburgh: Edinburgh University Press, 1990). I thank Hamid Dabashi for his help in compiling this brief checklist.

8   I hasten to add that these are excellent provocative essays. I am suggesting that they be supplemented by other histories. For the moment, the important examples may be Emily Apter, "Comparative Exile: Competing Margins in the History of Comparative Literature," in the Bernheimer volume, 86–96; and Aamir R. Mufti, "Auerbach in Istanbul: Edward Said, Secular Criticism and the Question of Minority Culture," in Paul A. Bové, ed., *Edward Said and the Work of the Critic: Speaking Truth to Power* (Durham: Duke University Press, 2000), 229–56.

9   In Deniz Kandiyoti, ed., *Gendering the Middle East: Emerging Perspectives* (Syracuse, NY: Syracuse University Press, 1996), 1–27.

10   Gayatri Chakravorty Spivak, "Acting Bits/Identity Talk," *Critical Inquiry* 18 (4) (Summer 1992): 770–73; "Ghost-Writing," *Diacritics* 25 (2) (Summer 1995): 78–82.

11   Spivak, "Acting Bits," 793–94; "Three Women's Texts and Circumfession," in Alfred Hornung and Ernstpeter Ruhe, eds., *Postcolonialism and Autobiography* (Amsterdam: Rodopi, 1998), 21–22.

12   Diamela Eltit, *The Fourth World*, tr. Dick Gerdes (Lincoln: University of Nebraska Press, 1995). Hereafter cited in text as FW, with page reference following.

13   Gayatri Chakravorty Spivak, "Unmaking and Making in *To the Lighthouse*," subsequently included in a revised version in *In Other Worlds: Essays in Cultural Politics* (New York: Methuen, 1987), 30–45.

14   Miller, *Others*, Princeton: Princeton University Press, 2001, 273–74.

15   Philip Foner, "Introduction" in José Martí, *Our America* (New York: Monthly Review Press, 1977), 24.

16   The OED's first index entry for Latin America is from 1890, the U.S. State Department's "Reciprocity Treaties with Latin America," but such a term enters official use when it has been around for a little while, of course. For its itinerary, see Angel G. Loureiro, "Spanish Nationalism and the Ghost of Empire," forthcoming in the *Journal of Spanish Cultural Studies*.

17   Gayatri Chakravorty Spivak, "Love, Cruelty, and Cultural Talks in the Hot Peace," in Pheng Cheah and Bruce Robbins, eds., *Cosmopolitics: Thinking and Feeling Beyond the Nation* (Minneapolis: University of Minnesota Press, 1998), 329–48.

18   Marx had spoken of this combination in connection with foreign trade in *Capital*, tr. David Fernbach (New York: Vintage, 1981), 3: 344–47.

19   For *mochlos*, see Jacques Derrida, "Mochlos; or, The Conflict of the Faculties," in *Logomachia: The Conflict of the Faculties* (Lincoln: University of Nebraska Press, 1992), 1–34.

20   Perry Anderson, *In the Tracks of Historical Materialism* (New York: Verso, 1983).

21   I am told that the "re" in *"repartir"* does not necessarily have the same force as the "re" in "redistribution." This does not interfere with the idea that the blood rushes *back* to the heart and is then shared out—a figure of exchange.

22   I have discussed this in Spivak, "From Haverstock Hill Flat to U.S. Classroom, What's Left of Theory?" in Judith Butler et al., eds. *What's Left of Theory?: New Work on the Politics of Literary Theory*, (New York: Routledge, 2000), 1–40.

23   Jeffrey Belnap and Raúl Fernández, "Introduction," in *José Martí's "Our America"* (Durham, NC: Duke University Press, 1998), 6.

24   One such poem is discussed by Julio Ramos in "Migratories," in Juho Rodríguez-Luis, ed., *Re-reading José Martí: One Hundred Years Later* (Albany: SUNY Press, 1999), 53–58.

25   W. E. B. Du Bois, *The Souls of Black Folk* (New York: Signet, 1995 [1903]); hereafter cited in text as SB, with page references following.

26   Johann Wolfgang von Goethe, *Faust*, tr. Walter Kaufmann (Garden City, NY: Doubleday, 1963), 145. Cornel West has tracked this passage to Emerson in *The American Evasion of Philosophy: A Genealogy of Pragmatism* (Madison: University of Wisconsin Press, 1989), 144.

27   Ashis Nandy, *The Intimate Enemy: Loss and Recovery of Self Under Colonialism* (Delhi: Oxford University Press, 1983).

28   Wole Soyinka, *Arms and the Arts: A Continent's Unequal Dialogue* (Cape Town: University of Cape Town, 1999).

29   Ifi Amadiume, *Male Daughters, Female Husbands: Gender and Sex in African Society* (London: Zed Books, 1987); V. Y. Mudimbe, *The Idea of Africa* (Bloomington: Indiana University Press, 1994). If in the case of Martí we had to circumvent the metaphor of woman-mother-earth proactively, concatenating Du Bois with feminism is, a more labor-intensive task. The Black European is not only class-fixed but gender-fixed as well. For deep background articulated, see Brent Hayes Edwards, "One More Time," *Transition* 89 (2001): 88–107, a review of David Levering Lewis, *W.E.B. Du Bois: The Fight for Equality and the American Century, 1919–1963* (New York: Henry Holt, 2000), which discusses Du Bois's sexuality in some detail.

30   John Guillory, "The Sokal Affair and the History of Criticism," *Critical Inquiry* 28 (2) (Winter 2002): 501. The next passage is from the same paragraph.

31   Northrop Frye, *Anatomy of Criticism* (New York: Atheneum, 1968), 27–28, 71–128.

Gerard Holden

WORLD LITERATURE AND WORLD POLITICS: IN SEARCH OF A RESEARCH AGENDA (2003)

GERARD HOLDEN (B. 1955) EARNED A PhD in International Relations from the London School of Economics, and has worked at the universities of Sussex (UK) and Frankfurt am Main (Germany). He currently lives in Frankfurt, and does research on, and publishes on, world politics, world literature, world cinema and world cricket.

The 2003 article we here reproduce is one of the rare attempts to link politics, or perhaps more correctly political science, in this particular case international relations, and world literature. Holden critically reviews a number of instances of the use made of literature in what is now known as the "aesthetic turn" in IR (International Relations). He finds most of them defective in one way or another. Specifically, he guards against what he calls the "cavalier" use political scientists make of literature when they grapple with it. Instead, he argues, they should pay more attention to what literary scholars do with literature, and with specific literary works. Still, he thinks that there might be a fruitful field for interdisciplinary study here. More recently Holden published another article: "World Politics, World Literature, World Cinema," (*Global Society* 24:3, 2010), which goes over some of the same ground he covers in his 2003 article, but which also tries to go further, looking at the work of some of the major contributors to the ongoing debate on world literature, such as Moretti, Damrosch, Spivak and Lawall, and also turning the argument around and partly criticizing scholars of world literature from an IR or world politics perspective.

Since the date of Holden's article here reproduced, the aesthetic turn in IR has expanded considerably, and now extends to writing on the politics of literature, the cinema, visual art, music, photography—just about all artistic fields, in fact. Literature is thus only one area of interest, and there has not been much examination of world literature as a distinct issue. In general terms, Holden thinks, this development is a symptom of a dissolution of boundaries between the social sciences and the humanities, though this is more true of IR scholarship in some places (e.g. the UK) than in others.

Looked at from a literary studies perspective, Holden's 2003 article may function as an eye-opener to literary scholars, suggesting to them ways other than those they are most familiar with, or used to, to look at literature in relation to what lies perhaps immediately outside but not necessarily beyond it.

Gerard Holden, "World Literature and World Politics: In Search of a Research Agenda," *Global Society* 17 (2003) 3: 229–52.

> "It is a work very broad in its scope," Herr Settembrini said thoughtfully, "and will require much consideration and wide reading. Especially," he added, and his gaze seemed to lose itself in the immensity of his task, "since literature has regularly chosen to depict suffering, and even second- and third-rate masterpieces treat of it in one form or another. But what of that? So much the better!"
>
> Thomas Mann—*The Magic Mountain*

Introduction

The idea that the study of literature should be among the concerns of International Relations (IR) has arrived in the discipline, or at least at some points on the spectrum of IR scholarship.[1] This is not an entirely new development, but it has recently gathered pace with the publication of a special issue of *Alternatives* on "Poetic World Politics" in 2000, and of a special issue of *Millennium* on "Images and Narratives in World Politics" in 2001. Roland Bleiker edited the *Alternatives* special issue, and has given this development a name by christening it "The Aesthetic Turn in International Political Theory" in his introduction to the *Millennium* special issue. This turn goes beyond prose fiction and poetry, the primary concerns of the present article, to include a number of other fields such as the cinema, visual art, music, and architecture.

This development merits discussion of a sympathetically critical, or perhaps critically sympathetic, nature. There seems to be a danger that the new turn will be ignored or dismissed by its opponents, who are likely to demand that it prove its credentials in relation to certain specified or unspecified standards of good IR theory, while being uncritically celebrated by its admirers and/or adherents. This article does not seek to reply to the first challenge; if this kind of charge is levelled, the decision on whether to respond must be left to the proponents of the aesthetic turn themselves. It is more concerned with the second (potential) problem, and attempts to engage IR's literary turn on the terrain it has itself chosen to occupy, scrutinising its explicit and implicit claims about the relationship between literature and (world) politics and arguing that they are not as self-evident as some of the IR authors involved appear to believe. I do this in three stages. The second section takes the form of an overview. I summarise briefly the intradisciplinary currents that have led IR to this point, arguing that there are a number of different sources of IR's interest in literature and that these cannot be subsumed under any one theoretical tradition. The third section compares and contrasts the work of Christopher Coker with that of Bleiker and a number of scholars with similar approaches, and argues that these authors tend to use literature to bolster views they already hold about world politics. In the fourth section I introduce additional material from the field of literary scholarship, first reviewing and criticising IR's reception of the work of the Russian literary theorist Mikhail Bakhtin and then using the work of two other literary scholars, Gabriel Josipovici and Franco Moretti, to explore further and challenge some of the positions taken by literary IRists.

My general approach is sympathetic to the interdisciplinary concerns of the IR authors whose work I discuss. However, there is a tendency on the part of these scholars to use the literary field for their own purposes without reflecting its complexity adequately, and in particular to oversimplify in relation to certain aspects of aesthetic experience and pleasure. I suggest that some of the IR scholars active in this area have been too selective about the assumptions on which their forays into unfamiliar territory rest, and that in some respects the onus is on IRists to clarify their positions and to strengthen the case for using fictional and poetic texts to illuminate or even transform world politics. This does not mean endorsing the views of those who are likely to reject this development on other grounds, but it does amount to an argument for greater caution on the part of IR scholars moving into fields that have their own pre-existing identity and autonomy. Literary scholarship has already occupied some of the territory IR scholars are seeking to move into, is aware of a number of the problems that arise, and deserves more sustained attention.

The boundaries of a discipline

> "Did you say you were leaving tomorrow?" he asked.
> "Yes," I replied. "That's the plan anyway."
> Magnus Mills—*All Quiet on the Orient Express*

International Relations sees itself as a discipline on the move. In the past something of an insecure field, a younger sibling within the social sciences and not even assured of an autono-mous institutional existence outside political science in some of the countries in which it is pursued, IR has in recent years seen a growing number of arguments to the effect that no natural boundaries separate it from other fields of scholarship. Some of these arguments suggest that the whole idea of a distinct sphere of "the international" is an artificial construc-tion, while others rely on claims about changes that are seen to have occurred at some fairly recent stage of world history and which render any distinction between the domestic and the international otiose on empirical grounds. Whatever the merits or demerits of the specific arguments involved, the outcome seems to be that at least part of the broad community of scholars dealing with world affairs sees itself confronted with a reality in which everything— politics, economics, warfare, social life, technology, culture, religion—is considered equally relevant to its concerns, and boundaries between fields of human activity and thus between academic disciplines appear to have become porous or disappeared. Reactions to this situa-tion can vary from a degree of alarm (if there is no sphere of human activity that can be uncontroversially identified as "the international", what exactly is it that IR scholars do?) to renewed self-confidence accompanied by the belief that IR is something like a universally competent meta-discipline and so the branch of intellectual endeavour best equipped to deal with this situation.[2] The term "world politics" is widely used to signal resistance to the idea that the field does or should restrict itself to a concern with relations between states ("nations"). And, depending on how one defines "culture", a case can be made for the view that world literature is a component of world politics and should figure among the concerns of whatever (inter- or meta-) discipline is responsible for the latter.

The concept of world literature has its origins in the European humanist optimism of the late 18th and early 19th centuries, in the idea that individual national literatures would in future fuse into a higher and more complete whole.[3] At that time it was a predominantly German concept. On several occasions during the 1820s, Goethe expressed his belief that the age of *Weltliteratur*, a kind of cosmopolitan conversation between national literatures that would bring the different nations together, would soon arrive—partly, and paradoxically, as a result of the wars of the Napoleonic period which had, he believed, made the nations of Europe more aware of each other.[4] Some 20 years later, Marx and Engels took up the concept in the *Communist Manifesto*. In the famous passage praising the revolutionary achievements of bourgeois civilisation, they spoke of a development in which: "The intellectual creations of individual nations become common property. National one-sidedness and narrow-mindedness become more and more impossible, and from the numerous national and local literatures there arises a world literature."[5]

Today, the term is more likely to be used to refer to the totality, or the best, of past and present global literary production. In German, the expression still has distinctly normative connotations; an enthusiastic book reviewer might say *"Das ist Weltliteratur!"*, and author and publishers will be delighted. More frequently, however, the term is used in English to denote the subject matter of comparative literature, a field of such potentially vast proportions that even giving a rough characterisation of its remit is fraught with difficulties. Franco Moretti, a literary scholar to whose work I shall return below, points out that the term "comparative literature" is something of a misnomer for a field that seeks to take responsibility for the whole of world literature: there are no experts on world literature, only people who specialise in more or less well-defined corners of the field. Nevertheless, he says, world literature does now exist as something like a planetary system, rather as Goethe and Marx/Engels prematurely envisaged it.[6] As soon as one acknowledges the impossibility of covering the whole field, controversies about the established literary canon and its justification inevitably arise. Moretti points out that scholars who select the existing canon for further discussion leave "the great unread", the 99.5% of world literature that lies outside the canon, to gather dust on the library shelves. Even attempts to construct an alternative canon cannot solve this problem, and can at best hope to reduce the great unread to 99% of the total.[7] Rather like IR, therefore, comparative literature has to confront the problem of what to include and what to leave out.

"Culture" is notorious for having the capacity to mean everything and nothing. The literary theorist Terry Eagleton has made some characteristically pithy comments on this problem:

> It is hard to resist the conclusion that "culture" is both too broad and too narrow to be greatly useful. Its anthropological meaning covers everything from hairstyles and drinking habits to how to address your husband's second cousin, while the aesthetic sense of the word includes Igor Stravinsky but not science fiction . . . [which] . . . belongs to "mass" or popular culture.[8]

Since IR's literary turn does include science fiction it can be absolved from this particular part of Eagleton's charge, but in other ways IR has done its bit to add to the confusion surrounding "culture". The insertion of "culture and international relations" into IR's agenda has taken a number of forms. Some of this literature has used anthropological and/or sociological understandings of culture or identity in order to illuminate or recast familiar fields such as foreign or security policy. A second category goes further and seeks to make questions of identity and identity-formation central concerns of IR, and has been remarkably successful (if we wanted to find a new title for the discipline reflecting its diversity and current preoccupations, we could perhaps consider renaming it "This, That, and the Other"). Samuel Huntington's "clash of civilizations" thesis shaped large parts of the disciplinary debate in the late 1990s, and reappeared in the public debate after 11 September 2001. Parts of the voluminous literature on globalisation have also used terms like "world culture", though some of these authors have been insufficiently aware of the full implications of the term.[9] One other body of literature that should be mentioned separately is the feminist literature, partly because feminism's questioning of conventional boundaries between the public/international and the private poses a radical challenge to disciplinary autonomy, and partly because there is a clearly identifiable line of succession from the early work of Christine Sylvester to her recent contributions to the aesthetic turn.[10] Feminist concerns have had a particularly strong influence on IR's engagement with the cinema.[11]

Even before the emergence of "culture and international relations" and the globalisation literature, attempts to relate world literature to world politics cropped up in some unexpected places; it is impossible to do much more here than mention some of them briefly. One was Martin Wight's *International Theory: The Three Traditions*, presented in the form of lectures in the 1950s but only published in 1991.[12] Wight refers to literary sources throughout the book, and suggests at one point that judging the actions of statesmen is more akin to literary criticism than to scientific analysis. He encourages students of international relations to read literature to help them appreciate the moral quandaries of statecraft: "Hardy's *Dynasts*, *Gulliver's Travels*, and political novels such as *War and Peace*, *Nostromo*, *Darkness at Noon*, *Nineteen Eighty-four* and others."[13] Wight's comment was later taken up by James Der Derian in the course of his attempt, with the help of literature and literary theory, to set up a dialogue between classical international theory and challenges to that literature.[14] Benedict Anderson's *Imagined Communities* has for some time been among the most influential works in the literature on nationalism.[15] One aspect of Anderson's work that is only infrequently mentioned, though Sylvester draws attention to it, is his use of novels written in societies under or emerging from colonial rule to illustrate how a consciousness of an alternative, independent political order could come into being (in the Philippines, Mexico, and Indonesia). At the beginning of the 1990s there were a—surprisingly small—number of commentaries on the controversy over Salman Rushdie's *The Satanic Verses*,[16] and one can also mention an interesting cluster of contributions by two senior German political scientists and peace researchers, Ekkehart Krippendorff and Dieter Senghaas, who have examined the political aspects and implications of works of literature and musical compositions.[17] Another relevant sub-field which emerged during the 1990s is the literature on the cultural history of the Cold War. This has produced books which include Frances Stonor Saunders's *Who Paid the Piper?*, a study of the actions of the CIA front organisation, the Congress for Cultural Freedom, in the 1950s–1960s, and is represented in *Alternatives* by Sylvester's article on abstract art and in the *Millennium* special issue by Fred Halliday's advocacy of an anthology on the subject.[18] In 1995 the critic and novelist Malcolm Bradbury published an article in *International Affairs* on "The Arts in and after the Cold War".[19]

Some philosophers and political theorists have also addressed the potential contribution of literature to ethical and political projects; special mention should be made of Martha Nussbaum and Richard Rorty.[20] Nussbaum argues that literary texts can provide privileged insights: "[C]ertain truths about human life can only be fittingly and accurately stated in the language and forms characteristic of the narrative artist."[21] Rorty takes a slightly less categorical view, arguing on the basis of his rejection of a correspondence theory of truth that there is no epistemological difference between theoretical physics and literary criticism. Rorty consequently treats intellectual history as the history of metaphors, and considers fictional and non-fictional texts to be of potentially equal value for the reformulation of philosophical questions. The most valuable texts are, he says, those that help us to become less cruel in our relations with others; he singles out Nabokov, Orwell, and certain writings of Derrida which can be classified neither as literature nor as philosophy. Within IR, Hayward R. Alker shares Nussbaum's view of the power of literature.[22] Alker sees his own work in terms of the pursuit of Karl W. Deutsch's ideal of a "philosophic synthesis of the sciences and humanities",[23] which he believes could eventually lead to "a more humanistically understood interdiscipline of International Studies".[24] He argues that a wide range of classical, literary, and philosophical texts contain potentially emancipatory narrative resources which can be revealed with the help of methods that include computerised textual analysis and structuralist literary interpretations (as applied, for example, to fairy tales; Alker quotes Roman Jakobson's suggestion that a fairy tale fulfils the role of a social utopia).

Alker can be seen as one of the forerunners of IR's literary turn. At the same time, these philosophical and theoretical works present problems which reappear in IR's recent engagement with literature. The most fundamental question that arises is that of the similarities and differences between textual categories normally considered to be distinct: the philosophical, historical, social-scientific, fictional, and poetic. Rorty and Nussbaum have both been accused by literary scholars of naivety in their treatments of literary works and literary theory. For example, they pay too little attention to whatever it is that is specifically literary about literary texts, and are strangely confident that reading novels will produce the responses they consider desirable. Nussbaum even seems to equate the relationships we form with characters in fiction with our relationships with real people.[25] One could add that if one privileges literary texts to this extent, one needs to explain what value is added by academic commentary on those texts; Nussbaum's (and Alker's) statement, quoted above, rather suggests that there is not much point reading the books in which it appears. This is a question to which I shall return.

Roland Bleiker has offered an account of IR's aesthetic turn that is partly persuasive and partly misleading. He argues that the turn to aesthetic concerns can be traced back to the postmodern critiques of positivist international theory that began to be written in the 1980s, and that this has developed in the last few years into a search for insights into world politics to be found in both "high art" and popular culture.[26] There is clearly a good deal of truth in this. From the late 1960s onwards, ideas that originated in European philosophy and literary theory became influential in literary studies, cultural studies, and subsequently in the social sciences in the United States and the rest of the English-speaking world, from where they found their way into IR. For most of the 1980s and 1990s postmodernist or poststructuralist IR scholars bracketed literary-theoretical questions as such because, even if they employed eclectic methods including tools from the literary field, they were more interested in other things—US identity and foreign policy, the gendered nature of international or strategic discourse, the construction of domestic/international politics, and so on. Increasingly, however, it appears that a small number of IR scholars (and some of them are indeed the same people) really are interested in imaginative literature and its relationship to world politics, which means that historical and theoretical issues from the literary field can no longer be bracketed out. However, it is not empirically the case that only postmodernist scholars are interested in literature and politics, and there is no theoretical reason to believe that only postmodernists have anything interesting to say on the subject. One only has to look at the list of contributors to *Millennium*'s special issue to find several scholars who are not remotely postmodernist (Anthony Smith, Chris Brown, Halliday). Furthermore, the shift to aesthetic concerns also seems to be related to the fact that some of those involved are now *ex*-postmodernists, though it is hard to put one's finger on the precise significance of this no doubt momentous development.[27] The point to be emphasised is that there are a number of different impulses behind IR's decision to head off into literary territory.

Schools of thought in literary IR

> Monsieur Jourdain: Et comme l'on parle, qu'est-ce que c'est donc que cela?
> Maître de philosophie: De la prose.
> Monsieur Jourdain: Quoi!
>
> Moliére—*Le Bourgeois gentilhomme*

A series of books by Christopher Coker represents the most sustained attempt so far by an individual IR scholar to explore the relationship between twentieth-century literary and political history.[28] Coker's work incorporates a wide range of philosophical and literary sources in its elaboration of a set of theses about Western consciousness and global politics during the 20th century. This body of work has received little attention within the discipline, even from other scholars interested in the same issues. However, because so little notice has been taken of it, Coker's work has not been exposed to critical scrutiny. For both of these reasons, I devote the first part of this section to a (necessarily brief) account of it before moving on to Bleiker's work.

Coker began this series of publications with a book on the role of historical myths and imagery in US foreign policy. He describes his general method as "impressionistic", a way of using literary references to illuminate the recent history of Western historical consciousness. Two books followed in which literature was allotted a more central role in the analysis (*War and the 20th Century* and *War and the Illiberal Conscience*), and these have been followed by two further books in which literature is less central but still present as a point of reference (*Twilight of the West* and *Humane Warfare*). In *War and the 20th Century*, Coker argues that the experience and representation of war provided the narratives via which the West sought to understand its experience of the 20th century, and a range of literary sources, many of them from European modernism, are used to support this. The argument is developed in *War and the Illiberal Conscience* with the help of an examination of illiberal thought, treated as part of the response to modernity. This is coupled with a critique of the Western liberal outlook for being unable to take others' ideas seriously and failing to recognise that attempts to create order can easily lead to greater disorder. In his two most recent books Coker examines the philosophical basis of the Atlantic community and the West's changing attitude to war, arguing first that the West needs to engage the Islamic world and Asia in new forms of dialogue now that the end of the Cold War has removed the basis on which the West had previously found meaning in history, and then that the West's current attempt to sanitise war and deny its cruelty is an essentially dishonest undertaking reflecting a loss of meaning in the West's military relationship with the rest of the world.

Coker is well read and is well equipped to relate literature to political history. Most readers of his work will find themselves constantly noting down promising references to sources dealing with aspects of cultural and philosophical history, not to mention numbers of novels they have been intending to read for a long time. Part of the time the impressionistic method works well, for example when Coker argues that some of the most insightful writers of the late 19th and early 20th centuries (Nietzsche, Kafka, Musil) identified or anticipated totalitarianism and the breakdown of European civilisation, and that those of them who lived to see it realised that the outbreak of World War I was a symptom rather than the cause of that breakdown. Coker stresses that he is not claiming that artists have a privileged access to the truth. He does, however, appear to believe that first-rate authors have had the most profound insights into 20th-century history, and also to believe that this is what makes them first rate; gifted but thoroughly illiberal writers (such as Jünger, Céline, and Pound) have, he says, had as many profound insights as liberals. The posited connection between literary merit and historical insight can be seen clearly in Coker's discussion of the British World War I poets, who, he argues, were not only historically blinkered (mistakenly believing that the working-class soldiers fighting the war all saw it as meaningless), but also rather second rate.[29] One has the feeling that important questions are being begged here, since it is not clear why literary merit and historical insight should be associated with each other in the first place. There are other occasions on which the method works less satisfactorily, and the mixing up of statements by fictional characters with comments drawn from philosophical or psychological sources begs the further question of the relationship between these genres. At one point Proust's Robert de Saint-Loup is uncomfortably sandwiched between the French historian Marc Bloch and Michael Herr writing about the Vietnam War. And Coker is not always a careful reader. In *War and the 20th Century*, for example, he makes a small but significant mistake about the plot of *The Magic Mountain* (it is not the case that Thomas Mann's hero, Hans Castorp, dies at the end of the novel—we do not know what will happen to him), a mistake which is corrected in *War and the Illiberal Conscience*. But the correction seems to be made by accident, and is the consequence of citing a secondary source rather than the original text.[30] Discrepancies like this are troubling, as is the fact that if one carries out a thorough check of Coker's footnotes, a substantial proportion of the literary references appear to have been taken from secondary sources, so that he is frequently dependent on others' interpretations.

The main thread connecting the stages of Coker's arguments, both those that refer directly to literary works and those that do not, is his Nietzscheanism. Coker values Nietzsche as a source of critique of the West's own civilisation and a thinker who at least points the way to the revaluation of values the West needs now that the Cold War is over. I think it is not unfair to say that, much of the time, Coker's literary interpolations appear as illustrations or confirmations of a thesis drawn more directly from a philosophical or other source. This is not itself problematic, though Coker generally avoids engaging with questions of literary theory. When one finishes reading Coker one is therefore stimulated but not quite sure how central literary analysis really is to the enterprise, and also uncertain about the foundations of the literary analyses and judgements offered.

In Bleiker's work, one finds that some of the literary-theoretical arguments are more explicit but the final destination of the argument is not dissimilar. I think one could almost speak of an "*Alternatives* school" of literary IR, consisting of Bleiker and several other authors with similar approaches (Sylvester, Michael J. Shapiro, Costas M. Constantinou, and possibly Der Derian). However, this group is internally quite diverse in some respects (Sylvester has written as much about painting and sculpture as about literature, and Shapiro has written on the cinema), and claims to have identified a new school can lead to unnecessary controversy that fails to advance understanding of the issues at stake. In what follows I do not assume that Bleiker can speak for others who may not share all his views but, as I have already pointed out, Bleiker himself has presented the aesthetic turn as a common project of a certain group of scholars (without naming names). He is also the most prominent and prolific member of the group. In speaking of this group, I therefore refer to "Bleiker and his colleagues".

In a nutshell, Bleiker's argument is that critical or dissident voices in IR become trapped in methodological dilemmas when they engage in critique of orthodox theories, because this means accepting the broad discursive framework of those approaches—their preoccupation with power politics and associated political practices.[31] The remedy, argues Bleiker, is to "forget" the object of critique and adopt an aphoristic or poetic style in writing about world politics which recognises that there is no point striving for a coherent and bounded representation of the whole field. The developments in world politics that are of most interest are "transversal struggles", forms of dissent that cross existing national boundaries and challenge the existing spatial logic that frames international relations, and aesthetic rather than mimetic representation is the appropriate way of addressing such developments. "The aesthetic turn reorients our very understanding of the political: it engenders a significant shift away from a model of thought that equates knowledge with the mimetic recognition of external appearances towards an approach that generates a more diverse but also more direct encounter with the political."[32] In a similarly programmatic statement introducing a volume on *Challenging Boundaries* co-edited with Alker, Shapiro speaks of moving beyond state sovereignties to examine the "global politics of contested spaces and contentious identities", using literary and other sources to do this.[33] Shapiro argues elsewhere that there are no firm boundaries dividing fictional from non-fictional texts.[34]

It follows in Bleiker's view that poetry, with its recognition of the inseparability of aesthetic form from political substance, is the best way of identifying alternative visions and practices in the "thinking space" thus created. He suggests that poetry can perform four distinct political functions. Sometimes it is directly political and engaged, though this kind of activist poetry is not always very effective; it can redescribe world-political realities in such a way as to permit a more inclusive and dialogical approach; it can provide alternative perspectives on mundane occurrences that are not usually classified as "international"; and it can provide a historical memory of events that can only be inadequately captured in conventional historical narratives. He also says that poetry can do what critical international theory seeks to do by questioning the prevailing structures of the world and opening up space for alternatives. It is not clear whether Bleiker believes that poetry alone can perform these functions. At one point he refers to some of the prose classics of Russian literature as forms of historical memory that are more effective than conventional historical narratives, and at another point Orwell's *Animal Farm* is mentioned as a particularly effective critique of communist totalitarianism. If one takes Bleiker's book *Popular Dissent, Human Agency and Global Politics* as the most authoritative statement of his position, it appears that not only poetry but also aphorisms, the essay, the novel, and various forms of dialogue can serve as discursive forms of dissent. Elsewhere in his *Alternatives* introduction, though, Bleiker suggests that poetry provides us with insights which cannot, in a fairly literal sense it seems, be translated into prose. The latter is associated with orthodox IR theorists and practitioners.[35] This is a distinctly odd twist to the argument: "prose" appears to take its place alongside realism and positivism in a triumvirate of heresies that have been anathematised. Bleiker himself has published readings of the work of Paul Celan, of Pablo Neruda, and of the Prenzlauer Berg poets, who were active in East Berlin during the late 1970s and 1980s; these contributions suggest that he really does believe what he appears to say about the superiority of poetry to prose as a form of linguistic dissent.[36] It should be said, though, that these are impressive pieces of commentary which show Bleiker's approach at its best.

Bleiker's view appears to be shared by at least some of the contributors to the *Alternatives* special issue on poetic world politics, some of which themselves take a poetic form.[37] However, the fact remains that Bleiker and those who take this view are thoroughly *bourgeois gentilhommes* who write orthodox academic prose most of the time and do not, presumably, address their students in iambic pentameter. In Bleiker's *Millennium* introduction this view is not mentioned, though it is not explicitly retracted. This essay only goes as far as to advocate aesthetics as a problematisation of representation that will make us "more modest about our claims to know the realities of world politics".[38] The *Millennium* special issue contains a broader range of contributions than its *Alternatives* predecessor, with a shift away from the literary and towards the visual, and with the diversity of the aesthetic turn reflected by authors who seem to share something close to Bleiker's perspective (Sylvester, Shapiro, Der Derian, Iver B. Neumann, Constantinou) appearing alongside others who do not (Smith, Brown, Halliday). Here, items on visual art and the cinema outnumber the purely literary contributions, and there is no contribution specifically on poetry. A special category of articles on science fiction deals with both literary and cinematic forms of the genre. These contributions make a good case for a political reading of science fiction, though they are rather hard going for anyone who is not an aficionado.

Refreshingly, Bleiker does not subscribe to the widely held view that "critical" scholars are some kind of disciplinary aristocracy (or, in terms of science fiction, more advanced life forms). At one point he says that the term "critical" is a piece of "semantic self-righteousness" which "assumes that everything but itself is uncritical".[39] Quite right. An acknowledgement on these lines from someone in or close to the "critical" camp was long overdue, though it has to be said that Bleiker himself employs the label "dissident" in much the same infuriating way. But there are other problems with Bleiker's position. As I have already suggested, I think his basic view of the relationship between poetry, prose, and politics requires clarification. It appears to rest on the claim that poetry has an inherent capacity to problematise the representational functions of language and that (most?) prose fiction lacks this capacity. If this is what Bleiker believes, it is quite simply wrong. He surely cannot believe that *all* poetry does this in a politically desirable way, in other words that there is no such thing as—for want of a better term—reactionary poetry. Even more importantly, the novel has a considerable capacity for self-parody. The canon of European prose fiction contains numerous works which themselves play with such ideas as the unreliability of literature, its imperfect correspondence to the world, and the potentially disorientating consequences of taking it too literally—Cervantes's *Don Quixote*, Sterne's *Tristram Shandy*, and Austen's *Northanger Abbey*, for a start. And even if 19th-century realist novels functioned differently, the rise of modernist prose towards the end of that century brought with it an even more radical questioning of the novel's capacity to represent the world (see next section).

Bleiker and those who hold views close to his do not hesitate to make their theoretical and political preferences clear, and they also go further than Coker in attributing privileged insights to the authors of poems or other literary texts. They derive theoretical inspiration from Nietzsche, from Theodor Adorno as an advocate and exponent of aphoristic writing, from the Russian literary theorist Mikhail Bakhtin (of whom more in a moment), and from postcolonial theorists such as Edward Said and Gayatri Chakravorty Spivak. These authors therefore rely much more heavily than Coker on contributions from cultural and literary theory. The political sympathies of most of the contributors to the *Alternatives* special issue are clearly with postcolonial subjects and other marginalised actors, and the literature selected encourages the exploration of hybrid identities, dialogue in politics and literature, and the conscious use of poetry as a moral resource (by, for example, the Mexican Zapatistas and Indian resisters opposing the construction of a missile base[40]).

I now turn to some further objections to the work of these authors. The problem is not that Bleiker and his colleagues do not make orthodox aesthetic judgements, as they are under no obligation to do so. Nor does any difficulty arise from the intermingling of "high" and "popular" culture, which is perfectly legitimate and is further justified by the attention paid to the cinema, the art form which has perhaps done more than any other to blur the distinction. Rather, the problem is that these authors constantly make what one could call political-aesthetic judgements about both high and popular culture which are, once the reader has got used to the genre, almost without exception formulaic and predictable. Literary and other works will receive a stamp of approval as long as they are perceived as challenging conventional representations and identities, and fostering diversity, hybridity, and respect for the other; those which are perceived as failing to do these things will be found wanting. It appears that there is a foolproof method for deciding which works belong in which category, and little or no room for ambiguity. One could indeed argue that these authors were more consistently poststructuralist when they were analysing international relations using literary tools than they are now that they have begun to write about literature as such. Because they have a clear idea of the function they want literature to perform (the destabilisation of conventional identities), it is not in their interests to argue that the meaning of a literary work is indefinitely deferred, as a consistently deconstructionist approach would suggest. They now want to be able to specify unambiguously which works are destabilising and which are not, and in a number of cases (for example the postcolonial works) they decide this on the basis of intentions attributed to the authors of those works.

Bleiker's apparent poetry/prose dichotomy is the most obvious example of this, but the phenomenon is equally noticeable outside the literary contributions. Shapiro finds conveniently that all the films and musicals he discusses confirm his pre-existing political-aesthetic views because they can either be classified as "critical" and "progressive", and so approved of (*Lone Star, Kansas City*), or have the undesirable quality of reconfirming conventional identities or narratives and so deserve condemnation (*Oklahoma!, Father of the Bride II*).[41] Thus the awesome firepower of Shapiro's theoretical arsenal (Kant, Deleuze, Derrida, Foucault,

Lyotard) is deployed to no more effect than to divide films into "progressive" and, well, *not* progressive.[42] And it is impossible not to notice that the authors and artists for whose work Sylvester expresses most enthusiasm tend to be female (the Zimbabwean author Nyamubaya, Louise Bourgeois, Margaret Atwood, Ruby the elephant). After a while, the reader has a pretty good idea of what to expect; these authors may want to challenge conventional views of the political, but their own views of what is politically-aesthetically desirable are fixed. Even when Bleiker and his colleagues do approve of a book, poem, or film, this does not seem to be because they have enjoyed it very much. Although they are theoretically in favour of irony and playfulness, their work has in practice all the light-hearted frivolity of a Fassbinder retrospective. (To avoid misunderstanding: I am a great admirer of Fassbinder's films.)

This is, I think, a serious shortcoming in any attempt to integrate aesthetics and (international) politics. Pleasure matters, and it is also quite possible to have pleasurable aesthetic experiences that are not in harmony with one's own political convictions or instincts. As a prime example of how a gifted critic can explore a work that presents these problems I would point to Edward Said's discussion of Rudyard Kipling's *Kim*, which is *the* novel of British imperialism but nevertheless a thoroughly good read.[43] Bleiker and his colleagues do not seem to have this kind of aesthetic experience, or if they do they are not telling us about it.[44] But Coker's treatment of illiberal authors, and Brown's account in *Millennium* of Iain M. Banks's science fiction (Brown likes Banks's novels but not his liberal/socialist utopianism), show that the experience is common. Ekkehart Krippendorf writes insightfully about Wagner, whose music is perhaps the most difficult case of all in this respect. He suggests that anyone who has political objections to Wagner would be well advised not even to begin to listen to his music, so great is its seductive power. And while we are on the subject of questionable sentiments expressed in memorable music, what about The Band's anthem, "The Night They Drove Old Dixie Down"?[45] (A useful reminder, incidentally, that the sentiments expressed in a song need not be those of the songwriter or singer.) In sum: there are a number of authors and other artists one would not necessarily want to sit next to at dinner at the BISA Conference (Jünger, Céline, Pound, Kipling, Wagner, the list goes on . . .), but this does not have much bearing on the quality of their work.

The majority of the IR scholars whose work has been discussed in this section use literature to support or illustrate political or philosophical views they already hold. They are entitled to do this if they wish, but they cannot explain why their readers should share these views if they do not already do so. Coker equates literary merit with historical insight, and Bleiker and his colleagues equate it with the destabilisation of orthodox identities. In neither case is the assumption provided with adequate support. The selection of some works rather than others is not in itself problematic and is indeed (as I argued above) inevitable, but it is important that authors should be aware of the limits of their own samples and the partiality of their own visions. The authors I have dealt with up to now also write at times as though they consider themselves to be creating a tradition of politically aware literary scholarship from scratch, which is misleading. Equally curiously, these authors seem determined to ignore each other. As far as I can see, Coker and Bleiker do not mention each other's work, even though they share philosophical inspiration (both are Nietzscheans), and Coker and Shapiro even have some literary tastes in common, both being admirers of Don DeLillo's novels. If one takes the core of Bleiker's own position to be the belief that poetry, and poetry alone, is capable of having the desired effect on existing identities, an even more fundamental problem arises: why should we then bother to write and read academic articles, in prose, about the matter?

However, in concluding this section it is worth drawing attention to Bleiker's comment that aesthetic IR does not "supersede the need for more conventional social scientific enquiries".[46] He has therefore left the door leading to the rest of the discipline open, and one hopes it will not be slammed shut by those on the other side of the threshold. My own response to the more narrowly literary concerns of IR's aesthetic turn is not to assert that these authors have got things wrong, but to argue that the selectiveness of their respective approaches leaves them unable to appreciate alternatives. Casting the net wider will reveal a richer range of traditions of analysis in the area where literature meets politics than either Coker or Bleiker and his colleagues have recognised.

Bend it like Bakhtin: perspectives from literary studies

The person, be it gentleman or lady, who has not pleasure in a good novel, must be intolerably stupid.

Jane Austen—*Northanger Abbey* (Henry Tilney, hero, speaking to Catherine Morland, heroine)

A good place to start is with the presence in the IR literature of Mikhail Bakhtin. For a number of reasons, some good and others less so, Bakhtin seems to have become IR's literary theorist of choice. Of the scholars I have already mentioned, Bakhtin is cited by Brown, Neumann, Der Derian, Bleiker and several other *Alternatives* authors, Coker, Shapiro, and a number of contributors to Shapiro and Alker's collection including David Campbell.[47] Other IR authors who use or cite Bakhtin include Andrew Linklater, Peter Mandaville, and Xavier Guillaume (probably the fullest single treatment), though these authors do not examine his work on literature—indeed, they barely mention it.[48] Bakhtin's writings are widely recognised as one of the most important bodies of work to have survived Russia's tormented intellectual history in the 20th century. He was known to Soviet readers during his lifetime (1895–1975) as a literary scholar, the author of books on Dostoyevsky and Rabelais, though he thought of himself primarily as a *myslitel* (thinker or philosopher) and also wrote widely on the human sciences, the philosophy of language, and aesthetics. Bakhtin has become immensely influential since the 1980s throughout the fields of Western literary and cultural theory, and the most important transmission mechanism explaining his presence in IR is probably to be found in the writings of Tzvetan Todorov. Todorov's *The Conquest of America* introduces Bakhtin briefly into an exploration of the encounter between the Spanish conquerors and the indigenous population of America, and the subsequent destruction of the indigenous peoples, their cultures, and their societies. Bakhtin serves here as shorthand for dialogism, a different way of dealing with alterity.[49]

Although Bakhtin is clearly more than "just" a literary theorist, it is that aspect of his work that is most important in the present context.[50] His theory of the novel stresses "heteroglossia", the fact that the novel is made up of a system of official and unofficial languages interacting with one another. In Dostoyevsky's polyphonic or multi-voiced novels polyphony is a dialogue between discourses, a dialogue without any privileged, authoritative authorial meta-language. Here, all the competing points of view are presented as powerfully and profoundly as possible, characters enter into dialogue with the author and he with them, and no one has the last word: "One could say that Dostoyevsky created a new artistic model of the world."[51] This is contrasted both with the monological way Dostoyevsky wrote as a journalist or publicist and with Tolstoy's monologic novels, in which the characters may enter into dialogue with each other but the author's voice dominates. Another important concept, especially in Bakhtin's work on Rabelais, is the idea of carnival, a festive outburst of laughter that provides a temporary challenge to official culture and the established order and which Rabelais represents by means of "grotesque realism". Bakhtin uses the term "novel" not just for literary works of the modern era but also for works of Antiquity and the Middle Ages; the novel flourishes, he says, in eras in which stable verbal-ideological systems are disintegrating and speech diversity is intensifying. The 19th century is seen as such an era, and the impact of capitalism on 19th-century Russia provided the unstable conditions in which Dostoyevsky wrote his novels.

Bakhtin is introduced by IR scholars in a variety of ways. Brown does little more than reproduce some comments from the glossary provided by Bakhtin's translators.[52] Neumann, Guillaume, and Der Derian consider him—reasonably enough—a theorist of radical alterity and the self/other nexus. Campbell uses Bakhtin's "philosophical anthropology" to develop the idea of a political "prosaics" of everyday life. Bleiker's *Millennium* article seems to treat Bakhtin as the guiding spirit of the whole aesthetic turn in IR, appealing as it does (though without mentioning Bakhtin by name) to the need for "dialogical understanding" and "carnivalesque challenges".[53] But if Bleiker wishes to invoke Bakhtin in this way, he has all the more reason to clarify his position on the relationship between poetry and prose; Bakhtin is not entirely consistent on this point, but most of the time he states clearly that lyric poetry is *not* dialogic in the sense in which he applies this term to the novel. Coker, for his part, makes a series of elementary bibliographical and biographical mistakes about Bakhtin. The second edition of Bakhtin's book on Dostoyevsky was published in 1963, not in the "late 1950s", and it was an expanded second edition, not a republication; the book is not a study of "one of Dostoyevsky's novels", but deals with the whole spectrum of Dostoyevsky's novels and shorter fiction; Bakhtin was not exiled to Kazakhstan for "a large part of his life", but was exiled there for six years before being permitted to live in different towns in the Russian Federation.[54] To make matters worse, Coker misunderstands Bakhtin. Bakhtin was interested in the consciousness of Dostoyevsky's heroes, not in heroic consciousness as something that might be manifested on the battlefield. A philosopher less interested than Bakhtin in what happens on the battlefield could scarcely be imagined.

Most of these authors single out the idea of dialogue, but one has the feeling that Bakhtin is being wheeled on to support the author's views about dialogue and global identities before being wheeled off again, and that these IR scholars have taken just enough from Bakhtin to suit whatever purposes they have in mind. No attempt is made to compare his work with that of other literary scholars, which might establish its superiority as literary theory. Insufficient attention is paid to the idea of carnival, even though it is almost as important as dialogue within the scheme of Bakhtin's writings on literature.[55] There is also insufficient appreciation of Bakhtin's concern with the differences between the novel and other kinds of writing. I would exempt from these criticisms Shapiro, who has read Bakhtin carefully and suggests some contemporary artists whose work conforms to his model of literature (DeLillo's novels, and implicitly Robert Altman's films), and Louiza Odysseos, who uses Bakhtin as, it seems to me, he should be used: to help elucidate an autonomously posed question, relating in this case to classical comedy.[56] Nevertheless, most of these appropriations of Bakhtin by IR scholars are also uncritical, in the perfectly straightforward sense of the word: there is never any consideration of the possibility that Bakhtin might have been wrong about anything. Bleiker is almost an exception to this rule, as he gives Bakhtin a rap across the knuckles for not noticing that Rabelais treats women as faceless objects.[57] Unfortunately, this rests on a misinterpretation of the Rabelais passage cited.[58]

A number of complexities of the field of Bakhtinistics are left untouched by these IR scholars. Caryl Emerson's study of *The First Hundred Years of Mikhail Bakhtin* shows how, in both Russia and the West, he has been seen to have something to offer to every camp: in post-Soviet Russia, to liberal neo-humanists, philosophers of religion, nationalists, and even nostalgic Marxist-Leninists; in the West, to multiculturalists, deconstructionists, feminists, and Marxists—to which we can now add literary IRists. Emerson also shows that one theme of the Russian reception of his work has been a debate about whether or not dialogue and carnival conflict with each other (Bakhtin introduced the carnival motif into the second edition of his Dostoyevsky book, but it sits uncomfortably alongside the analysis in terms of dialogue).[59] In addition to this debate, not everyone agrees that Dostoyevsky's novels are polyphonic,[60] and Todorov argues that Bakhtin's attempts to distinguish the epic from the novel are incoherent. Emerson traces the interpretive battles within the "Bakhtin industry" and the "legacy wars", and suggests that, in general: "Russians read Bakhtin as a culturologist rather than a politically acute multiculturalist".[61] Emerson herself is a stern critic of the "cult" of the master, of his perceived relevance to everything, and of attempts to recruit him for radical political causes. She reports the weary comment of a colleague on "the completely out-of-control genre of 'Bakhtin and Brussel Sprouts'",[62] and clearly does not consider him to have been a political thinker. Emerson is, however, encouraged to observe that by the mid- to late 1990s it was no longer possible to speak of a division between "Russian" and "Western" Bakhtinistics.

Just as Bakhtin is more than a literary theorist, so literary scholarship consists of a good deal more than Bakhtin. Any good literary theory reader or introduction to the field[63] will guide IR scholars through the history of different theoretical traditions, from the Russian formalists who have influenced Alker, via the liberal humanist tradition that saw the study of (English) literature as the "supremely civilizing pursuit",[64] and on into the range of structuralist and poststructuralist, psychoanalytic, Marxist, feminist, postcolonial, and new historicist approaches available to students of literature and hence, if IRists wish to take a literary turn, to IR as well. As we have seen, the postcolonial and to some extent the feminist and poststructuralist traditions can be identified as influences on Bleiker and some of his colleagues, and before the ascendancy of Bakhtin, Said was probably the most frequently cited literary scholar within IR—though this judgement might depend on whether one treats Derrida as a philosopher or a literary theorist. It may well be that the absence of any discernible Marxist influence in IR's literary turn (unless one unconvincingly classifies Bakhtin as a Marxist) is another indication of the decline of Marxist thought in Western academia.

Rather than make a doomed attempt to do justice to the whole of this literature, I will now single out two literary scholars whose work helps us to explore further some of the issues raised by Coker and Bleiker. Any such selection may appear arbitrary, but the objective is to reinforce the suggestion that there are alternatives to the approaches we have seen so far, not to demonstrate that they are wrong. Of the scholars I have chosen one, Gabriel Josipovici, would normally be considered an unpolitical critic, while the other, Franco Moretti, relates literature more directly to history and politics. Both have important things to say about the nature of literary representation and the functions of fiction.

Gabriel Josipovici's work provides a literary-historical perspective that helps us to engage with Bleiker's position on representation.[65] Josipovici begins by explaining the beliefs held by medieval Christian authors about the relationship between their writings and the world. When Dante wrote the *Divine Comedy* at the beginning of the 14th century, he considered himself to be creating a work to imitate a universe that was itself a book written by God. Anyone reading the poem would join the author on a journey towards salvation. Even by the time of Chaucer in the late 14th century this belief had begun to weaken, and by the 16th century (Rabelais) it had almost completely disappeared. Josipovici is no admirer of the traditional novel of the 18th and 19th centuries, which, he argues, tried to deny the artificiality and autonomy of fiction and to pretend that there could be a direct correspondence between the world and the words written by a novelist: "One could say that the traditional novel tries to make us forget that what we are reading is only a book."[66] Josipovici takes particular exception to Dickens, whom he accuses of sentimentality, bathos, and ludicrous plots. He therefore ignores both the disingenuous realist novel and postmodernist works which mistakenly conclude, he says, that the impossibility of correspondence between the book and the world means literary texts can be nothing more than games played with the reader.[67] The most significant literary works for Josipovici are, alongside Dante and Shakespeare, modernist, anti-representational "anti-novels" written by authors who knew that their books were just books rather than mirrors of the world. In these works it is the presence of the author in the text, and not the author as a historical person, that engages the reader's attention. There is no salvation at the end of a modernist novel, only—most notably in Proust, Kafka, and Beckett, the authors to whom Josipovici returns repeatedly (and in some respects rather repetitiously[68])—the possibility that individual readers will be able to recognise the patterns of their own lives and eventual deaths.

One could perhaps object that Josipovici has too narrow a conception of literary modernism. Malcolm Bradbury and James McFarlane, for example, offer a more political reading, seeing modernism as "a celebration of the technological age and a condemnation of it".[69] However, Josipovici himself clearly believes that it is a mistake to treat fiction as a way of illuminating global history or politics, which is Coker's approach. He shares some of Bleiker's reservations about mimetic prose, but clearly—and surely rightly—rejects the view that prose fiction cannot problematise the representational functions of language. Furthermore, once the book has been cut loose from the world in the way Josipovici describes, it is doubtful whether literature can be reattached to alternative political projects in the way authors such as Rorty and Bleiker wish to see. For Josipovici, reading is a much more private and potentially more unsettling experience than either Coker or Bleiker would allow. This does not preclude the possibility of aesthetic pleasure, though Josipovici is only marginally concerned with psychological explanations for the popularity of realist fiction; he rather loftily suggests that those who prefer it to modernist writing are simply mistaken. But just as one can enjoy a novel without approving of its political implications, so too can one be simultaneously entertained and disturbed.

Other critics proceed differently. Franco Moretti's work addresses some of these issues from a perspective that Moretti himself terms "materialist", and which is indebted to Marxist traditions of literary scholarship. His main contribution consists of his attempt to provide something like a systematic account of the relationship between world literature, or at least a significant section of it, and world history.[70] Moretti starts from his own area of expertise, West European narrative fiction published between 1790 and 1930. He develops a "sociology of literary forms", which he explains with the help of ideas imported from economic history, in the form of world-system theory, and to a lesser extent from biology, in the form of a Darwinist analogy applied to literary evolution. The task of literary history, he argues, is to explain how certain aesthetic forms that were originally created as experiments eventually come to be accepted as the norm, and this requires us to attend to the historical framework within which rhetorical conventions function. The *Bildungsroman* of the late 18th to mid-19th century (classically represented by Goethe's *Wilhelm Meister* novels) was the symbolic form adopted by European culture in response to the shocks of modernity and the French Revolution, dramatising the conflict between the ideal of individual self-determination and the demands of socialisation. While the realist novel emerged from the era of the French Revolution, European modernism was associated with the age of imperialism. The world-system model is used to explain the fact that outside its historical core, England and France (the "narrative superpowers" of the 19th century), the modern novel first arose not as an autonomous development but as a compromise between an English or French formal influence and local materials. This process, he argues, can be seen at work in the literary history of Eastern Europe, Southern Europe, Latin America, and other regions.[71] Moretti argues further that the European novel ceased to innovate during the course of the 20th century, and Europe now imports new literary products from Latin America and from English- and French-speaking countries in Asia, Africa and elsewhere (there is an obvious affinity with postcolonial analysis here).[72]

In his most ambitious book, *Modern Epic*, Moretti looks in detail at a category of works that have become the "sacred texts of the western world".[73] These works, he says, are more than novels. They reveal important things about the West's capacity for violence and drive to dominate the world, and they are all polyphonous and flawed masterpieces with indecisive endings that do not conclude the text or fix its meaning. Most of them were produced in the semi-peripheries of the Western world, which means everywhere outside the Anglo-French core in this period. Among these locations are German-speaking Europe (Goethe's *Faust*, Musil's *Man Without Qualities*, plus Wagner's *Ring*), America (Melville's *Moby-Dick*), Ireland (Joyce's *Ulysses*, not, of course, actually written in Ireland), and, now that the old European core has lost its significance in the age of *Weltliteratur*, Latin America in García Márquez's *One Hundred Years of Solitude*. For some reason Moretti appears not to think much of Proust, which leaves a large Proust-shaped hole at the centre of his treatment of the sacred texts of the modern West. It is clear that Proust does not fit the model: *À la recherche du temps perdu* was written in France, tells us nothing about global capitalism, and has a perfect ending. But all this is a problem for Moretti, not for Proust.

Moretti challenges Bakhtin on a number of points. The ironic multiplication of different points of view within the novel leads, he suggests, to skepticism rather than an open, flexible response as Bakhtin claims, and the Bakhtinian belief that heteroglossia generates dialogue cannot be sustained. If the text contains numerous heterogeneous languages, how can dialogue between them be possible? Monologues and misunderstandings are more likely, as is typically the case in the English comic novel.[74] Moretti argues further that it is not the novel, in which everyone lives in the same period and speaks the same language, that is the truly polyphonic literary form of the modern West, but rather the epic, in which there is no present and voices from the past and future coexist and permit multiple interpretations of the work (he shows this particularly well in the cases of *Faust* and *Ulysses*). Russia, he says, produced the undeniably polyphonic novel of ideas, a curious hybrid form somewhere between epic and novel, but this was an exception to general European rules of literary evolution. In essence, then, Moretti says that Bakhtin's model, developed on the basis of the Russian novel, cannot be applied to the European novel as such. (In defence of Bakhtin, one could argue that the master did not think his model applied to all novels, though he does treat Dostoyevsky's works as the purest form of imaginative literature and something to which, by implication, other novelists should aspire.)

Moretti insists that his conception of literature is neither deconstructive nor liberating. The main function of literature, he says, is to secure consent and to reconcile individuals to the world they live in and its prevailing cultural norms, and to do this in the most pleasurable way possible. This can be achieved by the use of reconciliatory, conventionally happy endings, frequently involving marriage in the realist novel, or alternatively through unhappy endings which the reader accepts because there appears to be no alternative. Moretti does not intend this to be read as an application of Freudian orthodoxy to literature, since he argues that Freud treated art and culture as purely repressive and failed to understand the importance of aesthetic pleasure in providing adjustment to the existing order—though Freud does help to explain why our desire to attain this feeling of adjustment is so strong.[75]

What follows from this? Certainly not any kind of imputation that Coker or Bleiker should abandon what they have been doing up until now and take their agenda from Josipovici or Moretti. I am not sure that either Josipovici or Moretti is right about the traditional novel. How many realist novelists seriously try to convince their readers that they are not reading a novel? And when I read and enjoy Balzac or Dickens, in what sense can I be said to be giving my consent to early French capitalism or the industrialisation of Britain? In addition, the different parts of Moretti's account (admittedly written over a number of years) do not fit together very well. If the main function of literature is to secure consent, how can it be that a number of the works conventionally considered masterpieces function in such a way as to undermine that consent? Nevertheless, if traditional lit. crit. can be represented by a scholar of Josipovici's subtlety and the Marxist tradition can still produce a critic as readable and engaging as Moretti (the man even seems to enjoy reading literature), these bodies of work deserve the attention of literary IRists.

This section has argued that other traditions of literary scholarship can challenge IRists to reconsider their positions, and shown that they address directly questions of aesthetic experience that IR scholars interested in literature have tended to avoid. It is also noticeable that the apparently more "political" of my selected literary scholars denies that literature can have any kind of emancipatory function, while the apparently unpolitical one could be read as holding out the possibility of some kind of liberating experience attained via literature, albeit one that would be purely individual. Equally importantly, the work of these scholars does not undermine itself in the manner of some literary political scientists: it shows us that there are good reasons to read academic literary criticism at the same time as we read novels or poetry.

Conclusion

It has become almost commonplace in recent years to lament the way in which increasing specialisation in the academy has, it is said, been detrimental to creativity: sub-fields within disciplines barely communicate with each other, different social sciences develop in isolation, and social scientists do not speak to their colleagues in the humanities. IR has been strongly affected by this mood as its boundaries have become increasingly indistinct and scholars within the discipline have called for greater interdisciplinary openness and even for transdisciplinarity, the removal of existing disciplinary borders and distinctions. Although this article has not been unsympathetic to these aspirations, it has shown that IR's transdisciplinary excursions and incursions into the literary field are not as unproblematic as some of their advocates imply.

The article has identified a number of different ways in which (world) literature can be approached, some more and some less obviously "political": as a source of historical insight (Coker); as a way of destabilising conventional identities (Bleiker and others); as an inherently dialogic cultural form (Bakhtin—the argument applies to the novel but not to poetry); as something that reminds readers of their own mortality (Josipovici); as a pleasurable source of reconciliation with the existing social order (Moretti). This list is unlikely to be complete. The article has not argued that any one of these approaches is mistaken, but it has sought to show that none of them is self-evidently preferable to the others. I have suggested that claims made implicitly by IR scholars to the effect that they have created a new field of literary-political studies are misplaced, as the literary field is already diverse enough to be aware of issues relating to literary representation, to political aspects of literary history, and to the relationship between politics and aesthetic pleasure. I have also shown that it is even possible to disagree with Bakhtin. My cautionary message is that IR scholars should be more restrained in making claims about their capacity to innovate radically in this area, and should be more aware of and prepared to engage with the specific debates conducted within other disciplines. Some IR scholars have been rather cavalier in seeking to extend the purview of their discipline, have tended to select only what suits them from the field of literary studies, and so have failed to do justice to the complexity of the field they are moving into. There has been some very casual reading of Bakhtin.

Perhaps, therefore, true interdisciplinarity is an ideal fated to remain just out of reach. The field of world literature and world politics has nevertheless established itself, and anyone with an interest in interdisciplinarity should welcome this development. The range of literary works and questions with which IR *could* concern itself is vast, and in this sense the field cannot have "a" research agenda. As IR scholars proceed with their work in this area they will need to be mindful of two dangers. On the one hand, they may be tempted to try to cover the whole literary field, and their work may turn into a kind of general catalogue unable to say much about individual works (to say nothing of the problem of the great unread). If, as is more likely, they concentrate on a smaller selection of works, the selection process itself will involve political-aesthetic judgements. These are quite legitimate, but scholars need to remember that neither their own substitute canon nor the particular way in which they deal with the works selected can be authoritative. Relativism in respect of different approaches seems—so far at least—inevitable. In some respects the plight of scholars interested in this field is not unlike that of Thomas Mann's Herr Settembrini, an advocate of humanism and enlightenment who is resident on the slopes of the magic mountain. Settembrini is engaged in a struggle to shape the world-view of the naive young Hans Castorp, and has also been allotted the task of writing a survey of all those works of world literature in which the problem of human suffering is addressed. The purpose of this project, conducted under the auspices of the International League for the Organisation of Progress, is to contribute to human self-realisation and happiness. Settembrini sets about his task but is destined never to complete it. Like the other patients in Hofrat Behrens's clinic he is suffering from tuberculosis, which slows his progress, and when war breaks out in 1914 he departs to devote his remaining energies to the Italian war effort. But as my quotation indicates, Herr Settembrini does not allow himself to be daunted by the enormity of his task, and the affectionate irony of Mann's attitude to his characters does not deny them the right to undertake such ventures. The mere fact that we are unlikely to complete a project should not deter us from commencing it.

Notes

1   I would like to thank *Global Society*'s two anonymous reviewers for their comments and suggestions (though they will see that I have not been able to follow all of these), and Jarrod Wiener for agreeing to consider a manuscript of greater length than the journal would normally publish. The acknowledgement of an older debt is also in order. The seeds of the idea of interdisciplinarity as a set of mutually beneficial relationships between history, literature, philosophy, and politics were sown in my mind when I was an MA student (of Russian Studies) at the University of Sussex in the late 1970s. Many years later and having ended up in IR, I would like to take this opportunity to acknowledge my debt to those who taught me in that spirit and to express the hope that this article reflects at least some elements of that interdisciplinary ideal.

2   For a recent article which, perhaps unwittingly, gives expression to both of these reactions see Barry Buzan and Richard Little, "Why International Relations has Failed as an Intellectual Project and What to do About it", *Millennium: Journal of International Studies*, Vol. 30, No. 1 (2001).

3   "Weltliteratur", in *Lexikon der Weltliteratur im 20. Jahrhundert*, Vol. 2 (Freiburg: Herder, 1961); on the history of the concept of literature, see "Literature", in Raymond Williams, *Keywords: A Vocabulary of Culture and Society* (London: Fontana, 1983).

4   Reiner Wild, "Ueberlegungen zu Goethes Konzept einer Weltliteratur", in Hans W. Panthel and Peter Rau (eds.), *Bausteine zu einem transatlantischen Literaturverständnis* (Frankfurt am Main: Peter Lang, 1994).

5   Karl Marx and Friedrich Engels, "Manifesto of the Communist Party", in Lewis S. Feuer (ed.), *Marx and Engels: Basic Writings on Politics and Philosophy* (n.p.: Fontana, 1969 [1848]), p. 53.

6   Franco Moretti, "Conjectures on World Literature", *New Left Review* (II), 1 (2000).

7   Franco Moretti, "The Slaughterhouse of Literature", *Modern Language Quarterly*, Vol. 61, No. 1 (2000).

8   Terry Eagleton, *The Idea of Culture* (Oxford: Blackwell, 2000), p. 32.

9   Two examples: John Boli and George M. Thomas, "World Culture in the World Polity: A Century of International Non-governmental Organization", *American Sociological Review*, Vol. 62, No. 2 (1997); David Held, Anthony McGrew, David Goldblatt and Jonathan Perraton, *Global Transformations: Politics, Economics, and Culture* (Cambridge: Polity Press, 1999), especially ch. 7, "Globalization, Culture and the Fate of Nations".

10   Christine Sylvester, *Feminist Theory and International Relations in a Postmodern Era* (Cambridge: Cambridge University Press, 1994); and *Feminist International Relations: An Unfinished Journey* (Cambridge: Cambridge University Press, 2002).

11   For example: Cynthia Weber, "IR: The Resurrection or New Frontiers of Incorporation", *European Journal of International Relations*, Vol. 5, No. 4 (1999).

12   Martin Wight, *International Theory: The Three Traditions*, Gabriele Wight and Brian Porter (eds.) (Leicester and London: Leicester University Press for the Royal Institute of International Affairs, 1991).

13   *Ibid.*, p. 258.

14   James Der Derian, "A Reinterpretation of Realism: Genealogy, Semiology, Dromology", in Der Derian (ed.), *International Theory: Critical Investigations* (Basingstoke: Macmillan, 1995). See also Der Derian's remarks on spy fiction in his *Antidiplomacy: Spies, Terror, Speed, and War* (Cambridge, MA and Oxford: Blackwell, 1992).

15   Benedict Anderson, *Imagined Communities: Reflections on the Origin and Spread of Nationalism*, revised edn (London and New York: Verso, 1991).

16   Ali Mazrui, "*The Satanic Verses* or a Satanic Novel? Moral Dilemmas of the Rushdie Affair", *Alternatives*, Vol. XV, No. 1 (1990); Reza Afshari, "Ali Mazrui or Salman Rushdie: *The Satanic Verses* and Islamist Politics", *Alternatives*, Vol. 16, No. 1 (1991); Fred Halliday, *Islam and the Myth of Confrontation: Religion and Politics in the Middle East* (London and New York: I.B. Tauris, 1996), pp. 123–27.

17   Ekkehart Krippendorff, *Politische Interpretationen. Shakespeare, Stendhal, Balzac, Wagner, Haŏek, Kafka, Kraus* (Frankfurt am Main: Suhrkamp, 1990), *Goethe. Politik gegen den Zeitgeist* (Frankfurt am Main and Leipzig: Insel, 1999), and *Die Kunst, nicht regiert zu werden. Ethische Politik von Sokrates bis Mozart* (Frankfurt am Main: Suhrkamp, 1999); Dieter Senghaas, *Klänge des Friedens. Ein Hörbericht* (Frankfurt am Main: Suhrkamp, 2001).

18   Frances Stonor Saunders, *Who Paid the Piper? The CIA and the Cultural Cold War* (London: Granta Books, 2000); Christine Sylvester, "Picturing the Cold War: An Art Graft/Eye Graft", *Alternatives*, Vol. 21, No. 4 (1996); Fred Halliday, "'High and Just Proceedings': Notes Towards an Anthology of the Cold War", *Millennium: Journal of International Studies*, Vol. 30, No. 3 (2001).

19   Malcolm Bradbury, "What was Post-modernism? The Arts in and after the Cold War", *International Affairs*, Vol. 71, No. 4 (1995).

20   Richard Rorty, *Contingency, Irony, and Solidarity* (Cambridge: Cambridge University Press, 1989), and "Introduction: Antirepresentationalism, Ethnocentrism, and Liberalism", in *Objectivity, Relativism, and Truth: Philosophical Papers Volume I* (Cambridge: Cambridge University Press, 1991); Martha C. Nussbaum, *Love's Knowledge: Essays on Philosophy and Literature* (New York and Oxford: Oxford University Press, 1990).

21   Nussbaum, *Ibid.*, p. 5; Nussbaum is, strictly speaking, attributing this view to Henry James and making it her own.

22   Hayward R. Alker, *Rediscoveries and Reformulations: Humanistic Methodologies for International Studies* (Cambridge: Cambridge University Press, 1996).

23   *Ibid.*, p. 3.

24   *Ibid.*, p. 182.

25   For these and other criticisms, see John Horton and Andrea T. Baumeister (eds.), *Literature and the Political Imagination* (London and New York: Routledge, 1996).

26   Roland Bleiker, "The Aesthetic Turn in International Political Theory", Introduction to Special Issue: Images and Narratives in World Politics, *Millennium: Journal of International Studies*, Vol. 30, No. 3 (2001).

27   James Der Derian, *Virtuous War: Mapping the Military-Industrial-Media-Entertainment Network* (Boulder: Westview Press, 2001), especially ch. 9; this may also apply to Bleiker himself—see Bleiker, "The Aesthetic Turn", *op. cit.*, pp. 522–23.

28   Christopher Coker: *Reflections on American Foreign Policy since 1945* (London: Pinter and John Spiers, 1989), *War and the 20th Century: A Study of War and Modern Consciousness* (London and Washington, DC: Brassey's, 1994), *War and the Illiberal Conscience* (Boulder: Westview Press, 1998), *Twilight of the West* (Boulder: Westview Press, 1998), and *Humane Warfare* (London and New York, Routledge, 2001).

29   Coker, *War and the 20th Century, op. cit.*, pp. 128–40.

30   Compare Coker, *ibid.*, pp. 45–46 with Coker, *War and the Illiberal Conscience, op. cit.*, pp. 64–65.

31   This summary is distilled from: Roland Bleiker, "Forget IR Theory", *Alternatives*, Vol. 22, No. 1 (1997), "Retracing and Redrawing the Boundaries of Events: Postmodern Interferences with International Theory", *Alternatives*, Vol. 23, No. 4 (1998), "Editor's Introduction" to Special Issue: Poetic World Politics, *Alternatives*, Vol. 25, No. 3 (2000), *Popular Dissent, Human Agency and Global Politics* (Cambridge: Cambridge University Press, 2000), and "The Aesthetic Turn", *op. cit.*

32   Bleiker, "The Aesthetic Turn", *op. cit.*, p. 511.

33   Michael J. Shapiro, "Introduction", in Shapiro and Hayward R. Alker (eds.), *Challenging Boundaries: Global Flows, Territorial Identities* (Minneapolis: University of Minnesota Press, 1996), p. xxii.

34   Michael J. Shapiro, *Reading the Postmodern Polity: Political Theory as Textual Practice* (Minneapolis and Oxford: University of Minnesota Press, 1992).

35   Bleiker, "Editor's Introduction", *op. cit.*, pp. 271–72, 276, 280.

36   Roland Bleiker, "'Give it the Shade': Paul Celan and the Politics of Apolitical Poetry", *Political Studies*, Vol. XLVII, No. 4 (1999), "Pablo Neruda and the Struggle for Political Memory", *Third World Quarterly*, Vol. 20, No. 6 (1999), and "Stroll through the Wall: Everyday Poetics of Cold War Politics", *Alternatives*, Vol. 25, No. 3 (2000). The case of the East Berlin poets is also examined in Bleiker's *Popular Dissent*.

37   The privileging of poetry is stated explicitly in Costas M. Constantinou, "Poetics of Security", *Alternatives*, Vol. 25, No. 3 (2000); and Anthony Burke, "Poetry outside Security", *Alternatives*, Vol. 25, No. 3 (2000).

38   Bleiker, "The Aesthetic Turn", *op. cit.*, p. 533.

39   Bleiker, "Redrawing and Retracing the Boundaries", *op. cit.*, p. 493.

40   Nicholas Higgins, "The Zapatista Uprising and the Poetics of Cultural Resistance", and Paul Routledge, "Geopolitics of Resistance—India's Baliapal Movement", both in *Alternatives*, Vol. 25, No. 3 (2000).

41   Michael J. Shapiro, *Cinematic Political Thought: Narrating Race, Nation and Gender* (Edinburgh University Press: Edinburgh, 1999), and "Sounds of Nationhood", *Millennium: Journal of International Studies*, Vol. 30, No. 3 (2001).

42   This may sound like an oversimplification, but it is not; see Shapiro, *Cinematic Political Thought*, *op. cit.*, p. 63.

43   Edward W. Said, *Culture and Imperialism* (London: Vintage, 1994), pp. 159–96.

44   Der Derian is the interesting exception who proves the rule. His book *Virtuous War* (*op. cit.*) captures very well (and entertainingly) the technological-aesthetic seductiveness of the products of the "military-industrial-media-entertainment network"—digitalised wargames, crisis simulations, and assorted mysterious acronyms. To protect his own virtue, Der Derian arms himself with theories of virtuality; thus, like Odysseus ordering the sailors to tie him to the mast, he is able to resist the allures of these sirens.

45   Some older readers may remember The Band. Those who do not are advised to avoid Joan Baez's version, which takes all the anger out of the song.

46   Bleiker, "The Aesthetic Turn", *op. cit.*, p. 510.

47   Chris Brown, "'Turtles All the Way Down': Anti-foundationalism, Critical Theory and International Relations", *Millennium: Journal of International Studies*, Vol. 23, No. 2 (1994); Iver B. Neumann, *Uses of the Other: "The East" in European Identity Formation* (Manchester: Manchester University Press, 1999); James Der Derian, "Post-theory: The Eternal Return of Ethics in International Relations", in Michael W. Doyle and G. John Ikenberry (eds.), *New Thinking in International Relations Theory* (Boulder: Westview Press, 1997), and "Act IV. Fathers (and Sons), Mother Courage (and Her Children), and the Dog, the Cave, and the Beef", in James N. Rosenau (ed.), *Global Voices: Dialogues in International Relations* (Boulder: Westview Press, 1993); Shapiro, *Reading the Postmodern Polity*, *op. cit.*; David Campbell, "Political Prosaics, Transversal Politics, and the Anarchical World", in Shapiro and Alker, *Challenging Boundaries*, *op. cit.*

48   Andrew Linklater, "The Changing Contours of Critical International Relations Theory", in Richard Wyn Jones (ed.), *Critical Theory and World Politics* (Boulder and London: Lynne Rienner, 2001); Peter Mandaville, *Transnational Muslim Politics: Reimagining the umma* (London and New York: Routledge, 2001); Xavier Guillaume, "Foreign Policy and the Politics of Alterity: A Dialogical Understanding of International Relations", *Millennium: Journal of International Studies*, Vol. 31, No. 1 (2002).

49   Tzvetan Todorov, *Die Eroberung Amerikas. Das Problem des Anderen* (Frankfurt am Main: Suhrkamp, 1985); for more detail, see Todorov's *Mikhail Bakhtin: The Dialogical Principle* (Minneapolis: University of Minnesota Press, 1984).

50   Mikhail Bakhtin, *The Dialogic Imagination: Four Essays*, Michael Holquist (ed.), Caryl Emerson and Michael Holquist (trans.) (Austin: University of Texas Press, 1981), *Problems of Dostoevsky's Poetics*, Caryl Emerson (ed. and trans.), Introduction by Wayne C. Booth (University of Minnesota Press: Minneapolis, 1984 [translation of 2nd edn of *Problemy poetiki Dostoevskogo*, published 1963]), *Tvorchestvo Fransua Rable i narodnaya kul'tura Srednevekov'ya i Renessansa* (Orange, CT and Dusseldorf: Izdatel'stvo "Antikvariat", 1986 [main text written 1940, first published 1965]), *The Bakhtin Reader: Selected Writings of Bakhtin, Medvedev and Voloshinov*, Pam Morris (ed.) (London: Edward Arnold, 1994), and "Dostoevskii. 1961g.", in *M.M. Bakhtin. Sobranie sochinenii T. 5. Raboty 1940-kh—nachala 1960-kh godov* (Moskva: "Russkie slovari", 1996 [written 1961, first published 1994]).

51   Bakhtin, "Dostoevskii. 1961g.", *op. cit.*, p. 369.

52   Compare Brown, *op. cit.*, pp. 228–29, with Bakhtin, *The Dialogic Imagination, op. cit.*, p. 428.

53   Bleiker, "The Aesthetic Turn", *op. cit.*, pp. 523, 526.

54   Coker, *War and the 20th Century, op. cit.*, pp. 44–46. For more accurate accounts see Todorov, *Mikhail Bakhtin, op. cit.*, and the Introduction to Bakhtin, *The Dialogic Imagination, op. cit.*

55   Bakhtin, *Tvorchestvo Fransua Rable, op. cit.*; Nikolai Pan'kov, "M.M. Bakhtin: Ranyaya versiya kontseptsii karnavala. V pamyat' o davnei nauchnoi diskussii", *Voprosy literatury*, 5 (1997).

56   Louiza Odysseos, "Laughing Matters: Peace, Democracy and the Challenge of the Comic Narrative", *Millennium: Journal of International Studies*, Vol. 30, No. 3 (2001).

57   Bleiker, *Popular Dissent, op. cit.*, p. 204.

58   According to the Folio edition of *Gargantua*, what Rabelais is doing in the passage in question is parodying a biblical idiom which omitted to include women and children in lists of those involved in a particular event. Of course, there is a good deal in Rabelais to which contemporary feminists may object, and this tradition is alien to Bakhtin. In this particular instance, though, Rabelais is making a point of *including* women, which is surely not bad for 1534. See François Rabelais, *Gargantua* (Paris: Gallimard, 1965 [first published 1534]), pp. 164–65.

59   On this point and for a detailed reconstruction of the Soviet and Russian reception of Bakhtin, see Caryl Emerson, *The First Hundred Years of Mikhail Bakhtin* (Princeton: Princeton University Press, 1997).

60   Louis Allain, "K voprosu o 'nezavisimykh golosakh' geroev v romanakh Dostoevskogo (tezisy protiv Bakhtina)", *Slavia Orientalis*, Vol. XLV, No. 1 (1996); S. Lominadze, "Perechityvaya Dostoevskogo i Bakhtina", *Voprosy literatury*, 1 (2001).

61   Emerson, *The First Hundred Years, op. cit.*, p. 69.

62   Caryl Emerson, "Review Article—A Bakhtin for the Twenty-first Century: Double-voiced, Double-faced, Face to Face", *Slavonic and East European Review*, Vol. 77, No. 2 (1999).

63   Philip Rice and Patricia Waugh (eds.), *Modern Literary Theory: A Reader*, 3rd edn (London: Arnold, 1996); Terry Eagleton, *Literary Theory: An Introduction* (Oxford: Basil Blackwell, 1983).

64   Eagleton, *Literary Theory, op. cit.*, p. 31.

65   Gabriel Josipovici, *The World and the Book: A Study of Modern Fiction* (London and Basingstoke: Macmillan, 1971).

66   *Ibid.*, p. 217.

67   Gabriel Josipovici, *The Lessons of Modernism and Other Essays*, 2nd edn (Basingstoke: Macmillan, 1987), *Text and Voice: Essays 1981–1991* (Manchester and New York: Carcanet & St. Martin's Press, 1992), and *On Trust: Art and the Temptations of Suspicion* (New Haven and London: Yale University Press, 1999).

68   Josipovici rarely writes about more recent fiction or new discoveries, though one of the exceptions, his essay on Georges Perec's *Life: A User's Manual* (in *Text and Voice*), is quite superb.

69   Malcolm Bradbury and James McFarlane, "The Name and Nature of Modernism", in Bradbury and McFarlane (eds.), *Modernism: A Guide to European Literature 1890–1930* (London: Penguin, 1991 [1976]), p. 46.

70   Franco Moretti, "Conjectures on World Literature", *op. cit.*, "The Slaughterhouse of Literature", *op. cit.*, *The Way of the World: The Bildungsroman in European Culture* (London: Verso, 1987), "Modern European Literature: A Geographical Sketch", *New Left Review* (I), 206 (1994), *Modern Epic: The World System from Goethe to García Márquez* (London and New York: Verso, 1996), *Signs Taken for Wonders: Essays in the Sociology of Literary Forms*, 3rd edn (London and New York: Verso, 1997 [1983]), and *Atlas of the European Novel 1800–1900* (London and New York: Verso, 1998). Moretti's *Atlas* is cited by Shapiro at one point.

71   Moretti, *Atlas of the European Novel, op. cit.*, and "Conjectures on World Literature", *op. cit.*

72   For a challenge to Moretti which criticises him for failing to address the problem of "the unavowed imperialism of English", see Jonathan Arac, "Anglo-Globalism?", *New Left Review* (II), 16 (2002), quotation from p. 44.

73   Moretti, *Modern Epic, op. cit.*, p. 39.

74   Moretti, *The Way of the World, op. cit.*

75   Moretti, *Signs Taken for Wonders, op. cit.*, especially the essay on "The Soul and the Harpy".

Chapter 24

Sarah N. Lawall

ANTHOLOGIZING "WORLD
LITERATURE" (2004)

ARAH N. LAWALL (B. 1934) IS PROFESSOR EMERITA of Comparative
Literature at the University of Massachusetts, Amherst. Her research interests combine literary phenomenology, poetry and poetics, surrealism, and the work of Yves Bonnefoy. She is credited with having introduced the so-called Geneva School of Criticism to the US audience with *Critics of Consciousness: The Existential Structures of Literature* (1968), in which she chronologically discussed the major works of phenomenologically inclined European literary critics such as Albert Béguin, Maurice Blanchot, Georges Poulet, Marcel Raymond, Jean-Pierre Richard, Jean Rousset and Jean Starobinski, as well as the first three critical works of the American J. Hillis Miller. She also contributed to the translation of works by a number of classical authors (a.o. Euripides). The phenomelogical approach to literature as an act, and not as an object, proved influential in the way Lawall later dealt with the concept and practice of world literature.

Lawall's work on world literature began in the early 1970s, when she was asked to review the third edition of the Norton anthology *World Masterpieces: Literature of Western Culture* (1973). From then on, she has been involved in the compilation of several editions of Norton anthologies, from the first one mentioned—whose title has been changed into *The Norton Anthology of World Masterpieces: The Western Tradition*— to *The Norton Anthology of Western Literature* and *The Norton Anthology of World Literature*. Her understanding of anthologies of world literature is indebted to, on the one hand, the role they play in the educational system and, on the other hand, the way the reader gives meaning to the works selected within the framework of the anthology itself and additional materials. As to the former issue, Lawall approaches anthologies of Western/world literature as a "literary genre" devised for a setting—undergraduate seminars on world literature—which is "a uniquely American institution" (1988: 53). As for the latter issue, in the same way that Lawall stressed the relevance of phenomeno-logical aesthetics in René Wellek's literary-theoretical principles, she shows great concern for what one may call "intercultural phenomenology", that is, the problems posed by a horizon of expectation which "moves outward to embrace unfamiliar cultures" in anthologies of world literature.[i]

All these issues are discussed by Lawall herself and other contributors in the book she edited in 1994, *Reading World Literature: Theory, History, Practice*, whose Introduction begins by highlighting the individual and collective experience of reading world literature: "For the individual reader, it promises vicarious experience and personal growth as well as the excitement of an aesthetic voyage among masterpieces. For society and its educational institutions, world literature offers a pleasurable way to prepare broadly informed, self-confident, and adaptable citizens" (Lawall 1994: 1). "Anthologizing 'World Literature' " identifies and discusses three key issues related to such anthologies, namely, the editorial challenge, the task of the anthologist, and the phenomenological and hermeneutical changes operated by the anthology of world literature.

Sarah Lawall, "Anthologizing 'World Literature'," *On Anthologies: Politics and Pedagogy*, Ed. Jeffrey R. Di Leo, Lincoln: U of Nebraska Press, 2004, pp. 47–89.

> "I seek a form ..."
>
> —Rubén Darío

> "It's difficult to imagine a form to fit such content."
>
> —Richard S. Pressman

Anthologizing "world literature" is a unique editorial challenge with its own special history. First, it is burdened by pedagogical associations with a narrowly Western canon and by a critical history that runs from Goethe's national stereotypes engaged in privileged conversation to the idealist implications of Great Books. Second, theoretical attempts to define the anthologist's task run into the extraordinary ambiguity of the terms world and literature (Lawall, "Reading World Literature"). More objective terms have been proposed: *globe* for *world* and global literary studies for a newly scientific approach based on cultural data. Yet the subject matter is still unclear, and globalization—as Ian Baucom notes—tends to impose static paradigms and a methodology that does not allow for relational dynamics. The inevitable selectivity of the anthology format draws attention to gaps in both global and "world literature" coverage, and the anthology's table of contents is also scrutinized for its relevance to "literary" standards vis-à-vis various forms of cultural production. Finally, world literature anthologies are still anthologies: they extract individual texts from their original settings and reassemble them as a collectivity produced for a contemporary audience. The result is often seen not as the passionate exchange of eager voices that Goethe envisaged but as an academic construction with a manual-like facade of authority that chills inquiry and critical speculation.

So much for the bad news. In contrast, I prefer to see anthologies as a theoretically interesting form whose potential for opening up discourse has yet to be sufficiently explored; moreover, I believe that the academic anthology, situated at the intersection of public and private readings, of tradition and cultural change, best embodies this potential. Such an anthology's various constitutive parts—its visibly constructed table of contents, preface, and editorial apparatus (footnotes, headnotes, extended essays, ancillary materials); its self-reflexive identity (always aware of its situation vis-à-vis the audience); and finally its virtual

---

i   Sarah Lawall, "René Wellek and Modern Literary Criticism," *Comparative Literature* 40.1 (1988): 3–24; Gerald Gillespie, "Crossing the Millenial Divide in the U.S.A," *By Way of Comparison. Reflections on the Theory and Practice of Comparative Literature* (Paris: Honoré Champion, 2004) 157–73 (168).

reality as a paradigm enacted differently in each classroom—bring to the surface a web of communicative relationships that might otherwise remain obscure. The academic anthology is the anthology at its most typical, to adapt Shklovsky's term for a form that lays bare its own devices, and the world literature anthology is its most typical example. The very diversity of world literature materials raises issues of sameness and difference and of the relationship between different modes of understanding. Readers require new information—and categories of information—as they encounter unfamiliar settings and perspectives and pursue questions of social and personal identity. Taking advantage of that initial curiosity, editors can explore formats that will encourage inquiry, investigate the various uses of contextual information, and open up routes for speculation and critical analysis.

The question is how to do it, and how to find a format that illuminates and raises questions without proposing hidden and limited answers: what materials to choose, where and how to juxtapose them, what systematic relationships to bring to the fore to encourage critical perspectives, and how to avoid both the comfort of traditional arrangements and the lure of a format that promises diversity but instead narrows avenues of inquiry. I don't mean that there is only one formula, but rather that there are pitfalls and possibilities to consider in any proposed structure, and they are worth exploring in both historical and theoretical context. My own experience in editing an academic anthology comes chiefly, but not entirely, from working with Norton's world literature series; I joined the anthology in 1977, after responding to a request to critique the current volume (more on that later). While I am convinced of the actual openness and effectiveness of a work-centered collection (that is, a collection of texts in which the aesthetic function is predominant) in communicating cultural as well as aesthetic patterns, I am well-aware of the critiques directed against such a focus. Other anthologies, ranging from late nineteenth-century to contemporary multicultural collections, have chosen to foreground cultural voices, often making greater use of excerpts in order to sample a larger variety of texts. The aims are not exclusive—we do need to find ways to bring out the cultural embedding of a text, to read it as part of a broad continuum of texts and contexts, and constantly to seek "new questions and new ways in which the literary and nonliterary texts alike can be made to read and rework each other" (Johnson 15). The challenge for a work-centered anthology is to make sure that the analytic focus on individual works also recognizes, in theory and in practice, their relationship to contexts and patterns of reference. The challenge for a representational anthology is not only to validate its categories ("As the years pass we discover more categories of human beings demanding to be heard") and to interrogate the presumed transparency of each cultural "voice" but also to organize material without resorting to static paradigms and broad historical generalizations. A brief look at some early collections that foreshadow the contemporary world literature anthology shows the extent to which historical perspectives, aesthetic assumptions, changing cultural values, and a strong tradition of auto-didacticism intertwine. It may also illuminate changes taking place in literary anthologies around the middle of the twentieth century.

These early examples are not academic anthologies in the modern sense—that is, constructed for use in the classroom during a conventional academic year—but they already have a place in educational history. They date from 1885 to 1901, before the era of mass education, and are part of a proliferation of collected works made possible by the lifting of perpetual copyright in Britain. Jonathan Rose has described the broadly educational role played by such volumes in *The Intellectual Life of the British Working Class*, noting that the author of the infamous 1886 list of the "Hundred Best Books," Sir John Lubbock, was an adult educator and president of the Working Men's College and that the books on his list inspired and radicalized generations of British autodidacts (128–31). In the United States the populist publisher John B. Alden claimed to "inaugurate a Literary Revolution" by selling low-cost editions directly to buyers (Korey 3). The American anthologies edited by Alden, Charles

D. Warner, and Harry Thurston Peck are quasi-educational multivolume editions of selections aimed at a broad commercial audience: that is, "the great body of the reading public" reading at home (Alden I: 9). In their prefaces the editors discuss principles of selection and arrangement, the status of literature vis-à-vis other forms, the anthology's cultural aims, and the editors' belief that such anthologies are a new phenomenon important for modern society. The volumes are not organized to develop these principles, however, and the editors differ in the importance attributed to such a project. As might be expected, the very lack of organization and the editors' sense that certain issues do not need to be addressed reveal the power of unspoken assumptions.

Diversity is important in these collections, and it is apparently easy to come by. *Alden's Cyclopedia of Universal Literature* (1885–91) is subtitled *Presenting Biographical and Critical Notices, and Specimens from the Writings of Eminent Authors of All Ages and All Nations*; as the editor reassures us, it provides "a complete survey of the literature of all ages and of all peoples" (1: 7). (Non-Western writers are almost completely missing.) Charles D. Warner's *A Library of the World's Best Literature, Ancient and Modern* (1897) "draws upon all literatures of all time and of every race, and thus becomes a conspectus of the thought and intellectual evolution of man from the beginning" (iii). Harry Thurston Peck further defines the scope of his *Masterpieces of The World's Literature, Ancient and Modern* (1898) in 1901 by changing the title: he drops the word literature (while keeping masterpieces) and expands the title to *The World's Great Masterpieces; History, Biography, Science, Philosophy, Poetry, The Drama, Travel, Adventure, Fiction, etc. A Record of the Great Things That Have Been Said and Thought and Done from the Beginning of History*. The interchangeable titles—universal literature, world's best literature, masterpieces of the world's literature, the world's great masterpieces (but not of literature)—demonstrate not only that literature is a cover term but that the real anchor point is the "history of human culture and progress" (Alden 1: 7) conveyed by representative human voices.

The notion of representative voices—or of cultural ideas embodied in such voices—continues to be a recurrent theme in world literature and in culturally oriented anthologies. It evokes Goethe's 1827 description of world literature as a conversation between representative national figures, Lionel Trilling's assertion that the best subject matter for freshmen is "the great, resounding ideas of the ages" from Homer to Dostoevsky (373), and the "Great Conversation" that is Robert Hutchins's organizing principle for Great Books of the Western World (1952). Contemporary authors often use the personalized overtones of "voice" to designate various cultural groups inside the larger global heteroglossia: *Voices from Afar: Modern Chinese Writers on Oppressed Peoples and Their Literature* (1980); *Voices: Canadian Writers of African Descent* (1992); *Voices from an Empire: A History of Afro-Portuguese Literature* (1975). "Voices" constitute a slippery *editorial* concept, however, insofar as they obscure the editorial process and suggest unmediated cultural expression—transparent speech replacing textual ambiguity. Representing authoritative speech, they recall Harry Levin's description of the early canon's reliance on "*auctores*: authors designated as authorities . . . and collectively accepted to constitute the authorized body of knowledge" (354). In such anthologies the voice you hear is the one the editor hears: an effect particularly visible in these early anthologies that focus not on texts but on the presumedly direct expression of numerous authors. It has sometimes been noted that the earlier anthologies include more women and people of color than their mid-twentieth-century counterparts. Despite this apparent openness, the selections usually echo each other and social stereotypes as well: the passages by women in Warner and Peck, for example, ran to themes of piety, domesticity, and patriotism.

The two most ambitious editors, John B. Alden and Charles D. Warner, have different editorial missions and approach their tasks differently. The former wishes to edit a volume from a historical or objectively cultural point of view; the latter limits his selections to those with "distinct literary quality." Alden selects a greater variety of forms while stressing an author's personality and social history; Warner explores editorial strategies to make his more traditionally literary list accessible to the reader.

Alden's Cyclopedia of Universal Literature is an interesting attempt to combine canonical and noncanonical authors inside a neutral format that avoids editorial bias but leaves room for a picture of cultural evolution. Alden aims to avoid the triviality of collections of "'Elegant Extracts' or 'Gems of Thought' culled from writings which have come to be classics in their various languages." Instead his authors are included because they "have made a distinctive mark in the history of human culture and progress," and he offers biographical sketches followed by extracts "sufficient to give an adequate representation of the characteristics of the authors" (1: 7). This swerve from a belles-lettres convention (the "elegant extracts" he derides) toward cultural history is evident from the beginning, when the title's "universal literature" is followed by more neutral or scientific terms *(specimens, writings, extracts)* set in historical context. At times Alden adopts the language of historical relativism. "Greatness," for example, that staple of anthologies of the "best literature" and of "masterpieces," is for him a relative concept that can be measured by context and historical influence: "The names of some men will appear who were great, not absolutely, but only relatively. Such men, for example, as Diderot, Erasmus, and Paine, whose works exerted a powerful influence in their own day, and thus upon aftertimes, although had they appeared in an earlier or a later century they would soon have been forgotten" (1: 7). Such promising theoretical issues are unfortunately not explored. Alden never explains any of his evaluations, which range from literary-historical judgments like the previous to expressions of moral sympathy that contradict his historical principles. The first volume of his anthology (Abbott to Arnold) ends with four passages from Thomas Arnold (1795–1842), an English educator and historian, of whom Alden concludes that "Thomas Arnold was beyond doubt a man much greater than any or all of his published works" (1: 478).

[. . .]

Unlike Alden, Charles D. Warner confronts many of these editorial issues in his *Library of the World's Best Literature, Ancient and Modern.* Warner has a somewhat easier task, in that he has unified his list by restricting it to "literature" and to other writers ("philosophers, theologians, publicists, or scientists") who have "distinct literary quality" or profound influence on literature. He does not ask "What is literature?" or question his global coverage ("all literatures of all time and of every race" [iii]) but relies on a consensus of European and American "writers and scholars, specialists and literary critics" to decide what is best and to edit appropriate entries. The collection thus becomes "in a way representative of the scholarship and judgment of our own time" (v), a new editorial dimension made clear by the exceptionally long signed introductions to individual authors (some with a reproduction of the critic's signature). These scholarly and interpretive essays constitute a good portion of the anthology: in the first volume twenty-one pages are devoted to Abigail Adams's letters, with six pages of introduction; Accadian-Babylonian and Assyrian literature receive ten pages of introduction for twenty-three pages of text; eight and a half pages of Aeschylus are accompanied by over nine pages of introduction. Warner insists on the novelty of this arrangement, whose emphasis on critical perspectives enables his forty-five volumes to fulfill their cultural mission as a "conspectus of the thought and intellectual evolution of man" (iii). It contrasts sharply with the conservative format of Harry Thurston Peck's *The World's Great Masterpieces,* in which each entry is preceded by a short biographical paragraph whose ending sentence assesses the writer's complete work.

Warner was a prolific and popular writer with a strong interest in the relationship of text and audience. Author of *The People for Whom Shakespeare Wrote* (1897), he also co-wrote *The Gilded Age* (1873) with Mark Twain and was editor of the *Hartford Courant* for thirty-three years. The preface to A *Library of the World's Best Literature, Ancient and Modern* is the work of a popularizer: he introduces his collection as a "household companion" intended for "American households," including "persons who have not access to large libraries" (iii–iv), and mentions its educational value. The latter claim is certainly advertising, but it also reflects the recently flourishing extension movement in adult education: indeed, the scholarly and explanatory tone of the editorial apparatus goes far toward making Warner's series a forerunner of contemporary academic anthologies. [. . .]

Warner echoes other editors of the period by describing his anthology's mission in terms of cultural evolution and the "contemporary achievement and tendencies in all civilized countries." In practice, however, he differs by consistently focusing on "literary qualities" rather than on vague ideas about cultural progress. A writer himself, he insists that the anthology's "general purpose is to give only literature" (v) and concludes that the comparative study of "the older and the greater literatures of other nations" will give the American public "a just view of its own literature, and of its possible mission in the world of letters" (vi). Given this aim, it is not surprising that the various headnotes are so full and interpretive or that Warner chooses sizable or complete entries rather than a greater number of smaller excerpts. "The attempt to quote from all would destroy the Work for reading purposes, and reduce it to a herbarium of specimens" (iv), he says, explaining that a list and "comprehensive information as to all writers of importance" (nowadays, "coverage") will be relegated to later volumes (in fact, volumes 42–43). Contemporary readers may not agree with all of Warner's choices, but they will recognize his unusual willingness to lay out for discussion basic editorial issues of organization, selection, the scope and nature of editorial apparatus, and intended audience. These topics continue to be factors in the creation of the contemporary academic anthology and generate, in each instance, its unique editorial presence.

Such an editorial presence is veiled in the *Harvard Classics: Dr. Eliot's Five-Foot Shelf of Books*, which was produced by a singular team of President Charles W. Eliot of Harvard, an eminent educator and scientist; the publisher P. F. Collier and Son, which proposed the project (and was, incidentally, the first to sell books to the public by monthly subscription); and the scholar who did the real work of editing: William A. Neilson, a professor of English at Harvard and future president of Smith College. Collier's was in no hurry to recognize Professor Neilson's hand; his name is omitted from the title page and from their publicity booklet, which advertises opportunities for ambitious readers to acquire a Harvard education under the "personal guidance of Dr. Eliot" (Eliot, Analysis 17) and to read the texts along with Eliot's own "intimate personal comment" (25). Eliot himself was more forthright in his introduction to the series, when he explained that Collier's had promised him "a competent assistant of my own choice" and that he had "secured the services of Dr. William A. Neilson, Professor of English in Harvard University": "I decided what should be included, and what should be excluded. Professor Neilson wrote all the introductions and notes, made the choice among different editions of the same work, and offered many suggestions concerning available material. It also fell to him to make all the computations needed to decide the question whether a work desired was too long to be included. The most arduous part of his work was the final making up of the composite volumes from available material which had commended itself to us both" (Introduction 11).

The *Harvard Classics* are a mixed phenomenon. They are generally considered a conservative canonical relapse on the part of President Eliot, a liberal educator and scientist who had pushed through an elective curriculum at Harvard (Levin 357). Certainly Collier's, when it proposed to implement Eliot's public statements that a five-foot shelf would hold enough books to give "a good substitute for a liberal education" to anyone reading "but fifteen minutes a day" (Eliot, Introduction 10), intended a commercial rather than a canonical revolution. Eliot's introduction also echoes the vaguely phrased cultural optimism of earlier anthologies, with tributes to "the upward tendency of the human race" (7) and the evolution "from barbarism to civilization" (3). On a practical level, however, his educational beliefs lead him to propose a variable reading model that works—at least potentially—against any single or hegemonic interpretation. The all-important last volume, with its *Reader's Guide*, lists, indices, and Eliot's general introduction, foreshadows modern instructor's manuals or even a database search by computer in its care for the integrated use of material throughout the series. Eliot sets forth a reading program whose different options emulate his elective curriculum and encourage self-directed learning: two themes that permeate his many lectures on university education (Eliot, *Harvard Memories* 53–57). Nor does he shy away from discussing editorial problems and solutions: he explains principles of selection in some detail and outlines diverse routes into the material (by chronology or reverse chronology, by subject, by comparison and contrast, by an individual search that uses the index to explore issues raised by any one work). All selections are to be complete and, however diverse, must possess "good literary form." Eliot reserves his greatest enthusiasm for the "encounter with the mental states of other generations" (Introduction 7) and recommends, at one point, a comparative approach that contrasts "different social states at the same epoch in nations not far apart geographically, but distinct as regards their history, traditions, and habits" (8). This belief in the intellectual power of comparison and contrast is supported by a range of interdisciplinary readings (works by Darwin, Faraday, Kelvin, and Pasteur, for example, and a volume of American historical documents) and is governed by the system of selected paths. Collier's publicity, touting the novelty of this pedagogical organization in contrast with previous alphabetically ordered anthologies, asserts that this orderly reading makes the fifty-volume set effectively "one great book" and leaves the mind "with a well-defined impression instead of merely a jumble of facts" (Eliot, *Analysis* 32–33).

    [. . .]

    Despite Eliot's stated intention to present "ample and characteristic record of the stream of the world's thought" (Introduction 4), the geographic scope of his selections is much more limited than that of other anthologies: for example, Warner's anthology or even (since Eliot consciously addresses an English-speaking American audience) Chicago educator Richard Moulton's 1911 description of "world literature from the English point of view." Eliot is not really interested in a broader "world" literature, however, but wishes to explain to his American audience the European tradition from which they presumably came; he intentionally includes "a somewhat disproportionate amount of English and American literature" (about half) and emphasizes issues important for American social history (Introduction 5). The true innovation of this otherwise local and conservative series lies in the way it focuses attention on the reader's active participation and organizes different ways to make the masses of reading material accessible. The organization of Hutchins's *Great Books of the Western World* is closely modeled on the *Harvard Classics*: billed similarly as a way to acquire a liberal education, volume 1, *The Great Conversation*, includes an outline entitled "Possible Approaches to This Set" (85–89); suggests assignments in "Ten Years of Reading" (111–31); and recommends pursuing individual interests via a large index of cross-referenced terms and "great ideas" called the *Syntopicon* (volumes 2–3), produced by associate editor Mortimer J. Adler and his staff. The contrast between Eliot's exploratory reading program and the *Harvard Classics'* editorial tendency toward closure exemplifies a familiar tension between objective and interactive approaches: between texts viewed as units positioned inside a cultural canon or the same texts seen as part of a communicative paradigm emphasizing the reader. It is a tension that continues throughout the twentieth century, from early multi-volume collections aimed at a large commercial audience whose image is diversified only through a few social stereotypes to smaller anthologies created for use in the classroom and shaped by changing curricular and demographic expectations.

For a long time there was no shortage of anthologies through which English departments could offer a survey of Western literature—a course that was considered "world literature" in that it crossed national boundaries and extended beyond the English literature survey. The first single-volume academic anthology to attempt global scope was Philo M. Buck's *Anthology of World Literature*, published in 1934 and based on his classes at the University of Wisconsin. Buck (whose childhood was spent in India) included Indian, Chinese, and Japanese literature in his classes (Alberson 50), a pattern he hoped to reproduce in book form. His preface summarizes a struggle between various perspectives: a desire to go beyond European tradition, the difficulty of deciding on principles of inclusion and exclusion, a dislike of extracts, a critical and pedagogic intention to focus on great works, and—latent but decisive—the anthology's mission to illuminate the history of Western ideas. This last principle corresponds not only to the book's need to fill its curricular niche (as a literary counterpart to courses in Western civilization) but also to the editor's wish "to discover, not the author's manner, but the matter of his thought—his philosophy of life, and its significance to life today" (Buck [1934] v). Wryly, Buck reviews the usual reasons for including a non-European author: "Shall it be his 'human interest,' or shall it be any of the supposed 'influences' upon our present day thought? Really these are practical questions and difficult to answer." Rejecting extracts on the grounds that they are "fragments only from which to reconstruct the idea" of a whole work (Buck [1934] vi), he must make space by other means. He decides to exclude British and American literature because it is already well-represented in high school and college: a pragmatic choice that unfortunately isolates the one tradition and obscures any more integrative concept of "world" literature. It persists in many curricular patterns today. Translations, especially the translation of lyric poetry, are a "pestilent difficulty." As to literary types, they are "more or less of an accident" and of secondary importance: Shakespeare would be a novelist today, and Buck provides an index of types at the end for those who wish such a grouping.

Buck focuses on works, but works as ideas. He minimizes notes and biographical information to an extraordinary degree: Dante "lived in the Middle Ages—that period of saints and chivalry" (330), and Dante's vision is compared to that of Petrarch and Boccaccio. More factual historical background is relegated to the end of the volume, to a "Chronological Chart" that categorizes each entry under "Author or Work," "Date," "Nationality," and "Historical Background" in a single row across four columns. Unable to include Asian literature as much as he would like, Buck uses the chart to evoke the missing global context: "Asoka Emperor of India" appears on the same line with Plautus ("250–184 BC, Roman") and "Constantinople Captured by the Turks" along with François Villon. Ultimately, Buck's principle of selection limits his non-Western entries to those that have had a "vital influence" on European tradition: to one section out of fifteen groupings of texts. His concluding pages reinforce the Western perspective by extending "the great tradition" down to present-day European authors—Proust, Joyce, and Pirandello—and to the effects of modern science on Western representations of character and consciousness. The anthology's 1940 revision shows how contemporary historical pressures influence both anthology construction and editorial statements of belief. This revision (reprinted in 1951 and 1961) extends its global scope by adding a great deal of lyric poetry in translation. Conversely, it narrows the volume's intellectual and analytic horizons by eliminating the last section on literary criticism and by reverting to a conservative image of "the symphony of Western culture" (Buck [1951] vi). The classroom mission is clear: Buck's prefatory "confession of faith" states that "it is well that in at least one college course, open to all, there be a reassessment of the ideas that have made human civilization" (v). His revised conclusion (newly subtitled "Some Problems Today" and following nineteenth-century European lyrics instead of literary criticism) no longer emphasizes Pirandello as an example of stylistic ambiguities mirroring "a new age of realistic experiment" with its "current of consciousness—any consciousness" (Buck [1934] 1005). Instead the rewritten second half presents Thomas Mann's *The Magic Mountain* as a moral response from a revitalized humanistic tradition that preserves "the moral world of man's conscience" and rejects "the treason of the intellectual . . . exhibited in an allegory of a sanatorium inhabited by painters, musicians, writers, and theorists – all shut off from the world of life and action" (Buck [1951] 1101). Yet Buck's work overall modifies the Western anthology format in several ways: first, by insisting that world literature should include works from around the globe; and second, by displacing biography as an interpretive tool and moving closer to the interpretation (if not the analysis) of texts.

By the middle of the twentieth century a consistent set of beliefs and practices had emerged that would shape—and continue to shape—anthologies of "world literature." These midcentury beliefs are quite specific when it comes to exploring a work's status in cultural terms but have otherwise little to say: there is certainly no literary analysis or interest in pedagogy. The projected audience is generic-American (of presumed European background) and, for a classroom anthology, is the generic-American English-speaking student taking common-core courses in "Great Texts of Literature" and "Western Thought and Institutions." Stith Thompson's *Our Heritage of World Literature* (1938), for example, addresses readers of "our native English" and excludes foreign authors "felt to be exotic" in favor of "those really significant to us of the English-speaking world" (5). (The eminent folklorist also includes several essays of cultural analysis, notably Matthew Arnold's "Hebraism and Hellenism.") The anthology's educational mission is to give this generic student a perspective on human evolution from barbarism to civilization, with special emphasis on Western tradition as the foundation of twentieth-century America. Global representation is preempted by the community's need to display a common Western heritage, and the role of the editor is prescriptive, framing and conveying that heritage in terms of a history of ideas. It is understood that the writers are male and, for the most part, European. Texts themselves are transparent and have no separate identity to require annotation or analysis (which Robert Hutchins rejected as "vicious specialization" in his preface to *Great Books of the Western World* [1: xxiv]). Selected to illustrate the editor's vision, these texts are more usefully extracts, which have the added advantage of leaving room for more entries. A reader has no way to emerge from the editor's grand design without leaving the anthology, for all facets are subsumed under a single and prescriptive interpretation of culture. When Dagobert D. Runes writes, in his *Treasury of World Literature* (1956), that he would like to include more Asian works but must exclude certain ones because "some of our Eastern friends write with a decidedly Oriental mannerism" (vii), he clearly does not intend to discuss those (literary) mannerisms or that (cultural) Orientalism with the reader. This lack of attention to a work's formal identity, or to the way its structures embed and convey layers of meaning, leaves the way clear for superimposed opinions—opinions with nothing to challenge them so long as they coincide with the reader's expectations.

If I have emphasized the prehistory of contemporary world literature anthologies, my excuse must be that many critics (especially those connected with new anthologies) seem to believe that the world literature anthology began in 1956 with the first edition of *The Norton Anthology of World Masterpieces* and that the future consists solely in reacting to this presumed Origin. It will be more productive, I believe, to examine the way that the Norton anthology itself responded to contemporary cultural and literary-critical practice and the way it has continued to evolve along with the rest of modern intellectual history. [. . .]

When the editors of the first Norton anthology of world literature proposed their manuscript to two large publishing houses in the 1950s, the table of contents displayed a familiar emphasis on Western tradition, and the works included were well-known as literary "masterpieces." The editorial approach did not stress the rise of Western culture, however, and shifted attention to the examination of works. After a preliminary acceptance, Prentice-Hall and Harcourt Brace became worried that the anthology would not be marketable unless sizable changes were made to bring it in line with current practice. The differences were fundamental and could not be negotiated: the encouragement of critical thinking and literary analysis instead of prescribed outlines of cultural history; a focus on imaginative literature instead of the transmission of Great Books; a preference for complete works instead of myriad extracts; and—aimed specifically at classroom teaching—an unprecedented amount of information about the texts: analyses of works, textual annotations, and individual bibliographies. The preface to the first edition (reprinted in the following three) reveals the editors' impatience with current practice: "We have not tried to cover the entire history of the West in print, and have avoided filling our pages with philosophy, political theory, theology, historiography, and the like" (Mack et al. [1956] 1: ix); "In every instance, we seek to go beneath the usual generalizations about periods and philosophies" (1: x). It is, in other words, a rebellion *against* the vague cultural generalizations of preceding anthologies and a revisionary discussion of Western literary tradition (as it was then conceived) *by means of literary criticism.* A similar rebellion occurred in the pedagogical format, for the editors drew on their experience as practicing teachers to accompany the texts with factual, explanatory (and intentionally noninterpretive) footnotes. Control of interpretation thus passed from the unexplained pronouncements of an oracular editor to the classroom interaction of teacher and student, who discussed a single text and body of information. Unwilling to compromise, the editors (Maynard Mack, Bernard Knox, John McGalliard, Pier Pasinetti, Howard Hugo, René Wellek, Kenneth Douglas) looked further and found a small, employee-owned company, W.W. Norton and Co., that was willing to take the gamble. Oddly enough, it appears that one factor in the anthology's acceptance was an innovative format that the publisher, George Brockway, wished to try: instead of the conventional double-column format characteristic of current anthologies of literature—and the Bible—he proposed that the literary texts appear in more readable single columns (Kenney). The first edition of *World Masterpieces* (with the limiting subtitle *Literature of Western Culture*) came out in 1956.

Although there are visible connections between the new anthology's literary-critical approach and New Criticism's focus on texts, distinctions must be made between a critical revolution with bases in English and the separate disciplinary focus of world literature. Theoretical issues peculiar to world literature (for example, the principles of selection for an international book list, the accuracy and readability of translations, the contextual information necessary for teaching texts from other cultural and linguistic traditions) were not important for English studies. In addition, the editors came from various disciplines—English, classics, Italian, French, and Slavics and comparative literature, most of which had little to do with New Criticism. The only editor who had visible connections with New Critical theory was René Wellek, whose coauthorship of *Theory of Literature* (1949) has obscured the fact that he was primarily an intellectual historiographer with a background in phenomenological aesthetics and Prague structuralism. Wellek's literary-theoretical principles were established (and published) before he came to this country; he was not a literary critic, and—although sympathetic with the work-centered approach—he criticized New Criticism when it ignored a work's dialectical connections with history (Lawall, "René Wellek").

Instead the anthology's editorial principles broadly reflect the Kantian tradition of the work's autonomy as an aesthetic structure. Articulating that tradition inside the current curriculum, and devising a format that would illustrate the principle of literary autonomy, were the main tasks of the first edition: "Our introductions—in consonance with the scheme of the book—emphasize criticism rather than history. While providing all that seems to us necessary in the way of historical background (and supplying biographical summaries in the appendix following each introduction), we aim to give the student primarily a critical and analytical discussion of the works themselves" (Mack et al. [1956] 1: x). History was to be separated from criticism, so that historical perspectives did not become, imperceptibly, evaluation, and the critical introductions for each period were collected in a separate section. The table of contents' conventional division by centuries was replaced by literary-historical terms: section introductions used and explained concepts like Renaissance, Neoclassicism, Romanticism, Realism, and Naturalism. Literary-critical analyses considered the author's life and thought only insofar as they were (broadly) relevant to the selected work, and each concluded with a brief introductory discussion of the text. Relegated to the end was a short section titled "Lives, Writings, and Criticism": brief paragraphs in very small print that outlined basic facts of biography, dates and titles of works, and a recommended critical bibliography. Immediately thereafter, the literary selections appeared in sequence without further comment. This striking separation of literary-critical perspective and biographical data is clearly a device calculated to rebalance habits of interpretation that had been heavily weighted in favor of historical explanation. Occasionally awkward (especially the small print), it disappears later when the need to draw attention to the text is less urgent.

The preface to the first edition (reprinted as a statement of principles along with later prefaces through the fourth edition) addresses issues of "world" coverage with visible discomfort. The anthology does not include the literatures of the Far East because it would not be pedagogically possible, given the current curriculum: "the principal aim of a course in world literature" (presumably, the common-core literature or humanities course) is to "bring American students into living contact with their own Western tradition." To include a different tradition—especially one requiring "extended treatment" to be comprehensible— would defeat that aim and confuse the student. Thus the editors must content themselves with providing unusual variety under the subtitle's "Literature of Western Culture": "English, Irish, American, Russian, German, Scandinavian, French, Italian, Spanish, Portuguese, Latin, Hebrew, and Greek" (Mack et al. [1956] 1: ix). In fact, given the prevailing emphasis on the Big Four of modern European languages—English, French, German, and Russian (languages that were also favored in contemporary comparative literature studies)—this catalog is already a step toward curricular diversity. It clearly does not satisfy the editors' ambitions and thus echoes and prefigures similar struggles to represent global traditions.

It may seem odd that the preface to *The Norton Anthology of World Masterpieces* does not stress the concept of masterpieces, either as T. S. Eliot's "ideal order" or as a list of culturally approved Great Books. Not that the concept is missing, but it appears only as a conventional backdrop for the study of autonomous works. Thus the preface discusses how works of imaginative literature are to be approached, how such works mediate historical experience, and how the range of selected readings was decided. The emphasis is technical or procedural: "masterpieces" appears only as a title and in a single reference to the fact that it is difficult to find good translations of "the great masterpieces of the classical and modern foreign languages" (Mack et al. [1956] 1: x). This is not to say that the selections are not also considered (master) works from the traditional Western canon, whose relation to cultural hierarchies has repeatedly been demonstrated. Yet, in the history of world literature anthologizing, the preface marks an important shift away from editorial approaches that define works as signs of cultural progress "from barbarism to civilization." These works are presented as aesthetic objects whose structures of meaning merit critical examination, and the anthology's editorial apparatus is organized to carry out that critical principle. In practice, individual editors differ in the degree to which they examine literary structures or situate works inside intellectual and cultural history. (Compare the adjacent section introductions by René Wellek and Kenneth Douglas.)

The editors themselves were a group of seven friends from a variety of disciplines, with a shared interest in literature and in teaching: four taught at Yale, and the others at Berkeley,

UCLA, and the University of Iowa. This editorial group structure was itself unusual. The conventional pattern for world literature anthologies was (and, to a certain extent, still is) to have one or two academics—often with a preponderantly English training—preside over a collection and, when necessary, farm out individual assignments to specialists who subsequently had no connection with the anthology. The Norton editors already represented a broad range of expertise, and they undertook the anthology as an ongoing responsibility. They included a classicist, a prize-winning fiction writer from Italy, a literary historian and theorist from Prague who taught Slavic and comparative literature, a specialist in French literature, and three specialists in different periods of English literature. Many had previously published translations, and all were interested in issues of language use. Except for general editor Maynard M. Mack (whose "Note on Translation" appeared at the end of each volume), each was responsible for a section of the anthology. The editors wrote the period introductions as well as headnotes, footnotes, and bibliographies for individual works, and they compared available translations with an eye to accuracy, literary quality, accessibility, and likelihood of success in the classroom. It is hard to overestimate the importance of their role as teachers, for it gave them a practical sense of the linguistic and cultural information needed to approach foreign works and of questions likely to be raised in class. This combination of broad scholarly expertise and pedagogical experience made the anthology an immediate success in the classroom—it *worked*—and its success was measured by a rapid rise in adoptions and by the closeness with which later anthologies modeled their offerings on the Norton's table of contents.

How and why does an anthology change? "Market forces" is an answer frequently given, and of course the market (another word for teachers, perhaps) is part of the continued vitality of any classroom text. In my own experience with the Norton world literature anthologies, change has come partly from teachers' suggestions and reactions to existing volumes and partly from the editors' own sense of developments in their field or of works they have found interesting to teach. It is a lively interaction, and the prefaces to individual editions often give a glimpse into debates behind the scene. [. . .]

My personal knowledge of Norton editorial practice dates only from the mid-1970s, when I was one of a number of people asked to review the third edition and recommend improvements. Teaching French, Francophone, and comparative literature in a curricular framework that did not include "world literature"—the course was "owned" by the English department—I had never seen the anthology. As a comparatist and inveterate tinkerer with course syllabi and handouts, I was fascinated with the scale of the project and delighted with its focus on complete works: it contrasted with the only teaching anthology I had used, which was a popular survey of French literature that contained myriad short excerpts and, at one point, asked muddled students to choose between the philosophical attitudes of Voltaire and Rousseau. Reviewing the Norton anthology as something of an outsider, I made various suggestions and also objected to the frequently personalized discussion of twentieth-century authors, which seemed at odds with the editors' principles. I could not, for example, agree that André Gide should be introduced with references to a serpent and a statement that "even those favorably disposed to Gide will be ready to admit that the quality of deviousness distinguishes his character" (Mack et al. [1973] 2: 1359). (Rereading the introduction, I still disagree but now recognize a carefully composed "teacherly" essay designed to elicit student interest in "The Return of the Prodigal Son" as a human document.) In 1977 I was invited to become editor of the twentieth-century section and, before long, was working on other aspects of the anthology, meeting regularly with Maynard Mack and the Norton editor in charge of the series. I became general editor with the seventh edition of 1999.

I have described my initial contact not for its intrinsic interest but because it is an example of the relative openness through which the anthology has evolved. Each new editor—including myself—brings different critical and pedagogical expectations, creating an ongoing dialogue with current practice that achieves its own dynamics and helps define the way the anthology will move. From the first edition of *The Norton Anthology of World Masterpieces: Literature of Western Culture* in 1956 to the second edition of the "global" anthology (now called simply *The Norton Anthology of World Literature*) in 2002, these editorial dynamics have articulated changing concepts of "world" literature in ways that relate, more or less openly, to contemporary developments in literary theory, criticism, and cultural history. [. . .] The competing claims of "world" and "Western" texts, the proportions of innovation and tradition, the search for better translations, the style and substance of editorial introductions, and the best way to implement user suggestions are all issues included inside the larger topic of the anthology's dual role as both a transmitter of the "common heritage" and an introduction to the larger world in which that heritage is situated. The image of an "unchanging masterpieces anthology" may be useful as an oppositional debate tactic, but it is unreal and ahistorical in fact. A materialist critic might indeed profit by examining the publishing history of world literature anthologies: in this conglomerate-bound age, Norton is still, and uniquely, a small employee-owned company with its own evolving tradition of world literature; more typically, a large multinational corporation like Pearson, which owns two large publishing houses (Prentice-Hall and Longman) can make the market choice to package both a conservative anthology of Western world literature and a "multicultural" global textbook arranged along opposite lines. World literature anthologies, individually and jointly, also experience the dynamics of institutional change.

The fifth edition eliminated the previous anthologies' division of parts and began to reunite literary analysis with its cultural matrix. Individual works did not appear in unbroken sequence, evoking Eliot's ideal order, but were presented separately and prefaced by extended headnotes that newly included biographical and cultural information and were followed by the relevant (now annotated) bibliographies. Section introductions were reserved for a general intellectual-historical survey of the period that was organized to suggest social, philosophical, and thematic contexts for the coming selections. These changes did not mean that the emphasis on literary analysis had lessened, but rather that a format had been devised to incorporate historical information insofar as it illuminates literary analysis—which always concluded the headnote. The hermeneutic circle was clear, but expanded.

Changes in the fifth edition entailed further consequences. The new headnote format made it easier to point out different dimensions of the text, but, by focusing on individual selections, it also diminished the notion of an overarching cultural framework—whether "Western" or "world"—and remained open to different ways of viewing intertextual relations. This was a period of complex change in the teaching of literature: over fifteen years critics had demonstrated the cultural narrowness of current literary education, for which they blamed New Criticism, political conservatism, and T.S. Eliot's image of an ideal order of masterworks. Their attacks referred almost exclusively to the teaching of English and American literature and were exemplified in books like Louis Kampf and Paul Lauter's *The Politics of Literature: Dissenting Essays on the Teaching of English* (1972), Lauter's *Reconstructing American Literature: Courses, Syllabi, Issues* (1983), and Judith Fetterley's *The Resisting Reader: A Feminist Approach to American Fiction* (1983). The multiplicity of world literature, or even the linguistic diversity of American literature (discussed later, in Werner Sollors's *Multilingual America*), was not a topic, and issues raised by world literature were not addressed. The world literature anthology, built around the critical analysis of works from various linguistic and cultural traditions, would need to find its own route.

[. . .]

There are now two separate anthologies: one, the global or properly "world" literature anthology; and the other, the classic anthology of the Western literary tradition. The

Expanded was an "expanded" sixth edition in a literal, bookish sense, inasmuch as it contained (thanks to a different format and new paper) the earlier edition's Western texts together with an equal number of pages of non-Western works. Here function drives form: the book was designed to be usable for either the "Western" or "world" literature class, since no one knew how many teachers would move to a broader syllabus or how many were committed to teaching the Western tradition (which remained, in many institutions, a mandated part of the curriculum). It was a very chunky two-volume set: I once suggested that it be packaged with optional wheels, and certainly the increased weight of our increasing contents pointed the way to the next edition's separation into six smaller and handier volumes. In another sense, however, the book was not "expanded," for it was not produced by the same group of editors. New permanent editors came from various non-Western disciplines (if we except Native American literature, also included in the current Western anthology), so that their scholarly and pedagogical perspectives would bring to the global edition a certain critical distance from the "literature of Western culture." They were John Bierhorst (Native American literature), Jerome Clinton (Near Eastern), Robert Danly (Japanese), Abiola Irele (African and Caribbean), Stephen Owen (Chinese), and Barbara Stoler Miller (Asian literatures, followed after her death by Indira Viswanathan Peterson). Like the first editors, they would assume ongoing responsibility for different sections of the new anthology: in this case for major non-Western literary-cultural traditions.

The word major implies both format (a simpler, broader, and perhaps more coherent organization) and point of view. It is clearly only one option among many: other anthologies, especially those emphasizing varieties of cultural experience, have selected excerpts from numerous sources (much as did early, culturally oriented anthologies) as a more equitable representation of global experience. The format is a spatial necessity for Norton, however, given the anthology's commitment to whole works or large coherent units; it also echoes the critical principle stated in the first preface, that only complete works give adequate representation of aesthetic and cultural content. Finally, the "major" format reflects a pedagogical conviction that too much fragmentation is confusing in class. As the preface puts it, "Students of all dispositions and capacities retain more of value from an acquaintance of some depth with a few literatures than from a shrapnel burst of many" (Mack et al. [1995] 1: xxi). Yet this was only the first of several format decisions that had to be made, each with potential impact on the reader's understanding of world literature.

The most obvious challenge was to find an organization of materials that would be comprehensible for the reader (teachable in class) without merely imitating Western chronological and generic models. At first this turned out to be less difficult than expected, since the various section editors came to the table with cluster sequences that reflected canons established inside their own non-Western areas. (Anyone teaching "foreign" literature in the United States has firsthand experience of its discrepancies with English literary history and terminology.) These clusters, eventually called "sweeps" to express movement through history, intersected throughout the volumes in broadly chronological order, thus preserving the self-awareness of different cultural traditions while offering readers the broad chronological perspective of "world" literature. They were, in the words of the preface, "continuities from a single cultural tradition enabling students to reach at least a modest familiarity with its characteristic forms of expression before moving on to the next" (1: xxx). The dates of the first and last entries determined the chronology for each cluster, and the cluster dates determined the anthology's material division. No attempt was made to provide an overarching cultural interpretation, whether the early anthologies' "intellectual evolution of man" or modern socioecononomic patterns echoing globalization theory. Yet that very separation of sweeps raised other pedagogical issues: how to avoid an atomistic approach, which puts a great burden on the teacher and easily leads to confusion in the classroom; how to suggest coherent structures without prescribing critical perspectives; and how to mediate inevitable conceptual differences between world-views that derive from different cultural and linguistic traditions. I do not claim that we have resolved all these questions, nor am I sure that they can be resolved, but the attempts to resolve them have a certain pragmatic as well as intellectual interest.

[. . .]

The Western and the global anthologies were formally separated with the seventh edition of 1999, which was specifically rededicated to exploring the internal variety of the Western literary tradition. Three new editors—William G. Thalmann, Lee Patterson, and Heather James—added works from diverse literary and cultural traditions to the Ancient World, Middle Ages, and Renaissance sections or revised the presentation of current selections. Their introductions, headnotes, and analyses drew new attention to the interrelationships of aesthetic and cultural history and to interwoven and often competing structures of cultural meaning. Missing or additional passages were inserted into excerpted long works to restore their realistic representation of contemporary life and issues (Rousseau); a group of narrative poems was organized to bring out its underlying examination of diverse images of love and gender (Ovid); new genres such as fantasy (Lucian, Ariosto) and intimate journals (Dorothy Wordsworth) were represented; and pronunciation glossaries were provided, at once an aid to classroom discussion and a reminder of linguistic and cultural difference. Four clusters of poems from medieval, Romantic, Symbolist, and Dada-Surrealist periods reestablished a missing element in literary and cultural history, from the diverse picture of medieval society given by poems written in Arabic, Judaic, Welsh, Spanish, French, Provençal, Italian, English, and German, to the shaping influence of Romantic, Symbolist, and Dada-Surrealist world-views and experimental forms. Such changes are for the most part invisible, but—like the process of excerpting and arranging in the first place—they open or close the horizons of world literature for the anthology's readers.

The seventh edition's complementary global anthology appeared in 2001–2. Based on a thorough revision of the expanded edition, it introduced two relatively simple format changes that had further implications: the metamorphosis of two chunky books into six slimmer volumes and the change in title from *The Norton Anthology of World Masterpieces: Expanded Edition* to *The Norton Anthology of World Literature*. The six smaller volumes have many practical advantages: they are more easily handled and lighter in the backpack; separately available, individual books can supplement other courses; and the separation itself responds to many teachers' desire to spend more time with selected sweeps. Yet the format of smaller individual volumes may also direct attention away from broader literary interaction and the global premise of "world" literature. Partly for continuity, and partly with this fragmentation in mind, the six volumes are initially packaged in two boxed sets. The new title simplifies and clarifies by eliminating two words: *expanded* and *masterpieces*. *World* is a more logical descriptor than *expanded*, which it replaces; *masterpieces* was dropped because the term's accumulated cultural baggage fits neither the anthology's original statement of its mission nor contemporary users' (and editors') perceptions of what they are doing. *Masterpieces* suffers from overlapping methodological and cultural connotations: on the one hand, it refers to a model of technical or artistic excellence (proof in the guild system, of having mastered the techniques of one's trade), and on the other, it indicates cultural approval or—in recent political criticism—complicity in a system of master-slave power relationships permeating European patriarchal and colonialist history. The traditional Western canon of masterpieces is further implicated in such critiques as part of a campaign to export Eurocentric literary, linguistic, and educational capital throughout the world and thus to dominate cultural imaginations (Guillory). As a consequence the term *masterpiece* has become so tied to disputes over the cultural significance of the Arnoldian tradition that it is a hindrance to approaching any text included in that canon.

[. . .]

Although I am best acquainted with the workings of the Norton anthology, my subject throughout has been the specific enterprise of the academic world literature anthology with its various antecedents and special position in American educational history. As Jeffrey R. Di Leo remarks in his prefatory note to the 2000 *symplokē* issue on anthologies, *The Norton Anthology of World Masterpieces* has become a standard reference point—a foil—for recent discussions that situate anthology practice in cultural and ideological context (5). Often, like many foils, it takes on a separate and mystified life of its own, so that it has seemed useful to historicize its position in relation to previous attempts and to speculate on common challenges that any anthology—including those oriented differently—encounters as part of anthology construction.

One element that seems often missing from critical discussions is an awareness of the dynamic interrelationships among teachers, editors, publishers, and institutional practice that go into the creation of an academic anthology. A consistently successful anthology (and I do not mean merely the Norton anthology) is the result of a check-and-balance system in which critical principles are matched with workable format choices, keeping in mind curricular niches; teacher demand; classroom viability (whose classroom? what students? with what needs? in what institutions?); and, of course, such mundane but crucial factors as publishing costs (permissions, paper, volume, advertising, distribution) and availability of texts: some are simply not available, some are not translated or translated poorly, some are impossibly expensive, some allow only a limited number of lines to be anthologized. Often the most inspiring proposals await practical execution, or so it seems when the theoretical arguments are presented in great detail but other parts of the discourse remain undeveloped. Despite the many new publications on pedagogy, the least developed aspect—and certainly the one most difficult to predict—is the world literature anthology's interaction with the diverse and changing world of student readers. They remain for the most part a rhetorical abstraction in discussions of anthology reform. Those who will use the anthology, for example, are "the student," "the American student," "today's students" (possessing "the naiveté of students"), "the teacher," and "the contemporary American audience"—all oddly universalized figures, blind partners defined by their role as either consumers or transmitters of critical principles: "The student can gain entry into this conversation only by acknowledging the scholarship of its members. His or her questions should concern the terms of the discussion, its assumptions and its conclusions" (Graff and Di Leo 114). The theorist is usually "we": "We won't do better in presenting the newly expansive world of world literature until we do a better job of clarifying just what we mean to accomplish by presenting 'the literature' of 'the world' for a contemporary American audience" (Damrosch, "World Literature Today" 7). Karen L. Kilcup is right to ask, "Who are 'our students' and . . . who are 'we'?" (Kilcup 43).

Global world literature raises particular problems for anthologists, starting with the scope of its selections and including the need to present the material in an informative way that proposes structures of understanding but does not prescribe them. This is always a balancing act. Most anthologies move immediately to limit the field: by period, by theme, by language, by region, by excerpts. One anthology of literature by women has global scope but is limited to the modern period; another has chronological depth but is limited to the tradition in English; both are limited by gender. *One World of Literature* is restricted to the world of the twentieth century; *Global Voices* to contemporary literature of the non-Western world (both are interesting volumes, mentioned only to illustrate the practical difficulties of "world" coverage). Anthologies aiming for historical and global coverage often expand their scope by using numerous excerpts and minimizing editorial discussion. Excerpts, however, are always chosen for the way they fit into a selected anthology theme. Shaped by the editorial principles that selected them, they can only bear partial witness and lack even the intertextual openness of true fragments (Susini-Anastopoulos 194). It is always worth asking how such excerpts are chosen, how they are related to their parent texts, what exactly they represent, and whether we should accept the passages as transparent—as "voices" speaking directly across cultures. In the same vein: if the anthology includes guideline questions and topics for use in class, what critical perspectives do they reveal? (In my own quick survey these topics are almost always universal themes: but surely examples of "resisting" discourse are needed to preclude the overquick resolution of diverse materials.)

[. . .]

An interesting organization appears in the recent *Bedford Anthology of World Literature* (2003–), whose material is selected, arranged, and annotated to emphasize cultural themes. Each volume contains alternating sections of texts representing different traditions (for example, China, Japan, Europe, India) and smaller thematic units—printed on distinctive blue paper and collectively titled "In the World"—that group excerpts from a range of international texts. Imaginatively edited and produced, with a variety of illustrations and ancillary materials, this anthology has a mission to represent cultural themes on an international scale; it also exemplifies the tradeoff between a large proportion of representative excerpts and concomitant limits on the number of complete texts. A similar, although much more complicated and less colorful organization appears to govern the new *Longman Anthology of World Literature* (2004). Here, a series of differently thematized divisions groups texts to "build links within and between regions and periods." "Cross-Currents" are intended to "illuminate important transitions," "Perspectives" to "focus on literary and cultural issues," and "Resonances" to "provide responses or analogues to a work" (publicity letter from the editor). Both anthologies seek to provide viable approaches to cultural complexity and include a wide range of valuable material. The relevant questions have to do with the implications of the anthology form. If there are a great many excerpts used to gain breadth, then we have shifted attention to a higher, combinatory level while minimizing the time spent on rereading individual texts. Organizational implications become all the more important in this situation: What routes (going back to Charles Eliot) does the format open up for the user—and how easy is it to envisage thematic clusters other than those described? How prescriptive are the inset thematic sections: to what extent do they flatten the image of included works? If there is comparison and contrast, what cultural patterns do they imply? Who is compared to whom, and in what proportions: do the comparisons move outward around the globe, or are global references brought "home" to Western familiarity? Is binary comparison encouraged, or are multiple points of view concurrently brought to bear? David Damrosch has proposed to organize comparisons as "ellipses" between two poles, remarking that "contemporary America will logically be one focus of the ellipses for the contemporary American reader" ("World Literature Today" 10). While the strategy is indeed logical in relation to American curricular patterns, it also projects a mapping of the world in terms of two unified and stable subjects: *we* and *they*, bringing diversity once more under control. Damrosch's recent book *What Is World Literature?* develops more fully his image of an elliptical space—a force field of reading relationships—that defines world literature; he pictures a series of overlapping ellipses in which three or more foreign works are juxtaposed. At that point, "we triangulate between our own present situation and the enormous variety of other cultures around and before us" (300). These are thought-provoking metaphors for the geometry of reading, but as practical advice they recommend only the juxtaposition of multiple of texts. Issues of selection, coordination, and ideological implication recede into the background.

Anne Ferry has pointed out, in reference to English poetry, that anthologists are aware of shaping their readers' impressions and that "self-consciousness is another distinguishing feature of the anthology" (2). The self-consciousness required of a world literature anthology extends in many directions, of which the most obscure is surely the way that format and editorial apparatus reveal the anthologist's literary and cultural principles. Constructing a world literature anthology to express the diversity of global experience requires a rethinking of all editorial levels if we are to avoid unconsciously reinforcing local habits of mind and repeating the early anthologists' static paradigms. Not that anthologists have the final say: the choices they make will be further defined—altered and extended—when the book is used in class and becomes part of an institutional, pedagogical, and demographic matrix adapting the text to its own needs. [. . .]

Bibliography

Alberson, Hazel. "Non-Western Literatures in the World Literature Program." *The Teaching of World Literature (Proceedings of the Conference on the Teaching of World Literature at the University of Wisconsin, April 24–25, 1959)*. Ed. Haskell M. Block. University of North Carolina Studies in Comparative Literature 28. Chapel Hill: University of North Carolina Press, 1960. 45–52.

Alden, John B., ed. *Alden's Cyclopedia of Universal Literature, Presenting Biographical and Critical Notices and Specimens from the Writings of Eminent Authors of All Ages and All Nations*. 20 vols. New York: J. B. Alden, 1885–91.

Baucom, Ian. "Globalit, Inc.; Or, The Cultural Logic of Global Literary Studies." Globalizing Literary Studies. Spec. issue of *PMLA* 116.1 (2001): 158–72.

Biddle, Arthur W., ed. *Global Voices: Contemporary Literature from the Non-Western World*. Englewood Cliffs NJ: Prentice-Hall, 1995.

Black, Ayanna, ed. *Voices: Canadian Writers of African Descent*. Toronto: HarperCollins, 1992.

Buck, Philo M., ed. *An Anthology of World Literature*. New York: Macmillan, 1934.

—, ed. *An Anthology of World Literature*. 3rd ed. 1940. New York: Macmillan, 1951.

Damrosch, David, ed. *The Longman Anthology of World Literature*. 6 vols. New York: Longman, 2004.

—. *What Is World Literature?* Princeton and Oxford: Princeton University Press, 2003.

—. "World Literature Today: From the Old World to the Whole World." *symplokē* 8.1–2 (2000): 7–19.

Davis, Paul, et al., eds. *The Bedford Anthology of World Literature: The Eighteenth Century, 1650–1800*. Boston and New York: Bedford/St. Martins, 2003.

Di Leo, Jeffrey R. "Editor's Note." *symplokē* 8.1–2 (2000): 5–6.

Eber, Irene. *Voices from Afar: Modern Chinese Writers on Oppressed People and Their Literature*. Ann Arbor: Center for Chinese Studies, University of Michigan Press, 1980.

Eliot, Charles W. *Analysis of The Harvard Classics: Dr. Eliot's Five-Foot Shelf of Books*. New York: P. F. Collier and Son, n.d.

—, ed. *The Harvard Classics*. 50 vols. New York: P. F. Collier and Son, 1910.

—, ed. *The Harvard Classics*. Vol. 50, The Editor's Introduction: Reader's Guide; Index to the First Lines of Poems, Songs &. Choruses, Hymns &. Psalms; General Index; Chronological Index. New York: P. F. Collier and Son, 1910.

—. *Harvard Memories*. Cambridge: Harvard University Press, 1923.

—. Introduction. *The Harvard Classics*. 50 vols. Ed. Charles W. Eliot. New York: P. F. Collier and Son, 1910. 50: 3–14.

Ferry, Anne. *Tradition and the Individual Poem: An Inquiry into Anthologies*. Stanford: Stanford University Press, 2001.

Fetterley, Judith. *The Resisting Reader: A Feminist Approach to American Fiction*. Bloomington: Indiana University Press, 1978.

Graff, Gerald, and Jeffrey R. Di Leo. "Anthologies, Literary Theory, and the Teaching of Literature: An Exchange." *symplokē* 8.1–2 (2000): 113–28.

Guillory, John. *Cultural Capital: The Problem of Literary Canon Formation*. Chicago: University of Chicago Press, 1993.

Hamilton, Russell G. *Voices from Empire: A History of Afro-Portuguese Literature*. Minneapolis: University of Minnesota Press, 1975.

Hassan, Waïl S. "World Literature in the Age of Globalization: Reflections on an Anthology." *College English* 63.1 (2000): 38–47.

Hutchins, Robert M., ed. *Great Books of the Western World*. 54 vols. Chicago: Encyclopaedia Britannica, 1952.

Johnson, Barbara. *A World of Difference*. Baltimore: Johns Hopkins University Press, 1987.

Kampf, Louis, and Paul Lauter, eds. *The Politics of Literature: Dissenting Essays on the Teaching of English*. New York: Pantheon, 1972.

Kenney, Michael. "Norton Conquest with Nine Anthologies and More to Come, It's Still the 'Canon' for College Literature Courses." *Boston Globe*. January 12, 1997.

Kilcup, Karen L. "Anthologizing Matters: The Poetry and Prose of Recovery Work." *symplokē* 8.1–2 (2000): 38–53.

Korey, Marie E. "John B. Alden." *Publishers for Mass Entertainment in Nineteenth Century America*. Ed. Madeleine B. Stern. Boston: G. K. Hall, 1980. 1–7.

Lauter, Paul, ed. *Reconstructing American Literature: Courses, Syllabi, Issues*. Old Westbury CT: Feminist Press, 1983.

Lawall, Sarah N. "Canons, Contexts, and Pedagogy: The Place of World Literature." *Comparatist* 24 (2000): 39–56.

—. "Reading World Literature." *Reading World Literature: Theory, History, Practice*. Ed. Sarah N. Lawall. Austin: University of Texas Press, 1994. 1–64.

—. "René Wellek and Modern Literary Criticism." *Comparative Literature* 40.1 (1988): 3–24.

Lawall, Sarah N., et al., eds. *The Norton Anthology of World Literature*. 2nd ed. 6 vols. W. W. Norton, 2002.

—, eds. *The Norton Anthology of World Masterpieces: The Western Tradition*. 7th ed. 2 vols. New York: W. W. Norton, 1999.

Levin, Harry. "Core, Canon, Curriculum." *College English* 43.4 (1981): 352–62.

Lim, Shirley, and Norman Spencer, eds. *One World of Literature*. Boston: Houghton Mifflin, 1993.

Mack, Maynard M., et al., eds. *The Norton Anthology of World Masterpieces: Literature of Western Culture*. 4th ed. 2 vols. New York: W. W. Norton, 1979.

—, eds. *The Norton Anthology of World Masterpieces*. 5th ed. 2 vols. New York: W. W. Norton, 1985.

—, eds. *The Norton Anthology of World Masterpieces*. 6th ed. 2 vols. New York: W. W. Norton, 1992.

—, eds. *The Norton Anthology of World Masterpieces, Expanded Edition*. 2 vols. New York: W. W. Norton, 1995.

—, eds. *World Masterpieces: Literature of Western Culture*. 2 vols. New York: W. W. Norton, 1956.

—, eds. *World Masterpieces: Literature of Western Culture*. 3rd ed. 2 vols. New York: W. W. Norton, 1973.

Moulton, Richard. "World Literature from the English Point of View." *World Literature and Its Place in General Culture*. Norwood, MA: Macmillan, 1911.

Mukařovský, Jan. *Aesthetic Function, Norm, and Value as Social Facts*. [1936]. Trans. Mark E. Suino. Michigan Slavic Contributions 3. Ann Arbor: University of Michigan Press, 1979.

Peck, Harry Thurston, ed. *The World's Great Masterpieces; History, Biography, Science, Philosophy, Poetry, The Drama, Travel, Adventure, Fiction, etc. A Record of The Great Things That Have Been Said and Thought and Done from The Beginning of History*. 30 vols. New York: American Literary Society, [c.1901].

Pressman, Richard S. "Is There a Future for the Heath Anthology in the Neo-Liberal State?" *symplokē* 8.1–2 (2000): 65–67.

Rose, Jonathan. *The Intellectual Life of the British Working Classes*. New Haven: Yale University Press, 2001.

Runes, Dagobert D. Preface. *Treasury of World Literature*. Ed. Dagobert D. Runes. New York: Greenwood Press [1969, c.1956]. vii–ix.

Sollors, Werner, ed. *Multilingual America: Transnationalism, Ethnicity, and the Languages of American Literature*. New York: New York University Press, 1998.

Susini-Anastopoulos, Françoise. *L'Écriture fragmentaire: Définitions et enjeux*. Paris: Presses universitaires de France, 1997.

Thompson, Stith. Preface. *Our Heritage of World Literature*. Comp. Stith Thompson. New York: Dryden Press, 1938. 5–6.

Thorp, Margaret Farrand. *Neilson of Smith*. New York: Oxford University Press, 1956.

Rev. of *Timelines of the Arts and Literature*. By David M. Brownstone and Irene Franck. *Choice* 32.6 (1995): 911.

Trilling, Lionel. "English Literature and American Education." *Sewanee Review* 66 (1958): 364–81.

Warner, Charles Dudley. Preface. *A Library of the World's Best Literature, Ancient and Modern*. 45 vols. Ed. Charles Dudley Warner. New York: International Society, 1897 [c.1896]. I: iii–vi.

Chapter 25

Shu-mei Shih

GLOBAL LITERATURE AND THE TECHNOLOGIES OF RECOGNITION (2004)

S HU-MEI SHIH (B. 1961) TEACHES IN the areas of modern and contemporary Chinese literature, sinophone literature, Asian American literature, literary theory, feminism, Marxism and transnational studies in the Department of Comparative Literature at UCLA. Throughout her career Shu-mei Shih has been interested in the problematic relationships obtaining between Europe, or more broadly speaking the West, and the non-West. This interest speaks from her first book, *The Lure of the Modern: Writing Modernism in Semicolonial China, 1917–1937* (University of California Press, 2001), as well as from her numerous other publications, some of which, such as *Minor Transnationalism* (Duke University Press, 2006), have been realized in collaboration with her colleague Françoise Lionnet.

The article we here reproduce picks up on Shu-mei Shih's concern with East–West relations. The original idea of *Weltliteratur* was inherently Eurocentric, she claims. The recent return to this concept in our era of globalization risks continuing to mis-recognize the non-West through a number of Eurocentric interpretive strategies based on what Shu-mei Shih calls "omnipotent definitions." The result, she claims, is a Western-dominated "global literature" spiced up with some exotic exemplars from non-Western literature. Instead, she argues, the new global literature should be a continuously self-questioning enterprise interrogating its own underpinnings and claims to universalism.

Shu-mei Shih, "Global Literature and the Technologies of Recognition," *PMLA* 2004, 1: 16–30.

Recent interest in globalizing literary studies has largely involved attempts to locate conjunctures between contemporary literature and the economic formation of global capitalism and thereby to name a new literary structure of feeling—*structure* in terms of the organization of various literatures into a world system and *feeling* in terms of the literary production of new affects in new forms, styles, and genres.[1] Its precedent is the idea of "world literature," first articulated by Goethe in 1827 and recently recuperated. While many scholars resuscitating this concept offer a nominal apology for its Eurocentric origins, this Eurocentrism's constitutive hierarchies and asymmetries are seldom analyzed. Twenty-five years after Edward Said's *Orientalism* and the book's specific criticism of Goethe, it appears that the critique of

Eurocentrism in general has exhausted itself, that one only needs to show awareness of it because it is predictable.[2] Instead of working through the problem, one gives recognition to it, which serves as an expedient and efficient strategy of displacement, a tropological caveat, able to push aside obstacles on the path to globalist literary studies of global literature.

Fatigue with postcolonial critique and a fear of repetition are partly symptoms of academia's incessant search for new theories, paradigms, and ideas, but this ennui cannot dispense with the gnawing evidence that Eurocentrism, or, more accurately, Westerncentrism, still exists in old and new forms. Charges of repetition and yawns of familiarity, then, may be hazards one must anticipate in insisting on continuous dissections of Eurocentrism. As deepening economic and cultural globalization prompts new notions of global literature, it is as much in order to critique their politics as that of *Weltliteratur*. Crucial here are what may be called technologies of recognition that selectively and often arbitrarily confer world membership on literatures, whether national, local, diasporic, or minority. These technologies have largely operated alongside and within national, political, cultural, economic, and linguistic hierarchies. I would like to resituate the notion of technology, which Teresa de Lauretis wrested away from Foucault with a forceful feminist reinvention (1–30), in the transnational terrain of cross-cultural politics of power and in the national terrain of interethnic and intercultural politics of power so that it denotes the constellation of discourses, institutional practices, academic productions, popular media, and other forms of representation that create and sanction concepts. "Technologies of recognition," then, refers to the mechanisms in the discursive (un)conscious—with bearings on social and cultural (mis)understandings—that produce "the West" as the agent of recognition and "the rest" as the object of recognition, in representation.

In this essay I focus on two specific technologies of recognition, that of academic discourse and that of the literary market. They are not independent of other technologies, but they are exemplary in their seeming complexity and astonishing consistency. I identify five discrete yet intersecting procedures these technologies use. The first two modes of recognition I analyze below, despite their obvious limitations, are among the very few instances of engagement with non-Western and minority literatures outside area studies and ethnic studies scholarship, when all manner of other theorists continue to produce Eurocentric universalistic theories without taking responsibility for that which is seemingly distant. The seemingly distant is undeniably constitutive of Eurocentric universalism as we know it; hence, nonengagement with the non-West and with the minority is in actuality a "fantasy of distance," as Sara Ahmed terms it (167). To make an obvious and often displaced statement: what precedes recognition, and is more devastating than the politics of recognition, is sheer negligence or feigned ignorance. Negligence and ignorance of the other(s) are fundamental to the neocolonial production of knowledge and the global division of intellectual labor. They are masked by powerful silences that refuse to recognize the multiplex others by way of a simple disavowal whose mechanism has not been fully analyzed and that maintains and produces hierarchical knowledges across West–non-West, First World–Third World, and majority–minority divides. Silence and ignorance exacerbate these divides even before the Westerncentric politics of representation and recognition comes into play. On the margins of this centripetal production of knowledge and on the lower rungs of the hierarchy, a scholar working in non-Western and minority literatures often has to contend with scholars whose engagement—despite "good" intentions—falls short of the level they would exercise with their "own" areas of expertise. Their generosity is circumscribed by an uneven attention, a compulsion to apply less rigorous critical judgment to non-Western and minority materials than to canonical materials.

This essay posits, furthermore, an understanding of the Hegelian notion of recognition as but one mechanism for subjectivization among many, as opposed to seeing the notion as a primary dialectical process of subjectivity. Much scholarship on recognition assumes a Hegelian master-slave dialectic as the model for the relation between the self and the other, a model that limits subjectivity to a binary model of intersubjectivity of subjects and objects. But the subjectivity of the objects, if I may speak oxymoronically, is not defined in totality by their subjection to one master alone, even if we agree that subjection is a primary basis of subjectivity. Intersubjectivity is a field of relations not just to one subject or to one object but to multiple subjects and objects. The non-West is never singularly defined vis-à-vis the West, since many other factors come into play in the non-West's self-definitions. Similarly, the minor is never exclusively defined in terms of its recognition or lack thereof by the major, since the minor is related to many subjects and objects and, importantly, to other minority formations.[3] Something always exceeds recognition, whose technologies bind those awaiting recognition to the "pathology of oppression" (Oliver) and in turn undermine efforts to gain subjectivity in a chain of negativity. In other words, the mutuality that undergirds recognition is never total, for there are more than two players at any point. Dialogic intersubjectivity is also always among more than two. Although the West contributes to the non-West's sense of self and the major contributes to the minor's sense of self, however grave and definitive the contribution, there is always room for other relational identifications and identities and even for disidentifications.[4]

The five modes of recognition I identify here as belonging to academic discourse and the literary market—the return of the systematic, the time lag of allegory, global multiculturalism, the exceptional particular, and postdifference ethics—are not meant to be exhaustive but are intended to expose the fault lines of the variations of the world literature paradigm in late capitalist globalization.

The return of the systematic

How antisystematic poststructuralist thought successfully guarded the territory of its discourse at the boundary of the West perhaps makes an ironic story. Poststructuralist theory has served chiefly as an internal critique of Western thought and has not attempted to seriously confront the non-West. What implications poststructuralist thinking may have had for non-Western knowledges and other subjugated knowledges are beyond its range, and the history of the imperialisms and colonialisms that have made the seeming coherence of Eurocentric thought possible has also been largely absent from its field of vision. Poststructuralist theory exercised and strengthened the muscles of Western thought, rendering that thought even more able to reproduce itself through discursive self-criticism. Such theoretical self-criticism discovered aporias, contradictions, and instabilities of meaning in Western discourse, but these discoveries have been reinvested in Western discourse, proving its infinite complexity, which warrants even more scholarly attention. Self-criticism in this mode cannot be equated with the self-reflexivity that is critical of its own politico-economic condition of possibility, its Eurocentrism, and the limits of its representation (Spivak). Rather, self-criticism seems to have functioned as a form of narcissism.

Contrary to the antisystematic move of post-structuralist theory, where meanings in perpetual deferral are posited against totalizing narratives, various poststructuralist-inflected Marxist and other academic scholarship has striven to understand the non-West systematically. With a clear hint of exasperation, Said asked decades ago, "What was this operation, by which whenever you discussed the Orient a formidable mechanism of omnipotent definitions would present itself as the only one having suitable validity for your discussion?" (*Orientalism* 156). If we replace "Orient" with "the rest of the West," the question still stands for those who cannot be so simply dismissed as "Orientalists," and it allows us to see the extent of this strange procedure whereby antisystematic analysis is reserved for the West but "omnipotent definitions," broad generalizations, and the imposition of systems and structures are reserved for the non-West. If the West is modernist in the sense that it is critical of modern society, then the non-West is realist in the sense that it is reflectionist and cannot transcend its rootedness in society; if the West is postmodernist in the sense that it is fragmentary, complex, and indeterminable, then the non-West is modernist in the sense that it still retains a belated sense of purpose. Forever caught in the fallacy of temporal hierarchy and spatial distancing rather than the postmodern logic of simultaneity of time and compression of space, the non-West is mired in structuralism through such methods as taxonomies, culturalisms, Third-Worldisms, and, in short, "omnipotent definitions."

The recent debate surrounding Franco Moretti's essay "Conjectures on World Literature" is one such site where we see the return of the systemic as the return of the repressed. Like a Benjaminian flash of history, the symptomatic reemergence of the world literature paradigm illuminates some underlying logics of representation and the discursive management of non-Western literatures. Or, to rearticulate this question by creatively applying Moretti's sociological methodology in the study of literature, world literature is operative as a concept today because it is an abstract of contemporary social relations in late capitalism, globalization, and the consolidation of the American empire. Indeed, Moretti begins his essay with an evocation of Goethe followed by Marx and Engels's famous statement about the necessity of world literature to overstep "[n]ational one-sidedness and narrow-mindedness," calling them ideals that comparative literature "has not lived up to" (54). Contrary to the cosmopolitan beginnings of Goethe, Marx, and Engels, comparative literature has remained largely centered on Western Europe, or, in Moretti's vivid description, on the river Rhine. Moretti's positing of the cosmopolitan ideal of Goethe, Marx, and Engels is immediately suspect, however: although the charge of Eurocentrism does not completely undermine what they had to say about world literature, it qualifies the presumed universality of their concept. The concept can be recuperated from them only after its Eurocentric roots are dealt with as constitutive failures. This simple oversight, I think, structures the many other oversights in the essay, where, good intentions aside, there is a tendency toward generalization and "omnipotent definitions" even as the author frequently admits his limited knowledge about literatures outside Western Europe. What is most curious is how these caveats become not so much obstacles as enabling mechanisms for sweeping generalizations.

As Moretti notes, the impulse to generalize a "literary world system"—Moretti's main argument is that the modern novel in the periphery rose between circa 1750 and 1950 as a "compromise" between Western form and local reality—is motivated by the desire to bring the concept of world literature to the level of "theory." In this theory, the novel is the privileged genre and a site of compromise among foreign form, local reality, and local form, which he specifically designates as "foreign *plot*, local *characters*, and then, local *narrative voice*" (65). If this can be called a theory, it is an astoundingly neat theory. Efrain Kristal's rebuttal to Moretti has shown how the novel was not the dominant genre in Spanish American literature during the period examined and how the cross-cultural fertilization was not limited to one-way traffic from the center to the periphery. A cursory look at Chinese literature would also have led Moretti away from taking one scholar's work in English as the authoritative last word on the Chinese novel and from taking the Chinese novel at the turn of the nineteenth century as representative of the entire period from 1750 to 1950. Any genealogy of the modern Chinese novel has to examine its relation with the classics of the genre, which include (if we limit the list to Moretti's period) *The Dream of the Red Chamber* (1791), *The Scholars* (1803), and *Flowers in the Mirror* (1828), as well as the late-nineteenth-century novels that Moretti refers to. *Xiaoshuo* (fiction) has been called by the same name from time immemorial to the present day in Chinese and "sinophone" literatures.[5] The modern classification of *xiaoshuo* distinguished its long form (the novel, *changpian xiaoshuo*) from its short form (the short story, *duanpian xiaoshuo*). This distinction marks the uniquely modern moment for

Chinese literature in the early twentieth century, because at this point the short story became the dominant genre, and it remained so up to the 1940s. The short story was also more obviously "Westernized" than the novel in early modern Chinese literature. For the Chinese case, then, the short story would have worked better as a genre to support Moretti's theory and, by extension, Fredric Jameson's, on whose invocation of the novel as the modern global form Moretti bases his argument ("Third-World Literature").

Even if one agreed with Moretti that modern literature in the non-Western world in general (not the modern novel per se) is a site of cultural hybridization, it would be difficult to see how this hybridization could be so neatly categorized as Western plot, local characters, and local narrative voice. There are many objections to this mechanistic division of labor. Problematic too is the impact-response model of active Western progenitors and passive non-Western recipients, as Kristal has also shown, as if literary agency were always one-sided. Furthermore, literary historians trace the genesis of *xiaoshuo* to the tradition of Buddhist stories that originate in India and central Asia as early as the seventh century. If only literary mixing involving a response to European literature deserves to be categorized as world literature, then we are again not far from Goethe's and Marx's Eurocentrism.

This critique of Moretti is meant to be not a nativist rebuttal of a general, comparative piece of work (which has its place in the study of literature) but a reflection on the persistence of the tendency to provide "omnipotent definitions," or more modest-sounding "conjectures," about non-Western literatures and to give them the status of theory. Even Immanuel Wallerstein (from whom Moretti borrows) has called his work on the world system a "perspective and not a theory" (129). Among the questions to be asked, then, are who is allowed to produce theory, who is allowed to call it theory, in which language is theory written, and what amount of work on a literature is necessary before one can generalize about it? Silence or withdrawal ("I cannot speak of you, or to you, because you are different") is not the answer. Silence assumes a cultural relativism where the West, still the primary referent, indulges in a "fantasy of distance" and refuses to "take *responsibility* for that distance and difference" (Ahmed 166–67). In other words, responding to otherness is not a zero-sum game of relativistic silence and problematic recognition but a matter of responsible attentiveness that works hard to give the non-Western reality, however hybridized, as much due as one can, surely beyond citing a couple of secondary sources as final words on a national literature and beyond citing secondary works on the late nineteenth century as valid for a two-hundred-year period. Perhaps the era of close reading is over, as Moretti announces in this essay and its companion, since close reading championed a small canon of Western texts, but we still need to attend carefully to the texts we study. Although situated in a structure or a system, a literary text also always exceeds its structure or system in the power of its effect and affect, which may be transhistorical and transspatial. If we take this power of a literary text as a given for the best of Western literature, as Wai Chee Dimock has done in a recent essay, then we should do no less for non-Western literatures. "Literature for the planet" (Dimock), "world literature" (Moretti), or "globalit" or "global literary studies" (Baucom)—whatever it is called—should be as complex and rich as all that constitute it.

The possibility of constructing a global literature today does not hinge on exercising a "maximum of methodological boldness," as Moretti calls for ("Slaughterhouse" 227). Rather, it requires a lot more hard work, work that is necessary, not optional.

The time lag of allegory

Perhaps no other megastatement about non-Western literatures struck a nerve of scholars working in those literatures as did Fredric Jameson's remark that all Third World narratives are "necessarily . . . national allegories" ("Third-World Literature" 69). Many criticisms and defenses ensued,[6] and in the meantime this "omnipotent definition" gradually became its own prophecy as select Third World writers and artists either found the definition applicable or, worse, produced national allegories to sell in the global marketplace. Some of the sensational trauma narratives about China's Cultural Revolution written in English by first-generation immigrants living in the United States, Britain, and France,[7] for instance, may be categorized as deliberate national allegorical narratives with an eye to the market, and so may the works of the much-criticized fifth-generation cinema from China, in which allegory was supposed to be the chief mode of representation. When the signified is predetermined, allegories are easier to write or create and to understand and consume. A predetermined signified is produced by a consensus between the audience in the West and the Third World writer or director. It is a contractual relation of mutual benefit and favor that works first to confirm the stereotyped knowledge of the audience and second to bring financial rewards to the makers of those cultural products. In other words, allegory works and sells because it makes the non-Western text manageable, decipherable, and thus answerable to Western sensibilities and expectations (sometimes even by way of the non-Western text's inscrutability). In the context of uneven cultural and economic development across the First and Third World terrains, allegorical representation may thus collude with the production and reproduction of global capitalism.

In a brief response to Aijaz Ahmad's criticism, Jameson explained that he wanted to point out "the loss of certain literary functions and intellectual commitments in the contemporary American scene," such as the capacity to link a personal story with the "tale of the tribe" and with the "political role of the cultural intellectual" ("Brief Response" 26). The loss of such functions and commitments prompted Jameson to look to the Third World, where he finds them in plentitude. Unwittingly identifying the Third World as an embodiment of the self's past is a form of nostalgia, even though Jameson intended a critique of the First World. Indeed, one kind of allegory places in the past the paragon of virtue or that which has been lost in the present. This, for instance, was a primary mode of allegory in classical Chinese literature—namely, using the past to satirize or comment on the present (*yigu fengjin* or *yigu yujin*). The backward-looking of allegory, in this instance, parallels the backward-looking of nostalgia: in both, the referent or object is no longer. In a different context, Madhu Dubey has aptly described such First World nostalgia as the "romance of the residual."

Allegory is only one kind of meaning-producing form, and it is also but one of the hermeneutical codes we can bring to the reading of texts. Clever readers can, I would suggest, interpret any text as an allegory, as long as they labor to do so. The temporal gap between the literal and the allegorical meaning of a text is then the designated field of interpretive labor. In the end, it is in the politics of allegorical interpretation as value-producing labor—who has the privilege of doing it, who is forced to do it, who has the luxury not to do it—that the nostalgia of the First World theorist becomes legible and can be fruitfully critiqued. The time lag of allegorical meaning production in the movement from the literal to the figural evokes the belated temporality of Third World culture in modernity.

A central contradiction in Jameson's essay that has not been pointed out relates to the issue of interiority. Since Max Weber, scholars working in Chinese and sinophone literatures have been beset by the charge that the Chinese lacked interior lives because they did not have the concepts of sin and guilt, did not experience dynamic motivation, and passively adhered to exterior ethical codes of conduct and ritual. Hence, when they read Jameson praising Chinese literature for overcoming psychology—that is, sublimating psychology to national politics and history to the extent that the private is superceded by the public, the individual by the collective—they cannot help but feel a sense of déjà vu. Granted that Jameson intends to criticize what he calls "placeless individuality" and alienated psychologism in Western literature (85), constructing Chinese literature in terms opposite to them returns it to the old stereotype, albeit with a twist. The implication is that psychology and the libido in Chinese literature are to be read politically, since the individual as such does not exist. Scholars would argue, however, that modern Chinese literature was created by authors *after* Lu Xun, who serves as Jameson's archetypal Third World writer, as much as by Lu Xun himself. The early-twentieth-century Chinese romantics and modernists after Lu Xun dug deeply into the space of interiority, thanks partly to Freud. The split between Freud and Marx that Jameson proposes as characteristic of First World literature was an influential formula in Chinese literature after Lu Xun and, for the most part, contemporary with him. The formula applies to Chinese as well as Western literature because, unfortunately, cultural colonization and hybridization had already taken place in Lu Xun's China and the danger of essentialism was already operative there, even then.

It is also instructive to remember Gayatri Spivak's critique of the national-allegory model in her analysis of Mahasweta Devi's work—there are spaces and practices that cannot be interpreted by the nexus of colonialism, nationalism, capitalism, and their interrelations or reversals. Perhaps Devi intended her stories to be national allegories, but an attentive critic would be well advised to ignore her intention. Perhaps Lu Xun meant to write national allegories, as Jameson's ready equation of Lu Xun's character Ah Q with China suggests, but are we not supposed to be looking for polysemia, discontinuity, and heterogeneity rather than equivalence? The gap between the ideal of polysemia and the practice of monosemia is, perhaps, an allegory of the relation between the First World theorist and the Third World text.

All representations are representations; all interpretations are interpretations. I understand the limits of representation and interpretation in the radical split between the signifier and the signified and their dissociation from the referent. But the other side of the stereotype is not an anarchic proliferation of unanchored and irrelevant meanings and representations. If stereotyping is inevitable in cross-cultural representations (Chow 73), then we might ask for whom it is inevitable, why it is inevitable, and what are its consequences for Third World texts. Most important, we need to ask how it is implicated in the global division and hierarchy of intellectual labor, in which the First World theorist is situated and in which Third World diasporic scholars triangulate and mediate First World "theory" and Third World "reality" by variously and vicariously exercising options of complicity, ambivalence, and resistance. As diasporic scholars become more and more "American," the continuum of identities and identifications shifts gradually—for some, dramatically—in emphasis and tenor. The diasporic has been "Westernized" to the extent of "becoming Western" (because not assuming to be so is irresponsible), so that the ethical imperative here is situated in a continuum from a critique of the First World from a Third World perspective to an internal critique: Third World diasporic scholars are themselves part of the problem, since the Western tradition is also their own.

The ethics of the becoming-minority of diasporic intellectuals from the Third World lies in destabilizing the binary relation between the West and the non-West by dereifying and complicating it, which involves overcoming stereotypes without falling into a sea of anarchic differences.

Global multiculturalism

One of the more devastating forms of stereotyping has been the culturalization of ethnicity, history, politics, and nation. Culturalism is the procedure by which everything melts into culture, so that politics of power can be usefully restricted to the realm of representation (or to a politics of recognition) without having to account for social, economic, and political consequences of power (or confront a politics of redistribution, in Nancy Fraser's terms) and without transforming objects into subjects (Oliver). A global multiculturalism is thus engendered, an extension of the American national model of multiculturalism. What is national in the Third World is turned into ethnic culture during minoritization after immigration, and, similarly, even those who are outside Western metropoles are metaphorically and oftentimes practically minoritized (Shih). In the new rainbowlike globe, each nation is supposed to represent one reified culture, with a set of recognizable traits, just as each ethnic minority community in the metropole constitutes one reified culture in an official multiculturalism. A certain color scheme on fabric, a certain style of clothing, a certain food item, a certain practice of everyday life, and a certain work ethic become the definitive traits of one nation and one culture, as nation and culture are equated with an agreed-on repertory of images and styles. Identity politics has unwittingly played into such reification of culture, as did Third World nationalisms with their passionate focus on constructing bounded national cultures and an identifiable set of national characteristics.

Arif Dirlik has usefully critiqued culturalism as not so much a cultural privilege as a "cultural prison-house," which effectively suffocates everyday transformative practices of culture and politics for ethnic minorities in the metropole and for Third World peoples. Culturalization now substitutes for racialization, so that the trauma of race and racism can be sidestepped and the political potential of rupture based on a clear delineation of racial oppression is disenabled. Race becomes culturalized to such an extent that it all but disappears, even though it continues to structure hierarchies of power. Similarly, Third World nationalisms become cultures to the extent that they are complicit with the global marketplace by selling culture as commodity, even when there are dramatic racial and economic inequities between the First and Third Worlds. Commenting on this phenomenon, Slavoj Žižek called multiculturalism the "cultural logic of multinational capitalism." By incorporating a "series of crucial motifs and aspirations of the oppressed" and "rearticulating them in such a way that they became compatible with the existing relations of domination," (global) multiculturalism transfers politics to the realm of the apolitical so that the economic ends of global capitalism are achieved (30). I will analyze this "postdifference" position in the next section, and suffice it to say here that many have seen the limits to culturalisms underlying the politics of recognition. It is also important to caution that in many previously colonized and semicolonized nations, culture was one of the primary categories in which colonial epistemology organized native knowledge for domination and management, through missionary and other colonial apparatuses of dissemination.

When literature crosses national boundaries, culturalism comes into full play. Particularly in the popular market, global and domestic multiculturalisms have dominated the ways in which the work of a non-Western or minority writer is read and sold. In Asian American communities, condemning writers who use self-orientalizing strategies to cater to the mainstream taste as "selling out" is an issue of, on the one hand, the burden of collective representation imposed on the individual writer,[8] and, on the other hand, the individual writer's complicity with the market, often through a use of stereotypes. The new subgenre of Chinese immigrant memoirs written in English about traumatic experiences during the Cultural Revolution in China, as mentioned above, is a less complicated and more direct expression of *ressentiment* with an important difference. Unlike much Asian American writing dealing with racialized existence in the United States, this subgenre deals with oppression in—and directs its *ressentiment* toward—China. The popularity of this subgenre is not unlike that of postcolonial studies, whose *ressentiment* was directed at a British colonialism far away in time and space from the United States.[9] In both cases, spectacles are safely enjoyed from a distance.

A ten-year political struggle in which culture was largely reduced to ideological correctness or incorrectness, the Cultural Revolution was as much about the misrecognition of
culture as about the codification and management of social practices. For example, gender
difference was seen as a culture of signs (clothing, manner, makeup, hairdo, etc.) and the
basis of gender inequality; therefore, eliminating gender inequality required discarding, even
repressing, all feminine signs. The failure of the Cultural Revolution as an ideal and the era's
human consequences show the futility of imposing a reified and essentialized definition of
culture.

The popularity of Cultural Revolution trauma narratives in the United States and
increasingly in Europe reproduces this reification in a reverse, bourgeois mode. This reversal
plays into the reification of culture as commodity (packaged as history and trauma, hence
national allegory), transforming harrowing human experience into literary spectacle waiting
to be turned into film. The thin generic division between literature and film dissolves before
the desire to maximize market potential, but this desire is masked cleverly by a moralism that
upholds Western liberal democratic humanism in opposition to the Chinese Cultural
Revolution's dehumanizations. In the end, in the self-ethnographies of the diasporic, the
political and the ideological melt into culture. This is a new form of exoticism, or traumaism,
which culturalizes wherever it goes.

There is a risk of collapsing the distinct meanings of the political for United States and
global multiculturalisms. The political does not translate easily across boundaries, since what
is political in one context is not necessarily political in another. One can discern the United
States-centric agenda in domestic and global arenas, and in typical colonial fashion, the
metropole's mode of managing its others is transported to the peripheries. However, the
struggles of minoritized peoples in the United States have fashioned a critical multiculturalism that challenges not only assumed monoculturalisms but also various managed multiculturalisms. When the word *multicultural* is hijacked by the mainstream society, its political
valence needs to be redefined to resist the displacement of political economy. So even in
domestic multicultural discourses, the content and accent of the political shift in time and
space. The political is meaningful and productive when it can shift alongside the maneuvers
of power by the dominant, not only to respond to new forms of domination but also to
engage in transformation. The political, in other words, is constituted by time.

For non-Westerners managed under the banner of global multiculturalism through
international film festivals, book awards, art exhibitions, and so on (not to mention the
corporate version of managed multiculturalism), critical articulations are more difficult, for
at least three reasons: the discourse of nationalism has been the primary mode of resistance
to Western domination, and this discourse unwittingly reinforces the culturalization of a
nation; critical awareness of the global management and reification of cultures is consequently lacking; and the ascendancy of the market has proved the selling power of culture as
commodity. To the extent that self-culturalization has become a chief mode of self-identity
in the global context, the tasks left uncompleted by nationalisms are finished by capitalism
without boundaries. Given the fluidity of geographic and electronic boundaries, what distinguishes one person from another may be the distinctions between one culture and another,
which then displace the differences in racial and historical experience. In the zone of the
global multicultural, at least we can all be color-blind and origin-blind and congratulate
ourselves on our liberal notions of the world as we head toward becoming neoliberal.

The point of criticism here is not that the cultural is inherently devoid of the political or
is divorced from the material but that the deployment of the cultural in managed domestic
and global multiculturalisms systematically purges it of its political potentialities. The divorce
of the cultural from the political was largely orchestrated to rechannel the social discontent
of domestic minorities and to expand global markets. When the cultural is separated from

the political and, for that matter, from the material (except in its market variety), it is denuded of its transformative power. This is another oppressive division of labor that severs what is relational into separate spheres (Butler 42). The devaluation of the humanities as irrelevant these days is the direct consequence of such a division of labor. It therefore comes as no surprise that minority studies in academia has been seen as largely a phenomenon of the humanities, even though much is being done in the social sciences, policy studies, health sciences, education, and economics.

The exceptional particular

If global multiculturalism fetishizes reified cultures as embodiments of difference, its oppo-site fetishizes mimicry, model minority, and belated sameness. Belated sameness is seen as proof of the universal validity of the self, the precedent, or the majority: for example, the rise of modernism in Third World literatures and First World minority literatures supposedly proves the universal validity of metropolitan modernism. When texts from these literatures are granted an au courant designation such as postmodernism, the assumption is either that the Third World has finally arrived or that postmodernism is a universal advanced category. Reacting to the withholding of such designations, Third World and minority critics and scholars resort either to nationalism (claiming that their literatures are unduly ignored) or to masochistic self-orientalism (viewing their literatures as not good or advanced enough). These familiar reactions are dictated ineluctably by the prison house of recognition.

For decades the Nobel Prize in Literature obsessed Chinese critics and scholars, who publicly lamented that no Chinese writer had been awarded it. The issue came to be regarded as a national insult, the result of exclusion and prejudice. When Gao Xingjian, an exile living in France, received the award in 2000, there was a general outcry from official and unofficial Chinese sources that the selection was politically motivated and meant to vilify China. Gao had been the target of official criticism during the "anti–spiritual corruption" campaign of the mid-1980s before his exile, had been blacklisted in China for his avant-garde literary views and practices, which defied Maoist doctrines of literature (Tam 3–4), and had, since his exile, written forcefully against Maoism's ideological domination of literature. The nationalistic Chinese responses were thus predictable. Indignation mixed with a desire for recognition can be glimpsed in such postprize publications as *Flexing Muscles with the Nobel Prize in Literature* (2002), in which Kenzaburō Ōe (the Japanese Nobel Prize winner of 1994) was recruited to confirm that the neglect of Chinese literature by the Nobel committee is an "injustice" (qtd. in Xie Huadong 202), and in the series *Walking toward the Nobel Prize*, distributed by a promi-nent Shanghai publisher showcasing the best of contemporary Chinese fiction for broader recognition.

What are not predictable are the new ways in which the politics of recognition is played out by the international literary prize, as well as the complications arising from Gao's status as an author who writes in Chinese while living in France. His major novels, *Soul Mountain* (*Lingshan* [1990]) and *One Man's Bible* (*Yige ren de shengjing* [1999]), were published in Taiwan while Gao was living in France, although the first novel was partly written before he emigrated from China. These works have been ignored by literary histories in China but are important examples of sinophone literature. There are two compelling issues here: the Nobel Prize's politics of recognition and the need to understand the sinophone as a productive, important, and historically specific category for literature.

The politics of recognition involves the granting of universality to the exceptional particular—that is, Gao's works are exceptional in that they, in their particularity, transcend the particular and approach the universal. This logic suggests that particular works cannot be universal unless they are exceptional. The granting of universality to exceptional cases is selective and has to be analyzed in terms of how the universal is defined and how a particular is selected for the granting. The exceptional escapes the logic of the particular and does not set a precedent because it is singular and nonrepetitive and hence does not open a path for other particulars. Granting universality to the exceptional particular—the singular—thus in no way compromises standards of the universal, nor does it threaten the guardians of the universal.

According to the official citation, Gao was awarded the prize "for an oeuvre of universal validity, bitter insights and linguistic ingenuity, which has opened new paths for the Chinese novel and drama."[10] The presentation speech by the Nobel Prize committee member Göran Malmqvist explains the four items mentioned in the prize citation—universal validity, bitter insights, linguistic ingenuity, and new paths for Chinese literature. The second and fourth terms are spatially and temporally specific, hinging on Gao's experience in Maoist and post-Maoist China (the story of the persecution and suppression of his creative genius), which produced "bitter insights" as well as Gao's contribution to Chinese literature as a national literature. Gao's persecution during the Cultural Revolution is mentioned in the third sentence of the speech, establishing that Gao's story is one of escape from oppression, whether the shackles of Chinese tradition ("Confucian orthodoxy") or of politics ("Marxist ideology"). The speech elaborates the first term of the description, "universal validity," by foregrounding Gao's relentless exploration of the "existential dilemma" and the "meaning of human existence," as well as "the nature of literature, the conditions of authorship and, first and foremost, . . . the importance of remembering and imagination for the author's view of reality." The third term, "linguistic ingenuity," receives only one mention, however, in connection with Gao's creative use of pronouns to represent subjectivity in multiplicity.

This simple summary shows a tension between the particular (what is historically and politically specific) and the universal (what is human or literary). There is a causal relation between the particular and the universal, because the particular leads to the incessant search for the meaning of existence and the meaning of literature. But the universal is so widely assumed that it is nearly a banal cliché—one could argue that all serious literature is a search for the meaning of existence and the meaning of literature. The major value-producing criterion here, then, is apparently not the universal but the particular: the exceptional, singular case of one particular with universal resonances. In the end, the national is alive and well as a category in the selection of the Nobel Prize in Literature, just as the national produced in China the negative reactions to Gao's award. The harness of the national binds the Nobel Prize and the negative reactions from China in a binary duel of wills.

Gao's diasporic life in France and his fluency in French, prepared by a degree in French literature, make no difference to the two parties' unwitting collusion in fetishizing the national. Nor are Gao's numerous writings (such as his Nobel Lecture ["Case"]) that reject all forms of domination, including the Maoist and post-Maoist political and ideological varieties from China as well as the consumerist variety in Western metropoles, properly registered. When would Gao be considered a French writer who happens to write in Chinese? Or a writer who happens to write in Chinese and may live anywhere in the world? The sinophone as an organizing category allows for an alternative theorization of such a writer because it transcends national boundaries; its raison d'être is a condition of exile, diaspora, minoritization, and hybridity that resists incorporation both into China and into the place of residence.

Sinophone writers from Indonesia and Malaysia have carried on this double resistance for a long time—on the one hand, writing in Chinese in hostile local conditions and, on the other, writing in a unique kind of Chinese hybridized by local experience and thus circumventing Sinocentrism. Many of these aspiring writers immigrated to Taiwan, a sinophone country lacking nation-state status and under the threat of China's containment, for college education and began theorizing this relation to their places of origin and to China and Chinese-ness. For the generations of Taiwan intellectuals, writers, and scholars mystified by what was until recently the Kuomintang's Sinocentrism (the decolonization of consciousness from Sinocentrism in Taiwan began in earnest in the late 1980s with the lifting of martial law), these theorizations by Malaysian- and Indonesian-born sinophone writers are instructive.[11]

Gao's male protagonist in *One Man's Bible* tells a German Jewish woman that he has no "ancestral land" (a Chinese expression for "nation"), that "China is very far away," and that he is "tired of writing about the trauma" of China (16, 286; my trans.). Addressing the protago-nist as "you," the narrator later says, "[Y]ou do not need this national label, it is just that you are still writing in Chinese, that is all" (300; my trans.). If we thus justifiably suspend the battle of the national for the sinophone, so that the national and the linguistic are no longer metonymies and mutually determining, then we can move on to critically engage the novels themselves, noting, to start, their singular achievements in form and language as well as their problematic representations of women and of ethnic minorities in China. The granting of universality to the exceptional particular by the Nobel Prize committee then will require closer readings of Gao's novels and plays, readings that draw on all critical categories rather than selected ones. The affirmation of Gao by the Nobel committee should be an affirmation of sinophone, not Chinese, literature.

Postdifference ethics

The four preceding sections on the politics and technologies of recognition critiqued the fetishization of difference (national allegory, multiculturalism, the national) and the return to sameness (the systematic and the universal) as determined by the logic of "re-cognition," the cognition of that which is already known and predetermined by political economy in mostly predictable ways.[12] I introduced a new category, the sinophone, inspired by the francophone and lusophone, though they have different histories, to shift the politics of recognition from that which is assumed to be known to that which needs to be learned by effort. The ethical here is therefore embodied in a dual critical perspective on the uses of difference and same-ness as reified, re-cognizable categories under the regime of recognition and as value-producing constructs serviceable to dominant universals. This section will caution, however, that not all differences are the same, not all critiques of difference can be collapsed, and a blanket rejection of difference is not called for.

A recent consequence of critiques of multiculturalism gone wrong or postcolonial theory gone mainstream is the development of what I would call postdifference ethics or ethics after difference. The more Marxian proponents of postdifference ethics reject differ-ence because of its perceived problems, such as identity politics and culturalisms, and dismiss it as an obstacle to collective resistance to capital. In reaction to what is seen as the late-twentieth-century celebration of difference (or *différance*) in Derridian deconstruction as well as in the philosophy of Emmanuel Levinas, a simultaneous resistance to difference and desire to transcend difference have developed in philosophy. This interesting convergence between a Marxian perspective and a new philosophy of ethics is echoed in some discourses emerging after postcolonial theory, declaring the exhaustion of difference and hybridity and urging a postdifference ethics.

For Alan Badiou, difference is a fact of every situation, since multiplicity and infinity are the law of being, simply, "what there is" (Hallward xxxvi). Otherness has "neither force nor truth" as an ethical category because it has produced identitarianisms and displaced class struggles, thereby serving conquering civilizations. Levinasian ethics is to be "purely and simply abandoned" as a "pious discourse" like religion and hence can no longer be considered philosophy. The ethical lies, instead, in being "indifferent to differences" (Hallward xxxvi) and in "recognizing the Same" (Badiou 25); then one can approach "truths," which are "the coming-to-be of that which is not yet." "The Same," in this scheme, is what comes to be, since difference is what there is already. A futuristic notion of truth therefore should dispense with difference as belonging to the order of the banal present and should search for four truths of the Same, which are science, love, politics, and art (Badiou 18–28).

Badiou's rejection of difference is premised on the assumption that no one is more or less different from another person than is anyone else, so he argues that there are "as many differences, say, between a Chinese peasant and a young Norwegian professional as between myself and anybody at all, including myself" (26). By thus flattening all differences as universal and qualitatively similar, he rejects the conditions of difference, which are undergirded by the political economy of race, gender, class, nationality, sexual choice, and so forth—that is, the coimplication of difference and inequality in a politics of recognition and redistribution. Abuses of difference are seen as fundamental to difference as a discursive concept and social fact; thus, difference is rejected in favor of returning to the Same and to the search for truths.

There are strong resonances here with post-identitarian discourses that seek to show that minority and Third World peoples are not "otherness machines" to be used to produce difference for exoticist consumption or managed multiculturalism. Recent Asian American literature, for instance, concerns overcoming ethnicity as difference (Asian Americans are Americans too), and recent prominent Asian films are also less exotic spectacles than they are gritty urban portraits (globalization has made us all more and more alike). There is widespread disenchantment with difference-producing stereotypes of all kinds and fatigue with the orientalism analytic. But this disenchantment among the minority or the marginalized is qualitatively different from the rejection of difference by the majority and the center. Not all articulation and rejection of difference is the same, as not all difference is the same. Some differences carry more cultural capital than others; some differences are less universal than others; some differences are more disempowering and hurtful than others. The minority's and the Third World's desire to overcome reified differences does not mean that there are no more differences or that history, culture, and all other categories of human understanding are universal.

The center's rejection of difference amounts to rejecting the political and other gains of critical multiculturalisms. The timing of the emergence of a postdifference ethics in France (where minority issues are becoming more and more visible) is suspicious. Nancy Hartsock once questioned, "Why is it, exactly at the moment when so many of us who have been silenced begin to demand the right to name ourselves, to act as subjects rather than objects of history, that just then the concept of subjecthood becomes 'problematic'?" (26). One can adapt Hartsock's query to ask, why is it that, exactly when so many of us have begun to mobilize productive and nonreified forms of difference for political struggle, just then the concept of difference becomes problematic?

Judith Butler has usefully analyzed the disparagement of difference as "merely cultural" by contemporary Marxist thinkers and reasserts the importance of difference as a constituent of struggle, noting that the "refusal to become re-subordinated to a unity that caricatures, demeans, and domesticates difference becomes the basis of a more expansive and dynamic political impulse" (44). She criticizes the orthodox Marxist distinction between the cultural and the material as the result of a "selective amnesia of the history of Marxism itself." It is capitalism that separates the cultural and the material, through abstraction; hence, the separation is the "effect and culmination of the division of labor" (42).

Such a problematic postdifference ethics practiced in literature will return us to the older paradigms of universalism, with records of violence—epistemic, cultural, and otherwise. The reaffirmation of literature does not mean a return to the kind of unity or truth that caricatures, demeans, and domesticates difference. It is not that there was an original unity or monoliterature before the proliferation of differences but that monoliterature or universal literature as such was always a construct of power in the existential reality of differences. A global literature should be not the old world literature spiced with exotic or exceptional representatives from the "rest of the West" but a literature that critically examines its own construction by suspiciously interrogating all claims to universalisms, while acknowledging that any criteria emerging from these interrogations will be open to new questioning. This will be a more open stance toward the future, one that goes out to and engages with the other without appropriating it and sees this relation, à la Levinas, as the site of ethics. An unconditional law of ethics, in this case, is thus all the more able to respond to otherness in its past, present, and future forms so that the political of the future is not foreclosed but given the space of becoming.

Notes

1   See, for instance, *Globalizing Literary Studies*, a special topic in *PMLA* (Gunn), and Palumbo-Liu.

2   A notable exception is Pizer, who critiques Goethe's Eurocentrism and points out the contradiction between his convictions in national literature and world literature. Said's recent remarks on Goethe and the concept of world literature have been more positive, however. Instead of criticizing Goethe's "romantic Orientalist vision," as he did in *Orientalism* (154), Said in 2003 held up *Weltliteratur* as the model for a tolerant humanism that sees "literatures of the world as a symphonic whole" ("Window").

3   The horizontal view of minor-to-minor relation is posited in Lionnet and Shih ("Thinking").

4   For the notion of disidentification in the constitution of Asian American subjectivity, see Lowe.

5   By "sinophone" literature I mean literature written in Chinese by Chinese-speaking writers in various parts of the world outside China, as distinguished from "Chinese literature"—literature from China. The largest output of sinophone literature is from Taiwan and prehandover Hong Kong, but throughout Southeast Asia there were many vibrant sinophone literary traditions and practices in the twentieth century. Numerous writers in the United States, Canada, and Europe also write in Chinese, the most luminary of whom is Gao Xingjian, the Nobel Prize winner in 2000. The imperative of coining the term *sinophone* is to contest the neglect and marginalization of literatures in Chinese published outside China and the selective, ideological, and arbitrary co-optation of these literatures in Chinese literary history. *Sinophone*, in a sense, is similar to *anglophone* and *francophone* in that Chinese is seen by some as a colonial language (in Taiwan). Sinophone literature, furthermore, is to be distinguished from the universalization of the Chinese written script during the pre-modern era in East Asia when scholars from Japan and Korea, for instance, could converse with Chinese scholars and each other in the Chinese written script by "pen talks" rather than speech. See the section "The Exceptional Particular," below.

6   Of the responses, the most provocative is Ahmad's.

7   Personal memoirs of brutality of life in Red China are so numerous that they almost constitute a subgenre. Anchee Min's *Red Azalea*, Dai Sijie's *Balzac and the Little Chinese Seamstress*, Anhua Gao's *To the Edge of the Sky: A Story of Love, Betrayal, Suffering, and the Strength of Human Courage*, and Ting-xing Ye's *A Life in the Bitter Wind: A Memoir* are but a few examples.

8   This is another way national allegory is required by cultural nationalists in minority communities.

9   Even though postcolonial critics like Spivak often refuse to connect issues in postcolonial studies with those in ethnic studies, postcolonial studies is more politically productive for the local terrain when in dialogue with ethnic studies. The works of Radhakrishnan (*Diasporic Mediations*) and of San Juan (*After Postcolonialism* and *Beyond Postcolonial Theory*) are eloquent examples of cross-fertilization. In the light of the global multiculturalism I describe, immigration, diaspora, and globalization have caused the postcolonial and the ethnic minority to become increasingly intermingled.

10 All quotations from the Nobel Prize committee are from the official Web site of the Nobel Foundation, located at http://www.nobel.se/literature/laureates/2000/.

11 See, e.g., Huang.

12 This definition of recognition as re-cognition is from Ahmed.

Works cited

Ahmad, Aijaz. "Jameson's Rhetoric of Otherness and the 'National Allegory.' " *In Theory: Classes, Nations, Literatures*. London: Verso, 1992. 95–122.

Ahmed, Sara. *Strange Encounters: Embodied Others in Post-coloniality*. London: Routledge, 2000.

Badiou, Alain. *Ethics: An Essay on the Understanding of Evil*. Trans. Peter Hallward. London: Verso, 2002.

Baucom, Ian. "Globalit, Inc.; or, The Cultural Logic of Global Literary Studies." Gunn 158–72.

Butler, Judith. "Merely Cultural." *New Left Review* ns 227 (1998): 33–44.

Chow, Rey. "How (the) Inscrutable Chinese Led to Globalized Theory." Gunn 69–74.

de Lauretis, Teresa. *Technologies of Gender*. Bloomington: Indiana UP, 1987.

Dimock, Wai Chee. "Literature for the Planet." Gunn 173–88.

Dirlik, Arif. "Literature/Identity: Transnationalism, Narrative and Representation." *Review of Education / Pedagogy / Cultural Studies* 24 (2002): 209–34.

Dubey, Madhu. "Postmodernism and Racial Difference." U of California Multicampus Research Group on Transnational and Transcolonial Studies. U of California, Los Angeles. 20 Nov. 2002.

Fraser, Nancy. "Rethinking Recognition." *New Left Review* ns 3 (2000): 107–20.

Gao Xingjian. "The Case for Literature." Nobel Lecture. 2000. *The Nobel Prize in Literature 2000*. 21 Aug. 2003. Nobel Foundation. 13 Sept. 2003 <http://www.nobel.se/literature/laureates/2000/gao-lecture-e.html >.

—. *Lingshan* [*Soul Mountain*]. Taipei: Lianjing, 1990.

—. *Yige ren de shengjing* [*One's Man's Bible*]. Taipei: Lianjing, 1999.

Gunn, Giles, coordinator. *Globalizing Literary Studies. PMLA* 116 (2001): 1–272.

Hallward, Peter. Introduction. Badiou vii–xlvii.

Hartsock, Nancy. "Rethinking Modernism: Minority vs. Majority Theories." *The Nature and Context of Minority Discourse*. Ed. Abdul R. JanMohamed and David Lloyd. New York: Oxford UP, 1990. 17–36.

Huang Chin-shu. *Ma hua wenxue yu Zhongguo xing* [*Malaysian Sinophone Literature and Chineseness*]. Taipei: Yuanzun wenhua, 1998.

Jameson, Fredric. "A Brief Response." *Social Text* 17 (1987): 26–27.

—. "Third-World Literature in the Era of Multinational Capitalism." *Social Text* 15 (1986): 65–88.

Kristal, Efraín. "Considering Coldly. . . ." *New Left Review* ns 15 (2002): 61–74.

Levinas, Emmanuel. *Otherwise Than Being; or, Beyond Essence*. Trans. Alphonso Lingis. Pittsburgh: Duquesne UP, 2000.

Lionnet, Françoise, and Shu-mei Shih, eds. *Minor Transnationalism*. Durham: Duke UP, forthcoming.

—. "Thinking through the Minor, Transnationally: An Introduction." Lionnet and Shih, *Minor Transnationalism*.

Lowe, Lisa. *Immigrant Acts: On Asian American Cultural Politics*. Durham: Duke UP, 1996.

Malmqvist, Göran. "Presentation Speech." 2000. *The Nobel Prize in Literature 2000*. 19 Dec. 2000. Nobel Foundation. 13 Sept. 2003 <http://www.nobel.se/literature/2000/presentation-speech.html >.

Moretti, Franco. "Conjectures on World Literature." *New Left Review* ns 1 (2000): 54–68.

—. "The Slaughterhouse of Literature." *Modern Language Quarterly* 61 (2000): 207–27.

Oliver, Kelly. *Witnessing: Beyond Recognition*. Minneapolis: U of Mnnesota P, 2001.

Palumbo-Liu, David. "Rational and Irrational Choices: Form, Affect, Ethics." Lionnet and Shih, *Minor Transnationalism*.

Pizer, John. "Goethe's 'World Literature' Paradigm and Contemporary Cultural Globalization." *Comparative Literature* 52 (2000): 213–27.

Radhakrishnan, R. *Diasporic Mediations: Between Home and Location.* Minneapolis: U of Mnnesota P, 1996.

Said, Edward. *Orientalism.* New York: Vintage, 1979.

——. "A Window on the World." *Guardian* 2 Aug. 2003. 14 Oct. 2003 <http://www.guardian.co.uk/>.

San Juan, E., Jr. *After Postcolonialism: Remapping Philippines–United States Confrontation.* Boulder: Rowman, 2000.

——. *Beyond Postcolonial Theory.* New York: St. Martin's, 1998.

Shih, Shu-mei. "Globalization and Minoritization: Ang Lee and the Politics of Flexibility." *New Formations: A Journal of Culture/Theory/Politics* 40 (2000): 86–101.

Spivak, Gayatri. "Can the Subaltern Speak?" *Marxism and the Interpretation of Cultures.* Ed. Cary Nelson and Laurence Grossberg. Urbana: U of Illinois P, 1988. 271–313.

Tam, Kwok-kan. "Gao Xingjian, the Nobel Prize, and the Politics of Recognition." Introduction. *Soul of Chaos: Critical Perspectives on Gao Xingjian.* Ed. Tam. Hong Kong: Chinese UP, 2001. 1–20.

Wallerstein, Immanuel. "World-Systems Analysis." *The Essential Wallerstein.* New York: New, 2000. 129–48.

Xie Huadong. *He Nuobei'er wenxuejiang jiaojin* [*Flexing Muscles with the Nobel Prize in Literature*]. Shanghai: Xuelin, 2002.

Žižek, Slavoj. "Multiculturalism; or, The Cultural Logic of Multinational Capitalism." *New Left Review* os 225 (1997): 28–51.

Chapter 26

Pascale Casanova

LITERATURE AS A WORLD (2005)

PASCALE CASANOVA (B. 1959) IS A French scholar and permanent visiting professor at Duke University who has also worked extensively with literature in radio broadcasting. Although she does not use the term world literature to describe the main interest of her work, her 1999 book *La Republique mondiale des lettres* (Eng. 2004 *The World Republic of Letters*) was an early expression of the renewed interest in the theory of world literature, along with the work of David Damrosch and Franco Moretti. Where one of Damrosch's main interests is to bring unknown works into conversation with the Western canon, and Moretti seeks to explain how genres, in particular the novel, influence other literatures, Casanova's work can be said to adopt an intermediate position. Influenced by the work of both world systems theorist Immanuel Wallerstein and sociologist Pierre Bourdieu, and recognizing the many kinds of domination which take place between national literatures, she has described the breaches in the obvious channels of influence, for example by devoting much attention to writers from the semi-periphery of the major European literatures.

Building on the theories of Bourdieu, Casanova makes a case for an international literary space which has developed its own standards, canons and values, and which operates separately from the national fields of literature, where the structure made up of genres, histories and dominant authors is very different and requires a cultural intimacy which is impossible to achieve in the international literary field. This also accounts for a split between authors who operate predominantly nationally and internationally.

Bourdieu's model also acknowledges the idea of the only relative autonomy of the literary field and takes economic factors into account in the description of the conditions of circulation. Thereby Casanova's approach resembles that of Moretti, but rather than focusing on genres, Casanova convincingly describes the importance of creating new positions in a literary field as one of the central dynamics in the history-making of the international literary space.

In "Literature as a World" Casanova presents the main principles behind her book. She also emphasizes the difficulty of finding the perfect model to account for all the complexities of the exchanges which take place in the world literary society. Nevertheless, the analysis of the historical conditions and structures of literary fields remains key to understanding why some authors and not others have made their way into the international literary canons. In recognition of the growing influence of the Anglophone world at the expense of the position once held by Paris, she argues that the Nobel Prize is one of the institutions that both demonstrate that there is a world literary space that has values of its own, but which also increase the risk of its domination by fewer literatures. Her essay thus concludes with an examination of successful authors from the periphery who have had a lasting influence on the literary centers of the world, which is also a call for diversity and for a tempered optimism about what literature can achieve.

Pascale Casanova, "Literature as a World," *New Left Review* 31 (2005): 71–90.

> *Customer*: God made the world in six days and you, you can't make me a damn pair of trousers in six months!
> *Tailor*: But sir, look at the world and look at your trousers.
>
> quoted by Samuel Beckett

> Far, far from you world history unfolds, the world history of your soul.
>
> Franz Kafka

Three questions. Is it possible to re-establish the lost bond between literature, history and the world, while still maintaining a full sense of the irreducible singularity of literary texts? Second, can literature itself be conceived as a world? And if so, might an exploration of its territory help us to answer question number one?

Put differently: is it possible to find the conceptual means with which to oppose the central postulate of internal, text-based literary criticism—the total rupture between text and world? Can we propose any theoretical and practical tools that could combat the governing principle of the autonomy of the text, or the alleged independence of the linguistic sphere? To date, the answers given to this crucial question, from postcolonial theory among others, seem to me to have established only a limited connection between the two supposedly incommensurate domains. Postcolonialism posits a direct link between literature and history, one that is exclusively political. From this, it moves to an *external* criticism that runs the risk of reducing the literary to the political, imposing a series of annexations or short-circuits, and often passing in silence over the actual aesthetic, formal or stylistic characteristics that actually 'make' literature.

I want to propose a hypothesis that would move beyond this division between internal and external criticism. Let us say that a mediating space exists between literature and the world: a parallel territory, relatively autonomous from the political domain, and dedicated as a result to questions, debates, inventions of a specifically literary nature. Here, struggles of all sorts—political, social, national, gender, ethnic—come to be refracted, diluted, deformed or transformed according to a literary logic, and in literary forms. Working from this hypothesis, while trying to envisage all its theoretical and practical consequences, should permit us to set out on a course of criticism that would be both internal and external; in other words, a criticism that could give a unified account of, say, the evolution of poetic forms, or the aesthetics of the novel, and their connection to the political, economic and social world—including telling us how, by a very long (indeed historical) process, the link gets broken in the most autonomous regions of this space.

So: another world, whose divisions and frontiers are relatively independent of political and linguistic borders. And with its own laws, its own history, its specific revolts and revolutions; a market where non-market values are traded, within a non-economic economy; and measured, as we shall see, by an aesthetic scale of time. This World of Letters functions invisibly for the most part, save to those most distant from its great centres or most deprived of its resources, who can see more clearly than others the forms of violence and domination that operate within it.

Let us call this mediating area the 'world literary space'. It is no more than a tool that should be tested by concrete research, an instrument that might provide an account of the logic and history of literature, without falling into the trap of total autonomy. It is also a 'hypothetical model' in Chomsky's sense—a body of statements whose working out (if risky) may itself help to formulate the object of description; that is, an internally coherent set of propositions.[1] Working from a model should permit a certain freedom from the immediate 'given'. It should, on the contrary, allow us to construct every case afresh; and to show with each one that it does not exist in isolation, but is a particular instance of the possible, an element in a group or family, which we could not have seen without having previously formulated an abstract model of all possibilities.

This conceptual tool is not 'world literature' itself—that is, a body of literature expanded to a world scale, whose documentation and, indeed, existence remains problematic—but a *space*: a set of interconnected positions, which must be thought and described in relational terms. At stake are not the modalities of analysing literature on a world scale, but the conceptual means for thinking literature *as* a world.

In his story, 'The Figure in the Carpet'—turning as it does on the aims of interpretation in literature—Henry James deploys the beautiful metaphor of the Persian rug. Viewed casually or too close up, this appears an indecipherable tangle of arbitrary shapes and colours; but from the right angle, the carpet will suddenly present the attentive observer with 'the one right combination' of 'superb intricacy'—an ordered set of motifs which can only be understood in relation to each other, and which only become visible when perceived in their totality, in their reciprocal dependence and mutual interaction.[2] Only when the carpet is seen as a configuration—to use Foucault's term in *Les Mots et les choses*—ordering the shapes and colours can its regularities, variations, repetitions be understood; both its coherence and its internal relationships. Each figure can be grasped only in terms of the position it occupies within the whole, and its interconnections with all the others.

The Persian carpet metaphor perfectly encapsulates the approach offered here: to take a different perspective, shifting the ordinary vantage-point on literature. Not to focus just on the global coherence of the carpet, but rather to show that, starting from a grasp of the overall pattern of the designs, it will be possible to understand each motif, each colour in its most minute detail; that is, each text, each individual author, on the basis of their relative position within this immense structure. My project, then, is to restore the coherence of the global structure within which texts appear, and which can only be seen by taking the route seemingly farthest from them: through the vast, invisible territory which I have called the 'World Republic of Letters'. But only in order to return to the texts themselves, and to provide a new tool for reading them.

Birth of a world

This literary space did not, of course, spring into being in its present configuration. It emerged as the product of a historical process, from which it grew progressively more autonomous. Without going into detail, we can say that it appeared in Europe in the 16th century, France and England forming its oldest regions. It was consolidated and enlarged into central and eastern Europe during the 18th and especially the 19th centuries, propelled by Herderian national theory. It expanded throughout the 20th century, notably through the still-ongoing decolonization process: manifestos proclaiming the right to literary existence or independence continue to appear, often linked to movements for national self-determination. Although the space of literature has been constituted more or less everywhere in the world, its unification across the whole planet is far from complete.

The mechanisms through which this literary universe functions are the exact opposite of what is ordinarily understood by 'literary globalization'—better defined as a short-term boost to publishers' profits in the most market-oriented and powerful centres through the marketing of products intended for rapid, 'de-nationalized' circulation.[3] The success of this type of book among educated Western layers—representing no more than a shift from train-station to airport literature—has fostered belief in an ongoing literary pacification process: a progressive normalization and standardization of themes, forms, languages and story-types across the globe. In reality, structural inequalities within the literary world give rise to specific series of struggles, rivalries and contests over literature itself. Indeed, it is through these collisions that the ongoing unification of literary space becomes visible.

Stockholm and Greenwich

One objective indicator of the existence of this world literary space is the (almost) unanimous belief in the universality of the Nobel Prize for literature. The significance attributed to this award, the peculiar diplomacy involved, the national expectations engendered, the colossal renown it bestows; even (above all?) the annual criticism of the Swedish jury for its alleged lack of objectivity, its supposed political prejudices, its aesthetic errors—all conspire to make this annual canonization a global engagement for the protagonists of literary space. The Nobel Prize is today one of the few truly international literary consecrations, a unique labora-tory for the designation and definition of what is universal in literature.[4] The echoes it creates each year, the expectations aroused, the beliefs stirred all reaffirm the existence of a literary world stretching across virtually the entire planet, with its own mode of celebration, both autonomous—not subject, or at least not directly, to political, linguistic, national, nationalist or commercial criteria—and global. In this sense, the Nobel Prize is a prime, objective indi-cator of the existence of a world literary space.[5]

Another indicator—less readily observable—is the appearance of a specific measure-ment of time, common to all the players. Each new entrant must recognize at the outset a reference point, a norm against which he or she will be measured; all positions are located relative to a centre in which the literary present is determined. I propose to call this the Greenwich Meridian of literature. Just as the imaginary line, arbitrarily chosen in order to determine the lines of longitude, contributes to the real organization of the world and makes it possible to measure distances and assess positions across the surface of the globe, so the literary meridian allows us to gauge the distance from the centre of the protagonists within literary space. It is the place where the measurement of literary time—that is, the assessment of aesthetic modernity—is crystallized, contested, elaborated. What is considered modern here, at a given moment, will be declared to be the 'present': texts that will 'make their mark', capable of modifying the current aesthetic norms. These works will serve, for a time at least, as the units of measurement within a specific chronology, models of comparison for subsequent productions.

To be decreed 'modern' is one of the most difficult forms of recognition for writers outside the centre, and the object of violent and bitter competition. Octavio Paz brilliantly set out the terms of this strange struggle in his Nobel Prize acceptance speech, the title of which is, precisely, *In Search of the Present*. He describes his entire personal and poetic trajec-tory as a frantic—and successful, as his receipt of the highest award testifies—search for a literary present, from which he understood early on that, as a Mexican, he was structurally very distant.[6] Texts granted modern status create the chronology of literary history, according to a logic that can be quite different from those of other social worlds. For example, once Joyce's *Ulysses* had been consecrated as a 'modern' work by Valéry Larbaud's 1929 French translation, winning the reviews and critical attention that had so far eluded it in English, it became—and remains, in certain regions of literary space—one of the measures of novelistic modernity.

Temporalities

Modernity is, of course, an unstable entity: a locus of permanent struggle, a decree destined for more or less rapid obsolescence, and one of the principles of change at the heart of the world literary space. All those who aspire to modernity, or who struggle for monopoly control over its attribution, are engaged in the constant classification and de-classification of works—with texts apt to become former moderns or new classics. The recurrent use of temporal metaphors in criticism, airily declaring works to be 'passé' or 'outmoded', archaic or innovative, anachronistic or imbued with 'the spirit of the times', is one of the clearest signs of these mechanisms' functioning. This explains, at least in part, the permanence of the term 'modernity' in literary movements and proclamations at least since 1850—from the different European and Latin American modernisms, through Italian and Russian futurisms, up to the various postmodernisms. The innumerable claims to 'newness'—'Nouveau Roman', 'Nouvelle Vague' and so on—adhere to the same principle.

Owing to the inherent precariousness of the principle of 'modernity', a work declared modern is doomed to become obsolete unless elevated to the category of 'classic'. Through this process, some works can escape the vagaries of opinion and disputes over their relative value. In literary terms, a classic stands above temporal competition (and spatial inequality). On the other hand, practices that are remote from the literary present, itself established by the whole system of consecrations at the centre, will be declared long out of date. For example, the naturalist novel is still being produced in the zones furthest from the Greenwich Meridian (whether peripheral literary spaces or the most commercial regions of the centre), even though it has not been considered 'modern' by the autonomous authorities for a very long time. The Brazilian critic Antonio Candido observed:

> what demands attention in Latin America is the way aesthetically anachronistic works were considered valid . . . This is what occurred with naturalism in the novel, which arrived a little late and has prolonged itself until now with no essential break in continuity . . . So, when naturalism was already only a survival of an outdated genre in Europe, among us it could still be an ingredient of legitimate literary formulas, such as the social novel of the 1930s and 40s.[7]

This type of aesthetic-temporal struggle is often waged through intermediaries who themselves have an interest in the 'discovery' of authors from abroad. The Norwegian Ibsen was consecrated as one of the greatest European dramatists more or less simultaneously in Paris and London, around 1890. His work, labelled 'realist', overturned all theatrical practice, writing, decor, language and dialogue, leading to a genuine revolution in European theatre. The international consecration of a playwright from a country that had gained independence only a short time before, and whose language was seldom spoken (and therefore seldom translated) in France and England, was secured through the actions of a few mediators—Bernard Shaw in London, André Antoine and Lugné-Poe in Paris—who themselves planned to 'modernize' theatre in their respective countries, going beyond the stale, established norms of vaudeville and bourgeois drama which held sway in London and Paris, and making their own names as dramatists or producers.[8] In the Dublin of 1900, Joyce in his turn made use of the prodigious aesthetic and thematic novelty of Ibsen's work in his struggle against Irish theatre, which threatened, in his view, to become 'much too Irish'.

Much the same applies to Faulkner. Having been lauded from the 1930s on as one of the most innovative novelists of the age,[9] Faulkner himself became a measure of novelistic innovation after receiving the Nobel Prize in 1950. Following his international consecration, Faulkner's work played the role of a 'temporal accelerator' for a wide range of novelists of different periods, in countries structurally comparable, in economic and cultural terms, to the American South. All of them openly announced their use (at least in a technical sense) of this Faulknerian accelerator; among them were Juan Benet in 1950s Spain, Gabriel García Márquez in Colombia and Mario Vargas Llosa in Peru in the 1950s and 1960s, Kateb Yacine in 1960s Algeria, António Lobo-Antunes in 1970s Portugal, Edouard Glissant in the French Antilles of the 1980s, and so on.

Seeing through borders

But why start from the hypothesis of a world literary space and not a more restricted one, which would have been easier to demarcate—a regional or linguistic field, for instance? Why choose to begin by constructing the largest possible domain, the one entailing most risks? Because to illuminate the workings of this space, and in particular the forms of domination exerted within it, implies the rejection of established national categories and divisions; indeed, demands a trans- or inter-national mode of thought. Once we adopt this world perspective, we can immediately see that national boundaries, or linguistic ones, simply screen out the real effects of literary domination and inequality. The reason for this is simple: literatures the whole world over were formed on the national model created and promoted by Germany at the end of the 18th century. The national movement of literatures, which accompanied the formation of Europe's political spaces from the beginning of the 19th century, led to an essentialization of literary categories and the belief that the frontiers of literary space necessarily coincided with national borders. Nations were considered to be separate, self-enclosed units, each irreducible to any other; from within their autarchic specificity, these entities produced literary objects whose 'historical necessity' is inscribed within a national horizon. Stefan Collini has demonstrated the tautology underlying the definition of 'national literature' for the British—or rather, English—case: 'only those authors who display the putative characteristics are recognized as authentically English, a category whose definition relies upon the examples provided in the literature written by just those authors.'[10]

The national division of literatures leads to a form of astigmatism. An analysis of Irish literary space between 1890 and 1930 that ignored events unfolding both in London (the political, colonial and literary power, in opposition to which the Irish space is constructed) and in Paris (alternative recourse and politically neutral literary power), or passed in silence over the trajectories, exiles, and various forms of recognition offered in the different capitals, would be condemned to a partial and distorted view of the actual stakes and power relations facing Irish protagonists. Similarly, a study of the formation of the German literary space from the end of the 18th century that overlooked its intensely competitive relationship with France would run the risk of completely misunderstanding its structuring engagements.

This is not to suggest that international literary power relations are the only explanatory factors in literary texts, or the sole interpretative instruments we can apply to them; still less that literary complexity should be reduced to this dimension. Many other variables—national (that is, internal to the national literary field), psychological, psychoanalytic, formal or formalist—have a role to play.[11] The point is rather to demonstrate, in both structural and historical terms, how many variables, conflicts or forms of soft violence have remained undetected and unexplained due to the invisibility of this world structure. Critical writing on Kafka, for example, is often limited either to the biographical study of his psychology or to descriptions of Prague in the 1900s. In this case, the biographical and national 'screen' prevents us from seeing the author's place within other, larger worlds: within the space of the Jewish nationalist movements then developing across central and eastern Europe; in debates between Bundists and Yiddishists; as one of the dominated in the German linguistic and cultural space, and so on. The national filter acts as a kind of 'natural' frontier which prevents the analyst from considering the violence of transnational political and literary power relations as they impact upon the writer.

World space or world-system?

The hypothesis of a world space, functioning through a structure of domination that is, to some extent, independent of political, economic, linguistic and social forms, clearly owes a great deal to Pierre Bourdieu's concept of the 'field' and, more precisely, of the 'literary field'.[12] But the latter has so far been envisaged within a national framework, limited by the borders, historical traditions and capital accumulation processes of a specific nation-state. I found in Fernand Braudel's work, and his 'world-economy' in particular, the idea and the possibility of extending the analysis of these mechanisms onto the international plane.[13]

I would stress, though, the distinction between the 'world structure' that I am proposing and the 'world-system', most notably developed by Immanuel Wallerstein, which seems to me less appropriate to spaces of cultural production.[14] A 'system' implies directly interactive relations between every element, every position. A structure, on the other hand, is characterized by objective relations, which can operate outside of any direct interaction. Moreover, in Wallerstein's terms, the forces and movements that struggle against the 'system' are considered 'anti-systemic'. In other words, they are external to the system and struggle against it from a position 'outside', which is sometimes hard to situate but can potentially be located on the 'periphery'. In an international structure of domination, the opposite is the case: the definitions of 'outside' and 'inside'—that is, the boundaries of the space—are themselves the focus of struggles. It is these struggles that constitute the space, that unify it and drive its expansion. Within this structure, means and methods are permanently disputed: who can be declared a writer, who can make legitimate aesthetic judgements (ones that will endow a given work with a specific value), the very definition of literature.

In other words, world literary space is not a sphere that is set above all the others, reserved exclusively for international writers, editors, critics—for literary actors manoeuvring in a supposedly de-nationalized world. It is not the sole preserve of great novelists, hugely successful authors, editorial produce devised for global sales. It is formed by all the inhabitants of the Republic of Letters, each of them differentially situated within their own national literary space. At the same time, each writer's position must necessarily be a double one, twice defined: each writer is situated once according to the position he or she occupies in a national space, and then once again according to the place that this occupies within the world space. This dual position, inextricably national and international, explains why—contrary to what economistic views of globalization would have us believe—international struggles take place and have their effects principally within national spaces; battles over the definition of literature, over technical or formal transformations and innovations, on the whole have national literary space as their arena.

The one great dichotomy is between national and international writers. This is the fracture which explains literary forms, types of aesthetic innovation, the adoption of genres. National and international writers fight with different weapons, for divergent aesthetic, commercial and editorial rewards—thus contributing, in different ways, to the accumulation of national literary resources required to enter the world space and compete inside it. Contrary to the conventional view, the national and international are not separate spheres; they are two opposed stances, struggling within the same domain.[15]

This is why literary space cannot simply be imagined as a world geography that might be grasped merely through a description of its regions, its cultural and linguistic climates, centres of attraction and modes of circulation, as Braudel or Wallerstein have done for the economic world.[16] Literary space should rather be conceived in terms of Cassirer's 'symbolic form', within which writers, readers, researchers, teachers, critics, publishers, translators and the rest read, write, think, debate, interpret; a structure which provides their—our—intellectual categories, and recreates its hierarchies and constraints in every mind, thus reinforcing the material aspects of its existence.[17] Differentially so, according to one's position within it (national, linguistic, professional) at any given moment. Literary space in all its forms—texts, juries, editors, critics, writers, theorists, scholars—exists twice over: once in things and once in thought; that is, in the set of beliefs produced by these material relations and internalized by the players in literature's Great Game.

This is another thing that makes the structure so hard to visualize: it is impossible to place it at a distance, as a discrete and objectifiable phenomenon. More: any description or analysis of its workings has to go *against* the vast mass of conventional thought about literature, against the given scholarly or aesthetic facts, and to reconceive every notion, every category—influence, tradition, heritage, modernity, classics, value—in terms of the specific, internal workings of the world republic of letters.

Accumulating power

The primary characteristics of this world literary space are hierarchy and inequality. The skewed distribution of goods and values has been one of its constituting principles, since resources have historically accumulated within national frontiers. Goethe was the first to intuit the direct link between the appearance of a *Weltliteratur* and the emergence of a new economy founded on the specific struggles of international literary relations: a 'market where all nations offer their wares' and 'a general intellectual trade'.[18] In fact, the world of literature provides a paradoxical sort of marketplace, constituted around a non-economic economy, and functioning according to its own set of values: for production and reproduction here are based on a belief in the 'objective' value of literary creations—works denominated as 'priceless'. The value produced by national or universal classics, great innovators, *poètes maudits*, rare texts, becomes concentrated in the capital cities in the form of national literary goods. The oldest regions, those longest established in the literary field, are the 'richest' in this sense—are credited with most power. Prestige is the quintessential form power takes in the literary universe: the intangible authority unquestioningly accorded to the oldest, noblest, most legitimate (the terms being almost synonymous) literatures, the most consecrated classics and most celebrated authors.[19]

The unequal distribution of literary resources is fundamental to the structure of the entire world literary space, organized as it is around two opposing poles. At the pole of greatest autonomy—that is, freest from political, national or economic constraints—stand the oldest spaces,[20] those most endowed with literary heritage and resources.[21] These are generally European spaces, the first to enter into transnational literary competition, with large accumulated resources. At the pole of greatest heteronomy, where political, national and commercial criteria hold strongest sway, stand the newcomers, the spaces most lacking in literary resources; and the zones within the oldest regions that are most subordinate to commercial criteria. Each national space, meanwhile, is itself polarized by the same structure.

The power of the richest zones is perpetuated because it has real and measurable effects, notably the 'transfer of prestige' through reviews or prefaces by prestigious writers of hitherto unrecognized books, or of works from outside the centre: Victor Hugo's enthusiastic reviews of Walter Scott, at a time when the first French translations of his novels were appearing; Bernard Shaw's reviews of the first productions of Ibsen's plays in London; Gide's 1947 preface to Taha Hussein's *Livre des jours*; or the complex mechanism of recognition through translation, as in the consecration of Borges when translated by Roger Caillois, Ibsen by William Archer, and so on.

Degrees of autonomy

The second constitutive feature of the literary world is its relative autonomy.[22] Issues posed in the political domain cannot be superimposed upon, or confounded with, those of the literary space, whether national or international. Much contemporary literary theory seems bent on creating this short-circuit, constantly reducing the literary to the political. A salient example would be Deleuze and Guattari's *Kafka*, which claims to deduce from a single diary entry (25 December 1911), not only a particular political stance—thus affirming that Kafka is indeed 'a political author'—but a political vision that informs his entire oeuvre. Taking up a mistranslated phrase in the French version of the *Diary*, they construct the category of 'minor literature' and attribute to Kafka, via a flagrant historical anachronism, preoccupations which could not have been his before the First World War.[23]

Autonomy implies that the events which take place in literary space are autonomous too: the watershed dates, manifestos, heroes, monuments, commemorations, capital cities, all combine to produce a specific history, which cannot be confused with that of the political world—even if it partially depends upon it, in a form that would require careful attention. Braudel, in his economic history of the world between the 15th and 18th centuries, notes the relative independence of artistic space with regard to the economic and hence the political. Venice was the economic capital of the 16th century, but Florence and its Tuscan dialect were intellectually in the ascendant. In the 17th century, Amsterdam became the great centre of European trade, but Rome and Madrid triumphed in the arts and literature. In the 18th century, London was the centre of the economic world but it was Paris that imposed its cultural hegemony:

> In the late 19th and early 20th century, France, though lagging behind the rest of Europe economically, was the undisputed centre of Western painting and literature; the times when Italy and Germany dominated the world of music were not times when Italy or Germany dominated Europe economically; and even today, the formidable economic lead by the United States has not made it the literary and artistic leader of the world.[24]

The case of the Latin American literatures would be further proof of the relative autonomy of the literary sphere, with no direct link, no cause-and-effect relation between political-economic strength and literary power or legitimacy at an international level. The global recognition accorded to these bodies of work, in the form of four Nobel Prizes, the worldwide esteem for their great names, the established legitimacy of their leading aesthetic model, despite the political and economic weakness of the countries concerned, show that the two orders cannot be confounded. To understand the conditions for the emergence of Latin America's literary 'boom', for example, we need to postulate the relative independence of literary phenomena.[25]

But if the literary world is *relatively* independent of the political and economic universe, it is by the same token relatively dependent on it. The entire history of world literary space—both in its totality, and within each of the national literary spaces that compose it—is one of an initial dependence on national-political relations, followed by a progressive emancipation from them through a process of autonomization. The original dependence is still there to some degree, related to the seniority of the space under consideration; above all at the level of language. Their almost systematic nationalization across the world makes languages an ambiguous instrument, inextricably literary and political.

Forms of domination

In literary space the modes of domination are thus encased within each other. Three principal forms exert themselves to differential degrees, depending on the position of the given space: linguistic, literary and political domination—this last increasingly taking on an economic cast. The three overlap, interpenetrate and obscure one another to such an extent that often only the most obvious form—political-economic domination—can be seen. Numerous literary spaces are linguistically dependent (Canada, Australia, New Zealand, Belgium, Switzerland, Quebec) without being politically subordinate; others, notably those emerging from decolonization, may have achieved linguistic independence but remain politically unfree. But subordination can also be measured in purely literary terms, independent of any political oppression or subjugation. It is impossible to account for certain types of exile, or changes in written language, temporary or permanent—those of August Strindberg, Joseph Conrad, Samuel Beckett, E. M. Cioran, for example—without hypothesizing the existence of strictly literary forms of domination, forces outside any power-political framework.[26]

The consequences of literary domination for the production, publication and recognition of texts require their own analysis. The inevitable primacy that literary studies accord to psychology, for instance—notoriously based on the incomparable solitude of the writer—often hinders an account of the unnoticed structural constraints that impinge on a writer's production of works, down to their choice of form, genre, language. Take Gertrude Stein: although feminist studies rightly insist on her biographical and psychological particularity, especially her lesbianism, they leave unmentioned her location in world literary space, as if this were somehow self-evident. Or rather, anything relating to her position as an American in Paris is mentioned only in a biographical or anecdotal context. Yet we know that the US was subordinate in literary terms during the 1910s and 1920s, and that American writers came to Paris seeking literary resources and aesthetic models. Here we have an example of specifically literary domination, taking place in the absence of any other form of dependence. A simple analysis of Stein's status as an expatriate poet in Paris—'immigrant' status being a clear sign of dependence—and the position of the American literary space within the World of Letters would help us understand why Stein was so preoccupied, as was Ezra Pound at the same juncture, with the 'enrichment' of a national American literature. At the same time, her interest in the literary representation of Americans—her gigantic *The Making of Americans* its most striking manifestation—takes on its full significance. The fact that she was a woman and a lesbian in Paris in the 1910s is of course crucial to understanding her subversive impulse and the nature of her whole aesthetic project. But the historically structured relation of literary domination, clearly of primary importance, remains hidden from the critical tradition. As if, as a general rule, there were always some particularity—important no doubt, but still secondary—that concealed the overall pattern of literary power relations.

This form of literary ascendancy—so unusual, so hard to describe, so paradoxical—can in some situations represent a liberation, compared to the aesthetic, or aesthetico-political, imprisonment of archaic spaces that are closed to innovation. Its power is exercised over every text, every writer in the world, whatever their position and however clear their awareness of the mechanisms of literary domination; but all the more, over those who originate from a literary space that lacks autonomy or is located in one of the subordinate regions of the World of Letters.

However, the effects of consecration by the central authorities can be so powerful as to give certain writers from the margins who have achieved full recognition the illusion that the structure of domination has simply disappeared; seeing themselves as living proof of the establishment of a new 'world literary order'. Universalizing from their particular case, they claim that we are witnessing a total and definitive reversal of the balance of power between centre and peripheries. Carlos Fuentes, for instance, writes in *The Geography of the Novel*:

> The old Eurocentrism has been overcome by a polycentrism which . . . should lead us to an 'activation of differences' as the common condition of a central humanity . . . Goethe's world literature has finally found its correct meaning: it is the literature of difference, the narration of diversity converging in one world . . . A single world, with numerous voices. The new constellations that together form the geography of the novel are varied and mutating.[27]

Multiculturalist enthusiasms have led others to assert that the relation between centre and periphery has now been radically reversed, and that the world of the periphery will henceforth occupy the central position. In reality, the effects of this pacific and hybridized fable are to depoliticize literary relations, to perpetuate the legend of the great literary enchantment and to disarm writers from the periphery who are seeking recognition strategies that would be both subversive and effective.

Modernismo as re-expropriation

Literary inequality and its relations of dominance provoke their own forms of struggle, rivalry and competition. But the subjugated here have also developed specific strategies which can only be understood in a literary framework, although they may have political consequences. Forms, innovations, movements, revolutions in narrative order may be diverted, captured, appropriated or annexed, in attempts to overturn existing literary power relations.

It is in these terms that I would analyse the advent of *modernismo* in the Spanish-speaking countries at the end of the 19th century. How to explain the fact that this movement, which turned the entire tradition of Hispanic poetry on its head, could have been dictated by a poet from Nicaragua, on the far reaches of the Spanish colonial empire? Rubén Darío, captivated from boyhood by the literary legend of Paris, stayed in the city in the late 1880s and, logically enough, was enthused by the French symbolist poetry that was just making its mark.[28] He then carried out an astonishing operation, which can only be called an expropriation of literary capital: he imported, into Spanish poetry itself, the very procedures, themes, vocabulary and forms lofted by the French symbolists. This expropriation was asserted quite explicitly, and the deliberate Frenchification of Spanish poetry, down to the phonemes and syntactic forms, designated 'mental Gallicism'. The diversion of this capital towards inextricably literary and political ends[29] was not, then, carried out in the passive mode of 'reception', and still less of 'influence', as traditional literary analysis would have it. On the contrary, this capture was the active form and instrument of a complex struggle. To combat both the political-linguistic dominance of Spain over its colonial empire and the sclerosis that was paralysing Spanish-language poetry, Darío openly asserted the literary domination exercised by Paris at that time.[30] Paris, both as cultural citadel and as potentially more neutral political territory for the subjects of other imperial or national powers, was used by numerous 19th- and 20th-century writers as a weapon in their literary struggles.

The problem at stake in the theorization of literary inequality, then, is not whether peripheral writers 'borrow' from the centre, or whether or not literary traffic flows from centre to periphery; it is the restitution, to the subordinated of the literary world, of the forms, specificities and hardships of their struggles. Only thus can they be given credit for the invention—often concealed—of their creative freedom. Faced with the need to find solutions to dependence, and in the knowledge that the literary universe obeys Berkeley's famous *esse est percipi*—to be is to be perceived—they gradually perfect a set of strategies linked to their positions, their written language, their location in literary space, to the distance or proximity they want to establish with the prestige-bestowing centre. Elsewhere, I have tried to show that the majority of compromise solutions achieved within this structure are based on an 'art of distance', a way of situating oneself, aesthetically, neither too near nor too far; and that the most subordinated of writers manoeuvre with extraordinary sophistication to give themselves the best chance of being perceived, of existing in literary terms. An analysis of works originating in these zones as so many complex placement strategies reveals how many of the great literary revolutions have taken place on the margins and in subordinated regions, as witness Joyce, Kafka, Ibsen, Beckett, Darío and many more.

For this reason, to speak of the centre's literary forms and genres simply as a colonial inheritance imposed on writers within subordinated regions is to overlook the fact that literature itself, as a common value of the entire space, is also an instrument which, if reappropriated, can enable writers—and especially those with the fewest resources—to attain a type of freedom, recognition and existence within it. More concretely and directly, these reflections on the immense range of what is possible in literature, even within this overwhelming and inescapable structure of domination, also aim to serve as a symbolic weapon in the struggles of those most deprived of literary resources, confronting obstacles which writers at the centre cannot even imagine. The goal here is to demonstrate that what they experience as an insoluble, individual state of dependence, with no precedents or points of comparison, is in reality a position created by a structure that is at once historical and collective.[31] As well as questioning the methods and tools of comparative literary studies, the structural comparativism of which I sketch the outlines here also seeks to be an instrument in the long and merciless war of literature.

Notes

1   Noam Chomsky, *Current Issues in Linguistic Theory*, The Hague 1964, pp. 105ff.

2   Henry James, *The Figure in the Carpet and Other Stories*, Harmondsworth 1986, p. 381.

3   See André Schiffrin, *The Business of Books: How the International Conglomerates Took over Publishing and Changed the Way we Read*, London and New York 2000.

4   See Kjell Espmark, *Le Prix Nobel. Histoire intérieure d'une consécration littéraire*, Paris 1986.

5   The recent award of the prize to the Austrian Elfriede Jelinek—unclassifiable author of violent and experimental prose works and plays, with a radical, and radically pessimist, political and feminist critical stance—is another example of the Swedish jury's total independence in making its choices and conducting its 'literary policy'.

6   'The modern was outside, we had to import it', he writes, for example. Paz, *La búsqueda del presente. Conferencia Nobel*, San Diego 1990.

7   António Cândido, 'Literature and Underdevelopment', in *On Literature and Society*, trans. Howard Becker, Princeton 1995, pp. 128–29.

8   The same 'self-interested use' of the foreign explains the case of the French Romantics cited by Christopher Prendergast—the former 'made use of' Shakespeare and the English theatrical tradition to establish themselves in the French space. See 'Negotiating World Literature', NLR 8, March–April 2001, pp. 110–11.

9   Sartre's famous article on *The Sound and the Fury*, 'La temporalité chez Faulkner', appeared in the *Nouvelle revue française* in June–July 1939; reprinted in *Situations I*, Paris 1947, pp. 65–75.

10   Stefan Collini, *Public Moralists: Political Thought and Intellectual Life in Britain, 1850–1930*, Oxford 1991, p. 357.

11   *Pace* Christopher Prendergast, I do not argue that the ideas of 'nation' or 'national' must necessarily be linked to that of 'literature'. Indeed, it was rather to distinguish them that my *République mondiale des lettres* (1999) proposed the notion of 'national literary spaces', i.e., sub-spaces which are themselves located within the world literary universe. These sub-spaces vie with one another, through the struggles of writers, not for national (or nationalist) reasons, but instead for strictly literary stakes. That said, the degree of literary independence relative to national conflicts and ideologies has a strong correlation to the age of the sub-space. Here the example of Wordsworth—whose œuvre cannot of course be interpreted purely in terms of international rivalry—is a perfect illustration of the fact that it is the oldest and best endowed national spaces which manage gradually to constitute an autonomous literature within their national enclosures, (relatively) independent of strictly literary stakes; that is, a depoliticized and (at least partially) denationalized space. See Prendergast, 'Negotiating World Literature', pp. 109–12.

12   On this point see Pierre Bourdieu, *Les Règles de l'art. Genèse et structure du champ littéraire*, Paris 1992.

13   Fernand Braudel, *Civilisation matérielle, économie et capitalisme—XVe–XVIIIe siècles*, 3 vols, Paris 1979, vol. 3, especially ch. 1, pp. 12–33.

14   Franco Moretti takes up the world-system concept in his 'Conjectures on World Literature', NLR 1, January–February 2000, and in 'More Conjectures', NLR 20, March–April 2003. It allows him first of all to affirm the unity and foundational inequality of the literary system he seeks to describe, a crucial, boundary-defining affirmation to which I wholly subscribe. On the other hand, it seems to me that his use of the Braudelian opposition between 'centre' and 'periphery' tends to neutralize the (literary) violence involved, and so to obscure its inequality. Instead of this spatial dichotomy, I prefer an opposition between dominant and dominated, so as to reintroduce the fact of a power relation. Here I should make clear that this does not imply a mere division into two opposing categories but, on the contrary, a continuum of different situations in which the degree of dependence varies greatly. We could, for example, introduce the category put forward by Bourdieu of 'dominated among the dominants' to describe the situation of the (literarily) subordinate within Europe. The world-systems use of the term 'semi-periphery' to describe this type of intermediary position also seems to me to neutralize and euphemize the dominant–dominated relation, without providing a precise measure of the degree of dependence.

15   In offering a comparative table of the 'institutions of regional, national and world literature in India', Francesca Orsini suggests that there are different and mutually independent 'levels' or 'spheres' within a single national literary space. I would argue that we are dealing with positions that exist only in and through the relations of power in which they hold each other, and not with a rigid, immutable 'system'. See 'India in the Mirror of World Fiction', NLR 13, January–February 2002, p. 83.

16   See notably Wallerstein, *The Modern World-System*, 3 vols, New York 1980–88.

17   Ernst Cassirer, *La Philosophie des formes symboliques*, vol. 1, *Le langage*, Paris 1972, especially ch. 1, pp. 13–35.

18   J. W. von Goethe, *Goethes Werke*, Hamburg 1981, vol. 12, pp. 362–63. See also Fritz Strich, *Goethe and World Literature*, New York 1972, p. 10.

19   The *Dictionnaire Larousse* gives two complementary definitions of 'prestige', both of which imply the notion of power or authority: '1. Ascendancy stemming from greatness and which seems to possess a mysterious character. 2. Influence, credit'.

20   More precisely, those that have been longest in the space of literary competition. This explains why certain ancient spaces such as China, Japan and the Arab countries are both long-lived and subordinate: they entered the international literary space very late and in subordinate positions.

21   Notably those that can lay claim to (paradoxical) national 'universal classics'.

22   On the notion of 'relative autonomy', see Pierre Bourdieu, *Les Règles de l'art*, Paris 1992, especially pp. 75–164.

23   Kafka's *klein*—suggesting simply 'little literatures'—was overtranslated by Marthe Robert as 'minor literatures', an expression whose subsequent fortunes are well known. See Gilles Deleuze and Félix Guattari, *Kafka. Pour une littérature mineure*, Paris 1975, p. 75; and my 'Nouvelles considérations sur les littératures dites mineures', *Littérature classique*, no. 31, 1997, pp. 233–47.

24   Braudel, *Civilization and Capitalism, 15th–18th century: Volume* III, *The Perspective of the World*, London 1984, p. 68; *Civilisation matérielle*, vol. 3, p. 9.

25   See the debate on this crucial point which has been taking place in Latin America since the 1960s, and which is well reconstructed by Efraín Kristal in 'Considering Coldly . . .', NLR 15, May–June 2002, pp. 67–71. Here we can clearly see that the role of agents of social and political transformation, notably attributed to writers of the 'boom', was largely illusory.

26   August Strindberg briefly became a 'French writer' between 1887 and 1897, writing *Le Plaidoyer d'un fou* and *Inferno* directly in French for the purposes of international recognition.

27   Fuentes, *Geografía de la novela*, Madrid 1993, p. 218.

28   In his *Autobiography*, Darío writes: 'I dreamed of Paris ever since I was a child, to the extent that when I prayed I asked God not to let me die without seeing Paris. Paris was for me like a paradise where one could breathe the essence of earthly happiness'. *Obras completas*, Madrid 1950–55, vol. 1, p. 102.

29   What Perry Anderson has called 'a declaration of cultural independence': *The Origins of Postmodernity*, London and New York 1998, p. 3.

30   Efraín Kristal's analysis of this point is very illuminating and entirely convincing. But he seems to believe that the idea of appropriation or diversion contradicts that of emancipation. Could we not on the contrary put forward the hypothesis that this initial diversion (necessary if it is true that no symbolic revolution can take place without resources) makes possible a creative renewal? After Rubén Darío had played the role of aesthetic accelerator, *modernismo* of course became an entirely separate Hispanic poetic movement, inventing its own codes and norms without any reference to France.

31   This is why I fully subscribe to Franco Moretti's affirmation, which could serve as a motto for a discipline still in its early stages: 'Without collective work, world literature will always remain a mirage'. See 'More Conjectures', NLR 20, March–April 2003, p. 75.

Chapter 27

Milan Kundera

DIE WELTLITERATUR (2005)

MILAN KUNDERA (B. 1929) IS a French-Czech novelist and essayist. His novels are read in most parts of the world, and in his essays he constantly returns to the theme of the nature of the novel and its importance to European and world literature. A sometimes extravagant essayist, he has produced a number of challenging descriptions of the relationships between different national literatures and the deeper values in the genre of the novel. The influence of the cosmopolitan spirit of the eighteenth century is a recurring element in his writing, while he at the same time acknowledges the importance of cultural diversity which nation-states help to preserve. His own background as an immigrant who has switched from the Czech to the French language informs his own writing on the subject as well as his involvement in the translations of his own novels.

In an earlier essay on the writings of Aimé Césaire, "Beau comme une rencontre multiple," Kundera argues that a complex semiperiphery of a nation can be a productive challenge to its writers, an issue which has been significant in his attempts to describe his own roots in a Central Europe whose borders are not as easily defined as those of Scandinavia. The complexities become even greater when we consider many of the post-colonial nations whose ties to the distant colonial powers continue to exert a strong influence on their literatures.

In the essay reprinted here, "Die Weltliteratur", Kundera defines two kinds of provincialism: one which he ascribes to the overconfident large nations which do not need the rest of the world, and one characteristic of the small nations which do not think that they have anything to offer the world. Both provincialisms are fallacies that need to be overcome. Additionally, he makes a claim similar to that of Pascale Casanova's that there are a number of writers who have fared much better in world literature than in their national context, which again makes the case for the existence of a world literary circuit.

Milan Kundera, "Die Weltliteratur," *Le Rideau*, Paris: Gallimard, 2005, pp. 45–72. English translation in *The Curtain: An Essay in Seven Parts* in the translation of Linda Asher, London: Faber and Faber, 2007.

Maximum diversity in minimum space

Whether he is nationalist or cosmopolitan, rooted or uprooted, a European is profoundly conditioned by his relation to his homeland; the national problematic is probably more complex, more grave in Europe than elsewhere, but in any case it is different there. Added to that is another particularity: alongside the large nations Europe contains small nations, several of which have, in the past two centuries, attained or re-attained their political independence. Their existence may have brought me to understand that cultural diversity is the great European value. In a period when the Russian world tried to reshape my small country in its image, I worked out my own ideal of Europe thus: *maximum diversity in minimum space*. The Russians no longer rule my native land, but that ideal is even more imperiled now.

All the nations of Europe are living a common destiny, but each is living it differently, based on its own separate experience. This is why the history of each European art (painting, novel, music, and so on) seems like a relay race in which the various nations pass along similar testimony from one to the next. Polyphonic music had its beginnings in France, it continued its development in Italy, attained incredible complexity in the Netherlands, and reached its fulfillment in Germany, in Bach's works; the upwelling of the English novel of the eighteenth century is followed by the era of the French novel, then by the Russian novel, then by the Scandinavian, and so on. The dynamism and long life of the history of the European arts are inconceivable without the existence of all these nations whose diverse experiences constitute an inexhaustible reservoir of inspiration.

I think of Iceland. In the thirteenth and fourteenth centuries a literary work thousands of pages long was born there: the sagas. At the time neither the French nor the English created such a prose work in their national tongues! We should certainly ponder this thoroughly: the first great prose treasure of Europe was created in its smallest land, which even today numbers fewer than three-hundred thousand inhabitants.

Irreparable inequality

The word "Munich" has become the symbol of capitulation to Hitler. But to be more concrete: at Munich, in the autumn of 1938, the four great nations, Germany, Italy, France and Great Britain, negotiated the fate of a small country to whom they denied the very right to speak. In a room apart the two Czech diplomats waited all night to be led, the next morning, down long hallways into a room where Chamberlain and Daladier, weary, blasé, yawning, informed them of the death sentence.

"A faraway country of which we know little. . . ." Those famous words by which Chamberlain sought to justify the sacrifice of Czechoslovakia were accurate. In Europe there are the large countries on one side and the small on the other; there are the nations seated in the negotiating chambers and those who wait all night in the antechambers.

What distinguishes the small nations from the large is not the quantitative criterion of the number of their inhabitants; it is something deeper: for them their existence is not a self-evident certainty but always a question, a wager, a risk; they are on the defensive against History, that force that is bigger than they, that does not take them into consideration, that does not even notice them. ("It is only by opposing History as such that we can oppose today's history," Witold Gombrowicz wrote.)

There are as many Poles as there are Spaniards. But Spain is an old power whose existence has never been under threat, whereas History has taught the Poles what it means not to exist. Deprived of their State, they lived for over a century on death row. "Poland has not *yet* perished" is the poignant first line of their national anthem and, in a letter to Czeslaw Miłosz some fifty years ago, Gombrowicz wrote a sentence that could never have occurred to any Spaniard: "If, in a hundred years, our language still exists. . . ."

Let's try to imagine that the Icelandic sagas had been written in English: Their heroes' names would be as familiar to us as Tristan or Don Quixote; their singular aesthetic character, oscillating between chronicle and fiction, would have provoked all sorts of theories; people would have argued over whether they should or should not be considered the first European novels. I don't mean to say they have been forgotten; after centuries of indifference they are now being studied in universities throughout the world; but they belong to the "archaeology of letters," they do not influence living literature.

Given that the French are unused to distinguishing between nation and State, I often hear Kafka described as a Czech writer (from 1918 on he was, indeed, a citizen of the newly constituted Czechoslovakia). Of course that is nonsense: Kafka wrote solely in German, need we recall, and he considered himself a German writer. But suppose for a moment he had written his books in Czech. Today who would know them? Before he managed to force Kafka on the world's awareness, Max Brod had to deploy enormous efforts, over the course of twenty years, and that was with the support of the greatest German writers! Even if a Prague editor had managed to publish the books of a hypothetical Czech Kafka, none of his compatriots (that is to say, no Czech) would have had the authority needed to familiarize the world with those extravagant texts written in the language of a "faraway country of which we know little." No, believe me, nobody would know Kafka today—nobody—if he had been a Czech.

Gombrowicz's *Ferdydurke* was published in Polish in 1937. It had to wait fifteen years finally to be read, and rejected, by a French publisher. And it took a good many years more for the French to see him in their bookstores.

Die Weltliteratur

There are two basic contexts in which a work of art may be placed: either in the history of its nation (we can call this the *small context*), or else in the supranational history of its art (the *large context*). We are accustomed to seeing music quite naturally in the large context: knowing what language Orlando de Lassus or Bach spoke matters little to a musicologist, but because a novel is bound up with its language, in nearly every university in the world it is studied almost exclusively in the small, national context. Europe has not managed to view its literature as a historical unit, and I continue to insist that this is an irreparable intellectual loss. Because, if we consider just the history of the novel, it was to Rabelais that Laurence Sterne was reacting, it was Sterne who set off Diderot, it was from Cervantes that Fielding drew constant inspiration, it was against Fielding that Stendhal measured himself, it was Flaubert's tradition living on in Joyce, it was through his reflection on Joyce that Hermann Broch developed his own poetics of the novel, and it was Kafka who showed García Márquez the possibility of departing from tradition to "write another way."

What I just said, Goethe was the first to say: "National literature no longer means much these days, we are entering the era of *Weltliteratur*—world literature—and it is up to each of us to hasten this development." This is, so to speak, Goethe's testament. Another testament betrayed. For, open any textbook, any anthology: world literature is always presented as a juxtaposition of national literatures . . . as a history of literatures! Of literatures in the plural!

And yet Rabelais, ever undervalued by his compatriots, was never better understood than by a Russian, Bakhtin; Dostoyevsky than by a Frenchman, Gide; Ibsen than by an Irishman, Shaw; Joyce than by an Austrian, Broch. The universal importance of the generation of great North Americans—Hemingway, Faulkner, Dos Passos—was first brought to light by French writers ("In France I'm the father of a literary movement," Faulkner wrote in

1946, complaining of the deaf ear he encountered in his own country). These few examples are not bizarre exceptions to the rule; no, they are the rule: geographic distance sets the observer back from the local context and allows him to embrace the *large context* of world literature, the only approach that can bring out a novel's *aesthetic value*—that is to say: the previously unseen aspects of existence that this particular novel has managed to make clear; the novelty of form it has found.

Do I mean by this that to judge a novel one can do without a knowledge of its original language? I do indeed mean exactly that! Gide did not know Russian, Shaw did not know Norwegian, Sartre did not read Dos Passos in the original. If the books of Witold Gombrowicz and Danilo Kiš had depended solely on the judgment of people who read Polish and Serbo-Croatian, their radical aesthetic newness would never have been discovered.

(And what about the professors of foreign literatures? Is it not their very natural mission to study works in the context of world literature? Not a chance. In order to demonstrate their competence as experts, they make a great point of identifying with the *small* (national) *context* of the literatures they teach. They adopt its opinions, its tastes, its prejudices. Not a chance—it is in foreign universities that a work of art is most intractably mired in its home province.)

The provincialism of small nations

How to define "provincialism"? As the inability (or the refusal) to see one's own culture in the *large context*. There are two kind of provincialism: of large nations and of small ones. The large nations resist the Goethean idea of "world literature" because their own literature seems to them sufficiently rich that they need take no interest in what people write elsewhere. Kazimierz Brandys says this in his *Paris Notebooks: 1985–87*: "The French student has greater gaps in his knowledge of world culture than the Polish student, but he can get away with it, for his own culture contains more or less all the aspects, all the possibilities and phases of the world's evolution."

Small nations are reticent toward the *large context* for the exact opposite reasons: they hold world culture in high esteem but feel it to be something alien, a sky above their heads, distant, inaccessible, an ideal reality with little connection to their national literature. The small nation inculcates in its writer the conviction that he belongs to that place alone. To set his gaze beyond the boundary of the homeland, to join his colleagues in the supranational territory of art, is considered pretentious, disdainful of his own people. And since the small nations are often going through situations in which their survival is at stake, they readily manage to present their attitude as morally justified.

Franz Kafka speaks of this in his *Diaries*; from the standpoint of a "large" literature, in this case German, he observes Yiddish and Czech literature: A small nation, he says, has great respect for its writers because they provide it with pride "in face of the hostile surrounding world"; for a small nation, literature is "less a matter of literary history" than "a matter of the people," and it is that exceptional osmosis between the literature and its people that facilitates "the literature's diffusion throughout the country, where it binds with political slogans." From there Kafka arrives at this startling observation: "What in large literatures goes on at a lower level and constitutes a nonindispensable basement of the structure, here takes place in bright light; what there provokes a brief flurry of interest, here brings down nothing less than a life-or-death decree."

These last words remind me of a chorus of Smetana's (composed in Prague in 1864) with the lines: "Rejoice, rejoice, voracious raven, you have a treat in store: soon you will feast on a traitor to our country." How could such a great musician ever offer up such bloodthirsty foolishness? Was it some youthful error? No excuse there—he was forty then. And actually, what did it even mean at the time, to be a "traitor to our country"? Someone joining up with commando bands to slit the gullets of his fellow citizens? Not at all: a "traitor" was any Czech who decided to leave Prague for Vienna and participate peacefully in German life over there. As Kafka said, what somewhere else "provokes a brief flurry of interest, here brings down nothing less than a life-or-death decree."

A nation's possessiveness toward its artists works as a *small-context terrorism*, reducing the whole meaning of a work to the role it plays in its homeland. I open an old mimeograph copy of some lectures on composition that Vincent d'Indy gave at the Paris Schola Cantorum, where a whole generation of French musicians was trained in the early twentieth century. There are paragraphs on Smetana and Dvořák, particularly on Smetana's two string quartets. What are we told? A single assertion, several times restated in different terms: this "folk-style" music was inspired "by national songs and dances." Nothing else? Nothing. A platitude and a misinterpretation. A platitude, because traces of folk music are found everywhere, in Haydn, in Chopin, in Liszt, in Brahms; a misinterpretation, because Smetana's two quartets are actually a highly personal musical confession, written under tragic circumstances: the composer had just lost his hearing, and these (splendid!) quartets are, he said, "the swirling storm of music in the head of a man gone deaf."

How could Vincent d'Indy be so deeply mistaken? Very probably he was unfamiliar with those works and was simply repeating what he had heard. His opinion reflected Czech society's idea about these two composers: to make political use of their fame (to display pride "in face of the hostile surrounding world"), it had pulled together scraps of folklore to be found in the music and stitched them into a national banner to fly above the work. The outside world was just accepting politely (or maliciously) the interpretation that was offered.

The provincialism of large nations

And what about provincialism in the large nations? The definition is the same: the inability (or the refusal) to imagine one's own culture in the *large context*. A few years ago, before the end of the past century, a Paris newspaper polled thirty figures who belonged to a kind of intellectual establishment of the day: journalists, historians, sociologists, publishers, and a few writers. Each was asked to name, in order of importance, the ten most notable books in the whole history of France, and from those combined thirty lists the paper compiled an honor panel of a hundred works. Even though the question as asked ("What are the books that have made France what it is?") might allow for several interpretations, still the outcome does give a rather good picture of what a French intellectual elite today considers important in its country's literature.

Victor Hugo's *Les Misérables* came in first. That will surprise a foreign writer. Never having considered the book important either for himself or for the history of literature, he will suddenly see that the French literature he adores is not the same one the French adore. In eleventh place is de Gaulle's *War Memories*. According such value to a book by a statesman, a soldier, would almost never occur outside of France. And yet what is disconcerting is not that, but the fact that the greatest masterpieces appear only farther down the list! Rabelais stands in fourteenth place—Rabelais after de Gaulle! In this connection I read an article by an eminent French university professor saying that his country's literature lacks a founding figure like Dante for the Italians, Shakespeare for the English, and so on. Imagine—in the eyes of his countrymen, Rabelais lacks the aura of a founding figure! Yet in the eyes of nearly every great novelist of our time he is, along with Cervantes, the founder of a whole art, the art of the novel.

And what of the eighteenth-, the nineteenth-century novel, France's glory? *The Red and the Black* stands twenty-second on the list; *Madame Bovary* is twenty-fifth; *Germinal* thirty-second; *The Human Comedy* only thirty-fourth (Is that possible? *The Human Comedy*, without which European literature is inconceivable!); *Dangerous Liaisons* fiftieth; poor *Bouvard and Pécuchet* come trailing in last, like a couple of breathless dunces. And some masterwork novels do not appear at all among the hundred elect: *The Charterhouse of Parma; Sentimental Education; Jacques the Fatalist* (true, only within the large context of world-literature can the incomparable novelty of that book be appreciated).

And what about the twentieth century? Proust's *In Search of Lost Time*, seventh place. Camus's *The Stranger*, twenty-second. And after that? Very little. Very little of what's called modern literature, nothing at all of modern poetry. As if France's enormous influence on modern art had never occurred! As if, for instance, Apollinaire (absent from this honor list) had not inspired a whole era of European poetry!

And there's something still more astonishing: the absence of Beckett and Ionesco. How many dramatists of the past century have had such power, such influence? One? Two? No more than that. Here's a recollection: the emancipation of cultural life in Communist Czechoslovakia was bound up with the little theaters that were born at the very start of the sixties. It was there that I first saw a performance of Ionesco, and it was unforgettable: the explosion of an imagination, the irruption of a disrespectful spirit. I often said that the Prague Spring began eight years before 1968, with the Ionesco plays staged at the little theater called On the Balustrade.

One might object that the honor panel I describe is evidence less of provincialism than of the recent intellectual orientation that gives ever smaller weight to aesthetic criteria: that the people who voted for *Les Misérables* were thinking not of the book's importance in the history of the novel but of its great social resonance in France. Of course, but that only demonstrates that indifference to aesthetic value inevitably shifts the whole culture back into provincialism. France is not merely the land where the French live, it is also the country other people watch and draw inspiration from. And those are the values (aesthetic, philosophical) by which a foreigner appreciates works born outside his own country. Once again, the rule holds: these values are hard to perceive from the viewpoint of the *small context*, even if it be the prideful small context of a large nation.

The man from the east

In the nineteen-sixties I left my country for France, and there I was astonished to discover that I was "an East European exile." Indeed, to the French, my country was part of the European Orient. I hastened to explain to all and sundry what was the real scandal of our situation: stripped of national sovereignty, we had been annexed not only by another country but by a whole other *world*, the world of the European East which, rooted as it is in the ancient past of Byzantium, possesses its own historical problematic, its own architectural look, its own religion (Orthodox), its alphabet (Cyrillic, derived from Greek writing), and also its own sort of communism (no one knows or ever will know what Central-European communism would have been without Russia's domination, but in any case it would not have resembled the communism we did experience).

Gradually I understood that I came from a "faraway country of which we know little." The people around me placed great importance on politics but knew almost nothing about geography: they saw us as "communized," not "taken over." Actually, hadn't the Czechs always been part of the same "Slavic world" as the Russians? I explained that while there is a *linguistic* unity among the Slavic nations, there is no Slavic *culture*, no Slavic *world*;

that the history of the Czechs, like that of the Poles, the Slovaks, the Croats, or the Slovenes (and of course, of the Hungarians, who are not at all Slavic) is entirely Western: Gothic, Renaissance, Baroque; close contact with the Germanic world; struggle of Catholicism against the Reformation. Never anything to do with Russia, which was far off, another world. Only the Poles lived in direct relation with Russia—a relation much like a death struggle.

But my efforts were useless: the "Slavic world" idea persists as an ineradicable commonplace in world historiography. I open the *Universal History* volume of the prestigious "Pléiade" series: in the chapter called "The Slavic World," the great Czech theologian Jan Hus is irremediably separated from the Englishman John Wyclif (whose disciple Hus was), and from the German Martin Luther (who saw Hus as his teacher and precursor). Poor Hus: after being burned at the stake at Constance, now he must suffer through a dreadful eternity in the company of Ivan the Terrible, with whom he would not want to exchange a single word.

Nothing beats an argument from personal experience: in the late 1970s, I was sent the manuscript of a foreword written for one of my novels by an eminent Slavist, who placed me in permanent comparison (flattering, of course; at the time, no one meant me harm) with Dostoyevsky, Gogol, Bunin, Pasternak, Mandelstam, and the Russian dissidents. In alarm, I stopped its publication. Not that I felt any antipathy for those great Russians; on the contrary, I admired them all, but in their company I became a different person. I still recall the strange anguish the piece stirred in me: that displacement into a context that was not mine felt like a deportation.

Central Europe

Between the *large context* of the world and the *small context* of the nation, a middle step might be imagined: say, a *median context*. Between Sweden and the world, that step is Scandinavia. For Colombia, it is Latin America. And for Hungary, for Poland? In my emigration, I tried to work out a response to that question, and the title of a piece I wrote at the time sums it up: *A Kidnapped West, or The Tragedy of Central Europe.*

Central Europe: What is it? The whole collection of the small nations between two powers, Russia and Germany. The easternmost edge of the West. All right, but what nations do we mean? Does it include the three Baltic countries? And what about Romania, tugged toward the East by the Orthodox Church, toward the West by its Romance language? Or Austria, which for a long while represented the political center of that ensemble? Austrian writers are studied exclusively in the context of Germany, and would not be pleased (nor would I be, if I were they) to find themselves returned to that multilingual hodgepodge that is Central Europe. And anyhow, have all those nations shown any clear and enduring wish to create a common grouping? Not at all. For a few centuries, most of them did belong to a large State, the Hapsburg Empire, which in the end they wished only to flee.

All these comments relativize the import of the Central Europe notion, demonstrate its vague and approximate nature, but at the same time clarify it. Is it true that the borders of Central Europe are impossible to trace in any exact, lasting way? It is indeed! Those nations have never been masters of either their own destinies or their borders. They have rarely been the subjects of history, almost always its objects. Their unity was *unintentional*. They were kin to one another not through will, not through fellow-feeling or through linguistic proximity, but by reason of similar experience, by reason of common historical situations that brought them together, at different times, in different configurations, and within shifting, never definitive, borders.

Central Europe cannot be reduced to "Mitteleuropa" (I never use the term) as it is called, even in their own non-Germanic tongues, by people who know it only through the Vienna window; it is *polycentric*, and looks different seen from Warsaw, from Budapest, or from Zagreb. But from whatever perspective one looks at it, a common history emerges: looking out from the Czech window, I see there, in the mid-fourteenth century, the first Central European university at Prague; in the fifteenth century I see the Hussite revolution foreshadowing the Reformation; in the seventeenth century I see the Hapsburg Empire gradually constructing itself out of Bohemia, Hungary, Austria; I see the wars that, over two centuries, will defend the West against the Turkish invasion; I see the Counter-Reformation, with the flowering of baroque art that stamps an architectural unity on the whole of that vast territory, right up to the Baltic countries.

The nineteenth century set off patriotism in all those peoples who refused to let themselves be assimilated, that is to say Germanized. Even the Austrians, despite their dominant position within the empire, could not avoid making a choice between their Austrian identity and membership in the great German entity in which they would be dissolved. And how can we not mention Zionism, also born in Central Europe from that same refusal to assimilate, that same desire of the Jews to live as a nation with their own language! One of Europe's fundamental problems, the problem of the small nations, is nowhere else manifested in so revelatory, so focused, and so exemplary a way.

In the twentieth century, after the 1914 war, several independent states rose from the ruins of the Hapsburg Empire, and thirty years later all of them but Austria found themselves under Russian domination: a situation utterly unprecedented in the whole of Central European history! There followed a long period of anti-Soviet revolts: in Poland, in bloodied Hungary, then in Czechoslovakia, and again in Poland, at length and powerfully. To my mind there is nothing more admirable in the Europe of the second half of the twentieth century than that golden chain of revolts that, over forty years, eroded the empire of the East, made it ungovernable, and tolled the death knell of its reign.

The contrasting paths of the modernist revolt

I don't believe universities will ever teach the history of Central Europe as a separate discipline; in the dormitory of the hereafter, Jan Hus will always be breathing the same Slavic exhalations as Ivan the Terrible. In fact, would I myself ever have made use of that notion, and so tenaciously, if I had not been rocked by the political drama of my native land? Surely not. There are words drowsing in the mist that, at the right moment, rush to our aid. By merely being defined, the concept of Central Europe unmasked the lie of Yalta, that deal-making among the three victors of the war, who shifted the age-old boundary between the European East and West several hundred kilometers over to the west.

The notion of Central Europe came to my aid on another occasion, too, this time for reasons having nothing to do with politics; it happened when I began to marvel at the fact that the terms "novel," "modern art," "modern novel," meant something other for me than for my French friends. It was not a disagreement; it was, quite modestly, the recognition of a difference between the two traditions that had shaped us. In a brief historical panorama, our two cultures rose up before me as nearly symmetrical antitheses. In France: classicism, rationalism, the libertine spirit, and then in the nineteenth century, the era of the great novel. In Central Europe: the reign of an especially ecstatic strain of baroque art and then in the nineteenth century, the moralizing idyllicism of Biedermeier, the great Romantic poetry, and very few great novels. Central Europe's matchless strength lay in its music which, from Haydn to Schoenberg, from Liszt to Bartók, over two centuries embraced in itself all the essential trends in European music; Central Europe staggered beneath the glory of its music.

What was "modern art," that intriguing storm of the first third of the twentieth century? A radical revolt against the aesthetic of the past; that is obvious of course, except that the pasts were not alike. In France modern art—anti-rationalist, anti-classicist, anti-realist, anti-naturalist—extended the great lyrical rebellion of Baudelaire and Rimbaud. It found its privileged expression in painting and, above all, in poetry, which was its chosen art. The novel, by contrast, was anathematized (most notably by the surrealists); it was considered outmoded, forever sealed into its conventional form. In Central Europe the situation was different: opposition to the ecstatic, romantic, sentimental, musical tradition led the modernism of a few geniuses, the most original, toward the art that is the privileged sphere of analysis, lucidity, irony: that is, toward the novel.

My great pleiades

In Robert Musil's *The Man Without Qualities* (1930–41), Clarisse and Walter played four-hand piano, "unloosed like two locomotives hurtling along side by side." "Seated on their small stools, they were irritated, amorous, or sad about nothing, or perhaps each of them about something separate," and only "the authority of the music joined them together. . . . There was between them a fusion of the kind that occurs in great public panics, where hundreds of people who an instant earlier differed in every way make the same motions, utter the same mindless cries, gape wide their eyes and mouths." They took "those turbulent seethings, those emotional surges from the innermost being—that is to say, that vague turmoil of the soul's bodily understructures—to be the language of the eternal by which all men can be united."

This ironic comment is aimed not only at music; it goes deeper, to *music's lyrical essence*, to that bewitchment that feeds festivals and massacres alike and turns individuals into ecstatic mobs. In this exasperation with the lyrical, Musil reminds me of Franz Kafka who, in his novels, abhors any emotional gesticulation (this sets him radically apart from the German expressionists) and who, he says so himself, writes *Amerika* in opposition to "style overflowing with feeling"; Kafka thereby reminds me of Hermann Broch, who was allergic to "the spirit of opera," especially to the opera of Wagner (that Wagner so adored by Baudelaire, by Proust), which he calls the very model of kitsch (a "genius kitsch," he said); and Broch thereby reminds me of Witold Gombrowicz who, in his famous text *Against Poets*, is reacting to both the deep-rooted Romanticism of Polish literature and to poetry taken as the untouchable goddess of Western modernism.

Kafka, Musil, Broch, Gombrowicz . . . Did they make for a group, a school, a movement? No; they were all solitaries. I have often called them "the Pleiades of Central Europe's great novelists," and, indeed, like the stars in the constellation, each of them was surrounded by empty space, each of them distant from the others. It seemed all the more remarkable that their work should express a similar aesthetic orientation: they were all *poets* of the novel, which is to say people impassioned by the form and by its newness; concerned for the intensity of each word, each phrase; seduced by the imagination as it tries to move beyond the borders of "realism"; but at the same time impervious to seduction by the *lyrical;* hostile to the transformation of the novel into personal confession; allergic to the ornamentalization of prose; entirely focused on the real world. They all of them conceived the novel to be a great *antilyrical poetry*.

Kitsch and vulgarity

The word "kitsch" was born in Munich in the mid-nineteenth century; it describes the syrupy leftover of the great Romantic period. But Hermann Broch, who saw the connection between Romanticism and kitsch as one of inverse proportions, may have come closer to the truth: according to him, kitsch was the dominant style of the nineteenth century (in Germany and in Central Europe), with a few great Romantic works separating out from it as phenomena of exception. People who experienced the secular tyranny of kitsch (an opera-tenor kind of tyranny) feel particular irritation at the rosy veil thrown over reality, at the immodest exhibition of hearts forever deeply moved, at the "bread drenched in perfume" Musil speaks of; kitsch long ago became a very precise concept in Central Europe, where it stands as the *supreme aesthetic evil*.

I do not suspect the French modernists of succumbing to the lure of sentimentality and pomp; but without a long exposure to kitsch, they had not had occasion to develop a hypersensitive aversion to it. Only in 1960, thus a hundred years after it appeared in Germany, was the word first used in France; yet the French translators of Broch's essays in 1966 and of Hannah Arendt in 1974 both still avoided the term "kitsch" and instead used the translation *art de pacotille* (cheap art), thereby rendering incomprehensible their authors' thinking.

Rereading Stendhal's *Lucien Leuwen*, the fashionable drawing-room conversations, I pause over the key words that catch the various attitudes of the participants: *vanité; vulgaire; esprit* (wit—"that vitriolic acid eating at everything"); *ridicule, politesse* ("infinite manners, no feeling"); *bien-pensante* (right thinking). And I ask myself: What is the word that expresses the worst *aesthetic reprobation* the way the notion of kitsch expresses it for me? It finally comes to me: it is the word *vulgaire, vulgarité*. "M. Du Poirier was a creature of the utmost vulgarity, a man who seemed proud of his crass, overfamiliar ways; thus does a pig wallow in mud with a kind of voluptuous pleasure that is insolent toward the spectator."

Scorn for the vulgar inhabited the drawing rooms of the time just as it does in today's. To recall its etymology: "vulgar" comes from *vulgus*, "people"; "vulgar" is what pleases the people; a democrat, a man of the left, a battler for human rights, is obliged to love the people; but he is free to disdain it haughtily for what he finds vulgar.

After the political anathema Sartre had cast upon Camus, after the Nobel Prize that brought down jealousy and hatred on him, Camus felt very uncomfortable among the Paris intellectuals. I am told that he was further distressed by labels of "vulgarity" attached to him personally: his lowly origins, his illiterate mother; his situation as a *pied noir* (a Frenchman from Algeria) sympathetic to other *pieds noirs*—people so "overfamiliar" (so "crass"); the lightweight philosophy of his essays; and so on. Reading the articles in which such lynching occurred, I note this passage: Camus is "a peasant dressed up in his Sunday best, . . . a man of the people with his gloves in his hand and his hat still on his head, stepping for the first time into the drawing room. The other guests turn away, they know whom they are dealing with." The metaphor is eloquent: not only did he not know what he was supposed to think (he disparaged progress and sympathized with the Algerian French) but, graver yet, he behaved awkwardly in the drawing room (in the actual or figurative sense): he was vulgar.

In France there is no harsher aesthetic reprobation than this. Reprobation that is sometimes justified but that also strikes at the best: at Rabelais. And at Flaubert. "The primary characteristic of *Sentimental Education*," said the famous writer Barbey d'Aurevilly on its publication, "is vulgarity, first and foremost. In our view, the world already has enough vulgar folk, vulgar minds, vulgar things, without further adding to the overwhelming number of these disgusting vulgarities."

I recall the early weeks of my emigration. As Stalinism had already been unanimously condemned, people readily understood the tragedy the Russian occupation meant for my country, and they saw me as wrapped in an aura of respectable sadness. I remember sitting at a bar with a Parisian intellectual who had given me much support and help. It was our first meeting in Paris and, hovering in the air above us, I could see grand words: persecution, gulag, freedom, banishment from the native land, courage, resistance, totalitarianism, police terror. Eager to banish the kitsch of those solemn specters, I started describing how the fact of being followed, of having police listening-devices in our apartments, had taught us the delectable art of the hoax. A friend and I had switched apartments, and names as well; he, a big womanizer who was regally indifferent to the microphones, had pulled off some of his finest exploits in my studio. Given that the trickiest moment in any amorous adventure is the breakup, my emigration worked out perfectly for him: one fine day the girls and the ladies arrived to find the apartment locked and my name gone from the door, while I was sending off little farewell cards from Paris, with my own signature, to seven women I had never seen.

I'd meant to amuse this man who was dear to me, but his face gradually darkened until finally he said, with the sound of the guillotine dropping, "I don't find that funny."

We remained friendly, but we were never friends. The memory of our first encounter serves as a key to understand our long-unacknowledged difference: What held us apart was the clash of two aesthetic attitudes: the man allergic to kitsch collides with the man allergic to vulgarity.

Antimodern modernism

"One must be absolutely modern," wrote Arthur Rimbaud. Some sixty years later Gombrowicz was not so sure. In *Ferdydurke* (written in Poland in 1937) the Youngblood family is dominated by the daughter, a "modern highschool girl." She is mad for the telephone; she disdains the classical authors; when a gentleman comes to call she "merely looks at him and, sticking a small wrench between her teeth with her right hand, offers him her left with total nonchalance."

Her mother is modern, too; she works with a "Committee for the Protection of Newborns," is active against the death penalty and for civil liberties; "ostentatiously offhand, she sets out for the toilet" and emerges from it "prouder than she went in"; as she grows older, modernity becomes the more indispensable to her as the sole "substitute for youth."

And papa? He too is modern; he thinks nothing but does everything to please his daughter and his wife.

In *Ferdydurke*, Gombrowicz got at the fundamental shift that occurred during the twentieth century: until then mankind was divided in two—those who defended the status quo and those who sought to change it. Then the acceleration of History took effect: whereas in the past man had lived continuously in the same setting, in a society that changed only very slowly, now the moment arrived when he suddenly began to feel History moving beneath his feet, like a rolling sidewalk: the *status quo* was in motion! All at once, being comfortable with the *status quo* was the same thing as being comfortable with History on the move!

Which meant that a person could be both progressive and conformist, conservative and rebel, at the same time!

Attacked as a reactionary by Sartre and his bunch, Camus got off the famous remark about people who had "merely set down their armchairs facing in the direction of History"; Camus was right, but he did not know that the precious chair was on wheels, and that for some time already everyone had been pushing it forward—the modern high school girls, their mamas, their papas, as well as all the activists against the death penalty and all the members of the Committee for the Protection of Newborns and, of course, all the politicians, who, as they pushed the chair along, kept their laughing faces turned to the public running along behind them and also laughing, knowing very well that only a person who *delights* in being modern is genuinely modern.

That was when a certain number of Rimbaud's heirs grasped this extraordinary thing: today the only modernism worthy of the name is antimodern modernism.

Chapter 28

Nirvana Tanoukhi

THE SCALE OF WORLD LITERATURE
(2008)

NIRVANA TANOUKHI (B. 1976) IS an assistant professor at the University of
Wisconsin-Madison. She earned her PhD from Stanford University and has held a
postdoctoral position at Harvard University. She has translated works of fiction from
Arabic to English, co-edited *Immanuel Wallerstein and the Problem of the World:
System, Scale, Culture*, and contributed an article on African literature to *The Routledge
Companion to World Literature*.

In "The Scale of World Literature", she draws attention to how the concept of world
literature may not deliver a new perspective on global literature if the way the world itself
is conceptualized is not scrutinized critically. Following in the tracks of Franco Moretti's
interest in the geography of the novel, Tanoukhi investigates the uses of cartographic
metaphors, reacting against the seemingly solid insights of mapmaking by drawing attention to how different scales make a difference.

Cultural geographies are not merely given, but rather are constructed and used
for different purposes. Tanoukhi points to how different such geographies appear
depending on the position of the observer, in particular whether one looks at a national
or regional cultural geography from within or from the outside. This is particularly
important when dealing with areas which have traditionally been labelled as part of
the periphery of world literature, such as Africa, and where the mapping of the cultural
geography should not only be based on the concepts of the center. This is where the
idea of the postcolonial novel has worked to produce overly simplified descriptions of
literatures which do not take literature's own way of producing different scales into
account.

Tanoukhi does not provide easy solutions to the problems she discusses, but expands
and refines the debate on how to handle the immense complexity world literature presents
with a request to reflect on the many, mostly implicit, uses of scale involved in the presentation of arguments about the geography of world literature.

Nirvana Tanoukhi, "The Scale of World Literature," *New Literary History* 39 (2008) 3–4:
599–617.

This is his home; he can't be far away.

—Sophocles, *Philoctetes*

The problem: literary space

Distance has long been a thorny issue for comparative literature. Whether one tries to expli-
cate a foreign text, map a course of influence, or describe an elusive aesthetic, there is the
problem of crossing considerable divides without yielding to the fallacy of decisive leaps. And
yet, a condition conducive to methodological malaise found consolation in a fixed literary
geography that justified comparison, ingeniously, with the very fact of incommensurability.
Impossible distances beg to be crossed *precisely* because they cannot be. And for crossings to
be attempted, each book, each author, each device—each canon, nation, or interpretive
community—would assume its rightful place. While comparative literature, it was said,
would occupy the space-in-between conventional places. And so, by a euphoric celebration
of displacement, the comparative method became unquestionably subversive: in practice it
exacted "shock value,"[1] institutionally it was a "thorn in the side,"[2] in ideological wars it prof-
fered a "symbolic weapon."[3] But really, may that not be overstating the case? I want to
consider why the comparative method, in the first instance, made a *cartographic* claim to
scale. Why dedicate a discipline to the task of charting zones, paths, and crossroads obscured
by strict adherence to "national traditions"—when logically, comparison depends for its
existence on the entrenchment of nation-based geography?

Comparison's cartographic commitment (and its poetics of distance) is worth examining
not only as a logical paradox, but as a possible key to the recent disciplinary revival of the
concept "world literature"—which I take to be the latest, most pronounced attempt to
diffuse the teleological thrust of "literary history" with a radically synchronic outlook. With
this slide from "literary history" to "world literature" the literary discipline makes a belated
entry into the globalization debates,[4] a time-honored, social-scientific inquiry into the time
and place of uneven development. But what kind of possibilities does this move open up for
comparative literary analysis, and what are the risks involved?[5] Here's my answer: on the one
hand, the discussion about literary globalization has already launched us, however slowly or
implicitly, on a disciplinary critique of the very concept *scale*, which by necessity moves us
away from metaphorical deployments of "space" toward concrete discussions about the materiality of literary *landscapes*. I suggest that the concept scale, properly theorized, would enable
a more precise formulation of the role of literature, and literary analysis, in the history of the
production of space. But, in the meantime, though such a critique seems imminent, "world
literature" threatens to become a hardened (albeit enlarged) image of the old literary history,
where *geography* evokes a figurative solidity that assumes the guise of materiality. My aim is
to hasten the literary critique of scale by making cracks in the geography of "world literature." The postcolonial novel—perhaps one of the most geographically constituted objects of
literary history—offers an ideal weak spot to get us started.

Man with a novel

A most interesting insight about the comparative view of the novel comes in an essay by the
cultural philosopher, Kwame Anthony Appiah, where he describes a particular geographic
outlook that makes futile both the writing of the postcolonial novel, and by extension, its
cultural critique. Appiah argues that so long as the novel is taken as a representative sample
of African culture, Western intellectuals are bound to drown in misconceptions about the

popular mentality of the continent. By "popular" he means nonliterate, which is why he proposes African sculpture as an alternate sample object of African cultural history.[6] *Man with a Bicycle*, a Nigerian sculpture, is presented as the epistemological antithesis of the African novel, an object whose cultural ethos eludes Western critics (suggests Appiah) precisely because they insist on approaching it *as a novel* (Fig. 28.1). Appiah reprimands the sculpture's critics and curators as follows:

> I am grateful to James Baldwin for his introduction to the [Nigerian sculpture] *Man with a Bicycle*, a figure who is, as Baldwin so rightly saw, polyglot—speaking Yoruba and English . . . someone whose "clothes do not ft him too well." He and other men and women among whom he mostly lives suggest to me that the place to look for hope is not just to the postcolonial novel, which has struggled to achieve the insights of Ouologuem and Mudimbe, but to the all-consuming vision of this less-anxious creativity. It matters little whom the work was made *for*; what we should learn from is the imagination that produced it. *Man with a Bicycle* is produced by someone who does not care that the bicycle is the white

Figure 28.1 Man with a Bicycle, Yoruba, Nigeria, 20th century. Wood, 35 3/4 in. Collection of The Newark Museum, New Jersey, Purchase 1977 Wallace M. Scudder Bequest Fund. Photo: Jerry Thompson, 1986.

man's invention: it is not there to be Other to the Yoruba self; it is there because
someone cared for its solidity; it is there because it will take us further than our
feet will take us; it is there because machines are now as African as novelists . . .
and as fabricated as the kingdom of Nakem.

(PP 357)

One cannot be surprised by Appiah's admiration for *Man with a Bicycle*, a contemporary
Nigerian wooden sculpture whose nonchalant protagonist stands firm, it seems, because he is
impervious to the anxieties of influence. We understand why he would draw force from such
a *man* lacking in hesitation, who grabs a machine simply because it works. In fact, the *man*
seems to be at such ease that we almost wonder whether he takes the bicycle, not simply, but
unthinkingly. His apparent comfort in the "solidity" of things resonates for us uncomfortably
with the primitivism of Claude Lévi-Strauss's *bricoleur* who can make do precisely because he
does not reflect. We are a little surprised by Appiah's effortless conflation (or confusion) of
the maker of the statue with the figure he carves out: the producer, "someone who does not
care that the bicycle is the white man's invention," and the wooden personage, "someone
whose 'clothes do not ft him too well' " (PP 357). For sculpture to be an improvement on
the novel—a "less-anxious" alternative, as Appiah says—the author and his hero must become
one, such that the "hope" of the creator passes into the happiness of his creature, showing the
"dark vision" of the novel to be gruesome in comparison. We're meant to see how, as a sculpture, *Man with a Bicycle* conveys in itself the "solidity" of its conception, a man's matter-of-fact
contentment in his clothing, regardless of whether they "fit" or not. As if to say that writing
a *novel*—imagine a hypothetical novel called *Man with a Bicycle*—about this man would have
been akin to using his clothes to tell his story, which would lead inevitably to a novel *about* his
clothes, because their fit, being imperfect after all, would have become a problem (or the
story) itself. At best, such a novel could be about the man's contentment *despite* his clothes,
which is already not the same thing. Because surely, in this case, the man would "care" not
only about his clothes, but also about the status of the bicycle as "the white man's invention,"
so on and so forth . . .

Is this true, then? That in a sculpture, bicycles (and borrowed clothes) can be mere
conveniences, while in a novel a mere bicycle (or ill-fitting clothes) must be a problem? Does
the postcolonial writer's "struggle" with the novelist's mantle truly brand the hero with an
anxious temperament, and by extension, the postcolonial novel with its "dark vision"? For
now, instead of asking *whether* this is true, let's look at Appiah's own inadvertent explanation
for *how* it's true. What is fundamentally historical about the postcolonial novel, he says, is its
foreignness to African soil (a premise that, as we shall see later, echoes comparative wisdom
on the subject). For this reason—unlike in the case of sculpture—the novel's geographic
displacement becomes the context by which it can be properly historicized. This is, for him,
the generic difference that escapes the interpreters of *Man with a Bicycle*, who mistake a piece
of wooden handiwork for a modernist work of "high culture," burdening it with residues of
the kinds of expectations we bring to a novel. And where do we see the critics making the
mistake? Well, observes Appiah, when they "contextualized [the sculpture] only by the
knowledge that bicycles are new in Africa" (PP 339).

To contextualize an African novel, then, is *not* exactly to historicize. What Appiah
captures is the peculiar "contextual" work done by a so-called "historical" detail, where the
bicycle's novelty serves as the seed from which springs a whole psychic landscape with which
the postcolonial novel is identified. One exhibit caption stresses the same detail to "explain"
the sculpture as follows: "The influence of the Western world is revealed in the clothes and
bicycle of this neo-traditional Yoruba sculpture which probably represents a merchant en
route to market" (PP 341). As for Baldwin, he observes that: "His errand might prove to be

impossible . . . He is challenging something—or something has challenged him" (PP 339). The critics' knowledge of the bicycle's novelty is of course far from random, it is a "fact" chosen to mark a particular location: "new in Africa," not elsewhere. Since Appiah is far from interested in making a case for the African novel, the extent of his claim is that each genre is decipherable by a hermeneutic—a logic of contextualization—to which it is individually suited. The claim *betrayed* by his line of reasoning is far more interesting: that a wooden bicycle is turned into a sign of novelty by *a way of reading*, which not only pulls together identity and landscape in *Man with a Bicycle* such that they become inextricable—but more impressively, they mystify the man's journey, turning garb and transport into hurdles along his way. It's a way of reading that elicits a novel's "dark vision": "His errand might prove impossible . . ."—a way of reading that prevents the *Man* from reaching his destination.

Even as Appiah seems to be corroborating a common view of the postcolonial novel as "anxious creativity," he illuminates the obscure makings of its landscape. By doing so, he has taken us where we wanted: the symbolically historical place that is Africa-of-the-Novel, where each object is potentially a hurdle and distance is the threshold of motion.[7]

Distance, scale, location

We must linger on the nature of distance, in light of places like Africa-of-the-Novel. "The making of place," says Neil Smith, always "implies the production of scale in so far as places are made different from each other; scale is the criterion of difference not between places so much as between different kinds of places."[8] Smith is inviting us, here, to enlarge our schoolish association of scale to maps. From the perspective of a human geographer, the fact that the distance between two adjacent neighborhoods of unequal wealth cannot be measured numerically necessitates an understanding of geographic scale as a process—a process that establishes distances dually: by differentiating places *qualitatively* and demarcating boundaries *quantitatively*.[9]

The cartographic sense of scale—of representation through mapping—is only one of three senses of the term that Smith lists in the revised entry for "Scale" in the *Dictionary of Human Geography*:

> *Cartographic scale* refers to the level of abstraction at which a map is constructed . . . therefore crucial in determining what is included and excluded in a map and the overall image a map conveys . . . [*Methodological scale*] is largely determined by some compromise between the research problem (what kind of answer is anticipated), the availability of data, and the cost of data-acquisition and processing . . . If these first two definitions refer to the conceptualizations of scale—cartographic and methodological—*geographic scale* is of a different order. "Geographic scale" refers to the dimensions of specific landscapes: geographers might talk of the regional scale, the scale of the watershed, or the global scale, for example. These scales are also of course conceptualized, but the conceptualization of geographical scale here follows specific processes in the physical and human LANDSCAPE rather than conceptual abstractions lain over it . . . Geographical scale is in no sense natural or given. There is nothing inevitable about global, national, or urban scales . . . These are specific to certain historical and geographical locations, they change over time, sometimes rapidly sometimes slowly, and in some cases a scale that operates in one society fails to appear in another.[10]

So, three senses of scale: *cartographic*, *methodological*, *geographic*—each accentuating a particular kind of limitation the geographer will encounter in practice. The first is epistemological
and recognizes the limits of looking through a particular frame. The second, empirical,
acknowledges the necessity of compromise with preexisting conditions of research. In both
cases, scale is, more or less, a matter of choice. But the third, more materialist definition of
scale—what Smith properly calls *geographic* scale—sounds more complex and elusive.
Though geographic scales are arbitrary, says Smith, they *emerge* (for the geographer) as objectifiable elements in the course of *following* the material processes that shape a landscape. It is
this very notion, implied here, of a scale-sensitive procedure—a procedure that "conceptual-
izes" by following—which, I think, carries significant consequences for the idea, method, and
perhaps the ethics of comparison.

Smith takes "space" to be the kind of seemingly simple, abstract category (not unlike
"labor") whose conceptualization, articulation, and manifestation in social life must be examined and understood within a history of intercourse between humans and the physical universe
of which they are part. "In the advanced capitalist world today, we all conceive of space as
emptiness, as a universal receptacle in which objects exist and events occur, as a frame of
reference, a co-ordinate system (along with time) within which all reality exists."[11] This,
Smith explains, is a particular conception of space that resulted from a distinction made by
Isaac Newton between *absolute space* and *relative space*: "Absolute space in its own nature,
without relation to anything external, remains always similar and unmovable. Relative space
is some movable dimension or measure of the absolute spaces; which our senses determine
by its position to bodies."[12] Thus, we may speak metaphorically of spaces that "connect,"
"house," or "anchor"—but only as a way of gauging the navigability of a situation: "Absolute
location is simply a special case of relative location, one in which we abstract from *the social
determinants* of distance (83, my italics). Smith gives the medieval city as an example: "In
Euclidean terms, the distance from the ground foor to the fourth foor of a city tenement may
be equivalent to the height of a tree in the primal forest beyond the city walls. But the same
distance between floors of the tenement can also be measured in terms of social rank and class
whereas the height of the tree cannot" (78). Though we could, of course, imagine a situation
in which the height of the tree itself would "matter" as the center of a social dispute or trans-
action.

As comparatists, therefore, we must approach "spaces" wherever we find them, as the
articulation of distance within a particularly spatialized system of social relations. In a landscape like Africa-of-the-Novel, we must reconstruct the process by which the space of the
postcolonial novel becomes differentiated, gaining the contours of a place and the fixity of a
cultural location. Only by following the dynamics of a landscape will we be able to unearth
"the social determinants of distance."[13] If we can indeed imagine a literary history that is
entangled in the history of the production of space, it is time for comparative literature to
develop both a critique of *scale*, which would examine the spatial premises of comparison—
and, eventually, a phenomenology of scale, which would help us grasp the actually existing
landscapes of literature. Let us begin with the first problem, by turning once again to the
postcolonial novel, and the "conceptual abstractions lain over it."

A sensitive genre

The postcolonial novel, it would seem, lacks the serenity that comes with provincialism. It is
a place-sensitive genre that supposedly *intuits* its geographic displacement as the condition of
its impossibility. "An anxious creativity," Appiah says; nor are most critics of the postcolonial
novel as generous. "Compromise," not "creativity," is the central trope in criticism of the

postcolonial (or "peripheral") novel, according to Franco Moretti.[14] This idea of compromise appears so prevalent in the secondary literature, Moretti goes further, that one would think it "a law" of literary evolution: "Four continents, two hundred years, over twenty independent critical studies, and they all agreed: when a culture starts moving towards the modern novel, it's always as a compromise between foreign form and local materials."[15] And nowhere is the "compromise" more evident, say his sources, than in the narrator's anxiety. "Which makes sense," for Moretti, since "the narrator is the pole of comment, of explanation, of evaluation . . . when foreign 'formal patterns' . . . make characters behave in strange ways . . . then of course comment becomes uneasy—garrulous, erratic, rudderless" (65). If indeed a law could be extracted, for him it would look like this: "foreign form, local material—and local form. Simplifying somewhat: Foreign *plot*; local *characters*; and then, local *narrative voice*: and it's precisely in this third dimension that these novels seem to be most unstable—most uneasy." Moretti takes compromise to mean something like "refunctionalization," the concept conceived by Viktor Shklovsky to describe formal adaptation to historical change. However, when he applies it to describe a process of adaptation to *geographic* change (when refunctionalization becomes a process of *domestication*), an interesting tautology arises. "Local form" is initially proclaimed the *synthesis* of "foreign form and local materials." But when "form" is simplified quickly into "narrative voice," it emerges a *symptom* of incomplete refunctionalization (of impossible domestication). For Moretti and his informants, as with Appiah, the postcolonial compromise with the novel's foreignness forecloses the condition in the symptom; the landscape in the detail; the "law" (60) in the "unit of analysis" (61).

But no matter how intriguing this idea of the postcolonial novel's impossibility, or how poignant this malaise of compromise, it takes an "anxious" genre to illustrate *methodologically* the possibility of the project "world literature." And to even have a debate, it helps (as I hope to emphasize) that the novel's comparative potential is a matter of disciplinary consensus. Moretti defends his "law" as a scientific abstraction of a ubiquitous critical repetition, but more importantly he authorizes it explicitly as an *empathetic* reformulation of the testimonies compiled. Even the fiercest critiques of Moretti's law do not question the *substance* of the secondary literature, nor do they contest his description of the object itself (the postcolonial novel). I take the thesis of "formal compromise," which has remained remarkably invisible in the otherwise intense debate triggered by Moretti's essay, to point to a theoretical status quo.

Objections to the law itself have been generally procedural, targeting either Moretti's disengagement from textual hermeneutics or the law's limited *cartographic* potential. On the one hand, we have the critics of "distant reading" who are most concerned with the displacement of hermeneutic authority, and perhaps the implication that they may be "mere" specialists to whom "close-reading" would be conveniently outsourced. For this reason, they raise the problem of secondhand information as one of reliability (not *objectivity* for instance). Their quarrel with Moretti is: "How do you know they're right without *seeing* for yourself?" as opposed to "What can one make of this *kind* of repetition?" Then there's the second group, who wants to beat Moretti at his own game, claiming that his seemingly ambitious model actually circumscribes the *full* cartographic potential of the comparative enterprise. Appropriately enough, this group offers recommendations on how to hone and refine the proposed model, while implicitly agreeing that the schematization of "literary space" is the greatest and most significant challenge of a "world literature."[16] Important questions are raised about how to balance the representation of centripetal and centrifugal tendencies or differentiate the portability of certain genres over others. But there is little self-reflexivity about the cartographic impulse and the logic that accepts "portability" as a category of comparison. Overall, the principle of "world literature" as a cartographic program that would adjudicate the scope of "foreign interference" resonates both with structuralist theories of "influence" (literary interference, dependence, debt, et cetera)[17] and also with *post*structuralist theories of "reappropriation" (literary resistance, subversion, cannibalization, et cetera).[18] Even Moretti's swift concession to his critics is a victory of sorts, for instituting that question that must remain the center of comparative controversy: "yes, 'measuring' the extent of foreign pressure on a text, or its structural instability, or a narrator's uneasiness, will be complicated, at times even unfeasible. But a diagram of symbolic power is an ambitious goal, and it makes sense that it would be hard to achieve."[19] (Here, we must mention a third ascetic group who reject this imperative of "diagramming" on principle, choosing to abstain altogether from comparative schematizations lest they should fall into the temptations of universalism. But even there, the category "mobility" resurfaces as a theoretical axis in the metaphors of "translatability" and translation.)[20]

The problem, to my mind, lies not in the nature of measuring. Nor, as Pascale Casanova has famously suggested, in the impossibility of measuring distances established "in the mind": "the structure [of literary relations is] so hard to visualize [because] it's impossible to place it at a distance, as a discrete and objectifiable phenomenon."[21] But rather, in the fact that as literary critics, we often *begin* with strong ideas about what needs to be measured—for me, this is the most compelling justification offered by Moretti for pursuing a new comparative science: that "we are used to asking only those questions for which we already have an answer."[22] But are we posing a new question when we set out to investigate the *extent* of "foreign pressure on a text"; "its structural instability"? It's not that such measuring endeavors are "unfeasible"; what is worse, they appear superfluous because the mystery is already solved: "a narrator's uneasiness." Between Moretti's tragic conception of formal compromise (the postcolonial novel's *yearning* for independence) and Casanova's more conciliatory version (of literature as the willful *realization* of a compromise: "the majority of compromise solutions achieved within this structure are based on an 'art of distance'"),[23] we have transformed the comparative concern with xenocentrism into something like Xeno's paradox, where the riddle of distance produces either the *need* or the *will* to shape compromises with literary laws of motion.

This kind of paradox, of course, increases the novel's fortune in "comparative" controversy.[24] Let me explain by turning back briefly to *Man with a Bicycle*. I began with Appiah's insight that the novel's anxiety derives, at least in part, from a mode of contextualization, which grounds an African hero by circumscribing his mobility. As to what makes the African novel itself *conducive* to this kind of reading, says Appiah, the problem lies with the author. Or more precisely, the African novelist's obligation to what he calls the "space clearing gesture": an explicit departure from intellectual predecessors without which an author in the modern Western sense cannot make a claim to distinction.[25] Because *literary* producers *must* assert an authorial status, says Appiah, the African novelist vacillates discontentedly between the national and Western traditions, hoping to claim a sensible parameter of influence. Baldwin, on the other hand, offers a clue which suggests that the novelist's problem lies elsewhere: "He's grounded in immediate reality by the bicycle . . ." and then, "He's apparently a very proud and silent man" (PP 339). Not only must the hero of our hypothetical novel, *Man with A Bicycle*, worry about his clothes and his bicycle. Unlike his wooden counterpart, he is not afforded the stoic stance of a sculpture. The novel seems to demand that the African hero speak, and it's the force of this imperative that unleashes (in the mind of the novel's critics) the question of what, if anything, *distinguishes* the utterance of a postcolonial hero— what makes the postcolonial novel amenable to comparison—or better, what opens it to *geographic* explanation. Moretti correctly identifies "voice" as a possible point of political convergence between the comparatist's moral and empirical ambition, on the one hand, and his informants' anxieties, on the other. But is the convergence real? What is the sociology of this term "compromise" so often repeated in the secondhand testimonies, and what is its theoretical hold on the comparative imagination?

New anxieties

The thesis of cultural compromise is much more than a law of literary history; it is the most powerful and lasting cultural program to originate from the development era and was devised by emergent postcolonial intelligentsia to resolve the contradictions of "transition" in what was then candidly called "the third world." Partha Chatterjee has provocatively described this agenda as "alternative modernity" to insist on the cognitive and political work expended by Asian and African societies to formulate an *independent* path of progress from colonial patronage to indigenous state-formation.[26] But, in a remarkable development, the synchronic connotation of an "alternative modernity" appealed to analysts of *contemporary* cultural forms who sought a way of describing an increasingly integrated cultural world without recourse to teleological narratives of "modernization." Adopted as an *analytical framework*, "alternative modernity" has proved immensely fertile, producing a rich descriptive literature that demonstrates the versatility and creativity of "local" forms, *despite* compromises with larger forces of homogenization. But the anachronism that belies this critical gesture is unmistakable. Is it really possible to borrow the cultural slogan of an era of economic optimism to *describe* the uneven world that emerged in its painful aftermath? This spirited body of work must neglect, as Jim Ferguson has observed, that the early postcolonial investment in cultural alterity lost currency when the prospect of economic progress became dim. That in fact, when economic *convergence* was no longer believed to be a historical inevitability, cultural alterity appeared more like the symptom (or even the cause) of permanent economic troubles. The language of alternative modernity thus disguises a real dissonance between an academic thesis that celebrates the periphery's specificity and a local outlook that experiences "specificity" as a mark of inferiority. Speaking of his colleagues, Ferguson says: "Anthropologists today, working to combat old stereotypes, are eager to say how modern Africa is. Many ordinary Africans might scratch their heads at such a claim."[27]

What is "accomplished," he asks, by saying that Africa is "differently" or "alternatively" modern? We could indeed ask this question of Moretti, whose eagerness to proclaim the postcolonial novel the "rule," not the "exception," recalls Ferguson's description of anthropologists. We must consider the possibility that "alternative modernity" is currently a powerful horizon of world-scale literary analysis, and that Moretti's conjecture on "formal compromise" is neither a coincidence nor an isolated move. The thesis of "formal compromise," says Moretti, "completely reverse[s] the received historical explanation of [influence]: because if the compromise between the foreign and the local is so ubiquitous, then those independent paths that are usually taken to be the rule of the rise of the novel (the Spanish, the French, and especially the British case)—*well, they're not the rule at all, they're the exception.* They come first, yes, but they're not at all typical. The 'typical' rise of the novel is Krasicki, Kemal, Rizal, Maran—not Defoe."[28] Moretti's goal of provincializing the European novel appears worthwhile, even to his harshest critics. First of all, he avoids placing novelistic traditions in a chain of influence that defines literary modernity as literary Westernization. Second, he reveals that the "path" to literary modernity is *normally* alternative and, by extension, that the European novel is in fact a deviation from the norm. None of this could have been done without fulfilling comparative literature's unflinching commitment to scale, "[Y]ou become a comparatist for a very simple reason: *because you are convinced that your viewpoint is better*. It has greater explanatory power; it's conceptually more elegant; it avoids that ugly 'one-sidedness and narrow-mindedness . . .'" (68). In short, by looking at the production of the novel "on a world scale" (66), you are able to reframe (if not redirect) the traffic of influence.[29] But what if Ferguson is right? If, as he suggests, the ethos of development is the historical condition that allowed the two terms "alternative" and "modernity" to be sensibly conjoined, what seems most troubling about the anachronistic redeployment of "alternative modernity" is that it *should* bear some *trace* of the actual decomposition that befell the paradigm of development, and which broke the once reassuring tie between cultural ascendance and economic progress. An immediate question for a program of "world literature" becomes: How indeed does the theoretical framework of alternative modernity manage to do its work without bearing such a trace? When Moretti moves from "description" to "explanation" without raising questions about the very sociology of "compromise," what exactly did he borrow from a bygone narrative of postcolonial transition that proved surgically extractible?

Here, we must go back to Chatterjee who, in his account of "alternative modernity" as paradigm of postcolonial transition, described more than an agenda that called for adapting foreign forms to local reality. Chatterjee's description is most vivid and convincing when he reconstructs a complex mode of cognitive mapping that splits social life into an external economic domain and an internal spiritual domain. This zoning of the national consciousness offered a society, for better or worse, a way "to choose its site of autonomy" amidst a project of cultural normalization.[30] And after staking out the spiritual domain as a zone of autonomy, "culture" was again conceived as a *place* where foreign and native elements are allowed to mix by way of careful but creative compromises and negotiations.[31] This intricate mapping of the social terrain allowed the intelligentsia to evoke two contradictory views of culture: looking *outward* from the spiritual domain, culture looked like a defensive space that needed to be protected and differentiated from the sphere of commerce; whereas, looking *inward*, culture looked like a space of experimentation and innovation.[32]

In recent deployments of "alternative modernity," the cartographic impulse is emulated but economics and culture are taken as antagonistic *agents*, not mutually differentiated *spaces*. Ferguson finds that in anthropology, "the application of a language of alternative modernities to the most impoverished regions of the globe has become a way of *not* talking about the non-serialized, detemporalized political economic statuses of our time—indeed a way of turning away from the question of a radically worsening global inequality and its consequences."[33] In the case of comparative literature, I believe the picture looks different. It's not that the "detemporalized economic statuses of our time" are ignored. Instead they are routinely evoked as the "real" material condition to which postcolonial societies respond with defensive acts of cultural creativity. We no longer have the tension produced by the forced separation of economics and culture within a national sphere, instead economic pressure is experienced as an external force of "foreign interference."[34] As we saw with *Man with a Bicycle*, political statuses have so hardened as an *African* "reality" that they've become the "objective" limit of a work's interpretation. And the more these statuses' detemporalization is asserted, the more literary production at the periphery is imagined, in this "context," as a mode of creativity under duress. In a place like Africa-of-the-Novel, where problems are chronic and solutions short-term, there is no time for literary *projects*, only literary "acts" of survival: generic re-appropriation, reversal, refunctionalization, subversion, the list goes on. This helps us better understand Casanova's *World Republic of Letters* as a particular kind of *place*:

> to speak of the center's literary forms and genres simply as a colonial inheritance imposed on writers within subordinated regions is to overlook the fact that literature itself, as a common value of the entire space, is also an instrument which, if re-appropriated, can enable writers—and especially those with the fewest resources—to attain a type of freedom, recognition and existence within it.
>
> More concretely and directly, these reflections on the immense range of what is possible in literature, even within this overwhelming and inescapable structure of domination, also aim to serve as a symbolic weapon in the struggles of those most deprived of literary resources, confronting obstacles which writers and critics at the centre cannot even imagine.[35]

"An inescapable structure of domination" that "enables [the most unprivileged] writers . . . to attain a type of freedom." An ingenuous logic, which leaves us with a literary universe whose internal differentiation into zones may be theoretically attributed (according to Casanova) to the uneven distribution of literary capital—but that is differentiated *from a methodological point of view* by a fundamentally unequal capacity among zones for *sustainable* modes of literary production: "large-scale" projects like forms, genres, or "literature itself" *expand* out of "Central" Europe, while "small-scale" endeavors like techniques, styles, or texts *transpire* locally.[36] In such a universe, where "writers within subordinated regions" are oppressed-and-freed by the task of "writing back," *a misplaced genre* like the postcolonial novel is the quintessential object of comparison. In theory, the postcolonial novel points us in two directions: either to celebrate the reappropriation of a Western genre on the periphery or lament the perpetual struggle borne of cultural colonialism. The framework of "alternative modernity" allows us to indulge both sentiments in a single interpretive procedure: first, we *describe* the periphery as a "region" of economic struggle; then we *explain* individual novels as local acts of resistance or appropriation.

The brilliance of this formulation is that it reconciles two contradictory horizons of comparison: on the one hand, economic accounts of a single world made of unequal and connected regions; and on the other, cultural accounts of multiple universes that are intelligible in their own right. While the first precludes *in principal* the notion of comparison (as Immanuel Wallerstein would put it, "You do not *compare* 'parts of a whole' "), it often defines "unequal" peripheral regions comparatively in terms of their relative location to the center.[37] And the second, while it considers location de facto a guarantor of specificity (an incomparability inviting comparison), it ignores the dependence implied by this state of separateness: "If separate, then *from* what?" But there's no need to dwell too much on such contradictions. These two approaches have coexisted peacefully by a tacit division of labor: ecumenical models fulfill the function of describing a lamentably homogeneous economic world, while localized models illuminate, through case-by-case analytical care, a multifarious cultural universe. One could say that the economistic view has served the congenial role of springboard for culturalist arguments. After all, "alternative," "critical," and "other" cultural modernities need to be championed *against* the existing menace of a "singular" economic modernity.[38] In the shadow of a consolidating neoliberal order, the comparative imagination shouldered the responsibility of illuminating "local" spaces of hope. Thinking back to the cognitive map drawn by Chatterjee, we could say that the "comparatist" has not only mastered the cartographic impulse, but also assumed the position of a transcendental witness who can look both inward *and* outward from culture. In this way, comparison can become a spatialized escape route from the teleological claims of a singular modernity. The comparative method can double-up, as it were, as antidote and supplement to periodization. But as a condition, "scale" would have to remain a fat, untheoretical concept—the geographic foil of a cartographic enterprise heralding spaces of its own creation.

Indeed, for a human geographer and theorist of scale like Neil Smith, the conceptual framework of alternative modernity is a particular instance of what he describes as "the metaphorical uses of space that have become so fashionable in literary and cultural discourse."[39] In terms that recall Ferguson's remarks about anthropologists of contemporary Africa, Smith describes a subtle form of ideological complicity that belies the liberal dispensation of spatial metaphors, even (and increasingly, it seems) in the most ethically disposed cultural criticism:

> Much social and cultural theory in the last two decades has depended heavily on spatial metaphors. The myriad "decenterings" of modernism and of reputedly modern agents (e.g., the working class), the "displacement" of political economy by cultural discourse, and a host of other "moves" have been facilitated by a very

> fertile lexicon of spatial metaphors: subject positionality, locality, mapping, grounding, travel, (de/re)centering, theoretical space, ideological space, symbolic space, conceptual space, spaces of signification, territorialization, and so forth. If such metaphors functioned initially in a very positive way to challenge, aerate, and even discard a lot of stodgy thinking, they may now have taken on much more independent existence that discourages as much as it allows fresh political insight . . . Metaphor works in many different ways but it always involves an assertion of otherness . . . Difference is expressed in similarity. Some truth or insight is revealed by asserting that an incompletely understood object, event, or situation is another, where the other is assumed known . . . To the extent that metaphor continually appeals to some other assumed reality as known, *it* systematically disguises the need to investigate the known [at hand]. . . . (63–64)

Smith's insistence that we "investigate the known" at hand implies an important shift in the ethical horizon of comparison. A metaphorical space like "postcolonial culture," when conceived as an operative counterforce to the "world-economy," indeed "disguises the need to investigate" the particular spatial relations that shape the landscapes of the postcolonial novel. It makes it impossible to recognize Africa-of-the-Novel as a differentiated *place* that embodies, in part, the ethical anxieties of the culturally permitting Western critic, national commentators, and the producers of novels. A literary critique of scale would regard Africa-of-the-Novel as a dialectically "motivated" *landscape* (to use a key term of formal analysis) where the so-called laws of motion, progress, and probability unfold according to a logic of spatial differentiation—or better, as an anthropologist would say, in a process of *scale-making*. What better program for a geographically enlarged literary history than to conceptualize the dialectic of lived time and lived space in and around literature—in order to understand the entanglement of literature in the history of the production of space. There can, of course, be no productive conceptualization of literary scale that can be limited to a single genre.[40] And yet, the novel seems to offer a ready opportunity to begin tackling directly the stakes of the "literary globalization" as a historical, theoretical, and ethical conundrum: by returning us to one of the most time-honored problems of comparative literary history—the problem of historical contextualization—this time, for the purpose of considering the geographic thinking that grounds comparative claims to context-dependency.

Instead, in the "world literature" debate, we witness distanciation, a notion that may well qualify as the commonsense of the discipline, undergo yet another "radical" revival. And the repetition suggests that the comparative imagination is hitting a chronotopic limit. Again we are told what every comparatist already knows: that by enlarging the frame of inquiry beyond the nation-scale, by stepping back, as it were, to revision the literary terrain from afar, one becomes privy to broader connections—clusters, homologies, specificities, exchange, trails of influence. This is a cultural geography that will continue to harden, as I have suggested, to make crossings possible. But also, in the midst of familiar provocations, globalization is presented as an impetus to rethink the "evidence" of literary phenomena and the relationship of the literary object to its milieu. And this is where, to my mind, the simple logic of distance begins to disintegrate.[41] We are at a juncture where we must pursue directly a literary phenomenology of the production of scale, which can begin to elucidate the diverse forms of entanglement between literary history and the history of the production of space— and the function of literary criticism as an intermediary poetics. By doing so, we leave behind what Smith describes as "the metaphorical uses of space." Unlike schoolchildren for whom scale is the relation between distance on a map and distance in reality, literary comparatists conceptualize scale as the social condition of a landscape's utility.

THE SCALE OF WORLD LITERATURE 313

Notes

1   Emily Apter, *The Translation Zone: A New Comparative Literature* (Princeton, NJ: Princeton Univ. Press, 2005). Apter's critique of comparative literature begins by examining the cultural and racial biases of the discipline's founders, most notably Eric Auerbach and Leo Spitzer.

2   Franco Moretti, "Conjectures on World Literature," *New Left Review* 1 (January–February 2000): 54–68. Moretti's short essay, and the wide response it has solicited from "comparatists" and "specialists" alike is significant, primarily because it allows us to gauge a critical status quo. Responses include, but are not restricted to: Christopher Prendergast, "Negotiating World Literature," *New Left Review* 8 (March–April 2001): 100–122; Francesca Orsini, "Maps of Indian Writing," *New Left Review* 13 (January–February 2002): 75–88. Efraín Kristal, "'Considering Coldly . . .': A Response to Franco Moretti," *New Left Review* 15 (May–June 2002): 61–74; Jonathan Arac, "Anglo-Globalism?" *New Left Review* 16 (July–August 2002): 35–45; Emily Apter, "Global *Translatio*: The 'Invention' of Comparative Literature, Istanbul, 1933," *Critical Inquiry* 29, no. 2 (2003): 253–81; Jale Parla, "The Object of Comparison," *Comparative Literature Studies* 41, no. 1 (2004): 116–25; Frances Ferguson, "Comparing the Literatures: Textualism and Globalism," *English Literary History* 71, no. 2 (2004): 323–27; Wai Chee Dimock, "Genre and World System: Epic and Novel on Four Continents," *Narrative* 14, no. 1 (2006): 85–101; and Gayatri Spivak's "World Systems and the Creole," *Narrative* 14, no. 1 (2006): 102 – 112, and her discussion of Moretti's distant reading in *Death of a Discipline* (New York: Columbia Univ. Press, 2003): 108. The list goes on.

3   Pascale Casanova, "Literature as a World," *New Left Review* 31 (January–February 2005). Casanova's application of Pierre Bourdieu's sociological construct of the "field" to describe a tightly knit international sphere of literary production that emerges in the seventeenth century and which gradually guarantees for literature "relative" autonomy from politics, has received general approval in U.S. and British academic circles, upon publication of an English translation, *The World Republic of Letters* (Cambridge, MA: Harvard Univ. Press, 2005), of her French book *La République mondiale des lettres* (Paris: Editions du Seuil, 1999). Terry Eagleton calls the book "a milestone in the history of modern thought" in *New Statesman*, April 11, 2005, and Perry Anderson says "*The World Republic of Letters . . .* is likely to have the same sort of liberating impact at large as Said's *Orientalism*, with which it stands comparison" in "Union Sucrée," *London Review of Books*, September 23, 2004. This has, so far, not been the case. Casanova's work has been more often lauded than engaged or discussed. Less favorable reviews include Christopher Prendergast's "The World Republic of Letters," in *Debating World Literature*, ed. Prendergast (Verso: London, 2004), 1–25, and Gayatri Spivak's "cautioning" to Casanova in "World-Systems and the Creole" (see note 2).

4   For a summary of this debate, see the introduction by Prendergast, *Debating World Literature*, vii–xiii.

5   Here I am not only counting those of us who hail from comparative literature; for many outside the "discipline" who espouse a comparative approach, comparison has come to be a horizon of interpretation and research.

6   Kwame Anthony Appiah, "Is the Post- in Postmodernism the Post- in Postcolonial?" *Critical Inquiry* 17, no. 2 (1991): 336–57 (hereafter cited in text as PP). Appiah's article makes a strong (and I think correct) argument about the limited relevance of a category like "postmodernism" to most of the postcolonial world, and he offers interesting observations about the "nativist" turn in prominent African writers. In this essay, I derive insight from Appiah's juxtaposition of novel and sculpture.

7   As a structure of narrative motivation, this landscape could not be any tighter; every "object" in it is explosive, a Chekhov's gun.

8   Neil Smith, "Contours of a Spatialized Politics: Homeless Vehicles and the Production of Geographical Scale," *Social Text* 33 (1992): 99. Smith's essay has been widely quoted and discussed in relation to "the scale question," which has been the center of renewed discussion among human geographers and beyond the field of geography, most notably in cultural anthropology.

9   For more on the scale debates in geography, and the critique of scale by human geographers, see Eric Sheppard and Robert McMaster, *Scale and Geographic Inquiry* (Oxford: Blackwell, 2003).

10 Smith, "Scale," in *Dictionary of Human Geography*, ed. Ronald J. Johnston et al., 4th ed. (London: Blackwell, 2000): 724–26.

11 Smith, *Uneven Development: Nature, Capital, and the Production of Space* (London: Blackwell, 1984), 68 (hereafter cited in text).

12 Newton quoted in *Uneven Development*, 68. Smith goes further to associate the "progressive abstraction of space from matter" in the history of the concept to the rise and consolidation of capitalism in *Uneven Development*, 69.

13   If we can argue that Edward Said was, in a manner, concerned with the mutual differentiation and intelligibility of the "Occident" and "Orient" as geographic *scales* in the Western imagination, then every instance in which the categories of "Orient" or "Occident" are pressed into service, what is evoked and enforced is a notion of cultural distance—the impossibility of reconciliation, or indeed, the inevitability of a clash of civilizations. See Said's critique of Raphael Patai's *The Arab Mind*, in *Orientalism* (New York: Vintage Books, 1987), 308–9.

14   Moretti uses "peripheral novel" to denote novelistic production outside central Europe, which includes what is widely referred to as "the postcolonial novel." I will use the latter term.

15   Moretti, "Conjectures," 60 (hereafter cited in text).

16   A most coherent and well-articulated project in this direction is that of Shu Mei Shih and Francoise Lionnet, whose goal is to challenge the statuses of "minor" and "major" literature by charting minor-minor and periphery-to-center movements. See *Minor Trans-nationalism*, ed. Lionnet and Shih (Durham, NC: Duke Univ. Press, 2005). Elsewhere, Wai Chee Dimock dismisses Moretti's use of "world-systems analysis," but takes on the "mapping of 'literature' as an analytic object" in "Genre as World System" (see note 2). Spivak notes this discrepancy in Dimock's critique, and gently guards against "unintended consequence[s]" in "World Systems and the Creole," 110.

17   For example: Fredric Jameson, "On Literary and Cultural Import-Substitution in the Third World," *Margins* 1 (1993): 11–34; Roberto Schwarz, *Misplaced Ideas: Essays on Brazilian Culture* (London: Verso, 1992); Itamar Even-Zohar, "The Laws of Literary Interference," *Poetics Today* 11, no. 1 (1990): 53–72.

18   The seminal text here is Bill Ashcroft, Gareth Griffiths, and Helen Tiffin, *The Empire Writes Back: Theory and Practice in Post-Colonial Literatures* (London: Routledge, 1989).

19   See Moretti's response to his critics in "More Conjectures," *New Left Review* 20 (March–April 2003): 73–81.

20   See Apter's *Translation Zone*, where she argues that Moretti "ignores the extent to which high theory, with its internationalist circulation, already functioned as a form of distant reading" (43); and Spivak's *Death of a Discipline*, whose "utopian" trajectory is remarked upon in a review by Roland Green (*Sub-Stance* 35, no. 1 [2006]: 154–59). In contrast, David Damrosch's claim, in *What Is World Literature?*, that "texts become world literature by being received into the space of a foreign culture," offers a pragmatic approach to translation, which acknowledges the privileged role of close-reading *in the second language* in the world circulation of literature (Princeton, NJ: Princeton Univ. Press, 2003), 283.

21   See Casanova's "Literature as a World," 82.

22   Moretti, *Graphs, Maps, Trees: Abstract Models for a Literary History* (London: Verso, 2005), 26.

23   Casanova, "Literature as a World," 89. The notion of "art" here magnifies the element of design on the part of postcolonial authors. Of course, Casanova contends, at the very same time, that such compromises are largely unconscious. All of this again casts the postcolonial writer as peculiarly artful and artless, a particularly "intuitive" or "instinctive" producer.

24   Pheng Cheah, who (among others) has noted the novel's centrality in accounts of cultural transition to "modernity," remarks in the context of a discussion of Benedict Anderson's work on Indonesia on the "placing of the novel at the threshold of the epistemic coupure between 'traditional' and 'modern' worldviews." *Diacritics* 29, no. 4 (1999): 8n5.

25   Indeed Appiah's "Man" could not be fit into Casanova's "literary" republic.

26   Partha Chatterjee, *The Nation and its Fragments* (Princeton, NJ: Princeton Univ. Press, 1993).

27   Jim Ferguson, "Decomposing Modernity: History and Hierarchy after Development," in *Postcolonial Studies and Beyond*, ed. Ania Loomba et al. (Durham, NC: Duke Univ. Press, 2005), 174.

28   Moretti, "Conjectures," 60–61 (hereafter cited in text).

29   The point here is not that Moretti's conception of scale is faulty, but more importantly that he, as others in the world literature debate, have thus far deployed the term scale untheoretically (speaking of literature or literary analysis on "the world scale," "the global scale," "the large scale").

30   Chatterjee, *The Nation*, 11.

31   "Language . . . became a *zone* over which the nation first had to declare its sovereignty and then had to transform in order to make it adequate for the modern world." Chatterjee, *The Nation*, 7 (my italics).

32   These two views of culture proved contradictory, Chatterjee shows, when "modern women" became anxiously perceived as the barometers of compromise. *The Nation*, 135–57.

33   Ferguson, "Decomposing Modernity," 179–80.

34   J. K. Gibson-Graham has offered a critique of a political economy, which increasingly endows "the economy" with the quality of an abstract and unchanging "Real." *The End of Capitalism (as We Knew It): A Feminist Critique of Political Economy* (Oxford: Blackwell, 1996).

35   Casanova, "Literature," 90.

36   In this logic, it matters little that some products are more far-reaching than others, because all modes of production are *aesthetically* equal.

37   This has long been Immanuel Wallerstein's position, and is expressed explicitly in relation to the comparative method in "Call for a Debate about the Paradigm," in *Unthinking Social Science: The Limits of Nineteenth-Century Paradigms* (Cambridge, MA: Polity, 1991): 237–56.

38   Anna Tsing explores the relationship between "modernization" and "globalization" as historiographical tools in her influential essay, "The Global Situation," *Cultural Anthropology* 15, no. 3 (2000): 327–60, where she proposes "scale-making" projects as an object of ethnography.

39   Smith, "Contours," 62 (hereafter cited in text).

40   It has been argued, with validity, that the novel's centrality in discussions of world literature and literary globalization must itself be scrutinized and explained. See note 4.

41   The term scale has recently attracted some specialists of American literature, such as Wai Chee Dimock and Lawrence Buell, who argue that what appears to be a national American literature can in fact be shown to be transnational; this is finally done by asserting the "multiculturalism" of a presumably homogeneous American canon. *Shades of the Planet: American Literature as World Literature*, ed. Wai Chee Dimock and Laurence Buell (Princeton, NJ: Princeton Univ. Press, 2007). Hsuan Hsu also introduces the language of "scale" to the debate among Americanists about regionalism, most recently reactivated by Sara Blair's article, "Cultural Geography and the Place of the Literary," *American Literary History* 10, no. 3 (1998): 544–67. Hsu associates scale with the ability of literary texts to negotiate the experience of belonging to geographic spheres of experience that vary in scope, and consequently chooses to examine instances where conventional geographic scales (such as the world, the nation, the home) are named and questioned, or when the word "scale" emerges in the discourse of American writers. Also see Ann Brigham's "Productions of Geographic Scale and Capitalist-Colonialist Enterprise in Leslie Marmon Silko's *Almanac of the Dead*," *Modern Fiction Studies* 50, no. 2 (2004): 303–31. Brigham draws widely from Neil Smith's work.

Chapter 29

Horace Engdahl

CANONIZATION AND WORLD LITERATURE: THE NOBEL EXPERIENCE (2008)

H ORACE ENGDAHL (B. 1948) IS A Swedish literary scholar and a member of the Swedish Academy, of which he served as the permanent secretary from 1999 to 2009. Prior to this he was culture editor at Sweden's leading newspaper *Dagens Nyheter* and worked as an independent scholar outside of academia. During Engdahl's tenure as secretary, the Nobel Prize was awarded to a number of writers who were politically controversial in their homelands, such as Turkey's Orhan Pamuk and the exiled Chinese writer Gao Xingjian, in addition to authors who wrote literature which bears witness to traumatic events, for example Hungary's Imre Kertész. His 2003 edited anthology *Witness Literature* includes a number of essays by Nobel laureates who reflect on the role of literature in relation to history and memory, and in his introduction Engdahl reflects on Elie Wiesel's idea that testimonial literature is a new and important wave in world literature in the twentieth century.

Having written on a number of other subjects himself, from hermeneutics to voice in romantic literature, Engdahl's essay "Canonization and World Literature" displays a wide range of approaches to the changing agendas in literature and the complexities of literary cultures. He counters Moretti's model of dominant waves in the literary system by demonstrating how diverse the field appears to be from the monitoring position of the Nobel Prize committee. At the same time, he also acknowledges the prize's limited influence on popular culture, and he traces the significant shifts in the criteria of the committee. These shifts are both the expression of shifts in a general trend in the criteria—which privileged humanist modernists at one point and writers dealing with traumatic events at another. But at the same time there has always been diversity in the criteria applied in each period, which makes it difficult to pinpoint precisely what Nobel literature is. According to Engdahl, this is as it should be, especially in light of the continued importance of an institution which has increasingly become identified as the most important arbiter of what counts as world literature.

Horace Engdahl, "Canonization and World Literature: the Nobel Experience," *World Literature, World Culture: History, Theory, Analysis*, eds. Karen-Margrethe Simonsen and Jakob Stougaard-Nielsen, Aarhus: Aarhus UP, 2008, pp. 195–214.

Is the writing of Nobel Prize winners different from that of other good writers? Sound scepticism answers: no, why should it be? In what way would a book be altered because its author has a new entry in his CV? But since a literary *oeuvre* consists not only in a body of texts but also in the mental preconditions for their reading, something undeniably changes as a result of the award.

Ivan Bunin, the Russian *émigré* writer who was awarded the Nobel Prize in 1933, described in his diary how after receiving the celebrated telephone call from Stockholm he was assailed by a counter-reaction, an instinctive suspicion. Walking home to his little house in Grasse, Provence, he began to have doubts and to believe it was all self-suggestion. But on approaching the house, at that time of day normally nestling unlit in deserted olive groves, he saw lights in every window and was brought back to reality. Everyone was there, waiting to congratulate him, and "[a] quiet sorrow settled on my heart", he writes (Bunin 39). He understood that his life was forever changed and his previous existence unattainable. It was the same for his writing. From that moment on, his work would be regarded as belonging to an elite order and ranked accordingly, whatever one might think of the order itself. His books still risked not being read but Bunin no longer risked being forgotten. The Nobel lamp would forever burn in the window of his authorship, like a quiet welcome.

Because of the attention that the literature prize attracts across the world and because of its prestige, the Nobel laureates have inevitably come to be seen as forming a kind of canon, which has provoked the critical reproach that many of the twentieth century's greatest writers are missing from the list, that it includes too few women, too few non-Europeans and too many mediocrities. I believe that the Academy members who commenced work in that first Nobel Committee of 1901 would have been terrified had they realized what they were about to set in train. Certainly in those first few years no one thought of the prize as a means to define a canon. Nor was the concept of a canon applied to contemporary literature. Alfred Nobel's will talks of rewarding a literary work published in the previous year and obviously refers to a single book, not a body of writing. The donor clearly intended the literature prize to act in the present rather than to crown masters for all time. But the Swedish Academy exploited the wording of the Nobel Foundation's statutes, stating that the phrase "during the preceding year" should be understood principally as a demand for the continued viability of a work; older works may therefore be rewarded, but "only if their significance has not become apparent until recently".[1] As things turned out, it immediately became a principle to consider the writing of a lifetime rather than an individual work. From the Academy's point of view, this was wise. Carrying out Alfred Nobel's orders to the letter would have greatly diminished the importance of the prize.

If canonization, then, was not the purpose of the prize, it was nevertheless apparent that the donor wanted it to have international reach. Literary prizes are generally limited to a single country or language. Why did Alfred Nobel bequeath to the Swedish Academy the daunting task of choosing prizewinners from the literature of the entire world? Nobel was a cosmopolitan with business interests in many countries. He spoke and corresponded in five languages. He is known to have said: "My country is where I work, and I work everywhere." But this is only half an explanation. Nobel's idea of literature was founded on a particular intellectual tradition. When he was in the process of drawing up his famous will, he was given by his friend Bertha von Suttner, the peace activist and writer, the first issue of *Magazine International*, a journal published by an international artists' union which began appearing in December 1894. His copy is preserved in the Nobel Library of the Swedish Academy. On the cover is a quotation from Goethe that Nobel could not have missed: namely, the famous passage from Goethe's conversations with Eckermann where the term "Weltliteratur" appears for the first time. The quotation goes as follows: "Nationalliteratur will jetzt nicht viel sagen, die Epoche der Weltliteratur ist an der Zeit, und jeder muss jetzt dazu wirken, diese epoche zu beschleunigen" (National literature has no great meaning today; the time has come for world literature, and each and every one of us should work to hasten the day) (Eckermann 214).

In his will, Nobel declared that it was his "express wish that in awarding the prizes no consideration whatsoever shall be given to the nationality of the candidates."[2] The prize is intended as an award for individual achievements and is not given to writers as representatives of nations or languages nor of any social, ethnic or gender group. There is nothing in the will about striving for a "just" distribution of the prize, whatever that could be. Such an aim would clearly contradict the donor's philosophy. What was vital for him was that the prize-winning author should have contributed to humanity's improvement ("conferred the greatest benefit to mankind"), not that the prize should flatter the self-esteem of one or other human herd.

The deficiency of a strictly nation-based concept of literature is evident from a mere glance at the list of prize-winners from 1901 to the present day. For several of the winners, exile, whether internal or external, has been the inescapable condition of their work. The reading public and literary opinion-makers in their home countries have generally preferred other writers to those selected by the Academy. In authoritarian or strongly traditional societies laureates have often been perceived as outsiders or dissidents. The issue of a writer's representativeness or authenticity tends to be voiced in terms of a suspicion of some sort of ideological crime. Two recent examples: in 2000, the Chinese government announced that Gao Xingjian was not a genuinely Chinese writer and congratulated France on the prize. Conservative nationalists in Turkey expressed similar sentiments in the case of Orhan Pamuk in 2006. They branded his work as being too strongly influenced by Western values. Oddly enough, the same demand for a writer to be loyal to his origins is voiced by Western intellectuals of the post-colonial school of thought. Critics of that leaning have argued that in giving the prize to writers such as V.S. Naipaul, Gao Xingjian and Orhan Pamuk, the Academy was actually rewarding European literature in an exotic guise, thereby joining forces with cultural imperialism.

But writing always in some sense means deserting one's kind. Great authors are quite often nomadic beings, hard to classify ethnically or linguistically. It is striking how many prize-winners, especially in recent years, have had uncertain or problematic nationalities. Beckett was an Irishman who wrote in French, Canetti a British subject of Jewish origin from Bulgaria whose literary language was German. The Brodsky who won the prize no longer called himself Iosif but Joseph and was bilingual as a poet. Nelly Sachs belongs to German literature but not to Germany – nor to Sweden, where she spent most of her life. Singer was anchored in Yiddish and in English, and his imaginative recreation of the vanished Jewish culture of Eastern Europe presupposed the distance of a foreign shore and a modern, secular society.

Two anecdotes: when Naipaul was given the prize in 2001, the British foreign service at first refused to accept that the award had gone to Great Britain. Congratulations were extended to Trinidad! But at the time Naipaul was born on that island, it was still part of the British empire and Naipaul, who moved to England early in life, has never been anything but a British subject, in recent times even knighted by the Queen. Despite this, the British ambassador in Stockholm only reluctantly and belatedly accepted this intensely English writer as a compatriot. And an even more sinister example: the first question I was asked by Hungarian journalists when Imre Kertész arrived in Stockholm to receive his prize was: why don't you give the prize to a real Hungarian instead of a Jew?

Going further back in the list of literature laureates, one finds the above-quoted Ivan Bunin, a stateless refugee with a Nansen passport. It has been my experience as a permanent secretary, when looking at the reactions to the announcement of the prize, that the hostile comments usually come from the writer's own country. Great authors are a great annoyance. Nations are happiest with their geniuses when they are dead.

Romanticism and world literature

Despite the time it took for the Academy's Nobel Committee to accept literary modernism, the Nobel Prize for Literature has from the very first been an expression of modernity. The preconditions for the award of the prize are the freedom of thought and the cosmopolitanism that are the progeny of the Enlightenment. In the field of scientific research, a kind of international republic of learned people developed as early as the seventeenth century, with Latin as its mother tongue. Bacon and Descartes were among the republic's legislators. Perhaps Goethe, in minting the term *Weltliteratur* in 1827, believed the time had come to establish a similar cross-border community for literature. Earlier, in her essays and novels, Mme de Staël had attempted to interpret the great European cultural nations for each other. Prejudices were destroyed and literary news was suddenly transported at a speed that not even modern media can match. This was the internationalism lauded by Georg Brandes in the first part of his *Main Currents of the Nineteenth Century*, "The Emigré literature" of which Mme de Staël is the heroine. If we study the relevant part of *Eckermanns Gespräche mit Goethe* it transpires that Goethe's "world literature" did not signify a huge compendium of all literature written by all peoples but rather the possibility of dialogue between different cultures through their great writers. In *West-östlicher Divan*, Goethe had himself set an example by playing with a double identity as a German and a Persian poet.

The intellectual underpinning for the views expressed by Mme de Staël and Goethe had been created around 1800 by the extraordinary circle of German geniuses that centred on the brothers Friedrich and August Wilhelm Schlegel and included Novalis, Schleiermacher, Caroline Böhmer/Schlegel/Schelling, Dorothea Veit/Schlegel and others. For the first time, the idea was expounded that Western literature comprised a spiritual whole with an autonomous, historical development. In his lectures, Friedrich Schlegel described literature as an enormous organism in which every part interacts with every other. In this magnificent historical-philosophical construct he found room for the poets of antiquity as well as those of the Middle Ages and of the new age, and for both the Roman and the German peoples. (There was as yet little coming from the Slavic peoples.) Thus he delineated what we regard as our Western canon, stretching from Homer to Goethe and onward. Sometime later, German scholars tackled the gigantic chore of charting the literary development of all civilized peoples even beyond the Western sphere. The first "history of world literature" appears to be Karl Rosenkranz's *Handbuch einer allgemeinen Geschichte der Poesie*, published in three volumes in Halle, 1832–33 (Pettersson 3).

Alfred Nobel, himself a decent amateur poet, was very much a child of Romanticism. His literary idols were Byron and Shelley, he read Goethe and Pushkin in the original languages, and he was friendly with Victor Hugo. His extensive library also contained writings by Mme de Staël, another reason to bring up her name. The numerous underlinings in his copy of *De l'Allemagne* testify to his interest.

In the nineteenth century, the humanistic belief in literature as a spiritual and transnational totality, found among the Schlegels, Mme de Staël and Goethe, conflicted with another concept of literature that originated with Johann Gottfried Herder and was based on the notion of *Volksgeist*, the individuality of nations. When Herder spoke of "the voices of peoples in poetry" he meant principally archaic voices that represented the spirit of these peoples at a time when they were still uninfluenced by a common civilization. In the nineteenth century, most of the countries of Europe created narratives of literary history that described their own country's writing as though it sprang from its own root, absorbing only superficial impulses from outside. Alien tendencies such as foreign influence on the mother tongue were seen as harmful.

It is clear that Alfred Nobel in his will takes a stand in the conflict between these two warring concepts. In his conception of a literature prize he chose the cosmopolitan view of literature and rejected the nationalistic view that dominated his era. His initiative aroused protest in his homeland. Sweden's King Oscar II tried to prevent the will from being implemented. The king wanted the Nobel Prizes to be given exclusively to Swedes and possibly Norwegians (who were also His Majesty's subjects at the time).

The birth of literature

Nobel's will and the statutes of the Nobel Foundation assume that the meaning of the word "literature" is commonly known and uncontroversial. The only explanation comes in a supplementary paragraph not found in the will, stating that the term "literature" shall comprise "not only belles-lettres but also other writings which, by virtue of their form and style, possess literary value."[3] The term *belles-lettres* ("schöne Literatur") was coined by August Wilhelm Schlegel to describe verbal texts created with an artistic intention as opposed to writing with a practical or theoretical aim. Thus the Nobel process employs an approximately two-hundred-year-old concept of literature that has only fairly recently been adopted outside the cultural sphere of Europe, even though today it seems to have achieved currency in most parts of the world. The concept is nonetheless neither obvious nor very ancient.

Although we often convince ourselves of the opposite, what we call literature was just as alien to Europe's ancestors, the Greeks and Romans, as it still is for ethnic groups in the Third World without a written language. The French scholar Florence Dupont demonstrates in her book *L'Invention de la littérature: de l'ivresse grecque au livre latin* (1998) how radically the poetry and narrative art of antiquity differed from what we call literature today. Romans did not read books – or if they did, it was not for pleasure. Their poetry was a function of convivial gatherings of friends and lovers. Their "novels" were really a kind of compendia for oral narrators.

Dupont traces the birth of the idea of literature to the curatorial approach to poetry taken by officials of the Hellenic archives. When Ptolemy Soter founded the museum and library of Alexandria, material had to be catalogued, so scholars divided the works into genres and attributed them to writers, at times rather arbitrarily. They made chronological lists that had authors following each other in a kind of genealogy of master and pupil; they supplied each with a biography; they decided that a work must consist of a single text, and they dated, edited and corrected the manuscripts to create unity among numerous versions and to remove the repetitions characteristic of oral forms of expression. Meanwhile, philologists began writing commentaries on the works and making value judgements of their authors. In the world outside the archives, everything continued as before. For Greeks and Romans, poetry was above all a vital element of parties and social occasions. The performance, not the text, was the poem's primary mode of existence. Poets' scrolls were not intended for a reading audience. And yet, an elite of ambitious Roman writers was affected by the archivists' curatorial approach. Their works could be described as updated classics. The *Aeneid* and Horace's *Odes* were originally museum texts transcribed by clerks for clerks, for the purpose of securing continuity between the Greek and Roman cultures.

This is not yet literature as we understand it. For something like our modern concept of literature to arise, the reader must first be invented. Not primarily in an exterior but in an interior sense: the reader as an element in the completion of the text. To achieve what we call literature, the author has to conclude a pact with a stranger who is granted a shadowy presence in his book: an unknown ally, at once distant and close, a "you" that can almost be mistaken for the writing "I". The change demands writers who break loose from the immediate community of society and who seek a confidant without individual features, with no real intimacy involved. The transparency of shared song is replaced by solitary reading, which acts as an initiation into the creator's singular universe. Having been but the imperfect registration of an event, the text from now on becomes an autonomous reality.

The source of this innovation is obscure. It happened through a number of successive mutations from antiquity via the Renaissance and further. Who were the pioneers? St. Augustine? Dante? Montaigne? Montaigne's *Essays* contain remnants of the old attitude: words as a minor game in the greater game of friendship. And then his closest friend, de la Boétie, died. Who am I now, the writer asks himself, when my friend no longer exists to see me? To its own gaze, the ego is a chaos of shifting phantoms. Writing becomes indispensable. The anonymous reader becomes the imagined other who allows the author to grasp who he is. Having at first regarded his readers as a species of intruder, Montaigne came to understand that only they could bestow on him an identity. The book became the guarantee of his self-identity, yet without forcing him to be always the same. In Montaigne's essays we thus witness, if not *the* birth of literature, at least one of its births.

Humanists created in literature a mental space removed from state affairs, a sanctuary in which they were able to converse with the great spirits of ancient times. Rhetoric was gradually replaced by hermeneutics. During the Renaissance, through writers such as Petrarch and Aretino, an image of the writer was formed that has lasted until the present day and that emphasizes uniqueness of the writing ego. Literature also required the growth of the written work as a legal category. Foucault and Derrida have stressed the parallels between literature and law and connect the genesis of literature with a moment in the history of justice. Literature's existence as a form is conditional on law, Derrida writes: "it did not become 'literary' until a certain epoch in the history of justice, when problems involving the ownership of works, the identity of a text, the value of a signature, the difference between creating, producing and reproducing and so on, were regulated" (Derrida 133). This took place in Europe between the end of the 1600s and the beginning of the 1800s.

Older definitions of literature often focus on written documents having the character of "utterances answering to high standards", that is, literary monuments of a canonical character. These are texts of normative content and exemplary style, not "imaginative literature" as we understand it. Thus, for example, poetry in the language of the Koran in Arab countries is still in part a demonstration of the ability to use literary Arabic (*arabía*), a language no one speaks as a mother tongue.

According to authorities on the subject, the Arabic concept *adab* carries much the same sense as eighteenth-century French *literature:* learning and good breeding. The current Japanese concept of literature came into being in the late nineteenth and early twentieth century. At the time, *Genji monogatari*, for example, was elevated to the status of a literary masterpiece. The generic word *bungaku* came into existence earlier but had another meaning. During the Meji period (1868–1912), it was reinterpreted on the model of Germany's "Nationallitteratur". Previously, what were known in Europe as literary genres had been bundled together with calligraphy, painting, tea ceremonies, the shamisen and so on as *yugei* (leisure activities), the antithesis of *bugei* (the arts of war). It should not be forgotten that there was a time when similar classifications were accepted also in our part of the world. I am thinking, for example, of the passage about pyrotechnics in the discussion of the fine arts in Claude Perrault's *Parallèle des anciens et des modernes* (1688). We once used to call the arts "embellishments to life".

A concept of literature that encompassed prose fiction appeared in Europe as late as the 1700–1800s, against some resistance. In other parts of the world, opposition was greater and more successful. Traditional Chinese poetic theory condemned fiction (Kaikkonen 39). A sharp distinction was made between books intended for the educated elite and books intended for the masses. Chinese *wenxue* encompassed poetry and scholarly essayism, which was associated with reflection and considered to be based on real experience. Fiction, on the other hand, was a lower category. The classification has a misogynist undertone. Folkloric sagas of the kind recounted by old women were especially despised. It would take a considerable time before it became possible to produce a coherent account of what we call the history of Chinese literature. The first was apparently written by a Japanese literary historian. The Mandarin class, China's literati, existed for a thousand years and the influence of that tradition is still tangible, though perhaps waning. Today, after a century of exchange with Western literature, Chinese writers of both sexes are proud to present themselves as novelists.

Criteria behind the Nobel Prize in literature

In *Comparative Poetics* (1990), Earl Miner claims that cultures other than the Western have generally based their understanding of literature on poetry. In the West, however, Aristotle's influence meant that the idea of mimesis became decisive for the understanding of what was literary, which led to the inclusion of other genres such as drama and narrative poetry. The Nobel Prize for literature basically rests on the Western concept of literature that took shape with the Brothers Schlegel. But thanks to the paragraph in the Nobel Statutes allowing non-fiction writing of literary value to be considered for the award, a relic of an older definition is preserved in the regulations. This clause has been exploited five times, twice for philosophers and three times for historians, of whom Bergson and Churchill respectively are the best known. This archaism may yet prove to be prophetic in a climate where the position of poetry and fiction is in relative decline and reportage, travel writing, witness accounts, autobiography and the essay seem to be gaining importance in the field of literature.

It is harder to tell what criteria of literary quality Alfred Nobel thought should guide the choices of the prize-givers. All he says in the words of the will is that the prize should go to "the person who shall have produced in the field of literature the most outstanding work in an ideal direction." No one has been able to establish indisputably what Nobel meant by "ideal direction."[4] In his book *The Nobel Prize in Literature. A Study of the Criteria behind the Choices* (1991), Kjell Espmark has analysed and classified the different stages of the Academy's work with the prize, a history that can also be traced in the collected edition of the Nobel Committee pronouncements 1901–50.[5]

The first Nobel Committee was a child of the nineteenth-century philosophical aesthetic that descended from Kant, Schiller, Goethe and F.T. Vischer. It interpreted Nobel's wording as "idealistic" direction, which implies that only edifying and ideally god-fearing writers should get the prize. The Nobel Committee of the time believed that great art should be comprehensible to a general audience and create harmony in the soul; it should be "soothing and liberating". The obscure and esoteric were rejected, as were "negative" tendencies of varying kinds. Georg Brandes was first proposed in 1903 but the Nobel Committee warned in a statement to the Academy of the Danish author's "negatively sceptical, totally atheistic and in ethical-sexual issues very adventurous and loose outlook", and bemoaned the "insidious sneer in the tone" of his texts, "that often robs the presentation of its quiet nobility." He did not get the prize, despite the dedicated support of Selma Lagerlöf in the Academy.

Maeterlinck was first criticized for his fondness for the abnormal and the masked, but in his case the Members reconsidered and gave him the prize in 1911. Swinburne was seen by the Nobel Committee majority as not sufficiently noble for a prize "in an ideal direction." As for Hamsun, he was judged by Per Hallström, a Member who was influential in Nobel issues, to use experimentation as a goal in itself, and Henrik Schück wrote in 1920 that what he found lacking in Hamsun's *Growth of the Soil* as well as in his other novels was "the culture, the well-reasoned world view and the humanity that I must demand in a Nobel Prize winner" (Svensén 1: 413). But the Academy's majority forgave him his experiments.

At times the Committee would acknowledge the greatness of rebuffed candidates yet still reject them. Tolstoy was an important author, it was conceded, but "anti-culture"; Ibsen "negative and bewildering", Zola "cynical". Or to name some Anglo-Saxon examples from the early years: in Henry James the Committee was disturbed by unclear motivations (the very feature of his work that now fascinates us), and by his tiring mass of detail, while Thomas Hardy lost the day because of his immoral heroines and because he was too deterministic and rebellious against God. Even though the Academy successively renewed itself and abandoned its defence of philosophical idealism, a few of these principles survived through the 1920s and '30s, together with a love of classical form and epic narrative. Reference was often made to "ordinary readers". The "universally intended Nobel Prize" should not go to "exclusive and unapproachable writing". Sinclair Lewis was chosen over Theodore Dreiser for his humour and more conciliatory spirit. Stefan George was too narrow and Paul Claudel perplexing. One Member spoke of "Valéry's lofty de-nature". The prizes to relatively "difficult" authors such as Pirandello and O'Neill are the exceptions to the 1930s focus on writers with broad influence such as Galsworthy and Martin du Gard. For a long time, a typical Nobel winner was an edifying and accessible writer rather than a misanthropic and demanding innovator. Sigmund Freud was proposed for the literature prize – a daring but not unreasonable idea. Freud was unquestionably one of the previous century's foremost essayists and perhaps unintentionally, through his case studies, an important novelist. The proposal was made in 1936 by a previous Nobel laureate, Romain Rolland. The Nobel Committee's report, signed by permanent secretary Per Hallström, was however extraordinarily tart. In part it said: "Freud appears, more than any of his patients, to be possessed by a sick and twisted imagination, which speaks volumes, since he has an abundance of unusually strange patients" (Svensén 2: 24p). That year the prize went instead to Eugene O'Neill.

The mid-1940s brought a re-alignment. A new generation of writers had been inducted into the Academy and took charge of the Nobel Committee. Valéry would have been awarded the prize in 1945 but died before the decision was finalized. But from 1946 the awards went to several prominent figures in modern literature: Hesse, Gide, Eliot, Faulkner. Key to the prize process was defining "the great precursors". The Nobel Committee adopted modernism's belief in literary evolution towards more and more advanced forms. A strange side effect of the interpretation of "precursors" was that for forty-five years (1946–91) it proved impossible to award the prize to a single female writer, with the exception of Nelly Sachs, who shared it with Samuel Agnon in 1966. Overlooked without compunction were Anna Akhmatova, Karen Blixen, Elsa Morante, Simone de Beauvoir and Marguerite Duras.

Simultaneously it was becoming less necessary for the prize-winners to represent a kind of positive humanism. Nihilists and pessimists such as Faulkner, Beckett, Golding, Cela, Naipaul, and Jelinek had been accepted. The wording "ideal direction" was ultimately interpreted as "serious writing", which is to say it lost what little directive power it may have possessed.

Pascale Casanova has claimed to see an aesthetic prime meridian cutting across the Swedish Academy, forming the ultimate standard for literary value in a "universal literary space" that stretches around the world. Judging from her book, *La République mondiale des lettres*, she considers this meridian to have originated in Paris before it became a global norm thanks to the prestige of the Nobel Prize. There is some truth in this. From the 1940s onwards, the Academy came to accept a set of literary ideals that have their roots in French modernism. But a central perspective of the kind suggested by Casanova would be too narrow to account for the variety that actually characterizes the list of Nobel prize-winners. To be sure, the standard-setting modernists – "the great precursors" in Österling's words – are there, but many writers in the 1950s and '60s were rewarded according to different criteria. I need only mention names such as Russell, Churchill, Mauriac, Laxness, Steinbeck, Solzhenitsyn, Böll, Singer, Gordimer, Morrison and Szymborska. To put it another way, the Academy has never won unanimous approval from any single intellectual camp, literary generation or trend. All regard some of the Academy's decisions as brilliant and others as bewildering or even disastrous. The list of Nobel prize-winners cannot be classified according to any one aesthetic creed or literary tradition. The English say: "Success makes strange bedfellows." This was never more apt than in the case of the Nobel literary laureates. But in my opinion, this diversity is the strength of the list.

For this reason we should not disparage the early twentieth-century Nobel Committees and Academy Members who judged literature from different criteria than our own. The greater part of our contemporary cultural establishment automatically and without much reflection belongs to the victorious church, that of modernism. It can be difficult to enter into the values of qualified literary judges of a previous epoch, who saw in the avant-garde a temporary disorientation with no relevance to the long-term development of literature. Reading the copious reports by Per Hallström, the long-standing chairman of the Nobel Committee and the Academy's permanent secretary between 1931 and 1941, texts that in their way are brilliant literary essays, one becomes aware that Hallström repeatedly slighted the very tendencies that underpinned the avant-garde: elitism, aestheticism and primitivism. In other respects, this reflected a more broad-minded attitude. For example, we might note that it was less difficult for the conservative officials in the Academy at the time to award the prize to women writers than it was later on, when the Academy was dominated by the boys of the modernist generation.

Why did modernism's values triumph in the West after 1950, despite its (continuing) unpopularity among the general public? Presumably thanks largely to the huge expansion of academic literature studies that resulted from the proliferation of universities. One consequence has been the circumstance touched upon by the English professor of literature Frank Kermode in one of his valuable essays on the concept of canon. Kermode says that the serious literary criticism of our day is the discussion in university classrooms. Recalling the notion of "the common reader", still the ideal for Virginia Woolf in her literary essays, he adds: "all the duties of the old Common Reader have now virtually devolved upon professional students of literature" (Kermode 51).

It may well be so. But the generations of Academy Members responsible for the Nobel Prize during the first forty years did *not* believe that great literature is written for university professors and their students. They believed it is written for, if not the ordinary reader, then at least the voluntary reader: admittedly an educated person but not someone who is forced to read for a living or to pass an exam. At the time, therefore, the criticism levelled at the Academy by the intellectual elite was not received with any great distress by the members. Today the situation is more difficult. There is no longer an educated general public to turn to when under fire from an avant-garde that in the meantime has conquered the institutions and become integrated into the tax-funded stipend economy. Currently, a publicly funded elite culture stands face to face with a mass public inspired by *Paradise Hotel* rather than Dante's *Paradiso*.

The Nobel Prize and the canon

Does then the list of literary Nobel prize-winners correspond to a reasonable canon of modern classics? I do not feel called upon always to defend my colleagues of the past, but if the issue is to be examined, we must recognize that it would have been chronologically impossible to give the prize to some of the twentieth century's greatest writers. As Kjell Espmark has pointed out, this pertains certainly to Proust, Kafka, Rilke, Musil, Kavafis, Mandelstam, Lorca and Pessoa, and in a fashion also to Brecht and Celan. Kafka's *oeuvre* was published posthumously as were the writings of Kavafis and Pessoa. Part Two of *A la recherche du temps perdu* was published in 1919 and led to Proust's breakthrough. Three years later he was dead, without having been nominated by the French or anyone else. *Duineser Elegien* was published three years before Rilke's death in 1926. Lorca's most important works, his plays, were written shortly before his death in 1936, and *Poeta en Nueva York* was not published until 1940. Musil's stature became apparent only with the publication of his collected works between 1952 and '57. He had died in 1942. Brecht was first proposed in 1956 and died the same year. Celan appeared in the 1960s and died in 1970. To add a Nordic example: Edith Södergran succumbed to consumption in 1923 in a corner of Finland cut off from the rest of the world before her poetry had attracted more than passing and mainly negative attention within that country's Swedish-speaking minority.

Another interesting observation is that almost all the giants absent from the list of prize-winners were overlooked by the proposers in their own countries. Virginia Woolf was never nominated and neither was Joyce. In Sweden, Strindberg was passed over by those eligible to nominate.

It is easy to become anachronistic when discussing literary values. An intellectual effort is called for to realize that writers such as Proust, Joyce, Kafka and Musil were initially marginal in the literary life of their respective countries, that their works only gradually, and posthumously, found their way to the centre, thanks to new critical methods and thanks to discoverers and followers among writers of subsequent generations. In the 1930s Proust was judged to be *passé*. His exaltation had to wait for *la nouvelle critique* to develop, in the 1940s and '50s, the analytical tools to tackle his novels. Kafka's reputation grew slowly, not reaching its present extent until the 1960s.

To win the Nobel Prize, a great author's career should resemble Thomas Mann's rather than Kafka's. We might deplore this, but it is hard to change. A Nobel Committee in 1840 would probably have awarded Victor Hugo and ignored Stendhal, if for no other reason than because the only observer with an overview of Stendhal's authorship, hidden as it was behind his numerous pseudonyms, was at that time the Austrian police. The Academy can draw comfort from the realization that it has sometimes discovered great writers ahead of the general public: Tagore, Faulkner, Singer, Milosz and Canetti to name a few.

Work on the prize means applying the canonical perspective to literature created in the present. It teaches how difficult it is to calculate the future prospects of a literary *oeuvre* or a critical principle. Not even every second author on the list can be said to have reached something like a canonical status, despite the unique prestige of the prize and the lengthy exposure it confers on the laureates – while several writers who missed out for various reasons have come to number among the great names of twentieth-century literature.

Canonicity is a function of forces that cannot be controlled and do not form a closed and identifiable system. Cultural authority is only one of these forces and perhaps not the strongest. The symbolic power that the Nobel Prize has accumulated over a hundred years is demonstrably insufficient to make an author canonical, but sufficient to arouse the curiosity of posterity. Confronted with the laureate's name on the list, people will for centuries continue to ask: Who's that? What did he or she write? The Nobel Prize guarantees an entry in encyclopaedias if not a presence in the living memory of literature. The Catholic system of sainthood incorporates a lower rank, where a person is not *sanctus* (sainted) but *beatus* (beati-fied). Let us say that Nobel prize-winners in relation to actual canonicity achieve something analogous: immortality of the second grade.

The Nobel Prize has possibly contributed to conserving the idea of Literature with a capital L – serious literature as opposed to literary entertainment. But is it a literature that is read? Let us look at the Top Ten Nobel laureates, as they appear in the list of books borrowed from Swedish public libraries in 2006 (the latest statistics I have been able to access):

1.   Selma Lagerlöf (Nobel Prize 1909) – 77,907 loans
2.   J.M. Coetzee (Nobel Prize 2005) – 39,812
3.   Ernest Hemingway (Nobel Prize 1954) – 34,931
4.   John Steinbeck (Nobel Prize 1962) – 34,808
5.   Orhan Pamuk (Nobel Prize 2006) – 34,306
6.   Rudyard Kipling (Nobel Prize 1907) – 33,666
7.   Harry Martinson (Nobel Prize 1974) – 25,250
8.   Doris Lessing (Nobel Prize 2007) – 24,328
9.   Pär Lagerkvist (Nobel Prize 1951) – 21,478
10.   Thomas Mann (Nobel Prize 1929) – 14,314

Elfriede Jelinek went from no loans in 2003 to 11,025 in 2004, having been named prize-winner late in that year; peaked on 29,458 loans in 2005, then fell to 12,315 in the following year. Naipaul, awarded in 2001, was still listed at 11,562 loans, but the curve has been descending since.

There is one point that we should not overlook when considering these figures. Selma Lagerlöf, the Nobel laureate most enjoyed by Swedish readers, is still in only 150th place among all writers. Literature of the Nobel Prize sort provides reading for a small section of the public, even if at times this section attains a decent size. The Nobel brand is strong, but if it has not been able to induce mass consumption over a hundred years, it is not likely to do so in the future either. The group of readers involved is perhaps similar in number to the group of opera-goers and even to some extent coincides with it.

The world literature system

In the current discussion of world literature, the idea of a centre and a periphery plays a prominent role. The Nobel Prize is generally seen as an expression of literary values characteristic of the nucleus of the Western cultural sphere, even if not everyone goes as far as Pascale Casanova in implying that it is actually a French prize awarded by Swedes.

An influential description of the inequality between centre and periphery is Franco Moretti's theory of diffusion. Moretti maintains that the life of literature consists of waves of influences flowing from the centre, disturbing local development. The result is a great degree of uniformity, as regions are progressively pulled into a common market of books and values. According to Moretti, the phenomenon was first observed in the wave of Petrarchism that washed across Europe during the Renaissance. In the eighteenth century, the poetry of all European countries was largely adapted to French models. But at the same time, the pattern from the centre was applied in different ways on the periphery, depending on local traditions. "The analytico-impersonal style of nineteenth-century France is replaced by judgment, loud, sarcastic, emotional voices, always somewhat at odds with the story they are narrating" (Moretti 118). The barbarism of the fringes is revealed in their inability to achieve the aloof aestheticism that characterizes the French attitude. The result is often plot from the centre combined with material and narrative voice from the periphery.

Moretti's argument, drastically paraphrased, is that literature is a special form of malevolence invented by the French that the rest of the world tries to learn with no definitive success. My thoughts are drawn to a passage in Edmond de Goncourt's diary where he talks about a conjugal quarrel between Alphonse Daudet and his wife, provoked by their divergent estimations of Montaigne: "The wife says that when her husband reads the essays, it is no longer the Daudet she knows, no longer the father of her children, he becomes harsh and unfeeling. And she protests at the meanness in Montaigne's philosophy, the selfish and unimaginative doctrines, the smutty pessimism that arises from the prose".[6]

But from the viewpoint granted by working with the Nobel Prize, the literary system appears far from unified and centralized. Every nation seems to have its own idea of world literature. There is no neutral ground or transnational vision shared by all. On the contrary, it can be seen everywhere that national canon pierces the international, not only in the sense that national writers are granted a special place but also in the slightly different choices of foreign classics. In Sweden, for example, more authors from the Nordic countries are canonical than in England or Italy. Alexis Kivi is a canonical author in Finland and Sweden, and Sandemose in Scandinavia but scarcely beyond. The phenomenon also includes older classics. Chekhov is a more canonical author in the West than in Russia while the opposite is true for Pushkin. For an observer from a small country this effect is especially obvious, while critics from the great nations are often convinced that the canon cherished by the academic elite of their own country is the universal one. This can be felt even in the writings of a highly sophisticated scholarly critic like Harold Bloom.

Yet it is evident that the Nobel Prize represents a unifying force in relation to the mass of local traditions. Pascale Casanova has even described it as a definitive proof of a universal literary consciousness:

> One objective indicator of the existence of this world literary space is the (almost) unanimous belief in the universality of the Nobel Prize for literature. The significance attributed to this award, the peculiar diplomacy involved, the national expectations engendered, the colossal renown it bestows; even (above all?) the annual criticism of the Swedish jury for its alleged lack of objectivity, its supposed political prejudices, its aesthetic errors – all conspire to make this annual canonization a global engagement for the protagonists of literary space.
>
> (2004, 147; 2005, 74)

As a member of the Nobel Committee, one cannot hope to take a purely theoretical view of the subject. "World literature" shifts from a descriptive term to something of a performative. Rather than designating the bulk of literary works existing world-wide, it signifies a context into which we hope to bring the winning *oeuvre*.

Notes

1   *Statutes of the Nobel Foundation*, § 2.
2   *Statutes of the Nobel Foundation*, § 1.
3   *Statutes of the Nobel Foundation*, § 2.
4   Sture Allén, former permanent secretary of the Swedish Academy, has analysed the passage from a linguistic point of view, but not even after his meticulous reading does Nobel's expression become anything like a workable criterion for the evaluation of literary art (Allén 1993, 135–41). For a brief summary of his view in English, see Allén and Espmark 7ff.
5   See Bo Svensén, ed. *Nobelpriset i litteratur. Nomineringar och utlåtanden* 1901–50.
6   Edmont de Goncourt, *Journal*, 7. Oct. 1884.

Works cited

Allén, Sture. "I idealisk rigtning." *Svenska Akademiens handlingar från år 1986*, vol. 19. Stockholm: Svenska Akademien, 1993: 135–41.

Allén, Sture and Kjell Espmark. *The Nobel Prize in Literature. An Introduction*. Stockholm: Norstedts Förlag, 2001.

Bunin, Iwan. *Ein unbekannter Freund*. Trans. by Swetlana Geier. Zürich: Dörlemann Verlag, 2003.

Casanova, Pascale. *La République mondiale des lettres*. Paris: Seuil, 1999.

—. *The World Republic of Letters*. Trans. M.R. DeBevoise. Boston: Harvard UP, 2004.

—. "Literature as a World." *New Left Review* 31 (2005): 71–90.

Derrida, Jacques *et al. La Faculté de juger*. Paris: Editions de Minuit, 1985.

Dupont, Florence. *L'Invention de la littérature: de l'ivresse grecque au livre latin*. Paris: La Découverte, 1998.

Eckermann, Johann Peter. *Eckermanns Gespräche mit Goethe*, vol. I. Ed. Ernst Merian-Genast. Basel: Verlag Birkhäuser, 1945.

Espmark, Kjell. *The Nobel Prize in Literature. A Study of the Criteria behind the Choices*. Boston: G.K. Hall & Co, 1991.

Kaikkonen, Marja. "Becoming Literature: Views of Popular Fiction in Twentieth-Century China." *Literary History: Towards a Global Perspective*, vol. I. Ed. Gunilla Lindberg-Wada. Berlin: Walter de-Gruyter, 2006: 36–69.

Kermode, Frank. *An Appetite for Poetry*. London: Fontana Press, 1990.

Miner, Earl. *Comparative Poetics: An Intercultural Essay on Theories of Literature*. Princeton: Princeton UP, 1990.

Moretti, Franco. "Evolution, World-Systems, *Weltliteratur*." *Studying Transcultural Literary History*. Ed. Gunilla Lindberg-Wada. Berlin: Walter de Gruyter, 2006: 113–21.

Pettersson, Anders. "Introduction: Concepts of Literature and Transcultural Literary History." *Literary History: Towards a Global Perspective*, vol. I. Ed. Gunilla Lindberg-Wada. Berlin: Walter de Gruyter, 2006: 1–35.

Svensén, Bo. ed. *Nobelpriset i litteratur. Nomineringar och utlåtanden 1901–1950*. Stockholm: Svenska Akademien, 2001.

Chapter 30

Mariano Siskind

THE GLOBALIZATION OF THE NOVEL AND THE NOVELIZATION OF THE GLOBAL: A CRITIQUE OF WORLD LITERATURE (2010)

MARIANO SISKIND (B. 1972) STUDIED AT the University of Buenos Aires, and at New York University, where he obtained his PhD. He teaches nineteenth- and twentieth-century Latin American literature, with emphasis on its world literary relations, as well as the production of cosmopolitan discourses and processes of aesthetic globalization, at Harvard. His research interests comprise nineteenth- and twentieth-century Latin American literature, travel writing, histories and theories of globalization, Marxism, deconstruction, and critical articulations of literature and philosophy.

In the article here included Siskind considers the novel, which in many ways has been the favorite genre of scholars discussing world literature, from various points of view. To begin with, he looks at the novel as indeed a world genre, spreading the idea of an originally European bourgeois order of things around the globe, especially so in the nineteenth century, and thus imaginatively paralleling the effective spread of such order as chronicled and/or projected philosophically, historically and economically by Kant, Hegel and Marx. It is precisely in this idea of a bourgeois order that the attraction of the genre lay also outside of Europe, whence it originated in its modern form. Siskind then looks at how the novel itself at the same time imagined the world as available to the European bourgeois, thus literarily appropriating the world for the consumption of its European, or by extension Western, readers. Finally, he reads recent theories of world literature, such as those of Moretti, Casanova and Damrosch as attempts to overcome the identity politics of preceding approaches such as postcolonialism or multiculturalism. Siskind closes with a warning, though, that pedagogical practice—at least in the United States—is not necessarily in step with these theoretical concerns and may in fact re-appropriate world literary texts for identitarian purposes. With its unusual breadth of reference, its firm but unobtrusive grounding in philosophy, economics and literary theory, and its level-headed discussion of what the contribution of "world literature" may be to the bringing into being of a more cosmopolitan world, Siskind's article usefully summarizes where the world literature debate was at when this volume went to press.

Mariano Siskind, "The Globalization of the Novel and the Novelization of the Global: A Critique of World Literature," *Comparative Literature* 62 (2010) 4: 336–60.

Kant and the global novel

In "Idea for a Universal History with a Cosmopolitan Purpose" (1784), Kant drafts the historiographic parameters for a re-conceptualization of a human history narrated from the point of view of the actualization of freedom in a cosmopolitan political formation that he imagines as a world-republic (*Weltrepublik*).[1] In this crucial essay, Kant articulates the passage from the conceptual universality of reason to its universal (that is, global) actualization in concrete cosmopolitan political and economic institutions, inaugurating what I have called elsewhere a "discourse of globalization." The discursive construction of globalization is a highly ideological operation that consists of naturalizing an assumed universality of reason that is in fact the result of a universalization of the cultural particularity of the bourgeoisie. More importantly, Kant's discourse of globalization translates the abstract and philosophical concept of the universal into its concrete geopolitical actualization in a world structured as a totality of meaning governed by modern reason. Kant's narrative of the global realization of bourgeois freedom (soon after perfected by Hegel through the concept of "world history") opens up, on the one hand, the interpretative horizon of globalization as the necessary spatial dimension of the project of modernity and provides, on the other, the epistemological structure for the economic, political, and military discourses of globalization that surround us today.

Here I am interested in underscoring, in addition to the cosmopolitical narrative of Kant's essay, an idea that, to my knowledge, has been overlooked by the many literary critics interested in the relation between literature and globalization. Towards the end of "Idea for a Universal History with a Cosmopolitan Purpose" Kant suggests that the novel could play an important role in the production of the discourses of globalization by imagining the world as a totality mediated by bourgeois culture. He concludes that "it is admittedly a strange and at first sight absurd proposition to write a *history* according to an idea of how world events must develop if they are to conform to certain rational ends; it would seem that only a *novel* could result from such premises" (51–52).

What I find striking about Kant's admission is his implicit disciplinary comparison between philosophic and novelistic discourses as he attempts to determine which one is the more adequate to tell the story of a modern world that should march towards the global actualization of rational freedom. He seems to be saying that although it might look like the novel is much better suited to accomplish this task it is a philosopher's job. But even if Kant considers that it is the philosopher who must *conceptualize* the process of globalization, his formulation concedes that the challenge of *imagining* the world as a reconciled bourgeois totality of freedom could fall to the novel[2]—the novel as the cultural formation that, during the nineteenth century, renders the historical process of globalization visible; the novel, or at least the imaginary potential of discourse contingently embodied in the novel form, as that which makes the process of globalization available so that reading audiences can work through the transformations they are experiencing at home.

During the second half of the nineteenth century, when bourgeois reason (through its economic, political, and cultural institutions) was thought to occupy every single region of the planet, the novel produced privileged and efficient narratives of the global formation of a bourgeois world. Because the novel was the hegemonic form that bourgeois imagination adopted in the nineteenth century, and because of the aesthetic and political force of the social totalities it was capable of constructing, most novels dealing with distant places produced powerful images of the globalization of bourgeois culture.[3] This is the specificity of the relation between the novel and the historical process of globalization vis-à-vis modern philosophy: if philosophy conceptualized the transformation of the globe as the realization of a totality of bourgeois freedom (Kant, Hegel, and Marx), the novel provided this philosophical concept with a visual reality, a set of images and imaginaries that elevated the fiction of bourgeois ubiquity to a foundational myth of modernity.

My goal in this essay is to propose two different but complementary models with which to think about the relation between the novel and the discourses of globalization. The first—*the globalization of the novel*—works not with particular textual formations but with the historical expansion of the novel-form hand-in-hand with the colonial enterprise of Western Europe. This concept will allow me to review the historical and theoretical parameters that have been used to study both the historical spread of the novel from Europe to the peripheries and the constitution, at the end of the nineteenth and throughout the twentieth century, of a global system of production, reception, and translation of novels.

The second model—*the novelization of the global*—focuses on the production of images of a globalized world as they are constructed in specific novels. I will read these figures, primarily, in novels by Jules Verne and a novel by Eduardo Ladislao Holmberg. As might be expected, the kind of images they create of travelers spreading modern bourgeois culture throughout the world and beyond, reaching even into outer space, are entirely different. While Verne was a professional novelist working in France and surrounded by imperialist discourses and a reading public imbedded in its state's mission *civilisatrice*, Holmberg was an amateur writer (whose first occupation was in the natural sciences) living in Buenos Aires, a large village (a *gran aldea*) at the threshold of becoming a city. Verne lived and breathed the experience of modernity; Holmberg's Latin American context was constituted by a desire for modernity itself.[4] The point I try to make is that the particular geopolitical determinations that marked each of these writers produced dissimilar imaginaries of the global reach of their bourgeois characters and plots. In Verne's novels, omnipotent bourgeois characters (based on the *topos* of the *bourgeois conquérant*) travel adventurously, around the entire world and beyond: the bottom of the sea, the center of the earth, the moon, Mars, and the sun. In Holmberg's *Viaje maravilloso del señor Nic-Nac al planeta Marte* (1875), however, the social position of the Argentine (and Latin American) bourgeoisie within the global economy of the discourse of adventure allows only for spiritual/immaterial/imaginary travel: the body of Nic-Nac never leaves his home, and only his soul (!) travels to Mars. I read these novels, which take their materials from discourses of adventure, science fiction, and spiritism, in relation to the hegemonic protocols of realism in order to try to broaden the concept of representation as it pertains to the world historical globalization of the European bourgeoisie.

Finally, in a coda to the main argument, I connect the interpretative models of the *globalization of the novel* and *the novelization of the global* that I'm putting forth here with the *rentrée* of the concept of world literature. Recently re-introduced to academic debate by Franco Moretti, Pascale Casanova, and David Damrosch, among others, this restored notion of world literature can be understood as an attempt to conceptualize the global ubiquity of the novel since the mid-twentieth century. In the final part of the article I analyze what could be called the cultural politics of world literature and the critical and pedagogical practices that are derived from this concept. I also examine its underlying claim to address, in academic practices, cosmopolitan expectations related to the production of a discourse about the world based on respect for cultural difference. In other words, my question in this closing section is whether world literature, as a concept and as a practice, is capable of becoming an effective cosmopolitan discourse.

The globalization of the novel

During the eighteenth and nineteenth centuries, the novel traveled from Europe to Latin America, as well as to other peripheries of the world, through the colonial and postcolonial channels of symbolic and material exchange.[5] Novels were appealing to a Creole class torn by the contradiction between its cultural and economic attachment to Europe and its desire for political autonomy. Local elites found in those narratives of subjective freedom the possibility of imagining and modeling identities independent from the colonial metropolis. Specific to the Latin American consumption of novels was the opportunity to grasp an experience of modernity that, for the most part, was not available to the reading Creole class in its everyday life, despite liberal aspirations that were beginning to be articulated as a political and cultural project.

Because of the kind of experiences that the novel afforded to the readers of the colonial and semi-colonial peripheries, Latin American intellectuals immediately realized the important role that the consumption, production, and translation of novels could play in the process of socio-cultural modernization. The Argentine Domingo F. Sarmiento was perhaps the most prominent writer and politician to propose that novels were an essential instrument for the modernization of Latin America. In *Facundo. Civilización y Barbarie* (1845) he argued that Latin America could leave its pre-modern backwardness if it imposed over its barbarian, natural being civilized/modern (that is, European) cultural practices and institutions. Modernization was a process of conversion (forced or voluntary—and, in any case, violent) enacted by reproducing European modernity in Latin America. Immediately after the publication of *Facundo*, Sarmiento traveled to Europe, North Africa, and the U.S. Walking through the streets of Paris, Sarmiento reflects that

> Las ideas y modas de Francia, sus hombres y sus novelas, son hoy el modelo y la pauta de todas las otras naciones; y empiezo a creer que esto que nos seduce por todas partes, esto que creemos imitación, no es sino aquella aspiración de la índole humana a acercarse a un tipo de perfección, que está en ella misma y se desenvuelve más o menos según las circunstancias de cada pueblo.
>
> (138–39)[6]

> The ideas and fashion of France, her men and novels, are today the model and pattern of all other nations; I am starting to believe that this which seduces us here and there, this which we think is imitation, is nothing but the inherently human aspiration to be close to perfection that develops itself according to the circumstances of each nation.
>
> (my translation)

Sarmiento defends a mimetic path to modernization by arguing that imitation is not the post-colonial condition of the periphery, but, in a Platonic turn, an inherently human feature. And he does not hesitate to prescribe precisely *what* aspects of modern European culture should be imitated: namely, discourses (ideas and trends) and cultural institutions, with the novel being the single example that he provides.[7] The importance of the novel as an effective modernizing institution has been studied extensively by Alejandra Laera in *El tiempo vacío de la ficción*, where she quotes a rare journalistic piece by Sarmiento, "Las novelas" (1856), in which he compares the degree of modernization of a given culture with the number of novels it consumes: "Caramelos y novelas andan juntos en el mundo, y la civilización de los pueblos se mide por el azúcar que consumen y las novelas que leen ¿Para qué sirve el azúcar? Díganlo los pampas que no lo usan" (qtd. in Laera 9; Candy and novels go hand-in-hand in the world, and the culture of a nation can be measured by the amount of sugar they consume and the novels they read. What is sugar good for? Ask the Pampa Indians who don't use it; my translation). Although sweetness, that surplus addition to the natural taste of food, can be considered a sign of gastronomic refinement, of civilization, its value as an inscription in

networks of modern consumption becomes especially clear, Sarmiento suggests, when juxtaposed to the sentimental and political education the novel provides—the novel as a universal
measure of modernity.

Through processes of formal and thematic imitation, importation, translation, and adaptation, the institution of the novel grew roots in Latin America during the nineteenth century,
and towards the 1880s novelistic production and consumption had become well established
(the same process takes place, with minor temporal variations, in colonial Africa, Asia, and
Eastern and Southern Europe).[8] Due to the global hegemony of modern-bourgeois European
culture (produced and reproduced in its colonial, postcolonial, and neocolonial links with its
peripheries) the novel was the first universal aesthetic form of modernity.[9] It is important to
bear in mind that the global preeminence of the novel-form among all other discursive genres
cannot be explained as the result of a supposedly universal need for narration: narration and
the novel are in fact incommensurable cultural practices. The universality of the novel-form
was the historical outcome of the formation (through colonialism, trade, and promises of
emancipation) of a world in which bourgeois culture was increasingly hegemonic, if not
forcefully dominant. Wherever one looked for modern desires (desire for self-determination, for identity, for material development and progress) one found novels. One could thus
define the novel in the periphery as modern desire formally enclosed and regulated.

Was there (indeed, is there), however, a difference between the European novel and the
Latin American novel, the Asian novel, the African novel, and so on? Well, yes and no. Yes,
one could point to the diverse formal and thematic aspects of individual works (something I
do in the next section, in which I conceptualize and analyze the idea of *the novelization of the
global*), whose difference was informed by, among other things, a geopolitically determined
experience of the process of globalization of modern institutions, practices, and values.
However, if one looks at the globalization of the novel-form as a modern and modernizing
institution, it becomes quite difficult to identify differences in terms of the institutional and
political function of the novel in these different locations. In other words, the world system
of novelistic production, consumption, and translation reinforces the dream of a global
totality of bourgeois freedom with Hegelian overtones—that is, a totality whose internal
heterogeneity (the formal and thematic particularity of the Latin American or African or
Asian novel vis-à-vis the European novel) is functional to the identity of the *global novel*. I
insist that the globality of the novel-form is the result of a historical process of global
hegemony—the product of the universalization of its bourgeois and European particularity.
In an interesting note in the *Prison Notebooks*, "Hegemony of Western Culture over the Whole
World Culture," Gramsci uses the very category he developed to analyze social formations
within national scenarios to consider the processes of globalization as the world history of the
West's hegemony over its cultural others:

> Even if one admits that other cultures have had an importance and a significance
> in the process of "hierarchical" unification of world civilization (and this should
> certainly be admitted without question), they have had a universal value only in
> so far as they have become constituent elements of European culture, which is
> the only historically and concretely universal culture—in so far, that is, as they
> have contributed to the process of European thought and been assimilated to it.
>   (416)

In this quotation, Gramsci is at his most Hegelian. He affirms that World Culture—the possibility of proposing the existence of a global cultural field—depends on the universal mediation of Europe. As global *hegemon*, European culture recognizes and incorporates the
subaltern aesthetic norms, forms, and practices that are central to the cultures of its others in

order to form a world cultural field structured around the predominant *nuclei* that governed the appropriations that gave it form in the first place—a global cultural field whose universality and relatively stable homogeneity is the result of the hegemonic mediation of European or North-Atlantic bourgeois culture. Thus, the periphery does not merely receive and absorb cultural mandates from the core based on an international division of labor and trade balance that favors the development of the First World; on the contrary, core/periphery relations are culturally mediated by a hegemonic production of consent in the margins of globalization.[10] This hegemonic cultural mediation can be read in the gap between the globalization of the novel and the novelization of the global—between capitalism's creation of "a world after its own image" (Marx and Engels 477) through the global expansion of its aesthetic and cultural institutions, and the local literary reappropriations and reinscriptions of that epochal process.

In this sense, and taking a cue from the way Gramsci understands hegemony, the operation of universalization that constitutes the discursive basis for the globality of the novel should not be understood as an instance of the periphery's cultural subordination to the core. Not at all. That is why I mention notions of "importation," "translation," and "adaptation," instead of thinking only in terms of "imitation," "implantation," or "imposition." The ideas of coercion and consent imbedded in the concept of hegemony presuppose an active agency on the part of peripheral cultures in the enterprise of the universalization of the novel. That is, in the nineteenth and early twentieth century the representation of the particularity of bourgeois European culture and its institutions as universal was an enterprise shared by intellectuals and practitioners both at the center and at the margins of a global discursive field that sanctioned the universality of the novel-form.

It would of course be easy to dismiss the universalization of the novel as cultural form and modern institution simply as a function of colonialism, to see globalization *only* as a new name for the same old colonial relations. But I think this would be a mistake. Although both processes coincide to some extent, the global expansion of modern institutions presupposes the universal realization of the promise of a political and cultural modernity, and—whether in the nineteenth century or today—the peripheries of the world have an intense desire for socio-political and cultural modernization (a desire represented in and by novels). In other words, the globalization of bourgeois modernity and its institutions in the nineteenth century implied *both* the threat of (neo)colonial oppression and the promise of emancipation. Looking at this aporia through the glass of the deconstructive dictum that Derrida first formulated in "Plato's Pharmacy" about the double meaning of *pharmakon* as medicine and poison, one could say that globalization is both the condition of possibility and impossibility of modernity (and of novelistic difference) in the margins of the universal.

The novelization of the global

The model of *the globalization of the novel* serves the purpose of explaining the role the novel-form played in the global expansion of modern culture and its institutions during the nineteenth century. The crisscrossing trajectories of infinite exchanges, importations, translations, and adaptations of novels (what I term *the global novel as cultural form*) make visible the spatial extension and intensity of the process of globalization. However, this explicatory matrix does not provide any insights into the different textual devices, strategies, plots, or characters that can be found in the great variety of novels that gave specific content to *the global novel as cultural form*. It is necessary, then, to formulate a hypothesis capable of accounting not only for the historical spread of a global form but also for the narratives of globalization as a discursive figure produced by a subset of texts usually concerned with lands and peoples far removed from Europe. If *the globalization of the novel* looks at the world as a global totality of bourgeois culture and makes sense of it as a system and as a world-historical process, *the novelization of the global*—the second and complementary way in which I am trying to conceptualize the idea of the global novel—traces the specific imaginaries of universalism that these novelistic texts forge, putting into circulation effective accounts of the global reach of the bourgeoisie in terms of the production and reproduction of discourses of universal adventure, exploration, and colonial profit.

Jules Verne's novels in particular provide a productive case study of the novelization of the globe. If spatial meaning is discursively produced (an idea Edward W. Said worked through with the notion of "imaginative geography"), or, to put it bluntly, if fiction is the way we apprehend, categorize, and represent the world, then Verne's novels can be said to have provided some of the most radical imaginaries of the transformation of the planet into a totality of bourgeois culture and sociability, producing a textual surplus that exceeded what is usually read as a mere fiction of colonialism.[11] The bourgeois characters in his novels travel across the five continents, remapping the world in an epistemology of adventure and exoticism (see, for example, *Cinq semaines en ballon*, 1863; *Voyages et aventures du Capitaine Hatteras*, 1864–65; and *Le tour du monde en 80 jours*, 1873). Furthermore, Verne even dares to send his bourgeois men beyond the surface of the earth into the unknown: to the moon (*De la terre à la lune*, 1865; *Autour de la lune*, 1870), to the sun (*Hector Sevandac*, 1874–76), to the bottom of the sea (*Vingt mille lieues sous les mers*, 1869–70), to the center of the earth (*Voyage au centre de la terre*, 1864). In the closing paragraphs of *De la terre à la lune*, the omniscient narrator channels the pride and fear J.T. Maston felt for his three friends in space: "ils s'étaient mis en dehors de l'humanité en franchissant les limites imposées par Dieu aux créatures terrestres" (243; they had put themselves beyond humanity, surpassing the limits imposed by the Creator on his earthly creatures; my translation). In Verne's novels there are no limits for the realization of the bourgeois dream of universal freedom: the utmost recondite corners of the universe expect the arrival of Verne's *bourgeois conquérants* (see Morazé). Contemporary readers saw in these novels their own *local* experience transformed into global adventures that underscored the intensity and excitement available to those individuals willing to embrace their bourgeois subjectivity and explore its universalizing potential. As a result, these narratives have to be read not just as performances of the discourses of globalization but also as a recreation and reinforcement of the conditions of possibility for the universal adventure of the European bourgeoisie.

The construction of images and imaginaries of globality, of the transformation of the earth by bourgeois desire, is a symbolic challenge that could not be completed in one novel. Therefore, it has to be reconstructed as a panorama by putting together the pieces found in many (if not all) of Verne's novelistic archive. Here are some of the narrative strategies that opened up the possibility, for novels and their readers, to imagine the earth (in fact, the entire universe) as a bourgeois playing field, ready and available for science, profit, and amusement.

(1) All of Verne's novels involve travels of some sort; in these journeys there is always at least one instance when the novel takes a step back to capture an image of space as a meaningful cultural totality. Because the eye's perception of the real is always fragmented, articulating those fragments to create a larger mental image of something we cannot apprehend except in successive fragments is a complex psychological and intellectual operation that Kant theorizes conclusively in *The Critique of Judgment*. Only an imaginative discourse can produce an image of the earth as a round significant whole that is in fact inaccessible to empirical perception. In *Autour de la lune* (1870), for example, Michel Ardan, the French astronaut of a crew of three (the other two are American), looks at the small window of the rocket and exclaims: "Hein! Mes chers camarades, sera-ce assez curieux d'avoir la Terre pour

la Lune, de la voir se lever à l'horizon, d'y reconnaître la configuration de ses continents, de se dire: là est l'Amérique, là est l'Europe; puis de la suivre lorsqu'elle va se perdre dans les rayons du Soleil!" (94; "Ah! my dear comrades, it will be rather curious to have the earth for our moon, to see it rise on the horizon, to recognize the shape of its continents, and to say to oneself, 'There is America, there is Europe'; then to follow it when it is about to lose itself in the sun's rays!"). This is the same bird's-eye perspective that Dr. Fergusson has in *Cinq semaines en ballon* (1863): "Alors l'Afrique offrira aux races nouvelles les trésors accumulés depuis des siècles en son sein. Ces climats fatals aux étrangers s'épureront par les assolements et les drainages; ces eaux éparses se réuniront en un lit commun pour former une artère navigable. Et ce pays sur lequel nous planons, plus fertile, plus riche, plus vital que les autres, deviendra quelque grand royaume, où se produiront des découvertes plus étonnantes encore que la vapeur et l'électricité" (88; Africa will be there to offer to new races the treasures that for centuries have been accumulating in her breast. Those climates now so fatal to strangers will be purified by cultivation and by drainage of the soil, and those scattered water supplies will be gathered into one common bed to form an artery of navigation. Then this country over which we are now passing, more fertile, richer, and fuller of vitality than the rest, will become some grand realm where more astonishing discoveries than steam and electricity will be brought to light). In addition to the clearly colonialist idea that Africa "will offer" its treasures to the new race of explorers, scientists, and colonialists, the view from afar and from above produces a clear hierarchy between the subject and the spatial (humanized) object of observation, producing a symbolic relation in which the latter subordinates itself to the will of the former. In their mappings (of planet Earth in the first example, of a whole continent in the second) Verne's novels represent space as an opportunity available for bourgeois exploration, adventure, and profit.[12]

(2) Given the positivistic inclinations of the French bourgeoisie during the second half of the nineteenth century, the effectiveness of an image of the world or universe as a homogeneous space that can be crisscrossed back and forth depends on its measurability. For example, the eighty days that Phileas Fogg gives himself to circle the earth (*Le tour du monde en quatrevingt jours*, 1872) signals the philosophical and scientific certainty that the earth can be apprehended in a predetermined amount of time. All that is required is a willful individual. Analogously, *De la terre à la lune* (1865) is a journey that is expected to be completed in exactly ninety-seven hours and twenty minutes, as the subtitle of the book indicates (*Trajet direct en 97 heures 20 minutes*); in fact, the obsessive preparation for the journey and the study of all the variables, scientific and economic, occupies almost the entirety of the novel, which ends right after the rocket is launched. In both cases, the possibility of measuring with scientific precision the course of the adventure reinforces the initial intuition that seizing the earth or the entire galaxy is entirely feasible.

(3) After having produced the images that trigger an imaginary of global availability, these novels also represent the actual process of taking possession of these "vacant" spaces. Verne sometimes invents characters who are straightforward representatives of state colonialism—for example, the members of the Gun Club in *Autour de la lune*, who propose the exploration of outer space "Pour prendre possession de la Lune au nom des États-Unis pour ajouter un quarantième état à l'Union! Pour coloniser les règions lunaires, pour les cultiver, pour les peupler, pour y transporter toutes les prodiges de l'art, de la science et de l'industrie. Pour civiliser les Sélénites" (63; To take possession of the moon in the name of the United States of America! It is to add a fortieth state to the glorious Union! It is to colonize the lunar regions, to cultivate them, to people them, to transport to them some of our wonders of art, science, and industry! It is to civilize the Selenites). But that is not the only path available. A more interesting one is the one chosen by those characters who do not advance their colonial agenda in the name of the nation state but rather in the name of

modernity, the universal and universalizing goal of bourgeois culture. That is why Verne's novels are populated by bourgeois businessmen, politicians, professors, *pater familiae*, scientists, and *bonvivants*—not only from France, but from most of the other Western European nations, not to mention the U.S., Russia, and virtually any country that might have had at the time a growing middle class. The *bourgeoisiefication* of the world: that is the key to understanding the transnational dimension of the philosophical and literary conceptualization of the process of globalization, even in the nineteenth century—the desire to produce a homogeneous bourgeois totality that eventually would coincide with the surface of the earth (and, in Verne, with the entire universe). That is why *De la terre à la lune*, perhaps the most striking novel within this corpus, closes with a sentence (spoken by J.T. Maston, the secretary of the Gun Club) that pays homage to his astronaut friends, who are venturing into outer space in the name of bourgeois civilization: "A eux trois ils emportent dans l'espace toutes les ressources de l'art, de la science et de l'industrie. Avec cela on fait ce qu'on veut, et vous verrez qu'ils se tireront d'affaire!" (244; "Those three men have carried into space all the resources of art, science, and industry. With that, one can do anything; and you will see that, some day, they will come out all right").

Jules Verne's novels usually have been read as the intersection of science fiction and adventure. Without trying to dispute these generic inscriptions, I would like to propose that, in order to underscore the political relation his narratives establish with the global expansion of bourgeois-modern institutions and practices, one needs to question their relation to the realist novel's hegemonic protocols of representation. In other words, what happens if we think of Verne's novels as a form of *oblique realism:* the construction of bourgeois reality, not necessarily as it appears to be, but *as it could be* if it were to actualize its potential? Unlike the Verne scholars who have spent a great deal of energy discussing whether Verne prophesied technologies that were going to be invented in the next century or simply imagined uses for the technology already available at his time, I propose to read Verne's novels in the margins of the realist novel's representational protocols: that is, as narratives that give us an insight into the world historical, universalizing role of the modern bourgeois subject, an insight that the realist novel, with its frontal attack on the *real* of bourgeois social relations and its fiction of transparency, could not afford to produce as evocatively. Through a fantastic/scientific detour, Verne's *oblique realism* taps into the *real* of the global imaginaries of European modernity: as such, it is a representation of the discursive conditions of globalization.[13] What Verne's singular realism represents, then, is not (not only, not necessarily) the concrete social formation of the turn of the century's middle classes, but the latent power of the ideology that sustains it.[14] This is the radical and productive ideological potential that the *novelization of the global* opens up for the late nineteenth-century novel: to imagine the world as the global space, determined by bourgeois culture, in which the novel, or rather the global novel, will inscribe itself.

The Latin American novelization of the global

The globalization of the novel and the novelization of the global are not two parallel or alternative critical roads. It is the critic who makes them intersect when reading comparatively novels produced or consumed at different locations on an uneven global field of production, consumption, and translation, thus mapping the ubiquity of the novel-form. In other words, to understand the relations between different aesthetic articulations of the novelization of the global at distant points of a global novelistic field (in this case, the material conditions of production of Verne's novels, on the one band, and those of Eduardo Holmberg's *Viaje maravilloso del Señor Nic-Nac al planeta Marte*, on the other), one needs to read diachronically the displacements of "outer-space novels" (the globalization of the novel) together with the actual images of the universe produced in each of these cultural locations (the novelization of the global).

Holmberg began publishing *Viaje maravilloso del Señor Nic-Nac al planeta Marte* as a serial in the Buenos Aires newspaper *El Nacional* on November 29, 1875. It tells the story of Nic-Nac, an aficionado of all kinds of scientific and pseudo-scientific disciplines and gadgets, who makes an appointment with a doctor in spiritism who has just arrived from Europe: "Aquel espiritista se llama Friederich Seele, o si queréis su nombre en castellano, Federico Alma" (39; The spiritist's name was Friederich Seele, or if you want his name in Spanish, Frederick Soul).[15] Nic-Nac develops a "spiritual" crush on the doctor and convinces Seele to teach him the technique of transmigration or *transplanetation* ("transplanetación"), which consists of fasting for extensive periods of time until the soul leaves the body to travel across the universe: "¿y si ahora tuviera la idea de lanzar mi espíritu a visitar los planetas?" (43; how about launching my spirit and visit other planets now?). After eight days of fasting, Nic-Nac collapses and, as his soul leaves his body, he sees from above a doctor trying to reanimate him. Soon after beginning his spiritual journey, Nic-Nac encounters Dr. Seele, who will be his guide in the voyage to Mars, a planet whose natural, socio-political, and cultural features turn out to resemble those of Argentina.[16] After his spiritual adventure, Nic-Nac (or, rather, his soul) returns to his body in Buenos Aires.

The most interesting trait of Holmberg's book is its structure. The narrative Nic-Nac writes to tell his story and authorize his spiritual space travels is framed by two paratexts by the apocryphal editor of Nic-Nac's manuscript. In the "Introduction," his editor refers ironically to the general reading public's relationship with paranormal phenomena and narrates an encounter with two young men who read out loud newspaper headlines stating that Nic-Nac has been admitted to a hospital for mental patients. Moreover, people in the street don't seem to agree on whether Nic-Nac's journey is real or imaginary, "unos negando el hecho, otros compadeciendo a su autor, algunos aceptando todas y cada una de las circunstancias del viaje" (30; some denying the truth of the event, others feeling sorry for the author, and some accepting every single detail of the circumstances of the trip). Similarly, in the apocryphal "Note of the editor"—"El editor toma un momento la palabra" (The editor briefly takes the floor)—that closes the novel, the fictionalized publisher of the book blames the deficiencies of the text on the fact that the author is insane—"¿Pero quién es Nic-Nac? ¿Dónde está? ¡Ah! ¡En una casa de locos!" (179; But who is Nic-Nac? Where is he? Oh! In a loony bin!)—and informs the reader of the psychiatric diagnosis: "manía planetaria" (180; planetary mania).

There are many things to compare in Verne's and Holmberg's novelization of the global (or, perhaps more accurately, of the universal or the *cosmic*)—among them, the huge disparity in the aesthetic quality of the novels (*Nic-Nac* is a poorly written narrative in terms of its style and plot).[17] Rather than focus on the uneven worth of the novels—which could be explained in terms of the individual talent of the novelists or the varying degrees of autonomy within the French and Argentine literary fields—I wish to concentrate on critical questions raised both by the immaterial nature of Nic-Nac's universal spiritual/imaginary journey and by the ambiguity and shadow of doubt that the text itself casts over Nic-Nac's first-person narrative. If in Verne's novels the universality of the traveling characters is determined by the fact that they take real trips with real consequences (within the plot), that is, that they transcend their respective localities (France, the U.S., or the Earth at large) in order to materialize their universal aspirations by making the universe *theirs*, how should one read the imaginary or spiritual nature of Nic-Nac's journey to Mars in Holmberg's novel? Or, to say it differently, how should one understand Nic-Nac's adventure to Mars when the universal predicate of his trip depends, not on leaving his country, but on leaving his own body?

Perhaps the most obvious possibility would be to interpret it in relation to Holmberg's marked interest in spiritism and paranormal phenomena, and his attempt to reconcile these practices with the hegemonic positivist creed—an attempt that was widespread in both Latin America and in Europe at the end of the nineteenth century.[18] However, Holmberg's intellectual curiosity about spiritism does not exhaust the differences between his novels and Verne's, nor does it explain his decision to narrate an imaginary/spiritual trip instead of a real one, as in Verne's case. The imaginary nature of Nic-Nac's travel might also be characterized as a novelistic option determined by the conditions of enunciation at the periphery—conditions that did not provide the symbolic and material resources available to Verne. Holmberg's choice would then be attributed to the marginality of a culture defined by the lack of a first-hand experience of the universalizing/globalizing potential of the bourgeoisie. According to this line of thought, Holmberg represented a spiritual voyage because it was all his marginal conditions of enunciation could afford. Nic-Nac's journey would thus have been triggered by a cosmopolitan desire to explore what lies beyond one's own location, but it would have to be considered a less consequential kind of cosmopolitan drive: a spiritual, immaterial cosmopolitanism, aware of its limitations and impossibilities.

But the assumptions behind these interpretations are not historically accurate. Towards the end of the nineteenth century, Latin American elites were in fact engaged in worldwide travels and explorations. And even if they were not inscribed in a world historical transcultural imperialistic process, they did not lack the experience of hegemony, since they were engaged in an internal colonization that would soon lead to the reaffirmation of liberal nation states. Holmberg, moreover, could easily have written an account of an actual trip to Mars by an Argentine astronaut in the same way Verne sent to the moon two Americans and a Frenchman. Why not? Verne's *De la terre à la lune* was published ten years before *Viaje maravilloso del Señor Nic-Nac al planeta Marte*, and it seems highly likely that Holmberg, who is usually identified as the first Latin American to write science fiction (see Prieto), would have read Verne's novel before writing *Nic-Nac*.[19]

Why, then, did Holmberg write a novel about a galactic voyage made possible by transmigration and *transplanetation* instead of modern technology and science? Was his decision structurally determined by the material conditions of Latin America in the context of worldwide processes of globalization? Or was it the result of his interest and belief in paranormal phenomena? Structural determinations (such as lacking a direct experience of technological modernity, or the cultural authorization of paranormal explanations) play only a limited role in a writer's creative decisions inscribed within the relative autonomy of the literary imagination. I want to suggest that there is no need to explain the nature of Nic-Nac's spiritual voyage by resorting to either subjective or objective explanations, because the novel itself, in its paratexts, defines the main character's travel as a pathological adventure:

> No, Nic-Nac no es un loco furioso, es un loco tranquilo. Y es tan cierto lo que afirmamos, que basta abrir el libro de entradas de aquel establecimiento para leer una partida en la que consta que el señor Nic-Nac padece de una "*manía planetaria*". El director del establecimiento, hombre instruido y observador incansable, ha manifestado que Nic-Nac es un ente original, afable, un tanto instruido, al que se le pueden creer muchas de las cosas que dice, exceptuando, empero, los medios de los que se ha valido para transmigrar de la Tierra a Marte y de éste a aquélla.
>
> (179–80)

> No, Nic-Nac is not a raving lunatic, he is crazy but calm. We are certain about this, and the records of the establishment confirm it in an entry stating that Mr. Nic-Nac suffers from "*planetary mania*." The director of the establishment, a learned man and indefatigable observer, has declared that Nic-Nac is an original,

affable, slightly educated being; one can believe almost anything he says except his references to the means he may have used to transmigrate from the Earth to Mars and back.

By stating that the main character suffers from "planetary mania," the *editor* returns Nic-Nac's experience to the scientific realm of psychiatric taxonomies, within the limits of which *trans-planetation* is a mental illness and not the possibility of a journey through the universe. The *editor* sets the record straight: anyone aspiring to reach the stars should develop the necessary technology, just as the members of the Gun Club did in Verne's *From the Earth to the Moon*; paranormal sciences do not lead to the realization of universality but to psychiatric confinement. At the end of the editor's note, the rational and instrumental relation with the world that had been broken by Nic-Nac's first person (delusional) narrative has been restored, and literary renderings of the universe as a totality of meaning are again mediated by realist representations à la Verne.

If Verne's novels are capable of producing effective images of the world as a totality of freedom mediated by modern social relations, it is precisely because they are confident about the place they have as novels (indeed as French novels) in the historical process of the global expansion of bourgeois institutions, values, and practices. What determines, in turn, *Nic-Nac's* "radical situational difference in the cultural production of meaning" (Jameson, "A Brief Response" 26)? *Viaje maravilloso del Señor Nic-Nac al pianeta Marte* does not even attempt to imagine a world unified under the hegemony of modern social relations. Instead, it puts forth an alternative universalist imaginary, only to negate it later, as if the marginal conditions of production of universality allow only for the demarcation of the limits of its impossibility.

At a historical juncture immediately prior to the inauguration of a new universalist horizon for Latin American culture marked by the discourse of *modernismo*, at a time when Latin American writers were primarily concerned with the exploration of the frontiers of their national or regional particularities (think of Ignacio Manuel Altamirano's *El Zarco*, Lucio V. Mansilla's *Una excursión a los indios ranqueles*, José Hernández's *Martín Fierro*, Francisco Moreno's *Viaje a la Patagonia Austral*, most of Ricardo Palma's *Tradiciones peruanas*, González Prada's first essays, and Machado de Assis's *Memórias póstumas de Brás Cubas*), Holmberg's *Nic-Nac* posed questions about the novelization of the global and the universal that few others in the peripheries of the world seemed to be considering: Can my characters travel the way Verne's characters travel? Can they produce with and through their displacements images of a reconciled and available modern world? Can they be identified as cosmopolitan, metropolitan, or colonial subjects, striving to inscribe themselves in the universal order of modernity? Verne's novels do not need to give affirmative answers to these questions because the answers are presupposed in the texts' confident belief in their universal discursive nature. The "radical situational difference" (Jameson, "A Brief Response" 26) of Holmberg's *Nic-Nac*—and, in fact, of any Latin American narrative being interrogated by questions better suited for a Dr. Fergusson, a Phileas Fogg, or a Michel Ardan—lies not in a hopeful affirmation of those questions, but in the recognition of a limit. It is this epistemological obstacle that might be taken to inform the conditions of enunciation of a marginal space, where the world historical affirmation of a teleological discourse of globalization is decoded as the "planetary mania" of a schizophrenic and the "spiritist fantasy" of a boorish and precarious proto-novel that nevertheless anticipates the cosmopolitan aspirations of the discourse of *modernismo*.

Coda: a critique of world literature

The twofold argument of this paper stems from a double anxiety: on the one hand, a question about how to conceptualize the role of literature—and of the novel in particular—in the production and reproduction of the discourses of globalization and, at the same time, the ways in which those discourses determine the imagination and its forms in the novel; on the other, uneasiness about the re-emergence in U.S. academic discourse of the concept of world literature as an attempt to address what I have chosen to call in this essay the global ubiquity of literary texts, the universality of the novel as a modern institution, and, thus, the formation of a global field of production, consumption, translation, and displacements of novels.[20] In this final part of the essay, I would like to interrogate, not the notion of world literature itself, but rather the critical practices, political implications, and picture of the global literary field presupposed by this concept.[21] I am not particularly interested in defining whether world literature is a tool meant to classify *world literary texts* and exclude others, whether it is a discipline and a way of reading (and thus the new paradigm for comparative literature), or whether it is the name of the historical formation of a space of symbolic exchange and circulation that exceeds particular national cultures; world literature entails, to a certain extent, all of these critical and pedagogical operations. Rather, I am trying to focus on the cultural and theoretical effects that the revival of the concept of world literature may have on the ways we conceptualize, imagine, and teach the global dimensions at stake in the novel. My concern has to do with the potential of world literature (world literature as the specific name of a field of study, a discipline, a pedagogical practice, and a canon) to illuminate or obscure the global layout of the hegemonic formation of the literary institution—an uneven process that determines both the world literary status of certain texts as well as the discourse of world literature itself. In short, the question I would like to examine in this last part of the essay is whether world literature serves the cosmopolitan purpose that is supposed to be constitutive of its critical and pedagogical horizon.

Behind the *rentrée* of the concept of world literature lies a commendable political goal: to imprint a universalist inclination on a U.S. educational system and cultural ambience that has become increasingly chauvinistic and that is seen (appropriately so) as a symbolic battlefield for the future of global citizenship. This aim of the new world literature, an aim with which it is difficult to disagree, is very much in line with the radical and controversial proposal of a cosmopolitan education for American students that Martha Nussbaum put forth over a decade ago in "Patriotism and Cosmopolitanism":

> As students here grow up, is it sufficient for them to learn that they are above all citizens of the United States, but that they ought to respect the basic human rights of citizens of India, Bolivia, Nigeria, and Norway? Or should they, as I think—in addition to giving special attention to the history and current situation of their own nation—learn a good deal more than is frequently the case about the rest of the world in which they live, about India and Bolivia and Nigeria and Norway and their histories, problems, and comparative successes? Should they learn only that citizens of India have equal basic human rights, or should they also learn about the problems of hunger and pollution in India, and the implications of these problems for larger problems of global hunger and global ecology? Most important, should they be taught that they are above all citizens of the United States, or should they instead be taught that they are above all citizens of a world of human beings, and that, while they themselves happen to be situated in the United States, they have to share this world of human beings with the citizens of other countries? I shall shortly suggest four arguments for the second conception of education, which I shall call cosmopolitan education.
>
> (6)

When understood as part of the larger project of a cosmopolitan education, the political worth of the concept of world literature becomes undeniable, especially when, as in the case of Nussbaum's proposal, the notion of cosmopolitanism is articulated as a desire for universal justice.[22] But is world literature capable of accomplishing this cosmopolitan goal, or, better yet, which conception of world literature, if any, could produce critical and pedagogical practices capable of accomplishing what Nussbaum proposes? Indeed, at least some discourses of world literature produce a canon *of global great books* that tends to repeat itself in anthologies or in syllabi that, even when paying lip-service to *combined and uneven development* and to the asymmetry of global power relations, too often reinforce romantic essentialisms (a remnant of Goethe's coinage of the concept of *Weltliteratur*) according to which the third world would specialize in the production of hyper-aestheticized national allegories that express their cultural particularities—for example, their frustrated dreams of modernity— while the metropolitan centers contribute truly aesthetic innovations.[23]

Some of the field's most prominent comparatists have been working for a decade now on re-defining world literature in relation to the heritage of postcolonial studies—a discursive articulation that has to some extent moved the theory of world literature away from the two major threats that still loom over the discipline: on the one hand, the postulation of world literature as an even playing field in which an idealistic sense of parity among the literatures of the world becomes possible—in other words, world literature as an equalizing discourse that rights the wrongs of cultural imperialism and/or economic globalization; on the other, the *expressive* logic according to which some works convey the historical or aesthetic experience of their cultures of origin and, therefore, become part of the corpus of a world literature comprised of a plurality of global particularities.

In the critical discourses of Franco Moretti, Pascale Casanova, David Damrosch, Haun Saussy, Emily Apter, Shu-mei Shih, and Wai Chee Dimock, among others, world literature has already overcome the menaces of expressiveness and ideological blindness to the political determinations that shape the discipline, thus earning the *post-* prefix that indicates its inscription in a *post-identity politics* discursive field. Their *world literatures* are, indeed, *post-world literary* reshapings of the concept and have, for the most part, begun to take care of the first of the two dangers I have just mentioned.[24] In all of these authors, the articulation of world literature with postcolonial concerns, poststructuralist discourses on identity (national or otherwise), and world-system theory results in an account of the global based on the consideration of the constitutive unevenness of social relations across the world or within a given cultural configuration (see, also, Bhabha, *Location* 12).[25] But this refashioning of the concept of world literature at the theoretical level cannot modify (at least not soon enough) pedagogical practices that, as all of these theorists acknowledge, seem to be lagging behind in a romantic mood. A quick review of world literature syllabi and most anthologies shows that the logic of representation and expressiveness is still at work, especially when one looks at the aesthetic features of the texts that have made it into the classroom and the canon and the relation that these traits establish with the imagined characteristics of the country or region for which these works are supposed to stand. As David Damrosch puts it, "In world literature, as if in some literary Miss Universe competition, an entire nation may be represented by a single author: Indonesia, the world's fifth-largest country and home of ancient and ongoing cultural traditions, is usually seen, if at all, in the person of Pramoedya Ananta Toer. Jorge Luis Borges and Julio Cortázar divide the honors for Mr. Argentina" ("World Literature" 44).[26] Thus, even though anthologies of world literature have expanded their coverage enormously, a great majority of the texts (especially when they come from peripheries of the Euro-American world) are included because the anthology presupposes an expressive relation between the text and the cultural particularity of its assumed origin.

A fitting example of these facts is the MLA series "Teaching World Literature." When I received the 2007 catalog of this collection in the mail—the series had at the time 95 titles and was planning to reach one hundred volumes during the following year—I read the brochure from cover to cover and found (not surprisingly) that in terms of its discursive heterogeneity the list did not quite follow the patterns of the post-multicultural global canon that is familiar in university classrooms across the United States (at least in comp lit classrooms). There were an overwhelming majority of nineteenth- and twentieth-century modernist works in English, a handful of the eighteenth-century British novels that mark (according to Anglo-critics) the rise of the genre, a few classics (the Bible, Homer, Euripides, Virgil), and several medieval and early modern canonical texts (Chaucer, Dante, Elizabethan theater and poetry, Molière). Frederick Douglass's slave narrative was the only inclusion that once might have been thought to stretch the limits of the literary institution. Moreover, although the series bears the name "Approaches to Teaching World Literature," there is only one text in a non-Western language (Japanese). Out of 95 titles, 65 are in different intonations of English, fourteen are in French, three in Italian (Bocaccio, Dante and—surprisingly—Collodi's *Pinocchio*), three in German (Goethe, Kafka, and Mann), three in Spanish (Early Modern Spanish drama, Cervantes, and García Márquez), three in classical Greek and Latin (Homer, Euripides, and Virgil), and one each in Russian (Tolstoy), Norwegian (Ibsen), Japanese (Murasaki Shikibu), and classical Hebrew (the Bible).

In his book *What Is World Literature?* David Damrosch puts forth a convincing argument about how much things have changed in terms of the scope of world literature in the U.S. during the last hundred years. If at the beginning of the twentieth century world literature anthologies and course syllabi "defined 'the world' unhesitatingly as the Western World" (124), Damrosch points out that during the 1990s several anthologies (among them, *The Harper Collins World Reader* and *The Norton Anthology of World Literature*) radically changed their approach to world literature, turning it into a truly global field that encompasses the whole world and all historical stages, from pre-1492 indigenous narratives from the Americas to postcolonial and postmodern literatures from every periphery of the Western world. (One should of course also include Damrosch's own *Longman Anthology of World Literature* among the publications that fulfill the postcolonial premise of a newly conceptualized world literature.) I shared Damrosch's optimistic outlook about a world literature that seemed to have overcome its previous conservative and narrow conception of what the *world* was until I encountered the "Approaches to Teaching World Literature" series, which, given the institutional weight of the MLA, cannot be taken merely as the residual presence of an archaic conception of the field but on the contrary appears to make visible the pedagogical practice of world literature in most U.S. universities, in striking contradiction with the way in which most progressive intellectuals theorize it.

Apart from the production and reproduction of the global hegemony of English, in the MLA's list the rationale for the inclusion of the English and French works responds quite straightforwardly to a dynamics of canon reproduction, the constitutive grounds for institutionalization. The same logic seems to apply to the Bible, the Greco-Roman classics, Cervantes, Lope de Vega, Goethe, Tolstoy, Ibsen, Kafka, and Thomas Mann. The three remaining texts included in the list—the medieval *The Tale of Genji*, supposedly authored by Shikibu, García Márquez's *Cien años de soledad*, and Achebe's *Things Fall Apart*—speak to underlying assumptions about what the margins of the West can contribute to the discursive field of world literature. What lies behind the choice of *The Tale of Genji*'s eleventh-century account of the misadventures of Japanese courtesans, *Things Fall Apart*'s 1958 history of colonial unrest in Africa, and *Cien años de soledad*'s 1967 magical realist genealogical allegory is the belief that these texts can be taken to express the Japanese, African, and Latin American historical experiences. Each of these cultures is thus reduced to a singular essentialized meaning: a traditional Japan that lives on in the West's imaginary, a tribal Africa that falls victim to the violent social restructuring of colonialism, a Latin America forever doomed to political unrest and the pre-modern identity of private and public domains. In the case of *Cien años de soledad*, the global best-seller came to represent and express what a large portion of the world's literary public assumed was the essence of Latin American culture and social history—a narrative metaphor for Latin America, and not necessarily Colombia, or tropical South America, or Santa Marta. Thus, the essentialist logic of expression can be read (a) as a romantic ideology that assumes that cultural particularity is contained most perfectly in the indivisible unity of the nation; and (b) as a discourse of globalization based on the coexistence of fixed regional identities and national institutions.

It goes without saying that none of the proponents of a *post-world literary* world literature would subscribe in their theoretical construction of the field to such a logic for the construction of syllabi, anthologies, and research agendas. But what might be an alternative—and presumably more adequate—method of determining the specific textual content for a critical and pedagogical *world literary* practice? In his "Conjectures on World Literature" Franco Moretti provides what I find to be the most convincing, if impractical, answer to this question. For him, world literature must live up to the universal promise implied in its name, and thus he proposes a passage from world literature to the literatures of the world—all of the literatures ever written anywhere in the world.[27] This new universal field would transform world literature into a necessarily collective enterprise with a very clear division of labor: on the ground floor, the specialists producing knowledge on particular literatures through close readings of texts and cultural contexts; on the upper level, the meta-discursive realm of *über*-comparatists such as Moretti, tracing, through what he calls "distant reading," universal trends and patterns that make visible the world system of literature as a global cultural totality. By proposing to read *everything*, Moretti avoids the danger of a world literature comprised of texts that are chosen and isolated because of their supposed capacity to express and represent their respective national or regional cultures of origin. Standing for Latin America, we would no longer have magical realism and *testimonio* only, but the entirety of the immensely heterogeneous aesthetic universe of the region.[28]

Nevertheless, even if the constitutive threats of the world literary practices were actually taken care of, what I consider to be the most important question at the center of these world literary anxieties remains unanswered: is world literature as a cosmopolitan project that aims at articulating cultural difference in order to foster emancipatory goals even possible? Can a discourse about, and a pedagogy of, world literature produce *the planet* that Gayatri Spivak has proposed, a figure that "overwrites the globe," a concept characterized by "the imposition of the same system of exchange everywhere . . . In the gridwork of electronic capital . . . drawn by the requirements of Geographical Information Systems" (72)?[29] This ethically normative dimension has marked the cultural and political urgency of world literature's historical task since Goethe: an aesthetic formation underscored by the cosmopolitan demand to overwrite unjust social relations on a global scale—be they colonial, warmongering, or generally oppressive—the cosmopolitan desire to overcome the restrictions and limitations of our own particular culture and our claustrophobic experience of it, and to affirm the necessarily universal nature of the promise of the cultural emancipation of the planet. World literature becomes, in short, a discourse capable of leading the way towards global peace, the project of a global culture (as the dialectical negation of the one-sidedness of local particular cultures) in which all the emancipatory potential of "culture" can finally be released. David Damrosch notes that nowhere have these grand expectations been more eloquently stated than by René Wellek, who proposed in "The Crisis of Comparative Literature" (1963) a discipline structured around *world literary* goals: "Comparative literature has the immense merit of combating the false isolation of national literary histories" (282–83). In the last paragraph of the article, Wellek expands this idea and goes on to establish the crucial role played by such a critical discourse in the production of cosmopolitan values and, thus, in the actualization of the abstract construction of the universal subject imagined by the Enlightenment:

Once we grasp the nature of art and poetry, its victory over human mortality and destiny, its creation of a new world order of the imagination, national vanities will disappear. Man, universal man, man everywhere and at all time, in all his variety, emerges and literary scholarship ceases to be an antiquarian pastime, a calculus of national credits and debts and even a mapping of networks of relationships. Literary scholarship becomes an act of the imagination, like art itself, and thus a preserver and creator of the highest values of mankind.

(295)

If the cosmopolitan echoes of Wellek's discourse still seem relevant and even urgent in the context of raging inequalities fueled in part by a process of economic globalization, it is, however, difficult to sustain his optimism about the humanistic potential of world literature. The problem I find with this genealogy of world literature (again: from Goethe to Wellek to many of the proponents of a renewed world literature today) is that it tends to see the literary world—*the world of* world literature—as a field where the different cultural singularities that otherwise define each other through violent ethical and economic antagonisms find a common discourse and enter into a dialogue that, supposedly, serves as a model for a global political agency. A humanistic world literature, in short, is capable of producing a reconciled world that is unthinkable outside of its confidence in the redeeming power of Culture.[30]

But in this world literature, "informed by a sense of the implicit parity between literatures" (Trumpener 198) and represented as a Habermasian public sphere for global dialogue, what seems to be lost is the opaqueness of cultural otherness and the intermittent failures of communication and global translation at stake in the hegemonic social relations that make up the aesthetic and cultural exchanges of world literature—that is, the hegemonic formation of world literature's disciplinary discourse and object, and the necessary delimitation of what falls in and out of world literature: what gets to be translated (and why, and through what specific institutional articulations), and what, therefore, reaches audiences (particularly in metropolitan academic centers) beyond the culture of origin of a given text.[31] Thus, a critical reading of García Márquez's *One Hundred Years of Solitude* with *a cosmopolitan purpose* should not transform the novel into an allegorical sign of Latin America's cultural particularity and so determine its world literary worth precisely in terms of its ability to represent the region, or, even worse, because of the exotic flavor it would provide—with its characters ascending to heaven amidst bed sheets—to the world literary canon. These usually complementary ways of arguing the paradoxical universality of *One Hundred Years of Solitude* depend on the (usually metropolitan) assumption that magical realism expresses something about the pre-rational constitution of Latin American societies that escapes the protocols of modern realist representation and, as such, reify a reductive and condescending perception of the complex aesthetic and political relations between Latin American aesthetics and the region's social structure. Sylvia Molloy lucidly explains this metropolitan fascination: "Magic realism is refulgent, amusing, and kitschy (Carmen Miranda's headdress; José Arcadio Buendía's tattooed penis)—but it doesn't happen, couldn't happen, here" (129).

A cosmopolitan approach attentive to the hegemonic forces at stake in cultural formations would insist that the global status of García Márquez's novel has nothing to do with a supposedly privileged relation to its culture of origin and instead investigate the material production of its globality. For example, it would ask questions about the globalization of magical realism through Africa, South East Asia, Eastern Europe, and the Chicano Southwest of the U.S.: When was García Márquez (and perhaps, also, Alejo Carpentier) translated in each of these locations? And how were his novels and short stories received? What were the existing local aesthetic traditions—as well as socio-cultural relations—that may have contributed to transforming magical realist narratives into a form of postcolonial interpellation (cf. Bhabha, "Introduction" 7)? How, and in what specific forms and instances, was magical realism appropriated and re-written? Were the traces of these global appropriations of magical realism obscured, or were they acknowledged in order to produce cosmopolitan forms of affiliation? And, in turn, how did García Márquez and other Latin American proponents and practitioners of a magical realist aesthetic respond to the global echoes (cosmopolitan and postcolonial, but also metropolitan) of their discourse?[32]

The twofold idea of the globalization of the novel and the novelization of the global that I am putting forth is an attempt to re-inscribe the debate on world literature in relation to these cosmopolitan goals, while also accounting for the historical universalization of novelistic writing, reading, and translation, and for the production of singular images and imaginaries of universality that reduplicate in specific texts the global discursive horizon of modern literary practices. Or to put it in slightly different terms: it is an attempt to apprehend the hegemonic making of the universality of world literature, while resisting the temptation to fall back on particularistic reaffirmations of national or regional cultural identities, and in fact preserving universality as the necessary horizon of cosmopolitan practices with an emancipatory purpose.[33]

In spite of their methodological differences, the most intelligent interventions in the debate coincide in thinking of world literature, not as a defined corpus, but as a way of reading, of making relations and imagining unexpected and non-national contexts that may illuminate new meanings in certain literary works. While writing this article and thinking about cosmopolitan discourses, I came to understand the task of the world literature to come in terms of the classical Marxist characterization of class as a social relation, that is, to see world literature precisely as a social relation, a cosmopolitan relation. The model of the globalization of the novel and the novelization of the global, with its emphasis on historical processes at a global scale and the production of global imaginaries, allows us to see world literature as a cosmopolitan social relation, as both a critical discourse and a concrete universal field of cultural exchanges constituted by structural, asymmetrical forces disputing the meaning of the global. In other words, the globalization of the novel and the novelization of the global foregrounds the constitutive tension at the center of the discourse of world literature: on the one hand, the cosmopolitan drive to represent a diverse globe as a reconciled multicultural totality; and, on the other, the equally cosmopolitan mandate to map the asymmetric interaction of hegemonic and subaltern cultural and economic forces that determine the unequal making of the globe, as well as the account of its historical formation. Our challenge is to acknowledge and re-articulate in our pedagogical practices and in the design of our research projects these complex cosmopolitan interpellations that point to opposing ways of symbolizing global differences, assuming that it is impossible to embrace the normative side of cosmopolitan discourses such as world literature before accounting for the global hegemonic relations that shape them. The desires for commodities and discourses "of distant lands and climes" (Marx and Engels 477) that constitute to this day our cosmopolitan subjectivities are at once the symbolic ground on which we hope to inscribe an intellectual emancipatory practice and a domestication of the world that reproduces the hegemonic relations that world literature may or may not address.

Notes

1   Eleven years after Kant prescribed the notion of a world-republic in "Idea for a Universal History," he opts in "Perpetual Peace. A Philosophical Sketch" (1795) for a federation of nations (Völkerbund) so as to balance the sovereignty of each singular nation with the ultimate and transcendental location

of power in the federation as universal and cosmopolitan determination of the global system of international treaties and agreements.

2   It has been pointed out to me that I am reading Kant literally here, that Kant was not referring to the novel as a genre, but to the imaginative constructedness of a discourse clearly opposed to philosophy conceived as a scientific disciplinary discourse. However, Kant did choose to refer to "the novel" as that which lies on the other end of philosophy and, in any case, invokes the workings of imagination embodied in the novelistic form as the space where the type of universal history he imagines might take place.

3   This is a dimension of the novel mostly overlooked in classical materialist genre theories, which have studied the novel as the aesthetic product of the rise of the bourgeoisie and the consolidation of the national state. This critical perspective is historically determined by a concern about the specificity of national cultures and hegemonic struggles within the context of the nation state (see, for example, Ian Watt or Raymond Williams). Unfortunately, the explanatory power of these theories has blurred the global dimension of the novel, as well as the possibility of thinking a history of the novel that could account for the ways in which the process of globalization has been reshaping the world for the past 200 years.

4   See Lucio Vicente López's *La gran aldea* (1884), a *costumbrista* novel about Buenos Aires in the 1860s and 1870s, the period immediately after the civil war and before the modernizing explosion of the mid-1880s and 1890s. That is the Buenos Aires in which Holmberg's novels are set.

5   I am referring here to the novel as the aesthetic form historically determined by the rise of the bourgeoisie and its need to represent its own world view and its place in modern societies. Recently, this concept of "the rise of the novel" has been criticized in order to point to a longer history of the novel that extends back to medieval chivalric and courtly narratives. Nevertheless, I still believe that the hypothesis of the novel as cultural artifact determined by bourgeois world views, put forth paradigmatically by Ian Watt in *The Rise of the Novel: Studies in Defoe, Richardson and Fielding* (1957), remains the most convincing description of the historical genesis of the novel form (*stricto sensu*) in Europe and in its peripheries. Watt's arguments, however, consider the novel as an institution at work only on a national stage. The point of this essay is to think about the role the novel plays on a larger, indeed global, scale.

6   There are many instances in Sarmiento's narrative of his stay in Paris in which he destabilizes the notion of France as the privileged location of the universal. He even depicts most of France's political leaders as excessively provincial. However, Sarmiento always restores France's place in the global order of modernity as the model to imitate. Thus, although Sarmiento arrogantly plays with the idea of his own superiority to one or another French intellectual or official, in the end France remains the center and origin of the modern world to which he aspires.

7   Although Sarmiento never wrote a novel himself, he used the compositional strategies of the novel to write *Facundo*: "We do not read Facundo as a novel (which it is not) but rather as a political use of the genre. (*Facundo* is a proto-novel, a novel machine, a museum of the future of the novel)" (Piglia 135). See, also, Sorensen, *Facundo and the Construction of Argentine Culture*, especially chapter 2, "The Risks of Fiction. *Facundo* and the Parameters of Historical Writing" (41–66).

8   Laera notes that in the decade from 1880 to 1890 one hundred novels were published in Buenos Aires alone, whereas in the previous decade the number of novels issued did not exceed two dozen (19).

9   Franco Moretti even goes as far as deducing "*a law of literary evolution*" (58) out of this process of global expansion of the novel form. Such a law would state that "in cultures that belong to the periphery of the literary system (which means: almost all cultures, inside and outside Europe), the modern novel first arises not as an autonomous development but as a compromise between a Western formal influence (usually French or English) and local materials" (58).

10 This cultural mediation complements Franco Moretti's "law of literary evolution" (see note 9) by contextualizing within a cultural-political (rather than aesthetic) discursive frame his idea that the novel of the periphery results from a compromise between Western form and local materials.

11 Given the symbolic power that literary discourse held in Western Europe during the nineteenth century, the power of Verne's narratives to promote and reinforce the discourse of globalization must have been huge. Indeed, the importance of the role of literature and, more generally, the world of the "arts and entertainment" of the Second Empire cannot be exaggerated: there was a very specific need in France to produce and consume images of a colonial world beyond the borders of the familiar, not only because of the expansive dynamics of bourgeois-modern society, but also—and most importantly—because of boredom with the economic stability and solidification of (recently instituted) traditions in the middle class (see Girardet, Blanchard and Lemaire, and Compère).

12   Another important strategy among the representational operations of appropriation is the *familiariza-tion* of the strange, uncanny, or sublime by means of analogy: the Orinocco is like the Loire (*Le superbe Orénoque*); the moon looks to Ardan, Barbicane, and Nicholl like the mountains of Greece, Switzerland, or Norway (*Autour de la lune*); on his way to the center of the earth, Lidenbrok discovers another "Mediterranean Sea" (*Voyage au centre de la terre*).

13   This is the point Roland Barthes makes in his reading of *Vingt milles lieues sous les mers* in *Mythologies*: "Verne appartient à la lignée progressiste de la bourgeoisie: son oeuvre affiche que rien ne peut échapper à l'homme, que le monde, même le plus lointain, est comme un objet dans sa main" (80; Verne belongs to the progressive line of the bourgeoisie; his work portrays the fact that nothing is strange to Man, that the world, even its most remote corners, is like an object in his hand).

14   Writing from his prison cell, Gramsci addresses the realist nature of Verne's narratives, explaining that their verisimilar construction of reality is assured by the hegemony of bourgeois ideology: "In Verne's books nothing is ever completely impossible. The 'possibilities' that Verne's heroes have are greater and above all not 'outside' the line of development of the scientific conquests already made. What is imagined is not entirely 'arbitrary' and is therefore able to excite the reader's fantasy, which has already been won over by the ideology of the inevitability of scientific progress in the domain of the control of natural forces" (367).

15   Holmberg was himself a physician but never practiced. In his vocation as a naturalist he wrote important works on flora, fauna, geography, and paleontology, in addition to his literary and travel writings.

16   Although the complete title with which the serialized novel was published at the end of 1875—*El viaje maravilloso del Señor Nic-Nac/En el que se refieren las prodigiosas/aventuras de este señor y se dan a conocer las instituciones,/costumbres/y preocupaciones de un mundo desconocido*—states that the nature of the planet Nic-Nac visits is unknown, he finds in Mars a mirror image of the changing face of Argen-tine society at the end of the nineteenth century. As Sandra Gasparini and Claudia Román explain in their edition of Holmberg's *El tipo más original y otras páginas*, "la década del 70 está atravesada, en la Argentina, por una gran cantidad de gestos fundacionales. Se crean academias, establecimientos educativos, museos, observatorios: se echan los cimientos de una modernidad, en cuyo marco se construirá la Nación" (191; the 1870s is a decade of foundational gestures in Argentina. Academies, educational establishments, museums, observatories are created: the grounds of a modernity out of which the nation will be built up).

17   Victor Vich has pointed out to me that a possible reason for the qualitative disparity between European and Latin American novels during the nineteenth century is that in Latin America the novel had a marginal place in the cultural and literary fields. Indeed, as Efraín Kristal explains, "In Spanish America poetry was the dominant literary genre, and the essay or sociological treatise was of far greater significance than the novel until at least the 1920s, if not later. . . . One would be hard-pressed to point to a single literary work, other than *María* (1867) by the Colombian Jorge Isaacs, as an example of a nineteenth-century Spanish American novel that was widely read within and beyond the national borders in which it was produced" (62–63).

18   Angela Dellepiane describes the circulation of discourses of spiritism in the 1870s and 1880s in Argentina. She documents the presence of books by Allan Kardec (pseudonym of Hyppolite Léon Denizard Rivail), a disciple of the German scientist and pedagogue Pestalozzi, who late in life devel-oped a technique to contact spirits and became famous as a medium; and Camille Flammarion, author of very popular works on spiritism and astronomy, as well as hack science fiction novels. See also, Antonio Pagés Larraya's 1957 edition of Holmberg's fantastic short stories. On the constitutive tension at the core of Holmberg's discourse, see Rodríguez Pérsico (esp. 383, 389), who argues that in Holmberg's novels the positivistic preeminence of scientific imaginaries in Latin America at the turn of the century is met with an ambivalent gaze.

19   Dellepiane (220) makes the connection by tracing the publication of Verne's novels in Buenos Aires between 1872 and 1875 in *El Nacional*, the same newspaper that published *Nic-Nac* in 1875.

20   For excellent accounts of the different implications of the concept of world literature in Goethe and beyond, see David Damrosch's *What Is World Literature?*, Cooppan's "Ghosts in the Disciplinary Machine," Prendergast's edited volume *Debating World Literature*, and, for a Latin American perspec-tive, Ignacio Sánchez Prado's *América Latina en la "Literatura Mundial."*

21   Even though the widespread polemic about the refashioning of world literature in the U.S. was re-ignited by the publication of Franco Moretti's "Conjectures on World Literature" in 2000, Fredric Jameson's "Third-World Literature in the Era of Multinational Capitalism" (1986) anticipated many of the lines along which the debate would be organized almost two decades later.

22 For a full account of the debate and different interventions that took place around Nussbaum's piece, especially in relation to her goals of cosmopolitanism and patriotism, see Nussbaum, *For Love of Country?*

23 There are exceptions, of course. For example, in two fairly recent and very interesting texts, Vilashini Cooppan and Katie Trumpener give detailed accounts of the creation of world literature and culture courses at Yale. However, I believe that the MLA series "Approaches to Teaching World Literature," which I analyze below, exceeds in its institutional weight any particular attempt at creating world literature syllabi that challenge reified notions of the world and the hegemonic forces that shape it.

24 In spite of her Franco-centrism (clearly an imperialist residue that tends to resurface when the French intellectual field thinks about the structural function of France in a network of global relations), Pascale Casanova's use of Bourdieu's theory of social spaces organized in (only) relatively autonomous fields structured by specific institutions and practices makes clear the uneven formation of a global literary and cultural field constituted by asymmetric symbolic power relations. At the same time, because her understanding of Bourdieu is overly rigid, her division of a world into a single core (Paris) and several peripheries, with the structural function of the periphery being the production of innovation and the role of the core the recognition and consecration of such innovation, is another way of essentializing the periphery. In fact, the idea that the third world produces aesthetic innovation and revolutionary ideas seems to be a common fantasy (in the Lacanian sense) of metropolitan cultures.

25 It is also important to note that the political economy of the transnational publishing world (what sells, what does not) determines in almost absolute terms what gets translated and so what is read in world literature courses. In other words, European and North American publishing presses translate, more often than not, works that tend to respond to the expectations of *northern* reading publics about what, for instance, Latin American or African literature is and should be. *Cien años de soledad*, as a global best-seller, has in particular come to represent what a large portion of the world literary public sphere assumes is the essence of Latin American culture and social history. See Denning.

26 For a commentary on world literature anthologies and the recent inclusion of García Márquez and Chinua Achebe in some of them as a result of the globalization of the canon of world literature, see James English (306–7).

27 I take the idea of a critical differentiation of *the literatures of the world* from *world literature* from Djelal Kadir's essay "Comparative Literature in the Age of Terrorism," although Kadir uses the concept to indict all proponents of world literature, Moretti included.

28 The two volumes of *The Novel*, Moretti's gigantically ambitious attempt to rethink the history of, and the theoretical perspectives on, the novel—a project he undertook after having proposed his "Conjectures on World Literature"—can be read as the practical application of Moretti's ideas in his famous article. Here, Moretti attempts to establish the novel as a site where a community of critics can produce a concrete and well-grounded discourse on world literature. Damrosch, on the other hand, sees in this infinite and absolute expansion of the horizons of world literature not the elimination of world literature's worst stigma, but the dissolution of the discipline's specificity and value: "If the scope of world literature now extends from Akkadian epics to Aztec incantations, the question of what is world literature could almost be put in opposite terms: What isn't world literature? A category from which nothing can be excluded is essentially useless" (*What Is World Literature?* 110).

29 *Planetarity*, as Spivak defines it, would be a possible specific content to the new comparative literature she envisions, a comparative literature based on a form of reading that recognizes in the opacity and the undecidability of the figure the contingency of each particular dis-figuration, never giving in to the hegemonic demand of transparency and full comprehensibility. Planetarity is the figure that needs to be dis-figured, that is ethically and politically deciphered. The planet, then, is the site where, perhaps, we will be able to inscribe a form of community ethically different from that figured by the globe of globalization. "When I invoke the planet I think of the effort required to figure the (im)possibility of this underived intuition" (72). This is the first challenge with which the category of planetarity presents us: that the planet does not yet exist in the hegemony of the discourses of globalization. World literature, then, could be thought of as the comparative critical study of the symbolic that would deliver *the planet* to us.

30 One of the most effective critiques of this totalizing paradigm is the idea of a globalization of difference put forth by Emily Apter in "Global *Translatio*: The 'Invention' of Comparative Literature, Istanbul, 1933," where she traces Leo Spitzer's construction of discourses of comparative and world literature based on "untranslatable affective gaps" (108) during his exile in Turkey: "Spitzer's explicit

desire to disturb monolingual complacency" (105) produces "a paradigm of *translatio* . . . that emphasizes the critical role of multilingualism within transnational humanism . . . a policy of *non-translation* adopted without apology" (104).

31   See in this regard Diana Sorensen's remarkable study of the institutions that made up the materiality of the 1960s *boom* of Latin American literature, a study that charts a possible future road for a world literature mindful of the importance of material exchanges and hegemonic relations.

32   Commenting on this proposal to read the universality of García Márquez's novel in cosmopolitan terms rather than in relation to its capacity to express Latin American culture in a global market of cultural commodified particularities, an anonymous reviewer of this essay noted that "*Cien años*, and magical realism more generally, can make us critical of such universalizing moves (the United Fruit Company is nothing if not cosmopolitan) but only if we read it figurally as a planetary novel." This approach to the novel at the level of its plot and rhetorical construction adds a dimension I had not included in my argument and, I believe, complements my attempt to reject a globality based on the politics of cultural expression.

33   Roberto Schwarz has written, along these same lines, that if the intention of unearthing the idea of world literature "is to question the universality of the universal and the localism of the local, then it could be a good starting point for further discussion" (98).

Works cited

Apter, Emily. "Global *Translatio*: The 'Invention' of Comparative Literature, Istanbul, 1933." *Debating World Literature*. Ed. Christopher Prendergast. London and New York: Verso, 2004. 76–109.

Barthes, Roland. *Mythologies*. Paris: Editions du Seuil, 1957.

Bhabha, Homi. "Introduction: Narrating the Nation." *Nation and Narration*. Ed. Homi Bhabha. London and New York: Routledge, 1990. 1–7.

—. *The Location of Culture*. London and New York: Routledge, 1994.

Blanchard, Pascal, and Sandrine Lemaire. "Exhibitions, Expositions, Médiatisation et Colonies." *Culture Coloniale. La France conquise par son empire*, 1871–1931. Ed. Pascal Blanchard and Sandrine Lemaire. Paris: Éditions Autrement, 2003.

Casanova, Pascale. *The World Republic of Letters*. Trans. M.B. DeBevoise. Cambridge and London: Harvard UP, 2004.

Chaperon, Danielle. *Camille Flammarion: entre astronomie et littérature*. Paris: Imago, 1998.

Compère, Daniel. *Jules Verne: écrivain*. Genève: Librairie Droz, 1991.

Cooppan, Vilashini. "Ghosts in the Disciplinary Machine: The Uncanny Life of World Literature." *Comparative Literature Studies* 41.1 (2004): 10–36.

Damrosch, David. *What Is World Literature?* Princeton: Princeton UP, 2003.

—. "World Literature in a Postcanonical, Hypercanonical Age." *Comparative Literature in an Age of Globalization*. Ed. Haun Saussy. Baltimore: Johns Hopkins UP, 2006. 43–53.

Dellepiane, Angela B. "Narrativa argentina de ciencia ficción: tentativas liminares y desarrollo posterior." *Actas del IX Congreso de la Asociación Internacional de Hispanistas*. Frankfurt am Main: Vervuert Verlag, 1989. 515–25.

Denning, Michael. "The Novelist's International." *The Novel*. Vol. 1. *History, Geography and Culture*. Ed. Franco Moretti. Princeton and Oxford: Princeton UP, 2006. 703–25.

Derrida, Jacques. "Plato's Pharmacy." *Dissemination*. Trans. Barbara Johnson. Chicago: U of Chicago P, 1981. 67–122.

English, James. "Prizes and the Politics of World Culture." *The Economy of Prestige. Prizes, Awards and the Circulation of Cultural Value*. Cambridge: Harvard UP, 2005. 297–322.

Girardet, Raoul. *L'idée coloniale en France de 1871 à 1962*. Paris: La Table Ronde, 1972.

Gramsci, Antonio. "Hegemony of Western Culture over the Whole World Culture." *Selections from the Prison Notebooks*. Ed. and trans. Quintín Hoare and Geoffrey Nowell-Smith. New York: International Publishers, 1971. 416–19.

—. *Selections from Cultural Writings.* Ed. David Forgacs and Geoffrey Nowell-Smith. Trans. William Boelhower. Cambridge: Harvard UP, 1985.

Hegel, G.W.F. *Elements of the Philosophy of Right.* Trans. H.B. Nisbet. Ed. Allen W. Wood. New York: Cambridge UP, 1991.

Holmberg, Eduardo L. "Carta de Eduardo L. Holmberg a G. Méndez." *El tipo más original y otras páginas.* Ed. Sandra Gasparini and Claudia Román. Buenos Aires: Ediciones Simurg, 2001. 9–13.

—. *Cuentos fantásticos.* Ed. Antonio Pagés Larraya. Buenos Aires: Hachette, 1957.

—. *Viaje maravilloso del señor Nic-Nac al planeta Marte,* Ed. Pablo Crash Solomonoff. Buenos Aires: Colihue, Biblioteca Nacional de la República Argentina, 2006.

Jameson, Fredric. *Archaeologies of the Future. The Desire Called Utopia and Other Science Fictions.* London and New York: Verso, 2005.

—. "A Brief Response" [to Aijaz Ahmad]. *Social Text* 17 (Autumn 1987): 26–27.

—. "Third-World Literature in the Era of Multinational Capitalism." *Social Text* 15 (Autumn 1986): 65–88.

Kadir, Djelal. "Comparative Literature in an Age of Terrorism." *Comparative Literature in an Age of Globalization.* Ed. Haun Saussy. Baltimore: Johns Hopkins UP, 2006. 68–77.

Kant, Immanuel. *Critique of Pure Reason.* Trans. Norman Kemp Smith. Houndmills, Basingstoke, New York: Palgrave Macmillan, 2003.

—. "Idea for a Universal History with a Cosmopolitan Purpose." "Perpetual Peace. A Philosophical." *Political Writings.* Trans. H.B. Nisbet. Ed. Hans Reiss. New York: Cambridge UP, 1991. 41–53.

Kristal, Efraín. "Considering Coldly . . ." *New Left Review* 15 (May–June 2002): 61–74.

Laera, Alejandra. *El tiempo vacío de la ficción. Las novelas argentinas de Eduardo Gutiérrez y Eugenio Cambaceres.* Buenos Aires: Fondo de Cultura Económica, 2004.

Marx, Karl, and Friedrich Engels. "The Manifesto of the Communist Party." *The Marx-Engels Reader.* Ed. Robert C. Tucker. 2nd ed. New York: W.W. Norton, 1979. 469–500.

Modern Language Association. MLA Approaches to Teaching World Literatures Catalog, 2007.

Molloy, Sylvia. "Latin America in the U.S. Imaginary: Postcolonialism, Translation, and the Magical Realist Imperative." *Ideologies of Hispanism.* Ed. Mabel Moraña. Nashville: Vanderbilt UP, 2005.189–200.

Morazé, Charles. *Les bourgeois conquérants.* Paris: Librairie Armand Colin, 1957.

Moretti, Franco. "Conjectures on World Literature." *New Left Review* 1 (2000): 54–68.

—. "On the Novel." *The Novel.* Vol. 1. *History, Geography and Culture.* Ed. Franco Moretti. Princeton and Oxford: Princeton UP, 2006. ix–x.

Nussbaum, Martha. "Patriotism and Cosmopolitanism." *For Love of Country?* Ed. Joshua Cohen. Boston: Beacon Press, 1996. 2–17.

Piglia, Ricardo. "Sarmiento the Writer." *Sarmiento. Author of a Nation.* Ed. Tulio Halperín Donghi, Iván Jaksic, Gwen Kirkpatrick, and Francine Masiello. Berkeley: U of California P, 1994. 127–44.

Prendergast, Christopher, ed. *Debating World Literature.* London and New York: Verso, 2004.

Prieto, Adolfo. "La generación del ochenta: la imaginación." *Capítulo: la historia de la literatura argentina.* Buenos Aires: CEAL, 1967. 457–80.

Rodríguez Pérsico, Adriana. " 'Las reliquias del banquete' darwinista: E. Holmberg, escritor y científico." *MLN* 116.2 (2001): 371–91.

Said, Edward W. *Orientalism.* New York: Vintage Books, 1994.

Sánchez Prado, Ignacio, ed. *América Latina en la "Literatura Mundial."* Pittsburgh: Instituto Internacional de Literatura Iberoamericana, 2006.

Sarmiento, Domingo F. *Viajes en Europa, Africa y América.* Buenos Aires: Editorial de Belgrano, 1981.

Schwarz, Roberto. "Competing Readings in World Literature." Trans. Nick Caistor. *New Left Review* 48 (Nov.–Dec. 2007): 83–107.

Sorensen, Diana. *Facundo and the Construction of Argentine Culture*. Austin: U of Texas P, 1996.

—. *A Turbulent Decade Remembered. Scenes from the Latin American Sixties*. Stanford: Stanford UP, 2007.

Spivak, Gayatri Chakraborty. *Death of a Discipline*. New York: Columbia UP, 2003.

Strich, Fritz. *Goethe and World Literature*. Trans. C.A.M. Sym. London: Routledge and Kegan Paul, 1949.

Trumpener, Katie. "World Music, World Literature. A Geopolitical View." *Comparative Literature in an Age of Globalization*. Ed. Haun Saussy. Baltimore: Johns Hopkins UP, 2006. 185–202.

Verne, Jules. *Autour de la Lune*. Paris: Le Livre de Poche, 2001.

—. *Cinq semaines en Ballon*. Paris: J. Hetzel, 1865.

—. *De la Terre à la Lune*. Paris: Le Livre de Poche, 2001.

—. *Le Tour du monde en 80 jours*. Paris: Le Livre de Poche, 2000.

Watt, Ian. *The Rise of the Novel: Studies in Defoe, Richardson and Fielding*. Berkeley: U of California P, 1984.

Wellek, René. "The Crisis of Comparative Literature." *Concepts of Criticism*. Ed. Stephen G. Nichols, Jr. New Haven: Yale UP, 1963. 282–95.

Further Reading

Alberson, Hazel S. 1960. "Non-Western Literature in the World Literature Program." *The Teaching of World Literature: Proceedings of the Conference at the University of Wisconsin*. Ed. Haskell M. Bock. Chapel Hill: University of North Carolina. 45–52.

Appiah, K. Anthony. 2001. "Cosmopolitan Reading." *Cosmopolitan Geographies. New Locations in Literature and Culture*. Ed. Vinay Dharwadker. New York: Routledge. 197–227.

Apter, Emily. 2006. *The Translation Zone. A New Comparative Literature*. Princeton: Princeton University Press.

— 2008. "Untranslatables: A World System." *New Literary History* 39: 581–98.

— 2009. "Literary World-Systems." *Teaching World Lterature*. Ed. David Damrosch. New York: The Modern Language Association of America. 44–60.

Arac, Jonathan. 2002. "Anglo-Globalism?" *New Left Review* 16: 35–45.

— 2007. "Global and Babel: Language and Planet in American Literature." *Shades of the Planet: American Literature as World Literature*. Eds. Wai Chee Dimock and Lawrence Buell. Princeton: Princeton University Press, 19–38.

Asong, Limus T. 2002. "The Impact of African Publishing on World Literature." Zimbabwe International Book Fair Trust, *The Impact of African Writing on World Literature*. Mauritius: Book Printing Services. 165–75.

Azarov, Yury. 1992. "Specific Interliterary Communities and the Comparative Study of Literature." *The Year's Work in Critical and Cultural Theory* 2.1: 295–302.

Baggesgaard, Mads Anders. 2008. "The World in Double Vision: Negotiations of Literary Autonomy in the Age of Globalization." *World Literature. World Culture*. Eds. Karen-Margrethe Simonsen and Jakob Stougaard-Nielsen. Aarhus: Aarhus University Press. 228–44.

Balakian, Ana. 1983. "The Pitfalls of the Definitions of World Literature." *Neohelicon* 10.1: 33–39.

Bassel, Naftoli. 1991. "National Literature and Interliterary System." *Poetics Today* 12.4: 773–779.

Beecroft, Alexander. 2008. "World Literature without a Hyphen: Towards a Typology of Literary Systems." *New Left Review* 54: 87–100.

Birus, Hendrik. 1999. "Main Features of Goethe's Conception of World Literature." *Comparative Literature Now. Theories and Practice. La Littérature comparée à l'heure actuelle. Théories et réalisations. Selected Papers/Contributions choisies du Congrès de l'Association Internationale de Littérature comparée, tenu à l'Université d'Alberta en 1994*. Eds. Steven Tötösy de Zepetnek, Milan V. Dimić and Irene Sywenky. Paris: Honoré Champion. 31–41.

Bleiker, Roland. 2009. *Aesthetics and World Politics*. Basingstoke: Palgrave Macmillan.

Block, Haskell M., ed.1960. *The Teaching of World Literature: Proceedings of the Conference at the University of Wisconsin*. Chapel Hill: University of North Carolina.

Braginsky, J.S., ed. 1983–89. *Istorija vsemirnoj literatury*, 6 vols. Moscow: Nauka.

Brown, Calvin S., 1953. "Debased Standards in World Literature." *Yearbook of Comparative and General Literature* 2: 10–14.

Cabo Aseguinolaza, Fernando. 2006. "Dead, or a Picture of Good Health? Comparatism, Europe and World Literature." *Comparative Literature* 58.4: 418–35.

Carroll, Michael Thomas, ed. 1996. *No Small World: Visions and Revisions of World Literature*. Urbana, Illinois: National Council of Teachers of English.

Casanova, Pascale. 2007. *The World Republic of Letters*. Trans. M. B. DeBevoise. Cambridge, MA: Harvard University Press.

— and Tiphaine Samoyault. 2005. "Entretien sur La République mondiqle des letters." In *Où est la literature mondiale?*, Eds. Christophe Pradeau and Tiphaine Samoyault. Vincennes: Presses Universitaires de Vincennes. 139–150.

Casas, Arturo. 2005. " 'Local,' 'Regional,' 'Nacional,' 'Mundial': Dimensões da História literária." *História(s) da Literatura. Actas do I Congresso Internacional de Teoria da literatura e Literaturas Lusófonas*. Ed. Maria da Penha Campos Fernandes. Coimbra: Almedina e Universidade do Minho. 89–110.

Daghlian, Philip B. and Horst Frenz. 1950. "Evolution of a World Literature Course." *College English* 12.3: 150–53.

Damrosch, David. 2006. "World Literature in a Postcanonical, Hypercanonical Age." *Comparative Literature in an Age of Globalization*. Ed. Haun Saussy. Baltimore: Johns Hopkins University Press. 43–53.

— 2008. "Toward a History of World Literature." *New Literary History* 38: 481–95.

— 2009a. *How To Read World Literature*. Oxford: Blackwell.

— ed. 2009b. *Teaching World Literature*. New York: The Modern Language Association of America.

Dimić, Milan V. 1991. "Friedrich Schlegel's and Goethe's Suggested Models for Universal Poetry and World Literature and Their Relevance for Present Debates about Literature as System." *Actes du XIe Congrès de l'Association Internationale de Littérature Comparée / Proceedings of the XIth Congress of the International Comparative Literature Association*, 5: *Littérature comparée, littérature mondiale / Comparative Literature, World Literature*. Ed. Gerald Gillespie. New York: Peter Lang. 39–50.

Dimock, Wai Chee. 2006. *Through Other Continents: American Literature across Deep Time*. Princeton: Princeton University Press.

— and Lawrence Buell. 2007. *Shades of the Planet*. Princeton: Princeton University Press.

Dong-il, Cho. 2006. "The Medieval Age in Korean, East Asian and World Literary Histories." *Interrelated Issues in Korean, East Asian and World Literature*. Seoul: Jimoondang. 67–79.

Ďurišin, Dionýz. 1972. *Vergleichende Literaturforschung*. Berlin: Akademie.

— 1974. *Sources and Systematics of Comparative Literature*. Trans. Peter Tkáč. Bratislava: Univerzita Komenského.

— 1984. *Theory of Literary Comparatistics*. Trans. Jessie Kocmanová. Bratislava: Veda.

— 1989. *Theory of Interliterary Process*. Trans. Jessie Kocmanová & Zdeněk Pištek. Bratislava: Veda.

— 1992. *Čo je svetová literatúra?* Bratislava: Obzor.

Elster, Ernest. 1901. "Weltliteratur und Literaturvergleichung." *Archiv für das Studium der neueren Sprachen und Litteraturen* 107: 33–47.

Epelboin, Annie. 2005. "Littérature mondiale et révolution." In *Où est la littérature mondiale?*. Eds. Christophe Pradeau and Tiphaine Samoyault. Saint-Denis: Presses Universitaires de Vincennes. 39–49.

Espagne, Michel. 1993. *Le Paradigme de l'étranger. Les chaires de littérature étrangère au XIXe siècle*. Paris: Cerf.

Even-Zohar, Itamar, ed. 1990. *Polysystem Theory*. Special issue of *Poetics Today* 11.1.

Gálik, Marián. 2003. "Some Remarks on the Concept of World Literature in 2000." *Koncepcie svetovej literatúry v epoche globalizácie / Concepts of World Literature in the Age of Globalization*. Eds. Ján Koška and Pavol Koprda. Bratislava: Institute of World Literature – Slovak Academy of Sciences. 91–106.

Gnisci, Armando. 1999. *Poetiche dei mondi*. Roma: Meltemi.

Goethe, Johann W. von. 1973. "Some Passages Pertaining to the Concept of World Literature." *Comparative Literature: The Early Years. An Anthology of Essays*. Eds. Hans-Joachim Schulz and Philip H. Rhein. Chapel Hill: The University of North Carolina Press. 5–11.

Guillén, Claudio. 1971. *Literature as System: Essays Toward the Theory of Literary History*. Princeton: University of Princeton Press.

— 1993. *The Challenge of Comparative Literature*. Trans. Cola Franzen. Cambridge, MA: Harvard University Press.

Hassan, Waïl S. 2000. "World Literature in the Age of Globalization." *College English* 63.1: 38–47.

Hillis Miller, J. 2000. "World Literature in the Age of Telecommunications." *World Literature Today* 74.3: 559–61.

Hoesel-Uhlig, Stefan. 2004. "Changing Fields: The Directions of Goethe's *Weltliteratur.*" *Debating World Literature.* Ed. Christopher Prendergast. London: Verso. 26–53.

Holden, Gerard. 2010. "World Politics, World Literature, World Cinema." *Global Society* 24: 381–400.

Jameson, Fredric. 1986. "Third World Literature in the Era of Multinational Capitalism." *Social Text* 14/15: 65–88.

Julien, Eileen. 2006. "Arguments and Further Conjectures on World Literature." *Studying Transcultural Literary History.* Ed. Gunilla Lindberg-Wada. Berlin: Walter de Gruyter. 122–132.

Kristal, Efraín. 2002. " 'Considering Coldly . . .': A Response to Franco Moretti." *New Left Review* 15: 61–74.

Lambert, José. 1991. "In Quest of Literary World Maps." *Interculturality and the Historical Study of Literary Translations.* Eds. Harald Kittel and Armin Paul Frank. Göttinger Beiträge zur Internationalen Übersetzungsforschung, 4. Berlin: Erich Schmidt. 133–44.

Larsen, Svend Erik. 2008. "World Literature or Literature Around the World?" *World Literature. World Culture.* Eds. Karen-Margrethe Simonsen and Jakob Stougaard-Nielsen. Aarhus: Aarhus University Press. 25–36.

Laird, Charlton. 1961. "World Literature and Teaching." In *Yearbook of Comparative and General Literature* 10: 66–69.

Lawall, Sarah. 1988. "The Alternate Worlds of World Literature." *ADE Bulletin* 90: 53–58.

— 1990. "Canons, Contexts, and Pedagogy: The Place of World Literature." *The Comparatist,* 24: 39–56.

— 1993. "World Literature in Context." In *Global Perspectives on Teaching Literature: Shared Visions and Distinctive Visions.* Eds. Sandra Ward Lott *et al.* Urbana: National Council of Teachers of English. 3–18.

—, ed. 1994. *Reading World Literature: Theory, History, Practice.* Austin: University of Texas Press.

Lukács, Borbála H. 1973. "Recent Comparative Research in the Soviet Union." *Neohelicon: Acta Comparationis Litterarum Universarum* 1.1–2: 367–375.

Madsen, Peter. 2004. "World Literature and World Thoughts: Brandes/Auerbach." *Debating World Literature.* Ed. Christopher Prendergast. London: Verso. 54–75.

Marino, Adrian. 1975. "Où situer la literature universelle?" *Cahiers roumains d'études littéraires* 3: 64–81.

Marx, Karl and Friedrich Engels (2009). *The Communist Manifesto.* Teddington: The Echo Library.

McFarland, Annette Catherine. 2008. "The Impact of World Literature in Secondary Schools in Oregon and Chile: A Comparative Case Study." BA Thesis. Oregon State University.

McInturff, Kate. 2003. "The Uses and Abuses of World Literature." *The Journal of American Culture* 26.2: 224–36.

Meyer, Richard M. 1913. *Die Weltliteratur in zwanzigsten Jahrhundert: Vom deutschen Standpunkt aus betrachtet.* Stuttgart: Deutsche Verlag.

Milner, Andrew. 2004. "When Worlds Collide: Comparative Literature, World-Systems Theory and Science Fiction." *Southern Review: Communication, Politics & Culture* 37.2: 89–101.

Miner, Earl. 1990. *Comparative Poetics: An Intercultural Essay on Theories of Literature.* Princeton: Princeton University Press.

Moretti, Franco. 2006. "Evolution, World-Systems, *Weltliteratur.*" *Studying Transcultural Literary History.* Ed. G. Lindberg-Wada. Berlin: de Gruyter. 113–21.

Neupokoyeva, I. G. 1963. "Metodologija komparativizma SSA i ee svjiaz's reakcionnoj sociologiej i estetikoj." *Problemy sovremennych literatur.* Moscow. 19–65.

— 1976. *Istoriia svemirnoi literatury: Problemy sistemnogo i sravnitelnogo analiza.* Moscow: Nauka.

Orsini, Francesca. 2002. "Maps of Indian Writing." *New Left Review* 13: 75–88.

Parla, Jale. 2004. "The Object of Comparison." In *Comparative Literature Studies,* 41(1): 116–125.

Pettersson, Anders. 2008. "Transcultural Literary History: Beyond Constricting Notions of World Literature." *New Literary History* 38: 463–79.

Pizer, J. D. 2006. *The Idea of World Literature: History and Pedagogical Practice.* Baton Rouge: Louisiana State University Press.

— 2007. "Toward a Productive Interdisciplinary Relationship: Between Comparative Literature and World Literature." *The Comparatist* 31: 6–28.

Prawer, S. S. 1976. *Karl Marx and World Literature.* Oxford: Oxford University Press.

Prendergast, Christopher. 2001. "Negotiating World Literature." *New Left Review* 8: 100–121.

— 2004. "The World Republic of Letters." *Debating World Literature*. Ed. Christopher Prendergast. London: Verso. 1–25.

Puchner, Martin. 2011. "World Literature and the Creation of Literary Worlds." *Neohelicon: Actua Comparationis Litterarum Universarum* 38.2: 341–48.

Ross, Kristin. 1993. "The World Literature and Cultural Studies Program." *Critical Inquiry* 19: 666–76.

Ruden, Sarah. 2004. "World literature in 1928." *The New Criterion,* 23: 50–53.

Ruffel, Lionel. 2005. "L'International, un paradigme esthétique contemporain." In *Où est la littérature mondiale?* Eds. Christophe Pradeau and Tiphaine Samoyault. Saint-Denis: Presses Universitaires de Vincennes. 51–64.

Saussy, Haun. 2006. "Exquisite Cadavers Stitched from Fresh Nightmares: Of Memes, Hives, and Selfish Genes." *Comparative Literature in an Age of Globalization*. Ed. H. Saussy. Baltimore: Johns Hopkins University Press.

— 2011. "The Dimensionality of World Literature." *Neohelicon: Actua Comparationis Litterarum Universarum* 38.2: 289–94.

Saverio Quadrio, Francesco. 1739. *Della storia e della ragione d'ogni poesia*. 4 vols. Bologna: Ferdinando Pisarri.

Schmeling, Manfred. 1995. "Ist Weltliteratur wünschenswert? Fortschritt und Stillstand im modernen Kulturbewußtsein." *Weltliteratur heute: Konzepte und Perspektiven*. Ed. Manfred Schmeling. Würzburg: Königshausen und Neumann. 153–77.

Spivak, Gayatri Chakravorty. 1988. *In Other Worlds: Essays in Cultural Politics*. New York: Routledge.

— 1999. *A Critique of Postcolonial Reason. Toward a History of the Vanishing Present*. Cambridge, MA: Harvard University Press.

— 2003. *Death of a Discipline*. New York: Columbia University Press.

— 2005. "Commonwealth Literature and Comparative Literature." *Re-imagining Language and Literature for the 21st Century*. Ed. Duangsamosorn. Amsterdam: Rodopi. 15–38.

Steinmetz, Horst. 1988. "Weltliteratur: Umriss eines literaturgeschichtlichen Konzepts." *Literatur und Geschichte*, München: Iudicium, pp. 103–43.

Strich, Fritz. 1946. *Goethe und die Weltliteratur*. Bern: A. Francke.

Thomsen, Mads Rosendahl. 2008. *Mapping World Literature. International Canonization and Transnational Literatures*. London: Continuum.

Tihanov, Galin. 2011. "Cosmopolitanism in the Discursive Landscape of Modernity: Two Enlightenment Articulations." In *Enlightenment Cosmopolitanism*. Eds David Adams and Galin Tihanov. London: Legenda. 133–52.

Tlostanova, Madina. 2005. "O concepto de 'literatura mundial' no tempo da globalización—unha mirada dende o espazo postsoviético." Trans. César Domínguez. *A Literatura Comparada Hoxe*. Eds. Anxo Abuín and César Domínguez. 2 vols. Santiago de Compostela: Universidade de Santiago de Compostela. 2:191–220.

Trumpener, Katie. 2006. "World Music, World Literature: A Geopolitical View." *Comparative Literature in an Age of Globalization*. Ed. Haun Saussy. Baltimore: Johns Hopkins University Press. 185–202.

Victor, Gary. 2007. "Littérature-monde ou liberté d'être." *Pour une littérature-monde*. Eds. Michel Le Bris and Jean Rouaud. Paris: Gallimard. 313–20.

Villanueva, Darío. 1999. "Claudio Guillén: la Literatura Comparada en y desde España." *Sin fronteras. Ensayos de Literatura Comparada en homenaje a Claudio Guillén*. Eds. Darío Villanueva, Antonio Monegal and Enric Bou. Madrid: Castalia. 13–19.

Vinck, José J. de. 1996. "Anthologizing World Literature." In *No Small World: Visions and Revisions of World Literature*. Ed. Michael Thomas Carroll. Urbana: National Council of Teachers of English. 34–40.

Vipper, Yuri B. 1985. "National Literary History in *History of World Literature*: Theoretical Principles of Treatment." *New Literary History* 16.3: 545–58.

Vossler, Karl. 1928. "Nationalliteratur und Weltliteratur." *Zeitwende* 4.1: 193–204.

Walkowitz, Rebecca L. 2007. "Unimaginable Largeness: Kazuo Ishiguro, Translation, and the New World Literature." *Novel* 40.3: 216–39.

Wang, Ning. 2011. "'Weltliteratur': From a Utopian Imagination to Diversified Forms of World Literatures." *Neohelicon: Actua Comparationis Litterarum Universarum* 38.2: 295–306.

Wellek, René. 1965. "Comparative Literature Today." *Comparative Literature*, 17.4: 325–37.

Yoo Hui-sok. 2006. "A Little Pact with the Devil?: On Franco Moretti's Conjectures on World Literature." *Studying Transcultural Literary History*. Ed. Gunilla Lindberg-Wada. Berlin: Walter de Gruyter. 133–143.

Index